Performance Management in Retail and the Consumer Goods Industry

Michael Buttkus • Ralf Eberenz
Editors

Performance Management in Retail and the Consumer Goods Industry

Best Practices and Case Studies

Springer

Editors
Michael Buttkus
Horváth & Partner GmbH
Berlin, Germany

Ralf Eberenz
Horváth & Partner GmbH
Hamburg, Germany

ISBN 978-3-030-12729-9 ISBN 978-3-030-12730-5 (eBook)
https://doi.org/10.1007/978-3-030-12730-5

This Springer imprint is published by the registered company Springer Nature Switzerland AG.
The registered company address is: Gewerbestrasse 11, 6330 Cham, Switzerland

Foreword

Performance management of companies in the retail and consumer goods industry must meet increasingly demanding challenges. These are driven by drastic changes in consumer behavior, more and more volatile market developments, and the ongoing transformation toward a fully digitized world in terms of private, social, and economic life.

In order to cope with these immense changes, new concepts across all corporate functions are essential—in the strategic orientation, in sales, in marketing, in production, in the supply chain, and also in controlling.

The customer with his needs and shopping motivation has moved into the focus of the companies. Through ever-larger amounts of data his customer journey is more transparent than ever, and from this, management-relevant, insightful, and reliable information can be generated. Analyses and recommendations for action are thus generated much faster than before. The demand for a much more flexible and specific design of planning processes and decision-making instruments is therefore significantly greater. As a result, they can be increasingly automated by modern systems. In addition to these cross-industry requirements, which are mentioned here as an example, the changes resulting from industry-specific business models must be mastered. The multitude of interconnections, new sales channels and their integration, high transparency of prices, the importance of brands for the sales success, the development of digital ecosystems and platforms, as well as the mastering of pressure on margins are just a few examples that illustrate how corporate performance management in the retail and consumer goods industry faces its own challenges but also great opportunities.

This book gives multifaceted insights and answers on these fundamental challenges, from both a holistic and a functional perspective. Experienced managers of well-known companies as well as industry experts from the management consultancy Horváth & Partners provide insights into their valuable experience. Successful practical approaches from various projects will be presented and worthwhile solutions will be designed. As a result, this anthology offers valuable approaches concerning innovative solutions.

The challenges for companies of the retail and consumer goods industry are very similar worldwide. Performance management systems used to manage these challenges are based on the Anglo-American or German management accounting philosophy. Since the perspectives on approaches differ in German and American understanding, especially with regard to controlling, this is particularly exciting. These differences will be presented in detail throughout the introductory chapter. Readers outside of Germany are offered special impulses and suggestions that are intended to cause critical reflection and discussion as a result.

I hope that this work will support many readers in getting started with and further developing performance management in the retail and consumer goods industry and that they will enjoy reading them. At the same time, I would like to wish all companies the courage and success for the application of the concepts described herein.

Horváth AG, Stuttgart, Germany Michael Kieninger
January 2019

Preface

Far-reaching changes are challenging the retail and consumer goods industry. Continuous globalization, demographic change, new possibilities through digitization, and the trend toward increased sustainability but also increasingly volatile political and economic framework conditions create enormous pressure for companies to adapt. Concomitantly, changes in consumer behavior can also be observed. Costumers are increasingly accessing the Internet using mobile devices and are using social media to inform themselves and to rate and buy products. Their shopping decisions are more spontaneous; they expect immediate delivery and all this at lowest prices, regardless of stationary or online concepts.

For the consumer goods industry, this represents great challenges but also great opportunities. Whoever manages to be the first to present the market with real innovations can stand out from the masses of competitive products. Whoever carefully maintains and continuously develops brands and directly and effectively addresses the end consumer can not only generate competitive advantages through improved advertising and communication but can also create lasting relationships with him. New technologies support addressing the customer, both target group specifically and individually. With every step taken before, during, or after the shopping of a product, customers leave behind personal data. Their data trail is growing daily, and with smart and responsible usage, companies can use this to come to a better understanding of the customer and to increase customer centricity.

But also in the case of retail, the consumer goods industry's great partner, market conditions are changing. An ongoing predatory competition and an uninterrupted trend toward internationalization create increasingly large retailing companies with constantly growing purchasing power. Consequently, the battle for the margin is increasingly tough. In addition, the borderline between industry and retail is less and less clear. Retailing companies are progressively switching to in-house production or are successfully establishing their own strong brands. For the industry, this means that additional competitors, that are their own customers at the same time, emerge. As a countermeasure, the industry is attempting to reduce its dependence on retail. Their own sales channels are established, be it online or stationary using "brand stores," "factory outlets," or "flagship houses." Consequently, retail is faced with new competitors through its suppliers.

However, despite all far-reaching and multilayered changes, the commercial target setting, namely that all companies must earn money, remains completely unchanged. This being said, the pressure on costs and prices remains high and will undoubtedly increase further. As a result, performance management is faced with more and more demanding requirements regarding efficiency and effectivity. With the growing complexity and increasingly rapid speed of change of business, better, more consistent, and faster information is required on all decision-making levels. From the preparation of fundamental strategic decisions and their maintenance to the support of daily operative problems, good processes, instruments, and information are more important than ever.

But what defines good performance management? Or rather: Which personal qualification, which organizational structure and which planning, forecasting, and reporting processes, which steering information, and which IT systems are necessary to ideally secure a company's growth and profitability? Naturally, the answers to these questions largely depend on the respective particular business situation and its specific challenges. Nonetheless, the publication on hand attempts to answer these questions with persuasive conceptual approaches and implementation examples that have been tried in practice for the retail and consumer goods industry and have relevance for many applications. In doing so, the aim is taking on different perspectives while contemplating this multifaceted subject matter, thereby offering an overview that is as broad as possible and offers profound approaches to holistic performance management. Consequently, we have divided the subject matter into six parts:

1. Controlling vs. Management Accounting—How German and Anglo-American-Understanding Differs
2. Something New on the Agenda—Challenges and Trends Controllers have to cope with
3. How to Approach Performance Management—Best Practice Concepts
4. Digital Performance Management—New Opportunities to Boost Efficiency
5. Planning, Forecasting and Management Reporting—Suggestions for Doing it the Smarter Way
6. Functional Controlling—Business-Specific Value Propositions

The first part, "Controlling vs. Management accounting—How German and Anglo-American Understanding Differs," discusses the fundamental differences between the German and Anglo-American understanding of performance management. **Larry White** discusses the terminological differences and explains potential advantages of the German approach. **Peter Kajüter** and **Moritz Schröder** analyze the differences between German and US-American cost accounting systems on an empirical basis, and in both contexts, cost accounting is characterized as the core of corporate performance management.

The second part, "Something New on the Agenda—Challenges and Trends Controllers Have to Cope With," introduces the greatest trends and challenges for the retail and consumer goods industry with **Ralf Eberenz**'s and **Maximilian Schröer**'s contribution that also maps out their importance for controlling. Subsequently, **Carsten Bork**, **Sascha Brosig**, **Walid Mehanna,** and **Stefan Tobias** offer a more detailed discussion on the special implications and opportunities offered by the digitization of corporate performance management.

Specific approaches for performance management are then suggested in the third part "How to Approach Performance Management—Best Practice Concepts." Therein, **Philipp Graf von Arnim** addresses the particularities of multichannel management in retailing companies and discusses how a stronger customer orientation can be reflected in controlling. Steering a combination of wholesale and retail businesses with a consistent set of key performance indicators is similarly challenging. **Bernd Seufert** illustrates how the METRO Group has solved this issue. The part is then concluded with an example project by the REWE Group. **Tino Eichler**, **Christoph Kremers,** and **Florian Werner** demonstrate the value contribution of a data-based management information system on the basis of a modern data warehouse.

Under the heading of "Digital Performance Management—New Opportunities to Boost Efficiency," we illustrate digitization's diverse opportunities in our fourth part. **Daniel Kittelberger** and **Lea-Sophie Allramseder** promote a comprehensive strategy for the digitization of steering processes in order to meet the danger in inconsistent island solutions. The basis to this end remains the ERP system.

SAP S4/HANA now also offers the option of controlling in real time. **Frank Poschadel** describes the preconditions under which this opportunity can provide real added value for management. In particular, **Kai Grönke**'s and **Sina Gieseking**'s contribution is dedicated to realizing efficiency potentials in the finance function. They examine the possible application of robots for the further automation of predominantly transactional finance processes. However, the potential of digitization exceeds the mere field of cost reduction. Decision-making processes can also be automated with the use of mathematic-statistical algorithms. **Mareike Clasen** and **Michael Milnik** illustrate how powerful machine-based forecasts already are today and how replenishment processes, for example, can be optimized. In conclusion, **Jörg Engelbergs** introduces a consistently digital business model with Zalando and maps out the particular controlling requirements necessary for its management.

We have given all relevant steering processes their own place in Part 5 "Planning, Forecasting and Management Reporting—Suggestions for Doing it the Smarter Way." We have dedicated three contributions to the most important aspect, namely, the organization of planning processes. In his contribution, **Michael Buttkus** highlights simplicity, robustness, and flexibility as the fundamental quality criteria of planning in a retailing environment. **Dominique Reuse**, **Mario Schoeb,** and **Ulrich Teuscher** supplement the discussion with the aspect of a planning process' length. Shortening the planning duration principally proves beneficial for the quality and the steering relevance of planning. This is proved by the practical example from REWE in the contribution by **Anna Thiel**. In it the fundamental realignment of company planning and the necessary implementation steps are covered. In his contribution, **Thorsten Lips** concerns himself with business prognosis or rather: forecasting. He illustrates how so-called predictive analytics approaches can meaningfully add to management assessments or even partially replace them. Finally, **Johannes Isensee** and **Angeline Schulmeister** indicate the great importance of the standardization and harmonization of performance indicators for an effective management reporting using the discounter PENNY as an example.

In the last part, "Functional Controlling—Business-Specific Value Propositions," we discuss the most important controlling functions in retailing and consumer goods companies. It is sorted according to organizational aspects and begins with strategy controlling. Herein, **Nikolai Brosch**, **Oliver Greiner,** and **Svenja Stöveken** address a holistic management approach for the development and controlling of a successful product and brand portfolio. They are followed by **Johannes Hofmeister** and **Björn Portner** who examine the influence of new technologies on *risk controlling*. All relevant trends and challenges for *corporate controlling* are introduced by **Ralf Eberenz** and **Stefan Behringer's** contribution. **Reto Andreoli** and **Beate Oberholzer** supplement this perspective with a practical example: the realignment of Swarowski's performance management system. With **Franziska Schmiedebach-Ullner**'s contribution concerning the requirements of controlling from marketing's point of view we open the discourse on *marketing and sales controlling*. An effective division of tasks between functions is thoroughly derived and then it is illustrated how a collective pursuit of targets can succeed. **Oliver Hupp** and **Franziska Rumpel** precisely explain current market developments and their effects on the allocation of marketing budgets to sales channels. Finally, **Carsten Moldenhauer** and **Henning Zwirnmann** illustrate in which way digitization has also entered marketing and use the example of the analysis of shopping behavior using mathematical models. **Heiko Schulte-Oversohl** addresses the specific challenges of sales controlling. He illustrates how tasks, instruments, processes, and personality traits of successful sales controllers are distinct. The part is concluded with two contributions concerning *supply chain controlling*. **Christian Daxböck**, **Jochen Kröber,** and **Markus Bergmann** give an overview on digitization potentials through supply chain steering, whereas **Dominik Fuchs**, **Matthias Haas**, **Julian Dombrowski,** and **Nicolas Göpfert** focus on the new possibilities created by SAP S4/HANA.

Our perspective throughout these contributions is strongly marked by the German language area. The relevant economic-historical, cultural, and academic preconditions represented in this paper have led to some manifestations of performance management that are not representative for other regions of the world. Nonetheless, many companies, as numerous product brands and company names can testify, are successful with these local steering concepts. Consequently, the approaches discussed in this paper are intentionally brought up for discussion in the Anglo-American area and are intended to motivate the reader to deal critically therewith. In order to do so, some terminological barriers must first be overcome. In Germany, management's support by corporate performance management is summarized by the "German" generic term *controlling*. *Controlling* is considered as all activities, processes, and instruments necessary to this end, but also the organizational function itself. Precisely translating this term to English is almost impossible, as in the Anglo-American area, different contents and different institutionalization have developed for management support. In this respect, the often-used translations of controlling—managerial accounting or management accounting—should always be met and used with caution. Hence we have deliberately foregone a standardization of the terminology used in this volume and have left it up to the individual authors to use the terminology they consider best. The underlying and ultimately significant content is discernible in the texts themselves in any case. For good measure, we have added footnotes in relevant cases to this end.

We would like to express our sincere gratitude to all the authors who have contributed to this book. Their enormous experience and expertise, as well as their willingness to publish practical examples, constitute this book's content value. They have contributed immensely to the practical relevance of this book while simultaneously offering conceptual impulses. Special thanks also go to **Larry White** who has repeatedly helped us with his deep understanding of and valuable insights into American and German controlling. We would also like to thank our editors **Cosima Gerlach**, **Caroline de Ladonchamps,** and **Kevin Rome,** our translator **Christian Bredow,** and in particular, **Philipp Graf von Arnim** for his in-depth and enthusiastic editorship.

Berlin, Germany — Michael Buttkus
Hamburg, Germany — Ralf Eberenz
January 2019

Contents

Part I
Controlling Versus Management Accounting: How German and Anglo-American Understanding Differs

Understanding the Benefits of German Controlling and Management Accounting

Larry White

Abstract This chapter explains the difference in the use of the term "controlling" as it relates to the management accounting profession in Germany and the USA. The author explains the benefits of the German controlling profession and its practices for managerial decision making, identifies some areas where the US and global accounting profession could learn from German practices, and traces the evolution of the differences that has led to the difference in the use of term "controller."

Keywords German controlling system · German controlling profession · US management accounting system · US vs. German perspective · Historical evolution of controlling · Historical evolution of management accounting

1 Do You Know the Difference? Between Controlling and Management Accounting in Germany and the USA

I strongly suggest you take this short quiz before you read this book:

1. Do you know what a controller does at a US company?
2. Do you know what a controller does at a German company?
3. Do you know that the two jobs are radically different?

If you answered NO to any of the three questions, you *need* to read this article before proceeding. This book contains some fascinating insights into the management of and the management accounting for retail and consumer product organizations, but to gain the full advantage of its insights you need to understand the German perspective and practices associated with controlling and management accounting. Don't be surprised if you don't know the difference; knowledge of German management accounting is not common in the USA.

L. White (✉)
Resource Consumption Accounting Institute, Suffolk, VA, USA

M. Buttkus, R. Eberenz (eds.), *Performance Management in Retail and the Consumer Goods Industry*, https://doi.org/10.1007/978-3-030-12730-5_1

German management accounting or, more broadly, the German profession of controlling is much more oriented toward operations and strategy and much less oriented toward financial accounting than US management accountants and controllers. This difference means many of the topics covered in this book are on the leading edge of enterprise performance management for the US accounting profession and accountants working in business.

Let's examine the two perspectives and look at the benefits of the German controlling approach and some deficiencies in the US approach. Finally, for those who are interested, the evolution of the two perspectives is discussed at the end of the chapter.

2 The Job of the Controller in the USA

The term "controller" is common in the accounting profession and business in the USA and much of the world. Investopedia defines the controller as: "A controller is an individual who has responsibility for high-level accounting, managerial accounting and finance activities. A controller typically reports to a firm's chief financial officer (CFO), although these two positions may be combined in smaller businesses. The duties of a controller include assisting with the preparation of the operating budgets, overseeing financial reporting and performing essential duties relating to payroll."

The work of the controller in the USA is dominated by accounting standards, regulations, and laws governing external financial reporting intended for the investment community and regulatory agencies. When financial information is presented or reported in any different form, it is often looked at with a certain level of suspicion and with requests for reconciliation to the regulatory financial statement figures. Non financial, operating information is typically outside the controller's span of responsibility except to the extent it contributes to a financial statement item. Even the budget process is often geared primarily toward predicting financial statement results. Operating information is generally viewed as lower quality information since, as far as most controllers know, it is not subject to the same controls and review as financial statement information. These perceptions are significant impediments for US controllers and management accountants when creating and using management accounting information to provide internal insights and decision support. However, these functions are where management accounting information is most needed to create sustainable economic value.

3 The Controlling Profession in Germany

The definition and perspective of a controller in Germany is very different. German controllers are generally not associated with external financial reporting or externally dictated financial or cost accounting standards. Their focus is on business intelligence to improve operations, competitive position, and internal business decisions.

German controllers are trained to create rigorous operational, revenue, and cost models that reflect the reality of the causal relationships among the resources, capacities, processes, customers, products, and services being modeled. The controlling body of knowledge is not part of the accounting curriculum. It is a separate university degree that teaches techniques and principles that guide collecting business intelligence and modeling their organization's operations to present business scenarios in operational and financial decision relevant terms.

In the long-established and well-documented area of costing, controllers create cost models in a manner that allows operating managers to understand how and where to improve the costs of operating resources and processes; how to project the financial impact of operating or capital improvements; and how to make marginal, incremental, and full cost strategic and operational decisions without a disconnect between the operating resources, the processes that consume the resources, and the cost information. This allows managers to accurately make timely adjustments to operating resources and processes to correct problems or seize opportunities. It also enables accurate projections of resource needs and costs based on demand scenarios. Managerial costing, as applied by German controllers, truly becomes managerial economics. Effective decision at all levels of management is how long-term, sustainable economic value is created in organizations. The results of decisions are eventually realized and reported in the external financial statements. The controlling profession has been aggressively moving beyond its costing roots and applying its body of knowledge more broadly with the goal of supporting the achievement of an organization's strategic goals.

German companies that use the controlling function most extensively are Germany's largest, most sophisticated, and globally competitive companies—think Siemens, Stihl, or Mercedes-Benz. German companies clearly see a competitive advantage from providing their managers with better information than their competitors to manage and control internal operations and costs. Research by the Institute of Management Accountants published in 2007 showed German managers were much more satisfied with the cost information they used than US executives.[1]

4 Benefits of the German Perspective

The benefits of the German controlling perspective and practices start with a broad focus on business intelligence and enterprise performance management, not just a focus on external financial reporting and basic accounting processes as in the USA. In Germany, the controlling department is not always associated with accounting and finance. It may be independent or associated with operations or general business management.

The skills the German controlling profession contributes to organizational management and decision making are the design, structure, and model operational and

[1] Krumwiede and Suessmair (2007).

financial business data in a manner that provides insights to further business success based on the strategy adopted. The responsibility of the German controller is to design the data, collection mechanisms, models, and reports that managers need to make decisions to achieve the organization's strategic goals and objectives. I have seen this referred to as "profit control mechanisms" but with equal emphasis placed on sales/market/revenue information and operational/cost information. The German perspective on controlling places a great deal more emphasis on planning and designing the intermediate objectives that will lead to successful achievement of strategic goals. Operating managers are clearly responsible for results, but controllers are responsible for designing and providing the information that will allow the operating manager to obtain timely feedback on decisions and take prompt adjusting actions if necessary to achieve goals. This generally includes designing data collection to support a range of possible competitive scenarios.

The German controlling function is much more focused on an organization's strategy and identifying the critical success factors (CSFs) and key performance indicators (KPIs) that it must achieve for the strategy to be proven correct or incorrect. The CSFs and the supporting KPIs are not just financial. The goal is to seek leading indicators to allow the earliest possible confirmations or adjustments. This typically means non financial data is the first input, and German controlling models, which are unconstrained by accounting standards, are designed to assess the financial impact in terms of clear cause-and-effect managerial economics. The external financial statements are some distance in the future, and high-quality decisions made as soon as possible will normally have a very positive influence at that future measurement point, with some timing-related exceptions associated with accounting standards and conventions.

Some examples you will see in this book include detailed discussions of how to measure the behavior and performance of customers and channels, with less discussion of measuring the associated financial result. This would be odd in a US management accounting text, but it illustrates the focus on leading indicators for German controllers. It also indicates their confidence in being able to build clear, causal models which will reflect the operations in financial terms that operating managers can use to take action to control profit outcomes.

5 Gaps in the US Perspective

The controller in the USA is trained to build financial models that align closely with generally accepted accounting principles. The perspective is that operational data is supporting input to a financial accounting model; somehow the obvious role of operational data as a leading indicator is often overlooked or considered someone else's responsibility. Causality, or cause and effect, is not a commonly discussed term or principle for the US controller; they are normally more concerned about how far they are deviating from accounting principles and standards. Operating and general managers (and even accountants) in the USA often use the terms "relevant" or "true" cost when seeking insight from finance and accounting information. What these words really mean is financial information other than what is in the financial accounting or management reports: in other words, financial information that can be causally related to operations or the decision at hand.

Increasingly, the work of the German controller is not done by the US controller's department due to its focus on regulatory financial reporting, but by a Financial Planning and Analysis (FP&A) department. These departments are often made up of general MBAs, accountants, and data analysts that do special analyses and projects. FP&A departments are nearly always part of the accounting and finance organization and frequently lack the operational focus and causal modeling knowledge and sophistication of the German controlling professionals.

There are US companies that imbed finance personnel in sales and marketing, operations, and logistics to enhance performance analytics. But there is not a professional discipline that has accepted the full range of responsibility for designing and communicating non financial and financial performance analytics to advise managers in an ongoing manner to support strategy execution. Management accounting is moving in that direction, but in the USA, academic support for management accounting is inconsistent and often a low priority for university accounting departments.

6 Need for Change in the US Perspective

Most organizations have realized on some level that managing by financial accounting statements is inadequate for decision support, planning, and control. A broader view of enterprise performance management is taking shape to encompass the increasing pace of change in business today—falling barriers to entry; more data and more processing capability; changing technology for products, services, and customer experiences and engagement; shorter, more frequent competitive and value creation cycles; and greater expectations and need for information and insight.

The German controlling profession may not have all the answers, but US organizations and, in particular, US financial and accounting professionals could benefit from detailed exposure to the German perspective—a perspective focused on business strategy, operations, causal analysis, and managerial economics rather than purely financial accounting conventions.

This book is not a panacea for US management accountants in retail and consumer products, but it will present a perspective that many, if not most, US finance and accounting organizations and accountants working in business haven't considered or been exposed to. It may also provide executive and operational management with the insights and knowledge to establish new expectations for strategic competitive information from their accounting and finance professionals and provide innovative CFOs a vision for new directions to create organizational value.

7 Evolution of US and German Management Accounting

It is remarkable that the German controlling body of knowledge and professional practices are largely confined to Germany and little known and rarely taught in other countries. Let's examine how the two different systems evolved in the USA and Germany.

The USA: Prior to the Great Depression of the 1930s, the focus of management accounting was on using accounting to improve management from the shop supervisor to the owner or senior executives. Industrial engineering and "scientific management," heralded by Frederick Winslow Taylor and Henry L. Gantt, were supported by costing that was calculated and recorded by modeling operational and physical relationships. In that era:

- Broadly averaged cost allocations of overhead expenses into product costs were considered sloppy, distorting, and misleading.
- Excess capacity costs were clearly identified.
- Accounting was expected to reflect the reality of how the business resources were consumed by processes and products.

However, during the Great Depression, management accounting's successful techniques were exploited by the federal government to regulate "fair and reasonable profits" and reign in profiteering by companies. The result was a host of regulations around costing practices and pricing to achieve social objectives, to the detriment of using management accounting for improving operational and cost efficiency

After World War II, the US economy boomed. Financial reporting standards and regulations focused accountants on linking costs to revenue in a general, more inaccurate way. Accountants began to neglect cause-and-effect relationships when allocating indirect and shared expenses to product costs since revenue, not the costs to increase revenue, was the major focus of the USA's growing economic prosperity. The rapidly expanding capital markets also focused on financial statement information and cost accounting adapted to provide convenient, but less insightful, costing methods.

In the late 1970s, US standard costing and production practices were shown to be insufficient to meet the operational, quality, and cost competition from Japanese imports. New costing methods, such as activity-based costing, throughput accounting, target costing for new product development, and other views of costing, started to emerge. However, they have not really gained momentum, and after the financial reporting scandals associated with Enron and WorldCom, legal pressure forced the accounting profession to focus on financial reporting and internal controls over financial reporting. Management accounting, as a body of knowledge, has remained a relatively minor discipline in the accounting profession even though 75% of US accountants work as accountants in business.

Germany: Capital markets were slower to develop after World War II and corporate financing was primarily private investment or bank financing. German controlling practices developed to demonstrate to sophisticated lenders that a business understood how to get the most profit from its limited resources and invested capital. Tighter capital availability also meant that business executives wanted to get the most from their resources to avoid refinancing trips back to creditors.

A part of German controlling is an approach to management accounting known as "grenzplankostenrechnung" (GPK), which means marginal cost planning and accounting. GPK adapted standard costing and flexible budgeting practices at the detailed cost center level to model the nature of resources consumption as fixed or proportional relative to changes in output (normally an intermediate output in a process rather than just a final product or service) and provide detailed marginal cost information. Arguments have been made that GPK is the result of a German cultural bias toward precision and control; however, there are sound historical and economic reasons for the development and use of GPK.

German controlling has found its costing methods extremely powerful and has seen limited benefit from any of the advanced cost methods developed outside Germany since the 1970s (e.g., throughput accounting, lean accounting). Controlling is not considered part of the accounting profession in Germany, and its professional body of knowledge has continued to develop in universities and professional controlling organizations. It has been moving beyond its costing roots and applying its powerful analytic approaches to the broader realm of enterprise performance management.

Reference

Krumwiede KK, Suessmair US (2007) Comparing U.S. and German cost accounting methods. Manag Account Q 8(3):1–9

Larry White is the Executive Director of the Resource Consumption Accounting Institute (www.rcainstitute.org). His professional activities include serving as a Member, Professional Accountants in Business Committee, International Federation of Accountants; Past Global Chairman of the Board, Institute of Management Accountants in 2004/2005; Past Member, International Public Sector Accounting Standards Board, International Federation of Accountants; and Past Member, Professional Certification Board of the Association of Government Accountants. He is the coauthor of the IMA Statement of Management Accounting titled "The Conceptual Framework for Managerial Costing." He is a columnist for AutomationWorld, a manufacturing industry magazine, and has written numerous articles for *Strategic Finance*, *Cost Management*, *Management Accounting Quarterly*, and other accounting and engineering publications.

Cost Accounting Systems in Germany and the USA: A Cross-National Comparison and Empirical Evidence

Peter Kajüter and Moritz Schröder

Abstract This chapter analyzes cross-national differences in the design of cost accounting systems between Germany and the USA—two countries that have a distinct cost accounting tradition. The comparison explores and summarizes several characteristics that make German cost accounting systems more detailed than US ones. It provides insights into national particularities and discusses mutual influences in the conceptual evolution of German and US cost accounting practices. Using empirical evidence from subsidiaries of anglophone multinational firms operating in Germany, the chapter identifies German cost center accounting as an interesting lever to improve the decision usefulness of US cost accounting.

Keywords Cost accounting systems · Cost center accounting · Cost type accounting · Cross-national differences · Financial reporting systems · Managerial accounting

1 Introduction

National specifics in accounting are well known for financial reporting: German GAAP differs from US GAAP, making it hard to compare financial statements prepared under the two national financial reporting systems. In recent years, of course, the adoption of IFRS and the convergence of national financial reporting systems with IFRS have led to a global standardization of financial accounting and

P. Kajüter
Chair of International Accounting, University of Münster, Münster, Germany

M. Schröder (✉)
Industrial Goods and High Tech, Horváth & Partners, Hamburg, Germany

M. Buttkus, R. Eberenz (eds.), *Performance Management in Retail and the Consumer Goods Industry*, https://doi.org/10.1007/978-3-030-12730-5_2

reporting. National particularities in managerial accounting[1] are less obvious, because this discipline is not regulated by law or by accounting standards. Still, different traditions in managerial accounting have emerged across countries over time due to various cultural, economic, and institutional influences. This is particularly the case for cost accounting, the historical core of managerial accounting. Especially cost accounting systems and practices in the USA/UK and Germany are distinct and have influenced the development of cost accounting in other countries.[2]

In general, national particularities in managerial or cost accounting might exist in three areas: (1) the adoption of accounting systems, (2) the design of accounting systems, and (3) the use of accounting systems.[3] First of all, globalization leads to a diffusion of the systems across countries. Multinational companies (MNCs) adopt the same concepts such as activity-based costing (ABC), economic value added (EVA), or balanced scorecard (BSC) around the world. Yet, national specifics are likely to survive as regards the conceptual design and the use of the systems. Such cross-national differences impair the comparability of information provided by management accounting systems in MNCs. Hence, MNCs face the challenge of whether to standardize their management accounting systems group-wide or to accept diverging systems in their domestic and foreign subsidiaries.

This chapter focuses on cross-national differences in the design of cost accounting systems. It first describes and compares major specifics of cost accounting in Germany and the USA (Sect. 2). After that, it provides empirical evidence about the design of cost accounting systems in foreign subsidiaries of anglophone[4] MNCs in Germany (Sect. 3). The chapter concludes with a summary and outlook (Sect. 4).

2 National Specifics in German Versus US Cost Accounting

2.1 Terminology

"Apparently straightforward terms tend to be defined differently in different countries."[5] This general observation is particularly true for cost accounting in Germany and the USA (and other anglophone countries). German cost accounting is based on the cost definition by Schmalenbach, who suggested to adjust the expenses from financial accounting by eliminating extraordinary items (neutral expenses) and

[1]The authors use the English word "managerial accounting" to translate the German term "controlling." Please refer to the discussion in the preface.

[2]Kajüter and Schröder (2017), p. 71.

[3]Moeschler (2012), p. 24.

[4]The term "anglophone" refers to the USA and five Commonwealth countries which are commonly covered in international research (Great Britain, Australia, New Zealand, Canada, and South Africa).

[5]Amat et al. (1999), p. 19.

adding imputed costs (opportunity cost such as imputed interest and imputed depreciation). This distinction between "costs" and "expenses" is uncommon in anglophone countries which define costs more generally as the value of resources consumed[6] and refer to financial accounting data. This basic difference results from different accounting systems. In Germany, so-called dual accounting systems prevail which have distinct databases for financial and managerial accounting. By contrast, so-called integrated accounting systems based on a general ledger dominate in the USA and other anglophone countries. According to Kaplan and Atkinson, this might result from economic reasoning: "(. . .) U.S. companies must have decided, sixty and seventy years ago, that the benefits of keeping two sets of books (. . .) were too costly relative to the benefits."[7]

Differences in terminology and underlying concepts cannot be solved by simple translation, because finding equivalent terms that have the same meaning in German and English is often difficult, if not impossible. Translating "Aufwand" by "expenses," for example, generally does not lead to a common understanding among German and US accountants. This is not only the case for the basic term costs, but for many other technical terms as well. There is no equivalent for "cost pool" in German, for instance, because cost pools have characteristics of cost types and cost centers. Moreover, "prime costs" as an expression for direct material and direct labor costs should not be confused with the more comprehensive German term "Primärkosten." Similarly, translating the German "Prozesskosten Rechnung" with "activity-based costing" may cause misunderstandings as the conceptual differences between the two cost accounting systems are not considered. Thus, national specifics in terminology impede the effective communication among accountants in MNCs and pose a challenge for researchers in conducting cross-country field studies.

2.2 *Conceptual Design of Cost Accounting Systems*

The conceptual design of cost accounting systems reflects the procedure of how costs are recognized, traced, and allocated to cost objects. According to this procedure, cost accounting systems consist of three main elements: cost type accounting, cost center accounting, and cost object accounting. The latter comprises product costing (cost unit accounting) and the operational income statement. National particularities in the conceptual design of cost accounting systems prevail in all three elements (see Fig. 1).

As regards *cost type accounting*, there are specifics in terms of recognition and measurement of cost items. German firms tend to recognize imputed costs in their cost accounting systems. Imputed costs such as imputed interest are an opportunity cost. Although opportunity costs are well known in US cost accounting, they are not

[6]For example, Datar and Rajan (2018), p. 49.

[7]Kaplan and Atkinson (1989), p. 9.

	Germany	USA
Cost type accounting	▪ recognition of imputed costs ▪ differentiation between primary and secondary costs	▪ no recognition of imputed costs ▪ differentiation between product and period costs (manufacturing and non-manufacturing costs)
Cost center accounting	▪ detailed cost center structure ▪ comprehensive internal service charges ▪ one or more cost drivers per cost center	▪ rough cost center structure ▪ few internal service charges ▪ one cost driver per cost center
Cost unit accounting	▪ job order costing: separate overhead charges for material and labor ▪ SG&A costs allocated to products	▪ job order costing: one overhead charge (manufacturing overhead) ▪ SG&A costs not allocated to products
Operational income statement	▪ separate internal income statement ("Betriebsergebnisrechnung") ▪ contribution margin statement with multiple layers of fixed costs	▪ income statement based on financial accounting ▪ contribution margin statement with one layer only

Fig. 1 Key differences between German and US cost accounting systems (adapted from Kajüter (2011), p. 106)

recognized in the cost accounting system as a regular cost item. Consequently, they are not allocated to cost centers and cost objects. Instead, opportunity costs may be part of special analyses prepared for decision making. Moreover, the classification of cost items differs. Despite similarities (e.g., classification according to resources, functions, traceability, variance with volume), there are specific cost categories in German and US cost accounting resulting from national particularities. While the distinction of primary and secondary costs is common in German cost accounting, due to a detailed cost allocation between cost centers, the differentiation of product and period costs (or manufacturing and nonmanufacturing costs) is common in the USA as a consequence of providing cost information for inventory valuation purposes.

Influenced by the German Flexible Plankostenrechnung ("GPK") *cost center accounting* has gained much more relevance in Germany than compared to the USA.[8] In the German literature, specific principles for establishing cost centers have been developed. Following these principles results in a quite detailed cost center structure with many rather small cost centers. This in turn facilitates a precise analytical cost planning and cost control in order to identify inefficiencies. Due to a strong focus on inventory valuation, such a detailed structure was not necessary in the USA. Thus, cost pools serve as a means for allocating indirect costs and cost variance analysis is not a part of US cost accounting systems but rather an element of

[8]Krumwiede and Suessmair (2007a), p. 7; Portz and Lere (2010).

responsibility in accounting and budgeting. At the same time, US firms generally have less but larger cost centers.

An extensive use of internal service charges also contributes to the larger number of cost centers in German firms. They distinguish between primary and support cost centers and apply internal transfer prices to account for services provided by support cost centers. Although this is also known in US cost accounting, it has a much lower relevance.[9]

Furthermore, differences in cost center accounting prevail in terms of the nature and number of cost drivers per cost center. While in traditional US cost accounting simple volume based cost drivers (e.g., labor costs) and only one cost driver per cost center is common, German cost accounting employs more sophisticated non-volume based cost drivers (e.g., m^2 or kWh) and, if necessary, more than one per cost center.

As regards *cost unit accounting*, German cost accounting differentiates between cost of conversion ("Herstellkosten") and total product costs ("Selbstkosten"). The former are determined as the subtotal of direct and indirect material costs and direct and indirect manufacturing costs. Adding sales, general and administration (SG&A) costs to this sum yields the total product costs. American job order costing differs here in two respects: First, indirect material and indirect manufacturing costs are usually allocated in one single step as "manufacturing overhead." Second, SG&A costs are generally not allocated to the product, but treated as period costs in the income statement. Hence, unit costs are not comparable if determined by different allocation methods of German and US cost accounting.

The *operational income statement* follows the function of expense method in both German and US cost accounting. However, in the dual accounting systems prevailing in German firms the operational income statement ("Betriebsergebnisrechnung") has a more pronounced role than in the USA. The operational income statement presents the operating income ("Betriebsergebnis") which can deviate from the net income in the profit or loss account due to differences in recognition and measurement of cost items. In the USA, the internal income statement is not part of cost accounting systems but rather of performance measurement in profit centers. Interestingly, the EVA concept pursues very similar ideas and objectives to the operational income statement in German cost accounting.[10] Financial accounting data is adjusted for internal performance measurement. By eliminating extraordinary items and other conversions, the "accounting model" is transformed into an "economic model." Moreover, cost of capital is deducted from operating profit. All these are elements of German cost accounting (eliminating some expenses to derive the costs; recognition of imputed costs). Hence, these concepts can be found in a similar way in US accounting, however, derived from financial accounting and not as a part of cost accounting systems.

---

[9]Zirkler (2002), p. 131.

[10]Wurl et al. (2001), Kajüter (2011).

Further differences prevail in the design of contribution margin accounting. Shaped by the decision-facilitating role of German cost accounting systems, detailed, multilayer contribution margin statements emerged. In contrast, rather simple one-layer contribution margin statements are common in the USA based on direct costing.

Overall, the design of German cost accounting systems is more detailed in all key elements compared to the design of anglophone cost accounting systems, which are rather pragmatic. The higher level of detail helps to capture a more precise picture of the resource consumption, but also requires more effort.

2.3 Cross-Country Influences and Convergence of Cost Accounting Systems

Fueled by industrialization, the growth of firms and increasing competition, cost accounting systems became a key management accounting instrument in both Germany and the USA during the twentieth century. Both countries developed a distinct cost accounting tradition that not only influenced cost accounting practices in other countries but also impacted on each other.

In the USA, the principles of scientific management led to the development of *standard costing*.[11] Due to the dominance of financial accounting, in particular since the crash of the stock exchange in 1929, cost accounting made little progress. Absorption costing dominated accounting practice, and the revolutionary idea of Harris (1936), *direct costing*, gained little acceptance. This situation persisted until the mid-1980s when Johnson and Kaplan criticized the state of US cost accounting systems with their influential book *Relevance Lost: The Rise and Fall of Management Accounting*.[12] As a solution, they suggested *activity-based costing*. This cost accounting system gained much attention internationally. It is presented regularly in anglophone management accounting textbooks. Still, its adoption in practice remained rather low, both in the USA and other countries. As a consequence, several approaches to advance US cost accounting have been discussed in the past 20 years, including *Time-Driven ABC*,[13] *Resource Consumption Accounting* ("RCA"),[14] or the German *Grenzplankostenrechnung* ("GPK").[15]

The German cost accounting tradition is based on the influential ideas of Schmalenbach.[16] After World War II, three competing cost accounting systems were developed by German academics in the 1950s and 1960s: *Flexible Plankosten- und*

[11] Harrison (1930).

[12] Johnson and Kaplan (1987), also see Cooper and Kaplan (1988).

[13] Kaplan and Anderson (2004, 2007).

[14] van der Merwe and Keys (2001, 2002).

[15] Sharman and Vikas (2004), Krumwiede (2005), Krumwiede and Suessmair (2008).

[16] Schmalenbach (1899, 1919); Schoenfeld (1990).

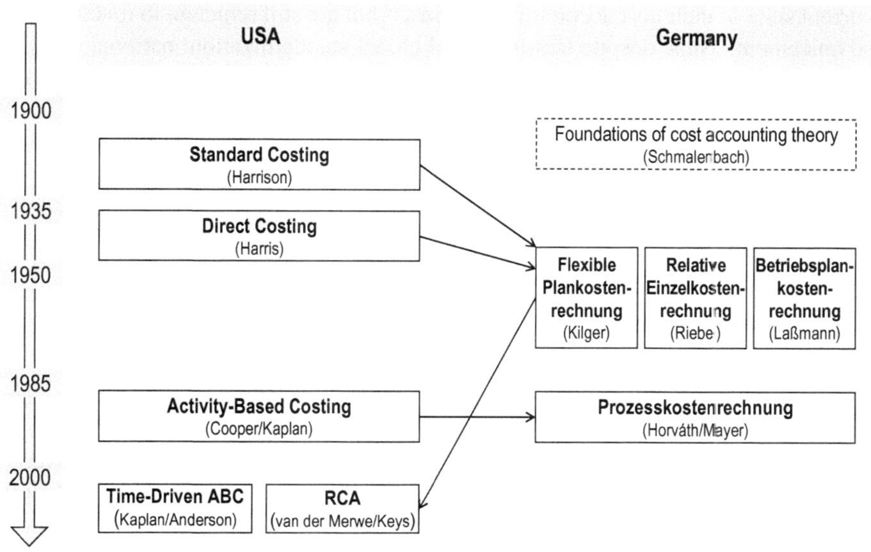

Fig. 2 Cross-country influences on cost accounting system development (Kajüter (2011), p. 110)

Deckungsbeitragsrechnung,[17] *Relative Einzelkosten- und Deckungsbeitragsrechnung*,[18] and *Betriebsplankostenrechnung*.[19] Each of them has a sound theoretical concept and is mainly designed for manufacturing companies. Moreover, they all emphasize the decision-facilitating purpose of cost information and therefore enable marginal costing. However, only Kilger's cost accounting system has been widely adopted in practice and has been implemented in the SAP software. As such, it has gained attention as "GPK" in the USA in recent years. In the 1980s and 1990s, the further development of cost accounting focused on single aspects, special applications, and the decision-influencing purpose. In addition, *Prozesskostenrechnung*[20] emerged as a German version of ABC.[21]

Figure 2 shows the cross-country influences between German and US cost accounting: While the development of GPK has adopted ideas of standard costing and direct costing, and ABC has stimulated the development of Prozesskostenrechnung, there is now also an influence of GPK on US cost accounting. As such, there seems to be some convergence in the design of cost accounting systems internationally. German MNCs increasingly abandon dual accounting systems and adopt integrated ones.[22] US firms, however, seem to be dissatisfied with the

[17]Kilger (1961).
[18]Riebel (1959).
[19]Laßmann (1968).
[20]Horváth and Mayer (1989).
[21]For conceptual differences with ABC, see Kellermanns and Islam (2004).
[22]Friedl et al. (2009).

current state of their cost accounting systems,[23] but are still reluctant to invest in their advancement. Thus, despite trends toward global standardization, national specifics remain. Anglophone cost accounting systems tend to be less detailed than German ones. The following section will provide empirical evidence in this regard.

3 Empirical Evidence on Cross-National Differences in Cost Accounting Systems of MNCs

3.1 Research Design

To identify cross-national differences in the design of cost accounting systems empirically, subsidiaries of anglophone MNCs in Germany as well as a control group of local German firms were surveyed from January to May 2013. Overall, about 500 anglophone and 500 German medium-sized firms with 150–2000 employees were contacted by phone and asked to participate in the survey. 109 anglophone and 104 German companies returned the questionnaire, yielding a response rate of 22% and 21%, respectively.

In doing so, each participant provided information on fifteen characteristics of a cost accounting system—for each of which a measure ("score") was developed. Three scores describe how cost type accounting is defined [(1) number of primary cost types, (2) recognition of imputed costs, and (3) application of a dual accounting system]. Six scores summarize the characteristics of the cost center accounting system [(4) applied principles for center formation, (5) number of primary and secondary cost centers, (6) identification of primary and secondary costs, (7) variance analyses on cost centers, (8) overhead allocation between cost centers, and (9) overhead allocation from cost centers to cost objects]. Another six scores characterize the cost object accounting system [(10) cost categories available for cost objects, (11) number of layers in contribution margin accounting, (12) design of operating income statement, (13) time reference of costs, (14) variance analyses on cost objects, and (15) types of cost objects].

Every score represents distinct characteristics of the cost accounting system. To form score (2) "recognition of imputed costs," for example, participants responded to the following question:

To what extent do you apply the following imputed costs

- Imputed depreciation?
  □ Not at all; □ In separate calculations only; □ As part of regular cost accounting.

(continued)

[23]Sharman (2003a, b).

- Imputed interest?
  □ Not at all; □ In separate calculations only; □ As part of regular cost accounting.

The score takes its maximum value of one if both imputed depreciation and interest are used "as part of regular cost accounting" as each answer adds 0.5 to the score. For each answer "in separate calculations only" 0.25 is granted. If "not at all" was selected, 0 is attributed. Hence, the score's minimum is zero. In a similar manner, all the other scores vary between zero and one. Thereby, a one indicates a rather detailed (German) design of the cost accounting system whereas a zero specifies a rather pragmatic (anglophone) design. The average of the three (six, six) scores for cost type (cost center and cost object) accounting is used to characterize the three main elements of the sample firms' cost accounting systems. Moreover, the average of all 15 scores represents the detail of the overall design of the cost accounting systems in the sample firms.

The anglophone and the German participants have similar characteristics. The companies' size, management functions (e.g., procurement, production, sales), implemented ERP systems, and the skill set of cost accountants do not vary significantly. There are no structural differences between the two samples that might impair the comparison of the cost accounting systems of the anglophone subsidiaries and the German control group.[24]

3.2 *Results*

3.2.1 Overview

Figure 3 shows the average scores for cost type, cost center, and cost object accounting as well as the total score summarizing all 15 sub-scores. The findings underline the above explanations empirically. Cost accounting systems in anglophone subsidiaries are less detailed than cost accounting systems in the domestic German control group (0.54 vs. 0.58).

This finding for the average cost accounting score is especially driven by the less detailed cost type accounting systems (0.40 vs. 0.51) and the less detailed cost center accounting systems (0.57 vs. 0.59). Because the score reflects German and anglophone cost accounting traditions, these results suggest that cost type and cost center accounting systems in the anglophone subsidiaries are shaped by their parent company's customs. In contrast, the cost object accounting cannot be distinguished statistically from German traditions. Potentially, the anglophone parent companies regard standardized cost types and comparable overhead allocation procedures (cost

[24]For a comprehensive description of the survey design, data collection procedures, and sample characteristics, see Schröder (2014) and Kajüter and Schröder (2017).

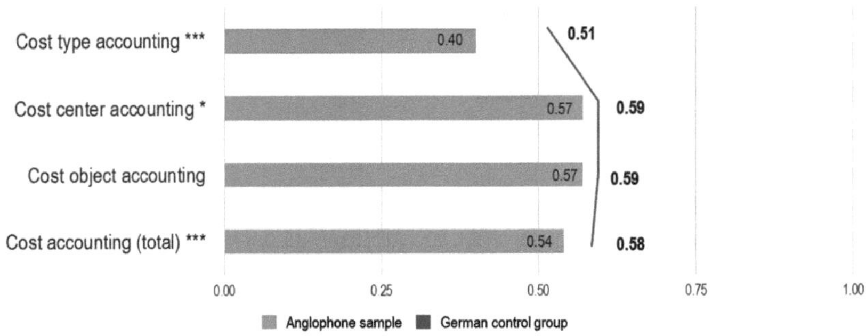

Statistically significant differences: *** = 1% significance level; ** = 5% significance level; * = 10% significance level

Fig. 3 Cross-national differences in cost accounting (Overview)

center accounting) as important for corporate control, but offer subsidiaries some discretion with respect to the local analyses of cost objects' profitability (cost object accounting).

A closer look at the empirical results in Fig. 4 reveals that all but one [(9)] of the seven significant findings for the sub-scores [(1), (2), (5), (6), (8), (9), (11)] support the expectation that cost accounting systems in anglophone subsidiaries are less detailed than cost accounting systems in domestic German firms. Curiously, the reversed finding for overhead allocation from cost centers to cost objects [(9)] does not appear to violate the prevalence of anglophone cost accounting traditions in the anglophone subsidiaries either. This finding results from a significantly larger proportion of anglophone firms that apply activity bases (27% vs. 13%) and time-driven activity bases (34% vs. 13%) to allocate costs from cost centers to products. Prior studies have revealed that anglophone firms tend to use activity-based overhead allocations more extensively than German firms do.[25]

These descriptive findings show that anglophone subsidiaries in Germany design cost accounting systems differently than domestic German firms. By presenting (1) selected underlying characteristics of the cost accounting systems, (2) the empirical explanations for these characteristics in the anglophone subsidiaries, and (3) the consequences for the performance of the anglophone-induced systems, the following paragraphs attribute the identified differences more conclusively to cross-national differences in cost accounting.[26]

[25]Askarany and Yazdifar (2012).

[26]For more detailed descriptive evidence, explanatory effects, as well as findings on the performance of cost accounting systems, see Schröder (2014) and Kajüter and Schröder (2014, 2017).

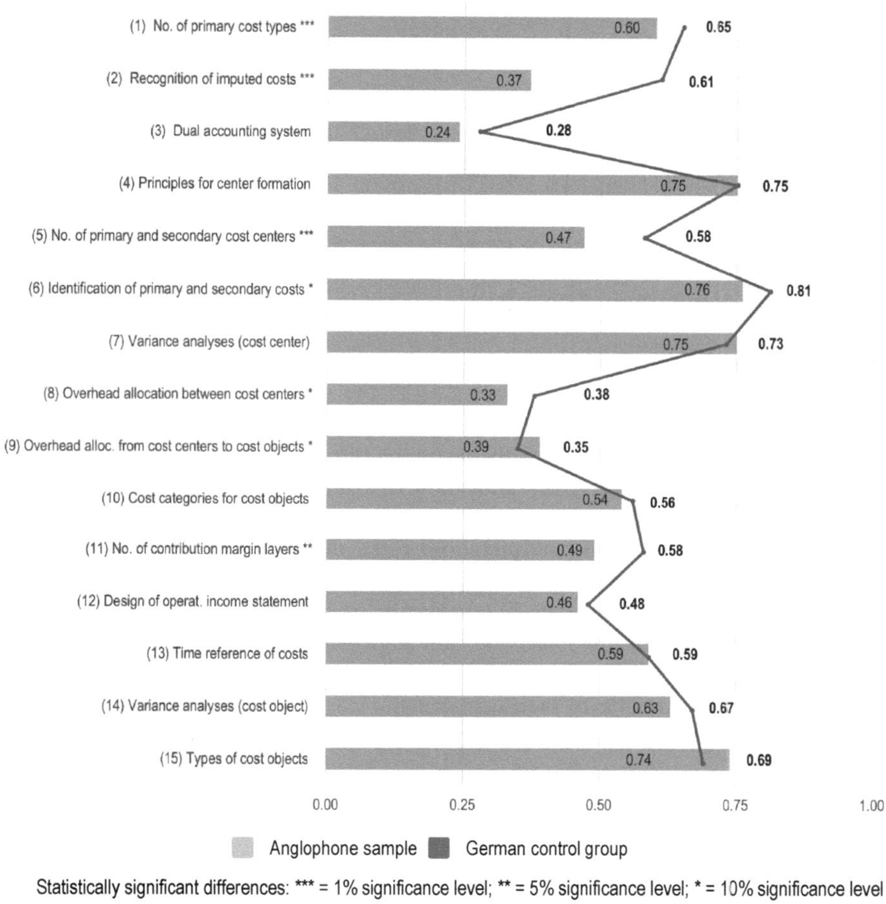

Fig. 4 Cross-national differences in cost accounting (Detail)

3.2.2 Cost Type Accounting

Figure 5 shows that anglophone firms have less primary cost types on average (177) than the German control group (220). Hence, the foreign subsidiaries appear to plan and control their resource consumption in a less detailed way than German firms. Moreover, German companies use imputed costs more regularly. Whereas 50% (44%) of the German firms use imputed depreciation (imputed interest) on a regular basis, only 24% (17%) of the anglophone companies do so. The latter rather consider imputed costs in separate calculations. 36% (32%) include imputed depreciation (imputed interest) in such analyses. Moreover, the anglophone firms also tend to fully disregard imputed costs more often.

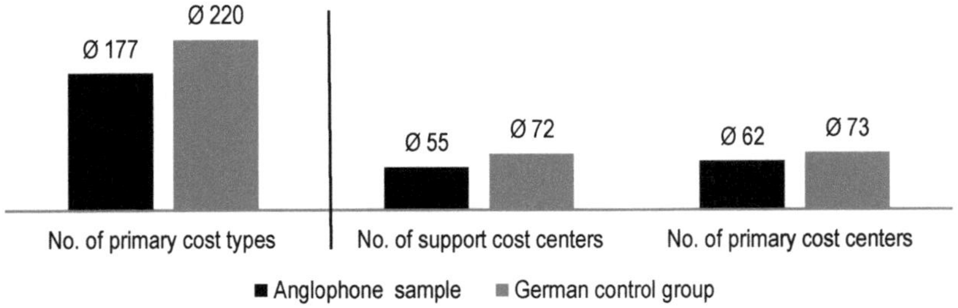

Fig. 5 Number of cost types and cost centers

3.2.3 Cost Center Accounting

The anglophone firms have on average less cost centers than the German control group (117 vs. 145). This is especially due to the significant lower number of support cost centers (Fig. 5). Hence, the allocation of overhead costs by internal service charges between cost centers appears to be less detailed in the anglophone firms. Two findings underline this interpretation: First, the total number of cost drivers (e.g., direct costs, m^2, kWh, kg, etc.) used in the anglophone firms to allocate costs between cost centers (on average five measures) is lower than in the German firms (on average seven measures). Second, the anglophone firms differentiate primary and secondary costs on about two-thirds of their cost centers, whereas their German counterparts do so on 74% of their cost centers.

3.2.4 Cost Object Accounting

Cost unit accounting also shows a stronger link between cost and financial accounting in the anglophone firms. 53% of the anglophone firms only allocate material and manufacturing costs to their products. SG&A costs are recognized as period expenses. Such an approach is less common in the German control group. Here, only 38% assign to their products mainly those costs that can also be used for inventory valuation according to GAAP.

Remarkable cross-national differences also exist with regard to the operating income statement. The anglophone subsidiaries focus more regularly on their (external) profit and loss statement only: around one-third refrains from using a complementary operating income statement. This is less common in the German firms (Fig. 6). Furthermore, the design of operating income statements also reflects a stronger link to financial accounting in the anglophone firms. In these companies, the line item structure of the operating income statement differs less from the one of the profit and loss statement compared to German firms. In line, the number of contribution margin layers within an operating income statement or separate

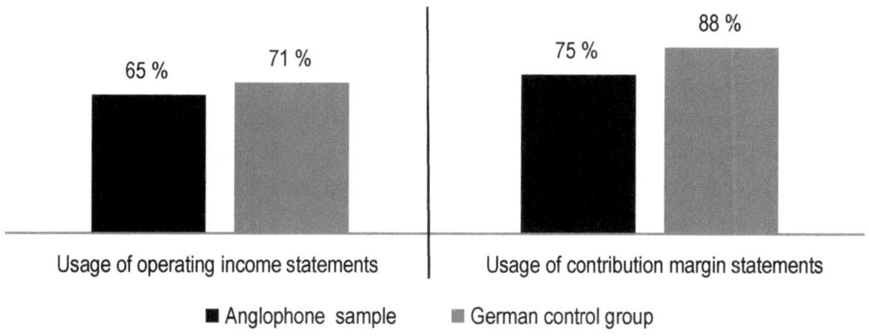

Fig. 6 Managerial income statements

contribution margin statement varies between the two samples. While the anglophone firms have two contribution margins on average before the operating income, German firms have three.

3.2.5 Determinants of Cross-National Differences

By using additional empirical data from the survey, the main factors that determine the less detailed cost accounting systems in the anglophone subsidiaries can be identified. The key drivers of the cross-national differences seem to be the personal involvement of the anglophone parent companies (expatriates and corporate managers' involvement) and accounting trainings through anglophone associations of management accountants like IMA or CIMA. In contrast, powerful ERP software (e.g., SAP) and the influences from local (German) managers tend to facilitate the establishment of a more detailed (rather German) cost accounting system in the anglophone subsidiaries. Economic factors such as company size or industry affiliation do not bias these findings.

Overall, there is sound empirical evidence that the identified differences in the design of cost accounting systems between the anglophone subsidiaries and the German control group are driven by the subsidiaries' affiliation to an anglophone parent. As such, the differences can indeed be explained by different national cost accounting traditions. The findings thus underline the existence of cross-national differences in managerial accounting.

3.2.6 Decision Usefulness of Anglophone Cost Accounting Systems

The survey data also allow us to derive some implications in terms of the decision usefulness of the implemented cost accounting systems. The local managers and their management accountants in the anglophone firms assess their cost information worse, the less detailed it is. Hence, cost accounting systems are perceived to be less useful for decision making if the systems reflect to a large extent anglophone cost accounting traditions. Additional analyses reveal that especially a greater detail in cost center accounting is a powerful path to improving the performance of the cost accounting systems in the anglophone subsidiaries. In other words, looking at German cost center traditions appears to bear potentials for improving anglophone cost accounting systems.[27]

Furthermore, the data show that an increasing level of detail yields a diminishing marginal positive effect. Apparently, once the optimal level of detail is achieved, adding, for instance, more cost centers or cost drivers does not provide additional benefits for decision making. Moreover, the data from the German control group suggest that exaggerating the detail of a cost accounting system can actually hamper its decision usefulness. Attributing high efforts toward running and maintaining a too detailed cost accounting system may make managerial accountants lose sight of their managers' information needs. Hence, the optimal level of detail for a cost accounting system must be chosen very carefully.

4 Summary and Outlook

Cross-national differences prevail in management accounting in general and in cost accounting in particular. At first glance, they are less visible than the differences between national financial reporting systems that are regulated by law or accounting standards. However, cross-national differences exist with regard to the adoption of specific cost accounting systems and their design and use. Especially Germany and the USA have their own distinct cost accounting traditions that have influenced the development of cost accounting in other countries as well. The conceptual arguments and the empirical evidence show that cost accounting systems in German firms are more detailed than those in their American counterparts. As a result, they provide more precise cost information. This does not necessarily lead to a superior performance because more detailed cost accounting systems also entail higher costs. Still, the empirical evidence suggests that US firms might improve their cost accounting systems by implementing some German specifics, such as a more detailed cost center structure.

Due to technological advancements, interesting developments can be expected in German and US firms in the next few years. The new SAP S/4HANA software moves toward an integration of financial and managerial accounting. As such, the new system can apply German traditions of cost center accounting or operating

[27]These findings support the RCA discussion in the US literature. The authors pointed out the importance of German cost center accounting for decision-making as well, e.g., Keys and van der Merwe (1999, 2001), van der Merwe and Keys (2001, 2002), Mackie (2006), Krumwiede and Suessmair (2007b).

income statements based on an integrated accounting system. The conceptual discussions from the RCA literature thereby gain in practical applicability.

References

Amat O, Blake J, Oliveras E (1999) Variations in national management accounting approaches. Working paper

Askarany D, Yazdifar H (2012) An investigation into the mixed reported adoption rates for ABC: evidence from Australia. New Zealand and the UK. Int J Prod Econ 135(1):430–439

Cooper R, Kaplan RS (1988) Measure costs right – make the right decisions. Harv Bus Rev 66 (5):96–103

Datar SM, Rajan MV (2018) Horngren's cost accounting – a managerial emphasis, 16th edn. Pearson, Toronto

Friedl G, Frömberg K, Hammer C, Küpper H-U, Pedell B (2009) Stand und Perspektiven der Kostenrechnung in deutschen großunternehmen. Zeitschrift für Controlling und Management 53(2):111–116

Harris JN (1936) What did we earn last month? NACA Bulletin:501–527

Harrison GC (1930) Standard costs: installation, operation and use. Ronald Press, New York

Horváth P, Mayer R (1989) Prozeßkostenrechnung – Der neue Weg zu mehr Kostentransparenz und wirkungsvolleren Unternehmensstrategien. Controlling 1(4):214–219

Johnson HT, Kaplan RS (1987) Relevance lost – the rise and fall of management accounting. Harvard Business School Press, Boston, MA

Kajüter P (2011) Kostenrechnungssysteme im internationalen Vergleich. In: Kajüter P, Mindermann T, Winkler C (eds) Controlling und Rechnungslegung. Schäffer-Poeschel, Stuttgart, pp 89–118

Kajüter P, Schröder M (2014) Kostenrechnung anglophoner Konzerne in Deutschland. Controlling Manage Rev 58(6):34–41

Kajüter P, Schröder M (2017) Cross-national differences in cost accounting of MNEs: empirical evidence from anglophone subsidiaries in Germany. J Int Account Res 16(2):71–100

Kaplan RS, Anderson SR (2007) Time-driven activity-based costing. Harvard Business School Press, Boston, MA

Kaplan RS, Anderson SR (2004) Time-driven activity-based costing. Harv Bus Rev 82 (11):131–138

Kaplan RS, Atkinson AA (1989) Advanced management accounting, 2nd edn. Prentice-Hall, Englewood Cliffs, NJ

Kellermanns FW, Islam M (2004) US and German activity-based costing: a critical comparison and system acceptability propositions. Benchmarking 11(1):31–51

Keys D, van der Merwe A (1999) German vs. U.S. cost management: what insights does German cost management have for U.S. companies. Manag Account Q 1(1):1–8

Keys DE, van der Merwe A (2001) The case for RCA: excess and idle capacity. J Cost Manag 15(4):21–32

Kilger W (1961) Flexible Plankosten- und Deckungsbeitragsrechnung, 1st edn. Gabler Verlag, Wiesbaden

Krumwiede K (2005) Rewards and realities of German cost accounting. Strateg Financ 87:27–34

Krumwiede K, Suessmair A (2007a) Comparing U.S. and German cost accounting methods. Manag Account Q 8(3):1–9

Krumwiede K, Suessmair A (2007b) Getting down to specifics on RCA. Strateg Financ 89:50–55

Krumwiede K, Suessmair A (2008) A closer look at German cost accounting methods. Manag Account Q 10(1):37–50

Laßmann G (1968) Die Kosten- und Erlösrechnung als Instrument der Planung und Kontrolle in Industriebetrieben. Düsseldorf
Mackie B (2006) Merging GPK and ABC on the Road to RCA. Strateg Financ 88:33–39
Moeschler M (2012) Cost accounting in Germany and Japan: a comparative analysis. Peter Lang GmbH, Frankfurt a.M.
Portz K, Lere JC (2010) Cost center practices in Germany and the United States: impact of country differences on managerial accounting practices. Am J Bus 25(1):45–51
Riebel P (1959) Das Rechnen mit Einzelkosten und Deckungsbeiträgen. Zeitschrift für handelswissenschaftliche Forschung, Neue Folge 11:213–238
Schmalenbach E (1899) Buchführung und Kalkulation im Fabrikgeschäft. Deutsche Metallindustriezeitung 15
Schmalenbach E (1919) Selbstkostenrechnung. Zeitschrift für handelswissenschaftliche Forschung 13:257–299 and 320–356
Schoenfeld H-M (1990) The development of cost theory in Germany: a historical survey. Manag Account Res 1:265–280
Schröder M (2014) Cost accounting in Anglophone subsidiaries: empirical evidence from Germany. Peter Lang AG, Frankfurt a.M.
Sharman PA (2003a) The case for management accounting. Strateg Financ 85:42–47
Sharman PA (2003b) Bring on German cost accounting. Strateg Financ 85:30–38
Sharman PA, Vikas K (2004) Lessons from German cost accounting. Strateg Financ 86:28–35
Van der Merwe A, Keys DE (2001) The case for RCA: understanding resource interrelationships. J Cost Manag 15(5):27–36
Van der Merwe A, Keys DE (2002) The case for resource consumption accounting. Strateg Financ 84(4):31–36
Wurl H-J, Kuhnert M, Hebeler C (2001) Traditionelle Formen der kurzfristigen Erfolgsrechnung und der "economic value added"-Ansatz – Ein kritischer Vergleich unter dem Aspekt der Unternehmenssteuerung. Die Wirtschaftsprüfung 54(23):1361–1372
Zirkler B (2002) Führungsorientiertes US-amerikanisches Management Accounting. Gabler Verlag, Wiesbaden

Prof. Dr. Peter Kajüter holds the Chair of International Accounting at the University of Münster (Germany). His research and teaching deals with current issues of both international managerial accounting and international financial reporting. As a member of several working groups at Schmalenbach-Gesellschaft and the Accounting Standards Board of Germany, he is actively engaged in the dialogue between academia and practice.

Dr. Moritz Schröder is Managing Consultant with Horváth & Partners for the Competence Center Industrial Goods and High Tech in Hamburg. His fields of activity are cost and managerial accounting as well as transfer pricing and performance management.

Part II
Something New on the Agenda: Challenges and Trends Controllers Have to Cope with

Current Challenges for Consumer Goods and Retail Companies and Their Implications for Controlling

Ralf Eberenz and Maximilian Schröer

Abstract This contribution describes the impact of current market trends and social developments on the controlling of the consumer goods industry and retail companies. For this purpose, current trends and developments are exemplarily demonstrated and the implications for selected controlling aspects of the considered industries are derived. The findings are then discussed and an outlook on the upcoming necessary changes and optimization for controlling organizations is given.

Keywords Controlling · Controlling functions · Digitization · Social developments · Trends retail · Trends consumer goods

1 Introduction

International retail companies and the globally operating consumer goods industry are subject to constant change. This change is characterized by economic and political influences as well as structural adaptations. Consequently, the situation of manufacturers and retailers is coined by demographic change, increasing commodity prices, and booming emerging markets as much as by growing globalization and an extensive digitization—to name only a few of the currently most relevant challenges. In addition to these global developments, region- or rather development-specific particularities exist. Accordingly, structural problems, declining surface productivity, and an increasingly difficult differentiation of product ranges create additional

R. Eberenz
Industrial Goods and High Tech, Horváth & Partners, Hamburg, Germany

M. Schröer (✉)
Retail and Consumer Goods, Horváth & Partners, Düsseldorf, Germany

M. Buttkus, R. Eberenz (eds.), *Performance Management in Retail and the Consumer Goods Industry*, https://doi.org/10.1007/978-3-030-12730-5_3

challenges in the highly developed markets. The increasing fusion of different sales channels—floor trade, online trade, etc.—also lead to an enormous pressure to adapt.

These changes have great differences in growth dynamics and development of profitability. The top 50 consumer goods companies have had difficulties adapting to changing conditions, which is evident in a decline in revenue of 0.7% in the year 2016. However, they have managed to increase their profitability through internal optimization. In contrast to established companies, new market participants with agile business models can manage an organic growth on the market and profit from population growth in particular.[1] Although the leading 250 retailers managed to avoid sales declines, their revenue growth of 4.8% (CARG) between the years 2011 and 2016 was merely sufficient for half the revenue growth of ten years previously.[2] Regional profiteers of this were mainly companies from South and Central America that successfully used dynamic growth markets. Apart from 2016's value-wise greatest consumer goods fusion of the beer industry by AB Inbev and SAB Miller, it was mainly Latin American retailing companies that could increase their revenue with acquisitions and organic growth.

In addition, there exists a fundamental "uncertainty of the future," resulting crises and the fluctuating political as well as economic environment of the last years. A focus on growth topics, concerning international expansion and further increased product innovations, must currently be accompanied by an especially thorough risk prevention. The management's task in this is better securing profits and market positions for uncertain times and retaining a capability to react in the case of unexpected events.

In this context, controlling[3] is increasingly moving into the spotlight. In times of dynamic markets and volatile economic framework conditions, a target-oriented, efficient, and in particular, a timely steering on the basis of current data is of great importance for the success of a company. But what constitutes successful controlling and which factors should be taken into account? The following contribution will initially take a close look at the current conditions and challenges relevant to both consumer goods and retail industry. In doing so, the focus will lie on challenges that are driven by both society and the market (see Fig. 1). Subsequently, this contribution will derive implications for controlling.

[1]OC & C Strategy Consultants (2016).

[2]Deloitte (2018).

[3]The authors use the English word "managerial accounting" to translate the German term "controlling." Please refer to the discussion in the preface.

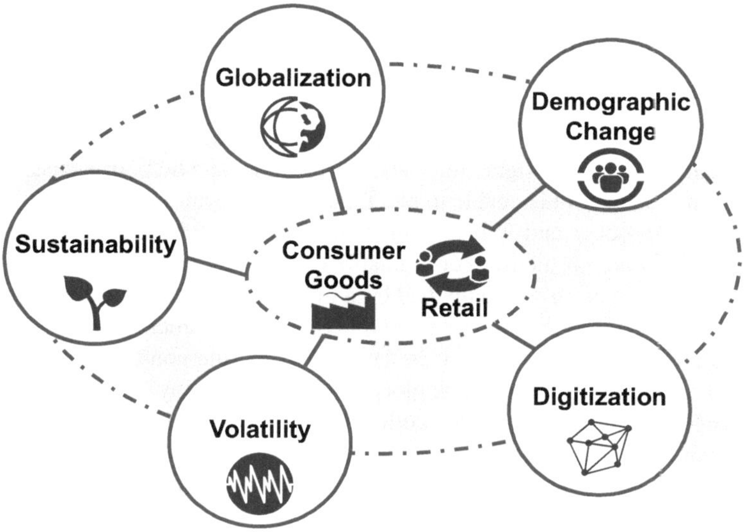

Fig. 1 Social and market-driven challenges

2 Current Developments Relevant for Both Industries

2.1 Globalization

The world economy's degree of globalization is constantly increasing. For producers as well as retailers, this entails an increase in international competition on established "home markets," but also the opportunity of international expansion to new markets. This creates lucrative sales markets—mostly in Asia—that will relieve the markets of the West of their position as consumer market of the world shortly.[4] This trend has amplified over the last few years; in many cases, local or, rather, smaller producers could increase their share of the market. The top 50 FMCG manufacturers have had little success on the new markets. In all BRIC states, they lost market shares to small and more agile competitors.[5] Consequently, the successful utilization of additional international market potential is a possibility but in no ways a matter of fact for established companies. This requires a (local) customer understanding and a demand-oriented and differentiated product range as much as target-group-specific sales methods. Contrary to the ongoing globalization, individual customers are actually increasingly individual and therefore also wish to be garnered with individual offers. Mass products that make equal sales all over the world are in demand; however, local conditions and customer expectations must increasingly be taken into account during the design and the marketing of products. In doing so, an

[4]See exemplary Unilever (2017).

[5]OC & C Strategy Consultants (2015).

internationally differentiated observation and comparison of markets becomes inevitable.[6] As a rule, the more global a company is, the more it must take the local preferences of its customers into account in order to reach a differentiated cognition with these.

Another factor crucial to success remains offering a customer the right product, for the right price, at the right time, and at the right location. If a customer has decided on a product, but is unable to purchase it at the location, then he will choose a competitor's product and will remember this supply shortage during his future purchasing decisions. If a customer is unable to purchase his product in the online shop as well, this casts an especially bad light on the manufacturer's and/or retailer's ability to deliver. Consequently, both manufacturers and retailers should secure their supply capability at all times. Over the last few years, the conditions for this have changed considerably. On one hand, globalization and thereby the resulting competition have led to a situation in which both manufactured goods and primary products can be purchased on the global markets at decreasing prices. On the other hand, the supply industry is characterized by only a few large providers. The dependency of the consumer goods manufacturer, in particular, has thus increased substantially and has reached a level at which manufacturers must ask themselves what they are willing to spend on delivery reliability in the future. If individual primary products are exclusively obtained from one supplier in one country, then natural disasters or political unrest can easily result in supply shortages and increasing costs of production. Companies should therefore focus the framework conditions and those of their supplier more intensely and develop a strategy on how to reduce risks and minimize their dependencies.[7] As a warning example you could mention the earthquake in Japan in 2012, during which the automotive industry came to an almost complete standstill.[8]

2.2 Demographic Change

The structure of the world's population is dramatically changing. A rapidly growing population with extreme regional growth differences and extremely different aging structures substantially change global political, military, and economic distribution of power. When regarding current projections for demographic developments, the extent of the influence of the "aging society" alone becomes evident. Today, only about 15% of the world's population lives in Western countries (North America and Europe), their relative share prospectively sinking further and the population size of Europe even shrinking in absolute terms.[9] Parallel to this development, the world's

[6]Horváth & Partners (2016).
[7]PWC (2010).
[8]United Nations (2012).
[9]OECD (2017).

population will continue to age, while this trend will be especially and surpassingly strong in Western countries.

In 2017, there were an estimated 962 million people aged 60 or over in the world, comprising 13% of the global population. Currently, Europe has the greatest percentage of population in that age (25%). Rapid aging will occur in other parts of the world; by 2050, all regions of the world will have nearly a quarter or more of their populations at ages 60 and above (except Africa). The worldwide number of older persons is projected to be 1.4 billion in 2030 and 2.1 billion in 2050 and could rise to 3.1 billion in 2100.[10]

Older people have different needs and expectations than younger generations. This is impressively supported by the results of a study according to which older people, for example in Germany, have a higher share of consumer spending with regard to their income than younger people.[11] This purchasing behavior offers great sales potential for retailers and manufacturers. In other regions, similar trends can be observed: the per capita spending of people aged 50 or over in South American countries was between 12% and 17% higher than the country average.[12] Until 2050, this age group will grow by up to 50% in South America.[13] Consequently, it is hardly a surprise that South American countries are already considered to be especially attractive developing countries for consumer goods manufacturers. Individual manufacturers have already tested and developed innovations that are intended to cater to the needs of the "aging society."[14] Many retailing companies are also currently considering this trend in their strategic planning. Age-specific product range design or home delivery concepts can be named as examples for this.

However, population is not only aging; it also exhibits various growth dynamics. As early as 2030, around 80% of the population with moderate income will live in developing countries.[15] The number of well-situated and purchase-willing consumers will lead to a veritable "consumer boom" in these countries. This can offer new opportunities for significant companies, as can be shown with an example from China: well-situated Chinese consumers love expensive Western luxury and status products. The profiteers of this are mainly European and North American consumer goods manufacturers of high-value durables. By this both manufacturers and retailers can simultaneously gain new customers, expand regionally, and compensate demand fluctuations of their Western core markets.

---

[10]United Nations (2017).

[11]If the average age group of people between 25 and 45 spends less than 45% of its total monthly income on private consumption, this percentage is nearly 60% for the over 65s, Statistisches Bundesamt (2018).

[12]Nielsen Company (2011).

[13]United Nations (2017).

[14]For cosmetics manufacturers, e.g., the "aging society" can roughly be divided into two groups: consumers who want to stay young and beautiful (down-aging) and consumers who want to age gracefully (age-pride). Following this classification, e.g., the brand Dove has launched a product line Pro-Age (age-pride), which is aimed at older women.

[15]OECD (2017).

2.3 Digitization

Apart from the restructuring of sales markets, the "digital consumer" also creates new requirements. The importance of this customer group is especially evident in Central Europe, where currently over 50% of customers are already regularly purchasing products online.[16] These consumers decide on purchases according to ratings on the Internet, share their experience in social networks, and research the sustainability and the social standards of the manufacturers. The importance of social media is clearly shown by the almost parallel development of Facebook users and Internet users in general.[17] There is no certain prognosis on which social media will have midterm success. However, it is very likely that this interactive form of communication's importance will continue to grow.

Accordingly, the Internet serves as the basis for the digital consumer. He may demand much, but he also offers enormous potential for a company's future success. Companies can use the knowledge gained on customers to respond to their needs more successfully and with their own products. Companies must also react to social networks with their products: they must find ways to defend and position their brand online.

The Internet is already the most important medium for consumers on the Western markets. In Asia, the availability of the Internet is also increasing rapidly and is currently surpassing that of Western countries.[18] The number of smartphone users who use their mobile device to access the Internet is also growing.[19] However, it is not only the mere number of online customers that is decisive for companies, but also that a great number of consumers are currently already making purchasing decisions on the basis of product reviews found online. Although, at the moment, this mostly has relevance to products with higher prices, customers are also increasingly making use of experiences and recommendations by other customers for day-to-day products. An increasingly large collection of data and Internet that is available at any time and any place have made researching and comparing products very easy for consumers. Consequently, shortcomings of the products and their manufacturing are more and more transparent and "googleable." Using a smartphone, information can be found out even when standing before a store shelf—e.g., by scanning the barcode—and the first shopping impressions and experiences can be shared directly with other potential customers. If the product is also available at a better price online, then the product will be purchased digitally—thus increasing the pressure on pricing. Furthermore, the delivery speed of online shopping has increased tremendously over the last few years. Amazon is currently already supplying many centers with products on the day of purchase itself.

[16]The UK leads this study with 78%, Eurostat (2017).

[17]In 2015, about half of the 3.1 trillion "online population" were Facebook users, Statista (2016).

[18]Internet World Stats (2017).

[19]eMarketer (2017).

Digital product evaluations remain subjective and can vary significantly from neutral test results. Over the space of only few hours, individual products or whole brands can suffer tremendous and lasting damage via social media. On the other hand, the Internet offers companies with a platform with which they can understand their customers better and satisfy their needs with new innovations. Most customers are willing to pay extra for a product tailored especially to them. With a targeted segmentation, higher margins can be realized despite the rising pressure on pricing. The digital "up-to-date" consumer—especially in emerging markets—will dominate the market in the near future. New mobile and digital payment methods will further increase customers' trust in online shopping and continue to drive the growth of M- and E-commerce.[20] Globally, the revenue of B2C E-commerce is increasing significantly and will almost double to 2100 Billion € between 2017 and 2022, while China is already the country with the greatest online revenue.[21] Not only China but the entire Asian region offers great potential for online distribution. The seven nations with the greatest E-commerce growth are all from this part of the world and an expected growth of 15% annually is projected.[22] The Internet is revolutionizing all channels of distribution and is met by reciprocal appreciation by the customer. In the course of this, online trade is also in motion and is removing borders between the markets. This removal is currently occurring in the European Union (EU), for example, where GeoBlocking is being removed. In the future, it will be possible to shop online without the restrictions of non-EU citizens or constantly being forwarded to the websites of one's own country. Such implications become very evident in the current situation in which 63% of the considered websites redirect or reroute potential customers rather than allowing them to make purchases.[23] On average, customers are also happier with products purchased online than with products purchased in store. Multiple sales channels not only change previously reigning market entry strategies, they also necessitate new approaches to better cater to customer wishes in M- and E-commerce and to improve customer binding. The customer himself aids this process, as he is rarely anonymous during M- and E-commerce. Online shopping offers new insights into the purchasing behavior and preferences of customers. From these, many new conclusions can be drawn for the future success of products as well as for innovations. Conventional distribution methods will not become obsolete through this; however, they will fuse with new approaches—with approaches that will blur the borders between manufacturer and retailer further. Direct distribution and own web shops allow the industry a direct sales contact to the end consumer, which, in turn, will further amplify retailers the development and sales of their private labels, which are already widespread. The aforementioned possibilities of digitization also entail that the previously extensively established entry barriers of globally acting

---

[20] Mobile- and Electronic-Commerce.

[21] Statista (2017a).

[22] Statista (2017b).

[23] European Parliament (2018).

corporations are more easily overcome or circumvented. New market participants are countering the global players' marketing budgets, scaling effects of production costs, and purchasing power with special customer proximity and agility—characteristics that are progressively gaining importance in our current day and age.

2.4 Volatility

Volatility is used as a risk measure and is oftentimes equated with risk itself. In its historical sense, volatility describes the previously observed deviations from a targeted or normal condition. In the past, the higher a volatility was, the higher the positive as well as negative deviations were from an observed mean value. Beyond the past, volatility can be used to attempt to describe evaluations concerning prospective trends. It is important to note that past volatility can only serve as indicator for future development and a comprehensive situation analysis is absolutely necessary for a prognosis. For detached from previous developments, one can never exclude the occurrence of significantly stronger or "diminished" outliers.

When considering the more recent past, it becomes clear that retailing and the consumer goods industry business is characterized by inconsistent and hardly predictable framework conditions that exhibit an increasing volatility over time. For companies, the challenge of adequately reacting to changes results from a complex structure resulting from political, social, legal, and technological changes. A concrete example that illustrates this is the varying purchasing behavior that is characterized by last-minute purchasing decisions, low product or brand loyalty, and rapidly changing interests, brands, and trends. This mix of uncertainties necessitates a rapid reaction to customer needs in order to prevent spontaneous sales declines. On the one hand, digitization supports or rather enables this customer behavior, as the growing transparency as well as anonymity of the online market fosters such behavior: never has it been as simple to compare the cheapest price, the newest technology, and current product and seller. On the other hand, digitization enables the raising and analysis of unprecedented amounts of data for companies as well as the quantitative and qualitative anticipation of prospective customer needs. Above and beyond digitization, changes in customer behavior are also fostered by the rapid emergence and vanishing of brands and trends. Apart from the factor of worldwide communication in real time via digital media, this increased pace of change can also be explained by physical interlinking, progressing through globally integrated international trade, international tourism, and increasing media.

The eminent challenge of volatile incidents lies in the quick reaction to prospective developments—regardless of their volatile and unforeseeable nature. If changes are recognized at an early stage and the reaction following is adequate, they can be used as a decisive competitive advantage. In this way, one's innovative strength, and thereby possibly also adaptions within the business model, can be used to weaken competitors and—depending on the degree of impact—even create an existential threat. In this way, companies are offered opportunities and risks for positioning on the market. In any case, due to the increasingly volatile changes, the standards for a company's flexibility are constantly raised and the success factor "ability to adapt" is gaining considerable importance.

2.5 *Sustainability*

Both retailers and consumer goods manufacturers are usually companies that can only be successful in the long term, if their product and/or company brands are maintained continuously. However, many customers have increasing misgivings against individual brands, if these do not meet the customers' requirements regarding social, ethical, or ecological standards. Companies have recognized this responsible customer and are attempting to take his demands into account. Customer requirements are primarily characterized by three aspects: saving resources, compliance with regulations and standards, as well as an increased transparency in company activities. However, for companies, meeting these requirements is complicated by customers' unwillingness to make concessions regarding price and service.

Society's interest in this matter is evident in many areas. Currently, in addition to regional appearances in social media, two million people follow the International Greenpeace account on Twitter in addition to three million users on Facebook. In order to meet requirements regarding sustainability, manufacturers and retailers are increasingly monitoring their own suppliers in order to prevent infringements in supplying countries. In the course of the global initiative Ethical Trade, for example, a code of conduct in which companies oblige their suppliers to follow certain mandatory regulations—e.g., for labor protection and level of wages—was developed. Well-known companies such as the Spanish corporation Inditex, one of the largest fashion providers through brands such as Zara, Pull & Bear, and Massimo Dutti, are a part of this initiative. H&M has committed to this code of conduct as well. Extensive responsibility reports are annually published by leading corporations and are intended to illustrate on which level social objectives were pursued or will be pursued and which motivation this social engagement can be ascribed to. For the "normal consumer" that does not read such responsibility reports, companies employ teams that look after digital brand maintenance, soften bad press, and attend to consumers through direct approach. The customer always wants to be taken seriously. Consequently, open admissions of guilt or the acceptance of criticism by the manufacturer are well-received. Already a few years ago, the pizza producer and delivery service Dominos Pizza released unfiltered criticism that they had received from customers on Times Square in New York. This open-minded interaction subsequently aided the company's turnaround.[24] Concerning all customer expectations, it is crucial that customers openly react to criticism and questions. A multitude

[24]Pizza Turnaround (2013).

of companies have recognized this customer requirement and are proactively reacting to questions and criticism on social media. The central platform for this customer dialogue is oftentimes constituted by the company's homepage.[25]

3 Implications for the Controlling of Retailing and Consumer Goods Companies

The aforementioned trends will continue to determine the framework conditions for consumer goods and retailing companies for the next years.[26] Companies will have to realign their strategies and risk managements and develop new approaches, especially in sales, marketing, supply chain, and also regarding their financial management, in order to successfully function on the global and digital markets. Likewise, controlling must successfully meet challenges resulting from changes and support management in its target-oriented planning, controls, and leadership. It should be designed in a manner that supports decision makers by providing information in an economically justifiable form,[27] but above it has to create the necessary transparency. Controlling must rapidly and flexibly act in a function- and process-spanning manner that meets the fast pace of the market. It is only in this way that it can live up to its task of supplying management with current and relevant information, holistically supporting decision-making processes and counseling in a target-oriented manner. These fundamental requirements must be met collectively by controlling and all available optimization potentials must be used.

We will illustrate the most important changes for controlling in institutional, procedural, and instrumental regard in an exemplary manner, using the most important controlling functions for retailing and the consumer goods industry.

3.1 Strategic Controlling and Risk Controlling

Strategic controlling is oriented toward long-term targets and success factors and serves the purpose of maintaining the company's existence. In doing so, its tasks concern the coordination of strategic planning, the control of target achievement, and thereto implemented measures. In this sense, strategic controlling must determine how a company should be structured to competitively act on the market in the long term. To this end, the aforementioned trends in strategy development must be taken into account and thereby the resulting opportunities and risks must be evaluated. If, for instance, end consumers increasingly transact purchases online and the stationary

[25]See, e.g., Nestlé (2018).

[26]Trendwatching (2018).

[27]Tietz (1993).

sales decrease constantly, far-reaching changes to the business model may result from such possibilities of digitization. For established retailers with an established infrastructure in stationary retail, this may constitute an existential threat, whereas it creates a significant opportunity for the provider of a customer-friendly online retailing platform.

In strategic controlling, apart from the cross-functional management of strategic risks (strategic monitoring) and the periodical reflection of the strategic orientation (monitoring of implementation), the control of framework conditions in particular plays an important role in preventing a misallocation of resources.[28] Shifting framework conditions result in the fundamental assumptions of the strategy pursued. If this occurs unnoticed, then new and also unrecognized risks are created by the continued pursuing of traditional strategies that now lack their substantive foundation. Therefore, an examination of assumptions should be used to examine whether or not an existing strategy remains realistic when regarding the specified trends. A timely questioning of the effects of trends such as globalization, digitization, and the aging society on one's own strategy enables an opportune adaptation or alteration. To a large extent, the instruments needed for this are already available. *Trend scanning models*, used for the evaluation of the effects of trends and cause–effect relations; *Porter's Five Forces Approach* for the analysis of industry structures on the levels of supplier bargaining power, customer bargaining power, competitor threat, substitute product threat, and competitive intensity of the industry[29]; *SWOT analyses* for the comparison of potential risks and opportunities with the strengths and weaknesses of one's own company; as well as the *representation of scenarios* for an overview of favorable and unfavorable business development are generally known and tried and tested.

Nonetheless, in many cases there is still a lack of adequate integration of strategic controlling and risk management with the operative management of the company. Planning and management processes, instruments, and contents are oftentimes not integrated between the strategic and operative levels, and in addition, they oftentimes are institutionally responsible in various departments. With the increasing speed of changes in the framework conditions, this leads to two significant problems. On the one hand, companies must strategically adapt to these changes increasingly often and rapidly. These adaptations can only be implemented successfully and timely with a functional integration into the operative management. On the other hand, many market changes are evident in day-to-day business. In turn, the resulting impulses can only be processed by strategic controlling, if they are passed on quickly and without falsification. Transparency and continuity of management will thus be even more important for a successful business development than it has previously been. Strategic controlling and risk management have to move inevitably much closer to operative management functions.

[28]Diederichs (2018), p. 266.

[29]Diederichs (2018), p. 268; Porter (1979).

3.2 Marketing Controlling

In marketing controlling, the positioning of the company toward the demand of the market is supported. This includes supplying the marketing function with management information, the analysis of the marketing budget with regard to efficiency and efficacy, as well as the support of marketing plans and controls regarding product range design, price positioning, target audience identification, and marketing mix design (promotional activities). Information supply, especially due to globalization, digitization, and demographic change as well, has to be far more differentiated than previously. The regional and age-group differentiation of target groups and their specific product ranges and sales channels entails the aspiration of depicting a business success in a similarly differentiated manner. The possibility of using additional miscellaneous data sources to this end, which include customer behavior, the effect of promotional activities, or competitive behavior, has increased exponentially with growing data availability. The use of big data in marketing controlling will therefore also increase significantly. In addition, the simultaneously growing volatility of markets through rapidly changing consumer behavior, competitor activities, etc., requires a more and more current supply of information with international consumer trends as well as scanner and market research data in order to adapt marketing activities accordingly. Therefore, the use of big data in marketing controlling will significantly increase. The thereto necessary interlinking of internal and external databases and the respectively powerful IT systems in reporting will consequently have to constitute an axiomatic standard of marketing controlling.

High demands regarding differentiation and process speed also apply to marketing planning. Here the influences are especially evident in the example of the marketing mix in retailing and industry: it is currently continuously changing due to shifts between online and offline activities. Additionally, communications platforms are not only increasingly gaining layers (social media, print, TV advertising, outdoor, events, teleshopping, etc.), but are also becoming increasingly personalized (customer journey, direct approach, personal nudging, etc.). Instruments that evaluate the cost and effect of alternative marketing measures both quantitatively and qualitatively, and then use the results gained for the conception of future marketing activities more rapidly, should be developed to this end.

All things considered, this leads to an evolving allocation of the marketing budget. Even more than previously marketing controlling must offer reliable evaluations regarding effectivity and efficiency of the assets used. This task was already insufficiently met in the past, and it has not gotten easier with the new and additional advertising possibilities and their simultaneous usage (blended marketing). Nonetheless, without an improved approach for evaluation the commercially smart handling of the enormous cost factor for retailing and the consumer goods industry will become even more questionable and the pressure on marketing controlling to react will become even greater.

3.3 Sales Controlling

The task sales controlling is faced with is supporting sales management with an adequate information supply, the analysis of the sales organization regarding efficiency and effectivity, as well as coordinating sales plans and controls. Furthermore, it supports activities such as distribution channel design, customer value analysis, price calculation, and product and customer profitability calculations. Regarding differentiation and topicality, the statements made in Sect. 3.2 regarding marketing controlling apply likewise. However, the implementation of new technologies seems to have even greater relevance. An example for this is the implementation of algorithm-based forecasting procedures for sales predictions. Such approaches from the field of predictive analytics already find diverse implementation and allow for an automatic sales forecast that comes to better and faster results than manual evaluation on a case-by-case basis. This suggests that retail in particular will be able to digitize substantial parts of operative activities of sales controlling with the enormous data available on all sales processes.

The digitization and globalization also change sales plans and controls. Multichannel retailers with very different customer interfaces, direct and indirect, offline and online, are necessary to meet the needs of individual purchasing behavior of different individual customers worldwide. The subsequent questions regarding customer value analysis will prospectively only be answerable using entire life cycles (customer life time) and with regard to not only *revenue potential* but also *data potential*. In future, a customer represents both a *cash flow* and a *data flow* and should be evaluated over the entire time span of a customer relationship. Facebook may suffice as an example to illustrate how valuable a customer's data can be on a case-by-case basis. However, sales controlling does not only have new questions in the B2C business. In the B2B business, for example, the role of local sales units also changes due to the ongoing globalization. Retailers acting worldwide naturally negotiate standardized purchasing conditions, but want to be serviced in a decentralized and country-specific manner. From the industry's standpoint, attendance of such global key accounts requires a balancing act between central and decentral task assignment or more boldly stated: between the postulates "one face to the customer" and "all sales are local." Consequently, creating incentives, management, and accounting for local sales organizations is increasingly difficult. How should centralized and locally adequate elements of a supply chain be allocated in an increasingly complicated international distribution of supply chains? Even upon neglecting the tax implications for an adequate profit distribution over the affected financial managements, this is becoming an increasingly large challenge.

3.4 Supply Chain Controlling

Supply chain controlling is faced with the task of steering logistic and manufacturing processes along the supply chain. In dependence of the respective business model procurement, warehousing, production and transport processes are relevant. Controlling is in charge of supplying supply chain management with information relevant for steering, the analysis of supply chain organization regarding efficiency and effectivity, as well as the coordination of supply chain plans and controls. In particular, the latter includes supporting delivery capacity, procurement planning, location and investment planning, and the working capital management. The complexity of these tasks is continuously increasing due to ongoing globalization of increasingly interlinked flow of goods. More and more often, controlling and the measuring of efficiency include multilayered international supply chains that include not only company-specific participants but also external cooperation partners such as suppliers, logistics service providers, and customers. Admittedly, digitization can also help: interlinked IT systems and databases facilitate the coordination of activities of all functions and/or participants involved and algorithms will prospectively, at least partially, take over demanding planning coordination, for example, in volume planning between sales and procurement.

Additional requirements arise from increasing volatility. On the one hand, many decisions through supply chain management have long-term binding effect. Location and investment decisions for production facilities or logistics centers are characterized by a large capital tie-up and a long life cycle. The more unsteady the conditions of such decisions are and the faster these can change, the higher the requirements for underlying calculations and assessments are. In addition to this, there exists an increasing concentration of the supply industry as well as an intensifying resource scarcity on the world markets. Both increases the sensitivity and thereby also the risks for a continuous delivery capability. Consequently, a much greater importance is ascribed to taking uncertainties, commitment periods, and the possibility of revisions into account and controlling must offer respective assessment processes. The flexibility of the supply chain should also be reevaluated for ongoing operation. Changing customer behavior leads to entirely new requirements regarding the availability of products and especially regarding fast delivery, which is further amplified by the possibility of online shopping. Today and despite constantly changing and increasingly individual product requests, the customer expects an "immediate" delivery and—when unsatisfied—a problem-free return. Supply chain is faced with increasing challenges regarding its flexibility, among them unchanged pressure on manufacturing costs and working capital. Production programs and distribution processes must be adapted to customer demands rapidly, but are still physical processes that can only be changed per se with a respective effort of time and capital. For the assessment of operative processes, flexibility as vital competitive factor, apart from revenue, cost, or profitability aspects, must therefore be focused much more strongly.

Finally, supply chain controlling will also be influenced by the increasing importance of sustainable economic activity. Out of all company functions, it is the supply chain, in both retailing and the manufacturing industry, which has the greatest influence on its ecological, ethical, and social "footprint." This function must widely account for working conditions of its own employees or those of the suppliers as well as the environmental impact of manufacturing, storage, and transportation. Adequately heeding these effects in strategic and operative target-setting and the subsequent assessment of commercial success is hardly pronounced to date. This is partially due to a still lacking internalization of the societal costs of sustainable actions,[30] but also because of underdeveloped methods for their reproduction in controlling's planning and reporting systems in comparison to cost and performance calculations. Currently, a holistic evaluation of the effectivity and efficiency above and beyond purely economic aspects remains far away. In order to meet these challenges, supply chain controlling will have to make efforts for special concepts and methods.

3.5 Corporate Controlling

Corporate controlling's task is supporting business management in steering the company in its entirety.[31] To this end, supplying the company management with information, planning and/or steering of corporate results, the coordination of different business areas, and the corporate-wide alignment of controlling in a methodical and procedural sense are paramount. In its role as interface between strategic and operative controlling functions, corporate controlling can be described as an "integration function." In this sense, the aforementioned implications for data supply also apply to corporate controlling. In case of doubt, the pressure for more rapid, relevant, and flexibly planning and reporting processes will be even greater than in other areas. Corporate planning in particular is very extensive, sluggish, and resource-consuming in many companies over time, which raises the question of the efficiency of this core process of controlling. However, new possibilities of digitization offer potential for corporate controlling as well. Improved data availability, computing capacities, and methodical approaches allow for significantly greater automatization and an improved integration of business areas into corporate controlling. Corporate planning can be improved significantly through this, and resources are released thereby that become necessary for the development of forecasting activities. Forecasts will increase relevance proportional to planning. In order to meet the flexibility and pace requirements set by the market, an (annual) planning process only is insufficient: instead, current developments should be captured by forecasts in short intervals that must be defined. Periodically updated, neutral interim

[30]Fritsch (2014).

[31]Behringer (2014), p. 20.

reports regarding the expected achievement of targets will gain significance with the increasing volatility of business.

Above and beyond one's own process changes, corporate controlling will be taxed as change agent for the other controlling functions and the company in general. The trends previously mentioned impact respective companies with varying intensity and speed. The same is true for the various functions within a company. Corporate controlling must recognize these developments as a whole and make interdependencies transparent. As corporate controlling function, it must secure the company's readiness to face impeding changes and must operationalize the reaction to this change. This means translating them into concrete target alignments and plans of action and monitoring its implementation. In most cases, these trends are far too abstract for companies to react to them with specific measures. Without an assessment of the changes in individual cases, a prioritization of measures, and a function-wide coordination of implementation, a successful support of leadership will not succeed. Many corporate controlling functions are still in the early stages of handling this task area.

4 Conclusion

The global challenges and trends in retailing and the consumer goods industry as discussed in this contribution are manifest and will influence their controlling functions. To which extent and in which form is dependent on the respectively specific company situation. Nonetheless, in conclusion, an attempt will be made to differentiate the relative concernment.

In Fig. 2, the level of influence of a certain change on the controlling function has been mapped out with the differentiation between strong, medium, and low influence. Naturally, strategic and risk controlling is influenced by all trends, as it must consider all of them with regard to content. We consider the evaluation of the influence on the local controlling itself, on operation and the instruments used with medium influence. This differs from marketing and also in sales controlling. In these cases, primarily globalization, digitization, and the increasing volatility of work content, planning and reporting processes, assessment processes, and system support will change substantially. The same is also true for supply chain controlling that must also take sustainability aspects into account in a much more explicit manner. To what extent this also leads to adaptations of the organization and personal qualification could not be elaborated upon within this contribution. However, it can be said that this is the case: at least with regard to digitization in controlling, there is convincing evidence.[32]

In corporate controlling, due to company-wide tasks and similar to strategic and risk controlling, all trends are influential. We assume that digitization and volatility

[32]Kirchberg and Müller (2016), p. 88.

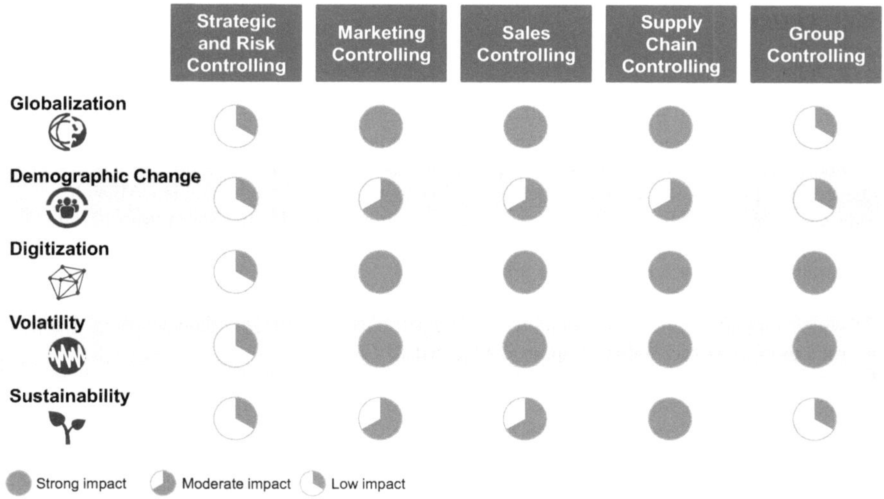

Fig. 2 The level of influence of selected market trends on controlling functions

have the strongest influence. The former offers enormous potential for the integration of steering across the borders of business areas and the latter forces a fundamental redesign of the consistently sluggish budget planning.

In conclusion, if one were to change one's perspective and observe the trends over all controlling functions, then it would become evident that the strongest influence, in relative terms, comes from digitization and increasing volatility. In the light of the core tasks of every controlling function, this seems plausible. Globalization, demographic change, and an increased orientation toward sustainability undoubtedly change many areas of controlling's work. In addition, however, the other two trends revolutionize controlling processes and instruments. The possibility of substantially automated leadership support will be achievable, and established planning and reporting processes no longer meet the requirements of an increasingly volatile business. It will be fascinating to observe how controllers will react to this in the years to come.

References

Behringer S (2014) Konzerncontrolling, 2nd edn. Springer, Berlin

Deloitte (2018) Global powers of retailing 2018, transformative change, reinvigorated commerce. https://www2.deloitte.com/content/dam/Deloitte/global/Documents/consumer-industrial-products/cip-2018-global-powers-retailing.pdf. Accessed 16 Feb 2018

Diederichs M (2018) Risikomanagement und Risikocontrolling, 4th edn. Vahlen, Munich

eMarketer (2017) Retail m-commerce sales via smartphone in the United States from 2014 to 2021 (in billion U.S. dollars). https://www.statista.com/statistics/276636/smartphones-us-retail-m-commerce-sales. Accessed 24 Feb 2018

European Parliament (2018) Parliament votes to end barriers to cross-border online shopping. http://www.europarl.europa.eu/news/en/press-room/20180202IPR97022/parliament-votes-to-end-barriers-to-cross-border-online-shopping. Accessed 24 Feb 2018

Eurostat (2017) Anteil der Online-Käufer in Europa nach ausgewählten Ländern im Jahr 2017. https://de.statista.com/statistik/daten/studie/153999/umfrage/anteil-der-online-kaeufer-in-europa-nach-laendern. Accessed 19 Jan 2018

Fritsch M (2014) Marktversagen und Wirtschaftspolitik: Mikroökonomische Grundlagen staatlichen Handelns, 9th edn. Vahlen, Munich

Horváth & Partners (2016) Branchenreport retail & consumer goods – Schwerpunkt: Individualisierung in Handel und Konsumgüterindustrie. https://www.horvath-partners.com/fileadmin/horvath-partners.com/assets/02_Kompetenz/Branchenkompetenz/PDFs/deutsch/161128_Branchenreport_Retail_CG_web_g.pdf. Accessed 3 April 2018

Internet World Stats (2017) Vergleich der Internetpenetrationsrate in Asien zur weltweiten Internetnutzung in den Jahren 2009 bis 2017. https://de.statista.com/statistik/daten/studie/39518/umfrage/internetpenetrationsrate-in-asien. Accessed 19 Jan 2018

Kirchberg A, Müller D (2016) Digitalisierung im Controlling: Einflussfaktoren, Standortbestimmung und Konsequenzen für die Controllerarbeit. In: Gleich R, Klein A (eds) Der Controllingberater, Konzerncontrolling 2020, vol 47. Haufe Gruppe, Freiburg and Vienna

Nestlé (2018). https://www.nestle.com/ask-nestle. Accessed 26 Feb 2018

Nielsen Company (2011) The global impact of an aging world, Diemen

OC & C Strategy Consultants (2015) The OC&C FMCG Global 50. https://www.occstrategy.com/en-us/news-and-media/2015/07/fmcg-global-50. Accessed 17 Feb 2018

OC & C Strategy Consultants (2016) FMCG CHAMPIONS – DIE PARTY IST VORBEI. https://www.occstrategy.com/-/media/files/insight-documents/de-insight-docs/occ_fmcg-champions-2016-die-party-ist-vorbei. Accessed 17 Feb 2018

OECD (2017) OECD-Wirtschaftsausblick, Volume February 2017. OECD Publishing, Paris

Pizzaturnaround (2013) The pizza turnaround. http://pizzaturnaround.com. Accessed 13 July 2013

Porter ME (1979) How competitive forces shape strategy. Harv Bus Rev 57(2) (March–April 1979):137–145.

PWC (2010) Genug für alle da? Wie gehen Händler und Konsumgüterhersteller mit Versorgungsrisiken um? https://www.pwc.de/de/handel-und-konsumguter/assets/studie-versorgungssicherheit-v09-ohne-kennwort.pdf. Accessed 3 April 2018

Statista (2016) Anzahl der Facebook-Nutzer und Internetnutzer weltweit in den Jahren 2004 bis 2015 (in Millionen). https://de.statista.com/statistik/daten/studie/245101/umfrage/facebook-nutzer-vs-internetnutzer-weltweit-zeitreihe. Accessed 28 Jan 2018

Statista (2017a) Ranking der Länder mit den höchsten Umsätzen im E-Commerce weltweit im Jahr 2017 (in Millionen Euro). https://de.statista.com/statistik/daten/studie/485047/umfrage/umsaetze-im-e-commerce-nach-laendern-weltweit. Accessed 26 Feb 2018

Statista (2017b) Die Top 10 eCommerce-Wachstumsmärkte. https://de.statista.com/infografik/8614/die-top-10-ecommerce-wachstumsmaerkte. Accessed 26 Feb 2018

Statistisches Bundesamt (2018) Laufende Wirtschaftsrechnungen Einkommen, Einnahmen und Ausgaben privater Haushalte. https://www.destatis.de/DE/Publikationen/Thematisch/EinkommenKonsumLebensbedingungen/EinkommenVerbrauch/EinnahmenAusgabenprivaterHaushalte2150100167004.pdf;jsessionid=AACD7579D71D6FD7DDB0949BE5C14F36.InternetLive2?__blob=publicationFile. Accessed 26 Feb 2018

Tietz B (1993) Der Handelsbetrieb: Grundlagen der Unternehmenspolitik, 2nd edn. Vahlen, Munich

Trendwatching (2018) 5 Trends for 2018. http://trendwatching.com/quarterly/2017-11/5-trends-2018. Accessed 28 Jan 2018

Unilever (2017) Umsatzverteilung von Unilever weltweit nach Regionen in den Jahren 2004 bis 2017. https://de.statista.com/statistik/daten/studie/254260/umfrage/umsatzverteilung-des-unilever-konzerns-nach-regionen. Accessed 26 Feb 2018

United Nations (2017) World population prospects: The 2017 Revision, Volume II: Demographic profiles: https://esa.un.org/unpd/wpp/Publications/Files/WPP2017_Volume-II-Demographic-Profiles.pdf. Accessed 16 Jan 2018

Prof. Dr. Ralf Eberenz serves as a senior advisor at Horváth & Partners and teaches business administration at the NORDAKADEMIE Graduate School in Elmshorn, Germany. He gained comprehensive practical experience in the consumer goods industry in various leadership positions at Beiersdorf. His major areas of expertise are strategic business management, management accounting, risk management, and mergers & acquisitions.

Maximilian Schröer operates as a Consultant with Horváth & Partners for the Competence Center Retail and Consumer Goods in Dusseldorf. Due to his previous professional employments, his consulting knowledge includes management accounting, finance, and organization with a focus on national and international retailers.

Digitization of Corporate Performance Management: Revolution or Evolution?

Sascha Brosig, Carsten Bork, Walid Mehanna, and Stefan Tobias

Abstract This contribution describes the change in performance management caused by digitization and corresponding consequences in various matters. In the first chapters, a fundamental change in the paradigm of business steering is addressed and additional new tools for business steering are elaborated. As a necessary basis for digitization, the entire topic of big data is discussed to build proper understanding, especially for the limits of big data. Digitization will not only change tools or data, but will also change the culture and required profiles for the finance department which will be highlighted in the last chapter.

Keywords Automatization · Big data · Digitization · Performance management · Scenario modeling · Predictive models

1 Digitization of Corporate Performance Management

There is no subject area that is momentarily discussed as hotly as digitization. The correspondingly resulting changes can be classified as comprehensive and interdisciplinary. Not only are single processing steps or processes changed, but the entire business models and value chains of companies are affected. Corporate performance management has to react to this on various levels and in different areas.

This contribution has been originally printed as Bork, C., Brosig, S., Mehanna, W.: Digitalisierung der Unternehmenssteuerung—Revolution oder Evolution? in Meyer, C., Pfaff, D. (2016): Jahrbuch Finanz- und Rechnungswesen, pp. 235–258, WEKA Business Media AG. Zürich.

S. Brosig (✉) · C. Bork
Controlling & Finance, Horváth & Partners, Frankfurt, Germany

W. Mehanna
Horváth & Partners, Stuttgart, Germany

S. Tobias
Controlling & Finance, Horváth & Partners, Stuttgart, Germany

M. Buttkus, R. Eberenz (eds.), *Performance Management in Retail and the Consumer Goods Industry*, https://doi.org/10.1007/978-3-030-12730-5_4

Digitization initiates a real change in the paradigm of corporate performance management. Consequently, previously established management processes must be questioned and re-understood. Employee's understanding of role, limits of process know-how, and technological barriers are broken down. Performance management reacts, along with accepting and establishing a respective foundation, successively to digitization and initiates changes in the steering instruments of companies.

First changes appear with the more intensive usage of stochastics or of machine control. Numerous companies are using first explorative approaches to make these possibilities accessible. The support for employees by new methodical approaches in performance management increases. Through digitization, new and operative performance management concepts are being established. A higher relevance of business and driver models in combination with the possibility of better using scenarios is being incorporated into performance management. Furthermore, the boundaries between processes and companies' value chain are shifting. The integration of business processes exceeding company boundaries is both a challenge and an essential advantage of this new performance management in companies.

The fundamental conditions of digitization are coined strongly through new technologies. Today, there are more possibilities than ever before for processing mass data and then harnessing them for companies. However, the limit of possibilities is far from being reached. Clear concepts and a defined governance structure are necessary for data processing. Not all available technological possibilities are also useful. In order to plan and implement a reasonable use of these technologies, a fundamental understanding should be built.

Apart from understanding, processes and technologies, the organization is also changing. New procedures, new roles, and responsibilities are the subject of discussion. In doing so, competences and responsibilities with adjoining operative areas will be broached—all the more reason why a clear picture of the future setup of finance organization should be developed at an early stage.

Whether digitization is consequently a megatrend, a revolution, or an evolution cannot really be determined momentarily. Nonetheless, the fact that all subject and technological disciplines of a company's finance organization are influenced by this and that this is accompanied with a new understanding, is indisputable.

2 Real Shift in Performance Management's Paradigm

Due to digitization, companies' business processes are undergoing significant change. The integration of business processes in particular, but also new services and the rendering thereof, will bring about a change of the supply chain and the necessary steering instruments.

Previous steering instruments were coined by backward-looking reporting on the basis of data history. Even in future-oriented steering processes, such as planning and forecasting, referencing the past oftentimes seems to have the greatest importance. Furthermore, forecasting is characterized by weaknesses in its implementation (e.g., political distortions), as for instance in situations in which it is important to give an unadulterated status of development. In the course of digitization, forecasting is given a greater importance. It is arranged in a more operative manner and has gained elementary significance in many company functions. Consequently, reporting the actual development has a lesser relevance to the management of operative functions.

2.1 Predictive Models Create Forecasts with High Quality and Accuracy

The need for steering information follows a clear development toward a proactive, future-oriented set of instruments. As a result, companies will be confronted with evaluating this outlook, in which respective procedures and models must be made accessible. This means:

- Operative predictive models are used more, on the basis of higher data granularity and a deeper understanding of business processes.
- Information on the *operative o*ptimization of individual circumstances or topic issues gains significance (case orientation).
- Depending on the steering focus, content undergoes change and may need to be realigned.
- Frequencies of data provision are not timed according to official reporting calendars.

This system identifies all those developments that will lead to highly probable results, using given parameters. Particularly the methodological competences necessary for this are challenging for today's management accountants.[1] If a forecast was previously made in all the management accountant's conscience, today, machine forecasts are created that determine the highest probability for a certain aspect, on the basis of mathematical procedures. On this basis, the responsible manager decides on how to best react to forecasting results, using additional measures (see Fig. 1).

The accuracy of these procedures will improve with increasing use. The manual process of creating forecasts is undergoing change and a further role, intended for checking the models and their results, stems from this.

[1]The authors use the English word "management accounting" to translate the German term "Controlling." Please refer to the discussion in the preface.

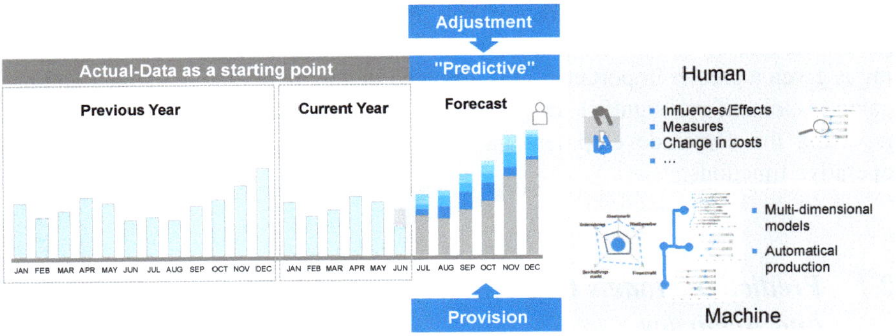

Fig. 1 Importance of forecasts in the course of digitization

2.2 *The Advent of Statistics in Performance Management*

The quality of data and methods used largely determines the quality of the results yielded. A distinctive task is securing the quality of the external "big data" database. However, the use of the correct algorithms as well as the constant optimization thereof is key: the development and maintenance of these complex models becomes a crucial factor of success.

Nevertheless, the key advantage of new digital steering instruments results from the combination of subject and industry-specific know-how, methodological competences, and entrepreneurial spirit of interdisciplinary experts and managers. In order to use these potentials to their fullest, cooperation is absolutely necessary. Data are analyzed according to contexts and dependences relevant to performance management, thereby creating the new discipline of data science. The interpretation and processing of the results will underlie management accounting and management. Results yielded by these models and their analysis show probabilities according to which departments steer and decide (Fig. 2).

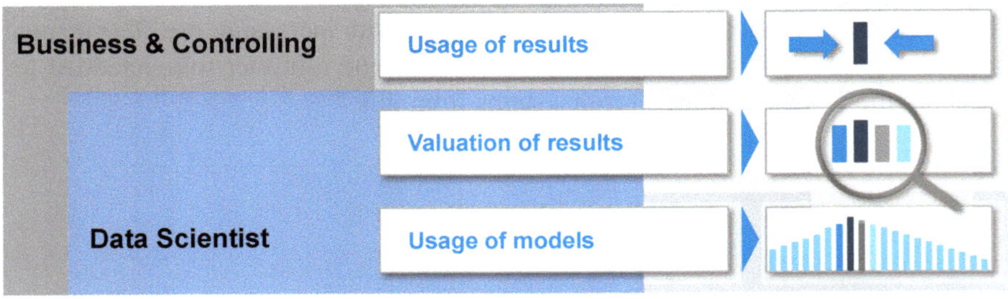

Fig. 2 Steering with probabilities: a new distribution of roles

2.3 *Operationalization: Altered Management Cycles and Content*

While past steering processes tend to focus on conventional reporting and planning processes, performance management will increasingly be operationalized. Steering contents will become significantly more operative and will substantially be based on operative forecasts and prognoses.

The necessity of better integrating operative topics within performance management asserts itself through familiarity with drivers and specific approaches of optimization. Predictive models make forecasts on the future development of drivers that are critical to success. Where necessary, these can then be supplied with specific measures. This explorative logic of optimization is integrated within reporting, is the subject of discussion in steering processes, and can be extended to other drivers if needed. In doing so, reporting aspects are taken up that were previously only considered in areas that were strongly operative. Instead of examining results, required actions, derived from the analyses of important drivers, were discussed specifically (Fig. 3).

Which articles display a high return rate? Which measures can be taken in order to reduce the return rate? Which level of return rate indicates a situation that is risky for the company's profitability? Predictive models are used to display conditions that may entail enormous risks (e.g., wrong product information or a poor readiness for delivery displays a high probability of an occurring increase of return rate).

The frequency of steering cycles is significantly raised. These topics are not discussed on a monthly or quarterly basis, but rather when they occur. Cockpits are being developed that can display data anomalies on a continuous basis. Responsible managers evaluate individual circumstances and prioritize and determine measures accordingly. Responsible task forces then implement these measures rapidly and promptly. Consequently, continuous gains in business productivity and efficiency are embedded in performance management. The resulting improved foundation for the optimization of business processes can then find application in all levels of the company.

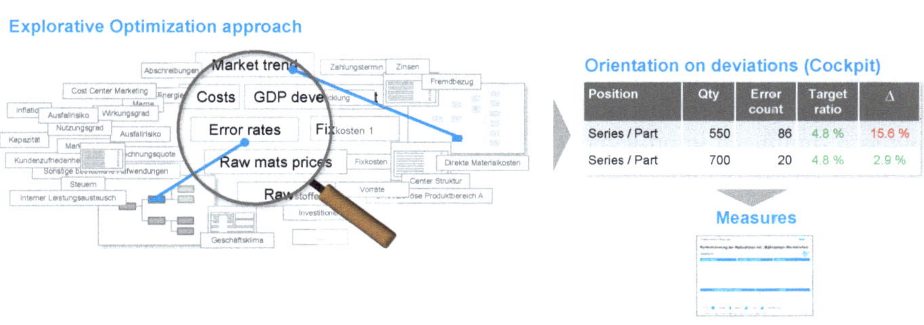

Fig. 3 Explorative optimization logics and the derivation of measures

2.4 Measures With Future Relevance Are Embedded Within Performance Management

On the basis of such analytical findings, the steering process can be launched. Specific measures can be identified to improve the results with the greatest probability toward the company's success. Product recalls, for example, can thus be prevented, as insights gained by analytical findings can lead to an early removal of the problem. The anticipation of risks is certainly only one field within the range of application of predictive analyses. Particularly in the sales department, aimed distribution measures can be initiated due to significantly higher customer transparency, thus further improving the company's success. For this purpose, altered processes will become necessary, in order to embed the orientation of measures within performance management more strongly.

2.5 Machine Performance Management: The Autopilot

Corporate performance management is increasingly being supported by advances made in automatization. In practice, typical examples can be found in data processing for reporting or within planning processes spanning various functions. Especially in these practical examples, it is evident that function-spanning dependences and correlations will play an increasingly large role. In the course of this, new technologies, such as rapid data processing, new tools, and big data approaches, are chiefly enabling new possibilities and paths of proactively facing corporate performance management.

In the past, simulations of various scenarios of potential company developments have already been conducted. This process was characterized by high personnel expenditure and could only react to changes with great effort. Due to the high personnel expenditure, simulations were oftentimes reduced to a minimum, thereby resulting in the loss of a certain degree of information and, consequently, the steering effect. Thanks to new technologies, simulations can be conducted with the use of automatisms, without great personnel effort. Especially in planning for retail, such approaches are already being used and implemented today.

Apart from automatization, new statistical approaches for the processing of historical data and the forecasting of future developments are finding increasing application. This combination of automatization and predictive approaches is emerging as a significant improvement of performance management overall.

In the course of digitization, operative decision-making processes are also changing, particularly due to the application of predictive analytics. On the basis of previously defined statistical approaches with value and risk limits, probability and forecasting results can be determined. These results can then serve as the basis for automatized decisions, such as sales forecasts or goods planning (see Fig. 4). Volume business has a substantial role in this. Especially for this, the use of automatisms and

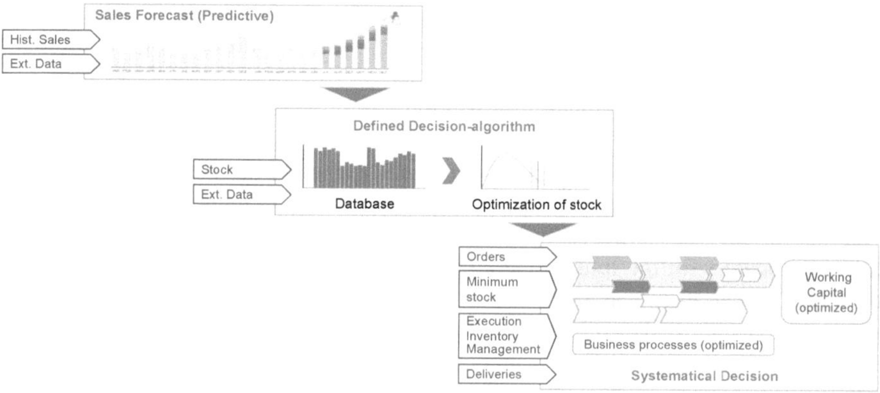

Fig. 4 Automated and function-spanning management

new statistical approaches is beneficial to supporting corporate performance management. For the application of new approaches, both technical and functional, the starting point regarding content is crucial. To this end, comprehensive data is absolutely necessary as factual basis, as well as consistent statistical approaches to differentiated and rapid decision making.

In order to summarize, there are four essential benefits to be gained from automatized and function-spanning performance management:

- Less effort spent on activities with low performance
- More precise results
- More automatization
- Optimization of business processes

On the basis of the aforementioned models, optimal decisions are prepared. Using their results as foundation, defined decision-making algorithms can come to quick, systemically automatized decisions. The automatization is one of the greatest levers of digitization and will also lead to automatization in decision-making processes that will reduce the necessity for human action.

Consequently, the heightening of value-added activities, precise results, and increasing degrees of automatization led to a significant optimization of business processes.

2.6 *Nothing Is Possible Without Seamless Data History*

Traditional reporting will continue to hold an important role in monthly or quarterly reporting processes. Especially complying with internal and external reporting requirements must continue to stay significant. Further, meeting requirements regarding content, structural and data quality of reporting, as well as its timely provision will continue to represent a factor of success for interior and exterior effect. Digitization will also lead to improvements in reporting, resulting from a continuous data supply and the heightened quality of data.

Within internal management, new methods using forecasts to function in a more future-oriented manner are moved into focus and will supply decisive information. In contrast, observing past data does little to add value. As has been exercised in the past, data history constitutes an essential element of future management. However, contrary to previous practice, which used fundamental business development to derive indicators for the future, operative and detailed databases are now consulted to predict developments in the future using mathematical procedures. Apart from the simple and linear trends, complex interlinking and dependences can prospectively be taken into account in decision-making situations. For this, operative details are decisive. A history of monthly values does not supply sufficient groundwork. Operative data, even up to single accounting records, is necessary in order for management to draw conclusions on the basis of new methods. Nonetheless, the human element remains important. Particularly as corrective measures against disruptive or irregular developments and effects, manual adjustments of the models, or rather the databases, are necessary.

The main benefit of this is reflected by significantly reduced efforts, resulting from the high degree of automatization with simultaneously higher accuracy. Decision-making processes become considerably more operative, resulting in apparent added value for the company. Coherences in the data and the integration of the database are leading to a new quality of information. In turn, significantly higher transparency regarding coherences leads to objective bases of decision making and thereby considerably improves the quality of management information. External data is taking on an important role and is undergoing an unprecedented commercialization. The availability of seamless data is increasing, and numerous companies offer the provision of services tailored to companies' needs. To continue being able to offer valuable services in management accounting organization, it is absolutely necessary to promote its integration with classic management accounting and performance management instruments.

3 Corporate Performance Management's New Approaches

3.1 Business and Driver Models Constitute the New Foundation of Performance Management

For some years now, practice has dealt with the development of driver-based performance management concepts. Numerous companies have already decided to establish this focused steering concept form. In doing so, the driver-based approach has been successfully implemented in reporting, planning, and forecasting. Driver-based steering approaches offer the following advantages in performance management:

- All significant drivers of all business models are focused.
- Business development is clearly discernible with the relevant drivers.
- Correlations of the business model are more transparent (business "logic" and "DNA")
- Foundation for the dialogue between all decisive levels of the company.

In this respect, driver-based approaches consistently find usage; they contribute significantly to improved communication between all business areas. In the course of the digitization of performance management, drivers are turning into crucial factors of success. Particularly with the configuration of predictive models, knowledge of the business' most important drivers and control levers is of vital value. Clear starting points of an optimization of a business can already be determined in the drivers. Using driver-based steering concepts, this can be used to derive clear-cut areas for the predictive analyses.

Previously drivers were mostly identified on the basis of logical correlations. These drivers were then mathematically verified in their prospective development using predictive models. While for one thing, existing driver models offer an excellent starting point for model-based analyses, predictive models offer a demonstration of whether changes in drivers actually correlate to the respective performance indicators. Self-learning models reliably supply the developments of individual drivers and recognize and use existing correlations (see Fig. 5). In this way, for example, self-learning models are applied to individual drivers (e.g., returns), or rather operatively underlying topic areas (e.g., predictive analysis on the reasons for returns). To this end, respective source data is consulted in order to determine correlations between drivers and internal and external factors.

The mathematical aggregation toward performance indicators of the steering concept takes place in connection with standard reporting. In doing so, the development of drivers and the relationship to these performance indicators can be demonstrated with proven reporting products. To this end, classical reporting content (e.g., profit-loss accounting, cash flow) and also balance scorecards continue to find application as steering instruments.

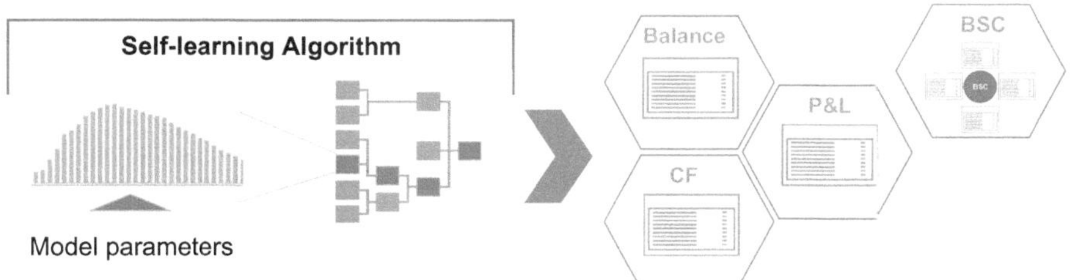

Fig. 5 Self-learning algorithms as indicators for the development of drivers

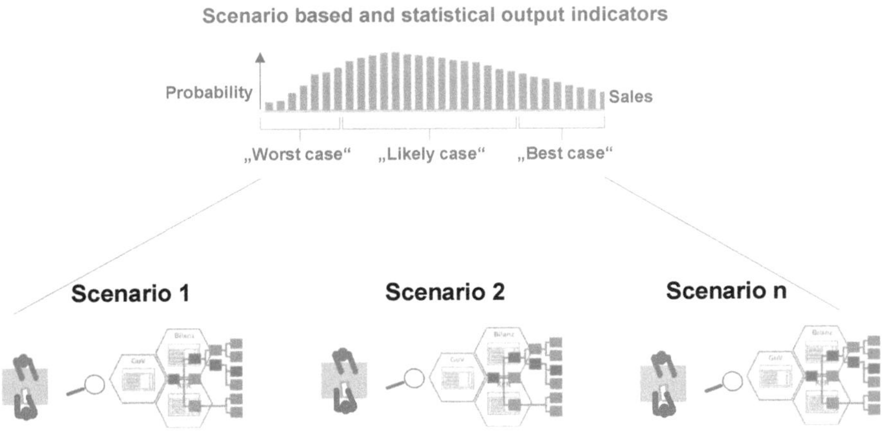

Fig. 6 Detection of scenarios based on important drivers and models

3.2 *Good Scenarios, Finally Manageable: Driver- and Model-Based*

Driver-based approaches offer an excellent basis for observing a company's different scenarios of development. Especially with scenarios, focusing on important drivers is the key factor of success to keep the complexity of scenarios low (Fig. 6).

These on-file models represent the results on the basis of probabilities. Different scenarios can be obtained using the models' parameter steering. Each driver is calculated using separate models. The corporate results can then be displayed, including its dependence on multiple drivers, and can be varied using the model parameters.

Displaying holistic scenarios by human performance is only possible to a certain degree—all the more reason why the focus has to be laid on a few input values. Scenarios will prospectively reach a new degree of quality. Simulations and scenarios that neither find acceptance, nor can be created in a satisfactory cost-benefit ratio, can be controlled by new technologies and predictive models.

3.3 *Performance Management: Now Really Across Companies and Across the Value Chain*

Digitization does not only start with individual processes. It is a change that should be understood company-wide. This entails an integrated steering of processes across companies and across the value chain. Furthermore, this networking does not end with the corporate boundaries, but rather goes beyond them.

Consequently, management accounting's role changes substantively. In the past, management accounting's focus oftentimes was laid on planning and reporting processes on financial information. In the future, it has to cover processes inside and outside the company: beginning with supplier integration, all the way to the evaluation of end-customer data and B2B integration.

Apart from management accounting's altered roles, processes regarding cooperation and integration between companies also change. In future (partially even today), various kinds of information are shared by companies and integrated in their own respective corporate processes.

In benefit analyses, the greater integration of the supply chain is a significant advantage that enables efficiency potentials through a supply chain without interfaces. This high degree of integration inevitably entails a vast basis of information which can in turn be used to optimize and deal with other topics.

4 The New World of Big Data

4.1 Internal and External Data with a High Degree of Detail

The basis of the statistic models is mostly granular raw data that can be aggregated to a key performance indicator when the information is demanded. The aggregation and transformation of data is no longer necessary to the previous degree, thereby maintaining the information content value for analysis and ensuring that the unlimited traceability of the data remains possible.

In order to fully utilize the potential of big data, access to diverse internal and external data is necessary. A prompt availability, even before a complete integration into a central data basis, is crucial to success. This encompasses both internal and external, as well as structured and unstructured, data sources, such as market and customer data (Fig. 7).

The single-circuit system is increasingly establishing itself as a standard in accounting. For steering, this entails significant advantages, as central data storage within an integrated business suite, such as SAP S/4 HANA Simple Finance, is unified and less fragmented. Elaborate comparisons between finance and management accounting are no longer necessary. The integrated data basis is also permanently available for analyses in real time.

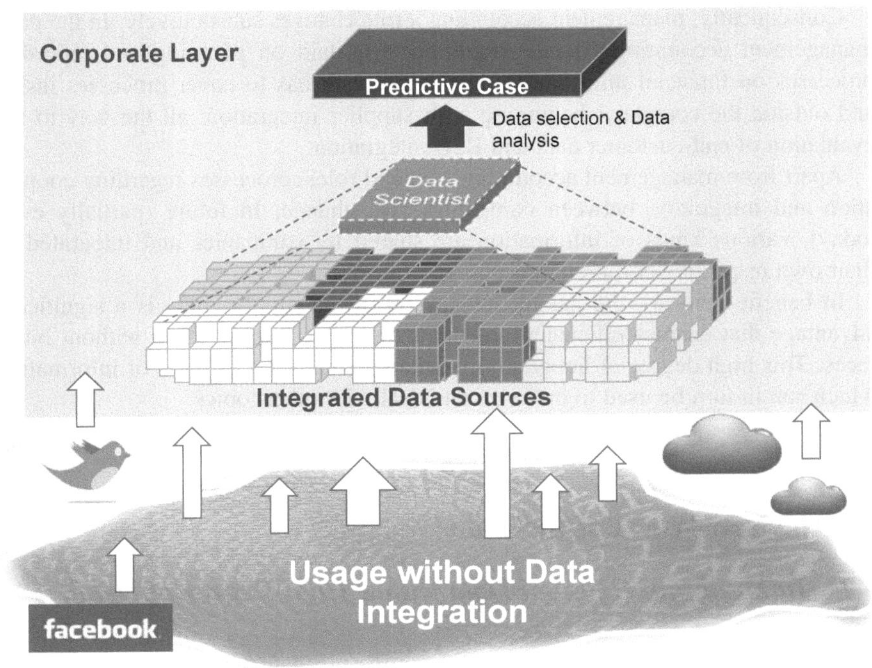

Fig. 7 Integration of internal and external data

4.2 New Data and a Strong Central Governance

As shown with the aspect of organizational changes of the finance function (c.f. Sect. 1 of chapter "Approaches for Steering Multi-Channel Retail Companies"), the integration of various data as well as gaining insights from these datasets signifies substantial competitive advantages for future corporate performance management. However, simply using unstructured datasets and expanding them in an uncoordinated manner will not suffice to lead to the desired benefits and therewith competitive advantages, as a certain standardization of the data structures will also be necessary in future.

Consequently, developing a strong governance role in the company that is charged with the following areas of activity, within big data approaches and the framework of digitization, will become necessary:

- Securing a minimum degree of standardization for the aggregated data
- Regulating the aggregation and usage of information
- Securing data security
- Securing an ethically appropriate usage of the data

In order to keep a data stock evaluable, keeping a minimum degree of standardization will remain indispensable, despite improved methods of analysis.

Consequently, regarding management relevant data, it should be determined both explicitly and proactively which minimum standardization is necessary and which grid should be used to integrate new (internal and external) data into existing data models (e.g., how should existing customer information be arranged within newly emerging segments).

Furthermore, a basic "qualification test" of the data with regard to analysis potential should be conducted in an upstream step. It should be noted that the full potential of this information is oftentimes only evident with the statistical analysis. Nonetheless, a central and sovereign function should still lay down fundamental rules for the acquisition, aggregation, and processing of information and also implement and sustain them.

In this process, a further important aspect is constituted by the securing of the data security. On the one hand, this function refers to the sub-aspect of unauthorized access of this data (from inside or outside), and on the other hand, it refers to the securing of a responsible handling of entrusted data. Consequently, the application of ethical norms and standards is of key importance when answering the question, whether or not everything that could be evaluated should be evaluated. Lastly, this presupposes the proviso that even a central governance function requires regular supervision.

All things considered, this central governance role targets the amalgamation of data potential under the mentioned rules and keeping data evaluable. Further, it should ensure that these can then be used to make better decisions for the purpose of the company as a whole or individual sub-areas.

5 The New Finance Function in the Digital World

In the course of digitization, working methods, processes, requirements and tasks of finance functions in companies change substantially. These areas of change mainly affect the qualification profiles of employees that oftentimes differ greatly from today's actual range of tasks. This raises the question of which role the finance function has in the company as well as the demarcation between its tasks and responsibilities and those of other areas.

5.1 Data Analysis: A New Field of Competences for Highly Trained Specialists

In order to be able to use the aforementioned potential of big data, a new and improved skill set is required: modeling, statistical analytical competencies, and capability in man–machine dialogue are often used to coin the competence profile which today is oftentimes circumscribed with "data scientist." Technological,

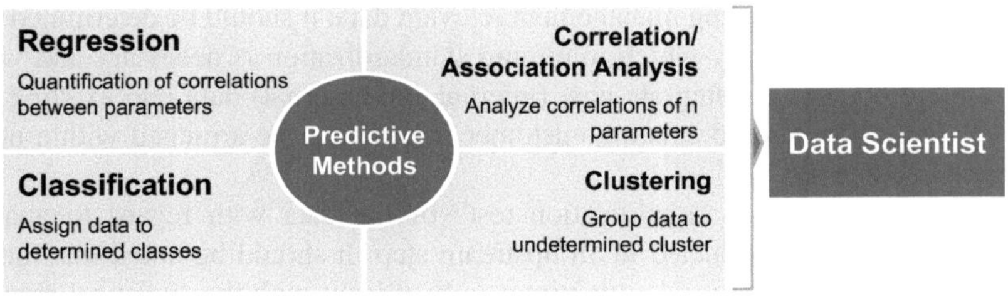

Fig. 8 Fundamental classification of Predictive Analytics Methods

mathematical, and analytical competences are all combined in this role. The methodological toolkit includes areas such as regression, correlation/association, classification, and clustering, as illustrated in Fig. 8.

Presently, these essential competencies are comparatively rare in company practice. However, the modeling and implementation of such analyses does not necessarily have to take place within the management accounting function. A "make-or-buy" decision as well as its organizational placement must be made company individually and under consideration of different strategic points of view. Nevertheless, comprehensive basics in stochastic methods and a sufficient professionality in model development and analysis are always factors crucial to success.

The preservation and expansion of management accountings business partner function lies in these data science competences. Key requirements that management accountants should meet at the least are solid evaluative competences regarding the new analysis instruments, understanding and coordination of this new process—from initiation to decision proposals for the management—as well as the validation and interpretation of the results for the management.

5.2 *Consequences for the Finance Function*

With regard to changes in the role of the finance function (as well as on the basis of the developments of the last few years), one can assume that it will develop toward the "guardian of the corporate financial performance" role even further and therewith also to a strengthening of the business partner role. Today CFO's role is increasingly turning into that of the Chief Performance Officer. The necessity of such a role is not the decisive new insight. However, if one were to compare this role, aspired to by the finance function, with the operative daily business in practice, one could note that processes of data mining, process and commenting reports, as well as the support of operative decisions mostly remain in focus presently (Fig. 9).

With digitization, new possibilities and tools are made accessible to increasingly automatize those operative processes and to turn special attention to understanding, monitoring, and consultation of operative business.

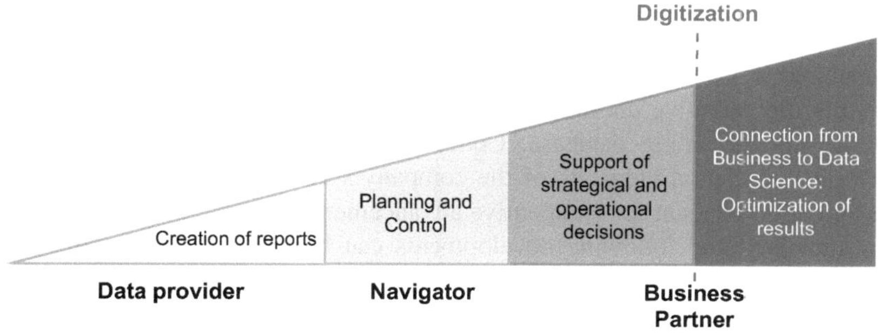

Fig. 9 Business partner functions in management accounting

The categorical division of transactional and analytical processes will also manifest itself in organizational structures: in "finance factories," tasks that can be standardized are bundled more strongly, in order to realize the respective economies of scale on the basis of a still high degree of efficiency pressure. On the other hand, analytical finance competences are bundled within data science centers that are concentrated on data analytics, the ongoing expansion of the data basis, as well as the derivation of new insights gained from the data stock in particular. Applying this, as much benefit as possible should be gained from the information, the "fourth production factor."

Especially relating to the internal positioning of these data science centers within company organization and its profiling, as opposed to that of other departments, respective development tendencies emerge. In the sense of securing data sovereignty, we expect these centers to be settled closely within the finance function. In conclusion, the factors of these units crucial to success can be seen in the aggregation and consolidation of all possible company-internal and external information, securing the obtained data's quality, the continuous cultivation, and expansion of the data basis and deriving the correct deductions on statistical methods and technological support.

The aforementioned organizational categorization of financial organization into "factories" and "data science centers" significantly changes the range of tasks of all employees of the finance function. Conventional standard tasks remain in "factories," which can however be increasingly automatized and replaced by machine automations. Approaches such as "fully automatized invoice auditing and posting" or the "centralization of all relevant transaction activities" are also automated and conducted in centralized manners. This automatization potential can realize significant savings in the finance function by a reduction of personnel requirement. In sum, this is not only true for all familiar accounting tasks but much rather for management accounting topics.

This new role of the "data scientist," as it has been described, is increasingly bundled in so-called data science centers or also "steering labs." The qualification profile in this role requires extensive knowledge in mathematical and statistical approaches and puts a strong emphasis on analytical abilities. These qualifications constitute the preconditions for the best-possible "exploitation" of a centralized data basis. Insofar as a management accountant acquires these skills, he/she can obtain the new role of business partner or work in close confines with data scientists in order to further the operative optimization of the company or to support strategic issues with the corresponding database. Consequently, these data science centers are developing as central elements of the company's value chain and the acquisition of information relevant for competitive advancements.

In summary, the following developments can be recorded for the role of the finance function:

- Management accounting and accounting are relieved by automatization and standardization (reduction of the personnel requirement for repetitive data processing).
- Data Scientists contribute mathematical and analytical abilities and take on a new role.
- Management accountants further the optimization of operative processes on the basis of analytical results and increasingly become a business partner.
- Factory approaches are expanded; analytical competences are made available centrally by data science centers.

6 Outlook: What's Next?

With increasing digitization, the digitization of "steering" will inevitably follow. This contribution describes the fundamental aspects of the forthcoming digital "steering." Apart from the transition toward a future-oriented steering, the next few years will be all the more important for the development of necessary fundamentals:

- Sustainably integration and improving internal databases
- Furthering the reduction of complexity in operative processes
- Improving master data quality
- Focusing and simplifying performance management through driver-based approaches
- Modernization of technological platforms for planning, forecasting, and reporting
- Embedding of new roles and skills within the organization
- Creating acceptance for the imminent transitions.

It is advisable to conduct a "digital maturity assessment" in order to determine the individual positioning and approach to the "digitization of steering." A clear understanding of goals and a roadmap are crucial to success. In doing so, all corporate steering instruments are examined and assessed, and according solution scenarios and target objectives are developed (Fig. 10).

Digitization will significantly change finance functions. Finance functions should ideally take first steps and develop a clear-cut positioning and approach.

Fig. 10 Roadmap "Digital Maturity Assessment"

Sascha Brosig operates as a Principal with Horváth & Partners in the Competence Center Controlling & Finance. His main consulting focus is the improvement of finance and controlling constellations and in particular processes within management accounting such as planning and forecasting.

Carsten Bork was a Principal in the Competence Center Controlling and Finance at the Horváth & Partners Office in Frankfurt am Main. For more than 14 years now, he had accompanied notable customers in the areas of retail, utilities, and consumer goods with the redesign of their steering tools and finance departments. In particular, solutions regarding planning and forecasting are emphasized in his consulting activity.

Walid Mehanna was responsible for the Business Segment Digital Solutions as a Principal with Horváth & Partners. As a computer scientist, he has been highly engaged with digital technologies for nearly twenty years and consults notable companies in the conception and implementation of business intelligence and big data solutions—always with the ambition of implementing actual trends. Apart from his project activities, he is coauthor of the book *Business Intelligence—Grundlagen und praktische Anwendungen* and shares his knowledge in lectures at the University of Stuttgart.

Stefan Tobias operates as a Partner with Horváth & Partners and is responsible for the Business Unit Planning, Reporting and Consolidation. He has been advising and supporting customers for the last 12 years regarding a holistic transformation within controlling and finance.

Part III
How to Approach Performance Management: Best Practice Concepts

Approaches for Steering Multichannel Retail Companies

Philipp Graf von Arnim

Abstract This contribution explains steering concepts for multichannel business models. In doing so, the scope and characteristics of single channels (stationary, print, and online) and the objective of a multichannel strategy are described first. Resulting challenges for management accounting are derived. The solution comprises the adaption of general steering dimensions with a focus on the customer perspective. Modern approaches for the steering of "customers" in a multichannel context are explained. Further typical performance indicators are highlighted to observe multichannel developments.

Keywords Customer centricity · Customer lifetime value · E-commerce · Performance management · Multichannel controlling · Omnichannel controlling

1 Introduction

For quite some time now, retail has been and is being determined by a high multichannel dynamic. Companies are using all possible channels to cater to the individual customer journey. In this digital age, E-commerce and Mobile-commerce are rapidly gaining significance. The Internet provides a maximum amount of information and mobile devices are enabling a continuous state of "being online." An increasing mobility and diversity of customer actions can be seen and these channels are practically asking to be used integratively. For example, information is found on the online shop, where the availability of the product in the nearest store is also confirmed. During the buying phase in the actual store, the customer is able to

This contribution has been originally printed as Graf von Arnim, P.: Lösungsansätze für ein Multi-Channel-Controlling, in Buttkus, M., Neugebauer, A., Kaland, A. (2016), Controlling im Handel: Innovative Ansätze und Praxisbeispiele, pp. 75–90, 2. Edition, Springer Gabler, Wiesbaden.

P. Graf von Arnim (✉)
Retail and Consumer Goods, Horváth & Partners, Hamburg, Germany

M. Buttkus, R. Eberenz (eds.), *Performance Management in Retail and the Consumer Goods Industry*, https://doi.org/10.1007/978-3-030-12730-5_5

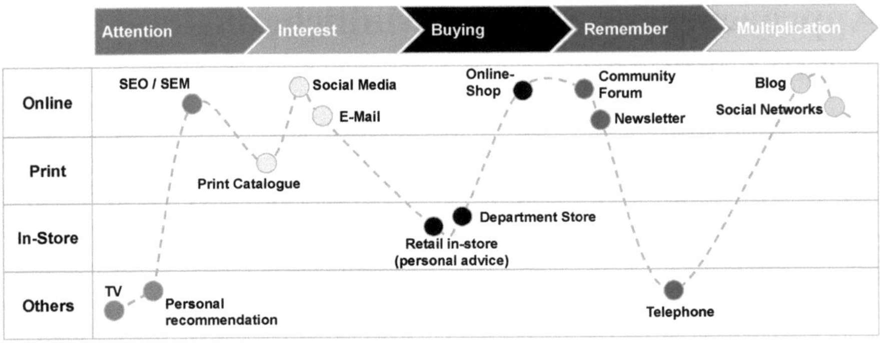

Fig. 1 Example of a customer journey

check further information and alternative options via his smartphone before he goes on to the transaction of an order. Throughout this process, the customer expects a range of services that is congruent throughout all different channels. Separately interacting and functioning channels have been outdated from the customer's point of view and the so-called channel-hopping has become a hygiene factor. The following graph shows the different phases of customer behavior and an exemplary customer journey that makes use of multiple channels (Fig. 1).

There are various retail companies that are progressively implementing an integration of these channels through the adaptation of their business models (e.g., OTTO, Sport Scheck). They are abandoning the concept of isolated and parallel channels and, as a consequence, are faced with assorted challenges in strategic as well as technical, procedural, and organizational aspects. Not only the sales and distribution function but also larger corporate functions such as supply chain or management accounting are influenced by this.[1]

This contribution will focus on steering approaches in a multichannel context. In doing so, the topic will be introduced generically but limited to the scope of significant channels (stationary, print, and online).[2] Subsequently, the primary focus will lie on the treatment of possible challenges and the demonstration of specific solutions.

[1]The author uses the English word "management accounting" to translate the German term "controlling." Please refer to the discussion in the preface.

[2]Other retail and operational types such as teleshopping or structural sales will not be considered.

2 The Fundamentals of Multichannel Retail

2.1 Defining the Objectives of a Multichannel Strategy

In the initial phase of a multichannel development, retail companies are faced with strategic questions of whether the expansion of existing channels is constructive or not, which channels are suited for a specific context, and how these are best arranged and developed. To solve these strategic questions, the main objectives of a multichannel strategy are essential. Three aspects should be emphasized:

1. A significant objective that must initially be named is the acquisition of new customers, as these may be reached through new channels. For example, an exclusively stationary concept will lose its regional limitation by opening an online shop. This opening of the online channel will consequently enable a regular adaptation of positioning in accordance with customer perceptions. For instance, some established companies are endeavoring to reach a younger and more online customer group. Further, opening new stores will promote publicity and advertise the company through physical presence.
2. A second objective is increasing the value of existing customers. It derives from the possibility of catering to the customer on multiple channels. This is not limited to a single additional sales opportunity but is much rather the opportunity of applying extra marketing activities to different phases of buying. As a consequence, the risk of losing customers to competitors can be reduced. The basis assumption is that customer value increases with the opening of additional channels and that this increase can be greater than the sum of all single channels combined.[3]
3. The third objective is aspiring toward a higher efficiency, which could possibly be set by a higher level of revenue (scaling effect). Moreover, it is possible to create synergies by the integration of channels. An example for this could be the possibility of collecting relevant customer data over all available channels, in order to appeal and cater to those customers.

It is worthwhile noting that these objectives are not universally valid and hence transforming from the existing business model to one governed by a multichannel concept is not necessarily appropriate or relevant. This is much rather a central strategic issue which the management should concern itself with and must be solved for each individual case. During this process, company-specific preconditions such as market positioning, competitive structures, and existing competences (concerning e.g. product range, employees) must all be taken into account.

[3] Rittinger (2014), p. 10.

2.2 *Functions and Specifics of Sales Channels*

After having defined the objectives of a multichannel strategy, it is now necessary to determine which suitable channels lead to the realization of these objectives and which concrete functions they will assume. In doing so, the specifics of these channels must be taken into account. Especially the shopping experience for customers can be very distinct and different demands can be met by the former. This is especially true for the comparison of stationary retail with distance retail (online and print). As clarification, the functions and specifics of the channels used will be generally defined below.

1. Stationary: The customer undergoes a comprehensive purchasing experience by being able to touch and try on the products and, in addition, can enjoy personal advice. Furthermore, multifarious possibilities of product staging are conceivable. The distributor is able to actively shape and configure prices; however, an automated and customer individual pricing is not possible in this channel. The direct approach to the customer is unincisive and usually occurs in the form of wide-ranging advertising media such as newspaper supplements. The local store participates largely through store traffic by pedestrians.

   Complete information concerning the customer's previous sourcing and purchasing trends is usually not accessible in stationary retail. Transaction information can only be collected after the buying process but is predominantly incomplete. For example, if the buying transaction is done with cash, relevant data such as the customer's name and address are not obtained.
2. Print: The customer receives the opportunity of rummaging through the range of products that a retailer offers by means of a catalogue. The possibilities of product staging are limited to the scope of its presentation in the form of imagery. The purchasing experience is almost completely unincisive: prices can be actively shaped depending on the catalogue, but they are and remain fixed after its printing. An alteration of prices only becomes possible with the next print catalogue (e.g., use of a newsletter).

   In this channel as well as the previous one, customer data concerning previous information and buying behavior is not collectable. However, in contrast to the store, complete transaction data and customer addresses are obtained.
3. Online: Throughout the online channel (e.g., online shops, apps), the customer has the possibility of accessing the product range without physically having to be present. The customer's buying behavior on the online channel correlates with that of the print channel but is generally less established. Nonetheless, this can be upgraded through personalization and the technical possibilities of product staging. Further, pricing is adaptable for each individual customer in the sense of dynamic pricing. The customer can be reached individually and pointedly through the instruments of online marketing (e.g., search engine optimization, search engine marketing, newsletters).

   The online channel can obtain complete transaction data and the company generally has more knowledge of the customer journey, although this knowledge is limited to this specific channel.[4] If the customer has used, is using, or will use other channels for information or buying purposes remains unknown. Nevertheless, it must be said that the online channel is well suited to the task of gaining customer data, which can in turn be used by the other channels. Insights gained from the clicking habits of customers in the online shop (e.g., an analysis of page views) could for example be used to shape product presentation in the physical store.

2.3 Structuring the Multichannel Strategy

After having defined and determined suitable channels, the next step is structuring the multichannel business model and actually defining this process. As previously portrayed, customers expect a strong integration of the aforementioned channels with a congruent and consistent range of services. In accordance with this, retail companies generally aim toward constructing an integrated channel concept and subsequently benefit maximally from these objectives.

Securing an effective and efficient multichannel concept in practical application is oftentimes subject to a development process and is further dependent on internal and external preconditions (e.g., technology). This development process could be described as in the following:

- After the decision of opening an online shop as a second channel with marketing function has been made, this channel can initially exist isolated—without linking to the established stationary capacity. For example, a new "E-commerce department" is created, which stays completely isolated from the preceding and present structure of the company.
- In the further course of this process, both channels are partially interlinked (crosschannel); e.g., the customer is given the possibility of ordering a product in the online shop and can collect it in a store nearby. However, this interlinking does not connect channels over all processes.
- During the evolution to a company led by an omnichannel, the customer's parallel usage of channels is enabled through a complete interlinking of all process stages. Through this all channels are linked completely in both a technical and organizational sense. For example, the customer can scan a QR code on a product and thus gain further information such as the delivery date in case of an online order.

The following graph attempts to illustrate and represent the previously characterized development from a single-channel concept to one governed by an omnichannel graphically (Fig. 2).

[4]Exceptions are possible results if the consumer were to delete his cookies.

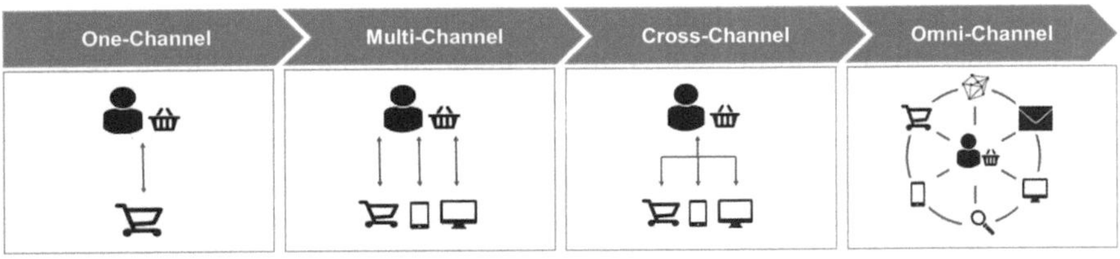

Fig. 2 Maturation process to an omnichannel approach (Raut 2014)

However, it must be added that not all companies envisage multichannel systems with equal channels. Oftentimes, single channels are credited with different roles.[5] For example, a concept that has previously operated completely in a stationary form will likely keep the stationary channel as the predominant one and merely use the online channel to function as source of information. The online channel's main objective in this situation is to motivate customers to buy a product in a stationary store.

In summary, it can be said that with the introduction of a multichannel strategy, positive target setting, customer ties and growth, as well as a higher grade of efficiency are to be expected. In this process, the objectives, the selection of suitable channels, and finally, the precise configuration all underlie company-specific preconditions, and therefore, it is necessary to consider each case individually.

3 Approaches for Steering Multichannel Retail Companies

3.1 Objectives of Multichannel Management Accounting

On the basis of the previously explicated multichannel strategy, a suitable management accounting concept must now be defined. This appears to be necessary in order to effectively and efficiently master the tasks of management accounting. The chosen state of development of the multichannel strategy can for instance influence the prioritization of channel observation within the management accounting concept.

This chapter will depict typical challenges that management accounting is faced with in a multichannel strategy and offer solution approaches. This process will be limited to the following aspects, which show a particular relevance to current practice:

- Prioritizing the observation of customers in management accounting
- Developing customer segmentation
- Prioritizing channel observation in management accounting concepts
- Crosschannel harmonization of data and KPIs

[5]Heinemann (2011), p. 15.

- Management accounting crosschannel cause–effect relationships
- Developing management accounting aspirations

3.2 Prioritizing the Observation of Customers in Management Accounting

Within a multichannel strategy, the addition of new channels alone creates new management accounting objects that supplement existing objects (e.g., regions, segments). Therefore, it is necessary to monitor the prioritization of these objects in a management accounting concept and where appropriate revise them.

The observation of the customer oftentimes gains significance in the process of opening an online channel, as this leads to previously inaccessible customer data becoming available. On this basis, it is possible to place the customer and his habits in the center of observation and adapt the management accounting concept accordingly. This seems to be especially advisable, if a change in customer habit is the trigger of change toward a multichannel strategy.

The most significant challenges of establishing customer observation in a management accounting concept are the collection of qualitative data concerning the customer journey along the channels. In practice, complete customer data concerning channels is rarely obtainable, which can limit a complete treatment of customer habits. However, there are different measures that can be taken in order to enhance the customer database. For instance, customer cards or surveys can be used in the stationary channel to secure customer data. Further, providing WIFI in stores can provide data on customer movement in the store. The print channel could use different product numbers than the online shop. If the customer uses the print product number to place an order online, it can be seen if the customer has gathered information from the catalogue during his customer journey.

Besides the aforementioned challenges of necessary data enhancement, the consideration and observation of customers can in itself be a new feature, which needs to be conceptualized. This is especially true for companies that have their origin in the stationary sector. In order to successfully conceptualize customer observation, the segmentation of customers into customer sections is a central challenge.

3.3 Developing Customer Segmentation

3.3.1 Customer Groups: Cohorts

There are different approaches to the segmentation of customers into customer groups. One approach outlines the observation of customer cohorts and originates from concepts of online retail. In this approach, customers are sorted into cohorts that correspond with their point of acquisition. A time slice could for example

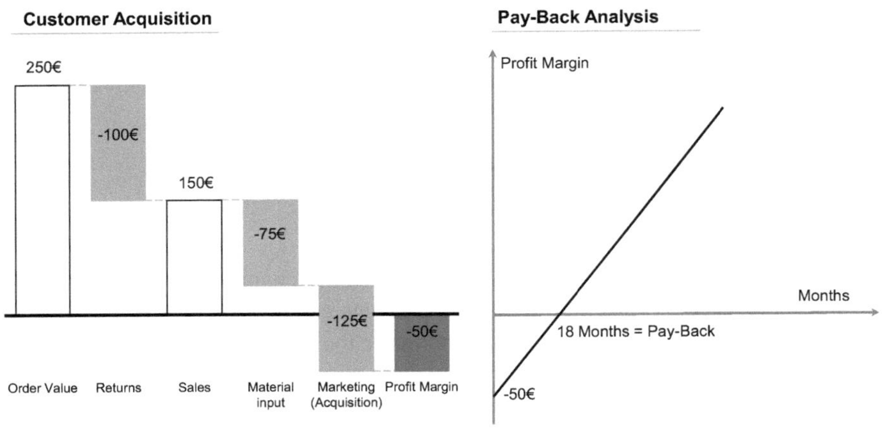

Fig. 3 Connection between customer acquisition and payback period

function as a cluster, so that all new customers of one month are defined as a customer cohort.

Relevant KPIs and these customer cohorts could together create a central element of assessing a company's development, as the customer lifetime value is oftentimes regarded as the central KPI. Customer lifetime value allocates all assignable costs and revenues to a customer cohort. Increasing the customer lifetime value should therefore be a significant objective of the company's development. The Payback period of customer acquisition can also be derived from the customer lifetime value. Observing customer cohorts in the context of payback periods is well suited to management accounting marketing activity. A possible marketing budget could for instance be derived from a target payback period (e.g., 18 months) suggested by management required to cover the costs of customer acquisition. This will then be allocated to specific marketing measures based on empirical values (Fig. 3).

3.3.2 Customer Groups: Frequency of Buying

A second approach to customer segmentation is grouping the customers in accordance with their buying frequency. This approach is oftentimes implemented by mainly print companies. The customers are typically subdivided into new customers, regular customers, and reactivated customers. As a rule, companies tend to define these customer groups depending on their specific situation. The following example depicts possible definitions for the aforementioned customer groups:

1. New customers: The customer was acquired in the ongoing season.
2. Regular customers: The customer was acquired at least two seasons previously and was active at least once in the last three seasons.
3. Reactivated customers: The customer has not been active over the last three seasons, but his/her last activity was within the last eight seasons.

In this process, a customer's activity can be derived from his/her revenue perspective. According to this perspective, the active customer is one that has created revenue over a relevant time period. The relation of the number of active customers in contrast with the amount of customers in total is oftentimes an important KPI.

Customer groups regularly have divergent manifestations of relevant indicators (e.g., product return ratio, average shopping cart, sales per order). For example, a higher product return ratio can be expected by a new customer as opposed to a regular customer. A change in the structure of customers can therefore have a decisive influence on business development. In this process, creating and observing customer groups aids the management accounting function. Furthermore, the development of customer groups leads to strategic aspects such as the categorization of the business model into different stages becoming embeddable. For example, business models with a high percentage of new customers will be designated to an early stage. In contrast, a high percentage of customers that need reactivating implies a saturated stage.

3.4 Prioritizing Channel Observation Within Management Accounting Concepts

As has been shown previously, an increase in the number of channels used is usually accompanied by the necessity of adapting the management accounting concept to this change. Apart from customer observation, interlinking channel observation with management accounting concepts being defined, it must thereafter be decided if, how, and by whom the channels are observed.

Defining channel observation within the management accounting concept is one of the central roles of multichannel management accounting, in order to secure efficacy and efficiency. In the initial phase of multichannel transformations, the channels can function as separately acting organizational units with partially parallel structures. Channel specific data is collected and indicators are defined and can be evaluated by decentralized management accounting units. In practice, the company's overall management accounting tends to ascribe too much significance to the observation of single channels and so neglects the influence that channels can have on each other. As a consequence, incorrect conclusions concerning revenue could be drawn from neglecting this influence. A channel that primarily serves for information purposes but is not used to order products can thus be underestimated in its economic value. Possibly, this channel can even have a negative profit margin so that its existence in general is questioned.

When embedding channel observation into management accounting concepts, it is important to use the precise configuration of the multichannel strategy as orientation. Focusing on single channels may be necessary during the early phases of the company's configuration. Especially if an established channel is enhanced by a second channel, this channel will, according to strategic considerations, have a

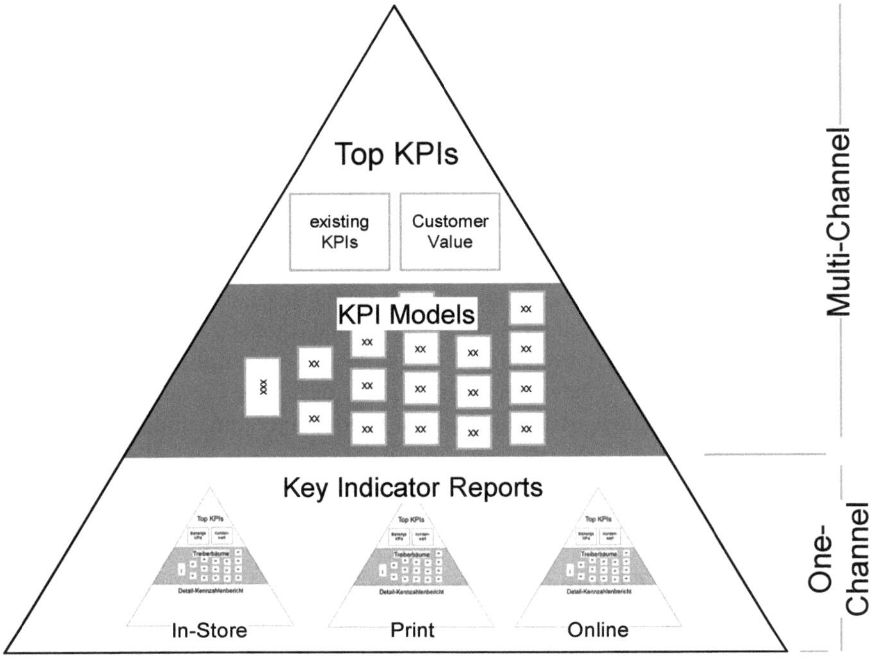

Fig. 4 Prioritizing channel observation

large part in the company's revenue in the long run (e.g., OTTO). The sales development of this new channel can become one of the management accounting concept's top KPIs. As a counterexample, a multichannel company with a stationary channel and an online channel, which merely uses the online channel for information purposes, will not need to embed channel observation into its management accounting concept.

For management accounting, it is advisable to observe channels subordinate to a holistic observation of the company. In the long run, the economic success of a multichannel company depends on the performance of the entire company and not that of the individual channels. This demand increases with the multichannel strategy's level of development or rather the integration of channels. In the sense of a pyramid structure, channel-specific management accounting is arranged beneath holistic top KPIs and KPI driver models and takes on an explanatory character (Fig. 4).

If observing the channels exhibits relevance to a management accounting concept, this channel observation should be linked with customer observation. In doing so, both general and channel-specific customer habits can be assessed, and this further augments the previously depicted approaches (cohorts, buying frequency). Possible customer groups for this approach are online-only customers and/or multichannel customers, and comprehensive connections and contexts should be included in target setting. A proposal made in literature is for example process cost accounting. This accounting method uses channel-specific and general overheads according to the process' grade of utilization by the customer.[6] Nonetheless, the multichannel context creates a considerable restriction for process cost accounting, as can be shown by the complexity of the customer journey: an aspect being that a crosschannel process such as "product search" is more or less pronounced, depending on the specific channel, and there are rarely complete datasets on this process. A pragmatic approach to observing multichannel contexts without complete knowledge of the customer journey is constituted by the three by three matrix featured in 3.6.

3.5 *Crosschannel Harmonization of Data and KPIs*

A crosschannel harmonization should be the goal of an effective and efficient multichannel management accounting. This is especially true for affairs that are comparable or identical in a crosschannel analysis and encompass data and their evaluation through dimensions and indicators.

As a result, one of the challenges that companies are faced with is that a multichannel strategy practically leads to an increase of objects in the dimensional model, business processes, and information systems. Apart from the rising amount of data, the quality of data obtained by each channel can be unincisive. This is especially true for customer observation, in which the online channel provides (almost) complete data and displays a high degree of relevance.

Furthermore, specific dimensions, indicators, and indicator systems are focused depending on the channel. This inevitably leads to so-called channel specifics. On the other hand, this could be a result of the circumstance that these channels may have been constructed separately. For the same issues and circumstances, completely different labels may have established themselves. The very same "average receipt" used in stationary retail may be named "average order value" in online retail. Clearly, a crosschannel harmonization is lacking.

For management accounting, additional data is important to gaining valuable information, but on the other hand, this data points toward an increasing complexity. In order to appraise the ever-growing quantity of data both efficiently and effectively and so turn it into a competitive advantage, the data must be merged into an integrated data warehouse, where it is managed and harmonized in the process. This harmonizing of data and indicators must be implemented in a comprehensive data model that can introduce unified labels and definitions. These should then be

[6]Schröder (2005), p. 271.

made obligatory for both the decentralized management accounting unit and the company's management accounting in general.[7]

3.6 Management Accounting Crosschannel Cause–Effect Relations

Apart from the previously described harmonization, it is necessary to control the complex and crosschannel cause–effect relations. This necessity arises through the specifics of channels, which influence the business development of multichannel companies regularly by way of structural effects. This challenge increases, if these relations are only describable in qualitative but not in quantitative terms (e.g., in case of the customer journey). The revenue correlation of channels to one another can for instance constitute a relevant challenge for planning and reporting. The question rises, to which extent channels cannibalize each other or produce a push effect. This lack of transparency evident in cause–effect relations complicates the allocation of success further.

The implementation of general indicator systems is recommendable in order to control crosschannel cause–effect relations. An indicator system can be defined as the illustration of the business model through quantitative and qualitative indicators which can be depicted by a KPI model.[8] Associated indicators are linked within the driver model in order to visualize these correlations. Management accounting business models with indicator systems enable the analysis of actual to budget deviations, with which purpose-oriented measures can be taken early on. Indicator systems are best derived according to the following principles:

- Alignment with the business model
- Sufficient interlinking
- Cascaded and balanced indicators
- Materiality and measurability of portrayed drivers

The basis of expanding indicator systems is a knowledge of the present business model, including the specifics of each channel and their interdependencies. These should be ascertained, assessed, and documented, thereby creating a central understanding within the company's management accounting for the increasingly complex relations.

In a multichannel indicator system, clusters for indicators of comparable circumstances should be created and allocated. "Conversion rate" in online retail and "ordering rate" in print retail should for example be allocated to the same level.

[7]For example, the "average receipt" (stationary sector), "average contract value" (print sector), and "average order value" (online shop) are combined by the term "average shopping cart." This general term can then be further specified by reference to the channel (e.g., "average shopping cart online").
[8]Reichmann (2001), p. 56.

Fig. 5 Example of a multichannel indicator system

Order / Information	Stationary	Print	Online
Stationary	70%	10%	15%
Print	15%	90%	25%
Online	15%	-	60%

Fig. 6 Exemplary values for multichannel indicators

Through this allocation, relocating figures in the indicator system is simplified and crosschannel developments and structural effects can be portrayed by comparable indicators.

Figure 5 depicts an example for an indicator system with a multichannel perspective.

An indicator system with consideration of multichannel contexts used in practice is the nine-field matrix. The nine resulting fields are respective to the three sales channels used by the company. (Two by two matrices are used by companies with two sales channels, resulting in four fields.) By means of this matrix, the imbalance between the sales channel to gain information (the customer has obtained information) and the sales channel to buy a product (or to place an order)—and thereby the customer journey—is depicted pragmatically. The correlations are portrayed as an example in the Fig. 6.[9]

This example shows that information obtainable by the customer in the store has the most relevance for creating revenue. 70% of all orders in the store are initiated through information obtained within the store. Print (15%) and online retail (15%) only push sales marginally. Online retail is essentially used as ordering media and only has a limited push on other channels. In this specific example, using the online channel to obtain product information has no influence on revenue in print retail.

[9]Schröder and Schettgen (2006), p. 44.

Information \ Order	Stationary	Print	Online
Stationary	In-Store-Purchase	Print-Order (In-Store)	Internet-Order (In-Store)
Print	In-Store-Order (Print)	Print-Purchase	Internet-Order (Print)
Online	In-Store-Order (Online)	Print-Order (Online)	Online-Purchase

Fig. 7 Example of multichannel indicators

On the basis of this observation, indicators that are taken into account by the management accounting concept can be defined. The following table contains a suitable example (Fig. 7).

As indicated in 3.4, insights gained from three by three matrices can be used to determine the customer lifetime value within each channel. In this process, revenue made by a customer within a sales channel is allocated to the different channels used during the buying process. In the earlier (nine-field matrix) example, 15% of the revenue created by the customer in online retail would be ascribed to stationary retail and 15% to print retail. Consequently, the customer worth previously calculated per channel is now enhanced by a multichannel context. This method can also be used for customer general profit margin calculations for each channel, and the results depict the actual performance of a channel within a multichannel context. Furthermore, the three by three matrix can provide management accounting with other valuable information (e.g., planning). The effect of increasing the marketing activity of one channel (e.g., opening a new store or raising the budget for online marketing) on the other channels can be approximated and taken into account as an additional factor.

However, it must be said that the circumstance of incomplete data concerning the customer journey has a negative impact on the applicability of the online channel. Nonetheless, the three by three matrix in particular can give a pragmatic approach toward depicting multichannel contexts. If a random sample of customers has been taken to examine the relations of information and ordering within the multichannel concept, then these can be used as premise-based assumption to these relations concerning all customers.

3.7 *Developing Management Accounting Aspirations*

A further aspect in shaping a multichannel management accounting is developing management accounting aspirations. Due to real-time data, there is an increasing demand for a higher speed of reaction and a shorter time span for decision-making processes. Management accounting should be proactive and take formative influence on business activity. The observation of past data, possibly in order to determine deviations of the present development from that of the preceding year or that of a plan, has decreased in favor of a future-oriented prognosis.[10] Automated analyses and a faster reaction time have become essential. By introducing dashboards and graphic representations of business development, resources for extensive cementation within reporting can be saved. As a result, demonstrating cause relations and courses of action can be focused. Within the organization of management accounting, establishing the role of the controller as business partner continuously gains relevance. In this sense, one could speak of a culture change in management accounting which is not referenced to the use of modern tools but also includes methods and standards.

The high dynamic of market or rather business development should be met with a high degree of flexibility. In this sense, resources should be planned efficiently and the degree of detail reduced reasonably to aspects that are relevant to management accounting. The application of business models, which can be used to simulate different developments and scenarios and thereby discover chances and risks, provides assistance to this end. Thus, in conjunction with the aforementioned driver models, cause and effect relations can be depicted and premises can be continuously adapted in the modeling process.

Furthermore, multichannel companies require a more intense interlinking of management accounting elements in the business. This is especially true if its channels are still functioning as separate units. This interlinking includes the networking of product managers in each channel. An agile crosschannel cooperation is key to the quality of management accounting.

4 Conclusion

Subsequent to the development of a multichannel strategy, a viable management accounting concept must be defined: the objective being a multichannel concept that is also embedded and incorporated in management accounting. In general, this makes an adaptation of the management accounting concept or rather the management accounting elements necessary. Due to the high value that multichannel concepts place on customer habits, it seems advisable to focus on observing the customer. To achieve significant results, the customers should be arranged into customer groups. Moreover, an observation of channels should be holistic in that it considers all available channels, and because of this holistic approach, the observation tends to have an explanatory character. The harmonization and interlinking of all channels as well as mapping cause and effect relations represent the central challenges of this development. The latter is best mastered by introducing a multichannel indicator system such as a three by three matrix.

---

[10]Micha et al. (2015), pp. 632–633.

In summary, there is no universally valid concept to arranging a multichannel management accounting. It is much rather essential to represent the company-specific and distinct multichannel strategy, and all its characteristics, within the management accounting concept. As the multichannel strategy is often subject to a development process, the management accounting functions must remain flexible and adaptable.

References

Heinemann G (2011) Cross-channel-management, 3rd edn. Springer Gabler, Wiesbaden

Micha MA, van Wahden J, Bruhn K, Felsmann D (2015) Erfolgreicher Aufbau und Betrieb von Cross-Channel-Projekten – neue, komplexe Herausforderungen für das Controlling. Controlling 27:630–637

Raut S (2014) Digital transformation impacting customer journey!! http://customerthink.com/digital-transformation-impacting-customer-journey/. Accessed 17 April 2016

Reichmann T (2001) Controlling mit Kennzahlen und Managementberichten. Grundlagen einer systemgestutzten Controlling-Konzeption, 6th edn. Vahlen, München

Rittinger S (2014) Multi-Channel Retailing - Prinzip, Konzepte und Erfolgsfaktoren. Springer, Saarbrücken

Schröder H (2005) Multichannel-retailing. Springer, Essen

Schröder H, Schettgen G (2006) Multi-Channel-Retailing und kundenbezogene Erfolgsrechnung. Thexis (4):43–47

Philipp Graf von Arnim operates as a Senior Project Manager with Horváth & Partners for the Competence Center Retail and Consumer Goods in Hamburg. He has broad expertise in the context of omnichannel retail, especially concerning the transformation of business models to omnichannel concepts with appropriate steering concepts.

Managing Retail and Wholesale Business by Performance Indicators

Illustrated by an Example of METRO

Bernd Seufert

Abstract Performance indicators are essential tools for the effective management and the efficient steering of business in retail companies. The selection of the right set and the correct use of performance indicators can help to foster the success of a business and to reduce the effort of managing a company. To ensure the positive effect of management by performance indicators, the chosen set of figures has to reflect the individual business model and has to be aligned with the steering logic of the company.

This contribution provides an overview on how to develop and apply the right set of performance indicators in retail business, as illustrated by an example of the METRO. The focus of the example is on the effective management of the brick-and-mortar business on the operational level by use of performance indicators. In this regard, the given example describes how to guarantee the comparability of performance indicators by respecting store, sales lines, and country-specific characteristics and by laying the basis for benchmarking and profound business decisions.

Keywords Operational management · Performance driver tree · Performance indicators · METRO · System of key figures · Wholesale business

An adaption of this contribution has been originally printed as Langer, T., Seufert, B.: Kennzahlen zur Steuerung im Handel: Veranschaulichung anhand des Beispiels der METRO Group, in Buttkus, M., Neugebauer, A., Kaland, A. (2016), Controlling im Handel: Innovative Ansätze und Praxisbeispiele, pp. 217–230, 2. Edition, Springer Gabler, Wiesbaden.

B. Seufert (✉)
Retail and Consumer Goods, Horváth & Partners, Hamburg, Germany

M. Buttkus, R. Eberenz (eds.), *Performance Management in Retail and the Consumer Goods Industry*, https://doi.org/10.1007/978-3-030-12730-5_6

1 Definition of Performance Indicators

1.1 Performance Indicators and System of Key Figures

Performance indicators are a set of measures that a company uses to document its performance and measure its success, development over time, and progress in relation to a specified goal. It is one of the most important controlling[1] instruments and also essential for the management and steering of a retail business. Classification of performance indicators can be made by different attributes and their respective characteristics.

The most common way to classify performance indicators is the statistical way in which absolute numbers and ratios are differentiated. A downside of absolute numbers is the isolated view and a lack of relation to other figures. With that, a reliable conclusion cannot be drawn that easily. This is also why ratios have a higher acceptance and information value.

Another possibility of segregating performance indicators is their classification into leading indicators and lagging indicators. Leading indicators anticipate future developments by detecting trends and structural changes. This kind of indicator is essential for companies' ability to generate competitive advantages, although it is hard to quantify them. On the contrary, lagging indicators already reflect existing or past developments.

Furthermore, financial and non financial key figures can be differentiated. Some of the most common performance indicators are based on financial data from income statement or balance sheet components and may also report changes in sales growth or in expense categories. Non financial key figures are measures used to assess activities that a company sees as important for achieving its strategic objectives. Typical non financial performance indicators include measures that relate to customer relationships, employees, operations, quality, cycle time, and the organization's supply chain or its pipeline.

Several further options for classifying performance indicators exist. Input performance indicators measure assets and resources invested in or used to generate business results. In contrast, output performance indicators measure the financial and non financial results of business activities. Qualitative performance indicators reflect a descriptive characteristic, an opinion, or a trait, while quantitative performance indicators show a measurable characteristic resulting from counting, adding, or averaging numbers.

Performance indicators can be joined in a system of key figures or in a driver tree. These concepts arrange figures by considering their logical dependencies and respecting the overall strategic target setting of the company simultaneously.[2] By creating transparency and making performance quantifiable, systems of key figures

[1]The author uses the English word "controlling" to translate the German term "controlling." Please refer to the discussion in the preface.

[2]Reichmann (2001), p. 56

and driver trees are a significant element in the performance management process of retail companies nowadays. Management based on figures provides the possibility of specifying performance indicators and of defining target values for them. Using the recognition of deviations from defined target values, countermeasures can be derived and implemented.

The definition and implementation of a system of key figures are challenging. In general, the linking of strategic and operational management has to be considered, and different data formats have to be connected. To take up the challenges in setting up a proper system of key figures, it is useful to start at the actual core of each company. This means first developing a business model-specific steering logic and then defining the steering-relevant performance indicators afterward.

In order to set up a business model-specific steering logic, the defined framework of the strategy has to be taken into account. These include, for example, the value proposition of the company, the defined customer interaction, and established earnings models. Furthermore, the defined steering logic has to consider the leadership approach and relevant management dimensions. These cornerstones of the business model are the foundation of identifying and deriving relevant performance indicators on a strategic level and lay the basis for steering, reporting, and planning.

1.2 Criteria for Performance Indicator Development

There exist hundreds of performance indicators to manage and steer business. In fact, it is not easy to choose the best matching indicators. The overarching goal of choosing the right performance indicators or set of key figures is to support and foster company success by also reducing the effort for management and the steering of the business. To be able to reduce this effort, performance indicators have to exhibit certain characteristics.

Performance indicators have to increase transparency for the management of the business. Linking the business model-specific steering logic and the framework of the strategy with the relevant performance indicators enables a strategy-consistent steering of the company. Furthermore, examining the specific calculation model of performance indicators indicates its drivers and thus gives the management the opportunity to influence them proactively at an early stage.

EBIT, one of the most common and most used performance indicators, is based on earnings figures such as turnover and cost of sales. A closer look at turnover shows that this measure is dependent on figures such as sold quantity and realized price. Furthermore, sold quantity and realized price also depend on external developments such as customer satisfaction or overall economic growth to a certain extent. Existing trends or public opinion can also have an effect on external developments. This simple example clearly shows the interconnection of external indicators, internal measures on operational level, and financial earnings figures and their impact on a company's performance indicators for strategic management.

The setup and concept of a system of key figures has to reflect the described interdependencies of performance indicators on strategic and operational levels.

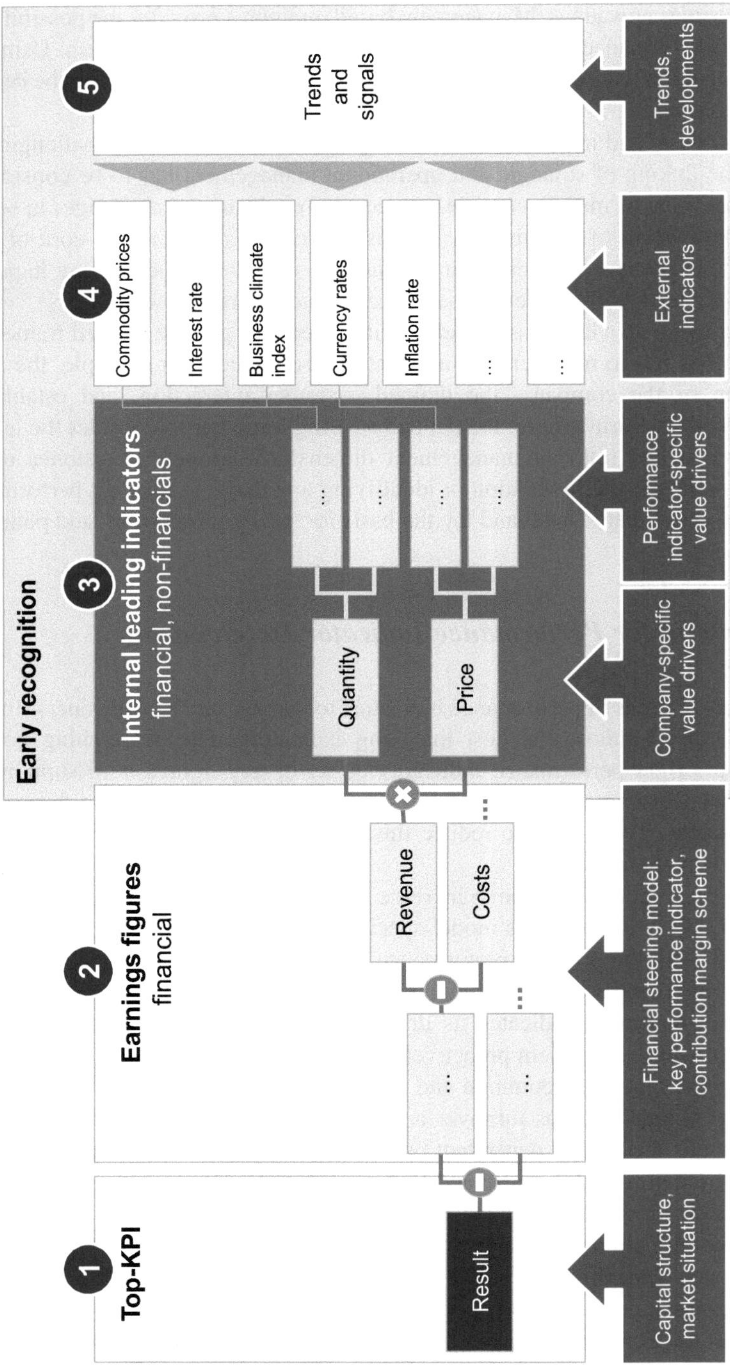

Fig. 1 Comprehensive system of key figures based on value drivers

Furthermore, it must point out the existing drivers for success. Respecting both requirements genuinely increases transparency for a business' management (Fig. 1).

Besides the connection of performance indicators and their drivers, figures have to deliver reliable data and high-quality information based on "single source of truth." Furthermore, it is also important to lay the foundation for an efficient data supply. In this regard, a fast availability of precise information, combined with low effort for coordination and preparation of data, is key and ensures acceptance throughout the company.

Ensuring that effective performance indicators are defined and an efficient data supply of precise information is established, management must also make sure to anchor the controlling instrument within the organization and to win employees' hearts and minds for the use of and understanding of the concept.

Promoting the concept within the organization can be supported by various actions. Employees and persons affected must absolutely understand how performance indicators are defined, the message they stand for, how to calculate them, in which frequency, and from which data exactly. It is also important that performance indicators are owned by one specific person. Measures need an owner to make sure they are reported and used for the benefit of the business. In this regard, performance indicators also have to inspire the right behavior and make obvious which actions are correct, to achieve better results. Furthermore, the measures must be tracked regularly and uniformly in order to be able to create transparency on development and progress.

Although important characteristics and criteria for the definition and selection of relevant performance indicators are well known, maintaining and adjusting a system of key figures remains a difficult and recurring task. Fast-moving markets and rising complexity, as well as new digital technologies like big data and predictive analytics, lead to changes in a company's strategy and its business model.

1.3 Performance Indicators in Retail and Wholesale Businesses

Competitive pressure due to financially sound retail and wholesale chains, consumer goods manufacturers opening own stores, stagnating revenue, and increasing costs requires fast response and high adaptability of retail companies. Furthermore, digitization results in strong market dynamics and aggressive pricing. The availability of relevant information for decision-making and therefore also the use of systems of key figures and performance indicators are increasingly gaining importance for retail and wholesale companies. In this regard, performance indicators have to be able to take industry specifics into account in order to support and enable target-oriented business steering.

In order to define the relevant performance indicators or to set up a system of key figures within the industry, it is necessary to observe the business model and strategic goals of the respective company. The need for an adaptation of the steering logic to the respective business model can easily be seen by a comparison of companies performing different concepts.

Value propositions made by discount companies focus on the excellent balance of price, performance, and proximity. In their comprehensive store network, discount companies offer a limited range of products, complemented by promotion articles for price-sensitive customer segments.

In contrast, the business model of organic food supermarket chains' core is offering a wide range of organic food articles. In selected stores, the ecological and sustainably cultivated products are sold to environmentally and quality-conscious customers.

While performance indicators like EBIT apply to both retail concepts, a huge difference in choosing the relevant measures for divergent retail concepts can be identified. Performance indicators such as share of promotion and share of own brand or customer traffic are more related to discount-oriented business models. Share of fresh articles, number of customer complaints, or purchase price trends can have higher relevance for organic food supermarket chains.

Nevertheless, respecting the retail concept to select relevant performance indicators is only one factor. Further elements, such as the financial structure of the company, market situation, and competitive strategy, must be considered as well. Moreover, the focus of the companies' steering logic can also vary significantly: from yield management and return-oriented management to value-based management.

Besides EBIT, the most common performance indicators in the retail industry used as key figures are turnover, gross profit, operating result, sales density, and labor productivity. With the intent of managing selected performance indicators proactively, influencing factors must be made transparent by their separation into their individual value drivers and respective calculation routines.

Linking financial performance indicators with retail concept-specific, non financial performance indicators can help create transparency on existing cause-effect relationships, thus fostering a company's ability to anticipate future developments with impact on business performance (Fig. 2).

Identification of trends and developments can be improved by taking external factors with impact on relevant value drivers into account. External factors arise from technological, sociopolitical, and economic developments such as changes in business climate, GDP per capita, customer's demand volume, supplier structure, exchange rates, and inflation rate. The integration of qualitative and even unstructured data enhances the forecast of future developments at an early stage.

Due to the importance of operational business, retail companies often focus performance indicators with reference to sales. This operational focus can lead to an oversized number of performance indicators on top management level, while a

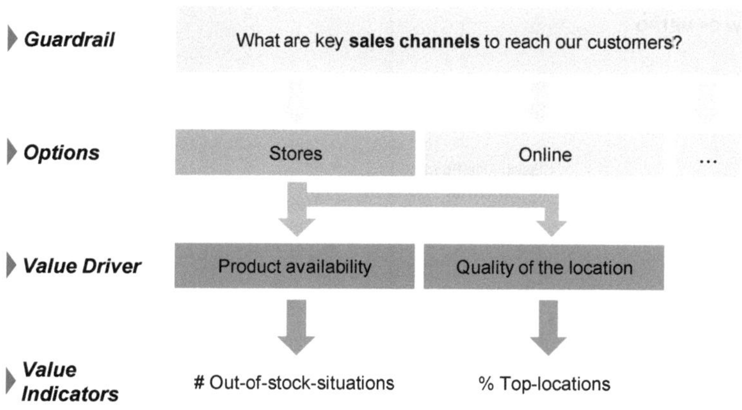

Fig. 2 Identification of business model and retail concept-specific drivers

lack of reference to current business strategy and unknown interconnections of performance indicators to its value drivers exist simultaneously. Moreover, in retail there is a strong focus of performance indicators on the corporate company or individual stores and less focus on separate functional areas like procurement, human resource, or IT. An efficient evaluation of performance indicators is hampered by non-standardized and non-harmonized definitions of figures across all levels of the retail company.

2 Operational Management Based on Performance Indicators at METRO[3]

2.1 METRO Business Model

METRO is a leading international specialist company in the wholesale and food retail sector (Fig. 3). The ultimate parent company is METRO AG, which acts as the central management holding company. It performs group management functions, particularly in the areas of finance, controlling, legal, and compliance. The central management and administrative functions of METRO are all anchored within METRO AG.

The group essentially consists of the two segments, METRO Wholesale and Real. The wholesale company METRO Cash & Carry operates 759 wholesale stores across 25 countries. The delivery business (food service distribution) is also part of this segment, with companies like METRO Delivery Service and the delivery

[3]Information such as values and names refer to the status of September 30, 2017.

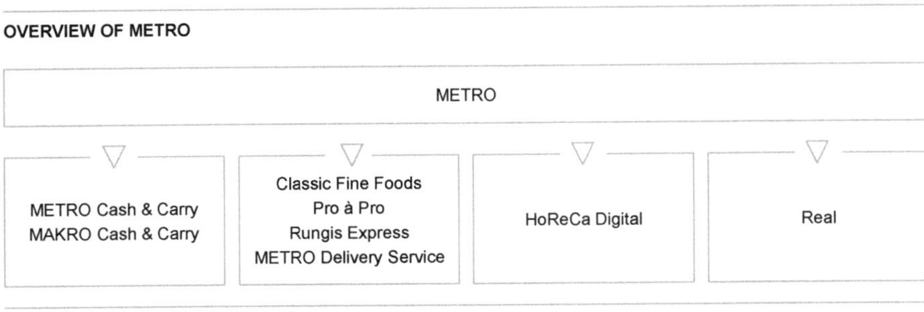

Fig. 3 Overview of METRO

specialists Classic Fine Foods, Pro à Pro, and Rungis Express. Real operates 282 hypermarkets across Germany.

Additionally, the business unit HoReCa Digital, founded in 2015, consolidates the group's digitization initiatives such as METRO Accelerator, powered by Techstars. This initiative sponsors two programs, lasting for 3 months each, and is aimed at supporting start-ups that are developing digitization solutions in the area of hospitality and retail.

Other service companies include METRO PROPERTIES, METRO LOGISTICS, METRO SYSTEMS, METRO ADVERTISING, and METRO SOURCING. These companies provide group-wide comprehensive services in the areas of real estate, logistics, information technology, advertising, and procurement to all group companies.

METRO Cash & Carry is a leading international wholesale trader and operates 759 wholesale stores under the METRO and MAKRO brands across 25 countries in Europe and Asia. Its more than 21 million commercial customers worldwide are mainly hotels, restaurants, catering companies, independent retailers, as well as service providers and authorities, to which the company offers a portfolio of products and solutions that has been tailored to their specific requirements.

In the area of food service distribution (FSD), METRO maintains a strong international presence with its METRO Delivery Service and the specialist companies Classic Fine Foods, Pro à Pro, and Rungis Express. Classic Fine Foods is an Asian fine-food delivery specialist. The company delivers products to premium customers, such as 5-star hotels and upmarket restaurants in Asia and the Middle East. Pro à Pro has been augmenting this area since February 2017. The company delivers products to commercial customers across France, in particular in the fields of corporate catering, canteens, and system catering. Rungis Express is an important food delivery company in Germany that mainly caters to HoReCa customers.

The group has pooled its digitization initiatives in the HoReCa Digital business unit. The initiatives include METRO Accelerator powered by Techstars. This start-up network supports international teams of entrepreneurs in the development of digital solutions for the HoReCa and retail sectors.

Real is an innovative food retail company in Germany, being a leading operator of hypermarkets with currently 282 stores. The hypermarkets are distinguished by a product range of around 80,000 individual products—many of them high-quality fresh-food products—and an attractive range of nonfood products. In addition to its brick-and-mortar retail operations, the company is also pursuing online sales. The integration of the Hitmeister online shop into real.de allowed Real to expand its online product range considerably. Since February 2017, it has been offering a very large product range.

2.2 *Performance Indicators for Operational Management of Brick and Mortar*

METRO is taking advantage of the opportunities arising from digitization and current mega trends in retail and wholesale. Real's overall strategic goal is to sustainably increase its customer relevance in Germany by expanding promising sales channels, such as online shops and click-and-collect services. METRO Cash & Carry, as multichannel supplier, combines its existing business with extensive food service distribution. Beyond that, management of the brick-and-mortar business and the optimization of the existing store network are important elements in METRO's strategy.

The right set of performance indicators supports strategy implementation by creating transparency on the operational level and by documenting its performance, measuring its success, development over time, and progress in relation to a specified goal. For instance, METRO uses a standardized scheme of financial performance indicators in order to calculate revenue-related operating result. Additionally, it serves as basis for the further determination of performance indicators on the operational level.

The revenue-related operating result of METRO is calculated by gross profit, deducted by handling costs. Gross profit is calculated by the revenue less cost of sales which consists of further components. Handling costs result from the sum of personnel costs, occupancy costs, central cost allocations, advertising costs, amortizations, and other costs. In general, these financial performance indicators and respective ratios are used to identify and evaluate strengths and weaknesses in different earnings and cost situations and are applied for internal comparisons of stores and the benchmarking of different sales lines (Fig. 4).

METRO enriches its performance indicators by adding non financial information to financial figures. Oftentimes, performance indicators and ratios are based on the number of full-time employees, number of checkouts, customer frequency, or size of sales area. As an example, revenue as a performance indicator can be enriched with further information and developed to a significant indicator with respect to efficiency and productivity. Typical ratios are "sales per employee," "sales density," or "average sales per transaction" (Fig. 5).

Furthermore, METRO analyzes and evaluates its financial performance indicators by breaking them down into their subcomponents. As an example, the performance

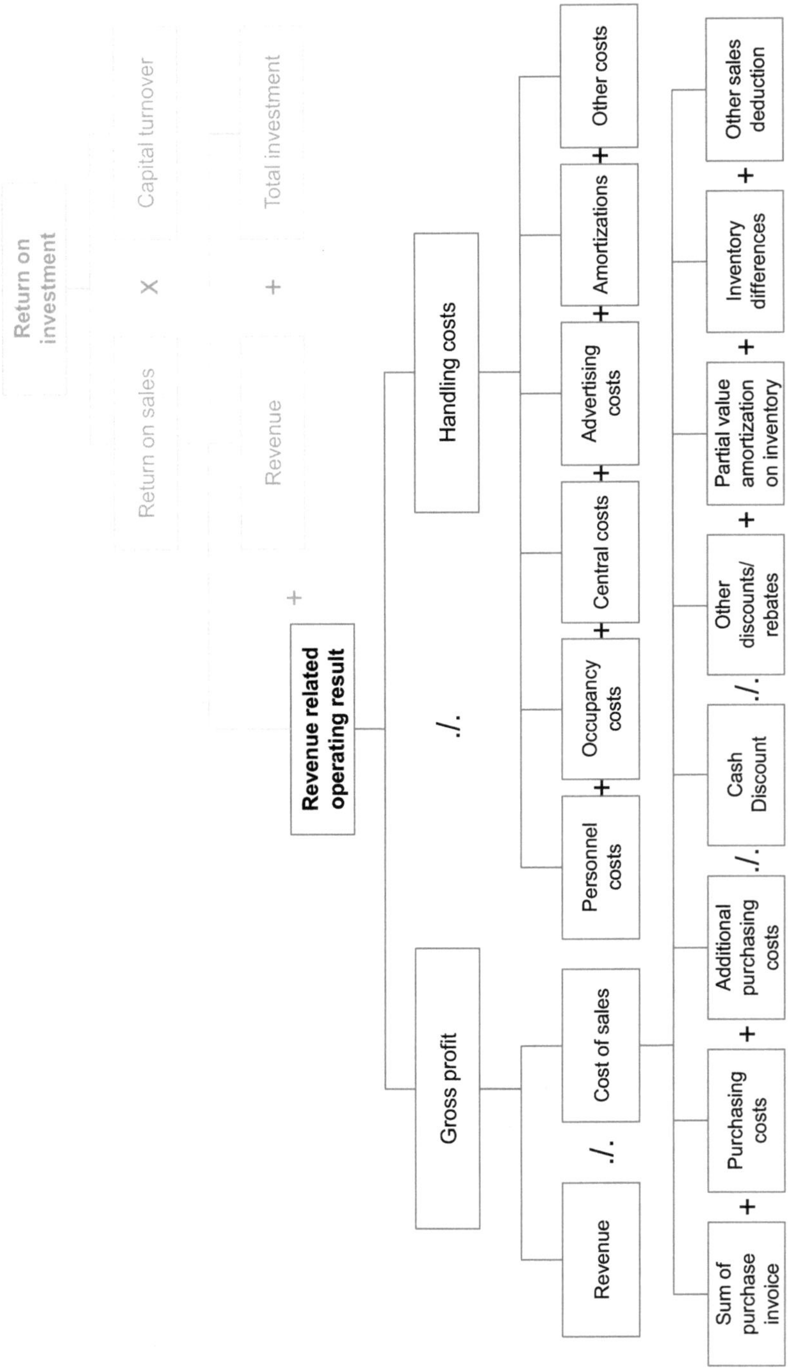

Fig. 4 Calculation of revenue-related operating result

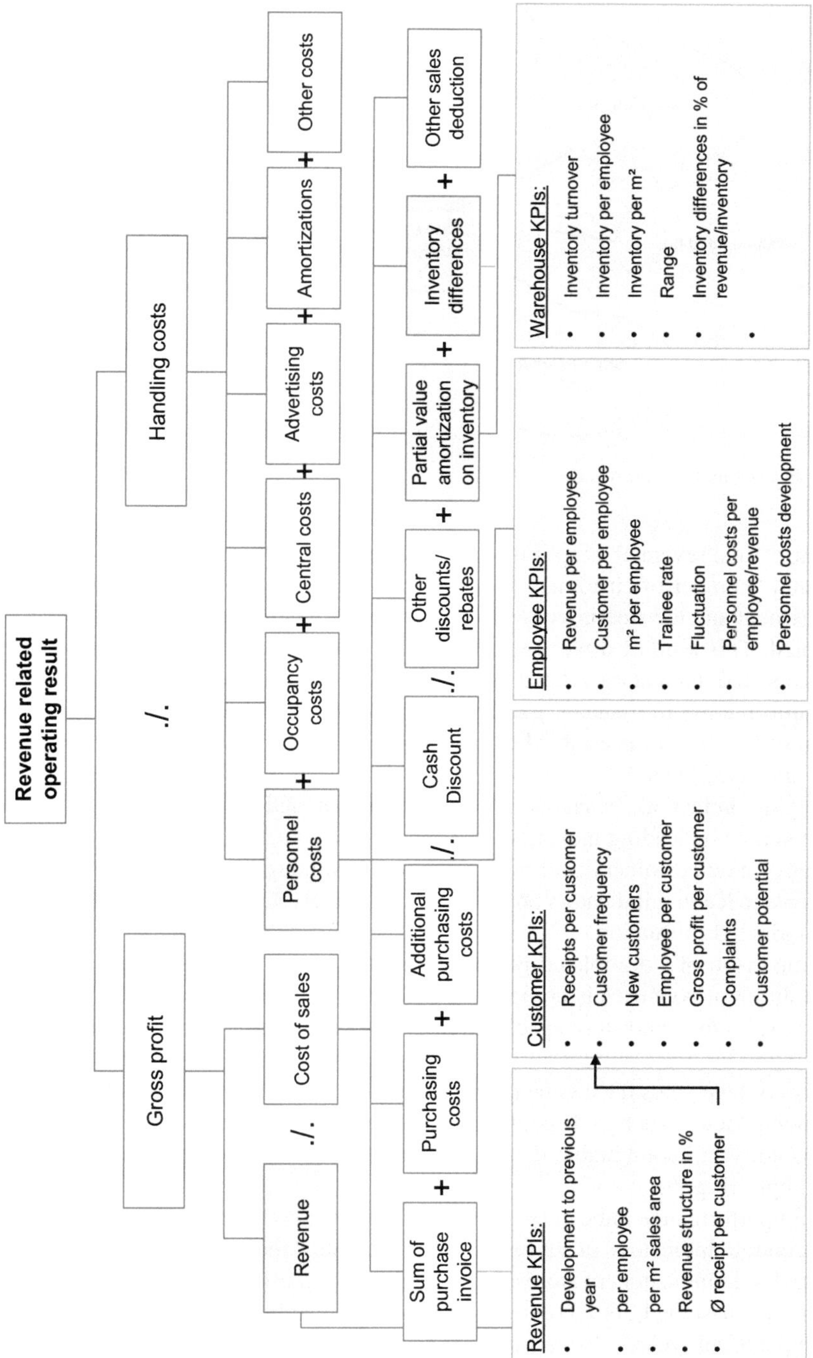

Fig. 5 Selected performance indicators for operational steering

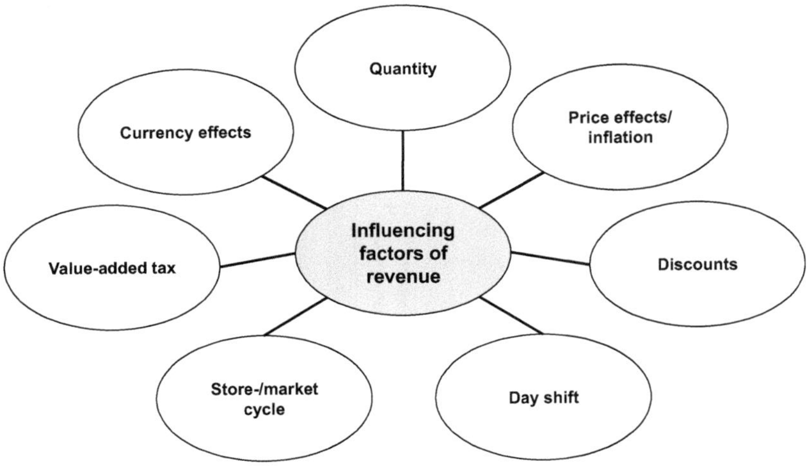

Fig. 6 Factors influencing revenue

indicator "total revenue" is split up into its value drivers "average sales per transaction" and "number of customers." In this way, important information that supports management and the steering of retail business on a detailed and operational level is generated. This kind of driver logic is also used for employee-related performance indicators and indicators related to warehousing performance. By linking value chain information to financial performance indicators, an integrated and consistent system of key figures is established, allowing for the evaluation and comparison of stores and sales lines.

Lagging indicators, such as sales development and sales per employee, are supplemented by leading indicators like employee fluctuation, customer complaints, number of new customers, and ratio of trainees. Although it may be hard to define and measure leading indicators properly, it is absolutely necessary for a balanced and future-oriented evaluation.

Comparison of store-related performance indicators across sales lines and even across different countries is complex. Consistency has to be ensured by respecting country, sales line, and store-specific framework conditions. Several data types such as deviating tax rates and inflation rate, currency effects, as well as varying public holidays or leap years have to be taken into account. Furthermore, sales line-specific influencing factors such as discounts and rebates have to be respected. To establish a homogenous and comparable data set, performance indicators have to be adjusted accordingly (Fig. 6).

Valid performance indicators on store level have to take the property's life cycle into account. Indicators of stores that were opened recently are not necessarily comparable to indicators of stores that are already well established. Therefore, stores have to be assigned into homogenous and comparable buckets such as "store opening current year," "store opening last year," "store closure current year," "store remodeling current year," "store remodeling last year," and "long-term

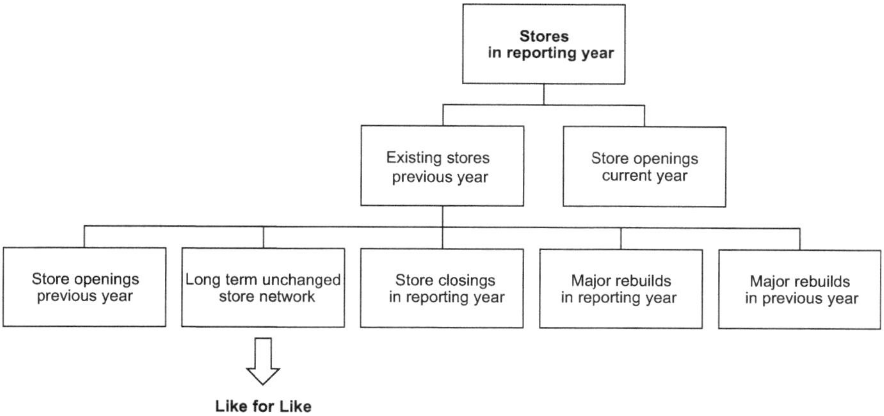

Fig. 7 Store life cycle

existing store network." In this regard, major store remodeling is characterized by the fact that the basic store format or layout has been changed significantly. For the comparison of performance indicators, the "long-term existing store network" is of particular interest, as it already represents a homogenous and like-for-like bucket of stores (Fig. 7).

Changes in sales can generally be explained by two factors: firstly, revenue changes due to changes in a store portfolio, such as openings, closures, or renovations, and, secondly, revenue changes in an unchanged store network. An exclusive consideration of the financial indicator "revenue" in a certain country would not provide explanatory factors about the change of revenue. However, dividing stores into the mentioned life cycles makes this possible. Further explanatory factors for the situation of the revenue can be measured by determining the operational performance indicators mentioned above, such as "sales density" in the various store life cycles in order to capture the development of area productivity in the inventory network compared to the recently opened stores. The classification of stores into different life cycles must be reviewed continuously and adjusted over time due to changes of the store portfolio with respect to openings, closures, or renovations.

In the following, the aggregation of the performance indicator "average receipt" of individual sales lines and the group performance indicator is described.

In retail sales lines, the amount of cashier processes is merely an indication of high or low customer traffic. The amount of cash processes is set equal with its "frequency." In contrast, in the METRO Cash & Carry wholesale business, it is possible to record the amount of purchases made by a customer through the use of loyalty cards. Purchases at various checkouts are added afterward. Therefore, the performance indicator "frequency" may possibly differ between the sales lines of

KPI: Customer productivity

- **In retail:** without customer card — Number of check outs as an indication for high or low customer traffic

  Frequency = Number of check outs

- **At METRO Cash & Carry:** with customer card — Purchases from different check outs are summed up

  Frequency = Number of purchases from one customer are detectable with the customer card

- **On group level:** Number of check outs are used for comparability

➢ Thereof the average ticket is calculated:

$$\text{Average Ticket} = \frac{\text{adjusted revenue}}{\text{number of check outs}}$$

Fig. 8 Consistent performance indicators on group level

retail and wholesale business when considering their definition and method of calculation.

However, on group level, consistency of the performance indicators has to be ensured. To achieve comparability on the METRO level, the indicator "frequency" is defined by the amount of cashier processes. This information is available across all sales lines and thus ensures a homogenous database (Fig. 8).

3 Conclusion

Performance indicators represent an essential instrument for comprehensive and effective management of retail and wholesale businesses. Financial information is combined with non financial information that considers value chain, product range, checkout, and sales area. In order to improve the comparability of the information, performance indicators have to be enriched by additional information and explanatory factors, such as life cycle of stores or further and specific information on country and sales line level. On this basis, consistent and significant systems of key figures, including leading and lagging indicators, can be developed.

This has been illustrated by respective performance indicators and systems of key figures for the management of brick and mortar at METRO and its sales lines.

Reference

Reichmann T (2001) Controlling mit Kennzahlen und Managementberichten. Grundlagen einer systemgeschützten Controlling-Konzeption, 6th edn. München

Bernd Seufert was a Principal with Horváth & Partners for the Competence Center Retail and Consumer Goods in Hamburg. Due to his professional employment, he possesses broad expertise and experience concerning various topics of German and international retail companies.

Enabling Data-Driven Management Information at the REWE Group Through a Value-Adding Integrated Management Data Warehouse

Tino Eichler, Christoph Kremers, and Florian Werner

Abstract This contribution describes the implementation of a value-adding integrated management data warehouse at the REWE Group under the program named ConCERT. ConCERT is the abbreviation for controlling, common, efficient, ready, and transparent. The program heads toward setting new standards for a modern controlling with business-focused and future-proof technologies as well as streamlined processes and organization. Besides providing front ends for planning and reporting, the program aims on setting up an integrated information management architecture to achieve a single point of truth. In this contribution you find information regarding the general benefits and use cases, as well as a description of the designed architecture for a single point of truth and of the agile project approach.

Keywords REWE Group · Single point of truth · Data warehouse · Merchandise management · Controlling · Business intelligence

1 Introduction

1.1 Basic Conditions for a BI Project at the REWE Group

REWE Group (REWE) is a leading diversified retail and tourism multinational with nearly 330,000 employees. It operates approximately 15,000 stores in 20 European countries. The cooperatively set up REWE Group is still built upon a network of independent retailers. In this group, strong brands such as the grocery chains REWE,

T. Eichler
Controlling & Finance, Horváth & Partners, Stuttgart, Germany

C. Kremers (✉)
Corporate Controlling & Development, REWE Group, Cologne, Germany

F. Werner
Retail and Consumer Goods, Horváth & Partners, Hamburg, Germany

M. Buttkus, R. Eberenz (eds.), *Performance Management in Retail and the Consumer Goods Industry*, https://doi.org/10.1007/978-3-030-12730-5_7

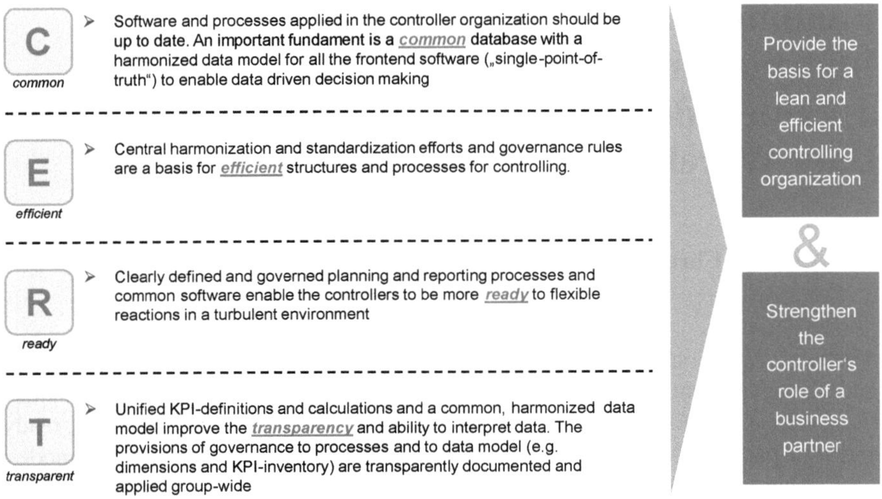

Fig. 1 ConCERT in a nutshell

BILLA, and PENNY and the tourism division, DER, Tjaereborg, and Jahn Reisen, are operated by largely independently managed companies.

Many of these companies try out new store concepts and brands. Often, innovative solutions are found, which is important to actively shape the market in today's fast-moving competition. But what is important for the business is a challenge for a streamlined and clear provision of management information. Fast solutions are at risk of leaving behind non-harmonized master and transaction data that are the heart of reporting and planning processes. Additionally, decentralized IT departments, differing processes, as well as historically grown decentral reporting and planning solutions in the hands of indispensable experts can harm data quality and affect efficiency.

To solve this challenge, the program ConCERT has been initiated which aims at anchoring new instruments for business steering within the REWE Group and its divisions. Within the program, the content of management information, architecture, processes, and organization is renewed and streamlined to give a new basis for current and future management requirements. The overall target of the program is reflected by the name ConCERT—an abbreviation for controlling, common, efficient, ready, and transparent (see Fig. 1).

The different issues are addressed by three sub-projects, reporting, planning, and data provision. According to the target definition of ConCERT, the sub-project data provision aims at setting up a single point of truth (SPOT) for delivering and processing high-quality information. For ConCERT the SPOT is the heart and data the lifeblood that keeps reporting and planning up and running. As there was no adequate SPOT for all the requested data that reporting and planning software can be integrated into, a new management data warehouse was required and thus defined as the project goal for the sub-project data provision.

1.2 General Benefits of a New Management Data Warehouse

On the one hand, making controllers fit for the future means shifting their activities from the time-consuming data scooping and comparing toward advising their customers—the management—as a business partner using relevant and adequate information. A management data warehouse will play an important role as it can make the controllers' work more efficient. On the other hand, the SPOT also helps the controlling[1] organization become more effective by getting access and gaining insights into all the requested information from a single source. When establishing a SPOT, data quality is one of the main issues that must be addressed, meaning data should be unambiguous and can be accessed in a timely manner and to the requested specification.

1.2.1 Merging Different Data Sources for Enhanced, Harmonized, and Seamless Analysis

The integration and harmonization of data from all sources into one data model is the main benefit of the management data warehouse. Integration aims at the structural fit of source system master data (including KPIs and hierarchies) into a common central data model, whereas harmonization aims at the semantic unification of data. A unique benefit is the logical integration of transactional data from several source systems with similar but non-congruent content. With this, we generate a common view on a specific domain by resolving data aggregations from transactional processes (see detailed examples in Sect. 2).

1.2.2 A Hub with Interpreter Qualities Ensures Central Control of Data Provision

Besides the gathering of high-quality data, a SPOT is suited to fulfilling important "hub-and-spoke" tasks. The data warehouse distributes the data needed for planning and reporting software as well as for data retraction toward source systems. In our case, we applied different views in the view layer for reporting and planning front ends, due to different business and software requirements. The reporting and planning front ends are provided with the required subset of the data models in which

[1]The authors use the English word "controlling" to translate the German term "controlling." Please refer to the discussion in the preface.

they need to realize their specific task. This aims at reducing complexity and modeling effort on the front-end side. For example, only those dimensions and KPIs required to keep data models of front-end systems small and high performance are provided. The same applies for the retraction of data (e.g., plan data) toward the SAP ERP systems.

1.2.3 Transformations Help to Solve Data Quality Issues but Need to Be Handled with Care

The management data warehouse can help to address data quality issues. Naturally a data warehouse can only improve data quality up to a specific limit, based on source system data quality and data availability. Even if this is possible, it is not the best way of improving data quality in the management data warehouse, as this approach lacks sustainability. Therefore data quality should be ensured primarily within the source systems. Only if this is not possible, due to technical, organizational, or processual reasons, transformations have to solve data quality issues. In our experience, the downsides of this approach have to be reflected carefully. Complex transformations can be cost drivers, are sometimes hard to monitor, increase the complexity of the data flow, and thus hamper the understanding of it. Transformations result in a deviation of the data compared with the data the users know from the source systems. Within the project we had to balance the decisions between cleansing the source systems and processes (long-time achievement) and setting up transformations to "repair" inconsistent data in the data warehouse (short-time achievement). Both approaches were applied within ConCERT.

1.3 The Underlying Technique

As many other typical finance IT architectures, REWE had also established a reporting based on a common database using SAP BW. The available SAP BW DWH covered several finance reporting requirements in separated modules but only a fraction of the newly defined requirements of ConCERT. Besides the nonavailability of data, the nonfulfillment of the reporting and planning requirements by the currently available front ends created the need for a new software technology on the user front ends. Based on this architectural front-end change, the technology provider for the data storage—the management data warehouse as ConCERT SPOT—also had to be evaluated.

Beyond the boundaries of the CFO area, there were already other technologies used within REWE. Especially Teradata, as an operational data warehouse technology, has to be mentioned here. Based on those basic conditions, a decision between SAP BW, Teradata, and other products such as MS SQL Server had to be made. The detailed requirements will be described in Sect. 3.1.

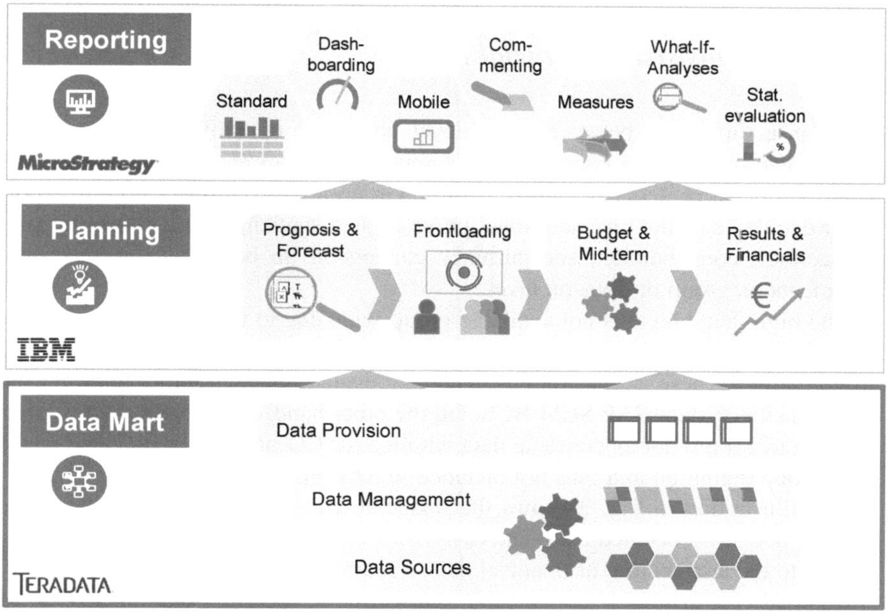

Fig. 2 ConCERT tool architecture

As result of the software evaluation process for the front end and data warehouse section, a best of breed architecture was defined. This consists of Teradata as management data warehouse, which is already used as an operational merchandise data warehouse, MicroStrategy as reporting front end, as well TM1 as planning front end (Fig. 2). All three tools have a clearly defined scope within the layer model of the ConCERT architecture, and together they generate a user-friendly, performant, and consistent platform for REWE. Details will be described in Sect. 3.

2 Practical Examples for Adding Value with the SPOT

From the early beginning, a clear vision of ConCERT was defined within the global controller community. This included the steering model, resulting harmonized global and division-specific KPIs and reporting structures, as well as an overall integrated information architecture. These decisions have formed the cornerstones of the SPOT content and functionality and the overall target for adding value to REWE.

2.1 Adding Value for Analysis by Creating Seamless and Consistent Financial Data

There is a difference between group-level and local operative controllers. The requirement of the local controllers is to report and analyze data at high level of detail (e.g., cost centers and cost elements). Group-level controllers need to report lower detailed data but face additional group-related challenges (e.g., intercompany transactions, consolidation, and currency conversion) to be able to make proper statements on group or division level.

The high-detail level is not available group-wide due to the existence of several ERP systems and due to missing access to operational transaction data for some group entities. These entities only provide aggregated financial information for the consolidation system SAP SEM BCS. On the other hand, the partner entities (self-reliant traders) provide operational data within SAP CO but are not included in the legal group definition and thus not included in SAP SEM BCS.

The illustration in Fig. 3 shows the financial data coverage of the two source systems SAP CO (detailed data) and SAP SEM BCS (aggregated data).

Due to the architecture of financial data, a seamless analysis from group level to operational cost centers is not possible. Furthermore, reporting data in SAP SEM BCS may differ from the aggregation of transactional data in SAP CO due to adjustments and period closing effects during the group reporting process. This is a main reason for inefficiencies in today's data analysis and reporting. Controllers need to know how different source systems operate in detail in order to compare and analyze information merged within one report.

The ConCERT management data warehouse integrates and harmonizes the data from both source systems as a hub-and-spoke. Thus the SPOT overcomes the

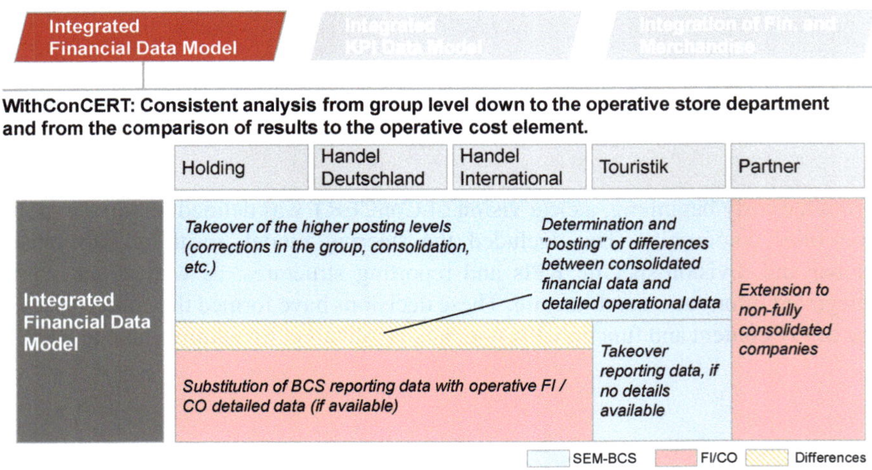

Fig. 3 Fragmented finance data in SAP data sources

limitations of system breaks and enables seamless analyses throughout all levels of detail. This enables a typical path for a business analysis of a group-level controller: he starts with the consolidated EBITA of the current period for the whole group. The top management wants to have a look at the segment details, where they find that a certain segment performs badly in comparison with the others. By stitching deeper into the data, the controller is able to identify the relevant deviations on financial performance drivers on entity level. This analysis can be detailed seamlessly down to cost center and cost element level. All of this is done within a single ad hoc analysis report based on the integrated ConCERT financial data model.

In addition the standard views on either SAP CO data or SAP SEM BCS will be still accessible and comparable to the source system. Further insights into the technique behind this approach are described in Sect. 3.3.

To give an example, the following financial KPIs are provided by the integrated financial data model (excerpt):

- Revenue
- Gross profit
- EBITDA
- EBT
- Investments
- Free cash flow

The integrated ConCERT financial data model acts as a true single point of truth for financial data. It allows variable reporting and analysis, covering data of all financial systems. Both group-level and local controllers use the same consistent and quality-proven data for different reporting requirements. A welcome side effect of this integration is a full transparency of SAP CO, SAP SEM BCS, and transition effects. Having one source and one front-end software to report this data does not only make things more transparent and offers better data quality—it also frees up the time that controllers may use in a more productive way.

2.2 *Adding Value Through Comprehensive Non Financials*

What is challenging for the financial data model also applies for the non financials. The data for all measures cannot be retrieved from one source only. Also, the detail—e.g., the hierarchy level of the organization—may be provided on different granularity. Some data can be found on a cost center level per month, others on higher levels of the corporate organization such as a consolidation entity or even on the level division and year. Furthermore, the level of data storage for identical measures may vary between divisions—or may not even exist for a certain division at all—and finally a certain entity may be provided with the same information out of different data sources with different granularity and quality. It is the management data warehouse's task to integrate and prioritize the source data and provide the single best-quality information for the downstream planning and reporting solutions.

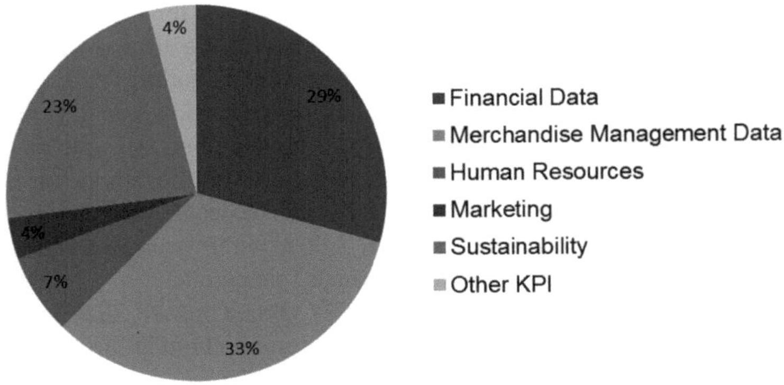

Fig. 4 Share of KPI per category of the KPI inventory

To give an example, the following KPIs are provided by the management data warehouse in addition to *top* financial data provided by the integrated financial data model (excerpt):

- # receipt, Ø receipt (like-for-like)
- Assortment inflation
- Private brand quote
- # Stores, # expansion, # closings
- Sales floor sqm, sales floor productivity
- Out of stock
- Mystery shopping results
- Sustainability figures like kWh/m^2

A common KPI inventory holding all relevant definition for financial and especially non financials is the basis for an implementation of measures, not only in the management data warehouse but also in the area of planning and reporting (Fig. 4). For the non financial KPIs, the complete and different sources were documented. To eliminate redundancies and inconsistencies and provide the best available data, the sources are prioritized. The main benefits of the non financial data model are the automatic usage of the best available data source which raises data quality and frees up time and the benefit of a unified nomenclature of originally different measure which is now presented in a common way.

2.3 Breaking the Frontier Between Finance and Merchandise Management Data

Often a true reporting frontier in retail corporations is the separation between accounting systems and merchandise management systems. At REWE, both data classifications are held in separate data repositories that must be used with different reporting front ends. This separation is historically grown and a typical case for retailers. In the past, (top-)management decisions on group level were mainly taken on the basis of accounting information, whereas more operational und functional units use merchandise management data for decision support. Two main aspects of merchandise management data are:

- Broader, more detailed information of key objects of a retailer, like logistics and stores
- More recent data due to almost real-time access and no constraints regarding the monthly closing process

This data offers more and new possibilities in data-driven short-term controlling, especially in today's dynamic markets, where deep knowledge of customers and store operations is crucial. So it is not surprising that more and more managers are interested in this information for their decision-making.

In ConCERT, we face this situation by merging the financial and the merchandise data for an integrated analysis via common reporting structures and additionally keeping the specific structures tied to either the financial or merchandise domain. Therefore, we use already-existing relationships between financial and merchandising data to automate the reconciliation effort within ConCERT.

The integration of merchandise management data already played an important role for the technology decision of the management data warehouse. For details see Sect. 2.1.

In the SPOT, the high-detail merchandise data can be retrieved by a store ID, which is the most common attribute for analysis in the retail market, and also a linking pin to the financial cost center element.

In the past, some static legacy reports have already combined merchandise management data with accounting data in a manual-sourcing approach, due to the lack of integration. With ConCERT it is now possible to apply drill paths from SAP periodic financial data to merchandise data with the use of one reporting front end. For example, the SAP-based turnover of a sales district can now be broken down by product categories, and ConCERT also facilitates further insights toward distributional actions and advertising effectivity. The usage of such an analysis is now much more efficient and reactive to ad hoc questions from the target audience. Apart from efficiency improvements and the benefits that come with more detailed real-time data, this integrated approach simplifies cross-domain analysis, where simplification is one further important step toward self-service reporting for managers.

2.4 Establishing Value-Added Methods

The previous sections focused on the assembling and cleansing of existing information from different domains and data sources. Great added value can be generated by creating real new information by adding logic to the existing data and structures. In the specific case of REWE, the grocery retail divisions with their huge store portfolio

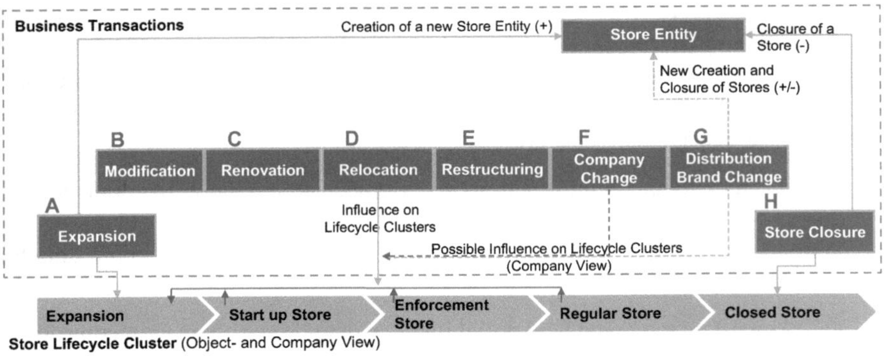

Fig. 5 KPI logic for changes within/of the store portfolio within the REWE Group

play a crucial role and request specific measures. By applying logic to master data, ConCERT provides full transparency toward the life cycle of individual stores as well as the entire store portfolio. Expansion, relocation, renovation, and store closure events (for details see Fig. 5) can be set in context to financial target ambitions. They are not only strategically important but also essential for stationary retailers' external reporting. Before ConCERT, these KPIs were collected manually via Excel upload from the divisions or even regions. This is the first time that REWE creates this event data in an automatic and integrated way and thus a big milestone, as it enables like-for-like analyses for the complete ConCERT financial and non financial data without additional manual efforts.

A new cost center attribute was established and integrated into the cost center creation workflows of the divisions. When creating new store cost centers, this attribute is filled automatically by defined criteria. Also the other attributes that are important for ConCERT are considered in the cost center creation workflow of the master data management systems.

3 ConCERT Architecture

3.1 Stable Operation Is a Key Requirement for a Software Decision

As mentioned in the previous section, there was the challenge of combining several requirements in a sustainable architecture. So the integrated data warehouse should not only integrate data from several source systems, harmonizing the diverse dimensional models and data structures in a common database, but it also has to provide several specific business functionalities to fulfill the different requirements (Fig. 6).

In the end, not all requirements can be fulfilled completely. So the challenge is balancing the requirements of ConCERT as a strategic project with a long-term

1 Typical DWH requirements

- Delivering a common and consistent data model with harmonized master data
- Delivering integrated transactional data on a common perspective without the source systems' constraints
- Bypass the organizational separation of structures and systems
- Separation of operative and analytical data spaces
- Archiving data and enable historical analyses

2 Operating the data warehouse

- Be a sustainable and flexible architecture
- Fit into the existing REWE IT landscape
- Work with IBM Cognos TM1 as planning frontend and Microstrategy as reporting frontend
- Be business user oriented from a change and run perspective

3 Requirements typical for a finance department

- Financial template structures for P&L, balance sheet and cash flow for different accounting standards
- Analyzing of legal consolidation effects, generation of mgmt. consolidation effects and creation of restatements
- Analyzing of posting levels and corresponding accounting effects
- Generating of periodic and cumulated YTD views
- Calculation of currency translation and enabling currency translation effect simulation

4 REWE management perspective

- Enable specific analyses as like for like or market view
- Integrate merchandise management information from several operational systems
- Overcoming system boundaries in the analysis

Fig. 6 REWE management data warehouse requirements

perspective. This means that usability and stability within a comprehensive and sustainable architecture is the key. Taking all of the requirements into account and with regard to the existing IT tools, there was a decision between:

- The established and existing finance architecture using SAP
- The merchandise data warehouse using Teradata
- Other software vendors, e.g., Microsoft

After a structured and transparent software evaluation, also taking existing technology capabilities at REWE Group into account, the decision was made for Teradata as management data warehouse. Even if Teradata does not offer comprehensive finance functionalities, it was chosen over SAP BW due to the IT strategy that aimed at establishing Teradata as common data warehouse for several requirements. The most important deciding fact was to have a better and easier integration of the already-existing merchandise data warehouse data. Due to the high-detail level, it was obvious that the volume of merchandise data within the corporation's merchandise data warehouse outclassed the financial data of the SAP BW by far.

This decision reduces business user orientation of the ConCERT architecture. However, it was accepted due to the fact that the data integration is more critical for the planning and reporting front ends.

3.2 *Enhancing the Typical Three-Layer Model for ConCERT*

Even though various approaches are described in the literature and differently delicate layer models can be found, most of them have a common structure. This

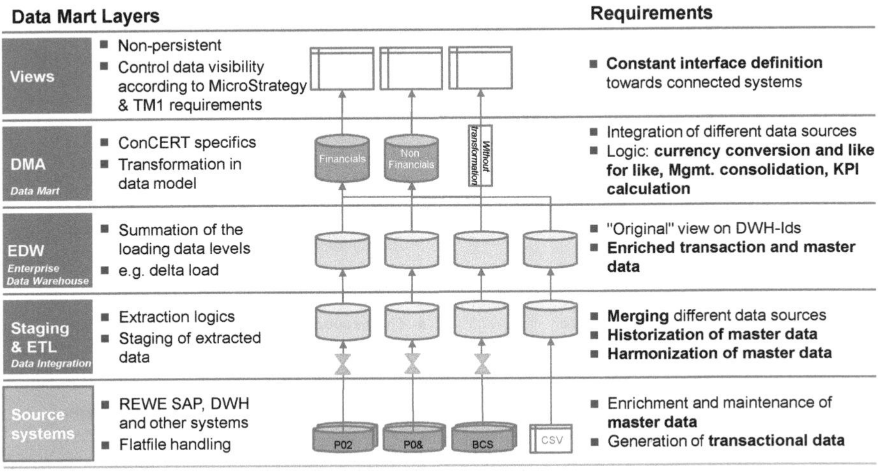

Fig. 7 Management data warehouse layer model

can also be found here. The ConCERT management data warehouse follows a three-layer approach and therefore respects common architecture principles combined with the fourth layer to fulfill ConCERT specific requirements based on the architecture (Fig. 7):

Layer 1 or staging is the data integration layer where source data from several source systems is replicated and stored persistently.

Layer 2 is the enterprise data warehouse (EDW) layer. Within the EDW, the master and transactional data is stored persistently and is available using the agreed and common ConCERT data model and nomenclature. The data is available in the required granularity and quality. Master data objects that must newly be defined or transformed are already available; and all relevant information is historicized.

Layer 3 is the data mart (DMA) layer, with persistent or virtual data stores for all relevant master and transactional data. The agreed and common ConCERT data model and nomenclature is used here as well. In addition, all functionalities or attributes which have to be represented in the data and have to be derived or calculated are already integrated here: as periodical and cumulated views or the store definition as described in Sect. 2.3.

Layer 4 is the view layer, which uses Teradata SQL views to provide the information required for planning and reporting. Further methods, e.g., dynamical currency translation, are calculated here. The data mart layer shows the finally required ConCERT information.

A special feature in the view layer is the consideration of specific front-end requirements (TM1 and MicroStrategy) on methods and data structures. We have to use a balanced and relational modeled hierarchy for MicroStrategy, while TM1 also tolerates unbalanced hierarchies, described as parent-child relationships. This layer is also used to connect source systems via data retraction as SAP ERP, which requires retracted plan data. Another structure is also expected, so data has to be split by the controlling area, which is no longer known in the ConCERT structures. Consequently, the management data warehouse masters technical and functional "dialects" and provides data that is already in the correct form in the view layer. Based on this fact, it is guaranteed that all front-end tools use the same data sets without additional effort in the front-end tools, even if these have to be prepared differently.

In addition, it is important to understand that within the complete ConCERT architecture, several data storages exist. So it is typical for a planning tool like TM1 that it uses its own analytical data space to store and to manipulate data as well as to create plan data. This is similar to MicroStrategy, where iCubes exist for data storage to increase performance for specific reports. Furthermore, there are also calculations within the metadata of MicroStrategy for specific reporting needs, if it is more convenient to be prepared outside the management data warehouse. To avoid modifications in the ConCERT data model, a strong governance is required and has already been defined to secure data quality and consistency.

3.3 Technical Features and Functions of a Modern Management Data Warehouse

3.3.1 Harmonized Data Model

As previously mentioned, the common ConCERT data model is one of the main advantages of the newly defined management data warehouse. It was defined in this manner in a very early phase of the project and throughout the project and the productive use of ConCERT it will be enhanced based on continually increasing requirements. All enhancements follow a defined nomenclature and are appraised by a governance function to guarantee stability in the nomenclature. This is essential to ensure parallel work on different components across different teams and front ends.

The harmonized data model not only focuses on the description of the dimensions and elements, but all technical names within the management data warehouse also follow an agreed nomenclature. This not only avoids errors in the connection of the front-end systems; it also ensures a quick orientation in the management data warehouse despite the enormous number of tables, dimensions, structures, and attributes (Fig. 8).

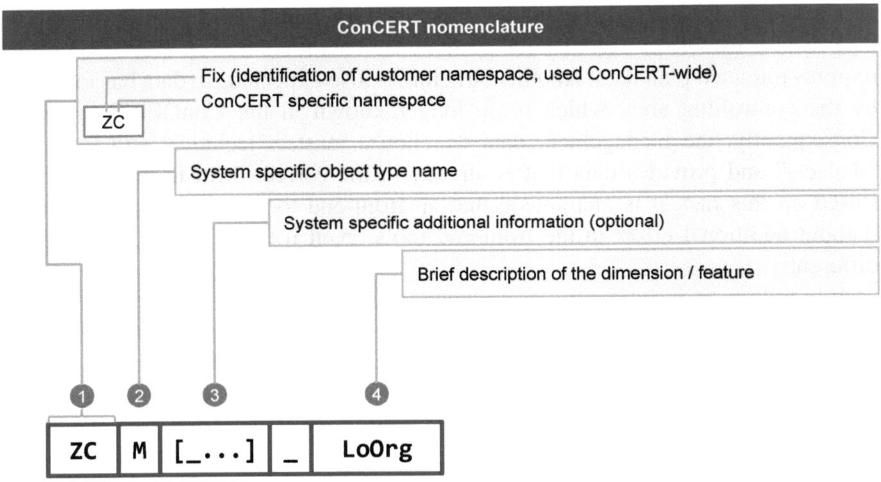

Fig. 8 ConCERT nomenclature

3.3.2 Integrated Financial Data Mart (IFDM)

Section 2.1 describes the added value of the IFDM. This is one of the main features of ConCERT concerning the finance data perspective. Furthermore, this is also one of the specialties of the described architecture, because unlike most data warehouses, this management data warehouse not only collects and aggregates data, it increases data's level of detail in an intelligent way by combining source systems.

In this case, there are low-detail data, based on SAP SEM BCS/BPS, and higher-detail data, based on SAP CO. But SAP CO does not contain adjustments based on the accounting principles and legal consolidation effects. Consequently, it is not possible to report group result and drill down to cost center or cost elements based on the source systems. To enable this type of analysis, the unconsolidated financial data from SAP SEM, which already contains adjustments (based on the consolidation preparation process), is replaced by more detailed SAP CO data on cost center and cost element level. The discrepancy of consolidation preparation adjustments between SAP CO and SAP SEM BCS (or more precisely between from SAP CO to SAP FI and from SAP FI to SAP SEM BCS) is identified and calculated automatically. This creates an adjustment booking within the management data warehouse to guarantee consistent data from group result to cost center. The group's system, SAP SEM BCS, provides the benchmark for this data.

From an organizational point of view, there is no system that covers all relevant entities (see Fig. 3). There are *non*-SAP ERP entities that are only contained within SAP SEM BCS; however, SAP SEM BCS does not contain nonconsolidated entities (e.g., self-reliant partners) that are partly available in SAP CO. ConCERT increases the amount of covered entities so the management data warehouse contains them all.

3.3.3 Integration of Planning Data and Non Financial Data

From another perspective, the integration of data within the management data warehouse is also challenging. From a planning perspective, there is the need to harmonize data. Even if TM1 already receives ConCERT data, there are several specific requirements within the planning process to change data composition. Thus, planning on different hierarchy levels and also within TM1 and other source systems as SAP CO is allowed. This necessitates a matching method of the different plan data to create a consistent set of data for reporting, as well as a separation of each different planning process and planning system up to the detail of each planning step. This issue was handled by a strong collaboration with the TM1 planning method to create correct plan data and an intelligent data model which enables separation of planning data, using specific dimensions such as "version," "plan version," and "year of planning." As result, a consistent and matched final plan version is available for reporting, and all relevant, temporary planning data can also be reported.

This concept differs from the concept of integration of non financials as described in Sect. 2.2. Here the result is only a unique value per KPI even if there are several data sources in parallel. Therefore, the database developer has created a prioritization table with all sources for the non financial data, where the prioritization of each source system per KPI can be maintained by the business administrator.

3.3.4 Monitoring and Validation

Monitoring and validation tasks have been defined in the management data warehouse. They are essential to keeping data quality and consistency. Due to the complexity of the methods and data models, there is a continuous risk of faulty master data or corrupt transactional data. For example, for the method of identifying the store as described in Sect. 2.3, it is essential that the attributes in the source system are maintained correctly. The same importance of source system master data exists for the creation of several reporting hierarchies such as the REWE organizational structure. Consequently, there are several validation processes defined that identify and report changed master data between the daily load processes and highlight changes if problems are expected, for example. Also, data sets that cannot be completely processed are separately stored and reported. So the guiding principle "consistent and correct data goes for complete data" is used.

On the other hand, there are also monitoring tasks or reports that show not only the non-processable data sets but also some specifically aggregated key figures or amount of processed data sets in order to obtain an indicator for data processing issues.

4 Procedure Model

Keeping things together is a main success factor for delivering a service that constitutes an interface to both data generation and analytical domain within a project environment in which stakeholders are widely spread over departments and divisions. Both conditions bring their own challenges that have to be considered adequately for a successful delivery on time, with quality, and in budget.

From **requirements'** point of view, a procedure model has to fulfill the following conditions:

- The management data warehouse has no end in itself—reporting and planning requirements are the main drivers of project activities.
- Sustainability and conformability are strong aspects of quality. The carrying out of solutions has to include selected measures on quality management.
- Different procedure models of other program stakeholders, such as the planning and reporting projects, are in place and have to be respected by the management data warehouse.
- Volatile requirements from other parties regarding content and time of delivery have to be accepted as a side effect of such a highly complex program with limited resources and widely distributed functional expertise.

To get things done, the project implemented a procedure model that is composed of classical project management approaches and influenced by modern agile approaches such as SCRUM. Due to the individual requirement scopes within the program, it was not possible to implement a "full-blooded" methodology. However, the mixture aims at providing stability and continuity for efficient progress achievement within a volatile and decentralized environment (Fig. 9).

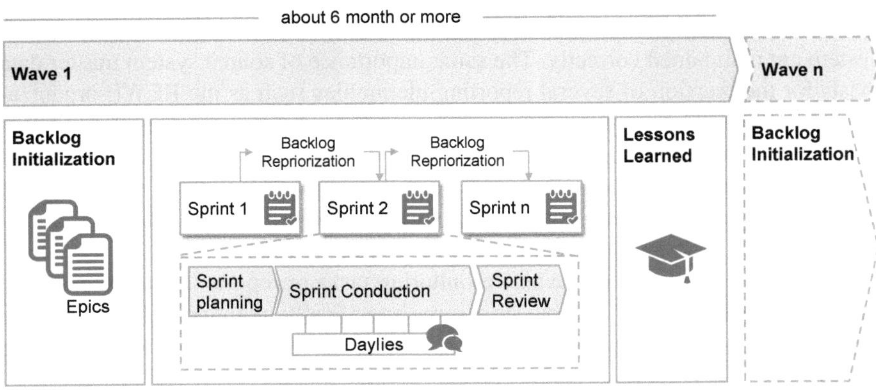

Fig. 9 Procedure model

4.1 Top-Level Schedule

The top-level scheduling is organized as a wave—6 months or more—that is often determined by go-live milestones of front-end projects such as planning and reporting projects. These waves are synchronized with other projects on program level, regardless of whether the other project also follows the wave approach or not. The reporting project, for example, also follows the wave approach; however, the planning project conducts a more classical and milestone-oriented procedure for most of the planning modules. This is due to the fact that go-live milestones are mostly bound to one certain point in time each year (e.g., budgeting).

4.2 Setting the Scene During Backlog Initialization

The initializing of a wave begins with a scoping phase. Each stakeholder introduces his requirements for data mart—called Epic—on a "bullet point level," also providing additional information on primary data sources and logical units. In the backlog initialization meeting, these Epics are then shared, explained, and prioritized between all stakeholders for maximum transparency and to identify synergies among them. Each Epic is then subdivided into sets of internal components. This is done in a standardized way in order to identify the required competence fields—e.g., data table definition, system interfaces, and logical units—and the skill level which is needed for the realization of the component. A rough effort estimation can be done considering different component suppliers.

This information, the available resources, and the priority determine the internal order for an initial Sprint assignment and a resulting overall "what's ahead plan." The results are then shared in a second backlog initialization meeting. The results are then shared in a second backlog initialization meeting. This is done in order to meet the milestones provided by projects which are not delivering in an agile (e.g., SCRUM) methodology. Due to a fixed resource planning scenario, almost every wave will have requirements that will not be realized because of missing resources. In addition, the chances and limitations of additional resources or special competencies for certain requirements are discussed and then decided on. Regardless of this, the non-realization of tasks with low priority is an accepted characteristic of the procedure model.

4.3 Sprinting to Deliver

With the scene being set during the backlog initiation phase, the Sprint section is initiated. A Sprint is a defined 3-week working period. It is a second level of scheduling over time in addition to the wave. The requirements assigned to the specific Sprint are subdivided into specific tasks, with updated effort estimation, and assigned to an employer for realization. In contrast to SCRUM methodology, the assignment of tasks to resources is not done by the members of the implementation team themselves, but each task is being assigned to a person whose skill level best matches the job to be realized. This is due to greatly differing skill sets within the implementation team.

If a component requires a functional concept paper, the paper needs to be provided 2 weeks before the Sprint's start date so that it can be quality-checked in order to ensure seamless and effective progress during the Sprint window itself.

The progress of a Sprint is tracked on the Taskboard. It lists all the tasks assigned to the Sprint and highlights their specific state (open, ongoing, done). The software platform JIRA is used for this tracking. The development process includes daily status calls in order to manage progress as well as to clarify issues during task realization. Each Sprint ends with a Sprint review in order to wrap up the achievements and nonachievements and to discuss lessons learned. It often happens that tasks are not completed during a Sprint, e.g., due to issues only becoming transparent during realization. In that case, other tasks with lower priority will remain "open" or "in progress" and will need to be continued in the following Sprint.

4.4 Nothing Is as Constant as Change

A reprioritization meeting is done before each new Sprint is started. The goal is readjusting the allocation of resources and tasks on the basis of newest information and requirements from the data mart team itself but also from the different stakeholders' points of view. Input for the reprioritization is gathered from the following three sources and shared among the participants during the meeting:

1. Sprint progress: Information about open tasks, nonachievements of the current Sprint, and general experience gathered during previous Sprint reviews.
2. New information from stakeholders: Changing requirements gathered during stakeholders' activities (e.g., progress of implementation of a planning module) or new requests from the stakeholders' clients (e.g., a new planning requirement which results in new data to be provided by data mart). This also concerns timing, e.g., a lack in progress of implementing a report leads to a later due date for required data provision by data mart.
3. Backward scheduling: A simple forecast that indicates if the remaining time and capacities of a wave cover the presumed effort of remaining requirements.

This information is then used to revise prioritization, resulting in a reassignment of requirements to future Sprints or the drop of requirements due to de-prioritization or due to requirements having become obsolete from stakeholder's point of view. The revised prioritization acts as a starting point for the next Sprint planning. The reprioritization meeting is a major success factor in this methodology. Not only does it consider nonachievement and deviation in time, but it mainly respects that stakeholders' requirements change due to new knowledge or internal replanning. It also ensures transparency and a common level of communication across all stakeholders, forcing and improving decision-making. In this way, resources are assigned with maximum effect for maximum client satisfaction.

5 Outlook

After all achievements and project work, the future has to prove the real success of the ConCERT management data warehouse. The architecture and basic conception have already been set up with the need for flexibility and reactivity toward future requirements in mind. Besides the technical aspects, the critical success factor is surely the organizational environment that cares about current operation and future development. Due to the fact that the data warehouse engages an in-between position from an architectural point of view and also due to its value-adding logical units, the dependencies toward the multiple source systems are highly critical. The data warehouse is indeed sensible toward changes in structure and content. A strong governance is thus required to take care of these. Every critical data object and source system process has been identified. Rules for, e.g., master data maintenance and changes in customization have been set up and need to be obeyed by decentralized units. Important central concepts and documents such as the KPI library—the conceptual basis for the implementation of measures in the data warehouse and the reporting layer—have to be covered by a strict governance. Furthermore, these conceptual cornerstones must also be made accessible to the organization for a good understanding of what is behind all the information. A wiki-like application with documentation from the functional and the technical perspective will be set up. A technical internal monitoring helps to identify inconsistencies in the provided source data in order to protect the subsequent processes against failures and data corruption.

In the end, acceptance is mainly achieved by fluent running and resilient systems. This is mainly achieved by people doing things the right way. After dissolving the project organization, daily operation has to be realized in a constructive collaboration model with clear activity split between IT and functional department and central and decentral. In addition, further development and fast reactivity toward additional or changing needs have to be anchored organizationally by providing a non-bureaucratic but still effective demand management. To cover the organizational challenges, a business intelligence competence center (BICC) will bring together the competencies and special expertise in a virtual organization.

Tino Eichler is a Principal with Horváth & Partners in the Competence Center Controlling and Finance. His consulting expertise lies in the area of management accounting, corporate performance management, planning, and consolidation with a focus on national and international project and program management.

Christoph Kremers is a Senior Project Manager and data architect in the Corporate Controlling & Development department of the REWE GROUP. He is concerned with the optimization and maintenance of group-wide controlling systems and processes. As a project manager, he focuses on establishing a new single point of truth for reporting and planning front ends.

Florian Werner is a Principal with Horváth & Partners in the Competence Center Retail and Consumer Goods. His consulting expertise includes management accounting, finance, and organization with focus on national and international retail and consumer goods industry companies.

Part IV
Digital Performance Management: New Opportunities to Boost Efficiency

The Digital Strategy: The Guide to Systematic Digitization of the Company

Daniel Kittelberger and Lea-Sophie Allramseder

Abstract The opportunities that digitization offers companies are unmistakable. One can almost speak of a digital gold rush. In fact, in many companies an actionist and uncoordinated image is evident in dealing with the possibilities of digitization: they approach the topic from a wide variety of directions and functions, but the individual efforts remain limited in their impact, as a comprehensive concept is lacking. The result is a digital patchwork carpet. Dealing with the creation of a dedicated digitization strategy can help to remedy this situation and catalyze the targeted exploitation of the potential that arises.

Keywords Digitization · Digital business model · Digital vision · Digitization strategy · Integrated strategy process · Key figures of digital targets

1 The Digital "Patchwork Carpet"

The digital revolution is one of the upheavals a company cannot avoid. Digitization is changing the world, not only technologically but also in the way we live and work. Hardly any area remains untouched by it, and the speed with which digital solutions are being disseminated exceeds the boldest expectations. Especially in commerce, consumers can easily get anything, anywhere and at any time.

But digitization is not a new topic. From a technical point of view, the term digitization refers to the conversion of analogue quantities into digital values for the purpose of storage and further processing. Seen in this light, digitization is "ancient."

An adaption of this contribution has been originally printed as Kittelberger, D., Greiner, O. Riepel, P. (2017): Die digitale Strategie—der Wegweiser zur systematischen Digitalisierung des Unternehmens, in Kieninger, M., Digitalisierung der Unternehmenssteuerung, pp. 19–32, Schäffer-Poeschel, Stuttgart.

D. Kittelberger (✉) · L.-S. Allramseder
Industrial Goods and High Tech, Horváth & Partners, Stuttgart, Germany

M. Buttkus, R. Eberenz (eds.), *Performance Management in Retail and the Consumer Goods Industry*, https://doi.org/10.1007/978-3-030-12730-5_8

The use and dissemination of information and communication technologies, for example, began more than 40 years ago. Methods and applications of digitization have been developing since the 1960s. Correspondingly, many areas in companies have long since been digitized to the highest degree, such as high-precision production machines or working with simulation models in development.

Since the turn of the millennium, however, digitization has gained a new quality. Today we live in a phase of "digital omnipresence": Possibilities in sensor technology, data processing, networking, and interaction between people themselves but also between people and things as well as between things under exclusion of humans (e.g., direct machine communication) have become fixed components of our present—and they will become even more so in the future.

Products are becoming increasingly digital, making them more attractive to end customers. Distribution channels are increasingly migrating to the Internet, so that the role of the classic, stationary retailer is put into perspective. New business models are increasingly based on digital networking. The production of services can be made increasingly efficient thanks to digitization. The control of the company and its partners can be made more precise thanks to greater transparency and predictability of events.

The opportunities offered by digitization are unmistakable. One can almost speak of a digital gold rush. But as with any intoxication, it is important to keep a cool head in order to make the most of opportunities and not to underestimate the risks. Digitization and the associated potentials have to be evaluated for each application case.

Not every application makes sense, and there is a danger of falling for a "digitization hype," without sufficient critical examination of the usefulness and cost-effectiveness. Especially in this new digital gold rush, it is difficult to find the right path. Better wait and see what works—and then catch up as quickly as possible? Or trying out a lot, knowing full well that there is the risk of sinking a lot of money? Or focus on individual specialist areas of digitization, but then carry them out at the highest level?

Unfortunately, in many companies, an actionist and uncoordinated picture is shown in dealing with the possibilities of digitization: The topic is approached from different directions or functions, but the individual efforts remain limited in their effect, because a comprehensive concept is missing. The reason for this uncoordinated approach is often cited as being the need for rapid action and the delimiting ability of the individual digitization measures.

The result is a digital patchwork carpet: many parallel digitization initiatives without a common thread or synergy. Worse still, because of the feeling that they are already "doing a lot of things," quite a few managers think that their company is already dealing with the topic sufficiently. A structured approach that ensures that all essential fields are considered adequately is lacking. Digital arrogance meets digital ignorance. Dealing with the creation of a dedicated digitization strategy can help to remedy this situation and catalyze the targeted exploitation of the potential that arises.

2 Yes to Digitization, but with Strategy

A strategy describes the behavioral pattern of an organization with which it should be successful in the future. This idea can be applied to digitization efforts: How should the company behave with regard to digitization in order to be successful in the future? The answer to this is provided by the digitization strategy.

In recent years, we have taken a closer look at a wealth of digitization strategies. We noticed that the basic structures of these strategies were very different: They ranged from superficial declarations of intent to the opportunistic listing of individual measures.

In our view, a better approach is to work on the digitization strategy with the same components as other strategies in the company. In accordance with the "integrated strategy process" of Horváth & Partners, this includes the clarification of the initial situation, the definition of a mission statement, the definition of the business model, the development of a target and key figure system, as well as the creation of a concrete action plan.

Of course, the digitization strategy is not in a vacuum. It is derived from the corporate strategy and contributes accordingly to its realization. In the following, the key points are presented which allow the topic of digitization to be anchored holistically in the corporate strategy (see Fig. 1)

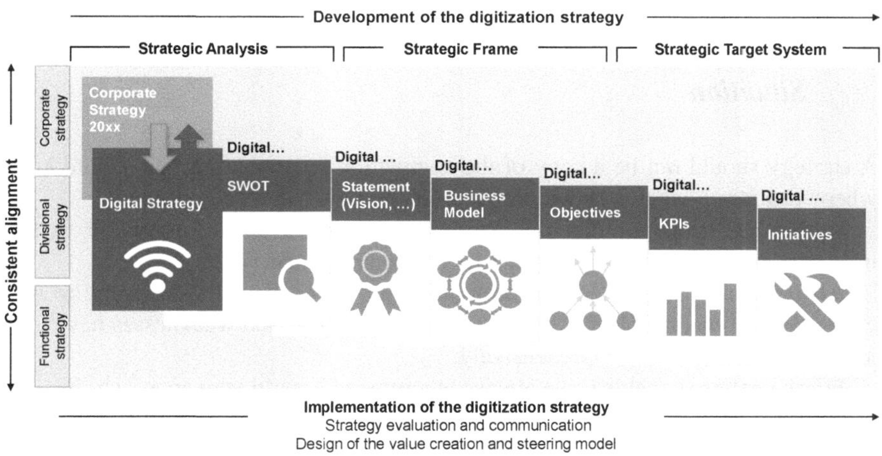

Fig. 1 The digitization strategy is derived from the corporate strategy and follows the same structure (© Horváth & Partners)

3 Some Thoughts About the Project Team

As part of the development of the digitization strategy, the depth and breadth of the topic should first be recalled. All functions of a company are affected by increasing digitization. Digital products require new knowledge and skills from development. For example: new business models presuppose major changes in marketing; industry 4.0 has great potential for change in production, logistics, and related functions. Digital "bots" can replace simple, low-value-adding activities in the areas of HR, controlling and purchasing. New collaborative (communication) technologies have a major impact on all employees, etc.

The diversity of participants resulting from the individual digitization activities shows that the project team must consist of representatives of the various functions of the primary and secondary value chain in order to ensure a holistic view. If necessary, representatives from participations must also be consulted if a decentralized management structure prevails. What sounds so self-evident can hardly be found in practice: Sales digitizes sales, production, controlling, etc. The silos work for themselves; the coordination of the interfaces is laboriously done ad hoc. However, it is precisely during the development of the strategy that an overarching view should be taken—with interdisciplinary representatives who are listened to in the company and have a desire for the future and change.

3.1 Analysis of the Market Environment and Internal Situation

A strategy should not be a copy of the competitor's actions: but you should know where you stand, what is or will be possible, and what customers expect.

Within the scope of the digitization strategy, it is also worthwhile to take inventory of your own company and its environment first.

All corporate functions and processes should be evaluated with regard to their current digital maturity level. Thus, individual strengths and weaknesses have to be identified quickly and comprehensively.

For the external analysis, we always recommend a multi-step approach. First the direct competitors and the direct competitive field, second the peer group (companies in similar industries or with similar business models), and finally the best in class for specific topics can be analyzed and combined to a holistic external picture.

The results are combined into a SWOT analysis. In addition to the SWOT analysis, a query of all running or already released digitization projects and initiatives from all areas and functions should be investigated.

The SWOT as well as the list of activities, which we cluster according to topics and subitems of the digitization strategy, forms the basis for the further steps. It should be noted that in the course of the next steps, the SWOT analysis will generally become more concrete and in some cases even broader.

3.2 *Development of a Digital Mission Statement as a Central Element of the Strategy*

The digital model is the emotional linchpin of a digitization strategy. Among other things, it enables a semantic clarification of the terminology (What does digitization mean, what kind of use cases are included in digitization vs., e.g., automation?), shows the digitization mission (What mission does digitization have?) and the digitization vision (What claim do we make with digitization?), and clarifies decision guidelines ("basic digital principles") and behavioral norms ("digital values"). As a rule, this digital mission statement is formulated on the basis of the corporate strategy or the mission statement formulated there, but with an emphasis on the role and task of digitization in achieving the overall strategy.

The table lists exemplary digital visions that have a different focus and emphasis (e.g., taking a leading role, changing the company, focusing on the customer or a general mission derived from the self-image of the company) (Fig. 2).

In addition to defining the digital vision as an emotional reputation for digitization, basic principles should also be clarified. These can, for example, adjust the company to whether the digitization strategy aims at an evolution of the existing business model in the sense of a logical further development or whether an absolute reorientation and thus a new fundamental business model is to be achieved. It is also

Company	Digital Objectives/Digital Vision	Focus
Otto Group	The best and most personal provider in the digital retail industry. We live close to our customers. We love innovative technology. We are passionate. We make digital future! [a]	**Leadership**
Rewe Digital	»By using digital possibilities we make everyday shopping easier through all channels. We increase the quality of life of our customers because they get all their daily needs from us - simply, anytime and anywhere." [b]	**Customer**
Carrefour SA	»Become the leader of the food transition by offering our customers, every day and everywhere, quality and trustworthy food at a reasonable price. To do this and return to a conquering dynamic, we must revamp our model, by simplifying our organization, opening ourselves up to partnerships, improving our operational efficiency, investing in our growth formats, building an efficient omnichannel model and developing our fresh and organic products offer, notably under the Carrefour brand" (Carrefour 2022[c])	**Transformation**

[a]https://www.otto.de/unternehmen/de/newsroom/dossiers/dossier_vision.php
[b]https://rewe-digital.com/ueber-uns.html
[c]https://www.powerretail.com.au/news/carrefour-digital-strategy/

Fig. 2 Digital objectives and digital visions in comparison

possible to clarify which innovation speed is considered appropriate and what weighting the creation of customer benefit vs. the increase of efficiency potentials has. Basic expectations of a "return on investment" can also be anchored in the mission statement.

Quite a few executives find it difficult to draw up mission statements, as this is all about formulating a still quite fundamental mentality with which the topic of digitization is to be addressed. Superficial statements without effect can actually be dispensed with. However, well-formulated models are strong guidelines that can be withdrawn time and again in concrete decision-making situations. We can only advise you to lay these foundations carefully.

3.3 The Digital Business Model

Digitization creates the possibility of new business models. But as part of the digitization strategy, however, it is first and foremost a question of the business model of digitization in the company as such.

A business model means the configuration of fundamental decisions, on the basis of which a business functions.

Business model collects all fundamental decisions on what should and should not be done in relation to digitization. To structure these fundamental decisions, Horváth & Partners has developed the "7-C model," which can also be applied to the digitization strategy. Here we distinguish between "use cases" and "enabler" (see Fig. 3).

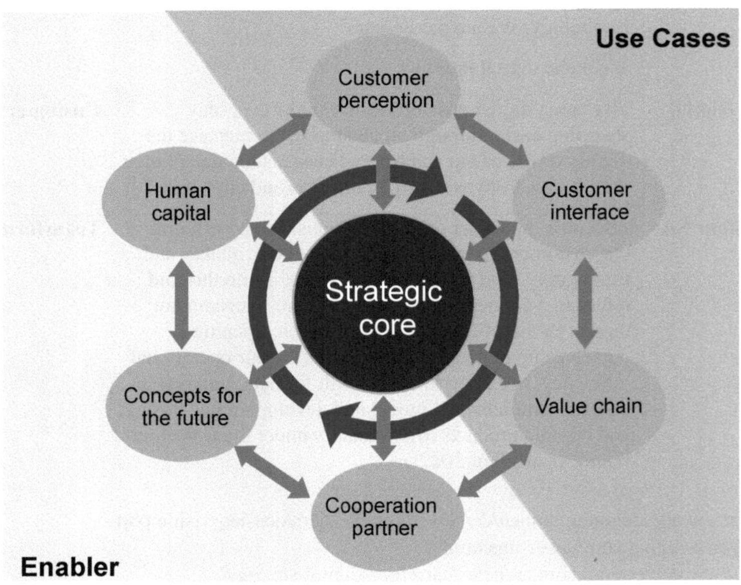

Fig. 3 The Horváth & Partners 7-C model subdivided by use cases and enabler (© Horváth & Partners)

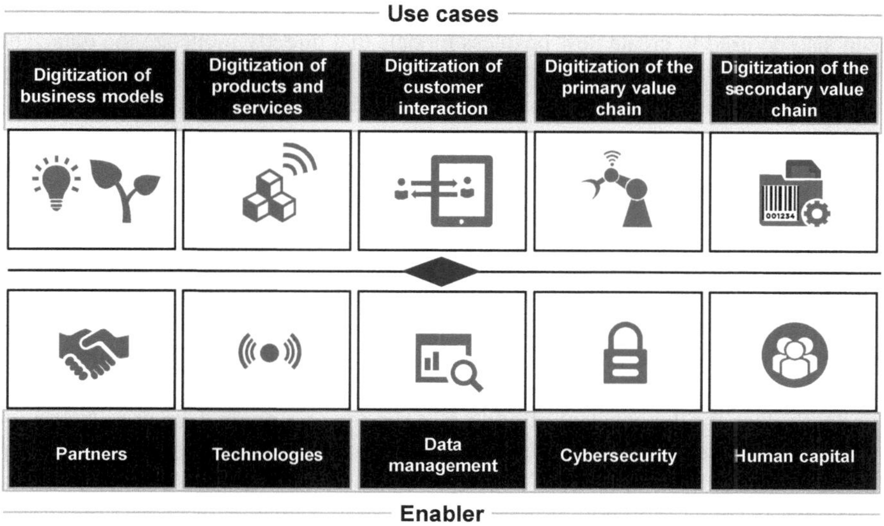

Fig. 4 Core elements of the digital business model according to Horvath & Partners (© Horvath & Partners)

Use cases represent the "active level" of the digitization strategy, i.e., the effect on sales through the digitization of products or the offering of new digital services; the effect on customer perception, e.g., through the use of digital marketing channels, or improved customer access, e.g., through own online shops; and the effect on efficiencies through the use of digital possibilities in the control and design of primary and secondary process chains in the company.

Enablers on the other hand, place the drivers of digitization in the foreground. As part of the development of concepts for the future, the main focus is on the technologies used (including IT infrastructures, sensors, connectivity) and the handling of data. In addition, the question arises as to how one's own human capital can be empowered to take advantage of the opportunities offered by digitization (e.g., competences, culture, mind-set) or how one should cooperate with which partners.

When developing the possible applications of a digitization strategy, the existing business model (see Fig. 4), the product portfolio, and other company-specific conditions are the decisive factors that determine the levers and the initial situation. Thus, the use cases that are relevant for a digitization strategy can differ greatly.

3.3.1 Digitization of Business Models

New business models arise when ways of expanding the existing offering by combining it with complementary services are found.

The newly generated data and insights from online shops, apps, and stores can on the one hand be used to expand the core business and offer new services as an extension to the already existing business model. On the other hand, this new data can also be used to create new business models that directly monetize the data. The sporting goods manufacturer Under Armour offers the Connected Fitness app platform. Within this app, customers are offered practical exercises and can also follow their own fitness routines. It primarily monetizes with premium versions and advertising. However, there are various possibilities to offer apps that allow retailers to monetize the generated data.

The example Software as a Service has already shown how effective this business model can be. Now, the trend is moving more toward Platform as a Service. Textbook examples for PaaS are Uber or AirBnB.[1] Another well-known example is of course amazon that offers distributors the possibility of connecting to a huge customer base. Another possibility in commerce are the so-called subscription-based business models. Within those business models, the customer pays weekly, monthly, or yearly fees for the constant offering of a service or a product, such as Netflix or Spotify. However, subscription-based business models can also be about physical products. The "dollar shave club"[2] is a start-up based in California that offers razors and other personal grooming products such as shave butter, shower gel, toothpaste, or hairstyle products to customers by mail. The consumer can buy onetime or the company delivers a starter kit and then ships the replacement blades on a monthly basis.

Another possibility in the range of the subscription-based business models, especially for food markets, could be a weekly delivery of different vegetables, fruits, and other products. Customers could possibly choose which products they want to include every week, or if they want the food market to include regional and seasonal products. The company Etepetete,[3] for example, offers organic vegetables or fruits that would not be sold in a supermarket due to their appearance and non-compliance with certain standards. However, customers can choose from different sizes of boxes and whether they want vegetables or fruit. The start-up then delivers the box to the front door every Friday.

With the launch of AboutYou, Otto has taken the next step in the direction of an ecosystem. AboutYou is more than a simple online webshop, but rather a marketplace with a connected ecosystem. The shop does not only involve third parties like developers and distributors but also other Otto services such as Hermes or Ratepay. This offers new synergies and opens the shop for new innovations.

---

[1] https://www.smartinsights.com/ecommerce/ecommerce-strategy/top-ecommerce-trends-inform-2017-marketing-strategy/

[2] https://www.dollarshaveclub.com/

[3] https://etepetete-bio.de/

3.3.2 Digitization of Products and Services

We have all gotten used to digital properties in our private environment: We can locate our smartphones, continually give (and read) reviews, easily connect digitally with like-minded people, or find the information we need in fractions of a second.

We transfer this experience to the equipment we work with, be it privately or professionally. On our vacuum cleaner robot as well as on complex machine tools in production. These experiences and expectations are constantly evolving. Accordingly, it is important to think consistently and innovatively through which digital enhancements make sense in the further development of one's own products. For example: the product must be able to send data in the future (e.g., to integrate the "fleet management" business model). Is it possible to make performance more individualized by using customer data?

However, retail only acts as an intermediary between the manufacturers of products and the customers. This implies that retailers only have limited influence on the products they sell. The logical consequence is, therefore, to bring new innovative services to the market in order to attract customers and retain them after their purchase. While innovative services before and during the purchase online, or in a store, are part of the customer interaction chapter (see Sect. 3.3.3), this chapter will especially highlight the importance of innovative additional services a retailer could offer its clients to complete the product range. One example for such services could be the renting of machines or other products. Customers might not be willing to buy huge machines they need once or twice a year. Therefore, renting them when they are used is a convenient and low-cost possibility for the customer. Renting those machines directly when they buy the rest of the products needed is even more convenient. For example: if a customer wants to build an outside barbeque, he would need the necessary materials, but also machinery to build the grill, such as a cement mixer. So, if the customer were able to rent the mixer where he buys the materials, this would be convenient for him. This is a point where construction markets, for example, could offer machinery for rent or they could enter a partnership with rental companies and offer their service in the stores. One example for such a partnership is the German construction market brand Hornbach.[4] Customers can also fulfil their long-cherished project dreams at low cost. In cooperation with the well-known partner Boels, the Hornbach rental service provides all the necessary machinery for this purpose: professional tools and machines that are not needed every day, but that are important if required. Other examples for rental services are Otto NOW and Tchibo Share. Otto primarily rents multimedia products, home electronics such as washing machines and sports devices for a fixed monthly payment. Tchibo has started its renting business with children's clothing.

---

[4]https://www.hornbach.de/cms/de/de/mein_hornbach/services/mietservice/mietservice.html

3.3.3 Digitization of Customer Interaction

New information and communication technologies lead to a lasting change in customer behavior. This presents companies with the challenge of establishing behavioral and contemporary forms of interaction with customers. How can new technologies be used to ensure that customer acquisition and retention are sustainable? After the treatment of the digital business model and the associated digital products and services, the next logical question is how to communicate these to customers.

In this case, digitization also offers a wide range of different approaches (see Fig. 5). However, it must always be ensured that existing (lucrative) customer relationships are not harmed by new forms of interaction. Customer interaction requires an analysis of the interaction behavior of the target customer group ("Customer Journey"). The field of tension between interaction behavior, existing customer relationships, and requirements from new digital business models must be brought into harmony.

However, companies with an online presence can no longer rely on sales simply because they are online retailers. The competition in this field has grown enormously, and online retailers have to find their own unique selling point.

The trends in this sector are especially the use of chatbots[5] to answer questions or to handle queries of customers. This allows retailers to save employees while the customers still feel cared about. The technology is getting better and better, so the skills of the chatbots are evolving. Another topic that has been a trend in the past but will be developed further in the future is in-store and off-store personalized advertising, as well as segment-of-one loyalty programs.[6] The prediction software will be

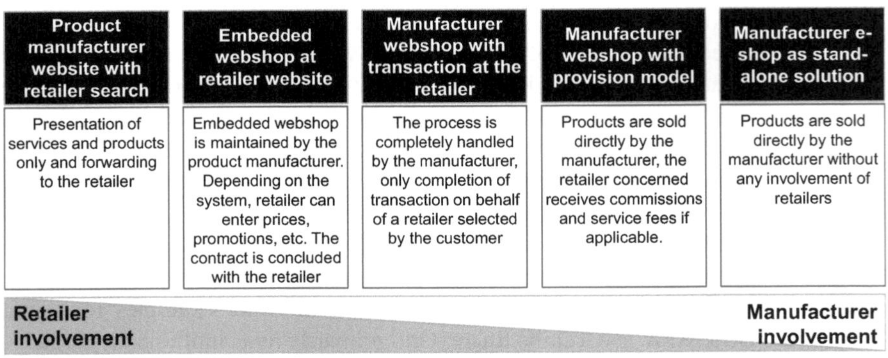

Fig. 5 Example of an application case of customer interaction—types of manufacturer E-commerce (© Horváth & Partners)

[5]https://www.smartinsights.com/ecommerce/ecommerce-strategy/top-ecommerce-trends-inform-2017-marketing-strategy/

[6]http://www.digitalistmag.com/customer-experience/2017/03/15/digital-future-of-retail-04964810

refined in order to offer precise and tailored recommendations of products or services. Via beacons or in-store Wi-Fi that capture all interactions, the customer journey of the client will be closely monitored in order to personalize marketing, based on history, context, and predictions for each client.

Another trend that online retailers should be aware of is the increasing use of voice-activated applications, such as Siri, Alexa, etc. For customers, shopping will become even more convenient since they can order products just by telling the device to do so.

Even though online shops are the best-known example of digitization in the retail sector, it goes much further today. Stationary retailers also need to offer their clients a unique experience in order to keep from losing them to the online competition, since Amazon, etc. are establishing stores and, therefore, are also playing an increasing role in the "real" world. At the same time, the model of click-and-collect will increase in importance. Customers can buy online and have all the advantages of an online webshop, such as higher stock, etc., but can also try the clothes on in-store.[7]

Another level of personalization can be reached with the use of augmented reality in-store. Through augmented reality configurators, mirrors, or apps, customers can see what the products will look like, which color or size, in real-time, and with zero effort. The clothing brand "American Apparel," for example, has introduced a new app, which—besides sending special offerings and product notifications—provides an "augmented reality experience" in-store.[8] Customers can scan barcodes or images and gain access to full outfits, change colors, and see additional videos or fashion advice.

Another huge trend is the use of smart shelves in retail. They know about the inventory, can reorder products independently, offer digital product information, and can automatically adapt prices according to customer preferences, digital and social patterns of the customer, as well as predictive financial models.

However, smart shelves are just the beginning of an increasing technologization in the store. Media Markt is one of the leading consumer electronics retailers in Europe and now leads its customers and employees into a new era of digitalization in their stores. In a pilot program, they have introduced a robot in one of their stores that supports the customer.[9] The robot, called Paul, can welcome customers, find products for them, lead them to the relevant shelf, or call a human employee, if the situation is too complex for it to solve. According to CDO Martin Wild, this robot will not replace employees but round off the store's service offering.

---

[7] https://www.zebra.com/content/dam/zebra_new_ia/en-us/solutions-verticals/vertical-solutions/retail/brochures/retail-study-2017-en-global.pdf

[8] http://fashionretailfuture.com/american-apparels-shopping-assistant/

[9] https://t3n.de/news/roboter-verkaeufer-media-markt-saturn-803296/

3.3.4 Digitization of the Primary and Secondary Value Chain

In the discussion about the digitization of the value chain, the automation of workflows must be dealt with in both the primary and secondary value chain (see Fig. 6). These are all kinds of hard- and software-supported automation of process steps that manifest themselves in cost reduction, time optimization, quality improvement, risk minimization, or general cost reduction (e.g., the use of robotics and automation in supply chain management and logistics or automation of reporting). In addition to these process-oriented potentials, there are also possibilities for managing the content of the company. At this point, the use of predictive analyses in particular should be mentioned, which, by integrating external data sources into logical prediction models, coupled with the corresponding computing power, allow a significant improvement in corporate management.

Prediction models of this kind can be developed for any business sector and can thus improve the control capability of the entire company by means of timely analyses.

Not only predictive analysis is a topic for the future, but also the use of blockchain in supply management. Walmart has used IBM Blockchain[10] to make its supply chain more transparent and to be able to trace its products at every step. Blockchain offers a shared ledger that is updated and validated in real time with each network participant. This allows visibility of activities and shows where the product is and in what condition it is, at any point in time. This offers unique transparency and traceability of products or assets, reduces fraud and errors, and increases consumer and partner trust.

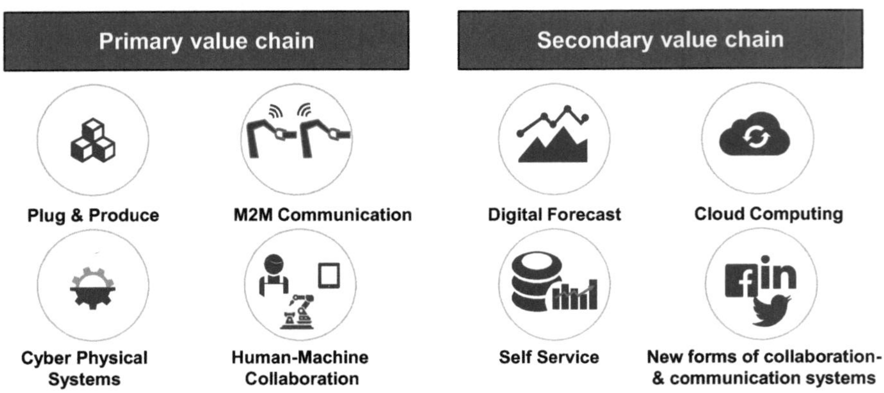

Fig. 6 Examples of use cases in primary (industry 4.0) and secondary value chain (© Horváth & Partners)

[10]https://www.ibm.com/blockchain/supply-chain/

Especially in this day and age, where consumers want more and more information on what they eat (where it comes from, how long it took to come to the supermarket, etc.), this system can be a helpful tool to attract customers and build up loyalty.

3.3.5 Derivation of Enabler

The identified digital options for action require prerequisites that allow the Enable companies to utilize their potential. Therefore, the next step will be deriving the necessary capabilities for the digital options for action. Capabilities include technologies (e.g., sensors or the Bluetooth transmission function), organizational requirements (e.g., the establishment of a "Chief Digital Officer" position for the coordination of digital measures), or knowledge (e.g., the creation of training places close to digitalization). By analyzing all the digital options for action with regard to required capabilities, it is possible to identify not only an individualized need for change or synergy but also, if clusters are repeatedly mentioned (cluster formation), an overarching need for change or synergy.

3.4 Anchoring the Digitization Strategy: Goals, Key Figures and Measures

In order to ensure that the digitization strategy is firmly anchored, the activities of the target and key figure definition, together with the derivation of strategic measures resulting from the evaluation of the options for action, complete the strategy process. The procedure in this phase follows the proven balanced scorecard logic. The digital corporate goals are derived directly from existing strategy documents (e.g., marketing strategy) and from the digital mission statement. For each digital target, appropriate key figures are defined as indicators of the achievement of the target and are stored with target levels in the form of target values. In this context, it often makes sense to check the values for consistency using a simulation model.

The options for action defined as part of the development of the digitization strategy are condensed into strategic measures by means of a prioritization process. For this purpose, the data recorded in the profiles of the options for action can be subjected to an evaluation grid, which measures the fit for the digitization strategy and the company on the basis of defined criteria. Digital options for action with a high degree of fit are converted into strategic measures and assigned to the previously derived strategic goals so that their implementation can be ensured by means of strategic measures or under- and over-coverage can be identified. Finally, an economic efficiency calculation must be prepared for the strategic measures before they are implemented.

4 Conclusion

Companies must face up to the issue of digitalization in order to keep from suffering any competitive disadvantages. However, one must not fall into actionism due to competitive pressure, but has to deal with the topic purposefully. The integration of digitization into the corporate strategy ensures a modern alignment of the company and allows the subject to be approached comprehensively and in a structured manner through the stringent process structure of the strategy development process. In this way, digitization becomes a potential risk factor that can be utilized to the full.

References

Die Bio Kiste mit krummen Gemüse und Obst (2018). https://etepetete-bio.de/. Accessed 15 Oct 2018

Digitalist Magazine (2018). http://www.digitalistmag.com/customer-experience/2017/03/15/digital-future-of-retail-04964810. Accessed 15 Oct 2018

Dollar Shave Club (2018). https://www.dollarshaveclub.com/. Accessed 15 Oct 2018

Fashion Retail Future (2018). http://fashionretailfuture.com/american-apparels-shopping-assistant/. Accessed 15 Oct 2018

Hornbach (2018). https://www.hornbach.de/cms/de/de/mein_hornbach/services/mietservice/mietservice.html

IBM (2018). https://www.ibm.com/blockchain/supply-chain/. Accessed 15 Oct 2018

Otto (2018). https://www.otto.de/unternehmen/de/newsroom/dossiers/dossier_vision.php. Accessed 15 Oct 2018

Power Retail (2018). https://www.powerretail.com.au/news/carrefour-digital-strategy/. Accessed 15 Oct 2018

Rewe (2018). https://rewe-digital.com/ueber-uns.html. Accessed 15 Oct 2018

Smart Insights (2018). https://www.smartinsights.com/ecommerce/ecommerce-strategy/top-ecommerce-trends-inform-2017-marketing-strategy/. Accessed 15 Oct 2018

T3n (2018). https://t3n.de/news/roboter-verkaeufer-media-markt-saturn-803296/. Accessed 15 Oct 2018

Zebra (2018). https://www.zebra.com/content/dam/zebra_new_ia/en-us/solutions-verticals/vertical-solutions/retail/brochures/retail-study-2017-en-global.pdf. Accessed 15 Oct 2018

Daniel Kittelberger operates as a Senior Project Manager with Horváth & Partners in Stuttgart for the Competence Center Industrial Goods and High Tech. His consulting experience is based on various projects in the digitization strategy, Industry 4.0, and other topics within the context of organization and operations.

Lea-Sophie Allramseder is a Consultant with Horváth & Partners in Stuttgart for the Competence Center Industrial Goods and High Tech. Her consulting experience is based on the development of new digital business models for service companies and by profound Industry 4.0 use case experience.

SAP S/4HANA: Performance Management in Real Time?

Frank Poschadel

Abstract For several years now, SAP S/4HANA made its way on to the agenda for finance and IT departments across various industries. Many companies are already in implementation, while other companies are in the phase of evaluating possible benefits. One of the most considered area of benefits is related to significant improvements in performance management with the goal of "real-time performance management." Based on practical experience, this contribution examines what benefits can be achieved specifically in the retail and consumer goods industry and what the prerequisites for this are. Our results: there are indeed substantial opportunities. However, achieving them requires a solid business design and harmonized and stringent processes and data structures in controlling and underlying business processes.

Keywords Condition contract management · Integrated financial performance management · Operational performance management instruments · Performance management process · Real-time performance management · SAP S/4HANA

1 The Path Toward Performance Management in "Real Time"

1.1 Increasing Performance Management Requirements

Products and services should be innovative and meet customer requirements, sold on the market for a good profit, and simultaneously create the foundation for further

An adaption of this contribution has been originally printed as Poschadel, F.: SAP S74HANA—Revolution oder Evolution in der Unternehmenssteuerung? in: Kieninger, M., Digitalisierung in der Unternehmenssteuerung, pp. 105–122. Stuttgart, Schäffer-Poeschel.

F. Poschadel (✉)
Controlling & Finance, Horváth & Partners, Hamburg, Germany

M. Buttkus, R. Eberenz (eds.), *Performance Management in Retail and the Consumer Goods Industry*, https://doi.org/10.1007/978-3-030-12730-5_9

company and market share growth. Customers are used to maximum transparency and global access to products and services via the Internet to search for the most favorable prices and conditions. B2B customers of every size have long since professionalized purchasing with the objective of sourcing goods and services under the best possible terms.

Especially in retail and the consumer goods industry, this results in a wide range of TTC (Trade Terms and Conditions) that, on the one hand, offer more flexibility in pricing toward the customer and, on the other hand, significantly increase the challenges and complexity for performance and profitability management. Typical examples for this are general or conditional volume or revenue-based discounts, dedicated promotions, additional BI-products, marketing and merchandizing materials, takeover of shop deliveries and warehousing, etc.

Meanwhile, (end-) customer requirements also constantly increase. Rather than standard products, in many cases, customized (or customizable) products, product bundles, or enhanced product features are expected. A well-known example is the Nike sneaker, which can be customized individually. Further, the width and depth of the assortment offered via online channels is greater compared to offline channels, due to the unlimited space in the front end. Besides this, expectations related to delivery (fast and convenient), availability (immediately on demand), and very high service requirements (always on) need to be considered.

Reacting to these requirements and simultaneously dealing with ongoing cost pressure from the operations side, including procurement, production, and logistics, lead to ever more complex value chains within a company's own organization and when cooperating with partners and suppliers. In addition, technological changes (e.g., digitalization, big data, Industry 4.0, Internet of things, etc.) lead to wide-reaching upheaval in value creation and in the interfaces to customers and suppliers.

To manage customer and product profitability and the profitability of the overall company in a sustainable way, companies require ever more precise knowledge of the following key elements:

- Which sales channel or marketing measure is suitable to realize the highest customer lifetime value?
- Which price is acceptable on the market and at which point can targeted cross-selling opportunities be used to realize additional profit margins as high as possible?
- Which real margins are we achieving with our products and customers?
- What are the real manufacturing and/or purchasing costs?
- Which points in the value chain provide hidden potential for optimization?

But this process is not just about achieving greater precision; it is also about more speed and a higher effectiveness and efficiency in the performance management process itself. The need of having reliable and transparent information available in real time and at any level of detail to be able to deal with competitive pressure leads to an enormous acceleration of management and decision-making processes in companies. Companies have very little time for detailed analyses of their own position and alternatives when reacting to customer requests with competitive and profitably product and service offerings.

1.2 Digitization of Performance Management Processes Provides the Basis

It is fairly evident that more transparency requires state-of-the-art finance and controlling[1] processes in all stages of a company's value chain. But what does "state-of-the-art" mean in this context? In the context described above, financial and non financial performance management information is only beneficial if it is as complete as possible, comprehensive, and available in "real time" and if it can be used to make operational decisions.

With regard to individual products sold to a retail customer, for example, convenience food offered for a certain period of time (e.g., during a football world cup), on the sales side, "complete" means that the real net sales are available, including all discounts, bonuses, and special trade conditions requested by the retail customer. On the cost side, "complete" means that all relevant cost items can be determined, including specific advertising, production and/or purchasing costs, real costs incurred for logistics, storage, return handling, payment costs, failures, defects, customs duties, etc. Own costs need to be considered at group costs, with elimination of any intercompany profit. The costs incurred for a product along the value chain should be recorded as precisely as possible and should be assignable to the product as "cost objects," even across several stages of production. Financial processes must therefore be closely connected to value chain processes and, in doing so, with the flow of materials. Ideally, they are fully identical.

For the underlying business IT systems (usually reflected within the "ERP systems"), this requires complete representation of all corporate sites and processes (e.g., sales, logistics, and service processes) that are as harmonized as possible and a connection to underlying operative systems, e.g., down to the level of the production facilities, warehouse operations, or transportation vehicles where possible. The many interfaces in all parts of a company that use the ERP system lead to considerable challenges in the process:

- Large volumes of data must be processed.
- Information from different sources must be scaled and standardized across the entire value chain (globally).
- If there are changes, for example, the introduction of new products or specific product bundles or special promotional merchandize products, the systems must be able to adapt quickly.
- With regard to the aforementioned challenge, it should also be possible to process everything as quickly as possible, in real time.

For consideration of the benefits of SAP S/4HANA, it is important to take into account that the ERP systems on the market are historically often based on "separate" data and databases. In the case of SAP, for example, in the classic FI/CO

[1]The author uses the English word "controlling" to translate the German term "controlling." Please refer to the discussion in the preface.

environment, the general ledgers and subsidiary ledgers with their financial accounting data are kept separate from the controlling data (CO, CO-PA, PCA, etc.). SAP took an initial step toward merging these areas several years ago with the "New GL" or new general ledger. This "separation" of data did not only occur for financial information but also in other areas such as the split in supplier and customer data.

In addition to the technical prerequisites, it is important to note that there is also such a thing as "too much information," which can quickly overburden the recipient and make target-oriented performance management, identification of measures, and decision-making almost impossible. This applies even more so, if financial information is not linked to basic operational and logistics processes or can only be identified and evaluated with limitations. In these cases root cause analyses are often only possible to a limited extent. Structured and user-friendly processing of information is therefore necessary to exploit the full potential of available transparency. In practice, a variety of methods and procedures, such as big data analyses, exception reporting, predictive analytics, analytical models, etc., are available.

However, these methods are limited if the data is extremely heterogeneous. Many companies do not have a broad and universally harmonized information base. In reality, systems "grew historically" and must often be merged within the reporting system in parts, often manually and at great costs. Fast and flexible adaptation of the system is not possible, and data is not actually available in real time, if it can even be made available at all.

1.3 What Are the Respective Key Changes for Performance Management?

For some time now, a "new" ERP system has been available on the market: SAP S/4HANA. It is to replace the previous SAP R/3 system, also known as SAP ERP. The promises and expectations associated with the new product are high. Business processes are expected to become simpler and faster. In addition to concepts like "digitalization," there is even the promise of real-time information provision. Further innovations, such as "BPC embedded" (Business Planning and Consolidation, a standard solution for planning, reporting, and consolidation) and SAP BW/4HANA (the well-known SAP data warehouse), are also integrated or closely tied in.

To begin with, the basis for this is technical improvement with a combination of a new storage algorithm with in-memory database technology. CPU and data-intensive evaluation and processing operations, such as order settlement, are directly performed in the HANA database and are thus significantly faster than they were previously.

In addition to the technical transformation, there are also content-related improvements with regard to business processes. The basic idea is to provide information for controlling, such as cost centers, orders, customers or sales channels, based on the general ledger account, that is, to remove the classic separation of the "FI landscape" from the "CO landscape." To this end, there will be an integrated posting document (a so-called universal journal) in the future. It will link accounting data to further information such as data from controlling, logistics, or sales management.

Integrated Posting Document in "Universal Journal"
To do this, all data is stored within a central table (a so-called "ACDOCA" table). This is accessed during every business transaction and is also available centrally for reporting purposes. Information is thus available in enhanced posting documents at the most detailed level so that they now not only contain accounting information but rather also include all relevant data for controlling and profit and loss accounts in controlling. This includes not only assignments to cost centers, cost objects, and profit centers but also detailed information with regard to products, customers, sales channels, etc. This entails significant advantages. Accountants and controllers work with an identical level of information, which leads to factual coordination between internal and external accounting. Complex reconciliations of financial accounting and controlling data, including lengthy coordination meetings, can be eliminated. Material valuation also becomes more flexible because different perspectives on the financial information can be taken ad hoc.

Although the practical use of SAP S/4HANA may offer a lot of potential for improvement, some of the discussed changes mean far-reaching changes to performance management concepts, controlling, processes, and the organization. Consequently, changing existing SAP systems to SAP S/4HANA is not a simple "technical system upgrade." This is especially due to historically grown and deeply segregated and often heterogeneous system landscapes, highly individualized and modified ERP installations, and often intensely experienced differentiation between accounting and controlling and the very specific and individually structured reporting processes that are thereby often performed manually. All these factors require more than a plain technical migration. The development of a finance target picture that structures different business management instruments and places them in relation to each other becomes very important; a detailed and integrated concept can be developed on this basis that, in addition to the technical dimension, also includes methods, processes, and the organization. Only then can a new era also be introduced in business management using SAP S/4HANA.

Besides the changes in finance and controlling mentioned above, many more changes are available with SAP S4/HANA. The focus of the following sections will lie on finance and controlling related topics. However, two areas are especially relevant for retail and the consumer goods industry – the introduction of the business partner concept and the replacement of the existing rebate management by the condition and contract management in SAP S/4HANA. Both topics will be evaluated further at the end of the next section.

2 Does It Change the Game?

How do the previously described improvement potentials present themselves in practice? For this purpose, the existing challenges in business and operational corporate management are evaluated with regard to improvements that can be achieved with SAP S/4HANA on the basis of specific examples. This is performed in three steps. First, we evaluate the effects of SAP S/4HANA on an overall (integrated) financial performance management on corporate (group) level. In a second step, we evaluate the effects on selected instruments for performance management on operational level, and, in a third step, we evaluate the effects from the new condition and contract management on performance management, specifically in retail and the consumer goods industry with focus on the trade terms and conditions (TTC) area.

2.1 *SAP S/4HANA for an Integrated Financial Performance Management*

Financial performance management has always been an essential part of any performance management model. Despite the fact that almost every company is facing the challenges mentioned above, improving the financial performance management capabilities has been on the agenda for many years. Among others, the typical objectives in this area are:

- Improving the convergence and methods of financial accounting and controlling
- Providing "one version of truth"
- Accelerating and increasing the efficiency of performance management and reporting and reducing complexity
- Increasing flexibility especially with regard to changes in the business

Based on our experience, several key elements for a state-of-the-art financial performance management can be identified. These elements are generally applicable – independent from the specific ERP system. However in SAP S/4HANA, these factors are even more important (see evaluation in next section).

It is important to understand that the objectives associated with an integrated financial performance management cannot be achieved with *one* individual element of a solution. Instead, it is important to carefully consider the available solution elements and to combine them in the best possible way.

Implementation of an integrated financial performance management approach is supported by an overall (IT) solution architecture in which the different levels of the systems are far more integrated. Key design principles, such as the harmonization of the data's origin or source (transactional posting in the ERP), consequently call for the transactional posting of (logistical) transactions in the ERP system with *all* required information for financial accounting and controlling in one harmonized, central posting document. This information creates the basis for financial reporting and performance management.

Especially in the context of multinational companies, parallel availability of financial information based on international accounting standards (e.g., IFRS) and the local valuation in the posting data are also contained therein. Delta posting logic typically replaces the account-based approach used today. The use of a parallel ledger combined with complete posting logic for IFRS and for local valuation is the intended solution for the future.

Leading management structure in many companies is based on a divisional or segmental view which needs to be reflected across the existing legal entity structure. In a SAP setup, profit centers are typically used to provide the basis for this purpose, and segmental allocation is derived from the profit centers. In addition, partner information for companies (partner companies) and segments (partner segments) are documented in posting documents.

In an optimized ERP setup, product and service charges will be settled between profit centers and segments that are based on the transfer price for transactions between legal entities and group costs for transactions within a legal entity or between segments. According to this approach, the posting of intercompany margins is avoided, or the incidental IC margins are separately posted as additional information within the transactions on dedicated accounts which are not considered for the consolidated profit and loss statements in the divisional view. At the same time, full reconciliation between the legal view and management view (division) within the individual companies is ensured.

Besides, managing functional costs has always been an important part of cost management and the underlying controlling. In SAP, the New GL already provides the option to combine the "internal" need for cost management by business function with the "external" or statutory requirement to provide functional costs for a P&L statement based on the cost of sales method. Technically, the common account-based solution, where accounts are split by functional cost areas, is replaced with the standard functionality for derivation of the functional areas. For this purpose, one-to-one assignments of the business functions to profit and loss account functional areas are required. This information is then assigned to an individual reporting line.

How does SAP S/4HANA now contribute to the aforementioned functional and IT-side elements of the solution? It becomes clear very quickly that the benefits associated with SAP S/4HANA can support the objectives on the business and IT side:

- Merging the transactional information distributed in today's SAP landscape in the "universal journal" in a document with the assignments required for financial accounting and controlling.
  - By merging the legal units view for accounting with the management units view (divisions, plants, functional areas, etc.) for controlling by depicting parallel stock valuation according to local view and group view

  - Assignment of relevant partner information for consolidation of the desired reporting views on the group and management unit levels as well as the defined business functions

- Integrated reflection of all cost accounting activities (e.g., allocations) for intra- and intercompany transactions in the "universal journal" so that the relevant reporting dimensions (legal units, management units, functional area/overhead areas, plants, etc.) are correctly released and charged, and, at the same time, there are no deviations between external accounting and controlling.
- Comprehensive validation capabilities between the different reporting views, based on posting in the ERP (and subsequent integrated consolidation methods) in real time.
- Reports in the legal units with all defined reporting requirements based directly on the transactions in the SAP system, without consolidation in summary tables of the general and subsidiary ledgers and CO-side computer units or in SAP BW.
- The new database technology also enables a significant acceleration of reporting and processing.

At the same time, however, there are two further important aspects that need to be taken into account. On the one hand, many of the aforementioned solution elements may have been implemented in the functions that were previously available in SAP. In particular, these include the new general ledger and the "material ledger" in which the described reporting requirements can be fully reflected in this practical example, supplemented with automated additional postings. The progressing integration of all required information in the "universal journal" is surely a consistent further development into a standardized and harmonized finance environment. But overall, using SAP S/4HANA is more of an evolutionary development step toward greater integration. However, this constitutes more of a "revolution" upon taking profit and loss accounts into consideration. This was previously also illustrated by using the new general ledger in a separate data inventory. In this case, the "universal ledger" creates the opportunity of also providing this information integrated within the data from financial accounting, among other things. The implications of SAP S/4HANA for this area will be considered in more detail throughout the next section.

However, the second aspect of this environment has a broader scope. The potentials that can be realized with SAP S/4HANA can only be achieved if important functional and technical prerequisites are in place. Significant changes on IT side are often needed to achieve a high level of standardization in the ERP systems.

2.2 How Are Operational Performance Management Instruments Affected?

As demonstrated, SAP S/4HANA provides a number of improvement potentials in the area of financial performance management on company or group level. The question as to how fundamental possible improvements through SAP S/4HANA are can be answered better when looking deeper into the instruments used for operational performance management.

As already described above, operational performance management must balance two important factors (comp. Fig. 1): management of individual areas within the company which in turn must be balanced with achieving an optimized overall performance of the company. On an operational level, performance management must therefore reflect two major perspectives in parallel:

- Management of market success and profitability along the market facing units
- Management of the value chain and the individual business functions and stages of the value chain (e.g., production sites, logistics, overhead functions, etc.)

SAP ERP has already provided an instrument for comprehensive management of profitability achieved on the market for several years with the CO-PA module ("Controlling Profitability Analysis"). This facilitates reporting and analysis of a variety of reporting dimensions (the so-called characteristics) such as product, customer, sales channel, region, etc. Originally, the CO-PA module was designed to be an instrument for sales performance management (that is, for measuring and managing turnover and margins achieved in sales). However, it was then developed further into a complete profitability statement in which, e.g., the associated overhead costs of the company or the individual market segment can be viewed using allocations. In the process, the CO-PA module is completely integrated in the logistical value flows. Two different approaches are generally available: "Account-based profitability analysis" based on accounts or cost elements and "costing based profitability analysis" in which the depiction of profit and loss accounting is based on the so-called value fields using imputed costs in many cases. Costing-based profitability analysis is particularly used in practice today.

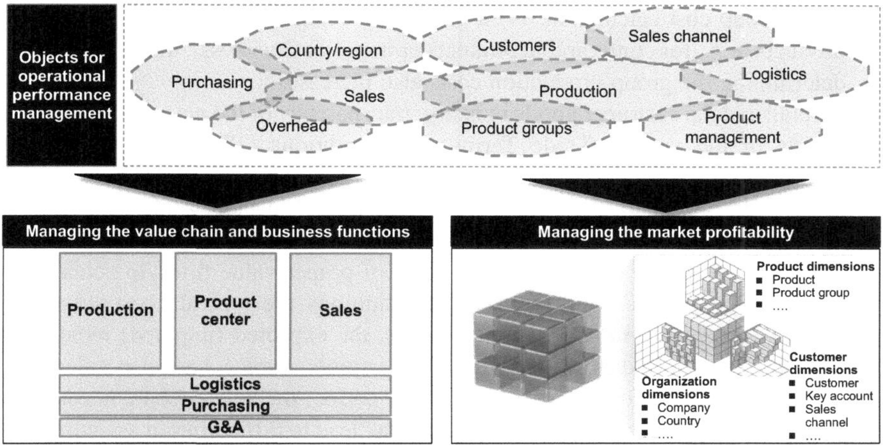

Fig. 1 Operational corporate management areas

But there are usually several challenges associated with using the costing-based CO-PA. These include:

- CO-PA creates its own data inventories with a high level of detail. This can often lead to a large number of data records, which can have a negative effect on performance, in particular during detailed analysis.
- For CO-PA, separate value flows must be established to transfer operational data from the logistical processes and objects (e.g., customer, sales orders, projects, cost centers, production orders, etc.). With an increasing complexity of the logistical processes, the complexity of the required value flows in the CO-PA increases, which initially increases the implementation effort. But far more serious is the increase in error susceptibility that also occurs when transferring data into the CO-PA during operation (e.g., due to faulty preceding processes or during changes in preceding processes), which can result in differences between accounting and CO-PA profitability analysis. Troubleshooting and corrections are then often complex and time-intensive. Confidence in the data is also undermined.
- When analytical profit and loss accounting is applied, turnover and production costs are based on the cost-of-sales view. Transitioning to the "total cost method" view, often used in accounting, is thus only possible in selected areas of profitability analysis. If imputed approaches are also used, e.g., for interest or amortization, this can cause further differences.
- The valuation of production costs is initially based on the valuation from the perspective of the local accounting area, that is, it possibly contains included intercompany margins. If profit and loss accounting is now to be performed based on group production costs, this is only possible if the turnover resulting from the external customers is always valuated with the group production costs it actually incurred, and this can also be reported in the CO-PA. Under certain technical conditions (using a single controlling area), this is possible for standard products using group cost calculation. With increasing complexity of the value flow and products (e.g., for configurable products or in project business), the complexity of determining the group production costs also increases.
- In retail and the customer goods industry, transparency of the net sales and margin effects of the various Trade Terms and Conditions (TTC) will be one key requirement. Reflecting all conditions correctly in CO-PA creates various challenges: On one hand, the number of "value fields" in the costing-based profitability analysis will increase, and it may reach its technical limitation. The bigger challenge, however, is related to the setup of proper value flows to actually fill these "value fields." Trade terms and conditions are typically maintained as "rebate agreement" in SAP. In these cases, the expected (imputed) rebates are calculated and posted as accrual with each customer invoice, later also reflected in CO-PA. At the end of the respective rebate period, the actual rebate needs to be reconciled with the imputed one, and this may lead to difficulties in assigning any difference to the right "characteristics" (e.g., customer, material, etc.). In addition, some "rebates" cannot be considered as sales deduction but need to be reflected as

cost line item. Again, assigning the right characteristics to these line items ("value fields") can be challenging, especially if the actual costs are coming in as supplier invoice.

- In the past, the development of CO-PA's own reporting functions was only very limited and not up-to-date with modern reporting tools. Appealing and user-friendly reporting was usually only possible using SAP BW and, if necessary, further reporting front ends.

How can SAP S/4HANA now contribute to addressing the previously mentioned challenges? First, it is apparent that all data is merged to one location (in a data record) using the "universal ledger." In the interaction with the changed technical structure and the "in-memory" technology, this leads to a significantly smaller database and, simultaneously, a simpler data model as well as faster access and processing times.

The previously existing separation of content from financial accounting and controlling is eliminated. All postings are executed relating to an account. Dedicated cost elements in the CO module no longer exist. The account-based profitability analysis in CO-PA thereby becomes the method of choice. To do this, the value posted to the account must be enriched with the required information (dimensions) for market segment profitability analysis. The usage of the costing-based profitability analysis will be less important in the future.

Three specific areas shall be highlighted at this point:

- Consistency between finance and controlling and more flexibility for detailed reporting of TTC: In SAP S/4HANA the accounting-based profitability analysis is the new standard for profitability analysis. This implies two major advantages: Firstly, financial accounting and controlling information will be based on the same data and can be accessed in "real time" as soon as the transactional posting has been created. A reconciliation will no longer be required. Secondly, limitations related to the number of "value fields" are no longer relevant. Individual Trade Terms and Conditions can be reflected in dedicated accounts posted with the invoice. For reporting purposes, these accounts can be grouped in a flexible way. In combination with the new Condition and Contract Management in SAP S/4HANA, more transparency on net sales and sales margins will be available. Nevertheless, it must be noted that the challenges in assigning any differences between (imputed) rebates with actual rebates in full detail to all relevant characteristics, as mentioned above, may still be a challenge.
- Availability of goods issue posting: The (standard) production costs could previously only be provided in the account-based profitability analysis with one account (goods issue) as a total. In costing-based profitability analysis, it was possible to create a breakdown of production costs, according to the cost component scheme at the point in time at which the turnover was posted. With SAP S/4HANA, the (standard) production costs are now also available in accounting terms within the outline of the cost component scheme. When applying the cost-of-sales method, a two-step posting can initially show goods in transit. These can later be reposted to be shown as COGS ("Cost of Goods Sold"). During the

posting process, the dimensions of profit and loss accounting are also assigned at the same time.

- This also applies for cost-object variances (production order). These were previously only available in account-based profitability analyses in one account (price difference account, "PRD") and could only be broken down further into costing-based profitability analysis. In SAP S/4HANA, the cost object variances in the SAP standard variance categories (input price variance, input quantity variance, scrap, etc.) are available as accounts. These are also assigned to the dimension of market segment profitability analysis.

Both of these aspects illustrate that a large step toward the identity of financial accounting and controlling can be achieved. However, it must be taken into account that much higher requirements must be placed on quality and completeness of the data, value flows, and the required derivation rules for market segment information, because the previous option (although not to be recommended) of correcting CO-PA data is no longer available or only available to a limited degree. In principle, derivation of the profitability analysis characteristics occurs in real time; that is, settlement runs (e.g., for cost centers, projects, or cost objects) are no longer needed to provide profitability analysis information.

Providing profitability analysis information based on group production costs, however, the same challenges that previously existed still remain.

Further significant improvements are the new "Fiori" interface and connection with further reporting tools (e.g., SAP Analysis for Office), both for analytical reporting and also for management reporting. More intuitive user interfaces in conjunction with direct access to posted transaction data in real time allow for faster and more flexible analyses and create the basis for "self-service reporting" up to the top management level.

The fact that different business functions require different performance management approaches due to their specific tasks must be taken into account when performance management instruments and tools are designed and implemented. Three different center types can usually be discerned (comp. Fig. 2).

In practice, the different management approaches also result in different requirements on the respective management instruments and the information required to that end. While the budget center is usually managed on the basis of a "simple" comparison of budgeted costs and actual costs, management of a performance center is more complex. This can be seen clearly in the example of a production plant. The "responsibility" of a production plant is to manufacture the required quantity of products at the agreed costs (that is, at the standard product costs). Furthermore, an additional direction from management is usually set, e.g., the development of a standard cost of goods over time. On the other hand, production is not responsible for "volume variances," for example, underutilization due to missing quantities resulting from too optimistic sales planning or from the effects of changing raw material prices. Production can be considered to be successful if the consumption variances it is responsible for are as small as possible. Ideally they equal zero.

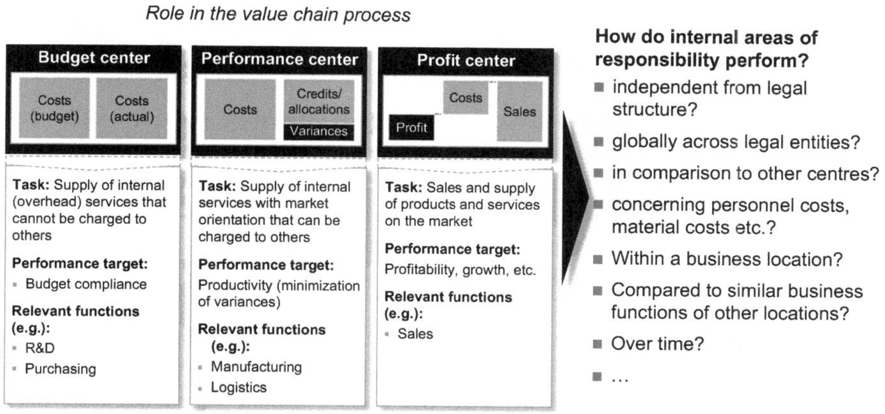

Fig. 2 Center types in the company

On the basis of this example, it can be seen that performance management of different business functions in today's SAP landscape must often access data from different modules. In the case of production management, these are the valuated output (change in inventory), the (actual) costs of production cost centers and production orders, and variances from cost centers and production orders. Profit center accounting creates the common basis in which the functional breakdown of the company is reflected and the individual elements of plant performance management are available at the account level. However, this itemization is usually not sufficient. So, for example, variance information is only posted in total to one account (price differences) so that additional information from other sources (in particular, cost center accounting and product cost accounting) must be added.

The "universal ledger" in SAP S/4HANA can significantly simplify things in this area, and a breakdown of the deviation categories can be derived according to accounts so that these are also directly available for reporting. Because profit center assignment and further assignments for controlling are posted, it is possible to perform a complete analysis on the basis of the "universal ledger" data.

While the technical availability or provision of the data is significantly simplified with SAP S/4HANA, the interpretation of the data and the interpretation of the variances, in particular, continue to remain complex. One of the greatest challenges lies in deriving the correct measures on the production side on the basis of the determined (financial) variances, for example. SAP S/4HANA can only provide the *technical* basis as the starting point for further analysis with regard to the causative products, machines, batch sizes, production sequence, etc. In future, complex (stochastic) models are additionally required here. They are used to determine the causes on the one hand and, on the other hand, to prevent or reduce possible deviations beforehand.

2.3 The Role of the New Condition Contract Management (CCM)

As in financial accounting and controlling, SAP S/HANA provides significant harmonization and simplification potential. The new "business partner" concept is one of these examples. In traditional ERP systems, the vendor master and customer master are maintained and stored separately, while the approach in SAP S/4HANA is the business partner approach. The central "business partner" now replaces the different suppliers and customers. However, each "business partner" can have multiple roles.

With the new condition contract management (CCM), a similar path is taken in SAP S/4HANA. SAP has replaced traditional rebate processing with the new "condition contract management" (CCM) module which is intended to bring together customer and supplier conditions in one place. To do so in the traditional approach, two things need to be in place: First, a rebate agreement needs to be created, specifying who receives the rebate payment, what criteria the rebate is based on (customer, customer and product, etc.), the validity period of the agreement, etc. To keep track of this, SAP creates separate condition tables for each customer billing document (invoices and credit/debit notes). Automatically posted accruals can be used to keep track of the accumulated value of a rebate for accounting and performance management purposes periodically. Final settlement takes place with the creation of the credit note for the customer.

The traditional approach has several disadvantages:

- The SAP table which stores rebate relevant invoices is huge, with a large number of data records.
- If changes in customer conditions are made, the table needs to be rebuilt, and this blocks access to this data.
- Only rebates related to customer sales documents can be processed.

In SAP S/4HANA, rebate conditions can be applied directly to the sales order invoicing data without the need for separate tables to store the condition data. Rebates can be applied to new customers, and previous business can be considered retrospectively. In a first step, condition contracts need to be created and released. However, sales invoices can be created before or after the condition contract creation. If the sales document is created after the contract creation, the accrual condition would be available in the SD sales order condition tab, but, if not, the rebate would be provided as part of the settlement process, and the rebate condition is available in the credit memo which posts the correct accrual amount to the respective accounts.

One of the key benefits of the new approach is the possibility of bringing together conditions on the sales side and the purchasing side. This can be relevant in cases where conditions are negotiated with the customer as part of the order to cash process, but "technically" the effect of this sales condition has to be processed as part of the purchase to pay process (e.g., when these costs need to be processed via a supplier invoice from a logistics provider).

3 Conclusion

A final evaluation of the initial question whether or not SAP S/4HANA is really changing the game must be provided in two parts. On the one hand, SAP S/4HANA can achieve significant improvements for creating the "transparency in real time" needed for corporate performance management. Information that is currently distributed is merged in one place, financial accounting and controlling are integrated much stronger, and information is available faster and in more detail and can be accessed more easily and more flexibly. This also applies for the Contract and Condition Management area as customer and supplier related information is managed 'in one place' what increases transparency. In addition the account-based profitability analysis provides more flexibility and (if needed) more granularity for analyses of customer- and supplier-related contract conditions.

However, more data and granularity do not automatically guarantee better management decisions. In reality, the transparency created for the recipient must be structured and provided in a recipient-specific manner. At the same time, however, the requirements on the quality of the accounting data and preceding transactional processes and value flows also increase. The experiences from today's SAP landscape demonstrate that high integration is both a promise and a commitment. Changing to SAP S/4HANA requires an even greater effort with regard to further improvement of process and data quality in most companies.

Nonetheless, the most important aspect in this context, the quality of the performance management model, remains unchanged. Even in the SAP S/4HANA landscape, the question of how management of the whole company and individual business functions should be performed in the context of a sound business management concept must be answered. Which instruments are necessary to this end and which prerequisites must be created in structures and processes? For the implementation of this concept, SAP S/4HANA enables new and more improved options than today's SAP landscape.

Frank Poschadel is a Principal in the Competence Center Controlling and Finance at Horváth & Partners and an expert in corporate performance management and cost/profit and loss accounting and reporting. He is responsible for both business and IT design and IT implementation for a variety of large projects in this context.

How to Use Robotics Within Finance Functions?

Sina Gieseking and Kai Grönke

Abstract This contribution describes how the current trend of digitization has gained entry into the financial department. After standardizing processes and implementing shared services, the CFO Organization 4.0 is all about using the potential of big data, predictive forecasting, and robotics. This contribution lists the advantages of these technologies and contains some application examples for accounting and controlling functions. In addition, new roles and functions accompanied by the transformation will be highlighted.

Keywords Robotics · RPA · Process automatization · Predictive analytics · Shared service center · CFO Organization 4.0

1 Future-Oriented Roles and Tasks of Financial Organization

Over the past years, processes in the production industry have been automated to a high degree, and on this basis, the entire industrial sector has been digitized heavily. Almost on a daily basis, media is discussing the challenges of digitization. However, the question of which effects "digitization" will have on the financial sector has not been entirely answered. Most recently, digitization's implementation in financial functions has only been put into practice to a very limited extent. Due to partly enormous investment costs, high complexity of processes, and lacking standardization, the financial sector still operates with many interfaces and media discontinuities to date.

S. Gieseking (✉)
Retail and Consumer Goods, Horváth & Partners, Munich, Germany

K. Grönke
Controlling & Finance, Horváth & Partners, Düsseldorf, Germany

M. Buttkus, R. Eberenz (eds.), *Performance Management in Retail and the Consumer Goods Industry*, https://doi.org/10.1007/978-3-030-12730-5_10

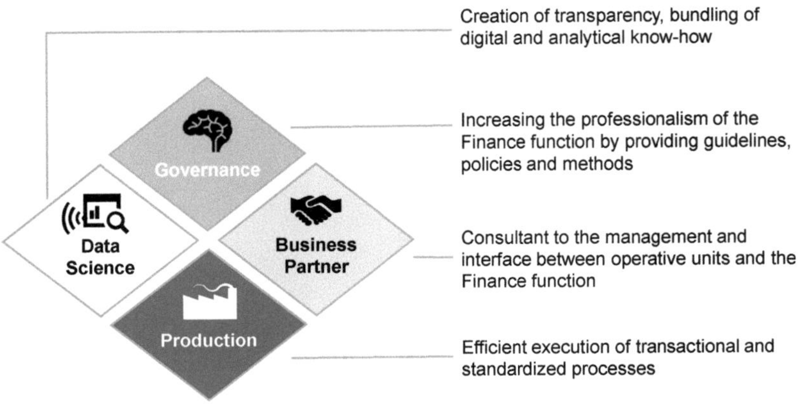

Fig. 1 Role model

Processes have been the focus of many transformation projects in the financial sector over the last years. The effectivity and efficiency of the financial sector has been increased using process standardization and the centralization of individual tasks in order to satisfy the rising pressure of costs and management's increasing demands. To this end, the tasks and responsibilities along processes were divided into different "roles" and, in many cases, re-embedded with regard to organization. Therefore, tasks were divided into "governance," "production," and "business partner." Recently, an additional role has established itself—with regard to future financial functions—with which all tasks in the field of "data science."

The role model illustrated in Fig. 1 serves as a grading pattern for all activities and responsibilities in the financial sector:

Governance: This role includes all tasks regarding the definition of group-wide standards, methods, and systems and secures their consistency and compliance. Consequently, it increases the professionalization of the financial sector and lays the foundation for all additional tasks in the financial function as well as the cooperation with up- and downstream functions.

Production: This role's tasks are usually embedded in service functions. In these, all transactions and standardized tasks and/or processes are bundled. Consequently, "production" focuses the generation, validation, and distribution of all data relevant for the corporate performance management.

Business partner: By bundling all standardized tasks within "production," the foundation for an efficient and effective analysis and support for decision-finding processes by the "business partner" is laid. With the business partner's role, management is given a partner with whom not only decisions are prepared and supported, but opportunities for improvement are identified and the implementation of change measures monitored. This role works as an interface between the financial department and the business segments as well as additional steering dimensions such as functions and regional subsidiaries.

This clear division of responsibilities enables both cost-optimized operating in financial organization and, simultaneously, the ability of offering the finance department's customers demand-oriented services in respective quality.

2 A Target-Oriented Transformation of the Financial Organization

The reorganization of roles and tasks and the concomitant changes to the distribution of tasks in financial processes generally lead to new forms of organization.

Over the last years, in many companies the bundling of similar processes has led to the emergence of service organizations. In these service organizations, tasks that were previously organized in a decentral manner are now centralized. The role model depicted in Fig. 1 supports a clear separation of tasks for the development of business service organizations with shared and expert service centers. Shared service centers increasingly take on transactional and repetitive tasks in a function-spanning manner, characterized by high volume and a generally high use of resources. In comparison, an expert service center focusses on a specific area of responsibilities and bundles the necessary expertise.

The general trend of shared service center organizations is going toward multi-tower organizations, in which the processes of multiple functional areas are conducted. Typically, tasks from the sectors of accounting, controlling, procurement, HR, and IT are bundled there: for example, auditing, payroll accounting, report creation, planning preparations, IT service hotlines, and more. The savings potential that can be gained from the transfer of tasks to a shared service center amounts to about 20–35%.

At the moment, many shared service center organizations are discussing and/or implementing additional transformation steps. On the one hand, the service portfolio of the organizations is expanded step by step, including additional functions and/or additional corporations into the service portfolio. This oftentimes entails an increased process orientation toward end-to-end processes such as purchase-to-pay, order-to-cash, record-to-report, or hire-to-retire. On the other hand, many companies are faced with the question whether or not additional saving potentials can be generated by transferring services. Several options have been discussed to this end: from transferring one's organization to a different, cheaper country to a transfer of services to an external service provider.

This so-called near- or offshoring, meaning the transferal of tasks to a foreign country or the outsourcing to an external service provider, also holds disadvantages. The controlling and monitoring of task execution through an internal service organization is made more complicated by this, for example, and multiple different languages and cultures can also constitute barriers and lead to misunderstandings that may be reflected in inadequate service quality. The savings additionally created through near- and offshoring can thus be neutralized to a certain extent.

3 Digital Financial Transformation

Compared to other functions, such as production, the finance department has initially exhibited a relatively slow development toward digitization. However, meanwhile, the various advantages of digitization and the constantly increasing cost pressure depict a holistic entry into digitization as the peerless possibility of both increasing efficiency and quality.

Since many finance departments have focused on the development of service organizations to increase the efficiency, the development of information and communication technology has strongly progressed. In addition, the rapid increase of available computing capacities has lowered the investment costs for storage capacities. A significant development is the generation, collection, and processing of big data by using new technologies. This development has been followed by changed demands in the finance department, both regarding data quality and the output generated.

Digitization's many advantages lead to previously optimized financial organizations that are now being developed further to digital financial organizations. Companies that had not previously introduced service organizations are now faced with the question of whether such a step can be skipped. However, digitization's advent necessitates a comprehensive "transformation-readiness" of the finance departments in order to make use of the opportunities offered by digitization to their fullest potential. In this process, transforming from an optimized service organization to a digital financial organization means significantly less effort than a direct transformation from a traditional financial organization to a digital one. This is due to the fact that in the former case, the necessary precondition for digitization and automation, the standardization of processes, has already been implemented.

A study conducted by Horváth & Partners confirms this trend and depicts additional significant drivers for digitization. The demand for financial organization's efficiency will increase. Routine processes that are based on clear decision-making rules will be downsized radically in the future.

In addition, performance management will be more future-oriented and be built upon new and previously unused data. Previously used methods, such as planning, reporting, or intra-year forecasting, will be developed further, partially replaced or supported by new technologies to this end.

These altered framework conditions are leading to a fundamental change in the roles within financial organization. Additionally, new competences and tasks arise that must be manned.

In order to support these trends and demands for financial organization, enabler and technologies for the implementation of digitization have been classified. In the following, especially the technologies, advanced analytics and robotic process automation (RPA) will be illustrated regarding their potentials for management improvement—or rather increase the efficiency (Fig. 2).

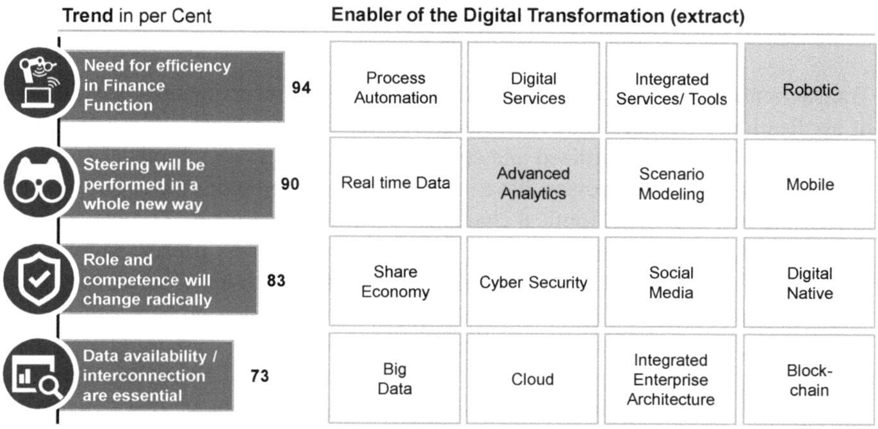

Fig. 2 Altered framework conditions within financial organization

3.1 *Future-Oriented Performance Management with Advanced Analytics*

For an effective and efficient corporate performance management, controlling supplies management with figures and data. At the moment, corporate performance management is based on planned and actual data that are analyzed and comprehensively evaluated by controlling. This inevitably implies a reactive-analytic evaluation that compares past development with the planned development and, however, is rarely capable of identifying errors in a timely manner and defining the corresponding measures for a future-oriented performance management.

Knowing what the company faces in the future would significantly improve performance management, as it could then occur in a significantly more target-oriented and proactive manner. The basis for a proactive forecasting evaluation is laid by (function-spanning) internal and external data, created by the advent of digitization. The advantage of the new management systems lies in the fact that apart from the usual structured data, now unstructured data can also be collected and processed. On this basis, a continuous and automatic search for patterns and dependencies takes place, while algorithms are simultaneously scouring through the data and evaluating them according to their probability.

In the course of the automation of corporate performance management, quantitative-statistical relations will replace previously known qualitative-theoretical cause-effect chains. This leads to a significantly greater accuracy of forecasting, thereby overcoming a typical weak point in planning and forecasting.

In addition, it signifies a great advantage that steering processes occur faster and more effectively with a significantly reduced commitment of resources. Advanced analytics allow a significantly improved forecasting of future business development.

3.2 Efficient Processes with Robotic Process Automation

Transactional process steps that are barely complex and recurring are classical fields of application for process automatization. As described in Sect. 2, these processes are usually already standardized and centralized within service organizations. In the course of this, first processes have already been automated. Optical document processing that uses OCR (optical character recognition) serves as a typical example of utilization in accounting. However, the weak point of past process automations lies in their technical limitations. For the most part, the execution of certain processes can only be carried out in an IT system. This means that a process can only be automated to the extent that it can be represented within an IT system. Process steps that occur in a different system cannot be taken into account by such systems—or rather, they must be automated separately. Entire process chains that extend over different IT systems cannot be automated using earlier technologies.

Robotic process automation (RPA) begins by tackling exactly this problem, since modern software robots function in a system-spanning manner and are capable of bridging boundaries between systems and applications even without complex interface programming. In doing so, these software robots operate on the level of a conventional user interface and replace human entries in various systems.

As shown in Figs. 3 and 4, a particularly large effect is realized through robotics solutions in transactional processes of intermediate complexity. They carry out autonomously recurring and rule-based processes based on structured data using specifically programmed software robots. In doing so, human process steps are imitated using prescribed decision rules; however, they are carried out significantly faster and more efficiently (see Fig. 5).

The benefit of RPA is evident: unlike humans, robots are operational 24/7. Productivity can be increased massively by this. Process steps are seamlessly documented and thus enable an auditing that can be processed easily. In addition, efficiency and process quality can be increased for task execution with a minimal error rate.

Meanwhile, the disadvantages present themselves in the form of implementation and recurring maintenance costs. Processes must be prepared and standardized for their deployment with RPA. Apart from the implementation effort, employees must simultaneously be trained for their cooperation with the software robots and be familiarized with their introduction and maintenance.

A great development potential exists for financial organizations, as employees will be relieved of transactional tasks and can be deployed for more complex tasks. The demand placed on the finance department—namely, prospectively functioning more clearly as business partner—can consequently be met more suitably. On the other hand, with the release of employee capacities and transaction volumes, an estimate of 30% of additional FTE and costs can be saved. Consequently, "roboshoring" represents a real alternative to nearshoring, offshoring, or outsourcing. Simultaneously, new competencies must be established in the finance department. Section 4 summarizes the necessary changes.

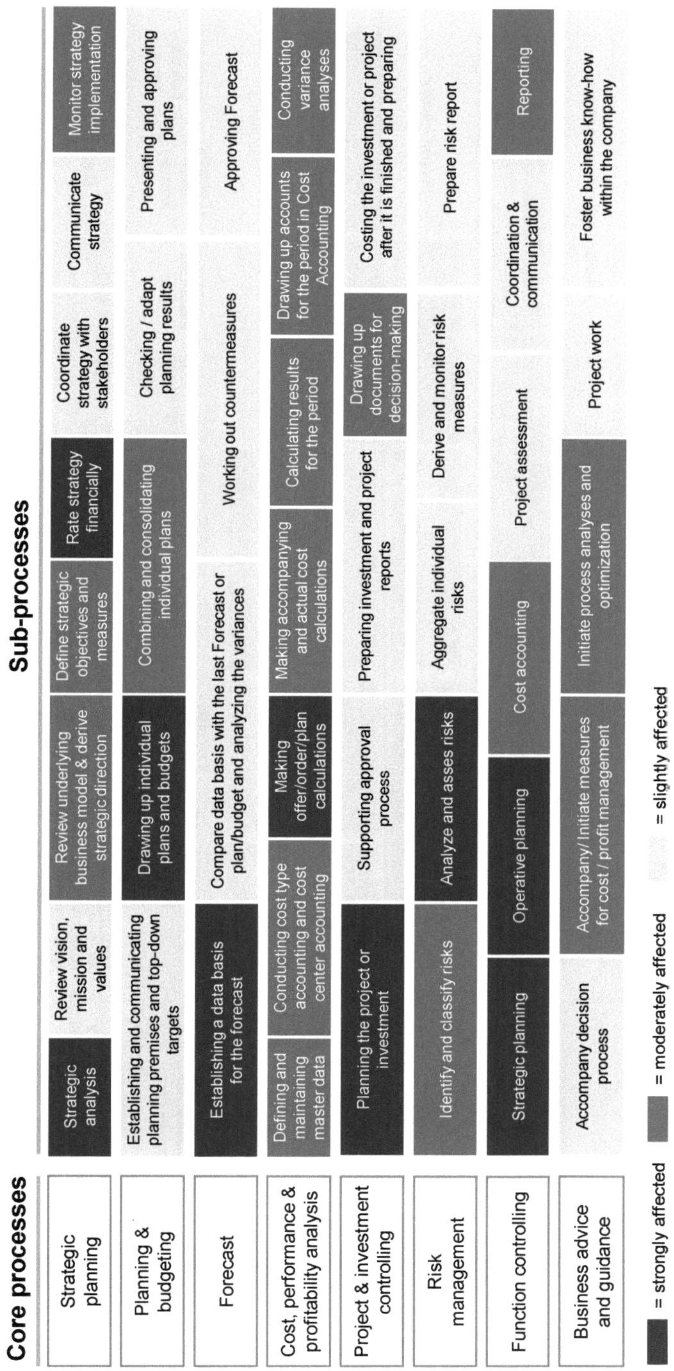

Fig. 3 Effect of digitization on typical controlling processes

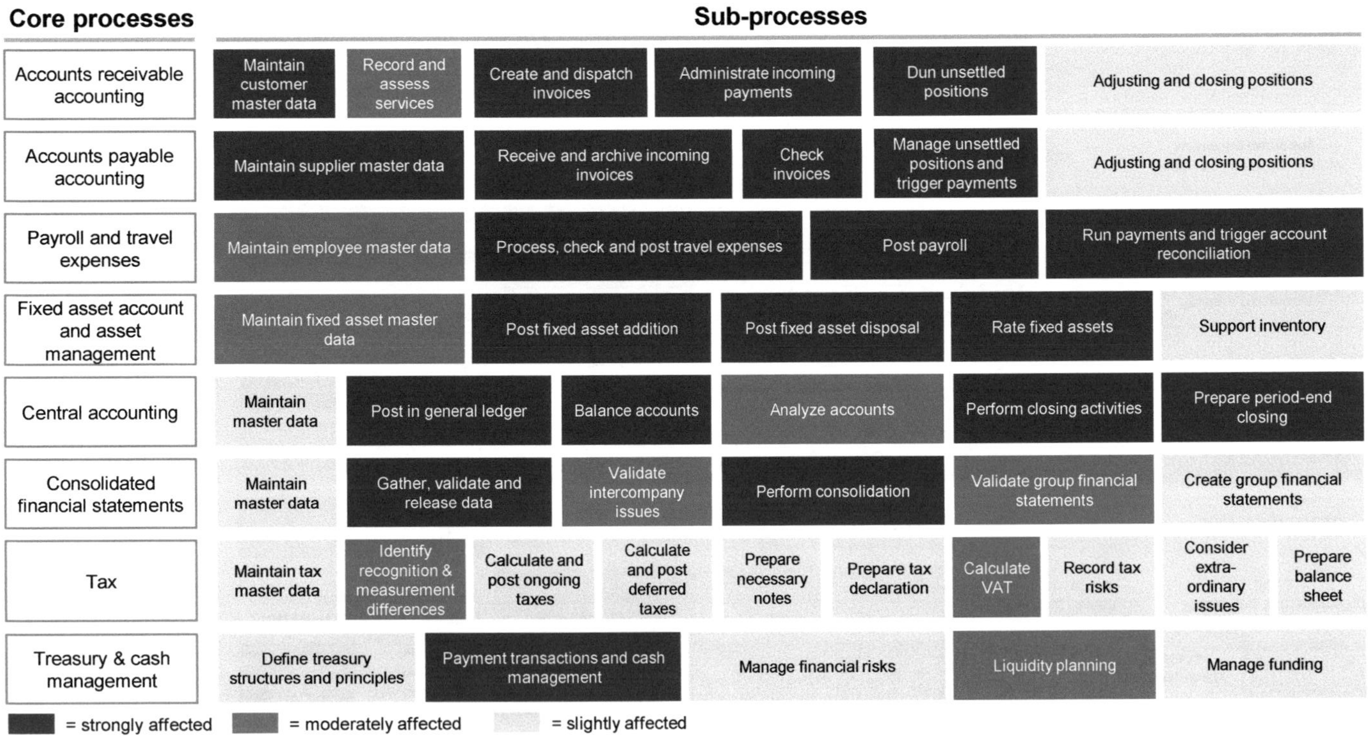

Fig. 4 Effect of digitization on typical accounting processes

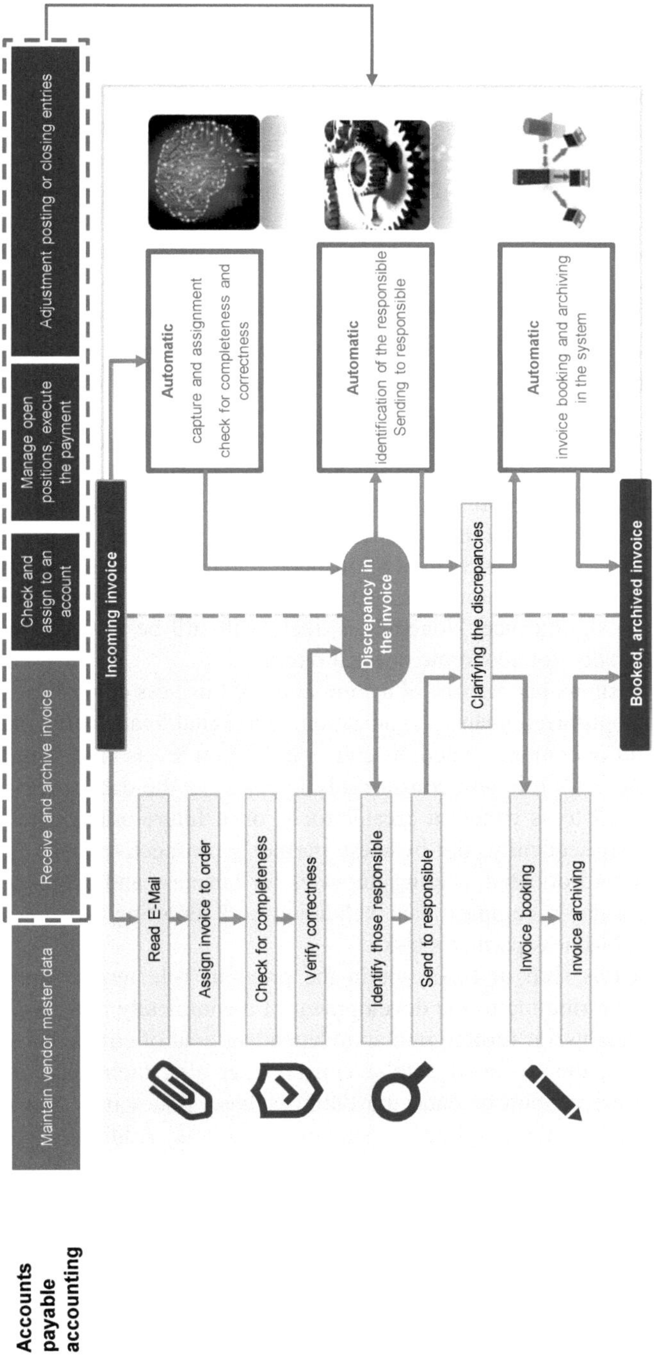

Fig. 5 Comparison of a manually (left) and RPA (right) conducted process

4 The Altered Role Model of Digital Financial Organization

At first sight, the release of resources in the wake of digitization and process automatization may seem like a loss of employment for many employees in financial organizations. Sure enough, many tasks are partially or completely taken over by artificial intelligence in corporate performance management or software robots. Nevertheless, a demand for employees in the finance department remains, albeit with changed role profiles. The "uninhabited finance department" will not exist in the future either. However, many activities that are still carried out by employees will be executed by machines tomorrow.

Concomitantly, the role *governance and leadership* is gaining significance. Not only the transformation and standardization mentioned above must be regulated and monitored. The extensive requirements and responsibilities of data analytics also arise. Simultaneously, governance tasks are improved, since with the help of RPA-based processes, a seamless documentation is facilitated. Consequently, employees can focus on the definition and implementation of standards, thereby contributing to a greater professionalization of the finance department.

The production tasks of the finance department, such as the accounting of business transactions and the creation of financial statements and reports, will largely be supported by RPA and automation technologies. Therefore, the role "production" will decrease in significance. Nonetheless, there will still be tasks in the role that cannot be automated for economic or legal reasons.

While the business partner role of a corporate and business controller is strengthened within an optimized finance organization, in a digital finance organization, it is developed at all operational functions and organization levels. The significance of the business partner's role will considerably increase, as the data processed by the new methods and tools enable a greater focus on a future-oriented performance management. Consequently, the business partner's prospective tasks will be the creation of forward-oriented steering impulses for business and complex analysis. In the future, today's complex data validation and reporting will no longer be included in the business partner's tasks.

Apart from this shift of tasks within the previous role model, the advent of digitization is contributing to the development of a completely new role profile: in this way, data analysis is turning into an independent field of competence of highly qualified experts, the so-called data scientists. Inter alia, their tasks include the collection and preparation of data, translating subject issues into data models as well as developing and adapting evaluation algorithms. Additionally, they will extract previously hidden knowledge and visualize results, thereby creating greater transparency. Consequently, the role of the data scientist bundles digital analysis know-how with technological knowledge regarding system and software innovations and takes on the systematic evaluation of relevant steering information. The competence profile of these data scientists therefore includes mathematic-statistical proficiencies, the ability of developing complex models as well as strongly developed IT skills (Fig. 6).

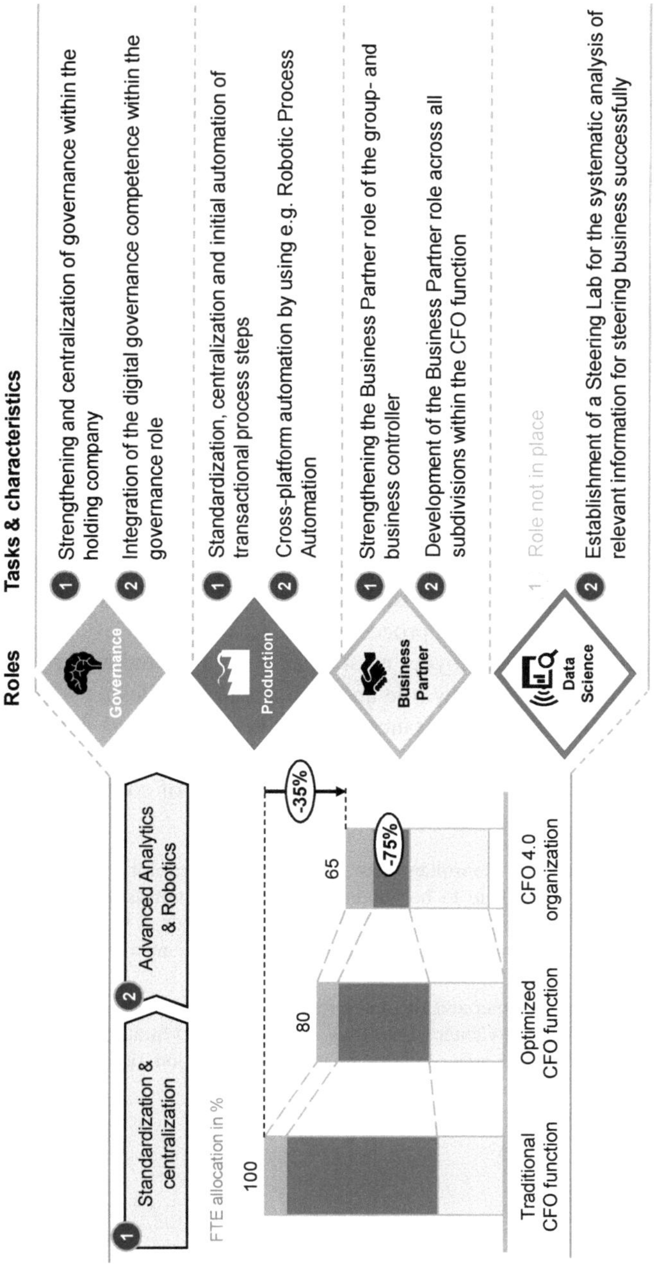

Fig. 6 Altered roles in the transformation process

Simultaneously, the new role necessitates the construction of a new organization unit that will be ascribed with the role: the "Data Science & Steering Lab." It will be located in line with the usual areas of the finance department such as accounting or controlling. The tasks of this unit are generally derived from the different functions that the Steering Lab is intended to comply with:

As *data enabler* it provides methods, systems, and processes for analyses of high-quality data.

In the function of *platform providers*, it develops, implements, and operates organization units necessary for "world-class" data analyses.

In the form of *analytics consultant*, the Steering Lab identifies, creates, and operates the "best in class" IT applications for analysis and forecasting.

As *coach and trainer*, it develops and trains the finance department in the maintenance, provision, and utilization of high-quality analysis and steering applications.

In the function of *data evangelist*, the Steering Lab promotes and shares a culture for the creation and use of data in the finance department.

In summary, the advent of digitization implies a shift of tasks within the existing role model. The new role of the data scientist will be added, and as a consequence, the Steering Lab will be needed as a new organization unit. For employees these changes can be unsettling.

Consequently, a key task of the human resources department will be meeting employees' fears in a timely and constructive manner. This should take place before and/or during the transformation processes and with the help of a comprehensive change management. The employees must be actively involved as early as possible, and an understanding for the new role and competence profiles must be developed. In this process, it is of great importance that employees summon the willingness to cooperate with each other more closely within the new role models and a readiness to continuously keep learning in order to expand their field of competence.

Sina Gieseking operates as a Consultant with Horváth & Partners for the Competence Center Retail and Consumer Goods. Due to her studies and previous professional employments, she possesses broad expertise in the context of retail and consumer goods as well as process standardization, especially concerning the implementation of shared service center and process digitization.

Kai Grönke operates as a Partner and Head of Office Düsseldorf with Horváth & Partners. He is responsible for the Competence Center Controlling & Finance/CFO Strategy & Organization. His consulting experience lies in the area of digital finance transformation, organizational design, and performance management.

Big Bang Based Decision Automation

On the Implementation of Innovative Methods, Discovered by Top-Level Research, for Automatized Decisions in Replenishment, Price Optimization, and Campaign Management

Mareike Clasen and Michael Milnik

Abstract In the following contribution, an innovative artificial intelligence technology will be introduced. It was developed by international top-level researchers and has found successful application in retail for years now. Future events in complex business environments can be recognized and precisely assessed by this artificial intelligence, and the insights can serve as basis for founded decisions. Further, a high degree of automatization can serve to reduce strain on business operations, while simultaneously creating more efficient processes.

This contribution highlights the implementation of statistical models and procedures that take all influencing factors and their interdependencies into account to calculate forecasts. In addition, the economic advantage by including variable costs and business targets into the optimization will be portrayed in particular. The area of application, the replenishment sector, as well as many other examples will be introduced.

This contribution aims at an audience consisting replenishment, purchase, marketing, and sales experts and responsible persons, as well as all those that are interested in an individual assessment of their customers, but do not have the necessary experience or methods to process the data at their disposal.

Keywords Artificial intelligence · Automatization · Forecast calculation · Machine learning · Neuronal networks · Predictive analytics

An adaption of this contribution has been originally printed as Clasen, M., Milnik, M.: Vom Urknall zur Prognose, Buttkus, M., Neugebauer, A., Kaland, A. (2016), Controlling in Handel: Innovative Ansätze und Praxisbeispiele, pp. 177–192, Springer Gabler, Wiesbaden.

M. Clasen · M. Milnik (✉)
Blue Yonder, Karlsruhe, Germany

M. Buttkus, R. Eberenz (eds.), *Performance Management in Retail and the Consumer Goods Industry*, https://doi.org/10.1007/978-3-030-12730-5_11

1 Artificial Intelligence (AI) as a Part of the Technological Business Competence

The last study conducted by the WWF in 2015[1] showed that in Germany alone over 18,000,000,000 kg of foodstuffs go to waste each year. Worldwide these numbers go as high as 1,300,000,000,000 kg.[2] This corresponds to one-third of all foodstuffs produced for mankind.

Reading this example, one could pose the question of how such an enormous overproduction can be reduced, without endangering service level and product availability for customers. The saving potential is enormous.

One of the topics that are most hotly discussed in the logistics branch is that of so-called green logistics. What can retail do to contribute to the reduction of harmful emissions?

Online retailing is booming. But which customer still needs an additional catalogue, in order to shop online? Which products should be presented to the customer in the online shop as additional recommendations?

Price search engines and the many possibilities of purchasing via the Internet have increased market transparency for customers significantly. Consequently, the price of a product, but also the provider's service quality, become even more direct influencing factors of purchasing decisions. So how can distributors sell remainder of stocks, if these exist? Which price allows a high usage of my logistics chain and helps me reduce idle time?

An increasingly large number of providers with solutions and offers are focusing on these and similar questions. Their results are meeting great interest in the market, with terms such as "predictive analytics," "prescriptive analytics," "machine learning," or, especially over the last period of time, "artificial intelligence." A survey conducted early in 2017[3] posed the question of how "machine learning" will change the future of food retail. Eighty-eight percent of the 750 companies referenced believe that machine learning will change the future of the retail sector or is already changing it. Artificial intelligence has already arrived in the general mind-set and partially also in companies themselves. In a study[4] conducted by McKinsey, it was estimated that somewhere between 26 and 39 billion US dollars are being invested into the development of artificial intelligence. This was a triplication of investment volumes as opposed to 2013.

Intelligent applications support the analysis of large data sets with complex relations (see Fig. 1). In this process, the various steps build upon each other. Machine learning allows to create forecasts with predictive analytics, in order to answer the question: "What will happen?". In contrast, the term of artificial

[1]Noleppa et al. (2015).

[2]FAO (2015).

[3]Blue Yonder (2017).

[4]Bughin et al. (2017).

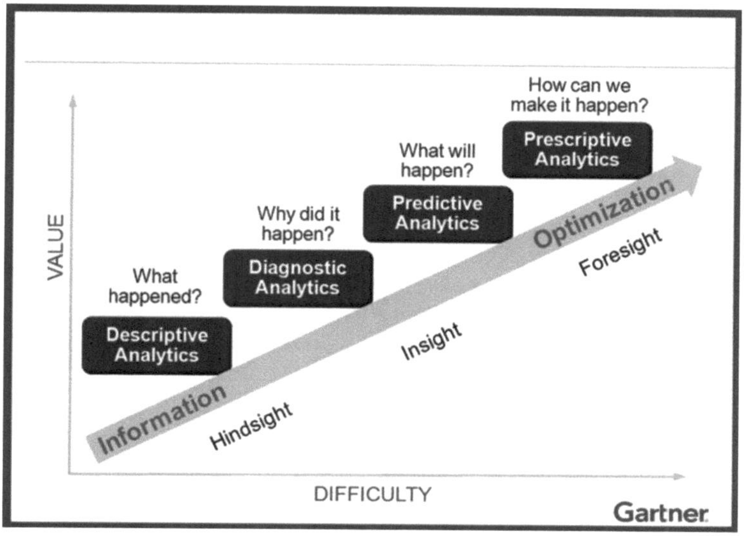

Fig. 1 Analytic value escalator (Manta 2009)

intelligence lies in the area of prescriptive analytics, answering the question "How do we reach a certain goal?". Intelligences make decisions in order to achieve those goals. With decisions for actions, a situation is created where processes and decisions can be automatized.

Applications around business intelligence are mainly focused on the visualization and analysis of historic data and require the user to make his own conclusions. "Although trend forecasts can be made by this to a limited extent, these are only reliable, if businesses and markets develop relatively homogeneously and constantly."[5] However, if future events such as predicted sales, likely customer or supplier behavior, are relevant for today's business decisions, then methods should be used to forecast those events. This is the goal of all approaches within "predictive analytics."

2 Daily Supply Chain Routine

Category managers and replenishers are periodically confronted with very complex problems. A multitude of aspects must be taken into account for each individual initial or reorder:

- How well will this product sell? How important is it? Does this product always have to be available, or is it a seasonal or highly fashionable product that needs to

[5]Beyer (2011).

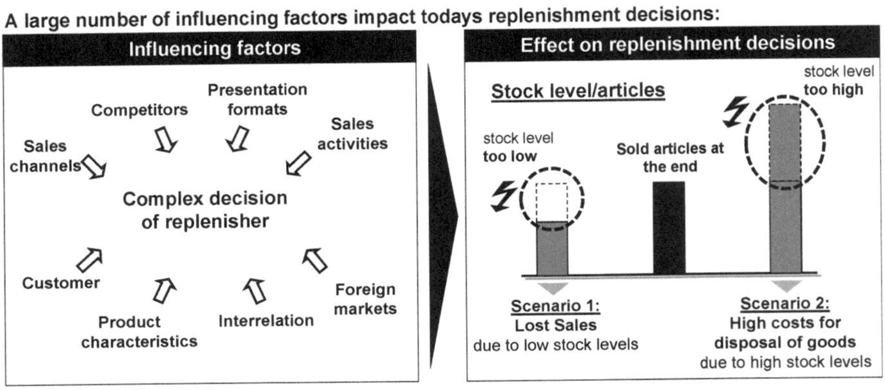

Fig. 2 Replenishment and inventory management

be available; or is the alternative of letting it go out of stock at a certain point in time more advantageous?

- When will the supplier deliver this product, if I place the order today? How long must the volume that has been ordered be available? Which sizes and colors should be ordered? In which store should the product be available? Can I even reorder this product later in the product life cycle?
- Is this product new to the product range? Which existing product could possibly serve as reference? Which of the product properties are the most relevant ones? Are products that have the same color more indicative than products using the same material?

This list illustrates only a small part of the complexity of the decision-making process concerning replenishment (see also Fig. 2). However, for a replenishment expert, a manual comprehensive analysis can only be conducted in very few cases, as each replenisher is responsible for a large number of products. Traditional methods, such as the often-applied rule of three, can yield relatively good assessments on an aggregated level. However, it is unable to take the multitude of influencing factors, existing on a single-unit level, into account. A precise forecast of future product sales on the lowest level, the so-called SKU ("stock keeping unit"), should be the precondition of each founded replenishment decision. The product level "product-color-size" (size can also include dimensions such as length and width) can be further subdivided into catalogues, stores, or even different locations within the stores. There are far too many possibilities resulting in the combination of these options to handle them manually or with traditional approaches. Furthermore, the dynamic in the retail sector is a critical factor, especially in crosschannel areas with various fulfillment possibilities. As opposed to the past, where most companies had to make decisions for "only" one sales channel, e.g., purely store or catalogue businesses, nowadays, online shops are used as main sales channel by most companies, and this makes the usage of the previously used methods difficult. Especially the interdependencies of separate channels such as the influence of advertising media or catalogues on online business are one of the biggest. In the fulfillment area, more and more possibilities for the end customer to receive products occur: Click&Collect, pickup stations, shipping, collecting in stores or delivery boxes, etc. All this has led to the underlying logistic becoming increasingly complex and demanding. Spreading products over the entire supply chain in an ideal manner has not become easier for employees. Recognizing relevant patterns and correlations that have influence on the sales volume of single products via various sales and fulfillment channels without using system support in extensive and partly unstructured data and then utilizing these for replenishment prove complex in this modern environment. This requires technology that is able to both recognize significant correlations in such an environment and make them useable.

3 The Origin of New AI Technologies and Their Application

Extensive data volumes and challenging circumstances are ideal prerequisites for the application of complex statistical methods. This section will make reference to new AI technologies that are very suitable to the aforementioned framework conditions. By combining diverse mathematical procedures, patterns and interdependencies within the available data volume are identified and can then be used to create probabilistic forecasts. We wish to illustrate this, using the example of the AI technology NeuroBayes. The high quality of NeuroBayes' forecasts can particularly be derived from the software's origin in research. While developing the forecast technology NeuroBayes, the intended areas of usage where not areas in the economy: scientific insights and gains in efficiency for international top-level research on elementary particle physics were targeted. Many of the general conditions of a particle accelerator are very similar to those in the economy: in a multitude of events, those relevant events (for the scientific analysis) must be recognized and separated from random events. Consequently, this leads to substantial efficiency gains with regard to processing time and the use of technical devices. In this contribution, we use NeuroBayes and its usages as an example for the application of machine learning algorithms in the economy.

In experiments, such as the LHC (particle accelerator in the European Center for Particle Physics CERN in Geneva that uses a subterranean tunnel system, spanning almost 27 km), 40 million packages, consisting of around 100 billion protons, collide per second. Over 5000 scientists from around the world are occupied with the processing of the resulting data. In 2011 alone, a data volume of over 15 million gigabytes was stored. The predominant part of this data volume merely consisted of statistical background noise complicating the scientific analysis. Within this bulk of data, tiny traces and patterns that could give insights to questions raised by scientists, concerning the circumstances and conditions directly after the Big Bang, the search for dark matter, as well as an explanation for the emergence of particle masses are searched for.

NeuroBayes was developed in this area of experimental particle physics and finds application in international top-level research in the most renowned particle physics research centers of the world: CERN (Europe), KEK (Japan), and Fermilab (USA). This technology is used by these centers to extract data sets that exhibit predefined and scientifically relevant characteristics from the aforementioned conditions (small interesting events in immense data volumes). At CERN during one of three major experiments, for example, 1 petabyte of data was generated per second, amounting to far more data than all telecommunication companies of the world create together. Since the initial idea for NeuroBayes, over 500 man-years have gone into its development and improvement. NeuroBayes is used by highly diverse top-level elementary particle physics research teams and is continuously being developed further and refined to these ends. Furthermore, for some years now, more and more commercial companies can profit from this powerful solution.

Over the last years, the rate of data generation has further increased by such experiments. In order to reduce data to a level where actual technologies can handle them, the Belle II pixel detector in the KEK (Japan) must cleverly decide whether or not data is relevant and useful during data acquisition. Useful, in this case, means that data is interesting physically and not merely part of statistical noise. To be able to handle the enormous data rate of the Belle II pixel detector, the NeuroBayes algorithm is no longer run as software on computers, but is rather implemented directly on the sensor module in the form of a hardware chip. This chip decides which parts of the sensor are read out. For this project, this means that algorithms for machine learning make eight billion decisions per second. This approach could be compared with a digital video camera that only reads out certain parts of the imaging sensor that contain new information, e.g., movement, in order to achieve a higher frame rate.[6]

Another example for the implementation of artificial intelligence is the automatization of scientific analyses. Traditionally, a physical analysis of particle physics experiments is conducted by a scientist. Nowadays, hundreds to thousands of scientists work on a similar, but on a more detailed level, different analysis during particle physics experiments. Using a meta-analysis, the mutual components of 1100 analyses were depicted in an automatized hierarchical reconstruction with 72 neuronal networks. The research of three doctoral candidates and the help of 72 artificial intelligences allowed to improve the analysis of 400 scientists over the course of 10 years by a factor of 2.[7]

As an individual development of artificial intelligences is particularly worthwhile where conventional statistical methods reach their limits, due to the complexity of the problem, the multitude of influencing factors, or the immense data volumes, their usage and implementation are especially interesting for sectors such as retail,

[6]Baehr et al. (2015).

[7]Feindt et al. (2011).

insurance, and fund management. Further, in business areas in which the best evaluation of one's customer is important, as, for instance, in the publishing industry, direct marketing, and banks—or, in general, in the area of customer retention—the use of algorithms is highly profitable. Additionally, optimizations for the manufacturing industry and the supply chain are possible.

4 Added Value Through Machine Learning

But what benefit does a technology used in experimental particle physics can possibly provide to retailers? Various tests for different use cases show that mathematical models can have the same performance as employees that have been working in this sector for years. Depending on the complexity of the problem, the application of previous experience on decision-making scenarios by mathematical models is much more reliable than that of the human brain. According to studies conducted in this field, the information processing capacity of the brain is limited and can consequently include no more than three influencing factors with the respectively correct emphasis on the decision-making process. However, sophisticated mathematical models can assess all relevant framework conditions on the basis of their "expertise" and use these with the correct priority and weights in the decision-making process. Mathematical procedures that mirror the way the human brain learns belong to the category of "self-learning" procedures. Pure prognostic, "predictive analytics," and the optimization or decision-making, "prescriptive analytics," are oftentimes not well differentiated. The borderline of research and application between those two is not fixed, yet, and they often overlap. Both are relevant to build an artificial intelligence system. Procedures of machine learning are commonly used mainly for forecasting.

As early as 1940, attempts of developing flexible, self-learning predictive procedures were conducted in order to analyze large quantities of individual factors and their correlations. First automatized learning processes of this type were developed during the late 1980s. All approaches have in common that they attempted the recreation of the biology of neuronal networks of the human brain (formulated in a strongly simplified manner). The advantages of these approaches lie in the fact that no functional correlations (such as the parametric approaches) must be developed manually for the creation of the predictive model and randomly complex correlations (even those highly nonlinear) could be learned. In doing so, the dependency and the weight of individual influencing factors are steadily adapted to changed framework conditions. However, the use of such technologies should not be used thoughtlessly, as data is oftentimes not prepared sufficiently for the use in the neuronal network, but rather feed into the model "in one go" and in the hope of reaching precise prognoses swiftly. Furthermore, if this artificial neuronal network is not used appropriately, the model can become "overtrained." This means that certain features of a certain time period or customer group are memorized bluntly. Without checking this model's general applicability, it will not work in daily operation. Also systematic changes in historical data need to be considered. For example, the German sales figures for cucumbers and tomatoes during the EHEC epidemic in the early summer of 2011 should not be used as the basis for forecasts for the coming year. This time period is clearly no longer characteristic due to the special event and should consequently not be generalized for other time periods. The mathematical model should be developed and tested on a broad data basis in order to avoid overtraining and reduce the negative impact of special events, thereby guaranteeing real generalizability. This is also applicable to situations such as breakdowns of online shops or batch recalls due to glass splinters found in jam. Consequently, it is still not recommendable to use machine learning approaches in an isolated manner without the respective expertise in the subject matter. However, from the combination of various statistical procedures with suitable control mechanisms and domain-specific expertise, a mighty solution can emerge, suitable for even the most complex business processes. In NeuroBayes' case, neuronal networks are linked with so-called Bayesian regularization processes, in order to reduce instances such as overtraining. In doing so, it can be ensured that only statistically relevant interdependencies are learned, others, however, systematically forgotten. This ensures that these do not influence forecasts in the future.

Another often seen issue is erroneous data. The example of the range of beverages offered by a food retailer, whose data warehouse system has recorded thrice the number of sales actually made, due to a data error, serves to illustrate the point. Depending on the predictive model, forecasts could lead—in an extreme case—to the assumption of a strong positive sales trend, leading to even more than the triple sales forecasts. Another example could be a single product that has had an average sales rate of 42 times a day over the last 2 years. Assuming that there are 5 open shopping days per week, a sales volume of about 22,000 is yielded for 2 years. If, due to a data error, 4200 is stored instead of 42 for a single day, the calculated average sales value rises by almost 20% from 42 to 50 pieces. Such a simple mean value model would systematically overestimate the true sales, and it would take years for such a system to stop making these mistakes. However, not only data errors but, also systematic effects must be handled sensibly by artificial intelligences: if there are regular influencing factors that are not tracked in the data, these must be taken into account as well as possible. If, due to local particularities, promotions are often held for a single article in a certain store, then the expectation should be that these periodic promotions are also recognized as such. If they occur in erratic intervals, then it should at least be included in the mean value calculation, even if the AI is not able to correctly locate the promotion's exact point in time. If there are discrepancies between forecasts and the truth, it will sooner or later become evident that data and business processes must be understood correctly and a solution must be found. In case of data errors, these can usually be corrected. Systematic effects can be solved by dialogue on how to provide the system with the necessary information or how this process can be integrated or taken into account otherwise.

These examples serve to demonstrate why generalizability and robustness are considered so highly when using predictive models and why commonly voiced criticism of such procedures in the past can undoubtedly be justified. Continuously providing high-quality forecasts can only be guaranteed with the combination of distinctly different statistical procedures and significant attention to details. If these procedures are to find use in the economy, then business processes must be reconciled with the use of predictive models, and the data and information flow must exhibit a high level of quality.

Another example for the implementation of machine learning is the adjustment of prices. Price optimization is a key strategic component that has influence on the profitability of entire retail companies. Nowadays, the price optimization process is influenced by enormous data and a multitude of influencing factors. Therefore, in order to secure lasting growth, it is absolutely necessary to face changes in the market with the strategic techniques of price optimization. Retailers must adapt to market pressure more and more rapidly. The competition is continuously changing the game with aggressive sales and marketing promotions. Companies have reacted by expanding their sales channels and the introduction of regional product ranges. However, this heightened complexity makes the determination of the optimal prices more complex and often entails that the product range manager only focuses on key products. Retail companies require to set the prices on the most granular level (per SKU, per store, per day) and need a strategic approach that makes the company stand out from its competition and supports increases in revenue and profit.

The retailer can obtain optimal price decisions for each product on a day-to-day basis, thereby increasing profit and revenue, with a solution based on machine learning for price optimization. This solution measures the influence of prices on the demand, the so-called price elasticity of demand. It is highly scalable, takes business strategies into account, and enables almost complete automatization. By taking competitive prices and other influencing factors such as weather or inventory levels into account, the solution can adapt to changes in the market quickly and automatically sets prices for each individual product and store.

Traditional systems usually implement general market concepts and pricing rules assuming certain customer behavior. In comparison, a solution using artificial intelligence supplies daily recommendations for thousands of products on the basis of precise measurements of the price elasticity of demand. Further, AI systematically reevaluates the optimal price changes, considers additional context factors (such as marketing promotions, inventory levels, obligation situations, and sales periods), and sets prices according to product life cycles. Price recommendations directly follow the set pricing strategy and are optimized on the basis of business-critical KPIs. As price optimization takes place with well-founded tests rather than with unfounded hypotheses, the solution can offer the best price decisions for retailers.

5 Setting Up Self-Learning Predictive Models

Using NeuroBayes as an example, we wish to illustrate the general structure of self-learning procedures. NeuroBayes consists of the intelligent combination of artificial neuronal networks with Bayesian statistics and a multitude of other statistical tools.

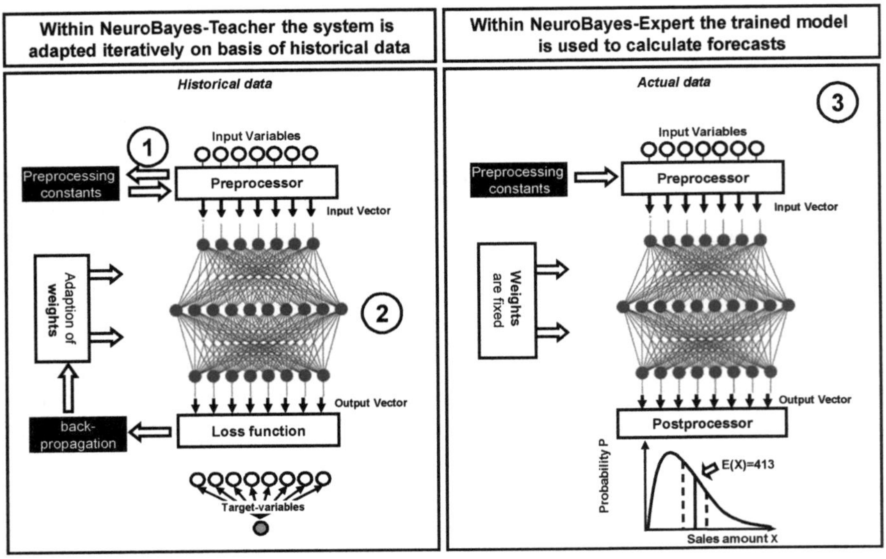

Fig. 3 Training and usage of neuronal networks

In order to derive precise forecasts from available data, three steps should be considered (see Fig. 3):

In the first step, the so-called preprocessing, the available data is analyzed, cleansed, and transformed to the correct shape intended for use in the actual predictive model. Forecasts are only ever as good as the data used for calculating them. During the preprocessing step, the available data is initially inspected for errors and incompleteness so that these, wherever possible, can be corrected. Following this step, the data is analyzed in order to create meaningful descriptive variables ("input variables"). This can be illustrated well with the sales data from the replenishment example. To learn which quantity of a respective product was sold during a certain time period in the past, variables such as "sales quantity during the last year" or "sales volume during the last week" for each individual product and for higher aggregation levels such as article groups, article of the same color, or articles of the same brand can be calculated. Additional variables concerning the revenue dynamics (constant, falling, or rising) can be calculated on different aggregated levels. However, if this aspect were to be ignored for crosschannel business, then a possible result would be that the dynamic of the online sector is hardly taken into account sufficiently. Another important task of this model development phase is the search for outliers that can be recognized and taken into account with an extensive data- and time-series analysis. Essential relations, as well as dependencies between individual influencing factors (especially linear relationships), are already taken into account by the aforementioned methods, before the application of neuronal networks. The use of neuronal networks is focused on the complex, partly highly nonlinear correlations between influencing variables and the "target" (e.g., the sales volume of a product). The preprocessed information is then used in the next forecasting step, saving (computing) time and at the same time improving the forecasting quality. In order to use all available data in an optimal way, all describing features, e.g., the size of a product, must be standardized (size S and ladies' size 36 should be interpreted in a similar way, after all). Moreover, all data fields existing solely in text format should be examined for relevant information by "text processing" and then reformatted into variables that can be processed by machine learning methods. After concluding this detailed data preparation phase, the data is fed into the neuronal network.

During the second step, relevant patterns and relationships are learned by the neuronal network. By presenting the historical data, in which the value that is to be forecasted (in the replenishment example: the number of sales per product and time interval) is already known, to the forecast model, the algorithm can by trained successively (see Fig. 3). In doing so, the weighting of the influencing variables defined in the first step is adapted and improved, until the model can extract the maximum amount of information from all available data sets on the relevant forecasting level (in the replenishment example: SKU/sales-channel level) and has "learned" the correct weighting and interdependencies in the model. The foundation for an actual usage of the first predictive model is laid with the completion of the second step.

During the third step, the fully trained model can be applied to new, current data, in which the actual and future value of the target is yet unknown and a forecast can be generated (see Fig. 4). In the case of NeuroBayes, the result of this calculation is a complete probability density distribution for the target quantity. For the previously illustrated replenishment example, this means that not only the expected product sales in the form of a single number is calculated, but also the uncertainty of this value.

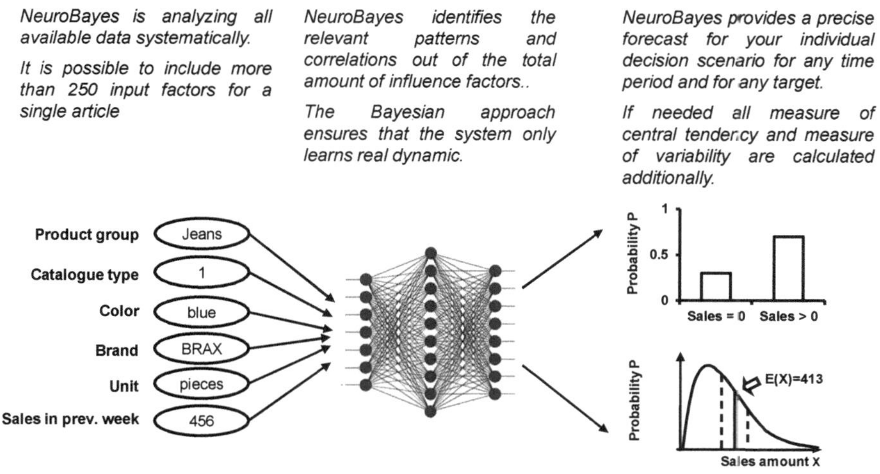

Fig. 4 Forecast calculation and probability density distribution

The probability density distribution can make statements concerning whether the true value will lie between, e.g., 50 and 100 pieces, with a probability of 99%, or make statements on the likelihood for a product of being a so-called fast seller, such as a probability of 15% for sales greater than 90 pieces. How this information can be used in a way to improve business KPIs will be demonstrated in the following section.

Using the aforementioned three steps that are automatized after the initial model development phase, the final model can dynamically adapt to new framework conditions and is consequently self-learning over time. This dynamic evolves simultaneously through two aspects. On the one hand, the recent history of a product or a customer can be included directly by a clever definition of input variables—in the replenishment example, this is achieved by the calculation of the cumulated revenue of the last week or the last month. With each purchase of a product, the forecast quality of future sales can be improved. On the other hand, training the algorithm regularly enables the model to adapt to new correlations within the data. Such new relations could, for example, be a change in customer behavior over time or possibly a different strategy by the company (e.g., slightly different marketing methods).

Naturally, for fast-changing industries like retail, this is extremely important. A predictive model, trained on the conditions 2 years ago, will rarely be able to describe the business processes and correlations of today.

6 Artificial Intelligence as a Fully Automated Replenishment Tool

In order to use artificial intelligence in an optimal manner, all other framework conditions, influencing the business processes, should be taken into account. In the field of replenishment decisions, precise sales volume forecasts per product for all relevant time horizons are extremely important and can be implemented by experienced employees and in a value- and business KPI-driven manner. Besides the forecast, there are various other, mainly logistical requirements (e.g., ordering schedule, minimum order quantities, maximum processing quantity in warehouses, promotional events) that need to be considered for the calculation of the optimal order quantity and the optimal point in time to place the order. As employee, having system support in these complex situations is very beneficial in most cases. Future product sales as well as shipping time on supplier level is fraught with great uncertainties. In order to cover the actual demand period in which a product must be available (meaning the time frame until the reception of the next order), a forecast model for shipping times should also be implemented in addition to the demand model. Another example for an often relevant forecast quantity is the average return rate of an individual product. Especially for retailers in the online sector, a return rate on individual product level of up to 80% and more is possible for certain assortments (e.g., textile). For an article that has an 80% return rate, a large fraction of the stock is not stored in warehouses, but is rather located in the supply chain and with the customers. For replenishment, this increases complexity significantly, and this proves the need for system support or an automatization of order processes.

Furthermore, the main characteristic of a good replenishment performance is that business-relevant key performance indicators (KPIs) are met or improved. Not only should revenue be maximized and costs reduced, customers need to be satisfied by high product availability. In this field of tension, finding the optimal order value and point in time to place the order is not easy. Elements of the cost function, such as "How much money am I paying excessively for an article leftover at the end of the season?" or "By how much am I valuing an article too little in terms of customer satisfaction?", wherever existent, should be combined with the aforementioned demand probability distribution to determine the optimal order value. If the cost of an additional article is less than the cost on customer satisfaction, then the ordered amount should be increased, rather than ordering the typically used expected value. If the product in question is a "never-out-of-stock" (NOS) article, the probability density function can be used to always reorder the right amount to have the product short only once a year on average. These values can only be calculated by the NeuroBayes algorithm because the probability distribution for each individual product is estimated. One of the greatest challenges for each individual decision is to find the optimal value for the present business objectives out of the calculated probability distribution. The more complex and diverse the objectives are, the more useful the additional implementation of simulations, which can be used to determine the expected KPI numbers at the end of a season, can be—the results of the simulation will be the basis to determine the optimal strategy for the company's KPIs.

But what is the optimal degree of automatization of such a software? Commonly, not all relevant influencing factors are available in the form of data. Consequently, it can be very useful to combine the yearlong knowledge of experienced employees with the statistical competence of such a tool. The extent of the cooperation between "man and machine," in the case of NeuroBayes, is exclusively dependent on the data situation and the wish of the company to integrate the software. Previously implemented solutions vary from an employee-supporting version by delivering indicative forecasts to fully automated replenishment installations. However, even a partial automatization can, dependent on the exact case, be quite sensible. A non-automatized tool can connect employees to the business process just as strongly, if not stronger, as it was before the integration of the new tool—the only difference being the decisions in replenishment are supported with precise proposals. A complete automatization is only useful when certainty exists that all relevant influencing factors are contained within the data and can therefore be considered or if decisions have a more short-term character, meaning that possibly faulty decisions can be corrected, or at least balanced, quickly by a later forecast and order run on the basis of latest data. In most, if not all, cases, striking a balance in which employees are relieved from complex decisions that can be calculated precisely by a proficient forecasting solution is beneficial. Generally, these make up the greater part of all decisions to be made. Employees can invest their time in all those areas, where the software is unable to calculate precise forecasts due to process-related reasons or external conditions. These so-called exceptions can be counteracted in a rule-based manner and can actively be presented to respective experts in the form of a proposal. This proposal can either be confirmed or adjusted. Thus, at any given time, certainty exists that software investments and experienced employees are integrated efficiently, simultaneously ensuring that the best possible values are used in the decision-making processes.

7 Customer Examples of Artificial Intelligence in Retail

How worthwhile the implementation of artificial intelligence can be has already been recognized by the multichannel retailer OTTO. The company has been using artificial intelligence for quite some time now in order to:

- Improve product availability
- Guarantee short delivery periods
- Optimize prices
- Reduce return rates

Especially the complex interdependencies between print and online channels can no longer be taken into account sufficiently by conventional methods. The implementation of modern AI solutions offers significant added value by an improved forecast quality. As early as the first year after its introduction, substantial potentials in revenue and cost reduction could be derived, as less products went out of stock, simultaneously reducing the remaining stock at the end of the season.

In order to excite and bind their customers, OTTO must offer a wide range of products at a competitive price as well as offer excellent service. Consequently, a high degree of product availability and short delivery periods are crucial success factors. In order to improve stock levels, fulfill increasingly high customer expectations, and adapt pricing to the company objectives, OTTO implements solutions for price optimizations. This has led to:

- Increased sales through more demand
- Maximized profit through intelligent pricing strategies

The English grocery retailer Morrisons has invested in an automatized replenishment solution in order to improve demand planning and to optimize product availability on the basis of customer behavior in each store. The emphasis was initially focused on long-lasting grocery, frozen products, and tinned foods and was later expanded to include fresh foods. In all segments, profitability was increased by a higher product availability at simultaneously reduced write-offs. In this way, the following achievements could be made:

- Reduction of out-of-stock situations by 30%
- Reduction of storage in stores by 2–3 days

- Revenue increase
- Reduction of write-offs
- Simplification and optimization of product replenishment
- Increase in employee productivity

Morrisons wanted to improve the customer experience in all stores. In doing so, offering customers the optimal product availability represented one of the greatest challenges. Prior to that, the supermarket chain relied on traditional ordering systems and manual orders by the employees of individual stores. This was time-consuming, caused inconsistencies from one store to the next, and was oftentimes inaccurate. Morrisons needed a solution for the most difficult aspect: finding the balance between an appealing product range and appropriate coverage of inventory. After implementing the new system, David Potts (CEO, Morrisons) attests that "The system is capital light, utilizing cloud technology and store specific historic sales data to forecast stock requirements. It is reducing costs and stock levels, while also saving time for colleagues, and providing a better offer for customers."

However, AI solutions are not limited to replenishment. This approach can be implemented in most situations where immense data volumes and multilayered influencing factors complicate, or even rule out, decision-making without system support. The replenishment sector in retail is only one of these areas. Especially in online shops, a multitude of various data is available that is collected, but often not used for processing and decision-making, nowadays—an ideal starting point for modern statistical methods. Who has not encountered recommendation machines, already in use by many online retailers, which offer customer recommendations as early as upon loading of the website and latest during the viewing and searching for products? The potential is immense. Not only the customer can be stronger engaged by good recommendations. Moreover, the additional revenue created by sales of fitting additional offers is mostly not connected with additional costs and is almost completely amortized. Nonetheless, this immense potential oftentimes remains (at least partially) unused. The combination of the full online-shop data with customer-individual purchasing history, as well as that of other sales channels, enables a comprehensive assessment of customer affinities and will deliver the best possible additional offers. Furthermore, the same models can be used to personalize the sorting order of products that are displayed when searching for products. AI solutions that can calculate the optimal recommendation in real time offer a clear competitive advantage in this situation.

Finding out which customer should be sent which advertising material or special offer via which channel and in which frequency is also very promising. The solution is a complex mathematical model which can yield the optimal composition of product offer, channel, and frequency for each customer and each advertising media, respectively, on the basis of the expected response probability or on the basis of the expected revenue created by the specific customer, naturally taking customer-individual purchasing and outfitting history into account. In this way, the advertising budget can be allocated in a target-oriented manner, as the same financial investment reaches the right customers. Alternately, the possibility of reducing costs by reducing the advertising-media usage exists, at the same time keeping the response rate at an appropriate level. All the aspects mentioned above can already be taken into account by individual models, as has already been proven by tests in the crosschannel sector.

The retailer SELGROS Cash & Carry dispatches brochures of up to one million customers every 2 weeks. Managing shipping was previously very cost consuming and used up a lot of work force as customer selection was conducted manually. Additionally, as not all dynamic and customer-individual influencing factors could be taken into account, advertising budget was not being used in an optimal manner. With a solution to target customers on the basis of artificial intelligence, customer-individual purchasing histories were evaluated, and then, using a machine learning algorithm, the purchasing probability and shopping cart size of each individual customer were forecasted, both with and without advertising media. With this method, SELGROS is able to make an optimal customer selection. Hence, only those customers receive brochures can thereby be positively influenced in their future purchasing decision. The following results were achieved:

- Substantial reduction of expenditures for advertising media at almost identical revenue
- Realization of ROI on the basis of directly calculable savings as early as after the first month of implementation

Distance sellers usually only want to offer those customers with an extended credit period, of which they know that they will actually pay their bills. This is also an ideal situation in which machine learning models can determine the debt default probability for each individual customer. Further, it could support the choice of the ideal payment arrangement for each individual customer (this has already been tested successfully by various companies, among others Bürgel Wirtschaftsinformationen).

8 Artificial Intelligence: A Competitive Advantage

Apart from the retail sector, there are various possibilities of implementing artificial intelligence, prescriptive analytics, and predictive analytics. In this manner, a model was developed for order placements in stock exchange trading. Axel Springer tested forecasts of customers canceling their subscriptions to identify future "cancellers"—the optimal foundation for an efficient customer relations management. Moreover, an ideal field of application for modern statistical procedures is insurance companies. For a large international reinsurance company, a model was developed that could forecast the amount of damage/cost probability of every insurance holder. For BVG, a new motor vehicle liability rate for young drivers was developed. Furthermore, issues such as fraud detection and business KPI-driven cross- and up-selling with regard to lapse rates and customer lifetime value are interesting:

Which "likely-to-leave customer" should I even strive to keep by offering customer loyalty programs?

Investments in the application of artificial intelligence are usually already profitable within a few months after its implementation. The potential that can be derived from the data of companies is immense and offers the opportunity for far more efficient processes. Significant effects of a well-introduced and superior AI solution in retail are among other things:

1. A procedural simplification of operative workflows:
   AI support enables employees to shift their focus to more relevant activities. Modern business intelligence tools often handle manual and automatic data acquisition, transformation, and aggregation procedures in central data warehouse applications. Systems with artificial intelligence recognize automatized patterns and connections for the support of processes in a productive business. The professional users are no longer professionals that must face complex Excel lists, but much rather pilots that steer data flows, business processes, and decision-making.
2. An improved data quality for performance and business management:
   A solution based on predictive models can forecast and take complex economic correlations and developments into account, thereby supporting management in decision-making processes by supplying a founded data basis. Performance management can supplement its oftentimes very simple reporting—usually implemented in Excel—with new solutions, above and beyond traditional reporting, and conduct reliable planning and forecasts.
3. A significant increase in productivity in operative core processes:
   This can lead to an improved inventory situation, a better service quality, an increase in the efficiency of marketing campaigns, and consequently an immense improvement of customer satisfaction.

The implementation of artificial intelligences is, in many respects, worthwhile, and through its innovative character, this application can offer a decisive competitive advantage. A study[8] conducted by the market-research company IDC verifies the added value of these methods: projects that make use of predictive analytics technologies could realize an ROI ("return of investment") of 145%—compared with an ROI of 89% realized by projects that do not consider forecasts.

References

Baehr S et al (2015) Online-analysis of hits in the Belle-II pixel detector for separation of slow pions from background. J Phys Conf Ser 664:092001. https://doi.org/10.1088/1742-6596/664/9/092001

[8]See Morris (2003).

Beyer M (2011) Das neue Business Intelligence. BI wird schlauer, mobiler und vorausschauender, www.cio.de. Accessed 18 Oct 2017
Blue Yonder (2017) Sechs Gründe, warum Lebensmittelhändler schnellere Entscheidungen treffen müssen. https://www.blue-yonder.com/de/Studie-Sechs-Gruende-warum-Lebensmittelhaendler-schnellere-Entscheidungen-treffen-muessen. Accessed 16 Oct 2017
Bughin J et al (2017) Artificial intelligence the next digital frontier? https://www.mckinsey.com/~/media/McKinsey/Industries/Advanced%20Electronics/Our%20Insights/How%20artificial%20intelligence%20can%20deliver%20real%20value%20to%20companies/MGI-Artificial-Intelligence-Discussion-paper.ashx. Accessed 16 Oct 2017
FAO (2015) Food loss and waste facts. http://www.fao.org/resources/infographics/infographics-details/en/c/317265/. Accessed 16 Oct 2017
Feindt M et al (2011) A hierarchical NeuroBayes-based algorithm for full reconstruction of B mesons at B factories. http://arxiv.org/abs/1102.3876v2. Accessed 16 Oct 2017
Gartner (2012) Analytic value escalator. https://www.flickr.com/photos/27772229@N07/8267855748/. Accessed 16 Oct 2017
Manta C (2009) Hintergrund BI. Besserer ROI durch predictive analytics. www.cio.de. Accessed 16 Oct 2017
Morris HD (2003) Predictive analytics and ROI: lessons from IDC's financial impact study, IDC
Noleppa S et al (2015) WWF Studie Das Grosse Wegschmeissen. http://www.wwf.de/fileadmin/fm-wwf/Publikationen-PDF/WWF_Studie_Das_grosse_Wegschmeissen.pdf. Accessed 16 Oct 2017
O.V. (o.j.) Cost of hard drive storage space. http://ns1758.ca/winch/winchest.html. Accessed 18 Oct 2017
Spies R (2011) Es wächst zusammen was zusammen gehört. Das Verhältnis von strukturierten und unstrukturierten Daten, IBM Management Forum. http://www-05.ibm.com/de/events/im-forum/. Accessed 18 Oct 2017

Mareike Clasen, Customer Success Director at Blue Yonder, is a graduated mathematician at the University of Hamburg. After several years of leading diverse predictive analytics projects in the retail sector (inter alia disposition, pricing, targeting, and customer creditworthiness), in the insurance sector, and in customer relationship management across all sectors, she is now Customer Success Manager for large multichannel companies in Hamburg.

Dr. Michael Milnik is Product Manager and Staff Data Scientist at Blue Yonder. He graduated in physics at the University of Karlsruhe. After being awarded with his master's degree from the London School of Economics in philosophy and history of science, he returned to the University of Karlsruhe as PhD Student of experimental particle physics. Following his doctorate, he switched from the University to Blue Yonder.

Performance Management of the Digital Pure Play Zalando

Jörg Engelbergs

Abstract This contribution describes how digitization is understood and lived at Zalando.

In the course of this treatment, the management accounting peculiarities in a digital environment, as well as the influence that digitization has on company management, will be shown. Furthermore, the development of digital business models and their influence on Zalando's performance management will be reflected. Lastly, specific performance management approaches of digital economies will be highlighted.

Keywords Big data · Digital business models · Digital economy · Digitization · Management accounting · Predictive analytics · Zalando

1 Introduction

Zalando is **Europe's leading online platform for fashion**. The enterprise originating in Berlin offers a wide-ranging selection of clothing, shoes, and accessories for men, women, and children.

Its product variety ranges from brands with international renown to local and fast-fashion brands and self-designed private labels; all in all, Zalando collaborates with almost 2000 brands. The product range is expanded and added upon by Zalando Lounge which enables registered members access to promotions and reduced prices. The stationary outlet stores, opened in Berlin, Frankfurt, and Cologne in the years 2012, 2014, and 2016, respectively, provide an additional sales channel for

---

This contribution has originally been printed as Engelbergs, J. (2017): Steuerung des digitalen Unternehmens Zalando, in: Kieninger, M., Digitalisierung in der Unternehmenssteuerung, pp. 245–257. Stuttgart, Schäffer-Poeschel.

J. Engelbergs (✉)
Controlling, Zalando SE, Berlin, Germany

M. Buttkus, R. Eberenz (eds.), *Performance Management in Retail and the Consumer Goods Industry*, https://doi.org/10.1007/978-3-030-12730-5_12

remaining stocks. The parent company Zalando SE was founded in Berlin in 2008 and is also based there today. Zalando's offering is tailored locally to the needs and demands of customers in 15 different European markets.

Zalando's logistics network enables efficient catering to all customers in Europe through five central logistics centers. The network is complemented by smaller international logistics sites in partnership with local service providers in Italy, France, and Sweden. In addition, the **centralized management** of the business areas purchase, logistics, and technology allows for the realization of scaling effects.

In order to offer a comfortable shopping experience, Zalando offers its customers free shipping and purchase returns with up to 100 days right of return, multifarious methods of payments, a free service hotline, inspiring online content, and personalized recommendations. The corporation is of the opinion that an **interplay of fashion, operative transactions, and modern information technology** plays a crucial role to success in this segment. Zalando is well established in these areas, and it is because of these competences that it can offer a convincing service commitment to both its customers and brand-name fashion partners.

Due to the aforementioned business activities, Zalando is typically and closely associated with digitization. How this influences the corporate environment, management accounting,[1] and especially business management will be described in the following. The next section will exemplify how digitization is understood and lived at Zalando. Subsequently, specific peculiarities of management accounting in a digital environment and its manifestation within Zalando will be highlighted. Both an insight and an outlook on the development of digital business models will follow before the final section emphasizes selected performance management concepts from digital economies that play a special role in this context or have strongly been influenced by it.

2 Digitization at Zalando

Digitization is understood by this contribution as the generating and transfer or rather the existence of information in digital form, in which information is available as discreet values in electronic form. The utilization on the basis of this information by communication and information technologies will also be considered a constituent of digitization.

In this way, digital information can be used as basis of a company's performance management. In a respective performance management approach, added value can be gained for the enterprise through a digitization of the supply chain and the accessibility of customer's in a digital environment.

[1]The author uses the English word "management accounting" to translate the German term "controlling." Please refer to the discussion in the preface.

2.1 *Customer Access in a Digital Environment*

Through digitization, new opportunities for companies to access their customers and prospective customers are possible. Especially for companies such as Zalando that employ e-commerce, this signifies that consumers can be reached through digital channels, such as country-specific websites for desktop applications and mobile devices, as well as apps in the mobile sector. These can then be used to make purchases.

Such opportunities of accessing customers span various areas: firstly, the general address of consumers and customers which shows a strong effect in the **internationalization** of the company and, secondly, the **recognition of individual customers** (**tracking**) and their guidance through his/her **multiple points of contact with the company** (**customer journey**). Both contribute to the special possibilities that digitization offers for the activation of customers. Thirdly, digitization creates an access to customers, as **interactivity** can be established through various means. It is this circumstance in particular that invests in controlling customer satisfaction and customer retention.

2.2 *Internationalization*

After the company's founding and the commencement of business activity in Germany, as well as first international activity in Austria 2008 and 2009, Zalando was able to access further European markets in short succession. In 2010, the Netherlands and France were added; in 2011 Italy, the United Kingdom, and Switzerland and in 2012 and 2013 Sweden, Belgium, Spain, Denmark, Finland, Poland, Norway, and Luxemburg were added. This swift expansion was largely possible due to the fact that Zalando's customers are primarily reached by digital channels.

Unlike in stationary trade, the necessity of establishing a branch network to open new markets does not apply to Zalando. It is **relatively easy to scale** market presence in a digital form, and this enables a fast expansion to new markets. Existing resources can be deployed pointedly for a necessary **local adaptation of market presence**. However, even if the (technical) transfer to a new country represents a relatively simple step, management should consider the fact that in heterogenic markets, such as in Europe, certain elements (e.g., customer preferences concerning methods and terms of payment) need to be adapted to local requirements. In this process, previously developed options can be transferred efficiently.

Zalando is a good example for demonstrating the extent and speed which such a scaling of digital business models can reach. As early as 2015, 7 years after Zalando's founding, the company counted around 18 million active users who had placed at least three orders using websites or apps. The implications of this simple scalability are, inter alia, relevant for strategic management accounting. Long-term planning is only useful in combination with **scenario planning**, as the ubiquity of customer access can easily reach enormous markets and growth developments do not necessarily follow clear-cut paths.

Performance management's focus should lie on a strong customer orientation since the change barriers between digital business models are typically low—and oftentimes only a mouse-click away. Management accounting can contribute majorly by assessing actions specifically by their contribution to the customer, as well as by equitably integrating customer satisfaction in performance management.

2.3 *Tracking and Customer Journey*

A further result of digitization, which is especially relevant to marketing management, is the possibility of identifying customers and tracking their contact points over their diverse points of contact with the company. While it is generally difficult to record how many customers enter a branch store in stationary trade, Zalando has a good overview of its customer frequency.

Customers are increasingly aware of the fact that they leave **digital footprints** during their journey throughout digital channels. Generally speaking, most customers do not object to this. On the contrary, many customers specifically use this possibility to actively identify themselves and store their data with logins or customer accounts, in order for companies to pointedly present their product range according to this information. In this respect, digitization leads to an increased expectation of **personalized product offers**. This is also true for other business areas that are classically interpreted as mass markets. Marketers use the available information in order to purposefully adjust campaigns and messages to specific customer groups. As a result, special offers can be made to customers that have not made any purchases over a certain period of time, or additional content or conditions can be unlocked.

Due to these purchase histories and in combination with respective contribution margin accountings, customer value contributions can be calculated over their respective lifetimes (**customer lifetime value, CLV**). Determining these value contributions becomes increasingly significant, if the **incremental increase of customer lifetime value** (iCLV) serves as basis. This equals the contribution margin of a customer's future transaction purchases that are placed on the basis of a specific measure and would otherwise not occur.

Management accounting should ensure that methods, aiming at assessing customer relations (e.g., customer-oriented contribution accounting, CLV, iCLV), are established within the company and are consequently consulted in decision-making processes. Further, introducing a **value-oriented customer segmentation** supports the company's ability to pointedly address those customers, who have relevance to the company's success and separate them from those whose purchasing behavior has little or no value contribution.

2.4 Interactivity

Zalando periodically surveys customer satisfaction, as this has a positive influence on financial aims such as revenue increase, profitability, and capital efficiency in the long run. Several of the company's key performance indicators (KPIs) relate to customer satisfaction; e.g., for instance, the **Net Promoter Score** is levied and communicated internally. The fact that **digital market research** offers considerably simpler methods of determining customer satisfaction further aids this procedure. Thanks to digital channels, both the systematic surveying of customers and the integration of customer feedback have become both possible and easier. For example, Zalando's customers can leave positive or negative comments on their purchase experience, immediately after placing an order. This feedback could then be evaluated systematically by **text mining** tools; and in this way, possible recurrent problems with processes or specific products could be recognized at an early stage and addressed in a solution-oriented manner.

A further possibility resulting from the digitization of information is the ability to distribute this data swiftly and broadly. This opens further additional opportunities for the customer to assess and rate a company's services and products or rather the company itself and also to examine other customers' opinions. Digitization has created a **culture of feedback**. Within this culture, customers can express their satisfaction publicly and thereby influence individuals that have no previous personal experience with the company or its products. In this respect, customer satisfaction management is more of a success factor than ever before.

This interactivity of feedback culture becomes evident in **online customer reviews**, for instance. These reviews offer the customer the possibility of transparently rating purchased products so that they are universally accessible. Digitization enables content to be shared directly and easily by customers themselves (**user-generated content** as generic term). In consequence, it is clearly visible that an increasing number of positive product reviews lead to a rise in sales volumes. Therefore, customer reviews can be accredited with an immediate influence on sales success.

Furthermore, digital channels offer a whole range of new possibilities of contacting the customer. In addition to classic forms of contact such as customer support over the phone or by email, in Zalando's case, options such as **chats** or making contact over **social media** are offered. In doing so, customers can enquire about their purchase order, delivery status, and terms of payment as well as pose questions to current trends or certain products.

Management accounting supports developments in this field through precise planning of measures in the development and expansion of respective channels of communication. Creating KPIs in contact with customers and **target sets** in customer support should also be regular functions. In the course of this and on the basis of **cost-benefit analyses**, an ideal service level should be set in order to accordingly alter the emphasis in the consideration of various points of contact.

2.5 Digitization of the Supply Chain

Since not all initial data is available in digital form, it is essential for companies transforming to a digital company to manage the transition from analog to digital data systematically. There are some elements along the supply chain that initially need to be recorded as electronic data. This becomes especially evident in the context of logistics, when using Zalando as an example. In this process, **goods are scanned** over multiple processing steps. Another area is registration of **product details** (e.g., material, color, structure), in order to offer consumers the best possible information on the respective product in the online shop.

2.6 Scans

From the placement of an order to its return, Zalando's logistics are a holistic process. Over 7600 Zalando employees ensure that goods deliveries are sorted, as well as finding orders quickly, packing them, and then dispatching them to Zalando's customers. Most of these employees have in common that they regularly scan articles' barcodes, thereby acquiring information regarding the order's location and/or condition.

As a result of this ongoing tracking, management accounting can determine the productivity of specific processing steps within the supply chain and then use the gathered information for performance management purposes in the context of **process cost calculations**. Furthermore, in the context of **benchmarking**, insights toward optimization initiatives can occasionally be gathered both company-wide and generally, for subunits within the company.

Management performance possibilities arise in the context of the optimization of walking routes in logistics centers. Hereby, a more economic operation, minimization of strain on employees, as well as the level of performance with respect to the customer (typically the speed of delivery) can be optimized pointedly.

2.7 Product Characteristics

Out of all of Zalando's functional areas, one stands for digital transformation like no other: content creation. The process of digital inclusion of products is allocated within content creation. The main focus lies on a product presentation which is both as realistic and as detailed as possible, e.g., 360° photos and photo or video footage of the products actually being worn by models. In the course of this digital inclusion, the process leading up to making these products available (upload) in the shop should be organized to function as quickly as possible, in order to ensure an early and long-lasting selling period.

How worthwhile well-digitalized data is can, for instance, be seen in the returns section. Zalando is continuously working toward improving the provision of information so that customers can make precise and fitting selections. Among other aspects, this affects the acquisition of data concerning size or characteristics of products. The better the quality of provided information, the lower the chance of customers returning products.

Product information is increasingly exchanged along the supply chain, as result of increasing digitization. Therefore, the continued development of data interfaces to vendors and the integration of data streams constitute relevant fields of development. This connection has developed in a manner that can allow a direct connection with manufacturers' warehouses. Physical boundaries no longer exist, as the entire product range is available on essentially unlimited virtual spaces. This is not only true for the presentation of the product range to the customer but also as early as warehousing.

There are various opportunities that management accounting can gain from the granular acquisition of products and their respective information. For instance, a versatile and **product-based contribution margin accounting** can be applied for the performance management of purchasing activities. Along the supply chain, stock keeping could be improved, in the case of a goal-oriented **working capital management**. Both of these opportunities can occur in ongoing business and not only on a particular date, as systems are continuously supplied with the necessary data.

3 Management Accounting in a Digital Environment

For a company's effective performance management, guiding the actions of key participants toward desired directions, by directly or indirectly influencing them, is imperative. Management accounting supports relevant processes in this context, by supplying incentive, planning, and performance indicator systems. Certain particularities of digital environments are the result of this.

Typically, a company in a digital environment has a vast data volume and corresponding possibilities of analyzing it. Nowadays, the collective term **Big Data** is oftentimes referred to in this context. Management accounting is faced with challenges that result from the characteristic "V"'s of Big Data, volume, velocity, and variety, to which, depending on the observer, more dimensions may be added. In the following, especially the first two subject areas will be discussed in the context of Zalando.

3.1 Granularity

As has been illustrated previously, Zalando acquires data at a very high level of detail. This enables the systematic depiction of information concerning individual products and thereby analyses on a very granular level. Selling a product creates a connection between a customer-oriented view (explicit allocation of a sold article to a customer) and a product-orientated view (explicit allocation commodity group) in the process.

This granularity is maintained within a **multilevel contribution margin accounting**, by allocating costs to articles. In doing so, directly assignable information such as data and product-specific discount is recorded on a primary level. On the following level, costs that can be allocated to orders are distributed to all articles within the order, according to keys that are in accordance with the principle of causation. Process-related costs, such as in logistics, for instance, are assigned to products according to insights gained from process cost calculations.

The digitization of various information offers management accounting additional options in the conception of allocation models and process analyses. In corporation with business intelligence teams, the following applies: available data must be linked intelligently, and automatic calculations must be implemented.

This results in an enormous advantage for management accounting, as the same data basis is accessible from a number of different perspectives. Differences resulting from different data sources do not occur, as both the purchasing department, primarily interested in a product group-oriented view, and the sales department, mostly focused on customer-oriented information, employ the same system. On the contrary, management accounting teams can analyze interfaces between the two areas and thereby record in which way customers and products are connected.

3.2 Speed

Not only the volume of available data, but also the speed with which data is processed and information can be made available, grows due to digitization. Zalando supports this with the use of **in-memory technologies**. These technologies enable a significantly faster analysis of data and opens new paths in the embedding of analyses in a company's performance management.

Over the last decades, economic cycles have shortened, or rather the pace of change and innovation has increased. In order to do this development justice, performance management systems made available by management accounting must be able to provide information faster. Simultaneously, this information must be adaptable for the purpose of depicting changes within the environment of the performance management system. This sometimes results in a need for reporting and analysis tools with **real-time functionality**. Zalando uses this, for example, in order to trace their sales success during dynamic campaigns or large-scale sales (e.g., so-called Cyberdays) for a single day and also to be able to adjust prices and product ranges immediately, in case the results fall short of target corridors.

Management accounting can help face these heightened requirements in decision-making support, by co-designing systems and tools, going through scenarios during planning, and identifying actions in dependence of these results. In case of emergencies, these measures are known and must "simply" be implemented.

4 Development of Digital Business Models

Digital economy is already one of the European Commission's most important sectors for innovation at present.

> The digital economy is developing rapidly worldwide. It is the single most important driver of innovation, competitiveness and growth, and it holds huge potential for European entrepreneurs and small and medium-sized enterprises (SMEs). Unfortunately, only two percent of European enterprises are currently taking full advantage of new digital opportunities. How European businesses adopt digital technologies will be a key determinant of their future growth. European Commission 2016

But how can the development of digital business models be controlled and supported by business accounting to the best of its potential? The next section will use Zalando as an example to show the development and change from start-up to grown-up. Subsequently, an outlook and an insight on the emergence of new fields of business and some of their particularities will be given.

4.1 From Start-Up to Grown-Up

A smaller start-up typically has no dedicated management accountant. It is only with increasing size of organization and structures that the functions of management accountings gain significance. This is why Zalando only employed the first management accountants several years after the business' creation. Tangibly, in course of building a start-up, profiles with a broad know-how and consequently flexible applications in order for management accounting to meet the fast changes of start-up environments are required. With the company's growing size, specialized profiles gradually become necessary, in order to apply risen requirements concerning utilized methods and processes.

This understanding of the increasing requirements management accounting is faced with also has relevance for situations in which a new business model emerges within an existing and established environment. Through precise differentiation of requirements in dependence of the level of maturity, it should be ensured that the business' growth area is not limited unduly. In consequence, special attention needs to be payed primarily to cash inflow and cash outflow in the early phases of an enterprise, whereas in grown-up structures, managing profit and loss as well as striking balances gains importance. A contribution margin accounting or profitability calculation may already be helpful to decision-making processes at early stages. However, an extensive budgeting process and cost allocations should only be added to the repertoire at a later stage. The ongoing assessment of which instruments are worthwhile and which are not applicable yet are among the crucial responsibilities management accounting should undertake during the development of start-ups into grown-ups.

Both the planning cycles and the tools utilized, as well as the degree of automatization, should all be developed in dependency of the business' path of development. During the early stages of an enterprise, it is advisable to use new models in a higher frequency, which consequently should be slim. In Zalando's case, short-term planning cycles were a key performance management instrument, especially during phases of strong expansion. Likewise, an easily accessible as well as flexible tooling with a small degree of automatization should be used initially. Typically, flexibility is more worthwhile than potential gains in efficiency, and consequently, start-ups regularly fall back on freely available (open-source) software.

4.2 New Business Fields

In the course of digitization, numerous new business models have formed. Especially platform and market place models profit from this development, as it has made the direct linking of customers possible. It is relatively **simple to scale** many of the corresponding business models, as a broad market can be addressed rapidly and it is relatively easy to achieve internationalization. Additionally, only slight investments in assets are usually necessary in order to support growth (asset-light business model). A further alternative business model that can often be found in digital economy is software as a service.

In this context, Zalando's central objective is "Connect people and fashion." In order to realize this objective, the company supplies the technological infrastructure necessary, within its platform model. In this process, new purely digital business models (**Pure Digitals**) are created or attached to the platform. This applies to the Zalando Media Solutions GmbH, for example, which enables insights into areas of digital marketing such as scope and consumer insights for brand-name partners. Another example is Tradebyte Software GmbH, which uses standardized interfaces to seamlessly connect manufacturers and brands with market places and retailers.

Consumers make contact with these new business models of the digital economy over different channels. More and more applications are no longer developed for desktop computers alone. A majority of usage occurs over mobile terminals, which leads to an increased focus on the mobile sites and apps being used. Management accounting can pointedly support this development, by regularly evaluating the appeal of specific channels and allocating resources and investing accordingly. A special feature of this is that consumers only install a limited number of apps and effectively use even less. Consequently, it is important to assess whether an investment into additional planning is worthwhile for the long run or not.

The regular emergence of new business models and the ongoing change in consumer behavior in a digital environment means that in Zalando's case, management must continuously question the allocation of resources. This becomes evident in shorter planning cycles, more frequent forecasts, and comparatively flexible budgets.

5 Performance Management Concepts in a Digital Economy

In the previous sections, the context of digitization was examined initially, and then it was demonstrated how the working environment in management accounting changes respectively and, lastly, how a connection between management accounting and the development of a company or rather new business models in this environment is created. In this context, Big Data was introduced as an issue. How Big Data and predictive analytics are embedded into a performance management environment will be demonstrated in the following. In conclusion, further special features of operating methods of the digital world that influence the conduct of employees and decision-makers and thereby also the company's management will be showcased.

5.1 Big Data and Predictive Analytics

The availability of data alone does little to add value. It is the generating of information and insights on the basis of this data that initially creates a valuable contribution to management and a company's performance management. The key prerequisite for this is a sufficient quality and granularity of data, in order to obtain useful information.

As there are various possibilities open for analytical purposes, due to the high granularity and variety of data, a **paralysis by analysis** may impend. This paralysis occurs, if decisions are not made due to newer, more in-depth, and alternative analyses being demanded and supplied. A company's efficient performance management should increasingly require the formulation of clear hypotheses and analysis tasks correspondingly. Management accounting has a substantial role in this process, as it regularly connects performance indicator systems with decisions made by management.

With increasingly sophisticated methods finding application in **predictive analytics**, computer-generated predictions, for example, increasingly gain importance. Zalando also uses predictive models that build on methods from the **data science area** for some individual applications, such as the prediction of product sales volumes or ordering behavior. In order to make the best possible predictions, the quality of different approaches is contrasted. As a reoccurring result, a combined approach of data models and human assessment (**man-machine approach**) yields the best outcomes.

Consequently, predictive analytics offer a starting point, and with its help, particularities of the upcoming development or structural change can be discussed and analyzed well. Especially in the context of performance management, these methods can be very helpful, as they contribute to a more conscious perception of correlations and the determining of measures that aid future development.

In order to be able to measure the success of measures or changes, **A/B testing** is oftentimes used within the context of digital economies. On the basis of being able to specifically identify customers and make tailored offers, alterations can be introduced for a group of customers, while a control group remains unchanged. Subsequently, effect and success of a certain measure can be evaluated precisely. On this basis, responsible managers can decide on the matter of expanding the measure to encompass all customers.

5.2 Working Methods in a Digital World

Compared with other companies, Zalando's employees are relatively young—a characteristic that many companies of the digital economy can exhibit. Practices in communication and interaction within the company change in accordance with this. Consequently, the usage and information distribution via short message programs or a company intern social network are among the most frequently used channels. In addition, the working environment changes due to the increasing demand of mobility (**mobile office, virtual office**) for the workplace and is therefore increasingly influenced by digital media. Zalando's management accounting has reacted according to these circumstances and has expanded their services as to include reports and data access, optimized for the use on mobile devices.

Furthermore, Zalando's management consciously differentiates between steering mechanisms that concern the "What?" and approaches of employee managements in the course of "How?." For steering and coordination, hence which objectives should be targeted ("What?"), **Objectives and Key Results** (OKRs) are applied company-wide. This concept is tied to the idea of SMARTer objectives (specific, measureable, accepted, realistic, terminated). The fact that these are constantly available to employees and not hidden within the individual target agreement of a single customer is remarkable in this approach. Additionally, there is no linkage with bonuses or individual payments.

Zalando assesses conduct, or rather the working method (the "How?"), of employees to evaluate their performance. Depending on the respective field, employees are categorized according to varying performance models that also serve as basis for feedback. In turn, this is also the basis for evaluating and determining possibilities of further advancement. This sector is also shaped by digital innovations, and so individual feedback can be provided anytime and anywhere, thereby making all information relevant to employee steering available.

Dr. Jörg Engelbergs is Controlling Vice President with Zalando. He regularly works with various teams within the company to develop management accounting in the digital environment and business performance management for digital business models.

Part V
Planning, Forecasting and Management Reporting: Suggestions for Doing It the Smarter Way

Corporate Planning in Retail Companies: Efficient, Robust, and Flexible

Michael Buttkus

Abstract The following contribution introduces essential elements of corporate planning as a central process of corporate performance management. The foundation for planning activities in the retail industry is outlined first, followed by a description of various forms of planning instruments, subjects, and processes. The contribution is concluded with possible solutions and examples for an efficient and flexible planning process in the retail industry. This is enriched by concrete examples from practice.

Keywords Corporate planning · Functional planning · Rolling planning · Planning process · Planning instruments · Retail

1 Introduction

Generally, corporate planning is a forward-looking activity that attempts to provide orientation for future entrepreneurial behavior.[1] Consequently, corporate planning instruments help to connect a company's vision with the desired or existing steering philosophy and therefore represent the steering instrument for strategic, financial, and operational corporate management as well as the incentive scheme and the required external communication.

Corporate planning normally represents a multifaceted instrument that at least selectively involves large parts of the organization. The following paragraph will

An adaption of this contribution has been originally printed as Buttkus, M. (2016): Planung im Handel—schlank, robust, flexibel, Buttkus, M., Neugebauer, A., Controlling im Handel: Innovative Ansätze und Praxisbeispiele, pp. 125–141, Springer Gabler, Wiesbaden.

[1]Steinmann and Schreyögg (2013), p. 144

M. Buttkus (✉)
Retail and Consumer Goods, Horváth & Partners, Berlin, Germany

M. Buttkus, R. Eberenz (eds.), *Performance Management in Retail and the Consumer Goods Industry*, https://doi.org/10.1007/978-3-030-12730-5_13

present typical planning instruments and describes the existing connections and interdependencies among them.

Strategic planning: Top management provides a general orientation and framework for future corporate development by planning qualitative and strategic measures as well as key performance indicators (KPIs).

Midterm planning (MTP): Expectations and objectives set in the strategic planning process are planned in greater detail and broken down to a shorter time frame. The MTP also bridges the gap between strategic and operational planning.

Budget: Detailed operational planning for the first year of the midterm planning that includes clearly defined objectives for operational action.

Projection (or forecast): The forecast is an honest assessment of the operational development and is often used to manage operational results, to identify gaps between forecast and budget, and to take appropriate measures.

Traditionally, these planning instruments play a significant role in most companies in the retail industry as they earn their margins by providing their customers with the right products, over the right sales channels, at the right time. Consequently, planning activities in the retail industry focus on merchandise management, finances, and investments.[2]

The components of merchandise planning can be classified in stock keeping units per product and location, price and supplier structure, brand portfolio, and purchasing data. All these aspects must be integrated into the financial planning activity. In practice, the level and extent of integration between financial planning and merchandise planning differ widely. In general, aspects such as price, volume, sales, and write-offs are integrated. The level of detail for product groups and single articles differs in practice, too. Moreover, merchandise management and financial management are operated by different IT systems. Typically, the financial planning process sets the framework for the corporate development. Consequently, merchandise management will not be examined in the following chapters.

At least for the stationary retail segment, administrative work is still regarded as unnecessary and inconvenient. Therefore, planning activities are often considered a necessary evil and receive little appreciation from retailers. Furthermore, planning activities in the retail segment are said to be expensive and do not add significant value. Finally, planning activities require enormous efforts due to an inappropriately high level of detail, the collaborative planning approach through the typical stationary retail hierarchies, a rather complex process management, and an insufficient technical support.

Planning in the retail industry is characterized by an abundance of available data, limited resources, highly heterogenic planning approaches, and steep hierarchies that, surprisingly, are not reflected in the planning processes.

[2]Guldin (2004), p. 174

2 Basics for the Planning Process in Retail Companies

Harmonizing the aforementioned planning instruments is critical for all companies in the retail industry, as the market is very competitive and saturated. Furthermore, it is generally characterized by small margins and stagnating sales, consequently leaving no room for imprecise planning and potentially incorrect decisions.

Example
Projections and plans are normally calculated with margins that are significantly lower than those expected and communicated. Consequently, to improve the financial result, a retailer decides to sell property. This has an impact on operational costs. At the end of the financial year, evidence shows that projections and plans were too cautious. Due to the incentive scheme, the entire organization generally plans very defensively and then tries to outperform the projections. In this example, it was not only unnecessary to sell the property, but also had a negative impact on the operational performance management.

Planning instruments in the retail industry must therefore reflect and support management structures and principles.

2.1 "Retail Is Detail"

It is no surprise that the entire industry and its participants follow the motto "retail is detail." Segments with particularly low margins earn their money by paying close attention to details. It is understandable that many companies meticulously track all value and cost-driving activities such as inventory discrepancies and changes in the product portfolio. However, it must be questioned whether those activities are critical for the overall success of the company. The retail industry is known to conduct detailed planned/actual data comparisons for personnel management purposes. A more constructive approach is using the principles of advanced budgeting[3] that focuses on key points and recommends the planning of less important issues in less detail, e.g., product groups and product lines. Companies that follow this approach generally plan budgets for entire regions (and shift the responsibility of executing them to those regions) and the most relevant global budgets instead of detailed budgets. In short, the profit planning activities must be output-oriented instead of input-oriented cost type planning.

[3] Horváth and Partners (2004)

2.2 "Retail Is Simple and Therefore Requires Simple Planning Activities"

In order to be successful, however, corporate planning activities in the retail industry require more than a focus on steering relevant aspects. The retail industry is a comparably simple and steady industry—complexity-increasing activities such as research and development (R&D) and production do not play important roles for the core business. Standardized purchase contracts and a simplified accounts receivables management also reduce complexity in the industry. The simplicity must therefore be reflected in all planning activities. As a result, the planning process in the retail industry must be very efficient and economical and should not include detailed coordination among retailers. Typically, most retailers face a certain seasonality that can be planned quite simply, and all participants know their business very well.

Consequently, the planning process does not require many coordination loops and can be designed efficiently using stringent assumptions and methods. These planning assumptions can easily be derived and utilized, e.g., the purchasing power development of a certain region can be used to plan sales, and the producer price index (PPI) from the Federal Bureau of Commerce can be used to derive the development of purchase prices. Planning assumptions and top-down targets represent a useful tool to make the planning process more coherent, i.e., starting with the steering philosophy that regulates central and decentral responsibilities for profitability and liquidity, to the strategic planning and the resulting measures that define the framework for the midterm planning, and then budget (operational planning) and forecast. An integrative approach strengthens the resilience of the planning instruments.

Furthermore, this approach also includes an ideal coordination among the different planning instruments. The planning of sales must necessarily be in line with the planning of cost of sales and gross margin and is connected to planning in logistics, procurement, expansion planning, and operational costs at the point of sale. Personnel deployment, real estate, marketing, IT, and governance represent other examples for individual planning in the retail industry and must be coordinated in order to obtain planning results with reasonable efforts that are fit to steer the company. Finally, the planning process should be supported by appropriate IT systems and can potentially become an embedded part of daily operations instead of the necessary evil. Even operational units in the retail segment can become familiar with planning activities as long as this adds value on all levels of the organization.

2.3 "Retail Means Change"

However, planning activities remain an attempt to anticipate the future, and that inherently entails certain insecurities and makes creating instruments that can react quickly to changes and new insights even more important. Planning activities must guarantee the ability to respond! Most retailers, at least prospectively, rely on their customers' volatile buying power. Changes in locational factors, order backlog, legal framework (e.g., can deposits, opening hours, interest rate barriers or IFRS requirements, etc.), and demographic changes must all be accounted for in the planning process. These changes can occur on a quarterly or even monthly basis. With the right planning process in place, these changes do not necessarily represent more effort. A rolling planning approach can cope with such sudden changes as the existing planning from prior periods only needs to be checked and adapted. Changes are only necessary if significant changes have come up that require an immediate adjustment of the existing planning. In practice, the underlying principle exists in many forms and differs for each company, depending on requirements and experience. A rolling approach that can be adjusted monthly or quarterly, but also semi-rolling approaches can be effective (see Fig. 1).[4]

By employing valid parameters such as consumer indices, forecasts, and typical seasonal cycles, the rolling planning process can be adapted flexibly. It also serves as a solid base for entrepreneurial decision-making in times of changing circumstances. The spectrum of reactions ranges from changing product lines, adjusting capacity and resources, changing prices, and purchasing policy to optimizing the supply chain and working capital. Besides constantly updating the existing planning, the rolling planning approach also requires planning one more planning period. Consequently, the focus of planning shifts from the year-end result to a constant outlook into the future.

3 Integrated Planning Instruments and Processes

The full spectrum of the aforementioned planning instruments can only rarely be found in the retail industry. Generally, very few retailers conduct strategic planning and engage in a structured strategy development. In most cases, retailers regard strategic considerations as part of the day-to-day operations of top management. Interestingly, this observation applies to all retailers regardless of the size of the company. Furthermore, financial and non financial KPIs are rarely determined or at least not communicated properly for a 5- to 7-year horizon. Consequently, many retailers have trouble defining a particular target for midterm planning and budget.[5]

---

[4]Rolling approaches typically also involve further adjustment requirements, for example, in the mapping of accounting effects over the turn of the business year or in the anchoring in the existing incentive systems.

[5]For reasons of simplification, the occasional combination of strategic planning and midterm planning should not be carried out here.

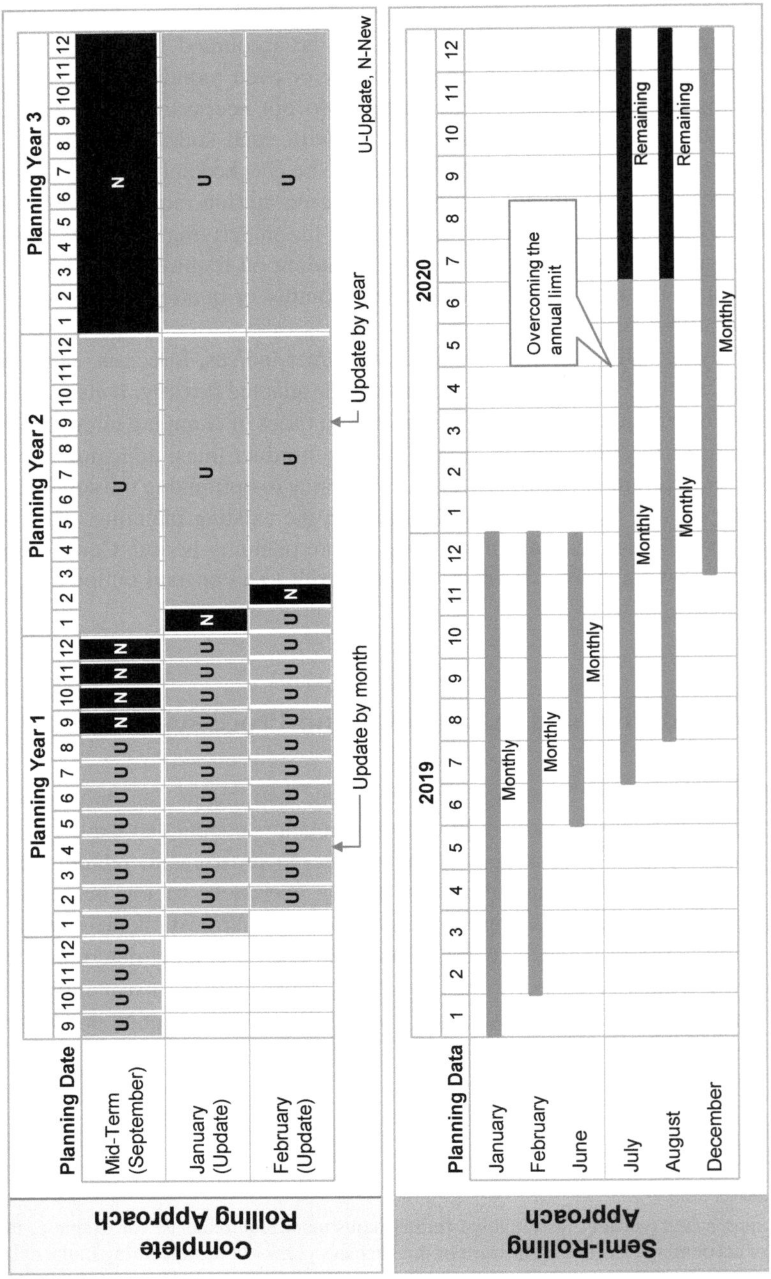

Fig. 1 Schematic illustration of rolling planning approaches

3.1 Planning Process

Lacking targets and assumptions result in comparatively inefficient and costly planning processes. For a traditionally organized retailer in the stationary retail segment, top management normally projects the future market and competitive situation, the development of prices, margins, and costs. The management of each country that the company operates in normally also engages in planning activities of their own, and without clearly defined and communicated targets and assumptions, these projections rarely match.

Generally, the projections of operating units and those of top management must not necessarily match. Many companies see such discrepancies as a value adding activity, since the process of comparing ambitious targets with projections from operational units helps to align all participants. This approach (top-down and bottom-up) is very popular. However, the definition and communication of targets and assumptions for the planning process are essential for an efficient and effective execution. Typically, the definition and the communication of targets and assumptions is performed by the top management in a top-down process.

Many retailers have confirmed a top-down approach. However, after observing this process in more detail, evidence shows that targets are not derived in a traditional top-down process after all, but are rather the result of a preceding bottom-up planning process in which particular departments provide their detailed assessment of the operational business development. This planning process is characteristic for the retail industry, as it increases acceptance for the resulting targets in the entire organization and uses operational business know-how to improve planning quality.

However, this planning process is highly inefficient, as preceding bottom-up planning processes are often performed under the radar and cannot be found in the official planning calendars. Additionally, it is highly questionable whether the quality of a strategic planning process should depend on a detailed operational planning process performed by operational units. The top management that is responsible for the strategic planning process has often gained experience in operational units and knows the business inside out. Furthermore, the day-to-day exchange between top management and operational units should be sufficient to evaluate the future orientation of the company. Admittedly, a lack of acceptance for top-down targets, assumptions, and expectations remains the biggest challenge for top management and must be secured at all times.

Example

An international food retailer intends to increase the quality and efficiency of its planning process. The existing midterm planning, with a horizon of 3 years, plays a significant role and represents an integrated strategic planning and midterm planning. The existing plan provides targets for the budget and ensures an efficient planning process. The targets are accepted on all levels

(continued)

of the organization and even grant a certain degree of freedom for individual sub-plans. Finally, planning content, processes, and templates are standardized to ensure a binding and standardized planning process.

Furthermore, the level of acceptance for the top-down planning process can be increased when top and middle management communicate and approve consistent targets, expectations, and assumptions. Such meetings are normally prepared by group controlling. Ideally, none of the participants demand a bottom-up planning from their segment in preparation for the meeting as the focus must remain on top-level strategy.

3.2 Coordinating All Planning Instruments

An integrated coordination of all planning instruments is essential for an efficient and effective planning process regardless of the selected planning approach.

The integration of all planning instruments can easily be established for companies in the retail industry. Typically, the stationary retail segment already has plans in place concerning the development of existing stationary stores over time. General expectations are recorded and contain various KPIs depending on the entrepreneurial situation. The expectations for new stores, other sales channels, and new ventures are recorded in a structured way (layer model or layer concept). These expectations are at least implicitly present and common. However, the extent to which these targets are communicated strongly depends on the company culture and the selected planning approach.

Another essential part of the planning processes (strategic planning and midterm planning) besides expectations is the underlying planning assumptions. It is critical for the validity of the planning process that the assumptions across all planning instruments are aligned regarding price, cost, and exchange rate development as well as specific market and sales channel developments. The planning assumptions are ideally recorded specifically as they can vary between units, e.g., regions or assortment groups. Furthermore, it is possible that certain assumptions only apply for a specific segment, e.g., a company in the retail industry also owns production units.

These assumptions and targets are critical for an efficient planning process and must be provided by central group functions to create company-wide transparency and enable the internal comparisons highly required in the retail industry.

The communication of planning assumptions and targets represents a very important step in the planning calendar and provides an integrated view on all applied planning instruments.

Integrating a forecast into the mix of planning instruments is another elementary step toward a comprehensive corporate management and planning process. The contribution "Shorter Planning, better Management" that can also be found in this book provides a practical example at Manor. Coordinated communication of planning targets, underlying assumptions, and planning instruments facilitate an efficient planning process. Additionally, a standardized calendar, structure, and procedure provide a high degree of transparency and make the planning process more comprehensible and comparable.

4 Planning Content

The planning content represents one more important building block toward an efficient and valuable planning process, i.e., the selected KPIs and dimensions that ought to be planned in the strategic planning, midterm planning, budget, and forecast.

4.1 Planning Content per Instrument

The general guideline for all planning instruments is that the longer the planning time frame, the less detailed the planning content should be. A strategic planning process in the retail industry typically includes six to ten financial positions, while a budget can easily involve more than 80 positions, regardless of cost types and centers. The underlying principle according to advanced budgeting[6] for the extent of the planning content is to plan steering relevant matters in more detail than less significant ones. The higher degree of detail is partly represented in the KPI selection, but also in the relevant dimensions (e.g., sales channels, formats, product groups, etc.), cost types, and centers (Fig. 2).

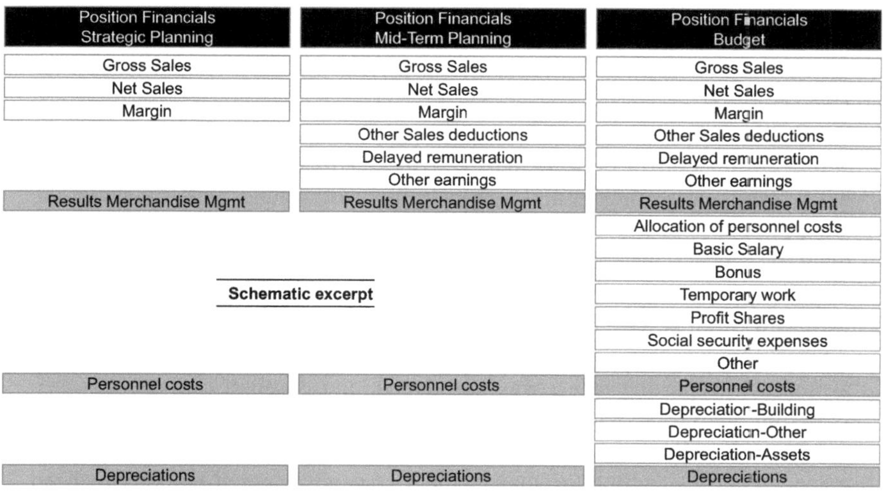

Fig. 2 Difference between planning content and planning instruments

[6]Brenner and Leyk (2004), p. 107

4.2 Differentiation Model to Increase Acceptance

The differentiation model is widely accepted; however, the final decision regarding the steering relevant content normally prompts intense discussions.

The definition of planning relevant content should be standardized for the entire company, although different format and country-specific regulations can require individual solutions. Differing planning requirements, multilayered and multichannel retailers, and integrated production units can be further differentiation factors.

The defined planning content must not only fulfill the principles of an efficient planning process, but must also receive a high level of acceptance among operating units. In the worst case scenario, a second unofficial corporate planning process is established, collecting apparently relevant details alongside the official planning process. Therefore, providing a model that not only satisfies the minimum requirements of the company, but also offers a certain degree of freedom and technical support when it comes to additional and individual details, is essential. This process requires a high level of technical support that is covered by all relevant planning tools.

Multinational companies, especially in the Anglo-Saxon area, are influenced by a trend toward a high level of detail, sometimes down to single accounts. Normally, a clearly communicated minimum requirement, paired with the option of adding more detailed individual planning, successively leads to companies limiting their planning content to the minimum requirement. In this case, top management must be strictly disciplined, and no further inquiries that exceed the scope of the minimum reporting requirement are allowed: this would significantly increase the risk of establishing an unofficial corporate planning process. Further analysis must be performed on the basis of existing actual data.

Example

For a global retailer, the level of planning detail varies greatly between the countries that it operates in. With experience, the planning process in Germany has become more efficient and now only includes around 25 KPIs, while the management in newly entered markets included more than 100 KPIs in their planning process. The more experienced management in Germany simply did not require the same level of detail to feel comfortable. Additionally, the management in newly entered markets wanted to demonstrate that everything was taken into account. To support the management in newly entered markets, a minimum reporting scope was introduced, and constant support was provided. Furthermore, a planning tool was provided that allowed planning in greater detail. However, the greater level of detail was not reported to top management. Over time the management in newly entered markets realized that a greater level of detail in the planning process does not necessarily

(continued)

increase the planning quality and was therefore successively reduced to the minimum reporting scope.

4.3 Cost Types and Cost Centers

Important matters are planned in more detail, while insignificant matters are planned in less detail. This general principle can also be applied for all cost centers that must be planned. In a strategic planning process, planning each cost center is hardly reasonable. Instead, depending on the structure, retailers focus on entities, regions, formats, and sales channels. A multichannel retailer that uses stores, online, catalogue, and wholesale as sales channels could, for example, plan online and wholesale in total and with little detail, while the other two essential sales channels, i.e., stores and catalogue, are planned on product line level and therefore in great detail.

The same principle applies to cost types that are normally not incorporated into the strategic planning approach and are summarized into cost type groups of the budget. These simplifications increase efficiency, but must certainly conform to the management structure and approach of the retailer.

It must be mentioned that all these simplifications cannot have any negative impact on the planning quality. Research[7] shows that when comparing planned and actual data on an aggregated level, the planning quality is at least equal to a more detailed planning.

5 Integrated Planning

All plans, but especially the budget, are composed of sub-plans that are executed by different operational functions. The budget therefore differentiates between segments that are planned by central or decentral functions and between planning dimensions, e.g., profit and liquidity planning.

5.1 Functional Planning

A holistic planning process always contains sub-plans from operational functions. There are comprehensive interdependencies among the plans for each function (e.g., administration, sales, human resources, procurement, logistics, etc.) that must

[7]Horváth and Partners Research (2010)

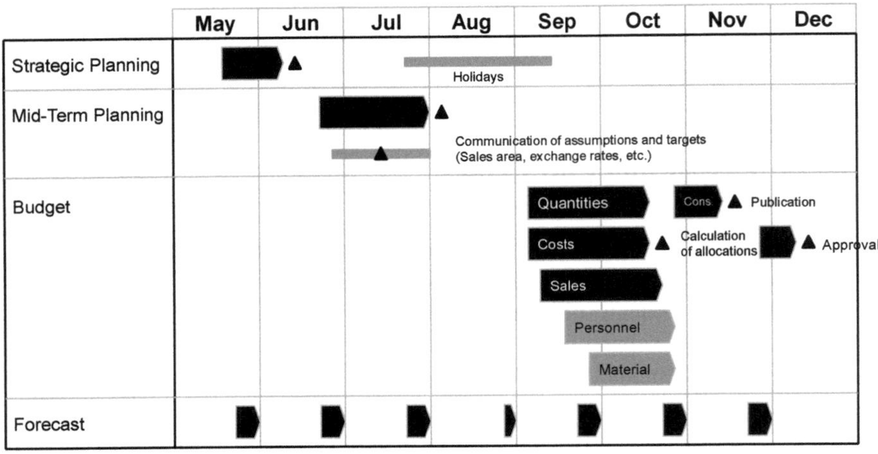

Fig. 3 Overview of planning processes

certainly be considered. Moreover, the interaction between centralized and decentralized functions must be coordinated carefully.

In the traditional organizational structure of a retailer, group functions supervise various organizations in different countries that normally consist of multiple regions and districts in which stores are combined. In most cases, these regions are responsible for planning sales, cost of sales, investments, store costs, personnel costs, administrative costs, and measures. However, superior planning instruments, assumptions, expectations, and targets must also be considered. Strategic measures, growth and investment measures, IT, marketing, and real estate are normally planned by central functions.[8]

In practice, there are usually differences in the distribution of planning responsibilities. The selected approach should reflect the management structure as well as the culture. The coordination of individual segment plans is carried out via detailed planning processes (see Fig. 3).

Depending on the state and orientation of the corporate development, it may be useful for retailers who are expanding or renovating to examine the investment plan separately. Especially, investments in new sales floor, i.e., in stores, can be planned easily and in a structured way. Standardized investment types are defined and ideally backed up by standardized numbers. On the basis of these standardized numbers, planning can be adjusted and the responsible manager can benefit from the company's prior experience.

[8]Sasse et al. (2006), p. 425

Example
A chain store with a highly standardized concept plans an expansion. Investments in new stores can be categorized into the following segments: individual city stores and small, medium, and large stores. Standardized investment plans are available for small, medium, and large stores, and the specifics can be entered into planning sheets and tools. In case the construction progress is delayed, the tool automatically proposes new deadlines. The planning tool is widely accepted due to the many planning features and also offers a constant update on investment plans for top management. The planning process for individual city stores is mainly based on experience and must be done manually.

5.2 Integrating Profitability and Liquidity Planning

Equally interesting, but much less common in day-to-day operations, is the integration of profitability and liquidity planning. A typical profitability or budget planning (P&L, balance sheet, cash flow, investments) is focused on the results-oriented steering of income/expenses, the individual reporting items (balance sheet, P&L, etc.), and the creation of controlling[9] options (plan/actual comparison). Typically, the focus of liquidity planning remains on cash flow-oriented steering objects such as cash inflows and outflows and the creation of reliable basic values for all finance and financing activities and liquidity management. For retailers that have financed their operational business mostly by extending their own payment dates and receiving their inflows immediately from their customers, the planning and steering of liquidity can be a deciding factor of success. Imprecise planning and unused liquidity lead to high financing and opportunity costs that can be avoided by employing an improved planning process. A proven concept to increase the quality of liquidity planning is to coordinate it with the budget. Wherever it is possible to coordinate the liquidity planning and budget planning beyond the manual top-line comparison, effectivity and quality of the planning can be increased significantly, building the foundation for an optimized liquidity allocation. An immediate monetary benefit can be realized (by identifying unused funds or additional financing needs).

Therefore, operational budget planning and liquidity/investment planning will be defined as an integrated planning cycle with coordinated methods (content, processes, frequency, level of detail, procedure, etc.). For the design of an integrated planning, the following four options are available (see Fig. 4).

[9]The author uses the English word "controlling" to translate the German term "controlling." Please refer to the discussion in the preface.

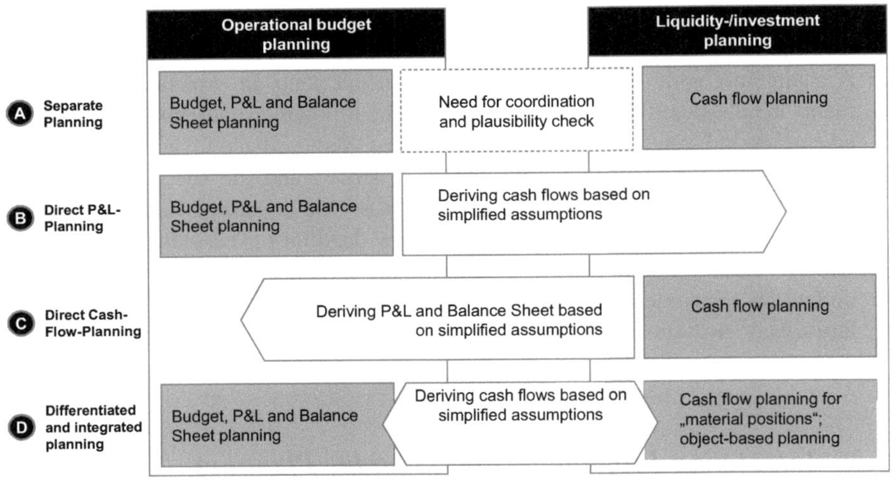

Fig. 4 Integrating budget and liquidity planning

Instead of having multiple planning solutions in place, the goal for all companies is to find a solution that is most compatible for the organization and can be established easily. A direct cash flow planning including a derived P&L and balance sheet is surely a unique case.

Especially for retailers, the required cash outflows for essential positions are well-known and can be planned easily. A differentiating option is therefore preferred: material positions are determined by existing contracts or proven seasonality cycles with existing payment conditions for cost of sales and sales. Immaterial positions will be added during the budget planning process. Methodically, this option is a very pragmatic mix that represents a renunciation from existing processes. Neither budgets, P&L, balance sheet, nor cash flows are planned in a conventional way, but are rather derived from planning content and times.

Such a differentiating procedure requires the support of a practical planning tool that guarantees a specific data entry and, consequently, an automatic transition to the planning tools. In comparison to separate planning tools, a more accurate planning process for cash flows is created at an acceptable level of detail regarding the P&L. Adaptation difficulties for the planner of the operational business can be solved through planning templates that enable a smooth transition.

6 Conclusion

Planning in the retail business is normally an easy task, since the most critical assumptions are widely known and represent a solid base for projections. Furthermore, the industry regularly employs a layer model that guarantees a high level of comparability for the corporate development of existing and new sales floors in the stationary retail segment. Repeating patterns increase the resilience of and act as a base for all planning activities, because the basic conditions normally remain stable.

Consequently, the most essential requirements for a highly efficient planning process in the retail industry are given. However, the quality of a planning process is not exclusively defined by the resilience of a business model. Incorporating these requirements into an efficiently designed planning process is essential. Therefore, an optimal and stringent coordination of planning instruments from strategic planning down to budget is required. Functional segment planning can include all parts of the organization, but must be coordinated accordingly in order to create a planning process that requires minimal effort.

The level of acceptance that the employed planning processes, methods, and systems receive from operational units is probably the most important success factor. Planning activities are normally carried out in greater quality when the operational units believe that additional value is added. The differentiating models mentioned above are able to meet the requirements of the operational units on all levels and secure the content, functionality, transparency, and rigor for the corporate planning process. Finally, reducing the level of complexity and detail to a minimum is critical.

Supporting systems play an important role, as the resilient assumptions can be transferred into the planning tool and help automate the process. This applies to cost distributions based on seasonality effects as well as to standardized life cycles of new objects and businesses.

Corporate planning in the retail industry can be efficient, robust, and flexible as long as the requirements can successfully be limited and controlled.

References

Brenner M, Leyk J (2004) Rollierender Forecast und rollierende Planung. In: Horváth & Partners (ed) Beyond Budgeting umsetzen: erfolgreich planen mit Advanced Budgeting, Stuttgart, pp 101–122

Guldin A (2004) Planung im Einzelhandel. Wie können Ganzheitlichkeit und Details verknüpft werden? In: Gleich R, Hofmann S, Leyk J (eds) Planungs- und Budgetierungsinstrumente. Innovative Ansätze und Best-Practice für den Managementprozess, Freiburg, pp 171–188

Horváth & Partners (2004) Beyond Budgeting umsetzen: erfolgreich planen mit Advanced Budgeting, Stuttgart

Horváth & Partners Research (2010) Research retail & fast moving consumer goods, internal source

Sasse A et al (2006) Unternehmensplanung und -steuerung. Einführung des Advanced Budgeting in einem Handelsunternehmen. In: Controlling-Berater, 03/2006, pp 425–438

Steinmann H, Schreyögg G (2013) Management-Grundlagen der Unternehmensführung—Konzepte, Funktionen, Fallstudien, 7 edn, Wiesbaden

Michael Buttkus is partner at Horváth & Partners, heading the retail and consumer goods competence center. He has extensive practical experience in the areas of performance management, management accounting and finance, strategic business management, and process and organizational management.

Shorter Planning, Better Management

Dominique Reuse, Mario Schoeb, and Ulrich Teuscher

Abstract The exceedingly dynamic environment in the retail industry represents significant new challenges for planning and steering concepts. During the course of a project focused on optimizing the planning and steering concept at Manor, the leading Swiss department store chain, new planning and steering instruments were implemented. Simultaneously, the time and effort required for preparing the existing financial budget was significantly reduced in order to free capacities for a new steering concept.

A key element of the new planning and steering process is the rolling forecast, which is prepared by the sales team on a quarterly basis and represents an honest evaluation of the company's performance. The forecast helps to identify changes in the business development and react accordingly by flexibly adjusting the resource management. New processes and instruments to determine and track binding measures and support a dynamic personnel planning process guarantee that gained insights are integrated into day-to-day operations. Our experience at Manor evidences that an improved planning and steering concept not only reduces the required time and effort for the preparation of the existing financial budget but also leads to measurable improvements in terms of revenue, margins, and costs.

Our approach to introducing new planning and steering instruments and our experience in the implementation process will be illustrated in this contribution.

Keywords Planning · Dynamic personnel planning · Forecasting · Budgeting · Planning process · Budgeting process

This contribution has been originally printed as Reuse, D., Schoeb, M., Teuscher, U. (2016): Kürzer planen, besser steuern, Buttkus, M., Neugebauer, A., Controlling im Handel: Innovative Ansätze und Praxisbeispiele, pp. 143–152, Springer Gabler, Wiesbaden.

D. Reuse
Manor AG, Basel, Switzerland

M. Schoeb · U. Teuscher (✉)
Horváth & Partners, Zürich, Switzerland

M. Buttkus, R. Eberenz (eds.), *Performance Management in Retail and the Consumer Goods Industry*, https://doi.org/10.1007/978-3-030-12730-5_14

1 Planning and Steering in the Retail Industry

The environment in the retail industry has become significantly more dynamic in recent years. Nowadays, consumers are generally well-informed about offers and price changes. New information and communication channels make pricing information more accessible and transparent and are one of the reasons why buying behavior has shifted toward one that is mobile, as consumers can quickly compare prices between vendors. Furthermore, globalization has changed the competitive landscape and is threatening the market position of many well-established companies as online shopping, outlets, and other alternative business models squeeze the margins of traditional retailers. In most cases, negotiations with suppliers have become more difficult and less reliable. Additionally, a shift to more liberal governments in many countries has introduced longer opening hours and therefore represents new challenges for personnel planning.

The planning process in the retail industry is traditionally a lengthy process and therefore contrasts the increasingly dynamic environment. Existing planning instruments are generally inflexible and very detail-oriented, and the yearly financial budget often plays a significant role in the planning process. Traditionally, the preparation of the financial budget is strongly influenced by the company's past performance as only minor changes are assumed. Moreover, the financial budget is often not only used for coordination, motivation, and target setting but also for forecasting purposes. Consequently, the financial budget must be adjusted repeatedly during the financial period to perform different functions.

This approach comes with significant costs as the comprehensive and lengthy adjustment process binds not only a significant share of management accounting[1] resources but also forces employees in the department stores to spend time on administrative tasks that they could otherwise spend on customer service or at the point of sale.

Furthermore, very detailed financial budgets are at risk of becoming irrelevant in increasingly dynamic environments, i.e., budget figures are possibly outdated by the time they are available for management. Additionally, a personnel planning that forecasts up to 15 months in advance must inevitably be modified multiple times per year.

Most planning concepts have not yet adapted to the rapidly increasing dynamic of the retail environment. Manor, the leading department store chain in Switzerland, has addressed this issue by collaborating with Horváth & Partners Management Consultants to develop a concept that includes new planning and steering instruments.

[1]The authors use the English word "management accounting" to translate the German term "controlling." Please refer to the discussion in the preface.

2 Starting Points for the Optimization of Planning and Steering Processes

By redesigning the planning and steering processes and instruments, Manor pursued the following three strategic guidelines:

1. Introducing new instruments to dynamically steer the business and actively exploit uncovered business potentials as well as promptly reacting to changes in the environment with appropriate measures. A key element of the new planning and steering process is the rolling forecast, which is prepared by the sales team on a quarterly basis and represents an honest evaluation of the company's performance. A systematic process to define measures and consequently track the outcome as well as a rolling personnel planning was designed and implemented based on insights of the forecast.
2. Consistent planning and steering instruments to help integrate the planning process into Manor's strategy implementation and set realistic goals for the Manor group. The content and the processes of the midterm planning were modified to create a link between strategy and operative budgeting processes. The resulting midterm targets are binding for the operative budgeting process. The timeline for all planning processes was aligned, and the total cycle time for the planning process was reduced significantly.
3. Significantly reducing the required time and effort for the preparation of the existing financial budget in order to free capacities for the new steering process of the business. Considerable improvements were accomplished by radically streamlining planning content and processes. The cycle time of the budget planning process in department stores was reduced to 2 weeks. The number of planning objects, e.g., product groups on the revenue and cost units and cost types on the cost side, was reduced by a factor of 100. About 1000 sales managers were relieved of all planning responsibilities, and the required time and effort for the group planning process was cut by more than 50%.

The key points of the new planning processes and instruments will be explained in the following chapter.

3 Forecasts: A Proactive Steering Instrument

Contrary to the top-down budgeting process, the forecast is a bottom-up steering instrument. Consequently, the sales team is directly responsible for the forecast, i.e., an honest evaluation of the company's future performance, as well as for the definition and tracking of countermeasures where deviations from the planning objectives are foreseeable.

The implemented forecast at Manor follows a predefined process consisting of five steps and is supported by an easily manageable IT system (forecasting tool) (Fig. 1).

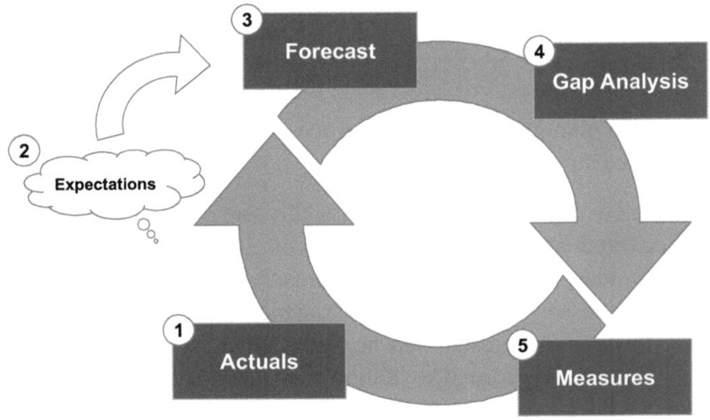

Fig. 1 Circle of forecasting

Based on available actuals from previous years (step 1) and expectations for essential revenue and cost drivers (step 2), the sales team, together with headquarters, forecasts (step 3) the revenue, margin, and cost development for all department stores. All individual forecasts are automatically transferred to the year-end income statement and can also be used for a rolling forecast of the next 12 months. By comparing forecast and budget, deviations can be identified easily (step 4) for all periods (current financial year, rolling 12 months). By deciding on effective countermeasures and including them in the forecasting tool, deviations from planning objectives can be avoided. Furthermore, the effect of countermeasures can immediately be quantified in the forecasting tool.

Hence, the forecast serves as a leading indicator for deviations from planning objectives and allows to push positive trends and reverse negative trends by deciding on appropriate countermeasures. The success of countermeasures and the accuracy of the forecast are tracked over time based on successively available actuals (step 1).

The forecasting process was designed in close collaboration with the sales team, and the product was pilot-tested in four department stores to tailor content, processes, and instruments perfectly to Manor's needs. The resulting solution enjoyed a high level of acceptance and was successfully launched in all department stores in Switzerland in 2010. During the course of the project at Manor, we identified the following factors for success:

– Focus on selected, but critical, forecast figures: Based on a materiality analysis (ABC analysis) and the existing steering requirements (impact on earnings and controllability), six cost and revenue figures were selected. The selected figures include net sales, personnel costs (directly forecasted by sales team), gross margin, and three major cost pools that are forecasted by central procurement and cost managers. All other revenue and cost figures are automatically updated based on trends. Therefore, management's attention is focused on a small set of forecast figures in order to minimize the required time and effort for the forecasting process.

- Appropriate forecast frequency and horizon: The forecast frequency and the number of months to be forecasted are determined based on a turbulence analysis that takes the dynamic of the environment and the required early warning period for countermeasures into account.[2] The forecast is prepared on a quarterly basis and includes four quarters of which two quarters are forecasted in detail (months and rayons), while the other two quarters are forecasted in less detail (quarters and sectors).
- Involve all responsible parties: Different hierarchy levels at headquarters and in the department stores are involved in the forecasting process at Manor. Generally, all managers directly forecast positions that they can influence in their department and define countermeasures in case deviations from planning objectives are foreseeable. Therefore, the forecast becomes an operative management tool for all responsible parties.
- Brief and efficient forecasting process: Due to the simultaneous preparation of the forecast by all involved parties and consistent IT support throughout the process, it was possible to cut the cycle time down to 7 days for the entire forecasting process, including consolidation and the definition of measures.
- Integrating the forecast into reporting: The forecast figures were consistently implemented into the existing reporting structure. All existing reports were complemented by an additional forecast column and now include a quarterly updated forecast on revenue and costs for individual department stores, regions, and the Manor group. The traditional comparison between budget and actuals is therefore complemented by a forward-looking comparison between forecast and actuals and therefore provides the opportunity to proactively steer the business.

4 Consistent Definition of Measures and Tracking

As mentioned earlier, the forecast is not an end in itself but rather a leading indicator to identify deviations from planning objectives. This enables management to flexibly adjust resources as long as the corresponding measures are methodically defined and implemented.

An individual and systematic process to define measures and consistently track the outcome was implemented at Manor for that purpose. The process is well connected to the forecasting process and supported by the planning tool. In the event of negative deviations from planning objectives (i.e., forecast > budget for costs, forecast < budget for revenue and margins), countermeasures to increase revenue or cut costs must be defined and coordinated with the supervisor and included in the forecasting tool.

[2]Brenner and Leyk (2004), p. 106.

The key to successfully implementing measures is regularly tracking the effectivity of all implemented measures. Consequently, the tracking at Manor is performed within the scope of the forecasting tool. The tool tracks the implementation status of all selected measures from design and implementation to completion or abortion and is subsequently discussed in regular meetings with the supervisor. By including a tracking process into the reporting structure, all measures taken by department stores and headquarters can be tracked in real time.

For the tracking to be successful, a number of requirements must be fulfilled, e.g., when designing a measure, the expected implementation costs and effect on revenue, margins, and costs must be included and are subsequently tracked over time based on successively available actuals. This allows Manor to consistently realize learning effects and increase the quality of the forecast.

5 Dynamic Personnel Planning

The regularly updated forecast also provides Manor with important information for implementing a dynamic personnel planning process. Based on the assumption that an increase in revenue at a constant level of customer service requires more staff, a forecasted increase in revenue is complemented by an increase in personnel costs. By connecting personnel planning to the dynamic forecast instead of the fixed financial budget, staffing can be adjusted flexibly (see Fig. 2).

Our experience at Manor evidences that sales managers assess a personnel planning approach that is based on the latest forecast to be very positive. All sales managers are responsible for the personnel planning of their respective division and

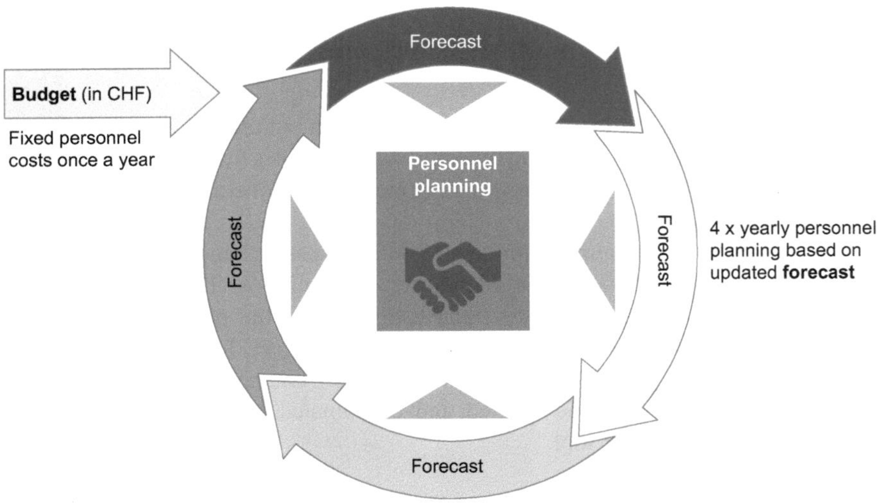

Fig. 2 Dynamic personnel planning

empowered to act as entrepreneurs within Manor. Therefore, each manager can flexibly react to changes within the scope of labor contracts and staffing policy at Manor.

6 Reducing the Required Time and Effort for the Budgeting Process

The availability of new steering instruments has enabled Manor to use the financial budget as a target setting instrument and subsequently reduce the required time and effort for the budgeting process. The financial budgeting processes and instruments were comprehensively modified by adhering to the approach described in Fig. 3.

Top-down targets set by management are broken down to lower hierarchy levels in the course of the budgeting process, while the monthly allocation is automatically generated by the forecasting tool. The allocation to individual department stores and products follows last year's actuals, but all automatically generated planning values can be amended.

The entire budgeting light process at Manor was completed during 4 weeks in late 2010, while department stores only required 2 weeks to complete the planning process. Numerous managers (e.g., product managers, head of administration, etc.) are only included in the target setting process of the budget and relieved of their other planning responsibilities.

The feedback we received after the first run was consistently positive. Even managers that were no longer part of the budgeting process gave positive evaluations as their steering requirements were compensated by their involvement in the forecasting process. The capacities that were freed by designing a leaner budgeting

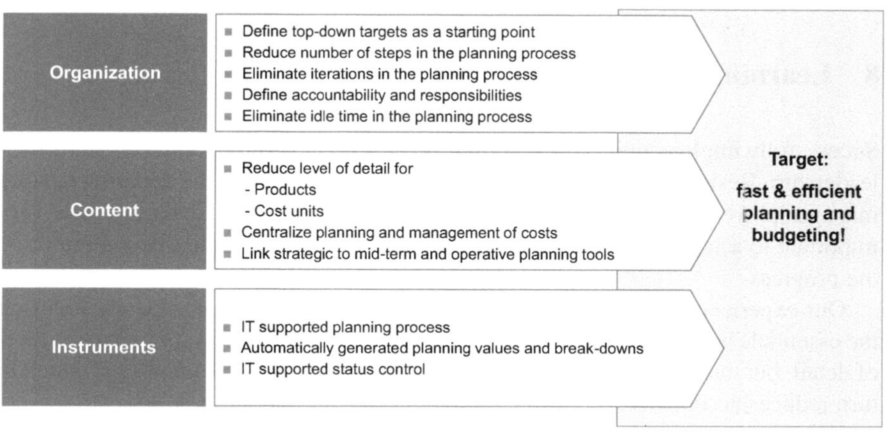

Fig. 3 Budgeting

process are estimated to considerably exceed the additionally required resources by the new forecasting process.

7 Product Rollout

At first glance, projects that change the planning and steering concept of a company are often seen as typical management accounting projects. However, our experience shows that the transformation often comes with considerable changes in the culture of the organization, e.g., several managers at Manor were relieved of their planning responsibilities but subsequently expected to become more autonomous as traditional tracking and planning responsibilities were substituted by more entrepreneurial freedom.

These changes require that all affected parties let go off their habits and apparent securities and put more trust in the company's employees and their capabilities. Only then can new processes and instruments reach their full potential.

The transformation requires a rethinking process and must be followed by intensive training and communication. At Manor this process was visualized in the form of a change map which was discussed intensely and ultimately followed by coaching sessions.

A change map is a training tool that illustrates changes by dividing the landscape into a current and a future state. The two states are represented side by side in the form of typical and sometimes exaggerated everyday situations and comments. The current situation is only hinted at as the change map clearly focuses on the target vision of tomorrow, which is illustrated by memorable symbols and comments. The change map can be drawn in smaller as well as in larger groups of affected parties and is an excellent tool to illustrate seemingly complex organizational, procedural, or technical issues in a comprehensible fashion.

8 Learnings and Factors for Success

Successfully implementing new planning and steering instruments always starts with leadership. Besides management and regional sales managers, the department store manager played a crucial role for the success of the project. Generally, it is very important to actively include management in the project and regularly communicate the progress.

Our experience shows that new planning and steering solutions ideally focus on the essentials instead of details. Planning solutions can certainly vary in in their level of detail, but more detail comes at the cost of understanding and simplicity, which in turn reduces acceptance.

Finally, changing the existing planning and steering concept always entails a cultural change that cannot be underestimated. Affected parties can react very differently to changes, and therefore offering intense support and constantly gathering feedback during phases of an organizational transformation is critical.

Reference

Brenner M, Leyk J (2004) Rollierender Forecast und rollierende Planung. In: Horváth & Partners (ed) Beyond Budgeting umsetzen – Erfolgreich planen mit Advanced Budgeting. Schäffer-Poeschel, Stuttgart, pp 101–122

Dominique Reuse was Head of Management Accounting with the Manor AG in Basel.

Mario Schoeb was a Managing Consultant with Horváth & Partners in Zurich and focused on accounting, management accounting, finance, and performance management.

Ulrich Teuscher operates as a Partner with Horváth & Partners in Zurich, where he directs in the areas of management accounting and finance. His consulting focus lies in the areas of management accounting, finance, and performance management.

Planning 2.0 at REWE Group: Identifying Potential for Efficiency and Optimizing Planning Processes

Anna Thiel

Abstract In a highly dynamic and competitive environment, retail companies are facing tremendous challenges. Not only in sales but also in management accounting, business processes have to be highly flexible in order to guarantee short reaction times. Due to the high degree of complexity in dealing with different countries, languages, and cultures, these challenges are even greater for internationally operating companies. As in other industries, the retailing business also has long-lasting planning cycles that often lead to a high planning effort and tie up numerous resources. Plans lacking the necessary flexibility and planning values that are outdated when finally approved are the result.

Being an international company in the food sector, the REWE Group also faces challenges concerning various and highly competitive markets within a dynamic retailing industry. It is for this reason that REWE has decided to initiate a comprehensive program improving processes in controlling and establishing a sustainable management control. One pillar of this program focuses on planning processes and overall planning. A holistic, flexible, and lean planning solution is meant to result in more efficient planning processes and to increase the quality of planning sustainably. While being separated in two phases, the program begins with the definition of a rough concept of the new planning solution. The second phase focuses on detailing the concept and implementing the defined processes as well as a new planning software.

Keywords Benchmark planning · Frontloading approach · Management forecast · Planning approach · Retail · Target setting

This contribution has originally been printed as Thiel, A. (2016): Planung 2.0 in der REWE Group—Effizienzpotenziale identifizieren, Planungsprozesse optimieren, Buttkus, M., Neugebauer, A., Controlling im Handel: Innovative Ansätze und Praxisbeispiele, pp. 153–175, Springer Gabler, Wiesbaden.

A. Thiel (✉)
Retail and Consumer Goods, Horváth & Partners, Hamburg, Germany

M. Buttkus, R. Eberenz (eds.), *Performance Management in Retail and the Consumer Goods Industry*, https://doi.org/10.1007/978-3-030-12730-5_15

1 Initial Situation and Objectives

Retailing companies are facing tremendous challenges nowadays. Increasing competition, stagnating or even decreasing sales, and increasing costs for staff, space, and equipment lead to a very demanding business environment. Changing customer behavior and highly dynamic assortments make it difficult to meet customer needs.[1] Due to the highly dynamic business environment and an aggressive price positioning of main competitors, retailing companies must have short reaction times and immense transition flexibility, in order to remain competitive.[2] As the controlling department[3] is meant to put the management into a position where it can make sound decisions, it faces challenges that are increasingly becoming more and more complex. Planning, management, and control must be adapted to the specific requirements of retail companies to be able to react on changing environmental conditions in a timely manner.

The challenging company environment necessitates planning processes that are leaner and more efficient. A shortening of planning processes oftentimes remains unrecognized, or is rather not appreciated enough, due to an increasing complexity and dynamics of the market. Many companies that have grown over the years claim a high level of detail in planning, preventing a greater efficiency of planning processes. Planning is often initiated very early during the fiscal/business year and lasts for quite some time, which does not meet the requirements of a highly dynamic business environment with a strong seasonal character. Resulting plans lack in topicality. Additionally, immense resources are tied up the longer a planning process lasts. Within a planning period, these resources typically lose sight of the day-to-day-business.

Due to highly dynamic business environments, budget figures hardly ever last very long. Operational plans as well as midterm and strategic plans have to be reviewed continuously and, if necessary, adapted to new findings and developments. Furthermore, an immense amount of necessary information is only available on a decentralized basis at regional or store management level. Regional and store managers usually know more about developments concerning expected developments in sales, staff, and customers. Assessments they make can be more profound than considerations of people that do not participate in the daily retail business. This is why retail companies often have distinct bottom-up planning processes and an extensive involvement of operational areas in planning. This results not only in long-lasting and complex planning cycles. It evolves into numerous discussions and

[1]Kispalko and Moretti (2016), 1.1; Möhlenbruch (2012), pp. 127–128.

[2]Kispalko and Moretti (2016), 1.3; Neugebauer (2016), 2.1.

[3]The author uses the English word "controlling" to translate the German term "controlling." Please refer to the discussion in the preface.

revisions, especially in the end of planning periods as budgets, planned on a decentralized basis, have to be combined with long-term and strategic goals of the company.

A necessitated modernized planning process aims at efficient and lean planning with a high impact on management. Overall, four requirements can be named to cope with highly dynamic business environments in planning[4]:

1. Short and efficient planning processes
2. Focus on substantial changes and strategic topics
3. Integration of diverse scenarios
4. Possibility of adaptions during the year

As the REWE Group is an internationally operating and diversified company, it also faces the named challenges especially in terms of higher flexibility in planning as well as shorter and leaner planning periods. The group is one of the leading retail and tourism companies in Germany and Europe. With 330,000 employees, 15,000 stores in 12 countries, and sales amounting to 51 billion €, REWE is one of the biggest retail companies situated in Germany.

The REWE Group is not only characterized by its internationality but also by a very high variety of distribution channels (Fig. 1). It has realized the necessity of improvements in management control and therefore also of a modernization of planning approaches. The planning project is embedded in a comprehensive program, aiming at identifying and using performance potential in management accounting and control. Corporate planning therefore undergoes a fundamental conceptual redesign and technical realignment. In its current state, the planning process is perceived as highly detailed and fragmented as well as very time-consuming. This is why conceptual work focuses on the reduction of procedural inefficiencies and an increase in systemic support.

The organizational structure of the REWE Group is very challenging, when considering the planning and steering approach. Six different business areas and numerous sub-organizations pursuing diverging business models have to be taken into account. Discount-oriented businesses such as PENNY differ from supermarkets like the known REWE stores in many business processes. This is intensified by cultural differences on the international market. Additionally, further business areas like DIY markets and travel agencies as well as differing interests of operative units, holdings, IT, and logistics increase complexity.

The complexity in planning, steering, and control processes must be reduced in order to cope with highly dynamic markets and therefore also meeting the requirements of the upper management. The planning effort has to be reduced on all levels while simultaneously increasing the quality of planning process and the resulting figures. As a result, the means of business steering become more important. Taking this objective into account, the first step was specifying the requirements of planning as well as the planning processes. Increasing transparency in existing processes and

[4]Kappes and Schentler (2012), p. 20.

Fig. 1 Distribution channels and brands of the REWE Group

identifying potential areas of improvement served as a fundamental basis for a comprehensive and efficient new planning approach. This leads—in a next step—to the following objectives and challenges of the planning project:

- The planning processes should be connected with strategic planning and, therefore, be aligned with strategic goals. Planning becomes an important means for steering.
- Planning logics and planning processes should be standardized within business areas that use comparable business models. Simultaneously, the fact that each business area is supposed to be and act highly individually has to be taken into account.
- Process-oriented thinking should be implemented on a permanent basis.
- Stable processes and organizational efficiency should be increased sustainably.
- Quality, transparency, and cycle times should be improved in the long term.

In conclusion, the main objective is the conceptual design of an integrated and holistic planning approach, with a high degree of harmonization and simultaneously taking the characteristics of the highly individual business areas into account. Furthermore, the efficiency and quality of planning has to be increased significantly.

Two main prerequisites for a harmonized planning approach were given while starting the project in the first stage: Capturing the processes in their current state showed that concerning the business areas in food and DIY retailing have similar planning processes. In most cases, these areas only differ in their level of detail and calculation methods. All business areas have sub-plans for investments and expansions, sales, and administrative, as well as logistics planning. These similarities are encouraged by an earnings calculation (EVDB calculation) that is compulsory group-wide and used by all business areas. This calculation scheme is not only used to calculate actuals; it is also the core element for planning and fundamental for reporting. As a common denominator for all business areas, it serves as a solid basis for a module-based harmonization of planning.

The new planning approach is meant to link different planning occasions such as budget, midterm, and strategic planning, as well as forecasting. This aims at increasing relevance and acceptance of each planning occasion. Based on this, the main objectives of the project are captured in a guiding picture and supplemented guiding principles, as they serve as a framework for the conceptual design of the new planning approach (Figs. 2 and 3).

The new planning approach consists of four mandatory planning occasions that will be explained in detail in the course of the following chapters. The *frontloading* process consists of target setting and a benchmark planning. These two planning occasions serve as a framework for other decentralized planning processes and ensure that planning will be oriented toward the operational and strategic goals of the group and the different business areas. *Budget planning* is the most important planning occasion that focuses on a comprehensive projection of the rest of the actual as well as the upcoming fiscal year. In the meantime, budget serves as a starting point for the *midterm planning* that includes two further fiscal years but on a less detailed level than the budget. Finally, the *management forecast* offers

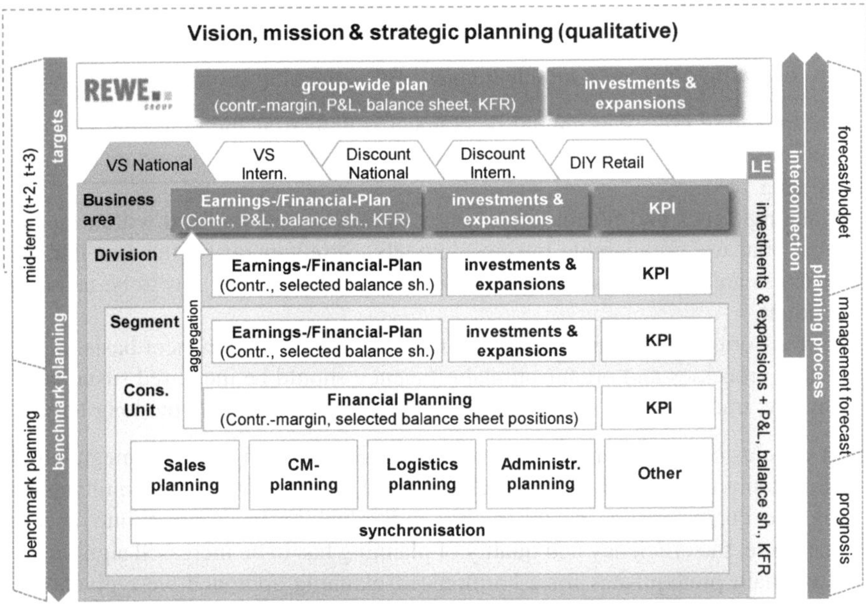

Fig. 2 Guiding picture of the new planning approach

1. All levels of the defined steering concept have to be taken into account. Each **level of responsibility** has to disclose the **required key figures**.
2. The **key figures** of the **steering concept** have to be reflected while **planning**. Planning depth have to be reduced considering **higher efficiency and effectivity**.
3. The planning process should be **more lean.** Only the **dimensions oftop KPIs** should be claimed that are clearly defined in the **steering concept** .
4. **Top-down targets** will be defined, reflecting profit responsibility. They are basis for **individual benchmark planning** of the business areas. To ensure flexibility, targets can be adapted top-down.
5. **Strategic aspects** should be taken into account during planning. Budget and mid-term planning have to reflect strategic planning.
6. **Explicit responsibilities for planning processes and interfaces** have to be defined (RACI). A time schedule has to be defined and is binding.
7. Aspects that are **not relevant for steering** will **not be considered** anymore or **determined on a central basis.** It has to be evaluated which KPIs should be planned.
8. The availability of planning has to consider **external reporting requirements**. Reporting requirements that are not relevant for steering are fulfilled efficiently.

Fig. 3 Guiding principles as a framework for planning

management a first indication regarding actual business development and possible deviations from the plan. The management forecast refers to a broader scope of time. Taking both effects that cause deviations as well as countermeasures thereof into account, this forecast also serves as a basis for planning and budgeting in upcoming periods. Additionally, business areas can decide to create a *prognosis* on a monthly basis, in order to control the target achievements in the actual fiscal year and increase the quality of planning.

2 Frontloading: Using Target Setting and Benchmark Planning to Ensure a Focused and Efficient Planning Process

In order to create a framework for efficient and focused planning for diversified and decentralized companies such as REWE, a top-down-oriented planning approach is necessary. This can be supported by a lean and focused frontloading process.

The basic idea of frontloading is to reduce time-consuming negotiations, numerous revision loops, as well as long-lasting coordination processes especially during the end of the planning period. Based on different assumptions and discussions during the beginning of the planning period, targets serving as a framework for decentralized planning are defined. This shift to the beginning of the planning period leads to higher efficiency in planning overall. The higher effort in the initial phase will usually be compensated by lower effort while planning. Typical loops during end phases of the planning process, necessary for aligning decentralized planning results with overall company objectives, can be reduced or prevented. Nevertheless, it is important for there to be no hidden bottom-up planning process to define targets. The frontloading process has to be premise-based and focused on central drivers in order to ensure success. Otherwise the potential of gaining efficiency cannot be used. Current developments and premises can be taken into account with the ability of reducing planning cycles due to a holistic and focused frontloading process: Planning values can be increased in actuality and quality. Additionally, resources are less tied up and can be used to pursue other activities.

In several companies, it can be observed that a focused frontloading is able to increase planning quality sustainably. Often the defined targets are designated to be "ambitioned but realistic"[5] and therefore can be met more often. A planning survey conducted by Horváth & Partners in 2012 proves that a top-down-oriented planning approach is able to reduce cycle times in planning sustainably (Fig. 4).

Additionally, frontloading processes can help avoid a planning that is too detailed at an early stage. Instead, strategical objectives as well as corresponding measures and effects can be taken into account during operational planning from the very beginning.

---

[5]Kappes and Schentler (2012), p. 20.

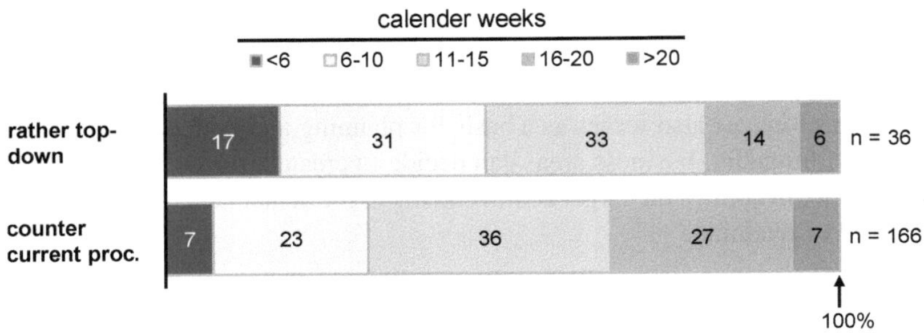

Fig. 4 Impact of a top-down planning approach on the duration of planning

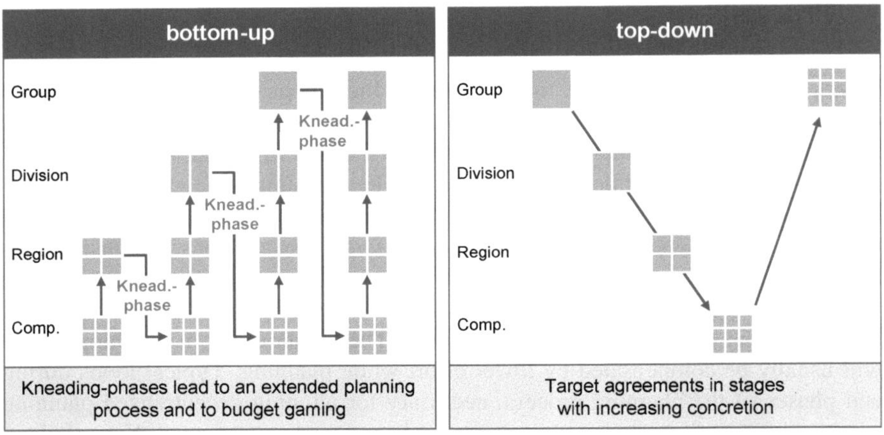

Fig. 5 A top-down planning approach reduces planning efforts and shortens planning cycle time

Furthermore, budget discussions are changing. A bottom-up planning process usually does not include any targets during initial phases. They tend to arise in discussions within the running planning process. Oftentimes, high efforts in planning coordination and numerous revision loops are necessary. As a result, decentralized areas are developing buffers, while centralized departments are reversing these again. These "kneading phases" can be very time-consuming, and resulting planning values often lack quality. A frontloading approach focuses target achievements and necessary measures. With the beginning of a planning process, precise targets are defined and are then substantiated on each level of planning in decentralized areas. Planning and related discussions focus on filling the gap between targets and planned values as well as on corresponding measures and their assessment (Fig. 5).

The designed frontloading process consists of two phases, in order to ensure the achievement of group-wide goals and to take into account the individuality of different business areas as well as the resulting strategic objectives. The first phase—target setting—is obligatory for all business areas. Based on bilateral

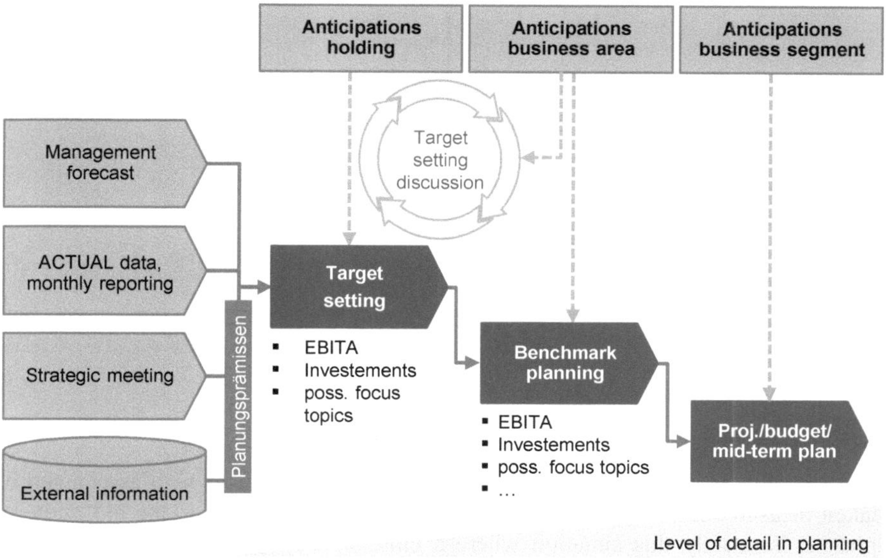

Fig. 6 The REWE Group's frontloading approach

discussions between the head of the business area on one and the corresponding key account on holding side, targets for selected key performance indicators are negotiated. The discussion should focus on two or three crucial earnings numbers that are important for steering. The discussion has to take place on a highly aggregated level, in order to avoid hidden bottom-up planning in preparation for the frontloading process. The subsequent planning phase, namely, benchmark planning, is optional for the business areas. As with target setting, the head of the respective business area can define targets based on discussions with subordinated units like countries or regions. If the respective business area does not aim at a discussion of targets with lower hierarchy levels, it is nevertheless mandatory to at least break down targets, in order to ensure the operationalization of targets on country or regional level. Where necessary, business areas can complement group targets with additional goals, in order to cope with the individuality of the business model (Fig. 6).

While benchmark planning is not mandatory for the business areas, a group-wide binding approach was defined for target setting. Target setting must be based on the midterm planning of the previous planning period. It serves as a connecting link between strategic and operational planning. As in many other companies, the REWE Group also used the midterm planning of the previous year as basis and starting point for the new budget, without this being reflected. However, when taking changing customer needs, hardly predictable seasonal deviations (e.g., weather conditions), and highly dynamic markets into account, the initial situation for planning may have changed in the meantime. Without reflecting these developments, past midterm plans cannot serve as a reliable basis for planning.

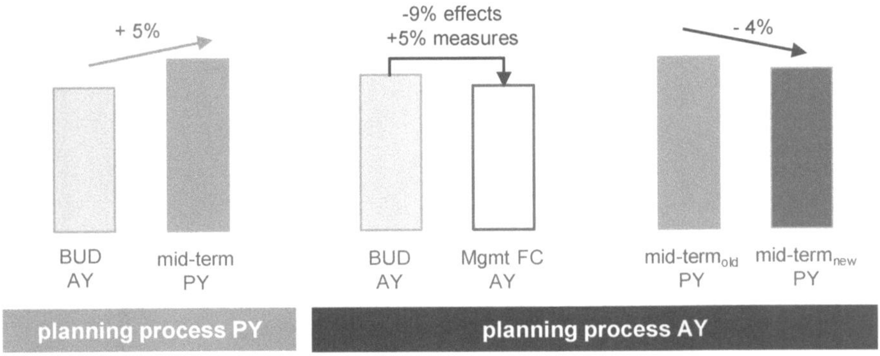

Fig. 7 Adjustment of midterm planning as a basis for target setting

If the new planning approach is followed, known effects as well as planned or taken measures are taken into account, and adaptions are made to the old midterm plan. It is exactly this situation where a close connection between management forecast and target setting is crucial. In conducting a management forecast, top management aims at identifying effects on the budget that were unknown previously and that may lead to plan deviations at the end of the current fiscal year. The effects identified earlier, as well as their impact on earnings, lead to adjustments of old midterm plans and therefore serve as a basis for target setting and the planning process as a whole. This approach is based on the following assumption: The midterm plan for the upcoming fiscal year is based on the last budget. If effects that occurred since the last planning period were known during that specific period, they would have been taken into account in budget and midterm planning. This is why old midterm plans are adjusted and subsequently used as the starting point for target setting. For all parties, this approach leads to an understandable and transparent basis that defines binding targets for business areas (Fig. 7).

Anticipated earnings effects and corresponding measures are planned and discussed, based on the adjusted midterm plan. A discussion that focuses only two to three key performance indicators is crucial. Furthermore, defined targets must not be differentiated further. The target setting aims at defining a framework for planning and is not focused on an itemization of expectations down to lower hierarchy levels. Expected earning effects and corresponding measures should be the main topics in target setting discussions between key accounts and the head of the business area. Some effects that have to be taken into account are defined group-wide and consequently must be considered by all business areas. These could, for example, be assumptions concerning the inflation or defined focus topics. Additionally, effects and measures that only affect one business area may be defined, in order to cope with the individuality of divergent business models (Fig. 8). The results of the target setting process are captured in a standardized document and are then presented to the executive board for a final approval of defined targets.

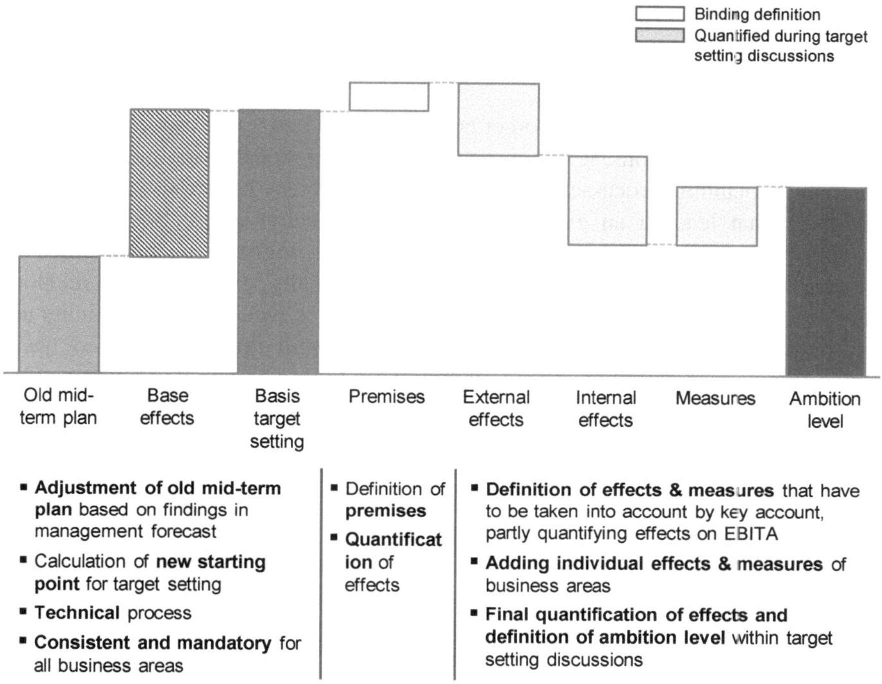

Fig. 8 Determination of the targets during the target setting process

Subsequently to target setting, benchmark planning is the second step of the frontloading process. It serves as the operational implementation of the defined targets and is mandatory for all business areas. How the benchmark planning is conducted can be determined by every business area individually. Using a discussion-based approach similar to the target setting process is recommended especially for internationally operating units. It is by this that quality and acceptance of the defined targets can be increased in different countries. Nevertheless, business areas can also merely break down the given targets to countries and/or regions. Benchmark planning is not limited to the operational business areas. Service providing units (e.g., IT and logistics) and administrative units also have to define targets. In administrative departments, these are mostly cost-related rather than earnings-based.

To ensure implementation, success, and acceptance of the previously described process, it is not sufficient to merely give support with an adequate IT system. It is rather important to increase the importance and meaning of targets in all business areas and planning units. The defined targets must be crucial in all budget discussions and presentations. Only with this change in the company's mindset, long-lasting coordination processes and correction loops can be avoided, thereby shortening planning cycle times.

3 Year-End Projections, Budget, and Midterm Planning: The Core Elements of Operational Planning

In the REWE Group, as in most other companies, the budgeting process, combined with year-end projections, is the core element of operational planning. In retailing companies, planning processes are usually characterized by numerous sub-plans and interfaces that lead to an excessively high coordination effort. Sales planning, administrative planning, category management, and logistics planning must be coordinated, just to name some of these. Additionally, intercompany relations must be taken into account to ensure that supplying as well as receiving units use the same planning values, for their plans to be built on a harmonized basis. Increasing company size and complexity normally lead to higher coordination effort and plan deviations. These can be explained only by insufficient coordination and do not have any business-related reasons.

The defined framework serves as basis for the REWE Group's new planning approach (Fig. 9). It combines all relevant sub-plans and focuses on important interfaces and dependencies. Planning processes of different sub-plans were captured and optimized on the basis of this framework. Due to the group-wide binding earnings calculation, planning processes and contents are comparable throughout different business areas. The implementation of a supporting IT system can therefore be based on a reasonably harmonized situation.

Targets defined through frontloading processes build the framework for detailed operational planning. For meeting the defined targets, this is mandatory for all business areas. Deviations are only acceptable in well-founded exceptions. They must be discussed in budget discussions and then be approved. To ensure that decentralized planning does not miss the defined targets, they are communicated to business areas, countries, and regions during planning preparations.

All sub-plans converge to the sales planning and finally to the earnings planning. Logistics planning, for example, leads to planned logistics costs—based on expected sales—which is one line of the earnings calculation and, therefore, a core element of sales planning. This is why expected developments in sales serve as a common and central basis for all sub-plans. To avoid sales, logistics, and category management generating expectations concerning sales development separate from each other, preparatory discussions for sales planning are institutionalized (Fig. 10). In addition to the named stakeholders, marketing and expansion experts are participating. The goal of these preparatory discussions is generating a common forecast for sales development on a percentage basis. The resulting figures serve as a starting point for all related sub-plans, just as quantity structures for planning all rely on assumptions concerning the development in sales. As investment and expansion planning is not limited to a fixed time period within the fiscal year but rather a continuous planning process, they can additionally serve as valid basis for sales expectations.

On the basis of common sales expectations, different sub-plans are constructed independently.

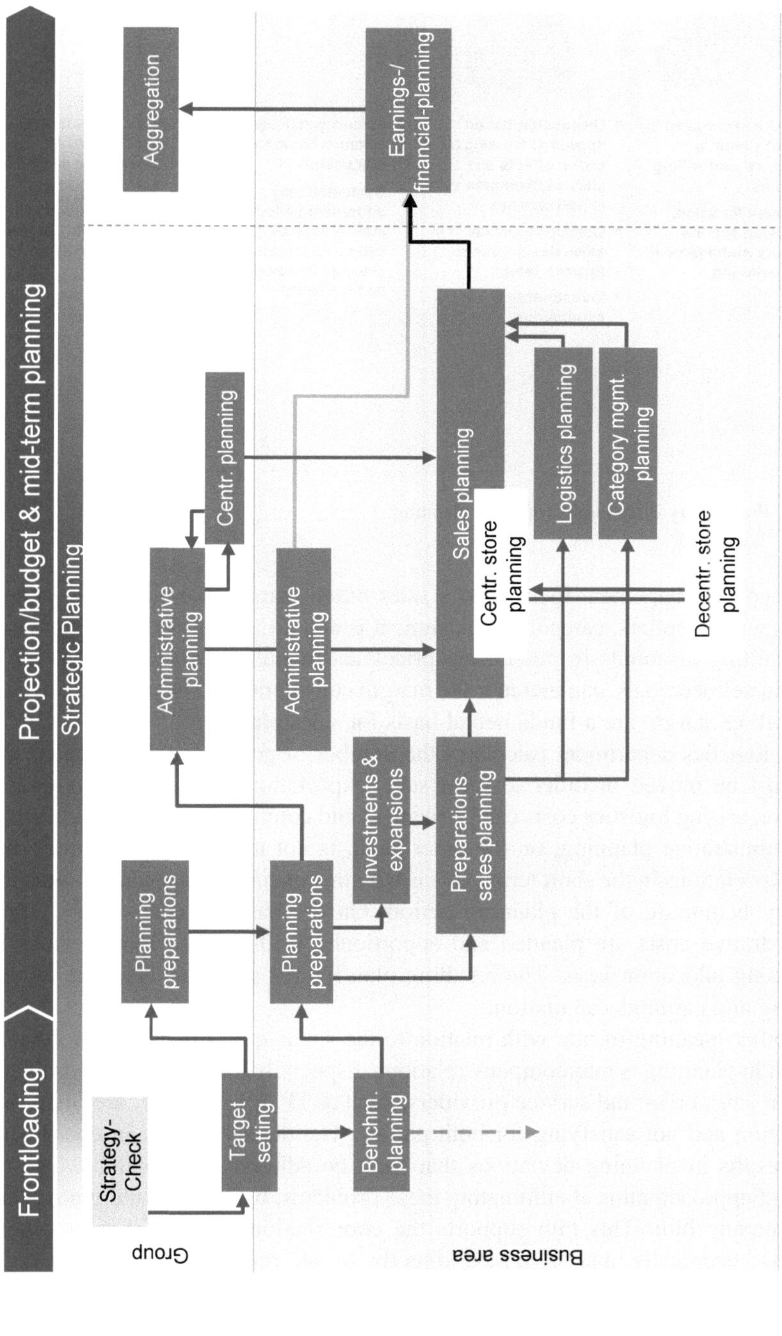

Fig. 9 Procedural framework for planning at the REWE Group

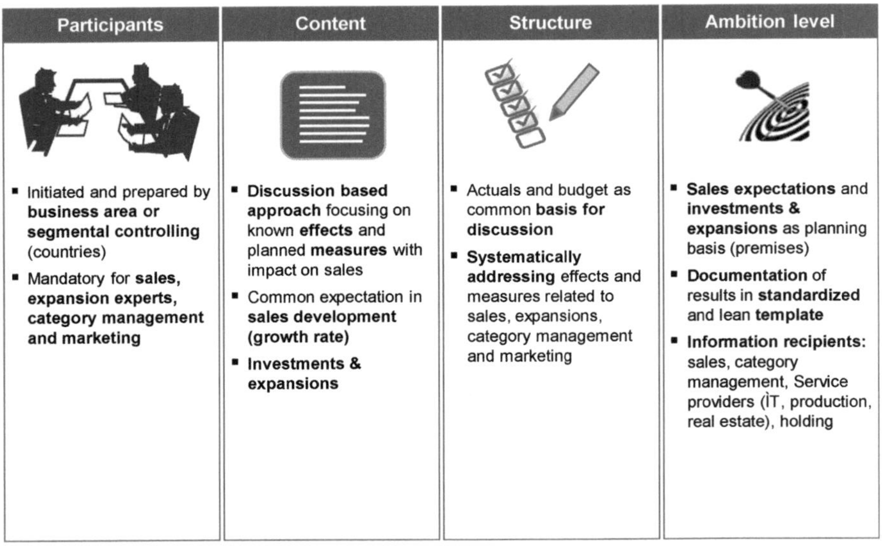

Fig. 10 Preparatory discussions for sales planning

Category management focuses on a sales-based margin planning. Due to negotiations with suppliers, category management is able to actively control the margin. The resulting discounts in purchasing prices and bonuses, which are paid out for reaching defined goals, can increase the margin considerably. The planned effects on the retailing margin are a fundamental basis for sales planning.

The logistics department calculates the number of goods or transportation units that must be moved in order to meet sales expectations. Based on this quantity structure, arising logistics costs can be planned and communicated to sales planning.

Administrative planning, on the other hand, is not influenced as strongly from sales expectations in the short term. This is why this planning occasion can start from the very beginning of the planning period. On the basis of cost centers, arising administrative costs are planned and apportioned to different business areas and units using allocation keys. The resulting plan figures are again relevant for sales planning and earnings calculation.

Another meaningful but, with relation to the status quo, oftentimes problematic element in planning is intercompany relations. Especially the necessary coordination between sales areas and service providers, such as IT or real estate, are often time-consuming and not satisfying for both parties. The described lack in coordination often results in planning deviations that must be adjusted or explained. The new planning approach aims at eliminating these problems, by implementing a so-called intercompany hub. This hub supports the coordination process of intercompany relations technically and is linked directly to all relevant business areas and sub-plans. On a procedural basis, it must be defined when a coordination between two parties must take place and which level of detail is necessary. Additionally for each intercompany relation, it must be defined which unit and its respective planning values will be followed, if the two parties cannot reach an agreement.

To further reduce the high planning effort, the REWE Group aims at avoiding an account-based planning. So far, accounts were used to cope with intercompany relations and to simulate a driver-based planning. Nevertheless, the resulting level of detail is far too high to ensure an efficient, lean, and flexible planning process. The company strives to intensify the driver-based planning by using real driver systems instead of different cost and profit accounts in the long run. This approach can additionally increase the quality in earnings planning. It shifts the focus to an effect- and measure-oriented planning rather than a sole collection of planning data. Furthermore, this improves planning transparency. In case of changing environmental conditions, driver-based plans can easily be adjusted to meet the challenges of the highly dynamic market environment of retailing businesses.

Following the completion of the operational sub-plans, sales planning can be finalized and combined with the earnings planning (Fig. 11). This plan is based on the group-wide binding earnings calculation, ensuring that earnings numbers are harmonized in all business areas. On this basis, planning processes and sub-plans can be harmonized and, therefore, also supported by an adequate IT system and planning software to increase planning efficiency.

Sales and earnings planning must be quite extensive and very detailed to cope with the high importance of sales and earnings numbers in retail businesses. However, financial planning will be simplified, in order to reduce planning effort significantly. In lower hierarchy levels, for example, only balance sheet positions

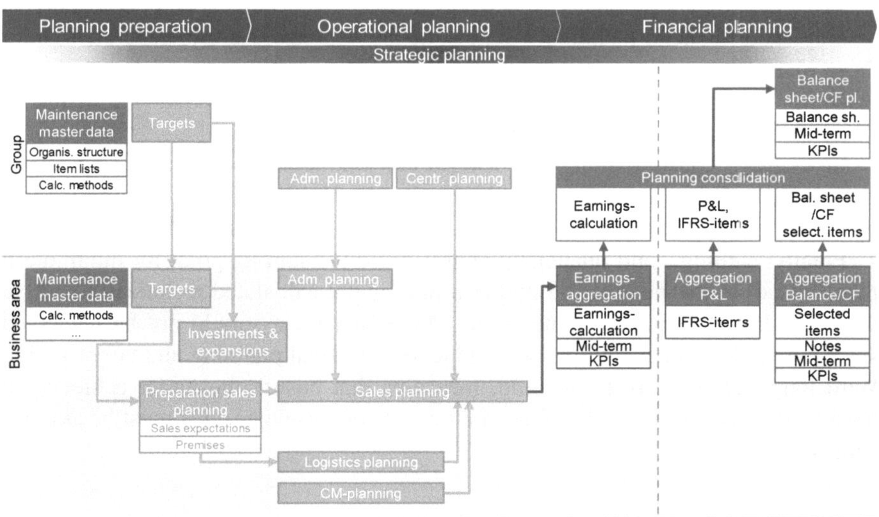

Fig. 11 Procedural context of earnings and financial planning

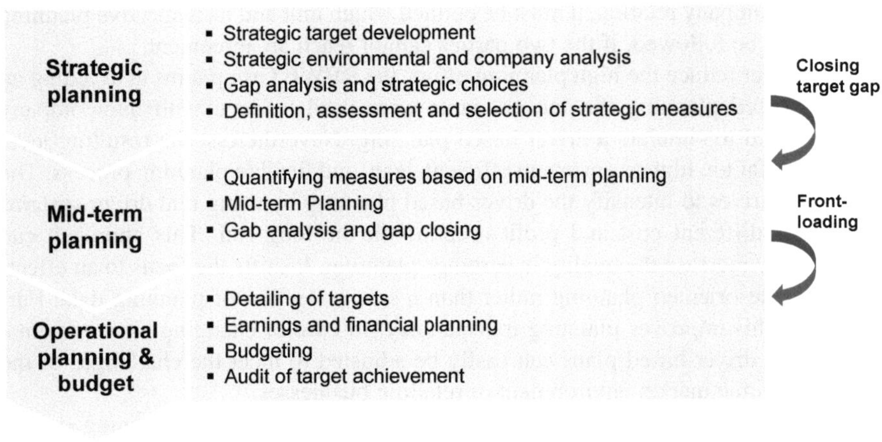

Fig. 12 Concept and objective of a target-oriented midterm planning

relevant for steering (e.g., items connected with the working capital) will be planned. Necessary items, ensuring a complete balance sheet for planning purposes, will only be planned top-down and on the level of legal entities. Lower hierarchical levels should not be involved in financial planning. P&L as well as cash flow statement will be calculated automatically and based on earnings and financial planning. There will be no planning effort involved for group and business areas concerning these planning occasions.

The planning of steering relevant key performance indicators is embedded in earnings and financial planning. As most of the data necessary is generated within these planning occasions, a large portion of relevant KPIs can be calculated automatically using existing planning data. Only a fraction must be planned manually, which further reduces the planning effort.

In terms of consolidation, only a legal consolidation of earnings and financial planning on group level exist. On all other levels, planned values are simply added up so that there is no planning consolidation on business unit at all.

Finally, earnings, and financial planning build the starting point for the midterm plan. Based on the budget, the midterm plan is pre-calculated technically and can then be adapted manually, if necessary. Nevertheless, it should not be neglected, since the midterm plan signifies the bridge to strategical planning and target setting. With long-term objectives in mind, measures that ensure the target achievement must be defined. Additionally, financial impacts of these measures must be assessed (Fig. 12).

4 Forecast and Management Forecast Building the Bases of Planning for the Upcoming Fiscal Year

Forecast (prognosis) and management forecast are not planning occasions in the proper sense of the word. They can much rather be characterized as steering instruments, used to control the achievement of defined targets during the year. Additionally, they serve as a resilient basis for target setting, for benchmark planning, as well as for planning itself.

A continuously performed forecast is an inherent part of modern management control. Comparisons between planned values and actuals are typically characterized as merely being an ex post control mechanism. In contrast, a comparison between planned and forecasted values enables the management to take countermeasures at an early stage during the year to avoid negative developments (Fig. 13).

In the REWE Group, business areas can decide to conduct forecasts on a monthly basis. A lean forecast, reduced only to the main earnings numbers of the earnings structure, is recommended and ideally supported by technical measures. A bottom-up planning process should be avoided, and only relevant changes with earnings effects should be taken into account. Additionally, countermeasures and the corresponding earnings effect must be defined and assessed. A monthly prognosis can serve as a solid basis for continuous control and steering of target achievement. Therefore, this prognosis becomes a central controlling instrument for all business areas.

Other than with the prognosis, management forecast is mandatory for all business areas and must be conducted once a year in May. The main objective is giving a first indication of target achievement early in the year. With high attention to the

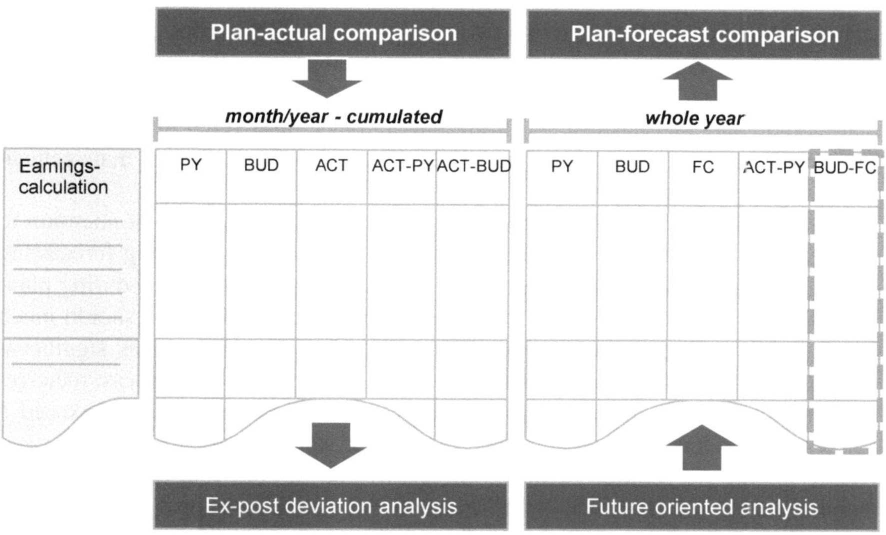

Fig. 13 Different objectives of plan-actual and plan-forecast comparisons

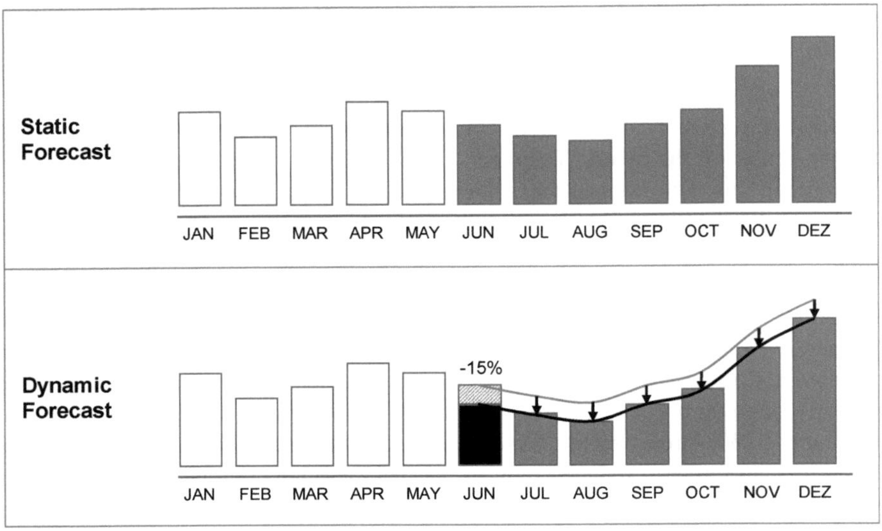

Fig. 14 Technical forecast as a discussion base

executive level, management forecasts enable the evaluation of business area development by the upper management areas on a harmonized basis. Consequently, management forecasts follow a group-wide standardized and harmonized procedure in terms of process and content.

The management forecast is conducted in an interview-based manner. The discussion takes place between the key accountant, on the one, and the head of business area partly supported by business area controlling on the other hand. A technical forecast is conducted in a two-step procedure as basis for preparation and discussion. In an initial step, a statistical forecast substituting the planned values of the past by actuals is generated. Subsequently, this data is enriched by key accounts that include data that has resulted from new findings, discovered in the meantime. The resulting dynamic forecast serves as discussion basis in the management forecast process (Fig. 14).

The jointly developed forecast focuses effect with a high degree of attention to management. Routine activities are not meant to be mentioned during forecasting discussions. These activities are normally predictable and anticipated during planning. Effects that reflect significant changes in business development should much rather be the subject of management forecasts. They are captured as significant deviations from budget and result in new, year-end figures. Nevertheless, management forecast should focus effects that have strategic meaning or that exceed a defined limit in terms of earnings effect. However, capturing significant effects and identifying the gap in target achievement is only one part of management forecasts. Another substantial issue is defining adequate countermeasures and assessing their respective earnings effects. Defined measures should go beyond daily business and enable the company to close the existing gaps (Fig. 15).

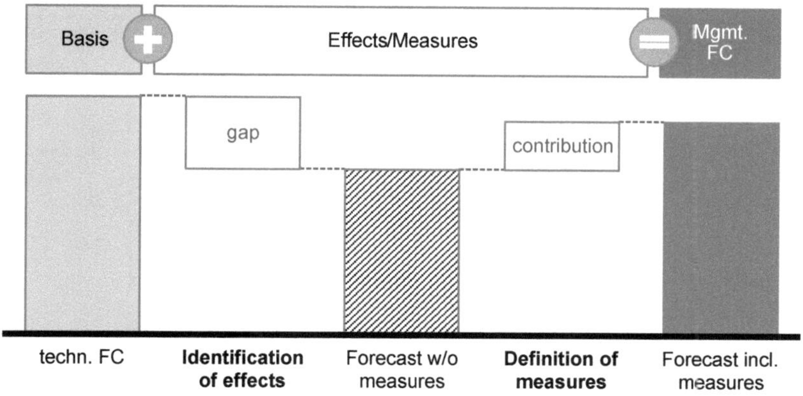

Fig. 15 Effect- and measure-based forecast

The fundamental basis for a lean and efficient management forecast with a clear focus on steering purposes is to restrict the discussion to the top management level and to discuss only two to three relevant key performance indicators. Due to similar content and approach, the management forecast has a close connection with target setting and can therefore serve as a reasonable starting point of the frontloading process for the upcoming planning period. Considering the fact that measures are often planned over a time horizon of more than one planning period, this connection between different planning occasions is even more important.

5 Planning Occasions and Sub-plans Merge into a Holistic and Integrated Planning Process

As previously stated, different planning occasions are connected to each other and embedded in an overall planning process. This leads to a holistic and comprehensive planning approach (Fig. 16).

Strategic planning and target setting are closely connected due to the yearly strategy meeting. This ensures that strategic objectives are reflected in operational planning. Additionally, the adjusted midterm plan that serves as starting point for target setting refers to a broader time horizon and therefore ensures sustainable orientation toward the achievement of strategic goals. Benchmark planning mainly seeks to operationalize targets on business area level. Hence, it serves as fundamental framework for operational planning. This top-down approach ensures that planning focuses on the achievement of targets rather than concentrating on the determination of planning values. The operational planning (budget) combined with a year-end projection is the core element of the planning process. Concurrently, the determined values serve as the basis for midterm planning and therefore also affect the upcoming planning process. The monthly prognosis is not mandatory for the business areas.

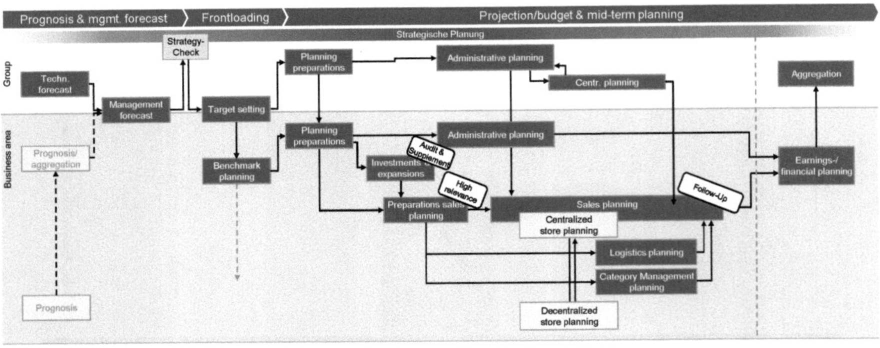

Fig. 16 Procedural framework for the planning approach of the REWE Group

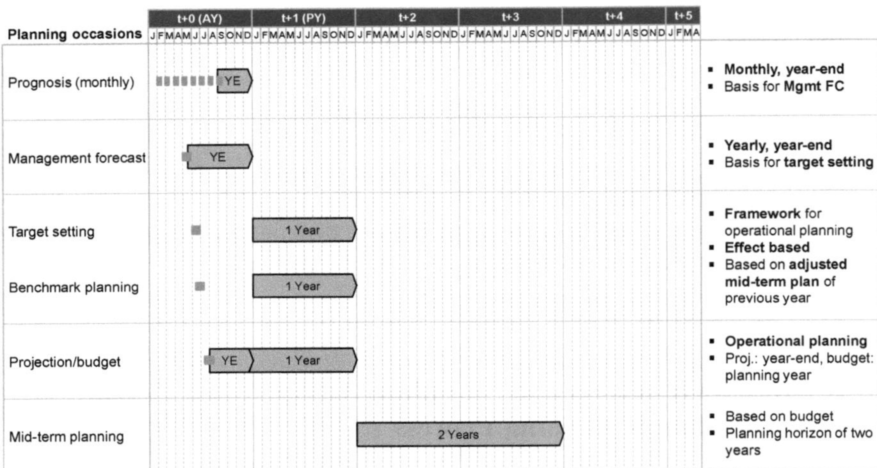

Fig. 17 Interaction of planning occasions

Nevertheless, it can serve as a valuable steering instrument throughout the business year by controlling the achievement of targets and by taking countermeasures if necessary. Furthermore, it can serve as solid basis for management forecasts that must be conducted once a year. The management forecast does not only provide top management with information concerning business development and target achievement as it also serves as basis for the upcoming target setting in terms of effects and measures (Fig. 17).

6 Conclusion and Outlook

The designed planning approach represents a holistic, flexible, and target-oriented process. This newly developed conceptualization exhibits many drivers of efficiency and enables a planning that is not only leaner but also enhanced in robustness and quality.

- The frontloading approach including target setting and benchmark planning constitutes a solid framework for planning and ensures a focused planning while taking into strategical issues into account.
- The high relevance of effects and measures enables planning units focusing on business development rather than on determination of values. This reduces planning effort and refocuses steering on earnings-relevant changes.
- The group-wide standardized earnings calculation, as most important output of operational planning, ensures harmonized planning and increases efficiency.
- Stopping planning account levels reduces the effort in operational planning substantially.
- Reducing financial planning to items relevant for steering, combined with a high degree of automatization, additionally leads to reduced effort on operational level.
- The intercompany hub and procedural changes simplify the coordination between supplying and receiving units and also reduces planning deviations.

To ensure a successful implementation and sustainable change in planning, technical changes as well as a comprehensive change management is necessary. New planning processes, as well as the lower level of detail in planning, must be accepted on all hierarchy levels. Especially planning occasions, such as target setting and management forecast that need to be discussed on a highly aggregated level, must be implemented step by step (Fig. 18).

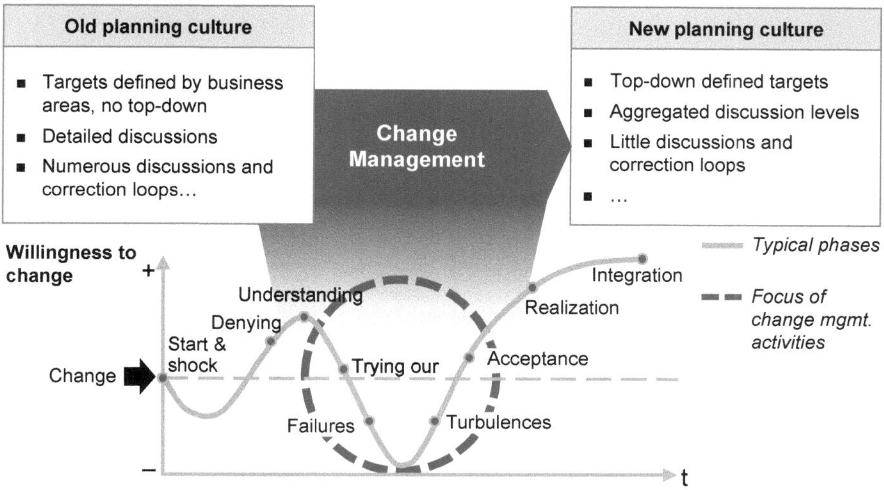

Fig. 18 Change management

References

Kappes M, Schentler P (2012) Planungseffizienz durch Frontloading. In: CFOworld 2012, pp 20–21

Kispalko S, Moretti V (2016) Aktuelle Rahmenbedingungen für das Controlling in Handelsunternehmen. In: Buttkus M, Neugebauer A (eds) Controlling im Handel, Part 1.1. Springer Gabler, Wiesbaden

Möhlenbruch D (2012) Wachstum durch Filialisierung im Einzelhandel. In: Zentes J (ed) Handbuch Handel: Strategien—Perspektiven—Internationaler Wettbewerb, 2nd edn. Springer Gabler, Wiesbaden, pp 127–149

Neugebauer A (2016) Typische Schwachstellen im Handel. In: Buttkus M, Neugebauer A (eds) Controlling im Handel, Part 1.2. Springer Gabler, Wiesbaden

Dr. Anna Thiel operated as Managing Consultant with Horváth & Partners for the Competence Center Retail and Consumer Goods in Hamburg. Her consulting experience is the result of extensive projects in the retailing industry, especially in a management accounting context.

Enhanced Sales Management: Using Digital Forecasting

Methods and Uses of Automated Forecasts

Thorsten Lips

Abstract This contribution is concerned with sales management based on digital forecasts. Estimating complex developments in companies is often characterized as an elaborate task. But as a result of digitization, there are new approaches for compiling automated and precise forecasts. The described approach in this contribution focuses on "Big Data" and "Advanced Analytics." Outlined application examples underline the practicality of new algorithm forecasts with a higher quality, even though every company has specific requirements that must be considered.

Keywords Advanced Analytics · Algorithm forecast · Automated models · Big Data · Digital forecast · Digitization

1 Introduction

Not long ago, digitization was considered the world-transforming megatrend. Today, companies have concrete projects promoting the digital age. Digitization is not a new phenomenon: what is new is the quality and extent of the digital revolution, as shown in "The Digitization of Just Everything."[1]

On the one hand, digital visions are being developed to significantly increase turnover and, on the other, to reduce costs. Examples from the new economy demonstrate that, after a setup phase, the companies maximizing their use of digitization generate significantly higher returns on capital than those of the old economy. However, it is unclear how traditional companies should act in practice so as to benefit from digitization, or more specifically, how they can significantly increase both revenue and EBIT. To clarify this point, four fields for the application of digitization within existing companies must be identified:

[1]Brynjolfsson and McAfee (2014), p. 57.

T. Lips (✉)
Strategy, Innovation & Sales, Horváth & Partners, Düsseldorf, Germany

M. Buttkus, R. Eberenz (eds.), *Performance Management in Retail and the Consumer Goods Industry*, https://doi.org/10.1007/978-3-030-12730-5_16

- Digital business models
- Digital products
- Digital processes
- Digital corporate performance management

The potential carried by each field is enormous. However, considerable investments are usually necessary for their realization, and profitability is often unclear beforehand. Digital products are complex and require an electrical engineering know-how that is often lacking in many companies. Horváth & Partners has implemented various customer projects showing that generating fast advantages through digitization in this area is possible, but only if the right concepts are chosen and specific know-how is applied.

Our approach for the automated and precise forecasting of events and developments focuses on "Big Data" and "Advanced Analytics." As a first step, specialists and managers are given important information for their actions using these forecasts. In further steps, processes can be improved and ultimately automated, thus supporting processes in all functions. The greatest benefits can be achieved if the sales department is used as starting point.

The human ability to predict the consequences of decisions made and the resulting situation is a core element of human intelligence. We are experts at recognizing and predicting simple and social correlations: We push the brakes, and the vehicle is slowed. We smile at someone, and the other person usually smiles back.

Complex projections of developments in companies are considerably more difficult. Our brain is not designed for the analysis of enormous amounts of data within a short period of time and simultaneously also deriving forecasts from this analysis. We are, however, experts at transferring our knowledge and experiences to other areas. When forecasting, we attempt to simplify tasks. The strategies chosen and mistakes made are described in detail by Daniel Kahneman's *Thinking, Fast and Slow*.

Consequently, estimating complex developments in companies is an elaborate task. Additionally, the effort stands in no relation to the result. Different experiences and underlying conditions, such as incentives, can lead to different forecasts, although the same initial data was used. Furthermore, a great deal of coordination is required to consolidate a forecast across different levels. This has two consequences. Firstly, comprehensive forecasts are usually performed periodically, only a few times a year. Secondly, periodic forecasts are rarely synchronized with operational decisions that are made continuously. As a result, it is not always possible for management to make operational business decisions based on forecasts. Critical discrepancies and unused potential are the consequences. For quite some time now, it has been clear that corporate management is more powerful if and when automated models are applied, as these are more capable of forecasting future developments.

Specialists often design simulations and models using Microsoft Excel, in order to generate "Business Forecasts." However, results do not always meet management's expectations. Reality is much more complex and more dynamic than the findings of static programs such as Microsoft Excel and other currently available simulation tools.

As a result of digitization, there are a few different new approaches for compiling accurate forecasts.

2 Using Digital Forecasts for Sales Management

2.1 General Statements to Digital Forecast

Digital forecasts are machine-calculated forecasts with improved accuracy that consider the increasing amount of internal and external information and use powerful statistical methods in order to predict a company's relevant developments. These are initially used to forecast the likelihood of events and, based on these, the performance of relevant sales ratios. As a further step, digital forecasts can connect prospective quantity and rating correlations in order to establish turnover and cost forecasts. As they are learning systems, which are increasingly more precise and reliable than traditional forecasts, digital forecasts can project up to five quarters. These are either calculated in real time or, as a minimum, on a daily basis. A distinction should be made between three forecast horizons:

- Horizon for operational decisions (sectoral, standard 1–30 days, very precise)
- Horizon for resource planning (sectoral, standard 31–90 days, precise)
- Horizon for corporate actions (sectoral, standard 91–450 days, reference values)

In order to avoid any misunderstanding, digital forecasts, as described hereinafter, are generated to predict developments that follow clearly recognizable trends or are foreseeable due to current trends. They are not designed to predict extraordinary developments like the Lehman breakdown or the VW emissions scandal.

2.2 Components of Digital Forecasts

The capacity of digital forecasts depends on three components: data, algorithms, and user interface.

Data

Digital forecasts are based on a huge amount of data that must first undergo "data cleansing." Data is the driving force of digital forecasts. In order to recognize the meaning of data, it is important to understand the change in paradigm, resulting from automatically computed forecasts. In conventional forecasts, complexity is reduced significantly by managers and specialists, and models are designed to select and aggregate information. In contrast, automatically calculated forecasts function differently. The more comprehensive and detailed the existing data is, the more precise their forecast.

Algorithms

Powerful algorithms compute desired forecasts using cleansed data. Different methods of digital forecasts are used, depending on the respective constellation. Some of the most important methods are:

- Extrapolation of time series with moving averages. Usually in addition to the modeling of season profiles
- Component models by Holt-Winters, using exponential smoothing
- Bayesian structural time series
- Box-Jenkins models
- ARIMA and SARIMA models (seasonal autoregressive integrated moving average models)

In general, there are different approaches for evaluating these methods and their usability.[2] In practice, their performance key characteristic is not formal complexity; it is rather the optimal dimensioning in three categories:

- Predictive power: Specifies how accurately the target variables are projected by the model
- Explanatory power: Shows the applicability of the model to explain cause-and-effect relationships comprehensibly
- Control power: Shows the response opportunities for people in power to react to predictions computed by the model

To obtain the best results from algorithms within the above dimensions during customer projects, the close collaboration of data scientists and department specialists is indispensable. Data scientists generate ideas and code algorithms accordingly. In turn, department specialists know the importance of different target variables, evaluate the performance of the models, and can support the acceptance of the models.

User Interface

The third part of digital forecasts is the user interface. Here, forecasts are made available to users. Digital forecasts have added value, as they are generated in real time. To this end, projections must be available via different mobile devices. Furthermore, one task of an interface is to provide a simplified presentation of complex issues. A good example of this implementation is provided by weather forecasts, offered by different online portals.

---

[2]Mertens and Rässler (2012).

2.3 *Procedure Model for Developing and Introducing Digital Forecasts*

In order to quickly establish and introduce forecasts in sales departments, a seven-step process has proven successful. This process is characterized by the following performance features:

- Modeling and prototyping are created to be flexible, so as to solve a company's specific problems both optimally and in a predefined period.
- The process is designed in such a way that the constructed models can be implemented directly in productive IT environments.
- The projects for modeling and introduction should be handled competently by management (Fig. 1).

1. *Use-Case Scoping*: Sometimes constructing and implementing digital forecasts can be extremely complex. This is why the goals and target functions of the digital forecast must be defined before the project begins. Furthermore, the available data must be clarified.
2. *Model Scoping*: Within the framework dictated by the use-case scoping, statistical models are evaluated and tested for usability. A comparison between alternative useful models and the framework conditions is also included. The first step is to analyze the data situation.
3. *Data Preparation*: This phase begins with the selection of relevant data from internal and external sources. Generating a basic understanding of data structures is possible with the use of simple analysis tools. Consequently, essential decisions can be made. The connection between cleansed data and the basic understanding of data structures, as well as internal and external data sources, offers the possibility of generating additional data. This task, known as "data enrichment," significantly improves the forecast model.
4. *Proof of Concept*: Adjusting and enhancing different models to the available data are the central tasks of this step. The assessment of models is based on the abovementioned dimensions of "explanatory power," "predictive power," and "control power." Conflicting goals in these dimensions must be identified and

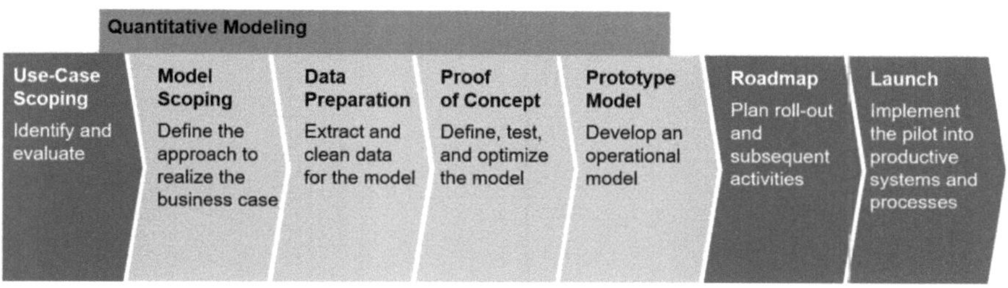

Fig. 1 Procedure model for developing and implementing digital forecasts

taken into consideration. Furthermore, an evaluation of prioritized models is included in this step, with former models serving as benchmarks.

5. *Prototype Model*: The development of an effective prototype model necessitates additional framework conditions, in order to reduce complexity. Model stability can be tested using data that was not taken into account during the setup of the model. Consequently, a smooth transition to live operation is ensured. A possible requirement could be an improvement in computing time. Simultaneously, an application is developed to enable the prototype model's results to be presented and illustrated to audience groups.
6. *Roadmap*: In general, many ideas for additional application possibilities and additional requirements concerning digital forecasting may be raised when compiling the roadmap. As a result, it is imperative to specify significant steps to achieve the business usage defined earlier in the process. Moreover, further development—after the transition to live operations—should be well planned and clear. The central elements of planning are:

   - Improvement of processes to realize defined usage (if necessary, changes in governance)
   - Technical implementation in product systems and their user interfaces
   - Instructions for users to use the computed forecasts productively
   - Generating and furnishing of know-how to enhance the algorithm

7. *Launch*: The smooth transition of algorithms to live operations is expected in cases of professional prototyping and planning during road mapping.

   The effort required for the management of alterations and adjustments, up until the previously defined (during the scoping phases) usage is achieved, should not be underestimated. Occasionally, serious resistance to automatically computed algorithms is offered. This has two causes. Firstly, automatically computed algorithms are able to create transparency, which results in reduced competences and less reporting freedom for managers and specialists, among other things. Secondly, digital forecasts are calculated in order to summarize the results of various events. This means that even an extremely good model could also fail in projecting individual cases. If managers or specialists were to repeatedly obtain inaccurate results, they could vehemently accuse the algorithm of being imprecise.

   Based on previous experience, professional change management is necessary for planned usage. In addition to supporting the management team, a learning curve should be planned for organization purposes.

3 Digital Forecasts: Application Examples

Application Example 1: Digital Forecast for Incoming Orders
Supported by Horváth & Partners—one of the leading consumer goods companies has developed a digital forecast for predicting incoming orders. Three goals were followed:

- Enhanced sales management (go/no decisions for supplies, depending on order probability)
- Better planning of incoming orders
- Effort reduction, by generating forecasts for incoming orders and implementing better management of the entire company

For rapid success, a first step was initially implemented in order to improve sales management. During the initial phase of the project, an analysis was conducted regarding the data that could be used in the forecast. It was found that very good forecasts could be generated by simply utilizing the available historical data from CRM and ERP. Even after 2 months, algorithms for the projection of incoming orders were available that were considerably more precise than previous models. The projecting capacity is shown in Fig. 2.

After the validation of this algorithm and to enable the productive utilization of the showcase "Digital forecasts for incoming orders," different modules were designed:

- A program set for automated data cleansing
- A program for the real-time computation and evaluation of incoming order probabilities in the event that sales opportunities are created or updated by salespersons

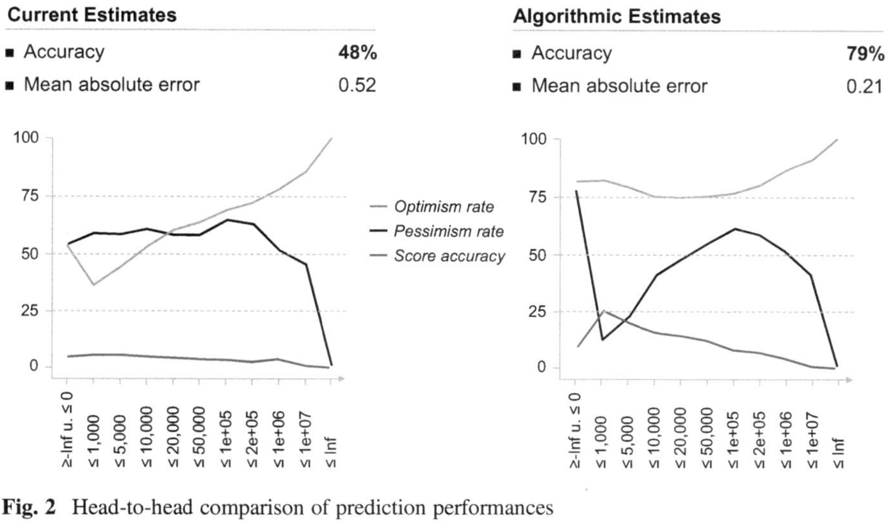

Fig. 2 Head-to-head comparison of prediction performances

- The optimized process and information model for the management of the sales processes with the additional data
- An analyzing concept, implemented in CRM, to support the decision process for sustainable management choices with calculated probabilities
- Assessments for sales coordinators to evaluate the quality of the algorithm (necessary for decision-making regarding optimization requirements)
- Technical concept for going live of the algorithm
- Schedule for going live
- Evaluation of additional expansion stages

On this basis, the model for calculating probabilities was implemented into the CRM model and went live. Salespersons were given help in evaluating the probabilities of opportunities. Consequently, decisions could be made concerning the generation of offers in sales. During this phase, integrating the computation of probabilities into the process model and the reporting in sales and FC was important. For this purpose, a communication model was applied, in order to motivate the relevant persons to use the calculated probabilities in their daily business as soon as possible. However, this did not result in a substantial reduction of manual forecasting.

In order to improve the algorithm, Horváth & Partners involved data scientists from the Steering Lab. After going live, in order to embed results and to rate both the quality and usage of the computed forecast, a structured learning phase was planned.

Application Example 2: Monthly Sales Forecasts and Predictive Forecasting
In the past, an international retailer had been required to manually generate a monthly sales forecast for the US market. Due to the complexity of the information, combined with special market features, it was often impossible to generate forecasts before the month end. In addition to this complexity, calculations were obstructed by the fact that a third of all products are sold within the last few days of a month. In cooperation with Horváth & Partners, the retailer strived to design a model that would enable the company to generate a daily prediction of the monthly results achieved by each product group. This included the following points:

- More accurate forecasts by taking account of nonlinear and unsecure coherences
- Faster available forecasts due to (partly) automated calculation
- Higher frequency, efficiency, and actuality of the forecast

To this end, a three-stage concept was introduced. The first stage included the definition of the pilot sector, the formulation of the conceptual framework, and the definition of different fallback scenarios. During the second stage, referred to as the implementation of the predictive forecast pilots, existing data was analyzed within an iterative process to enable the transformation of inconsistent and inconstant movements into fitting structures. The last stage was the definition of the forecasting goals and the roadmap, in order to integrate the pilot model into existing processes and systems.

A large number of different forecasting models were evaluated, and their results showed that a combination of two models was the optimal path. Traditional time

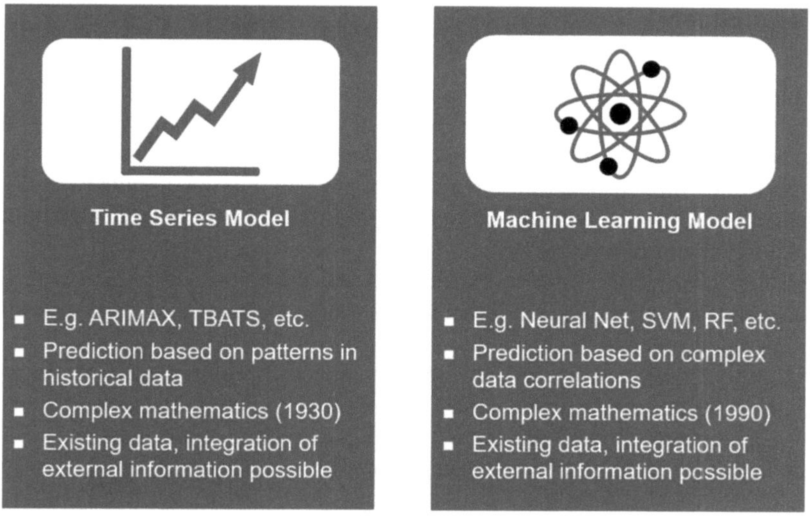

Fig. 3 Two possible approaches for modeling digital forecasts within sales

series models and machine learning approaches performed best for the forecasting of sales figures for different car models. Data patterns from the past form the basis of time series models, as patterns are found in historical data and then used to predict future patterns. The time series model performed significantly better when macro-economic factors were taken into account (Fig. 3).

Machine learning models were developed within complex mathematics during the 1990s. The algorithm focuses on complex data coherences and searches for the strongest similarities within the group. These are then used as classification rules, varied slightly using an iterative procedure, and tested using the elements within the group. A rule's quality is represented by a score, which is higher if multiple group elements verify the rule. To avoid false classifications, rules must be unusable for other groups. Rules rated with the highest scores should be run with test numbers.

Both methods were used separately to predict weekly sales and weekly sales structures. The forecast itself was generated using a weighted combination of separately calculated results.

A simple user interface for end users shows the major and most important information for an analysis of the projections and ensures transparency of the current and estimated sales situation. In this context, dashboards were implemented in order to show automatically generated overviews daily, a flexible breakdown according to different steering variables (e.g., sales regions), an interactive input, and flexible sales simulations.

The intuitive handling and the option to simulate the consequences of any additional adjustment resulted in high acceptance for the model.

4 Conclusion

The previously outlined application examples, as well as further projects by Horváth & Partners, underline the practicality of new algorithm forecasts. They meet demands that manually calculated forecasts cannot meet. The quality of their results is significantly higher (better, faster, and more precise). For the optimization of sales management, it is usually sufficient to base projections on the data yielded by well-curated CRM and ERP systems.

Furthermore, it is possible to expand and detail the forecast horizon with additional data from internal and external sources, thereby improving sales and operations planning processes as a whole.

Naturally, each and every company has specific requirements that must be considered during the implementation and introduction of digital forecasts. Nonetheless, experience proves that many companies within retail and the consumer goods industry would benefit immensely from the outlined approaches.

References

Brynjolfsson E, McAfee A (2014) The Second Machine Age: Wie die nächste digitale Revolution unser aller Leben verändern wird. Plassen, Kulmbach

Mertens P, Rässler S (2012) Prognoserechnung. Physica-Verlag, Heidelberg

Thorsten Lips operates as a Partner with Horváth & Partners Management Consultants, is responsible for the business segment sales, and has centered his client work on sales performance excellence approaches. His consulting experience spans multiple national and international sales optimization projects across all industries.

KPI Systems for PENNY Discount International

Johannes Isensee and Angelina Schulmeister

Abstract This contribution illustrates the project approach and key results of the introduction of a new steering and reporting system at PENNY International. In the course of the contribution, in particular, the central cornerstones of the project approach—harmonization of key performance indicators (KPIs), harmonization of the leadership and communication processes, as well as the standardization and centralization of the management reporting—are described in detail.

Keywords Corporate reporting · Key performance indicators · Management reporting · Performance management · Reporting concept · Penny

1 Requirements for Corporate Performance Management in Food Retailing

1.1 PENNY International

PENNY is an internationally operating German food discounter with branch stores in Germany and five other European countries. PENNY is a member of the REWE Group, situated in Cologne. After strong growth in 2017, the REWE Group achieved a total revenue of 57.8 billion Euro. Thereof, 72.3% can be attributed to foreign markets.

Within the REWE Group, PENNY's domestic and international businesses are distributed over two separate distribution channels. PENNY's international business (Discount International) generates a revenue of 4.2 billion Euro with over 1400 stores and is therefore one of Europe's leading discounters. PENNY's activities spread over Austria (290 stores), Italy (350 stores), Czech Republic (365 stores), and Romania (205 stores). In each of these five countries, PENNY is now established as a national discounter with country-specific product ranges.

J. Isensee (✉) · A. Schulmeister
Controlling & Finance, Horváth & Partners, Hamburg, Germany

M. Buttkus, R. Eberenz (eds.), *Performance Management in Retail and the Consumer Goods Industry*, https://doi.org/10.1007/978-3-030-12730-5_17

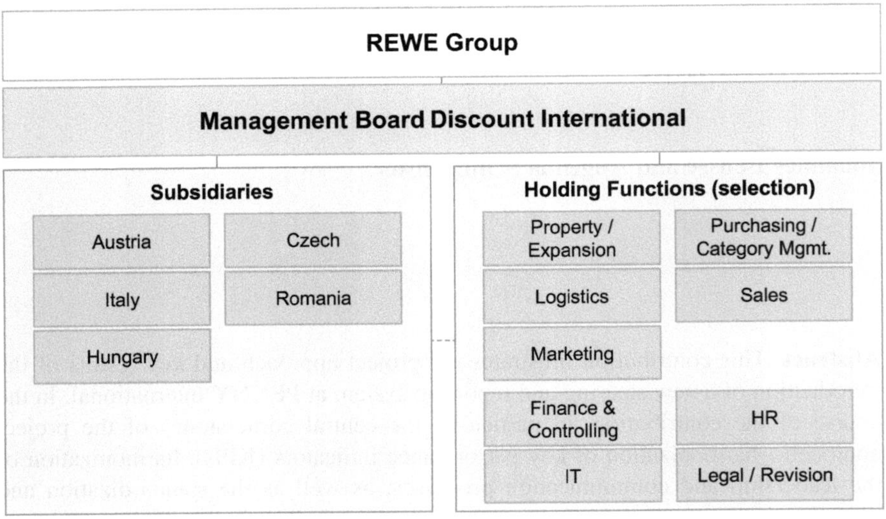

Fig. 1 Structural organization PENNY (Discount International)

The performance management of these five foreign subsidiaries is managed using the holding company "Discount International" (DCI). It is responsible for the countries' overall results and manages the operative foreign subsidiaries. For this, the management of each foreign subsidiary reports directly to the management board "Discount International." This holding company includes all relevant central functions in order to support all countries in accomplishing their operative activities. The aim is achieving transnational synergies and implementing uniform standards, without limiting country-specific particularities (e.g., the composition of local product ranges, etc.). PENNY's organizational structure is depicted schematically in the following Fig. 1.

1.2 *The Challenges of Transnational Performance Management*

A successful performance management of the foreign subsidiaries and the holding company necessitates the availability of relevant management information on company development for all five countries. In accordance with the holding company's operative claim to leadership, exclusively financial information is insufficient to this end. The need for reliable and uniform operative performance indicators—the value drivers of financial KPIs—ideally down to the level of individual stores in each country, is much more pressing. It is only in this manner that the countries' developments are made comparable and the success of measures can also be evaluated transnationally.

PENNY's previous international reporting was not yet able to meet this vision completely. As with many other companies, the centrally created management reporting was aligned with the financial information. Simultaneously, both the degree of detail and the creation effort resulting from heterogeneous KPI systems and historically grown, less integrated IT systems were relatively high. This starting point complicated not only an efficient performance management of the individual subsidiaries but also the reporting of the distribution channel Discount International to the REWE Group.

1.3 Project for Improving Performance Management and Reporting

The desire for a more effective performance management and a more efficient reporting process has moved PENNY International to a reconfiguration of the previous performance management approach, leadership and communications approach, as well as the resulting necessary management reporting.

The project initiated to this end was not only intended to increase the efficiency of PENNY International's performance management but also to create the foundation for the establishment of a corporate-wide data warehouse within the REWE Group, including uniform planning and reporting instruments. The following objectives were targeted during this project and are based on the aforementioned:

1. *Harmonization of the performance management concept, as well as the standardization* of relevant *key performance indicators (KPIs)*
2. Identification of *steering-relevant, operative KPIs* that depict the business model's central value drivers and serve as early warning indicators
3. *Harmonization of leadership and communication processes* on the basis of the new performance indicators and responsibilities (e.g., uniform performance review meetings)
4. Development of *standardized management reports* over all relevant levels for a simple, fast, and comprehensive data supply within leadership and communication processes
5. Centralization of *reporting processes* and *governance* (including interim implementation of reports until the beginning of the corporate project)

The project's objectives were formulated in a demanding but realistic manner. In this way, the total time effort for reporting was to be reduced significantly and consequently, more time gained for analytical and consulting activities within performance management. For the recipients of the reports, the reports should both gain validity and enable a timely and target-oriented performance management of all units. As all performance management levels (holding company and countries) should prospectively receive reports from one source, the effort spent on coordination and discussion concerning the "correct" data basis was to be reduced and, instead, more time spent on the discussion and passing of necessary measures.

The project for the implementation of this endeavor was designed for a time period of 6 months and can be structured into three phases:

1. *Analysis*: The initial phase was a sighting and evaluation of existing reports, leadership and reporting processes, as well as existing KPIs and their central and decentral definition. The information gained from this analysis then served as basis for the conception of a new performance management concept and reporting system. Parallel to an examination of the content, an evaluation of the established IT architecture as well as a coordination with the REWE Group with regard to prospective group requirements was conducted (concerning the new corporate processes and solutions).
2. *Design*: The design phase, or rather the concept phase, consists of two sub-phases. Firstly, the concepts for new KPIs (including responsibilities), leadership processes, and reports were compiled and coordinated. However, prior to the technical execution, or rather its implementation, a detailed examination of the feasibility of all new and altered KPIs per country was conducted.
3. *Implementation*: The implementation not only included the necessary local measures and their central steering so that foreign subsidiaries could meet new or altered KPI requirements. An interim reporting corresponding to the new structures was also drafted (Excel Interface), which was then to be replaced by the new corporate reporting.

A core team consisting of central and decentral experts from performance management, finance, IT, as well as selectively consulted representatives of relevant operative functions (e.g., sales, purchasing, logistics) was appointed for the implementation of the project.

2 A New Performance Management and Reporting Concept for PENNY International

2.1 *Performance Management Logistics and KPI Set*

The challenge of developing a KPI set lies in its limitation to those performance indicators relevant to the specific business model of the company. This not only requires the engagement with factors critical to success and the business model's processes but also a clear and coordinated understanding concerning use, intention, and definition of key performance indicators. To this end, clear criteria for the separation of pure performance indicators and the targeted "key" performance indicators are necessary.

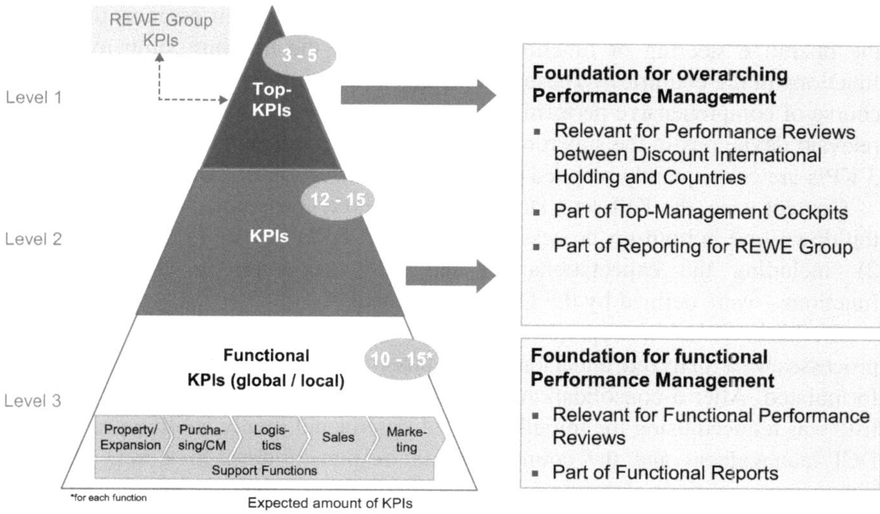

Fig. 2 KPI hierarchy with three steps

For PENNY International, KPIs constitute a number of parameters that are critical to the success of the strategic and operative performance of the company, are single units, or are measureable on the level of individual employees.

In doing so, these KPIs should meet the following criteria:

- The metric should force decision-making processes (in case of deviations).
- The metric is relevant for performance management (i.e., they have at least a target or budget value).
- The metric is measurable (with adequate cost-benefit ratio).
- The metric is influenceable and manageable by relevant individuals or teams.

On the basis of this understanding, a pragmatic KPI hierarchy on three levels was defined in order to structure the KPIs (see Fig. 2).

1. *Top KPI*: Three to five central indicators for the uniform financial performance management of PENNY International (in coordination with the REWE Group's requirements).
2. *KPI*: Significant financial and non financial parameters for the operationalization of steering the Top KPIs (Level 1) as well as for the evaluation of PENNY International's total performance.
3. *Functional KPI*: The third level includes explanatory, operative parameters as well as financial details per function (derived from a function's processes).

Top KPIs (Level 1) and KPIs (Level 2) should be made mandatory in each performance review between the holding company and the foreign subsidiaries. Consequently, they constitute the core of regular reporting (e.g., in form of a management summary or a KPI overview). Although functional KPIs (Level 3) have an effect on the superordinate Top KPI and KPIs, in their essence, they serve the operative steering of functions (e.g., between the holding company and its functions in the countries). These parameters should only be deferred to within the course of comprehensive performance reviews, if they signify operative drivers for relevant deviations in the superordinate performance indicators. In reporting, Level 3 KPIs are consequently mapped in the functional section of management reports.

Content-wise, the KPI set's structure on all three levels occurred in a combined top-down and bottom-up process. Initially, Top KPIs (Level 1) and KPIs (Level 2)—including the expectations for the most important Level 3 KPIs per functions—were defined by the DCI management.

On this basis and in cooperation with central experts of each function, the specific processes were analyzed, and a long list of possibly functional KPIs per function was formulated. After a consolidation and validation with the project team, this "long list" was reduced using the initially defined criteria and finally coordinated with the DCI management and the country-specific responsibilities. In a next step, the dimensions and their elements relevant to performance management were defined and coordinated for the set of KPIs previously passed.

Cascading over the respective management levels was key for the subsequent use and acceptance of the KPIs. As a result, especially in sales the performance indicators were cascaded over respective management levels in accordance with the criteria of accountability and controllability. Consequently, each of the roles in sales (from the National Sales Manager to the Store Manager) is measured exactly, using those performance indicators concurrent with their organizational competences (Fig. 3).

For the final result, a KPI set that is both transnational and harmonized across all functions (including definitions in KPI profiles), meeting both the PENNY business model's and the group's requirements, was achieved. The acceptance of the KPIs in

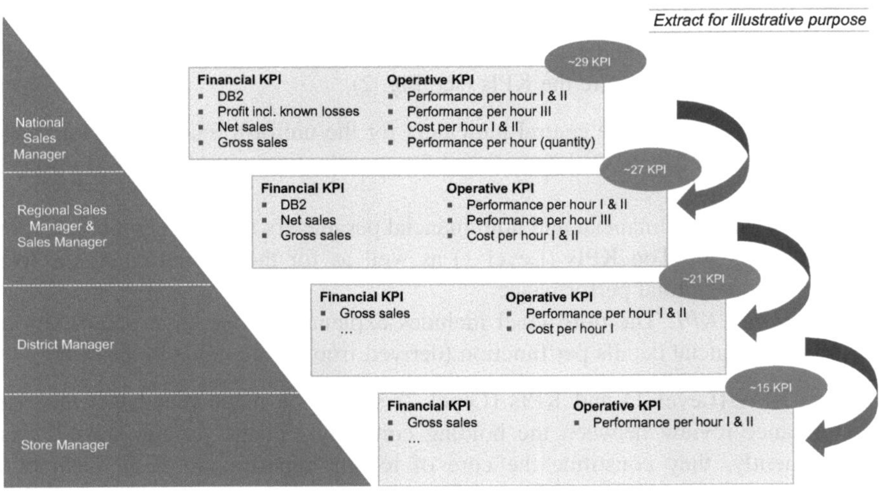

Fig. 3 Cascading of sales figures over management levels

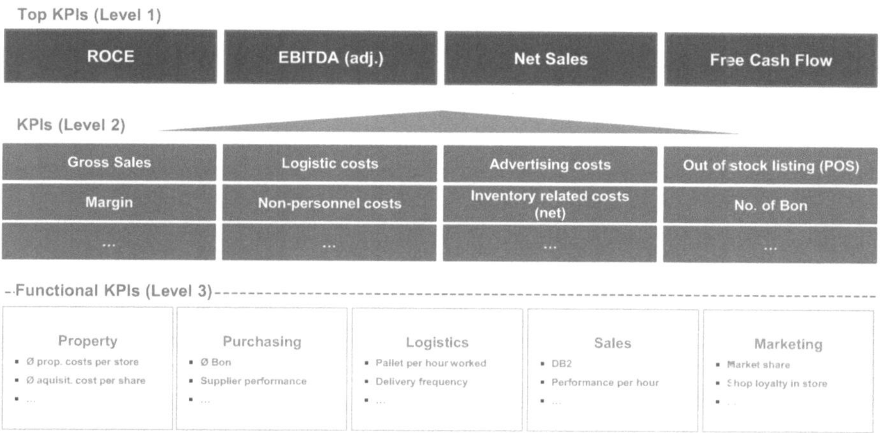

Fig. 4 New KPI set for PENNY (excerpt only)

the entire organization could also be secured with the preceding consent from all significant stakeholders.

In conclusion, the following illustration depicts some excerpts from the approved performance indicator set over all levels (Fig. 4).

2.2 *Harmonized Leadership and Communication Processes for All Countries*

The new KPIs and the reports, later to be based on them, were to support leadership and communication processes in a target-oriented manner. Standard reports can only support leadership and communication successfully, if they are supplied by relevant deadline and depict current topics.

However, before the single products of the standard reporting system were defined, the current leadership and communication processes were analyzed on all relevant levels and then almost completely harmonized.

In particular, this included communication:

1. Between REWE Group and the Management Board DCI
2. Between Management Board DCI and central functions
3. Between Management Board DCI and foreign subsidiaries
4. Between country management and local functions
5. Within local functions (especially sales: from regions and districts to markets)
6. Between central holding functions and local functions (e.g., central logistics with local logistics) (Fig. 5)

Who conversed with whom over which KPIs and to what point of time was defined in form of a calendar for each point of communication (Fig. 6).

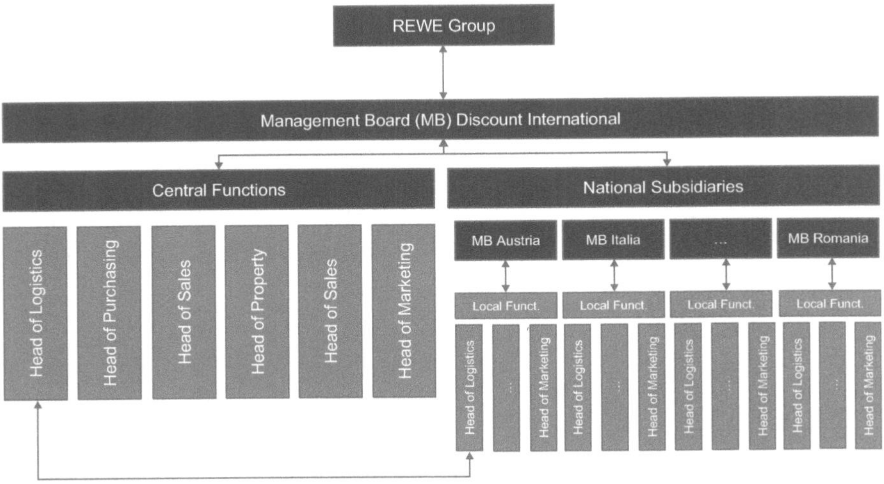

Fig. 5 Excerpt from the communications concept

	Meeting	Resp.	Participants	Frequency	Focus	Required / defined Reports
1.1	Monthly Performance Review	DCI Management	Country Management	Monthly	Pre-Result & Level 1+2 KPIs (prior month)	▪ Monthly Pre-Report (DCI + Countries) ▪ Monthly Mgmt. Report (DCI + Countries)
1.2	Weekly Sales Review	DCI Management	Country Management	Weekly (Mondays)	Short-term Sales KPIs	▪ Weekly Sales Report (DCI + Countries)
2	Functional Meetings	DCI Function Heads	Country Function Head	at least twice a year	Functional KPIs (Level 3 KPIs)	▪ Monthly functional reports

Fig. 6 Communication calendar and implications on report requirements (excerpt)

This communication concept signifies a mandatory minimum standard for performance reviews or rather the standard communication; specific ad hoc driven communication and/or leadership is not controlled by this. For example, apart from a monthly performance review, the concept consequently also intends a shortened weekly sales review.

In a next step, the amount of required standard reports as well as their necessary time of availability was derived from the sum of all regular points of interaction between relevant levels.

2.3 *Reporting Concept*

The reporting concept's task is transferring the defined KPIs, including the relevant dimensions and their elements, into reports that meet the requirements established by the communications concept. Accordingly, a uniform reporting concept covering all relevant levels of management was designed for PENNY International.

Apart from determining the recipients of the reports and their demand, relevant reporting types and formats, visualization and comment options, and the form of the reporting supply were defined for all processes necessary to reporting. Significant requirements were a uniform design as well as intuitive processing of information, enabling fast acquisition and comprehension. This requires a balanced relation of tables and graphs and/or the targeted implementation of visual elements in order to guide the recipient's attention to substantial topics/deviations. Short comments that are to the point should offer a better understanding of the recipient's attainment of objectives and respective recommendations of action from performance managers or rather from the countries.

As the implementation of reports only served as a temporary solution that was to be replaced by the subsequent corporate project, Microsoft Excel was predefined as tool for reporting. This means that reports were to be created using Excel and then "conventionally" distributed as PDF file. The reason for such a temporary implementation of an interim solution was to be able to realize quick wins in a timely manner, without being dependent on the progress of the group project. In this manner, on the one hand, the acceptance of the new solution was to be secured, and on the other hand, individual modules such as defined KPIs were functionally validated.

This implemented interim solution entails certain restrictions regarding reporting functions—such as individual navigation (drill-downs, links, etc.) and collaboration. In turn, these must be taken into account early on during the reports' development. Consequently, the selection of contents shown and their order ("flow") is co-created with the recipients in advance as, in contrast to freely navigable BI tools, they have no or very few possibilities for own analyses of drill-downs, etc. in the later phase. Naturally, current BI tools offer more functions and a greater degree of freedom with regard to individual recipient requirements ("self-service").

In accordance with the communication concept, weekly and monthly reports (including monthly preliminary reports) should be compiled for central and local report recipients. Figure 7 depicts an overview of the report products gained from the project. In uniform design standards, each product was first developed as mock-up in coordination with report recipients and then handed over for implementation.

Each individual package followed the same consistent structure; the design of each individual page is based on the uniform visualization standard. The aim of these reporting packages for management (or rather, DCI Monthly Management Report) is supporting management with comprehensive and holistic information on the development of each unit with an outline of the subordinate management level.

Using the management report on the DCI level as an example, the structure can be illustrated as follows. A KPI overview (Dashboard) shows the development of the Top KPIs (Level 1) and KPIs (Level 2) in an overview. Subsequently, details concerning financial performance followed by detail pages for each function with the defined Level 3 KPIs. This results in a monthly reporting package of about 40 pages for the DCI management board (Fig. 8).

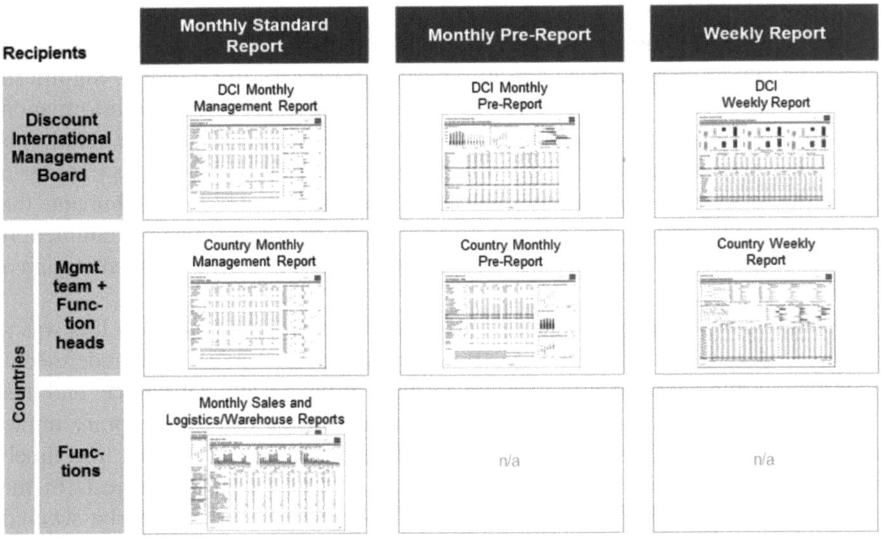

Fig. 7 Monthly and weekly report portfolio for central and local recipients

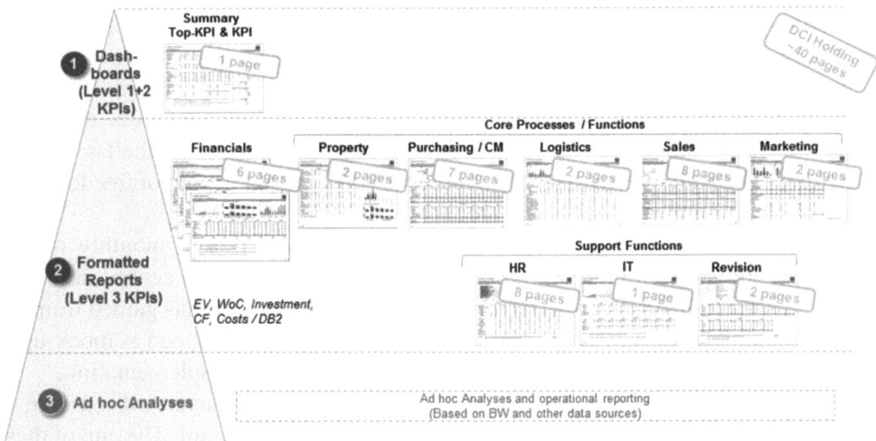

Fig. 8 Exemplary report package structure (DCI monthly management report)

Additional, especially spontaneous data requirements exceeding the scope of the standard reporting are covered by ad hoc analyses in the countries themselves or on a central level.

From the entirety of reporting templates, the data requirements per country unit were derived (KPIs, dimensions, deadlines, etc.) and then synchronized with the performance managers of the countries. The results showed that about 85% of all data requirements could be realized. For the remaining 15%, comprehensive or country-specific measures were defined in order to produce a complete "reporting capability" for the new concept.

3 Implementation and Use

3.1 Interim Implementation with Excel

As initially described, all compiled results support the subsequent implementation of a holistic corporate solution for data storage, reporting, and planning. Until such a corporate solution becomes available, reporting packages were originally implemented as interim solution in Excel including individual manual steps. In this process, reporting to recipients was in the form of PDF output, automatically sent per mail.

An Excel-based file, consisting of four essential elements, was created for each reporting product:

1. *Control Sheet*: Steering of the Excel file with all significant parameters and functions (adjusting the current reporting period, language option, configuration of page quantity (full package or single sections), print as PDF, individual or list recipients)
2. *Report Pages*: Uniformly formatted reporting pages including comment options (content derived from accounting pages)
3. *Calculation Sheets*: Calculation and/or processing of raw data for its depiction in the front ends
4. *Raw Data*: Inclusion of queries and manually recorded raw data depending on the source system

The reporting process as well as the governance through the now standardized KPIs and reporting formats reside with the central performance management. The companies are responsible for providing the data sets on schedule which must still be supplied manually.

3.2 Utilization and Outlook

With regard to performance management and reporting, PENNY International prepared itself for the comprehensive corporate reporting project with its KPI and reporting projects. The development of uniform performance indicators and reporting requirements including harmonized communication processes were a necessary first step toward an even deeper standardization of PENNY's five international companies; and new requirements made by the REWE Group could be taken into account directly.

Although the implementation of the temporary reporting solution still requires some individual manual activities in terms of data collection and processing and the PDF output format cannot keep up with the functions of a modern BI solution, first useful results could be gained from using the temporary solution, critical to the implementation of the new KPI system. Until the introduction of the corporate solution, further experience can be gained, and the system can possibly be adapted accordingly.

For management within PENNY International, concrete advantages and uses were yielded by the implementation of KPIs and reporting packages:

- Improvement of the companies' management through the integration of strategic, financial, and operational KPIs in accordance with the business model and critical processes
- Improvement of international comparability ("benchmarking") and analytical ability over all levels
- Specification of responsibilities and jurisdictions for the KPIs on each management level
- Reduction of the effort for reporting and the distribution of reports
- Improved data supply for management and simplified data processing through uniform and structured reporting packages
- Time gained for analyses and consulting activities in performance management

Johannes Isensee operates as a Principal with Horváth & Partners in the Competence Center Controlling & Finance. He is Head of the Business Segment Reporting and advises clients on the design of modern performance management concepts and reporting concepts, including their organizational and technical implementation.

Angelina Schulmeister operates as Consultant with Horváth & Partners for the business unit planning, reporting and consolidation. Her consulting focus lies in the field of management reporting.

Part VI
Functional Controlling: Business Specific Value Proposition

A 360° Portfolio Strategy in the Consumer Goods Industry

Eight Steps Towards a Holistic Management of Complex Product and Brand Portfolios

Oliver Greiner, Svenja Stöveken, and Nikolai Brosch

Abstract This contribution describes a solution approach to a holistic management of complex product and brand portfolios that has been tried and tested in the consumer goods industry. In light of the tension between an increasing product variety and a simultaneous increase in complexity, eight steps towards the development of a holistic portfolio strategy will be introduced. These range from its interlinking with the company strategy, over a market- and potential-oriented alignment of the portfolio, to sustainable steering approach.

Keywords Portfolio strategy · Portfolio management · Product portfolio · Brand portfolio · Product diversity · Resource allocation

1 Portfolio Strategy: Caught Between Diversity and Complexity: A Double-Edged Sword

> The unique depth and width of our assortment offers you a great variety of solutions. Our portfolio is integrated into a multitude of product lines and can therefore meet the most diverse requirements.

Today, such statements regarding one's own product and brand portfolios can be found commonly on the websites and advertising brochures of many companies. They show clearly that companies oftentimes attempt to react to increasingly specific customer requirements and increasing competitive pressure by expanding their product ranges.

O. Greiner · S. Stöveken
Strategy, Innovation & Sales, Horváth & Partners, Stuttgart, Germany

N. Brosch (✉)
Strategy, Innovation & Sales, Horváth & Partners, Munich, Germany

M. Buttkus, R. Eberenz (eds.), *Performance Management in Retail and the Consumer Goods Industry*, https://doi.org/10.1007/978-3-030-12730-5_18

Especially in the consumer goods industry, an explosive growth of the variety in product and brand portfolios can still be observed. A corporation such as the Nestlé AG comprises a portfolio of over 50 brands in Germany alone. Other companies such as Procter & Gamble, Beiersdorf or Henkel follow a similar strategy. This development is driven by the megatrend of individualization. This social development is leading to an enormous differentiation of individual ways of life and requires selfsame products. Many companies in the consumer goods industry react to this trend with a segmentation almost at the level of individual customers and production near the batch size one, as well as an increasing individualization of customer interaction. Nike, for example, offers their customers with individualization and the possibility of personally designing their desired shoes. With the resulting diversity of more and more products, variations and brands, companies expect the creation of new sales opportunities.

On the other hand, a customer-oriented acceleration of variety in a portfolio substantially impacts the underlying supply chain and boosts complexity costs. Each new product and every new variety causes costs in development, production, marketing and sales. Many companies are struggling with the consequences of such variety. The resulting complexity within the portfolio is difficult to manage. This is true for both new products and brands as well as those already introduced to the market. In addition, this complexity leads to an increasing lack of transparency in the portfolios of many companies. In this way, decision-making processes are decelerated, and the consequent alignment of the portfolio to rapidly changing customer demands can only be adjusted inertly. This can have fatal consequences in fast-paced markets.

In order to achieve a balance in the conflict area between market requirements and the complexity of the portfolio, a holistic approach towards the management of product and brand portfolios is necessary.

The portfolio approach of many companies (if it exists at all) oftentimes occurs without much strategy. True to the motto "because it has always been this way" or "whoever shouts the loudest", resources are distributed. A systematic orientation towards external market potentials or internal synergy effects occurs in the least cases. A holistic portfolio approach, originating from the company strategy, securing a potential-oriented alignment of the portfolio and its sustainable steering, only rarely finds application in earnest. Many companies lack:

- A derivation of the portfolio strategy from the overall corporate strategy in order to ensure a consistent alignment towards overarching targets
- A consistent alignment of the portfolio with market attractiveness and company fit in order to make full use of the overall potential
- A clear definition of strategic roles in the target portfolio in order to focus sales activities

- A clear positioning of individual products and brands in order to avoid cannibalization effects
- A systematic allocation of budgets and resources in order to avoid that resources are spread randomly
- A consistent steering for periodical tracking of portfolio performance and reacting to market changes

In order to meet these deficits, a holistic alignment of product and brand portfolios is essential. Due to the direct impact of portfolio decisions on the performance of the entire company, key parameters such as revenue, profit and customer satisfaction can be increased sustainably using a holistic approach.

2 Eight Steps Towards Achieving a Holistic Portfolio Strategy

This 360° approach to develop a holistic portfolio strategy is based on eight successive steps. In doing so, all portfolio activities are aligned with the corporate strategy using a strategic framework. On this basis the portfolio logic and portfolio specification are defined in order to maximize the potential of each product as well as the overall portfolio. Finally, the sustainable implementation of the portfolio strategy can be ensured using a steering model. In general, it should be noted that this approach is also suitable for the portfolio management of brands—not just products (Fig. 1).

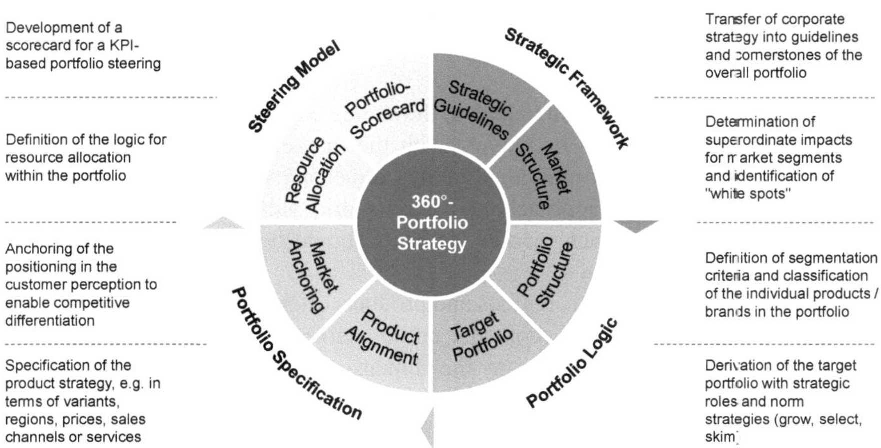

Fig. 1 Horváth & Partners' holistic portfolio management approach

2.1 *Strategic Framework*

The strategic framework functions as the portfolio strategy's starting point. On the one hand, it is constituted by strategic guidelines derived from the corporate strategy. On the other, first fundamental portfolio strategic decisions are made based on the market structure.

2.1.1 Strategic Guidelines

The close interlinking of all strategic activities and their concrete alignment with the corporate strategy are oftentimes neglected or half-heartedly implemented in practice. In our view, this signifies a severe mistake. The targeted success of the strategy can only be reached sustainably if the alignment of all strategic activities occurs in a way that is oriented towards a superordinate company strategy. Consequently, a sustainable interlinking with the corporate strategy is essential in the first step. In every good corporate strategy, fundamental decisions regarding the strategic core of the own business model can be found. In doing so, the target strategic core defines which products a company wishes to push to which target customers and in which target region. These superordinate cornerstones have to be identified and documented as central strategic guidelines. Exemplary formulations could be guidelines such as “focus on margin before volume”, “no products in the low-price segment” or “strengthening of international scalability”. These guidelines express clear dos and don'ts and offer orientation during the further design of the portfolio strategy and its individual aspects.

2.1.2 Market Structure

On the basis of the corporate strategy and the strategic guidelines derived therefrom, the portfolio should always be aligned with the market consistently. Hence, in a second step, an analysis of individual market dimensions along a so-called market grid takes place. In our approach, the market grid aids the determining of the strategic direction and which market segments should be pushed by the portfolio in particular (Fig. 2).

Which customer segments, regions and products offer the highest potentials? For the systemization of this question, the entire market is initially segmented into separate market cubes according to the dimensions product, geographic market and target customer. In doing so, the selection of dimensions and their subdivisions should be designed specifically to the company and/or industry. In the consumer goods industry, a variety-region matrix is oftentimes used, since according to our experience, both of these dimensions exhibit great relevance to most market players.

Within the market grid, an analysis for relevant market segments takes place. To this end, analysis criteria such as market development and competitive position are

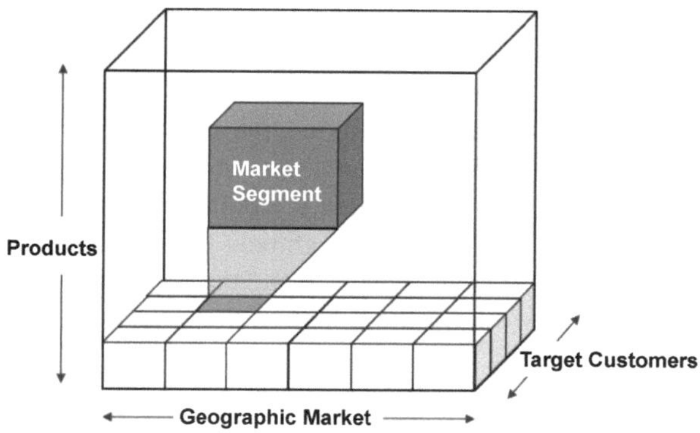

Fig. 2 Market grid rationale

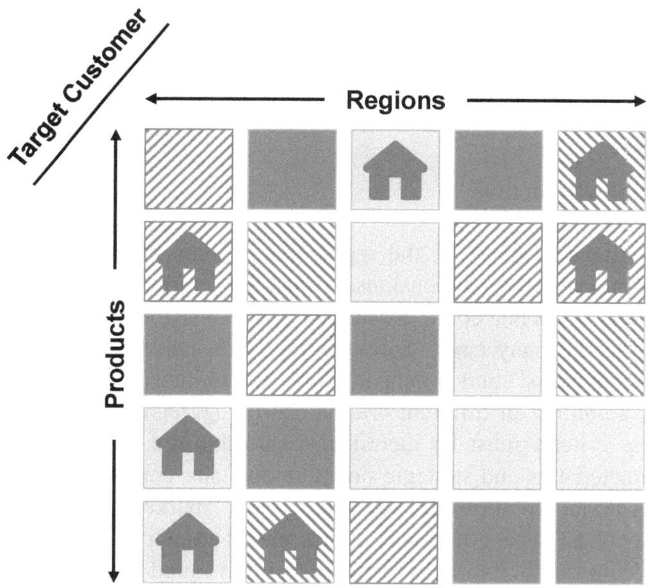

Fig. 3 Market grid analysis

primarily gathered. The arrangement of this analysis can reach from an expert assessment of the sales department to extensive market analyses. The analyses' results are represented using different colours for individual market segments. The traffic light colour scheme signifies the market attractiveness of the individual segments. Furthermore, this method also records those market segments the company is already represented in (Fig. 3).

Due to its high information density and its various perspectives from company, market and competitor perspective, the visualization via the market grid enables a compressed and easily understandable illustration of the initial situation. At a glance it is transparent, which market segments are attractive, in which segments the company is already active and where so-called white spots exist. On this base, central strategic directions can be defined systematically for individual product-region-customer combinations by interlinking the results from the analyses. For example, the "expansion of product *x* over all regions" or the "reduction of existing activities in the unattractive market segment *y*" could be forced. Via these strategic courses, a market- and potential-oriented alignment of the general portfolio can be guaranteed. Consequently, the strategic course and the previously derived guidelines serve as the strategic framework for the design of the overall portfolio.

2.2 *Portfolio Logic*

After determining the strategic framework, central questions regarding the arrangement of product and brand portfolios arise. According to which logic is the portfolio segmented and how do the products fit into it? What is the strategic role of individual products and which consequences result for the target portfolio?

2.2.1 Portfolio Structure

In order to reduce complexity, the segmentation logic of the overall portfolio is usually determined by two dimensions. A long list of criteria for determining these two dimensions exists that could possibly be used for segmentation. Our experience has proven that in many cases, a concentration on two key dimensions, namely "market attractiveness" and "company fit", is conducive. With these two key dimensions, a number of different criteria can be aggregated within an evaluation model. These criteria must be identified, evaluated and selected in light of the specific characteristics and strategic orientation of any company. For example, for a company with an ambitious growth strategy, the "market growth" and not "profitability" may be a typical criterion to define market attractiveness. This approach, in comparison with the limitation to two criteria often found in practice, can lead to a more balanced observation of the portfolio from various perspectives by taking multiple segmentation criteria into account, thereby offering a founded basis for decision-finding processes. According to our experience, five criteria for each of the two dimensions have proven themselves as benchmark for the optimal amount of criteria to be used in the evaluation model. If more criteria are chosen, the results will average out. However, if less criteria are chosen the observation of the portfolio will be too unbalanced (Fig. 4).

In accordance with the defined segmentation dimensions and criteria, a respective classification of individual products into the portfolio should take place. In practice, despite better judgement, this allocation for individual products oftentimes occurs according to rules of thumb and gut instinct that do not always correspond with reality of the portfolio. This is predestined to lead to inaccuracies and mistakes and

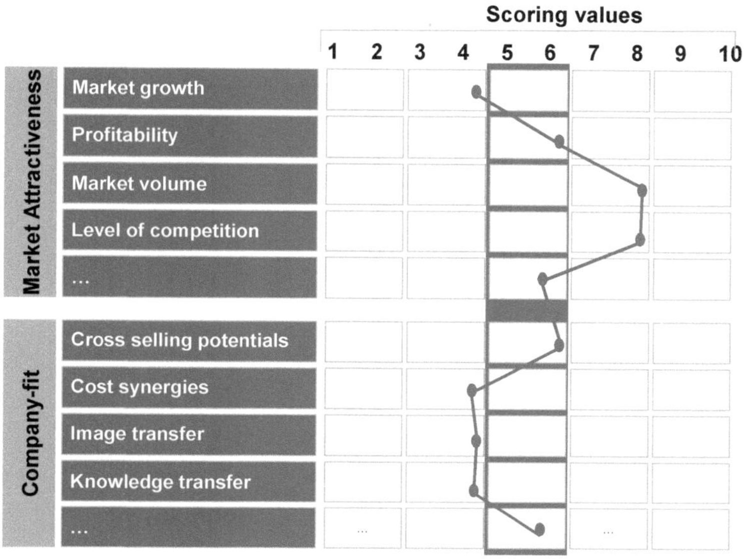

Fig. 4 Exemplary evaluation model

oftentimes has greater impact than most responsible persons realize. Empirically, greater added value is generated if a data-based evaluation is applied in order to ensure that the foundation for decision-making is both neutral and fact-based. Using a morphological cube, the individual products are then systematically evaluated according to their performance and potential. In this way, the exact position of each product in the portfolio can be determined using a scoring model. Where available, company's internal data as well as external data from market studies serves as data foundation. In workshops, these analysis solutions are then enriched with the specific expertise of the company.

2.2.2 Target Portfolio

After all products are arranged within the portfolio, the next step is deciding which strategic role individual products have, on the basis of the arrangement. The strategic role corresponds with the norm strategy that offers indicators for the long-term alignment of individual elements in the portfolio. In this process, three fundamental strategic roles can be identified (Fig. 5):

- **Growth:** The product exhibits a medium to high market attractiveness and a medium to high company fit. A growth strategy should be followed with investments above average.

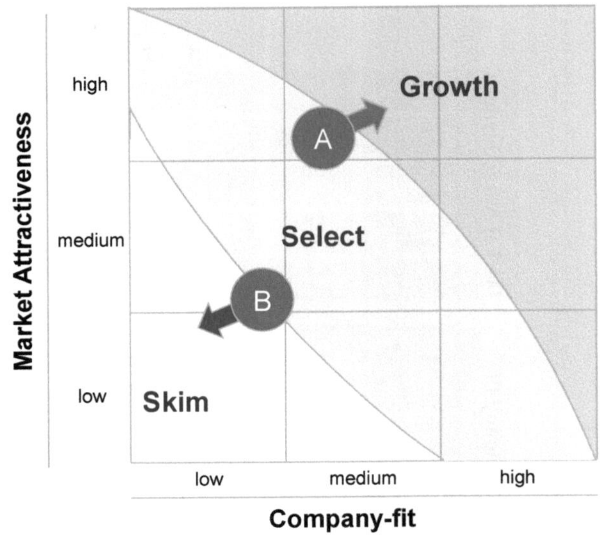

Fig. 5 Target portfolio with strategic roles

- **Selection:** The product exhibits a medium market attractiveness and a medium company fit. A selection strategy with purposeful investments should be followed.
- **Skimming-off:** The product exhibits low to medium market attractiveness and a low to medium company fit. A skimming-off strategy should be followed, and the level of investment should be reduced. An exit strategy should also be considered.

The target portfolio should be derived from these segment roles. In doing so, the future position of both existing products and those new products identified by the white spot analysis will be determined for the portfolio. It should be noted that the insights gained from the portfolio analysis merely serve as guidelines on which a management decision can be made.

2.3 *Portfolio Specification*

After the strategic framework has been set and the portfolio logic has been established, the further arrangement and specification of the portfolio follows. In order to make use of the full potential of individual products and brands, their positions within the portfolio and the market must be precisely aligned and placed.

2.3.1 Product Alignment

First the strategic roles of individual products as defined in the portfolio should be further substantiated. What is the concrete growth strategy for product A and how can the skimming-off strategy of product B be undertaken? In order to answer these questions, the individual products should be specified further within the portfolio. In doing so, a clear arrangement and differentiation regarding different objective characteristics of the product offering such as product variations/varieties, prices, target region, sales channels, packaging or services takes place. The relevant dimensions should be determined individually in light of the specific business model of every company. For example, the growth of product A might be targeted using an expansion of the product variations, while product B may be skimmed off with an increase in pricing and a reduction of the varieties. The overall results of product alignment are then captured using a concise fact sheet for each product.

2.3.2 Market Anchoring

In the sixth step, the specific position of products and brands should be refined and anchored in the market. The objective of market positioning is presenting one's own product offering to the subjective perception of the target customer in such a manner that it has preference over that of a competitor. The value proposition, the competitive positioning, the use of brands and the necessary communication should be considered to this end (Fig. 6).

Initially, the purchase-relevant value proposition, the particularities of the product offering and the underlying "reasons to believe" should be carved out for each product. While doing so, the value proposition may be based on technical, functional, value-based or experience-based characteristics. The significant elements of the value-proposition should then be arranged in relation to the competition. In doing

Fig. 6 Elements for market anchoring

so, a position should be found that is aligned with the specific situation-based needs ('need states') of individual customer segments and simultaneously positively separates the product from the competition. Especially in the sphere of the consumer goods industry, this is of great importance. Due to the overstimulation that a customer is exposed to by the mass of products and brands, positioning is increasingly gaining significance. Therefore, one should see to sufficient differentiation between products even in the own portfolio. In order to embed the established competitive positioning, the brand intended to transport the value proposition should be clarified. Apart from the use of existing brands, multiple-brand strategies for a more differentiated customer contact or the targeted expansion of a certain brand could be pushed. Following the clarification of brand usage, the foundation for communication should be laid in order to emotionalize the value proposition with advertising texts and graphics and promote it over all channels relevant to the target customers.

2.4 *Steering Model*

The last two steps deal with ensuring the sustainable implementation of the portfolio strategy using a steering model. A systematic and strategy-conform allocation of resources and steering based on key figures are necessary to this end.

2.4.1 Resource Allocation

Today, resource allocation oftentimes takes place on the basis of previous year values—"because it has always been this way" or according to the motto "whoever shouts loudest". Resource allocation is strictly derived from a concrete portfolio strategy in the least cases. Consequently, it mostly neither meets the present market's and competitors' requirements, nor does it support the company's strategic targets. Furthermore, resource allocation oftentimes lacks the necessary flexibility to realize ad hoc changes or special measures.

Therefore resource allocation should be a substantial building block in every portfolio strategy. Resource allocation should be consistently aligned with the target portfolio and the defined strategic roles. While the larger part of the resources would be invested in products with the strategic role of "growth", products with the strategic role "skimming-off" would receive no or very little resources (Fig. 7).

In addition, this approach bisects the budget. The first share is a defined fixed budget share per product. This fixed sum enables the planning security of individual product activities. A second variable budget share is defined for ad hoc measures or

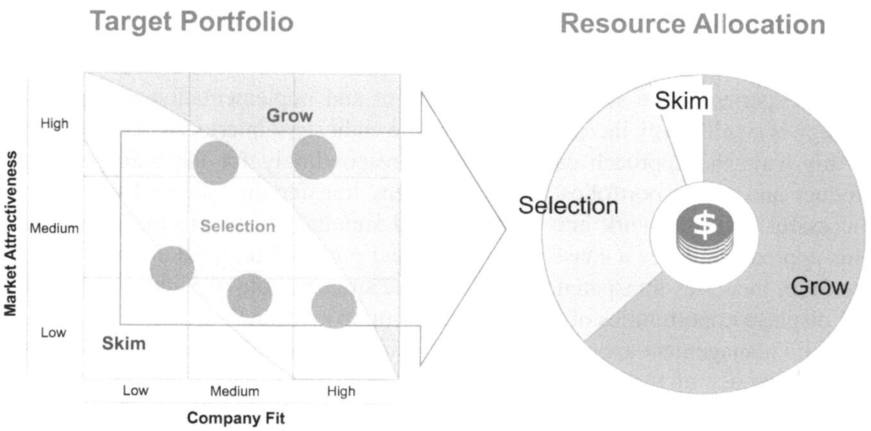

Fig. 7 Resource allocation

special measures. Products can then apply for this second budget share with their respective ideas. Consequently, special issues can be addressed while simultaneously maintaining the competition for good advertising campaigns and also ensuring very conscious budget decisions on this level.

2.4.2 Portfolio Scorecard

Many strategic actions have come to nothing because the implementation lost momentum. Therefore, the last step is laying a further important foundation for the sustainable implementation of the portfolio strategy. The integration of a portfolio scorecard constitutes an important success factor in closing the gap between strategy development and implementation and secures a holistic approach. To this end, specific targets are defined in the portfolio. The level of the set targets depends on the potentials defined by the market grid and the level of resource allocation. The more resources allocated, the higher the performance targets. Precise performance indicators and corresponding target figures are determined for the supervision and steering of the target achievement. Apart from financial performance indicators such as revenue growth or profitability, also non financial performance indicators such as brand strength should be integrated. Furthermore, a programme of measures for the implementation of the portfolio strategy is introduced. This includes among other things often-shunned measures such as the "implementation of an exit strategy". The progress of the implementation is then subsequently monitored using a KPI cockpit. The KPI cockpit is mainly limited to the significant performance indicators and thus ensures an efficient handling with concurrently high informative value. Last but not least, a periodical follow-up by the management team enables the company to react flexibly and quickly to changes in the market.

3 Conclusion

In our experience, the successful development and implementation of a portfolio strategy is significantly increased if each of the eight steps interlocks like cogs mesh. In this way, the approach can be used correspondingly for the management of product and brand portfolios. The eight steps transfer the essential elements of successful portfolio work into a holistic and simultaneously pragmatic approach. This approach enables a consistent market- and potential-oriented alignment of the portfolio, increases transparency regarding the strategic role of individual products and displays opportunities of reducing the complexity of the portfolio. This holistic portfolio management approach offers an escape from the tension between diversity and complexity of many portfolios and offers an immediate lever for positively influencing key performance indicators.

Oliver Greiner is a Partner with Horváth & Partners for the Competence Center Strategy, Innovation & Sales. He is one of the "thought leaders" in Germany for strategy work and the author of several books such as *Balanced Scorecard Implementation* and *Touchdown—How companies become unbeatable*.

Svenja Stöveken functions as a Senior Project Manager with Horváth & Partners for the Competence Center Organization, Transformation & Change. In combination with her previous employment as deputy general manager, she possesses profound knowledge in the area of strategy development and organizational transformation within the retail and consumer goods industry.

Nikolai Brosch functions as Managing Consultant with Horváth & Partners for the Competence Center Strategy, Innovation & Sales. His consulting expertise lies in the area of strategy development and execution across different industries with a special focus on corporate statement development and portfolio management.

Risk Management in Retail and the Consumer Goods Industry

Johannes Hofmeister and Björn Portner

Abstract In retail and the consumer goods industry, digitization has introduced the chance of selling individual products via central platforms both cost- and time-efficiently and suitable for mass markets. Risk management can only take up the inherent effects of digital transformation on a business model, if it reaches a new evolutionary stage. The future is fraught with new risks a modern risk manager must identify and manage. Consequently, it is not only the business model that must undergo a digital transformation but also risk management. The following contribution uses a practical example to illustrate why a performance-oriented risk management in retail and the consumer goods industry is necessary. Furthermore, it shows how intelligent algorithms are contributing to an improved risk intelligence in order to identify specific risks like changes in consumer behavior or trend environment.

Keywords Algorithms · Artificial intelligence · Digital transformation · Digitization · Performance-oriented risk management · Performance management

1 The Basics of Risk Management

Company-wide risk management is a comparably young discipline. Until the 1990s, risk management mainly focused on financial risks and risk hazards. The expectations were rather short-term and directed toward financial risks. In those days, the finance and insurance sectors were the pioneers of risk management. Additionally, various functions such as the accounting, treasury, or internal audit department mostly worked individually on their respective subject matters. An interlinking of information between the different departments did not take place. This only changed

J. Hofmeister
Controlling & Finance, Horváth & Partners, Munich, Germany

B. Portner (✉)
Controlling & Finance, Horváth & Partners, Frankfurt, Germany

M. Buttkus, R. Eberenz (eds.), *Performance Management in Retail and the Consumer Goods Industry*, https://doi.org/10.1007/978-3-030-12730-5_19

in the mid-1990s due to a combination of external and internal factors within the individual industries. Among the most important factors to be named were large company bankruptcies due to a lacking risk management, shorter product life cycles and faster innovation processes, internationalization of business activities, and worldwide deregulation in different sectors as well as the progressing development of IT systems.

In the following contribution, Sect. 1 illustrates the basics of risk management, which constitute the prerequisite for a risk-adjusted corporate performance management and its location in the organizational structure. Section 2 focuses on the digital transformation of risk management and its specifications. The implementation of risk management in today's digital age is introduced in Sect. 3, using a tangible example from retail and the consumer goods industry. Section 4 then summarizes the most important results and presents an outlook on coming developments.

1.1 Functions and Elements of Risk Management

In retail and the consumer goods industry, legal requirements for securing a risk management are only defined very vaguely and consequently leave a lot of room for interpretation. Moreover, there is no overall specification for risk management. The amount of regulations and requirements has almost doubled over the last years. In order to manage and monitor all relevant regulations and requirements, a company needs a suitable regulatory framework. The composition of this regulatory framework is the subject of governance systems. In this process, corporate governance is not only tasked with internal structures but also considers external relations with all stakeholders of the company (e.g., customers, suppliers, etc.). The monitoring aspects of governance systems have gained special significance through the large bankruptcy and fraud cases in the economy. Enron, WorldCom, and Arthur Andersen are only a few cases that made headlines with accounting fraud, corruption, and fraudulent behavior. In order to counteract such behavior, specific worldwide legal regulations were issued, and principles for the development of governance systems were formulated. Risk management in retail and the consumer goods industry initially derived from governance systems and has undergone substantial change ever since.

The complex risk landscape currently existing leads to increased challenges for risk management and forces the still young discipline to change:

- *Radical market changes:* International trade companies are at a crucial point in their reaction to drastic changes like Brexit or comprehensive economic treaties and trade agreements such as CETA.
- *Supply disruptions:* Supply chains in the consumer goods industry are becoming more and more complex with increasing customer-centeredness.
- *Cyberattacks:* The risks of data abuse, data theft, and data manipulation rise with the continuous digitization of processes.

- *Macroeconomic changes:* The low interest rate phase is especially challenging for financial institutions and has a negative influence on capital-intensive retail operations.
- *Political risks:* The increasing number of international and national crises (e.g., Turkey and Ukraine) impedes sales in the respective regions and contributes to a higher volatility in prices.

In order to manage such a complex risk landscape, a holistic and, above all, an opportunity-oriented best-practice risk management that contributes effectively to corporate performance management is necessary.

Such a performance-oriented risk management is aimed at recognizing market chances at an early stage and effectively managing risks in order to secure the company's continued existence. The definition of the term "risk" serves as the academic originator for risk management in business administration. In a narrower sense, risk is simply understood as the negative deviation from the expectation. In a wider sense, risk is understood as the deviation of the future development from defined target values. This encompasses both negative and positive deviations. Due to the fact that risk affects all decisions of a company, risk management generally always connotes the "management of opportunities." Performance-oriented risk management builds on this value proposition using the five following cornerstones:

- *Risk strategy:* Derived from the company strategy, it defines risk-specific target systems, principles, and measures.
- *Risk identification:* Extends planned situations by including risk aspects.
- *Risk evaluation:* Quantifies expected situations, considers correlations, and aggregates ranges of planned values.
- *Risk management:* Influences risk propensity by target agreements and compensation systems.
- *Risk controlling and reporting:* Adapts performance measurement instruments on the basis of risk development and creates an efficient and targeted reporting system.

1.2 Performance Risk Management: An Overview

Company strategy defines the basic orientation and strategic aims of a company as well as measures for their achievement. The *risk strategy* being derived from the company structure defines risk-specific target systems, principles, and measures. Consequently, the business model, strategic aims and strategic performance indicators must be congruent with the risk profile and the risk appetite as well as the defined key risk indicators.

Due to the aforementioned reasons a structured analysis of the risk landscape (*risk identification*) has to cover weaknesses and potentials relevant for business steering. To be able to conduct such an analysis, maintaining a risk inventory and developing standard strategies is necessary.

The quantification of risks (*risk evaluation*) plays a key role, as it can be used to locate risks and make them transparent. In this process, a uniform risk taxonomy simplifies communication across organizations.

To control risks a risk scorecard can be used which communicates risk indicators and derived indication of action (*risk controlling*). *The scorecard is designed* in a compact and topical manner via a control board, which is appropriate for targeted addressees. Subsequently, different approaches for risk reduction can be chosen with regard to the respective type of risk.

Finally, the risks are communicated via a directed reporting in order to improve the quality of decision-making in the entire company (risk controlling and reporting).

1.3 The Organizational Embedding of Risk Management

Risk management is a substantial element of a company's governance function and thus, is also embedded in the corporate structure. While the corporate performance is responsible for the risk management, it has much freedom regarding the placing of risk units. Generally, one should differentiate between decentralized and centralized risk management:

Decentralized risk management structures are characterized by risk measurements and monitoring taking place in the business areas. A significant advantage of this is the greater flexibility in risk management practices and the integration of risk management into existing processes.

Centralized risk management structures encompass a central risk unit which is responsible for playing through the risk cycle for significant risks. Here, especially the use of consistent approaches for company-wide uniform management of risks as well as concomitantly heightened efficiency and efficacy comes into effect.

In order to utilize all of the aforementioned advantages, Horváth & Partners' target solution follows a hybrid approach, consisting of both a decentralized and a centralized risk management. However, the organizational embedding of risk management should always be considered with regard to each individual corporation. Hence, the specific form of the organizational embedding may vary.

2 Digital Transformation in Risk Management

What does digitization mean for you? This central question has been posed to customers in innumerable meetings and workshops with very nuanced results. Digital transformation, in other words "digitally induced change in respective business models," is seen very critically by many people. While the so-called digital natives (0–18-year-olds) and the digital naturals (18–34-year-olds) see technological change as an opportunity to access new business areas, the "digital converted"

(35–100-year-olds) remain skeptical of digitization. Nonetheless, all of them can agree on one thing: Digitization will fundamentally change existing business models—be it in a positive or in a negative sense.

The ongoing digital transformation also offers new opportunities for risk management. Risk identification processes are becoming automated, and more time can be spent on the analysis of causes and the taking of measures. The amount of data and its granularity will steadily increase. Due to a high data density and high computing capacities available, intelligent algorithms are gaining significance for risk identification.

For Horváth & Partners' risk management and Big Data experts, digital transformation in retail and the consumer goods industry essentially means the opportunity of selling individual products, both for mass markets and cost- and time-efficiently via central platforms. In order to master this challenge, the digital transformation has to go hand in hand with the company culture. Consequently, a successful digital transformation requires a high degree of employees' identification with the defined digitization strategy.

The incubators of digital transformation are digital applications that enable customers to purchase products, inform themselves, or access after sales services. These applications are usually integrated into a digital ecosystem and offer manifold opportunities of getting in touch with the customer and understanding their needs. In order to make the applications as consumer-centered as possible, methods were developed that enable the bundling of all digital touchpoints on one platform.

To conclude, the digitization of the business model means that risk strategy and risk steering have to change, not only to secure the company's survival but also to ensure capital-effective growth.

2.1 *Digital Megatrends*

Over the last few years, one digital megatrend chased the other: "virtual reality," "artificial intelligence," and "blockchain"—to name only a few—were developed with an exponentially increasing speed, and many experts already predicted that the technology would change more over the next 15 years than it had over the last 50 years.

The influence of digital megatrends on risk management is substantial. The enormous implications of technological novelties are forcing companies to organize their processes in a more agile and thereby also a more adaptable manner. As a result, risk management is also evolving over time. The recognition of digital megatrends constitutes the foundation of its strategic focus and also determines the risk strategy. The final definition of norm strategies and their implementation mainly takes place in risk management: The quantitative methods for the identification of risks and the concomitant assessment of the risk impact classify measures and offer management the possibility of prioritizing and reacting in a timely manner. During this risk-based strategic realignment, classical risk management meets new digital methods.

Therefore, the aim of every company should be to clear a strategic path for the channeling and adoption of IT-driven innovations. In this process, the focus must always be two-dimensional, directed toward user-friendliness for the risk manager on the one hand and productivity—in the meaning of integration into the IT architecture of the company—on the other hand. A one-sided focus may have short-term usefulness in some cases; in the long run, however, a symbiosis between frontend and backend integration should always take place.

2.2 Algorithms for Risk Identification

Algorithms allow for the identification, measurement, and thus also the steering of risks. They constitute a central part of modern risk management, as the most complex and strategic questions are best answered with numbers and facts. In doing so, the machine-driven objectivity of algorithms helps us humans to make better decisions.

However, the well-advanced intelligence of machines also teaches us that a doctoral degree in computer sciences or mathematics is no longer necessary for creating and operating artificial intelligence. The entry barrier for the artificial intelligence market is as low as it has ever been before, and open-source libraries are already offering the most common code for free. *Argumentum a contrario*, this means that artificial intelligence has arrived in the age of digitization and integrated machine learning will soon become normality. Nonetheless, experience has shown that integrating this new technology into existing processes constitutes a great challenge. In risk management the statement "We could not see it coming" is still heard far too often, although early warning indicators have always existed. These warning indicators were either ignored or not recognized, due to a lack of appropriate methods.

The revolutionary potential of these new technologies becomes evident, if one focusses on Big Data and weak signals as early warning indicators. The increasing accuracy of risk models improves the robustness and consequently causes less costs through faulty or missing risk minimization.

The era of data warehouses is coming to an end. Static structures and limited interfaces are no longer up-to-date. In today's day and age, various kinds of information are accessible, and the speed of data acquisition and analysis marks the beginning of a new risk management. Rather than hoarding data in silo-like storage locations, all types of data can now be connected without changing their initial structures. Algorithms support the collection of classically structured data from databases and unstructured data in form of text documents in order to develop new and unprecedented risk indicators (Fig. 1).

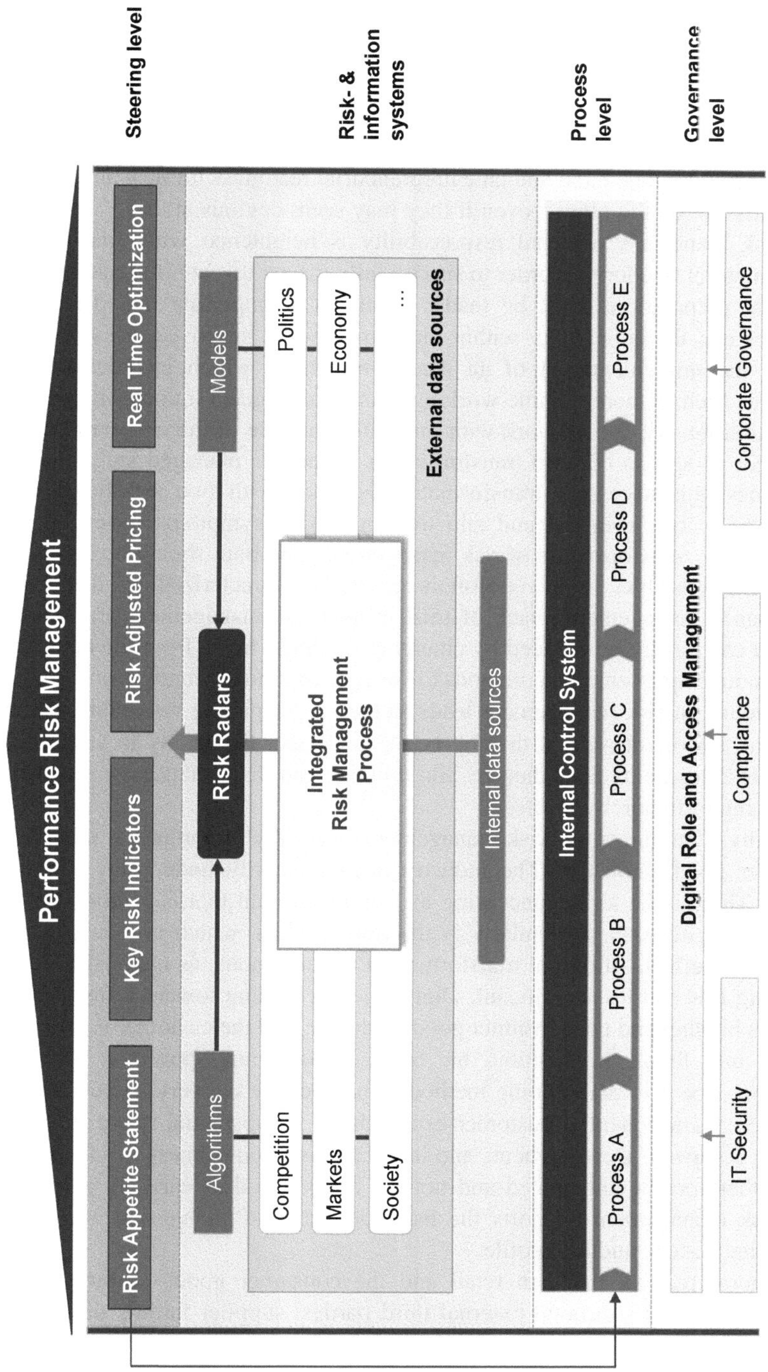

Fig. 1 Conception of a state-of-the-art performance risk management with emphasis on transparency, steering, and planning

3 A Practical Example from Retail and the Consumer Goods Industry

In order to create an innovative ecosystem within a company, some cultural preconditions within the organization must be met since, above all, digitization means one thing: change. To this end, risk managers must be given the freedom necessary for change on the one hand and an entrepreneurial readiness for new and controversial discussion on the other—even if they may seem devious at first.

A risk manager‘s personal responsibility is heightened with this new-found entrepreneurial freedom. In order to successfully master this cultural transformation, important preparations must be made: Firstly, it is important that the agility of processes and the collegiality within the company are improved. This is achieved through the implementation of an incentive system, which includes innovative incentives such as more flexible working hours and targeted training in quantitative areas. Additionally, the network with innovators outside of the company should be expanded, as such a cultural transformation cannot be managed single-handedly. Oftentimes, this necessary transformation is faced with two significant cultural inadequacies: risk aversion and silo thinking. Both symptoms have devastating impact on the transformation of risk management, and both should be counteracted as early as possible. Risk aversion is generally characterized by the corporate performance management's lack of trust in new risk management practices. Risk aversion can mostly be reduced by changing the focus away from the constant and monotonous improvement of methods toward the continuous innovation of methods. Silo thinking in risk management leads to the bigger picture remaining misunderstood and important aspects thereby being neglected. Especially in very complex companies, this holds great danger. Silo thinking can, for instance, be reduced by a downsizing of hierarchy levels.

So why is an innovative risk management especially important for retail and the consumer goods industry? The industry is momentarily undergoing a structural change. There is no topic concerning the future of retail that is as hotly discussed as that of digitization. Particularly in the middle class, which is focused on local markets, the effects of digital transformation are enormous, as national borders are becoming less and less significant. Digitization is leading toward a fusion of sales channels in retail and the consumer goods industry, and the customer is increasingly moving into focus. In addition, his basis of bargaining power is also further increasing—be it in determining method of payment or delivery. He decides when and where. Consequently, customer-centeredness is substantial to the success of a retailing company. Developments and implications of consumers' wants and needs should therefore be anticipated and noticed quickly and as early as possible. Big Data risk management supports the early detection of changes in a consumer's purchasing history and his profile.

Furthermore, risk maps in retail and the consumer goods sector are largely determined by risks through external third parties: supplier failure, disruptions of the supply chain, contract risks, debt defaults, or the quality of delivered products

Risk category	Risk area	Examples
Market risks	Trends	Growing number of online orders
	Competition and pressure on prices	Increasing client numbers among Peers
External risks	Negative press	Wrong and/or late communication
	Competition law	Limitation in expansion possibilities
Risks from core processes	Individual pricing	Dynamic Pricing
	Cost development	Raw material and energy prices
Risks from supporting processes	Supply chain	Quality of products and services bought in addition
	Financing and liquidity risk	Government crises in important distribution countries
Contract risks	Price maintenance	Remuneration of suppliers
	Contractual penalty	Warranty and goodwill claims

Fig. 2 Examples of risk categories and risk areas with Big Data dependency factor for retail and consumer goods companies—excerpt

have an enormous impact on a company's overall success. To reduce these risks, a holistic approach to risk management is required. Algorithms are capable of recognizing anomalies in publicly available data in local and international markets. Hygienic shortcomings, for example, are oftentimes published by suppliers. In order to counteract a possible food safety scandal, Big Data solutions can be used to identify such risks in a timely manner, as the algorithm can connect company-specific risks and potential risk drivers. In order to reduce risks, articles fraught with risks can be removed from the product range before the company has to suffer damage to its reputation (Fig. 2).

In the digital age, these insights are a key competence of strategic market orientation and risk reduction, as global networking is continuously increasing the speed of transactions and the risk manager's handling speed is becoming more and more important.

After a systematic and cultural foundation has been laid, the integration of Big Data solutions into an existing retail and consumer goods risk management can be administered with the following four phases:

Phase 1: Defining the risk network—The historical risk data of existing systems is collected and analyzed in a structured manner.

Phase 2: Validating the risk driver model—The interlinking of external, finely granular data with internal data enables a 360° perspective on all quantifiable risks.

Phase 3: Integration into risk management processes—Existing risk indicators are now expanded by a Big Data dependency factor. Following this method, liquidity indexes, for example, can be simulated and forecasted using external quantified market data from text documents.

Phase 4: Integration into the steering model—The key success factor of the expansion of risk management is its integration into the company's steering model. Interlinking risk parameters requires corporate performance management to resolutely implement them into its strategic orientation to be able to control the entire complexity of risk.

3.1 Semantic Data Analysis

How does semantic data analysis even work? And how can insights be gained from unstructured texts? These questions are posed by many risk managers that are integrating the new quantitative methods into their systems.

The answer to these questions is relatively simple: The first step is learning to understand the machinery of human language, and the second one is to evaluate the language used, using numbers. In doing so, one can determine whether, for example, the terms "retail" or "online sales" are used in a positive or negative context, by using artificial intelligence that bases its decision on reading out all articles available on the World Wide Web containing those terms.

Semantic data analysis aims at quantifying qualitative risk indicators (=key terms) out of text documents. Therefore, it is necessary to continuously expand the machine's vocabulary—similar to us humans. The positive or negative statements of the sets are finally scaled linearly (y-axis), and changes can be gathered on the time axis (x-axis), thereby identifying increasing volatilities or correlations (Fig. 3).

The key term "sustainability," for example, is increasingly gaining significance in the media, since customers place a higher value on organically manufactured

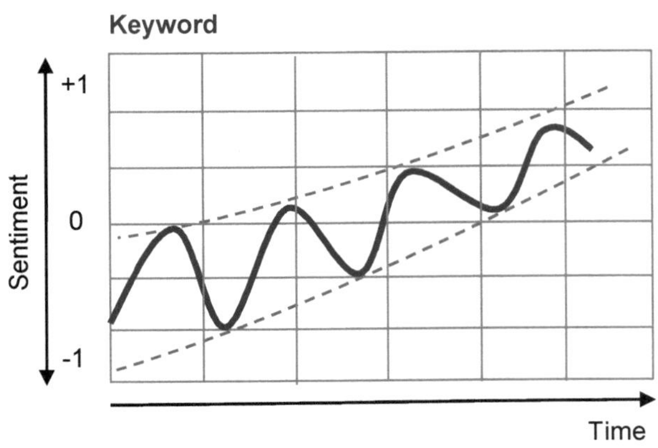

Fig. 3 Development of semantic data analysis

products. Since the Internet, mobile technologies, online trade, and social media channels influence consumer behavior strongly, it is important to understand how the public's opinion on sustainability changes on these platforms in order to react to market adjustments in a timely manner. Classic methods no longer suffice for this, as frequency and correlation analyses oftentimes do not allow for such conclusions. The main value of semantic algorithms lies in the actual evaluation of the topics: Data is coming to life and is entering in discussions with analysts—leading to completely new insights.

Other topics in risk management in retail and the consumer goods area such as interruptions in the supply chain, food scandals, quality defects, and currency fluctuations are previously being analyzed. Semantic algorithms are able to recognize changes in public opinion regarding the aforementioned terms. This improves the risk intelligence of modern risk managers on the one hand and becomes a competitive advantage for a company on the other hand, as a high rate of implementing measures for risk reduction is gaining significance. Partly this is because retail companies' existing price or performance advantages often only remain for a short time period, due to the currently perfect competition in the market, but also because global networking is contributing to an increasingly fast transfer of information. Another reason why a real-time risk analysis is absolutely necessary. Algorithms have to be implemented, as humans do not have the capacity of assessing such granular data in a structured manner and in so little time.

3.2 *Horváth & Partners Innovation: Business Radar Suite*

Very early on, Horváth & Partners had set itself the aim of not only developing risk management processes and concepts but also the respective solutions. In this process, three applications were created that utilize semantic algorithms for the detection of risks:

- The Global Risk Radar for the recognition of general risks
- The Global Treasury Radar for the recognition of liquidity risks
- The Global Innovations Radar for the recognition of innovation risks

All three applications have different features and functions and offer the possibility of making use of the advantages of Big Data technologies to the respective departments in risk management, treasury and innovation.

3.2.1 Global Risk Radar

In order to explore subject matters that were previously beyond the knowledge horizons, Horváth & Partners risk management and Big Data experts have developed a software named Global Risk Radar. This radar marks the beginning of a new era in the field of Big Data risk management. It offers unprecedented opportunities for the

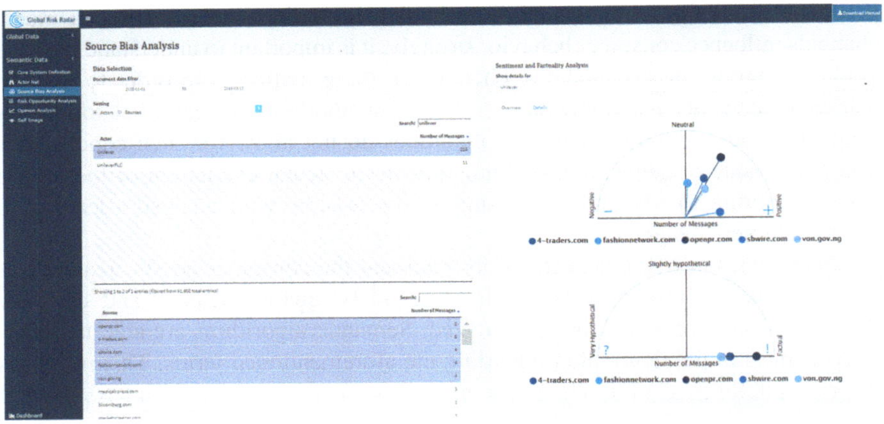

Fig. 4 The Global Risk Radar identifies drivers of the public opinion to grasp the brand value holistically

analysis of qualitative mass data and expands on the existing risks with a Big Data dependency factor, using semantic data processing. The Global Risk Radar marks the end of silo-like risk management. The Risk Radar objectifies the risk evaluation processes and offers a systematic perspective and the possibility of conducting competitive analyses in real time. The calculation of reputation and idiosyncratic risks enables a strengthening of one's own bargaining power and expanding of one's competitive position. The risks identified in the process can be considered in pricing, thereby improving the risk capacity (Fig. 4).

Risk managers can then communicate newly emerging risks at an early stage and thus contribute more to the company management. This improves the visibility of risk management in the company, especially in the global companies of the retail and consumer goods industry, as its market risk profile has been better understood as consequence. The new risks—those on which no reports exist—hold the greatest relevance for a strategic realignment.

3.2.2 Global Treasury Radar

The Treasury Radar is based on the same technology as the Global Risk Radar, although its functionalities are adjusted exactly to the treasury's requirements (Fig. 5). Among only a few others, liquidity planning requires the most expenditures in treasury. Especially in complex company structures, substantial resources are tied up. Nonetheless, planning quality and data quality are oftentimes lacking. This can be primarily tracked back to the circumstance that most planning is conducted manually and contains well-known weaknesses. A digitization of planning can help to compensate these weaknesses. The Treasury Radar was developed on the

Fig. 5 The Global Treasury Radar provides a global overview of treasury risks to improve liquidity planning

basis of Big Data in order to recognize liquidity risks at an early stage and to raise the treasury's degree of planning automatization.

3.2.3 Global Innovation Radar

Innovation is key to a successful company development. Horváth & Partners' Innovation Radar is the newest of these three solutions and is aimed at clustering, classifying, and identifying innovations in the market using patent data (Fig. 6). The database developed to this end, consisting of more than 5 million patents, and the complementary algorithm enable companies to reach a new level of innovation.

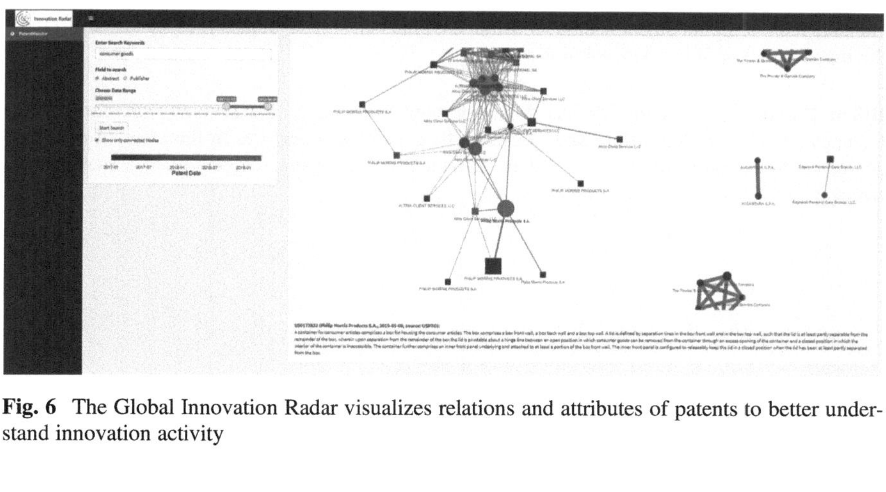

Fig. 6 The Global Innovation Radar visualizes relations and attributes of patents to better understand innovation activity

All three radars have their specific advantages—if applied together, their full potential can be reached. In our globally connected environment, risks should always be considered holistically.

4 Conclusion and Outlook

The past has shown that many companies react very differently to digitization and view its effects critically. Nonetheless, all can agree on one point—business models will change and, as a consequence, so will risk management standards. This means that the new generation of risk managers will have to reflect whether their methods are still congruent with their risk environment. In retail and the consumer goods industry, the application of modern methods for the identification of risks and the steering of such plays an important role, given that added value in this area is increasingly gained via digital platforms. The use of algorithms for the identification of market risks is very valuable in this industry, as the amount of data yielded by the platforms can increasingly only be controlled and structured by machines and no longer by humans.

The future will show that all those companies who possess an answer to the externally induced digital transformation will have a competitive advantage. On the one hand, this requires increasing agility in risk management processes and on the other hand a holistic view of all existing risk drivers. Corporate performance management is therefore well-advised to focus the integration of innovative solutions on risk management, as the speed of technological and macroeconomic changes is constantly increasing. Consequently, a first step in the right direction would be the interlinking of classic risk management procedures with new quantitative methods—since algorithms and their artificial intelligence will soon transform many existing applications and practices.

Johannes Hofmeister is a Managing Consultant with Horváth & Partners for the Competence Center Controlling and Finance in Munich. His consulting experience is based on the design and enhancement of digital business models within the financial service industry, especially concerning the transformation of big data solutions.

Björn Portner is a Senior Project Manager with Horváth & Partners in Frankfurt for the Competence Center Controlling and Finance. His consulting focus lies in the areas of risk management, digital business models, and performance enhancement, especially in a management steering context.

Corporate Controlling 2020: Trends and Challenges

Ralf Eberenz and Stefan Behringer

Abstract This chapter will discuss current trends of development and challenges for corporate controlling.

In the light of a holistic consideration of all design aspects inherent to a corporate controlling function, nine theses will be used to identify significant requirements of change.

Additionally, functional recommendations for dealing with changes that already have general relevance in the short term will be given.

The suggested theses are not derived empirically. They much rather deliberately reflect the authors' subjective observations.

Keywords Big data · Group controlling · Data analytics · Digitization · Operating model · Performance management

1 Current Tasks of Corporate Controlling

Each corporation's particular form of organization requires a particular approach to its corporate controlling.[1] This takes place in so-called group or corporate controlling departments.[2] Their specific activity is strongly dependent on the structure of the

An adaption of this contribution has been originally printed as Eberenz, R., Behringer, S. (2016): Konzerncontrolling 2020: Entwicklungstendenzen und Herausforderungen, Der Controlling Berater, Volume 47, pp. 18.

[1]The authors use the English word "controlling" to translate the German term "controlling." Please refer to the discussion in the preface.

[2]Behringer (2014), pp. 23–24.

R. Eberenz (✉)
Industrial Goods and High Tech, Horváth & Partners, Hamburg, Germany

S. Behringer
Controlling and Corporate Governance, Nordakademie, Elmshorn, Germany

M. Buttkus, R. Eberenz (eds.), *Performance Management in Retail and the Consumer Goods Industry*, https://doi.org/10.1007/978-3-030-12730-5_20

corporation. Group controlling focuses on the corporation as a whole, the various group functions, and the individual subsidiaries and investments.[3] Empirical studies show that it generally assumes cross-functional tasks concerning methods, processes, and governance, namely[4]:

- Group planning and reporting, especially group profit controlling
- Specification of standardized methods, guidelines, and information systems
- Coordination between business units, e.g., setting transfer prices
- Cross-functional special duties, e.g., business acquisitions or disinvestments
- Further development of the controlling organization, including people development

This examination will discuss the significant trends and challenges of group controlling. Its scope will be limited to such challenges as have become evident over the last few years and will increasingly determine its role and tasks in the near future. Nine theses will be introduced, using an *operating model* as regulatory framework for discussion. These are not derived empirically. However, they much rather represent subjective observations on the basis of their authors' personal management experience, various consulting projects, and relevant research activity.

2 A Regulatory Framework for an Operating Model

In this chapter trends of group controlling will be discussed on the basis of a general regulatory framework, a so-called operating model. This model describes substantial design aspects of an organization in a closed form (see Fig. 1). A primary target picture (vision), a description of the raison d'etre (mission), and the fundamental approach of group controlling relating thereto (strategy) can be used as initial points. They determine all the following design aspects substantially that are closely linked to the whole company. These three components are often expressed as a well-fitting combination but sometimes also as field of tension between the top management expectations and the group controller's self-conception.

Role models, responsibilities, and task areas connected with them can be derived from this basis. Typically, these can be separated into the following:

- Governance-Role (group-wide development and determination of controlling standards, guidelines, processes, etc.)
- Production-Role (providing information, reports, plans, etc.)
- Business-Partner-Role (business-related, decision-oriented support of management)

[3] Horvath et al. (2015), p. 406.

[4] Hahn and Hungenberg (2001), pp. 927–928.

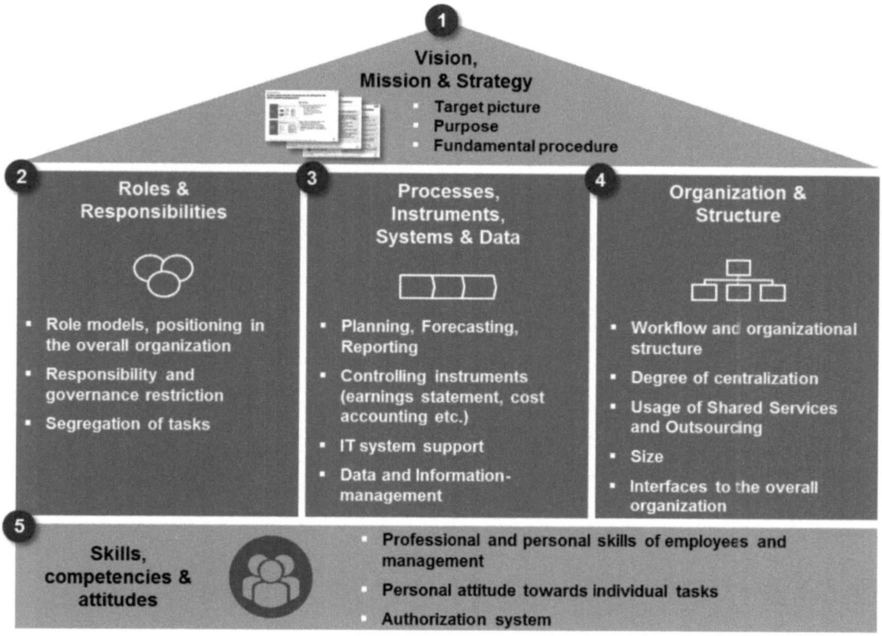

Fig. 1 The target operating model within a corporation

Each company must specifically decide which of these roles should take effect to what extent on corporate level. Nonetheless, the Governance-Role is by far the most common for group controllers, often in combination with the Business-Partner-Role vis-à-vis the group top management. Conversely, the Production-Role has a decreasing importance, as large corporates are increasingly outsourcing their transaction-oriented, quantitative information supply functions to shared service organizations or to external service providers.[5]

Apart from the previously mentioned roles and responsibilities, the design of business processes is key. Classically, planning, forecasting, and reporting processes as well as the conceptional design and the IT technical implementation of performance management instruments, e.g., revenue, cost, or profit statements, are determined on corporate level. Ultimately, this determines a large portion of the "products" group controlling offers to the company to support performance management. The responsible body is the controlling organization itself. Its size, structure, processes, and distribution of responsibilities to both centralized and decentralized as well as internal and external controlling functions must all be arranged in a manner that allows an efficient and effective operation. The basis for this is a respectively qualified team. The professional and, more importantly, the soft skills of management personnel and employees are decisive for any success.

[5]Eiselmayer and Kottbauer (2015), p. 25.

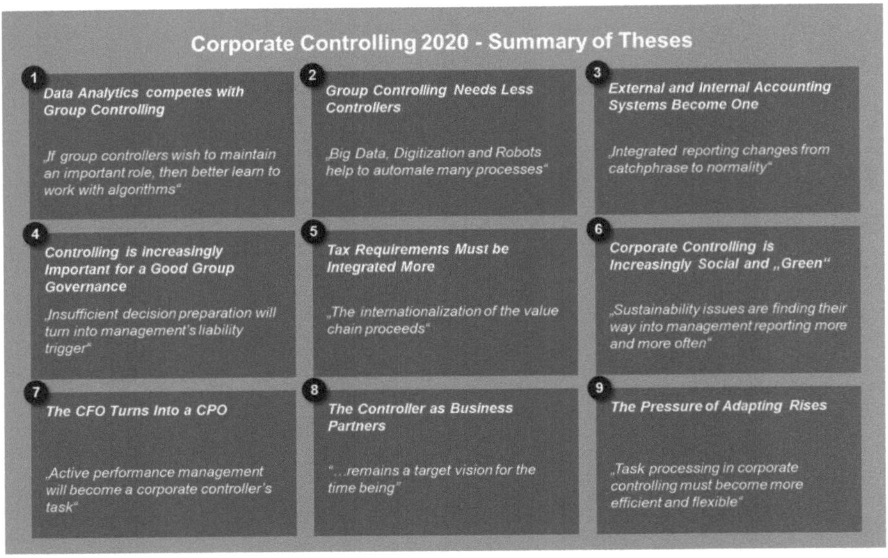

Fig. 2 Summary of theses

Furthermore, each team member's personal attitudes to their own role and their field of activity has great significance.

Both the combination of high professional expectations and the difficult personal balance of necessary proximity to the supported department and objective neutrality in particular create substantial problems for controllers. This is especially true, if the supervised area, as it is often the case with group controllers, is the executive board itself.

An operating model that is both consistent and properly integrated with the entire corporation equally secures the efficacy and the efficiency of a group controlling organization. Its deliberate and proactive development allows for a timely reaction to internal and external changes, without jeopardizing the controllability of the group or the efficiency of its corporate controlling function. Therefore, it seems appropriate to discuss the following theses (see Fig. 2) related to the operating model and to systematically demonstrate their possible implications.

3 Nine Theses on the Future of Corporate Controlling

3.1 *Thesis 1: Data Analytics Competes with Corporate Controlling*

> If group controllers wish to maintain an important role, then better learn to work with algorithms.

Competition is good for business. A trend originating in the Anglo-Saxon world is the provision of data scientists to some departments. Data science's aim is unveiling hidden information in large and unstructured data volumes by using analytical methods. Predictive analytics will therefore gain great importance to group planning; it attempts to recognize regularities and thereby predict future developments, by analyzing past data and possibly external data holdings.[6] This task is assigned to specialized departments in more and more companies, as statistical, analytical, and IT competencies are primarily necessary.

Consequently, competition that requires its own human and financial resources accrues from corporate controlling. Nevertheless, the role data science can play for performance management is much more decisive. Although the expertise of group controllers has previously played an important role, e.g., when checking the group's budget for plausibility, analytic prognoses generated by IT systems will increasingly gain importance. In light of this, they will represent a credible alternative for human evaluation.

Group controllers need to consider the fact that with automated prognoses, planning processes will be influenced implicitly. Prognoses have been generated by controlling to date, now, however, might be generated by machines and their algorithms. The prospects of such a development are clear: More reliable prognoses can be generated in shorter time. However, the risk is just as evident: If planning assumptions are deduced in a purely mechanical manner, the necessary connection to the business itself may be lacking. Thus, group controllers do not only secure their position by acquiring necessary mathematic-statistical competences in the fight for resources. They also can provide necessary business insights to be established in algorithms. A usage of the methods of data analytics that is too uncritical may lead to wrong decisions. Long years of experience gained by group controllers in their function of securing management rationality should not be lost merely because of automated options that are allegedly better. These methods need a qualitative input in order to be significant as well. Group controllers are predestined to provide this input on group level. Nonetheless, this role must be accepted and they need to brave the stony road of learning data analytics.

The increasing significance of data analytics could potentially lead to changes in many processes. For the future of corporate controlling, this means that competences, necessary for dealing with new methods and their application, must be acquired. This also impacts organizations. Data science competences must be embedded within corporate controlling units, even, or rather especially, if strong data science departments are established in the corporation.

3.2 *Thesis 2: Corporate Controlling Needs Less Controllers*

Big data, digitization, and robots help to automate many processes.

With the digitization of services or automated sales processes (usage of Internet shops, etc.), significantly larger amounts of data are created that can potentially be

---

[6] Buschbacher (2016), pp. 42–43.

used as aid in the decision-making process. In light of digitization, one can assume that this unstructured data could automatically turn into structured ones that management could also use to aid decision-making processes. Corporate controlling needs less employees to complete its tasks, and as a result positions could be eliminated.[7] Even if this change mainly influences operative controlling units, group controlling will still be affected indirectly.

The role of controlling as exclusive information provider is increasingly losing significance at all levels of a company. Simultaneously, the expectations set for the interpretation of provided information rise, which also raises expectations set for group controllers. However, automation carries a manual relief. For example, through the (technical) integration of external and internal accounting systems, reconciliations of both areas are not necessary anymore. The interpretation of an integrated accounting statement will increasingly gain significance; the very time-consuming analysis and explanation of differences in disclosure and evaluation will, however, lapse. As a consequence, corporate controlling will henceforth have to find new ways of justifying both its contribution to the business success and its number of employees.

The progressing automation and digitization will influence most processes, as is the case in both generating data and data processing. Thus, the organization will decrease in size but not in performance.

3.3 Thesis 3: External and Internal Accounting Systems Become One

Integrated reporting changes from catchphrase to normality.

Large companies' traditional organizations encompass an internal and an external accounting system. The internal accounting system (controlling) provides necessary information to management for business transparency and decision-making. The external accounting system's task is fulfilling the company's legal obligations for publicity and is confined to the narrow margin of legal compliance. However, both sides see the need for integration. Corporate controlling substantially uses external accounting data to feed their own reports. An understanding of the accounting rules and regulations, such as IFRS and USGAAP, is indispensable to a good group controller. This is especially true, as results are increasingly dependent on decisions made by the accountants. Group results are fundamentally influenced by the development of values by fair values and goodwill from acquisitions. As a consequence, result management without a close cooperation of controlling and accounting is impossible.

[7]Becker et al. (2016), p. 116.

On the other hand, the IFRS, for example, require the use of future-oriented cash flows to calculate fair values.[8] Cash flow planning is the domain of corporate controlling in which planning and forecasting are located. However, planning has to take the accounting standards into account, in order to ensure matching target and actual figures, as inconsistencies must not occur from different calculation rules or standard definitions. As a result of the increased importance of fair value assessment, accounting also absolutely requires the future-orientated information that corporate controlling can provide. The cooperation of controlling and accounting is institutionalized by IFRS in the so-called management approach.[9] This is further substantiated in the IFRS's framework: "published financial statements are based on the information used by management about the financial position, performance and changes in financial position of the enterprise."[10] Corporations are held to provide external investors with the same information that their own management uses as basis for its decision-making processes. The advantages for such an external investor are clear: He can comprehend decisions made by management on the exact same basis of information as the decision-maker himself.

Nonetheless, a company also has its advantages. The costs of acquiring information can be lowered, which should also be measureable in the reduced effort needed for the examination of annual accounts.[11] Consequently, group controllers have a co-responsibility in performance calculation and presentation. This presents an integration danger: If group controlling chooses their segments in a manner that is suited to external presentations, this can counteract the original function as "rationality anchor" of management.

Empirical studies show that integration is lived everywhere. However, complete integration remains the exception and not the rule.[12] Nonetheless, more and more companies will take the path of complete integration. It will no longer suffice to have accounting and controlling as separate silos. Instead, IT systems will contribute to internal and external accounting turning into an integrated department. A prominent instance that can be given as an example for this development is the newest ERP generation of SAP S4/Hana.

These changes in parameters affect roles and responsibilities, as definitions of tasks and responsibilities alter. Processes will therefore be affected, as IFRS-prescribed processes concerning business evaluation must be adapted. Systems will change and integrate the internal and external accounting. Further, organization will also be affected by this inevitable cooperation.

[8]Velte (2008), p. 133.

[9]Barth (2016), p. 529.

[10]IFRS Framework (2015), note 11.

[11]Lopatta (2011), p. 407.

[12]Weide et al. (2011), p. 63.

3.4 *Thesis 4: Controlling Is Increasingly Important for a Good Corporate Governance*

Insufficient decision support will turn into management's liability trigger.

The huge waves of regulations in the recent past, triggered by corporate scandals, the financial crisis, and a general skepticism against the management of large corporations by the general public, will exert an increasingly strong influence on corporate controlling. It is therefore predestined to take on a decisive as well as accountable role in risk management. An increased importance for the legal protection of the executive board and the supervisory board is also ascribed to reporting. Controlling is credited with a key role in protection against liability. Increasing regulation and a much stronger enforcement of present laws and legislations by justice will make this department ever more relevant.

The differentiation between infringements subject to liability and management mistakes will also gain significance. A wrong business decision is ruled by the business judgment rule in law. In Germany this is codified for stock-listed companies (AG) in § 93 (1) sentence 2 of the German Stock Corporation Act (AktG), although one can assume this also impacts limited companies (GmbH). Accordingly, the executive board has not breached its duties, if and when a member makes a decision for the benefit of the company based on adequate information.

An important criterion, which is a prerequisite for decision-makers to be able to invoke the business judgment rule, is "an adequate basis of information."[13] The German Federal Constitutional Court (Bundesverfassungsgericht) has summarized the business judgment rule in the following short form: A member of the board is legally not obligated to a successful decision, but rather to a diligent and prudent one.[14] This concerns the key function of controlling. Corporate controlling carries the primary responsibility of providing such information to the management of the group parent company to an adequate extent. It must take into account that the production of documents during decision-making preparations could be used as evidence in lawsuits.

However, this increased responsibility will even be rewarded: Legislators assume a rationality that is as objective as possible in its model for an adequate decision-making. Consequently, controlling's function of securing rationality gains significance. Corporate controlling should use its key competences and enforce its cooperation with compliance departments.

Implications in all elements of the operating model are to be expected: a controller's role will change and processes will be formalized. Both will not remain without impact on organization. Especially since not all documents produced by controlling are intended for exclusively internal purposes, legal expertise is becoming a key qualification of controlling.

---

[13]Graumann and Grundei (2015), p. 197.

[14]BVerfG from 23.6.2010–2 BvR 2559/08, NJW (2010), p. 3209.

3.5 Thesis 5: Tax Requirements Must Be Integrated More

The internationalization of the value chain proceeds.

The increased internationalization of supply chains and the accompanying complexity of corporates operating on a multinational level represent challenges to the management on the one hand and to an adequate organization that is also compliant with the tax law on the other.[15] The determination of transfer prices of group companies has immerged as the most important topic of international taxation practice. Two central issues face each other: a control concept to best support a corporate's performance management (management concept) and a compliant tax planning (transfer price concept). Both practically and theoretically, this results in an area of tension between business and tax perspective that has been solved insufficiently for most corporates. For example, the incentive effects of tax-compliant transfer prices might be possibly undesired by management, or the management perspective to consider a group of companies as a unit, opposed to the tax perspective, that separates all legally independent group companies into different tax subjects.

The transfer price issue is merely an example for ever-increasing restrictions to design adequate management concepts. International tax law as well as an increased enforcement through tax authorities will gain further influence, exceeding present hot topics such as the BEPS initiative of the OECD and the resulting regulations, granting federal governments more influence on the profit allocation of corporations. Securing the management concept of corporations without infringing tax regulation will therefore become an increasingly extensive task of corporate controlling.

On the level of performance management tools, processes, and IT systems, integrated solutions will get much greater significance. Consequently, profit and margin calculations must be designed in a manner that allows them to remain meaningful, despite continuously changing tax requirements. On the other hand, planning, forecasting, and controlling processes must reflect tax impact more strongly.

Corporate controlling functions and the tax department will close ranks organizationally. Jointly staffed transfer-price-offices, joint boards for financing questions, and projects to further develop a group's legal structure are respectively merely the beginning. In order to successfully work in such a constellation, the skill set of controllers must be developed further. On a professional level, they must develop an understanding of taxation aspects, as well as the ability of adapting their language to that of colleagues with a more juridical background. This is not always easy for a controller who is normally educated in his own business language and oftentimes very different to that of a legal expert.

[15] Eberenz (2014), p. 3.

3.6 Thesis 6: Corporate Controlling Is Increasingly Social and "Green"

Sustainability issues are finding their way into management reporting more and more often.

Sustainability is not a fashionable trend.[16] It is here to stay and will have an increasing influence on operational decisions. It is not only legislation that uses a continuous succession of new regulations that create greater transparency in the sector of sustainability. Nowadays, there are also investors, employees, customers, and the public who are immediately interested in the company and demand sustainable behavior directly and without compromise. For quite some time now, various initiatives on nongovernment levels have ensured pressure on companies to report their effects on society and the environment.[17] Transparency is inevitably greater. Greenwashing, such as many companies have or are engaged in, will be near impossible due to legal requirements. Legislation has set the guidelines with its mandatory introduction of the EU's CSR guideline that must be implemented since the end of 2016. According to this guideline, sizeable companies (more than 500 employees) or from important industries (banks, insurances, etc.) must hand in a declaration of non financial circumstances, such as their concept of diversity for management, administration, and supervision bodies.[18] With these pertinent duties of publication, the awareness of these key figures will also grow in management.

The ecological and social consequences of decisions must de facto be taken into account. Otherwise, there are many options for stakeholders to sanction the company. These developments absolutely require corporate controlling to dedicate itself to such questions. If this is neglected, other departments will fill this gap and play an ever-increasing role in decision-making preparations. Consequently, corporate controlling must open itself to the company's non financial sphere. This requires other instruments for data acquisition, other skills for analyses, and subsequently other competences for controllers.

Corporate controlling must integrate aspects of sustainable group governance on procedural levels. As a result, a controller's role will change. If the concept is taken seriously, then this will absolutely necessitate the consideration of "green" aspects in decision-making, which will in turn show in altered requirements for the competences of controllers.

3.7 Thesis 7: The CFO Turns into a CPO

Active performance management will become a corporate controller's task.

The CFO's area of responsibility is broadening from mere performance measurement to active performance management. A catchy term for this could prospectively

[16]Weber et al. (2012), p. 13.
[17]Hentze and Thies (2014), p. 43.
[18]Stawinoga and Velte (2016), p. 841.

be CPO, the Chief Performance Officer, who will primarily be accountable for the company-wide performance management process. This reaches from the organization and coordination of strategy development processes and the management of a necessary project portfolio all the way to the formulation of target agreements and incentive systems. The CPO substantially influences the allocation of capital, triggers initiatives to increase efficiency, and increasingly initiates and accounts for strategic company acquisitions and sales. Consequently, the CPO takes on an increasingly business transforming role that accompanies the expansion of his functional area of responsibilities. In summary, his responsibility increases.

A CFO's classic task area is not only enlarged by additional governance, compliance, or risk management tasks but also by strategic and operative subjects. Consequently, a greater focus on performance management competes with the other subjects and therefore requires an additional and varied support through corporate controlling. On one hand, this means a reallocation of resources within corporate controlling as to accommodate the support of performance management. This only succeeds without cost to other tasks, if sufficient efficiency potential can be raised. On the other hand, very interesting and near-to-business tasks are created for controllers, who are capable of leading, or co-responsibly supporting, strategic and operative restructuring processes.

The CFO's altered role will subsequently lead to a change in corporate controlling, up to a significantly larger determination of its objectives. However, the respective abilities, structures, and processes should not only be developed to this end internally. The cooperation with other functions must be readjusted externally as well, since an aspiration that is both action-oriented and more formative for business inevitably entails considerable conflict potential. Therefore, it is more important to develop an adequate strategy for corporate controlling and meticulously synchronizing it with the various other departments of a company.

3.8 Thesis 8: The Controller as Business Partners

. . .remains a target vision for the time being.

Despite the discussion on the role of controlling that has been going on for the past decades, and an equally long assentation of the accuracy of the target vision of their role as business partners, group reality remains otherwise. Although there is a measureable and gratifying trend toward business partnering,[19] there remain strong discrepancies between the actual and desired roles of controllers from management's perception.[20] More internal counselling, support, and change impulses and considerably less control and supervision are wished of controllers. They often come up

[19]Weißenberger et al. (2011), p. 331.

[20]Weber and Schäffer (2014), pp. 470–471.

short on their own expectations toward their role, as well as those of their business partners.

A further distinct approach to the target vision is existentially necessary as the progressing digitization and the increased competition due to other specialist functions massively threaten a controlling that does not comply with an accepted business partner role. If neither the range of tasks nor the controller's role constitutes a unique feature, then he comes dangerously close to becoming expendable to business success.

However, business requirements in this increasingly volatile environment in the foreseeable future will increase and change content wise. As a result, the challenges will correspondingly be greater and role expectations more situational. In future, corporate controlling will therefore have to develop further, in order to approach the role of business partner. Ultimately, this necessitates a change in all areas of the operating model. However, it is predominantly the controller itself who must adapt. Professional and personal skills must be developed, competences must be expanded upon or rather advocated, and the personal attitude concerning own tasks must be fitted with an adequate willingness for adaptation and reinvention. Only in this way can an increasing number of management accountants that approach the target vision business partner be ensured for the years to come. A comprehensive fulfilment of this aspiration remains distant for the time being, if not permanent.

3.9 Thesis 9: The Pressure of Adapting Rises

Task processing in corporate controlling must become more efficient and flexible.

The continuous efficiency pressure that companies exert naturally also affects the finance function and thereby also controlling. An increasing share of transactional activity in particular, such as the generation of reports, consolidation, or planning support, is being standardized, automated, and industrialized. Consequently, they can be processed much more cost-effectively. Outsourcing these processes to shared service centers or to an external service provider oftentimes opens further cost reduction potential. The trend of further efficiency enhancements remains unbroken and will also gain importance to the currently less focused group function.

An ability that is even more important than the improvement of the running business is that of adapting to new circumstances as quickly as possible. This flexibility of changing the business is a crucial factor of success in a dynamic and volatile business environment. For corporate controlling this means two things. Firstly, all processes and their supporting IT systems should be designed in a manner that allows for a fast and cost-effective adaptation to new, or rather differentiated, business requirements, despite all afforded standardization. This interplay can be demonstrated almost classically with the example of group-widely integrated, highly standardized but simultaneously expensive ERP systems. They are very efficient but barely flexible. Alterations are often lengthy and necessitate new investments, oftentimes even before the investments have been amortized. Finding a smart balance is always a greater challenge.

Secondly, the proportion of routine activities will continuously decrease with a simultaneous rise in project activities. Organizational flexibility means providing sufficient project resources in an ever-increasing number of cases. This can occur through an explicit differentiation of roles and tasks, if, for example, single controlling functions are exclusively established for business support and project activity and thereby separated from reporting, or rather governance, functions. Alternately, the cooperation with external service suppliers (consultants) can be developed to a certain extent, in order to avoid increasing fixed cost. The general trend to a project-oriented organization remains in any case and must be answered organizationally.

4 Conclusion

Corporate controlling will be faced with many challenges, looming in the near future. The competences expected of corporate controllers increase. Additional fields must be harnessed. The finance expertise conceded controlling with must be supplemented considerably. A good management of a company requires a much stronger integration of financial, technological, legal, and social aspects than ever before.

If corporate controlling adapts their operating model comprehensively, then there is a good chance of it becoming the deciding power of this integration process. Consequently, it will retain both a substantial role in the corporation and a complex and interesting task field. Nonetheless, the risk remains significant: If controllers are unable to master this development, they can easily be marginalized. Different departments such as data science, sustainability, or compliance are available for taking on controlling tasks. So what can controllers do in order to prepare for the challenges of the next years?

First of all, it must react to these developments and demonstrate an openness for new tasks. Investments in education and training will be of utmost importance. Only through individual competences can the department en bloc master these challenges. Controllers must also improve their image. Due to its diversity and importance, controlling as a task enjoys a high degree of popularity. This task must however be marketed well, both internally and externally. There is no other way of inspiring the brightest minds, especially top young professionals. Finally, it is controllers themselves who can do the most in order to simultaneously contribute to the company and strengthen their own position.

References

Barth (2016) Planung im Zusammenhang mit der Bilanzierung und Bewertung nach IFRS. In: Becker W, Ulrich P (eds) Praxishandbuch Controlling. Springer Gabler, Wiesbaden, pp 529–549

Becker W, Ulrich P, Botzkowski T, Eurich S (2016) Controlling von Digitalisierungsprozessen – Veränderungstendenzen und empirische Erfahrungswerte aus dem Mittelstand. In: Obermaier R (ed) Industrie 4.0 als unternehmerische Gestaltungsaufgabe. Springer Gabler, Wiesbaden, pp 97–117

Behringer S (2014) Konzerncontrolling, 2nd edn. Springer, Heidelberg

Buschbacher F (2016) Wertschöpfung mit Big Data Analytics. In: Schäffer U, Weber J (eds) Controlling & Management Review. Springer, Wiesbaden, pp 40–45

Eberenz R (2014) Zum Zusammenhang von Steuerungs- und Transferpreiskonzept. In: Plate G (ed) Nordakademie-Forschung für die Wirtschaft, vol 3. Cuvillier Verlag, Göttingen, pp 31–45

Eiselmayer K, Kottbauer M (2015) Trends im Controlling, Controller Magazine 2:24–25

Graumann M, Grundei J (2015) Nachweis einer "angemessenen Information" im Sinne der Business Judgement Rule. ZCG:197–204

Hahn D, Hungenberg H (2001) PuK Planung und Kontrolle, Planungs- und Kontrollsysteme, Planungs- und Kostenrechnung, Wertorientierte Controllingkonzepte, 6th edn. Springer Gabler, Wiesbaden

Hentze J, Thies B (2014) Stakeholder-Management und Nachhaltigkeits-Reporting. Springer Gabler, Heidelberg

Horvath P, Gleich R, Seiter M (2015) Controlling, 13th edn. Vahlen, München

Lopatta K (2011) IFRS und Controlling. In: Funk W, Rossmanith J (eds) Internationale Rechnungslegung und internationales Controlling: Herausforderungen – Handlungsfelder – Erfolgspotenziale. Springer Gabler, Wiesbaden, pp 515–538

Stawinoga M, Velte P (2016) Der Referentenentwurf für ein CSR-Richtlinie-Umsetzungsgesetz – Eine erste Bestandsaufnahme unter besonderer Berücksichtigung der empirischen Relevanz des Deutschen Nachhaltigkeitskodex (DNK). Der Betrieb (DB):841–847

Velte P (2008) Management Approach. Zeitschrift für Planung und Unternehmenssteuerung 19:133–138

Weber J, Schäffer U (2014) Einführung in das Controlling, 14th edn. Vahlen, München

Weber J, Georg J, Janke R, Mack S (2012) Nachhaltigkeit und Controlling. Wiley, Weinheim

Weide G, Hoffjan A, Nevries P, Trapp R (2011) Organisatorisch-personelle Auswirkungen einer Integration des Rechnungswesens – eine empirische Analyse. ZfbF 63:63–86

Weißenberger BE, Wolf S, Neumann-Giesen A, Elbers G (2011) Controller als Business Partner: Ansatzpunkte für eine erfolgreiche Umsetzung des Rollenwandels. Zeitschrift für Controlling & Management (ZfCM):330–335

Prof. Dr. Ralf Eberenz serves as a senior advisor at Horváth & Partners and teaches business administration at the NORDAKADEMIE Graduate School in Elmshorn, Germany. He gained comprehensive practical experience in the consumer goods industry in various leadership positions at Beiersdorf. His major areas of expertise are strategic business management, management accounting, risk management, and mergers & acquisitions.

Prof. Dr. Stefan Behringer is Professor of Controlling and Corporate Governance at the NORDAKADEMIE in Elmshorn and Hamburg.

Revision of Financial Performance Management Systems in the Swarovski Group

Redesign and Harmonization of Heterogenic Performance Management Logics

Reto Andreoli and Beate Oberholzer

Abstract Business models of companies may change over time, new models may arise, and existing models may become obsolete. Consequently, the challenge is adapting performance management systems to changing requirements. The *Swarovski* Group has had to meet this challenge and has decided to modernize the group-wide financial performance management system.

Keywords Heterogeneous business models · Performance indicators · Performance management · Revision process · Swarovski Group · Profit-loss accounting

1 The Initial Situation for the Revision of the Swarovski Group's Company Performance Management

A well-developed database with performance indicators is an important instrument and requisite for a company's management.[1] The *Swarovski Group* is active in business areas with varying business models and organizational structures. In such

This contribution has been originally printed as Andreoli, R., Oberholzer, B. (2016): Überarbeitung der finanziellen Unternehmenssteuerung in der Swarovski-Gruppe, Zeitschrift Controlling, Volume 11-2016, pp. 664–671.

[1]Behringer (2014), p. 89.

R. Andreoli (✉)
Corporate Controlling, Daniel Swarovski Corporation AG, Männedorf, Switzerland

B. Oberholzer
Daniel Swarovski Corporation AG, Männedorf, Switzerland

M. Buttkus, R. Eberenz (eds.), *Performance Management in Retail and the Consumer Goods Industry*, https://doi.org/10.1007/978-3-030-12730-5_21

a heterogenic environment, the concentration of performance indicators places additional requirements on the configuration of financial reporting.[2] Moreover, emphasis has shifted from B2B to B2C within the Swarovski Group. All this had led to a situation in which data available on group and business levels yielded insufficient data for an adequate performance management. The implementation of short-term requirements in order to reach a company objective, for example, could only be monitored inconveniently on all hierarchal levels. Key figures were also not continuously available in the areas of liquidity (e.g., operating cash flow) and value contribution (e.g., ROCE). Consequently, breaking down and retracing objectives in these areas were impossible. Moreover, this led to instances where missing information was levied by parallel data supply and the reporting process becoming more ineffective altogether.

1.1 The Swarovski Group

The *Swarovski Group* comprises *Swarovski Optik*, the manufacturer of precision instruments such as telescopes and binoculars; *Tyrolit*, the leading manufacturer of bonded grinding, cutting, sawing, drilling, and dressing tools and a system supplier of tools and machines for the construction industry; and lastly the business area *Swarovski Crystal Business* (SCB; see further explanations below). The Swarovski Group generated revenue valuing 3.36 billion euro in the year 2016 and engages approximately 32,000 employees. The company is owned by the families *Swarovski*, *Weis*, and *Frey*. All three business areas are run operatively by respective executive boards and are supervised by the advisory board which is constituted by six family members.

1.2 The Business Area Swarovski Crystal Business (SCB)

The business area SCB designs, manufactures, and sells highest-quality crystal and genuine gemstones and created stones as well as finished products such as jewelry, accessories, and lighting solutions worldwide. What started as a small crystal manufacturing business in Wattens, Austria, has grown to be a global group of companies. With a rich history and a culture of technological leadership, *Swarovski* is committed to growth and to maintaining its place at the forefront of design, creativity, and technological innovation. *Swarovski* products are available in about 170 countries, and the group has production sites in Austria, India, Liechtenstein, Thailand, Vietnam, Serbia, and the USA. Revenue generated by SCB in 2016

[2]Behringer (2014), p. 89, Niebecker and Kirchmann (2011), pp. 51–52.

amounts to 2.6 billion euro and was obtained with approximately 27,000 employees. The executive board of the business area SCB is constituted by five family members.

1.3 The Initial Situation for the Revision of Company Performance Management

For decades, business clients were the most important division within the business area SCB. Crystal products that are sold to B2B customers have always been self-produced. With entering the consumer goods business in the 1980s, *Swarovski* is now strongly represented in retail trade with 2,800 boutiques, of which 1,410 are run internally. Nowadays, consumer goods business represents the largest business area within SCB. Other units within SCB operate in segments such as genuine gemstones, created stones, lighting solutions, and traffic safety. Figure 1 illustrates the management structures within the business area crystal.

The developments in these business units resulted in performance management logics that no longer completely fit the altered business models and entailed an increase in both the heterogeneity of business models and the implemented performance management logics, especially due to the growth of a B2C business parallel to a traditionally strong B2B business, as well as different organizational structures within business units. It is in light of this setting that this contribution aims at demonstrating how an according project for the revision of company performance management could be designed and, in the course thereof, how the harmonization of performance management logics could also be facilitated. The initial situation of the *Swarovski Group* was illustrated to this purpose. In the following, project objectives and general conditions will be specified. Subsequently, the development of functional profit-loss accounting and the development of balance sheets, as well as their implementation in IT systems, will be analyzed as substantial components of this project. Finally, significant challenges of such a project will be discussed with experiences made by the *Swarovski Group*.

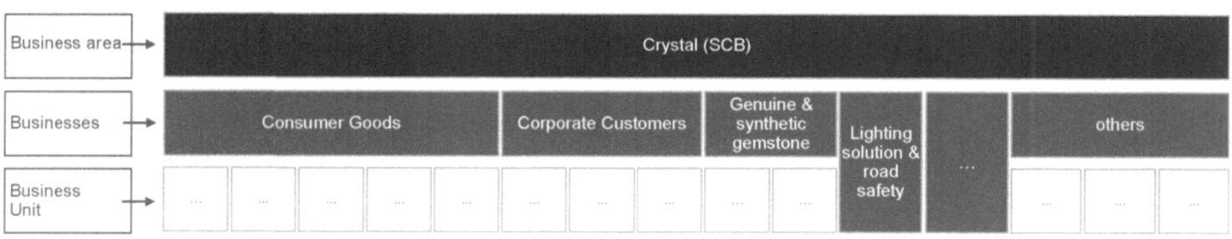

Fig. 1 Management structure of the business area, Swarovski crystal business

2 The Project's Background for the Revision of Financial Performance Management

The financial performance management logic was especially aligned with the requirements of the company client business, as well as production's performance management. The main area of financial performance management was a multilevel contribution margin accounting in which costs are allocated according to their function.[3] Essentially, this is largely based on a profit-loss account according to the cost-of-sales method as a result. For each business unit (see Fig. 1), a GM1 to GM was depicted, and GM4 was, respectively, only shown on business field levels. After GM4, no expenses (especially overheads) were allocated to the business segments, and no EBIT per business field or business unit was shown. Apart from details concerning investments in property assets, these were the only financial information available group-wide on a business field level. Within the business fields themselves, further operative information existing in reporting systems (e.g., Retail-KPIs, Revenue per Shop and Day, Cost Centers/Profit Center Information) was steered. Listed competitors usually disclose figures according to common profit-loss positions such as operating profit or EBIT. As the Swarovski Group did not have these performance indicators available periodically and in standard reporting, an external comparison (competitor benchmark) was complicated.

In order to create an external IFRS statement, legal units raised profit-loss,[4] balance, and cash flow accounting which then needed to be consolidated on group level in order to establish group financial statements. On the basis of this data, a large number of KPIs such as working capital indicators or free cash flow can be calculated. However, it was this transparency that was lacking for business fields and units.

Local companies usually report a profit-loss account according to the total cost method. Consequently, data was available on both a legal and SCB level, according to cost category. This necessitated the upkeep of an internal (multilevel contribution margin accounting) as well as an external reporting. Ultimately, the lack of transparency on business field level as well as on business unit level was the initiator of the project *SEFIR* (*Swarovski* enhanced financial reporting) launch.

[3]Coenenberg et al. (2016), pp. 226.

[4]IAS 1.10.

3 Project Objectives and Requirements for the Development of an Indicator Set

As the use of a performance management system absolutely necessitates supplying decision-makers with relevant and high-quality information,[5] the *Swarovski Group* project's main target setting consists of increased *transparency* on both business field and business unit level, thereby also providing management with financial indicators. This also gives management the opportunity to intervene and engage in *competitor benchmarking* more easily. The development of *continuously multilevel performance management logics* for the company should also include reaching a *standardization and harmonization of performance management logics*. In doing so, the central secondary condition was to not increase *complexity* further but on the contrary *reduce* it (see Fig. 2). To reach these objectives, an indicator set was developed (see Fig. 3).

In doing so, a substantial task was a comprehensive definition of a performance indicator repertoire, exceeding the dimensions of growth and profitability. The focus that had previously rested on SCB and revenue growth as well DB4 profitability should prospectively play an important role in the dimensions of investment, liquidity, and value contribution and thus lead to balanced relation between performance indicators and a holistic performance management. Depending on the management level, different performance indicators may be relevant. In the future, for instance, no free cash flow (FCF) of return on capital employed (ROCE) performance indicators are calculated and reported on the level of business units. The main reason for this is largely that balance positions such as production facilities or store fittings cannot be assigned directly to a business unit. This would lead to a very high

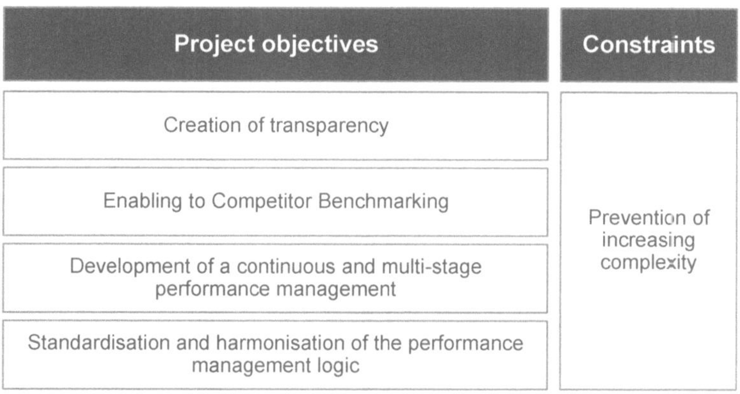

Fig. 2 Overview of project objectives

[5]Christ et al. (2016), p. 36.

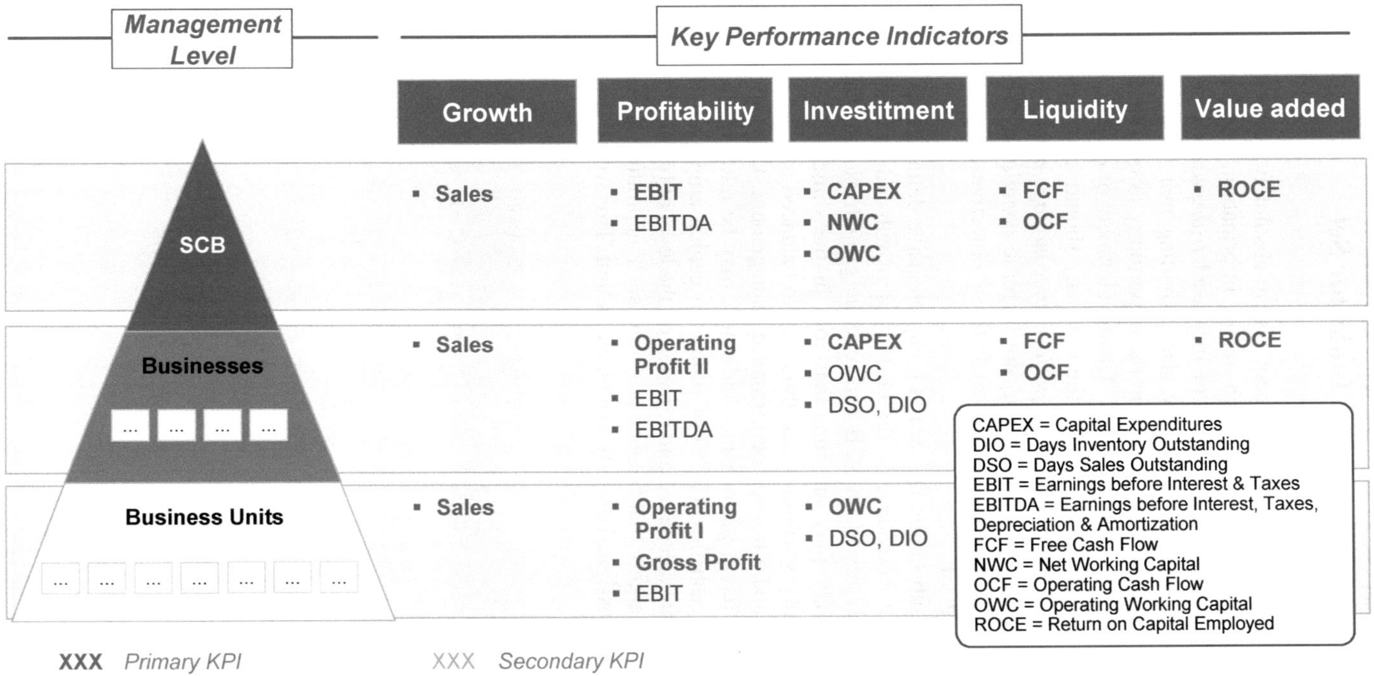

Fig. 3 Key performance indicators relevant for each management level

share of encoded positions and, consequently, to a highly limited significance of respective performance indicators. Conversely, strongly operative performance indicators such as Operating Profit I will play a subordinate role to SCB management. In order for performance indicators to fulfill their performance management function, they must be adaptable.[6] Therefore, it was important for *Swarovski* to define performance indicators per management level that were alterable by the respective management stage and that could be aggregated toward the top (Fig. 3).

A further target set consisted of merging the internal and external presentation of profit-loss accounts. In the future, a single harmonized view that aids the prevention of inefficient coordination and confusion is aimed at.

4 The Composition of Functional Profit-Loss Accounting

This new profit-loss accounting has high relevance for performance management logic. On one hand, certain performance indicators can be gathered from it (e.g., EBIT), and on the other, it serves as basis for the calculation of relation performance indicators (e.g., ROCE). In this form of presentation, a hybrid model using revenue and total cost methods is used. Nonetheless, the primary structure is dictated by the cost-of-sales method which has more international validity than the total cost method.[7] The costs are structured according to the functions sales and distribution and administration respective to the gross margin and are then further divided into appropriate sub-functions. The transparency of underlying cost drivers (viz., cost categories such as employees, rents, communication efforts, amortizations) was requested for performance management. Cost categories per sub-function were also included into this structure. This enables a representation of the profit-loss account according to the total cost method. The companies *Tyrolit* and *Swarovski Optik*—in contrast to SCB—will still be managed according to the total cost method. However, the crystal sector also gains highly relevant additional information to performance management, concerning how costs per sub-function can be decoded into cost categories. This transparency was preciously lacking in the business area SCB on both business field and business unit level.

In order to be able to utilize this newly formulated logic of indicator systems and profit-loss accounting for the performance management of their respective fields, responsible business persons have contributed largely to the project and have coined the structure significantly. It is because of this that a further element is needed to be integrated into the profit-loss account: the multiple stages that are known from contribution margin accounting. Consequently, before EBIT, three operating profit levels are levied to determine respective performance according to accountability (see Fig. 4).

[6]Küpper et al. (2013), p. 473.

[7]Reuter and Zwirner (2003), p. 622.

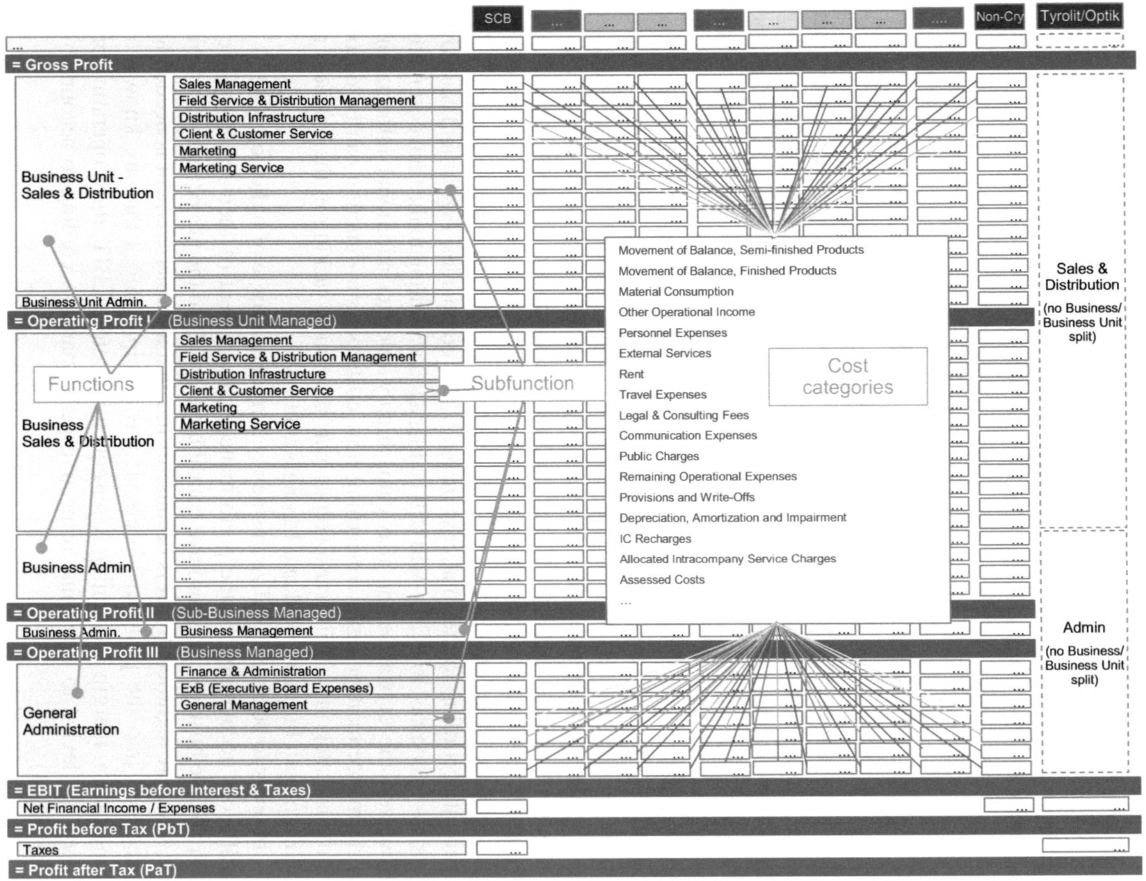

Fig. 4 Structure of the functional profit and loss accountant (extract)

In detail, this means that business unit managers are responsible for Operating Profit I, sub-business managers for Operating Profit II, and business managers for Operating Profit III and can directly influence their results up to this level.

Furthermore, an integration of the responsible business persons in question is important to the approval of this performance indicator system.[8]

The various business models and organizational structures within SCB lead to certain functions appearing repeatedly within the profit-loss structure (e.g., marketing or business management), in order to reflect respective accountability according to level. On the SCB level, these could be aggregated when necessary. For the account of EBIT according to business fields and units, overhead costs must be encoded. Encodings should only be undertaken, if and when costs (e.g., via distinctly assigned cost centers) are no longer directly assignable (e.g., costs of corporate functions). However, as cost responsibility is clearly identifiable with multilevel profit-loss accounting (Operating Profit I to III), cost allocation—which is oftentimes considered to be unjust—through keys will lead to less discussion. Keys are defined as budgeted revenue, in order to meet internal requirements (transparent and plausible, easy to understand/determine, constant, not in constant flux, and with little room for interpretation and influence). In non-operative companies (holdings, financial, or management companies), the planned group revenue is used as key.

The profit-loss positions following the EBIT level are no longer distributed on stores, as the taxation effort and especially financial results can only be influenced by business units on a marginal level—if at all—and the significance of the encoded results would consequently be very limited.

5 The Composition of Balances

Some of the newly formed performance indicators are directly derived from balance sheet positions (e.g., net working capital) or are partially determined by changes in balance sheet positions (e.g., free cash flow). Consequently, balance sheets should be subdivided according to business fields and business units. In this process, this subdivision would only be undertaken for balance sheet positions that are required for the calculation of defined performance indicators. That is to say, for the following balance sheet items:

- Trade receivables
- Other working capital
- Inventory
- Assets
- Fixed immaterial assets

[8]Küpper et al. (2013), p. 481.

- Goodwill
- Liabilities from supplies and services

As previously with profit-loss accounting, the underlying principle remains that the allocation according to business fields should primarily occur directly and only rarely and limited to situations in which this is not possible and utilize the revenue key for distribution purposes.

6 The Implementation Within IT Systems

The *Swarovski Group* effectively had two solutions for the implementation of the new performance management logic to choose from:

- Implementation within the ERP systems of local companies
- Implementation on group level by means of a reporting solution

The decision for a group-wide implementation on local ERP systems had many reasons, as this would yield better use in the long run. This is especially true, since only this solution approach ensures that the whole organization functions according to the same performance management logic. Nonetheless, this surely entails the disadvantage that its implementation takes longer and causes more expenses.

Most of the SCB business area's reporting units (mostly also a legal corporation) have *SAP* in use as an ERP system. Further, these corporations already have an interface for the consolidation tool *IBM Cognos Controller*, and most of the data is uploaded in an automatized manner. The environment of these finance and reporting systems as well as the respective data stream is depicted in Fig. 5.

Requirements that resulted from the project made the data supply mask significantly more extensive. This is largely due to the fact that reporting units not only demand a functional profit-loss account according to businesses and business unit but also the creation of a breakdown according to cost category according to sub-function. All the more reason why the demand of keeping efforts for local corporations as low as possible, by deducting this data from the ERP system via an automatized interface, is very distinct.

Reducing the complexity of the systems and reaching a greater consistency of data have been successful due to the elimination of contribution margin accounts for group purposes and thanks to the use of special ledgers in *SAP F1*. The most important changes in finance and reporting systems, as well as data flow, have been depicted in Fig. 5 using dashed lines.

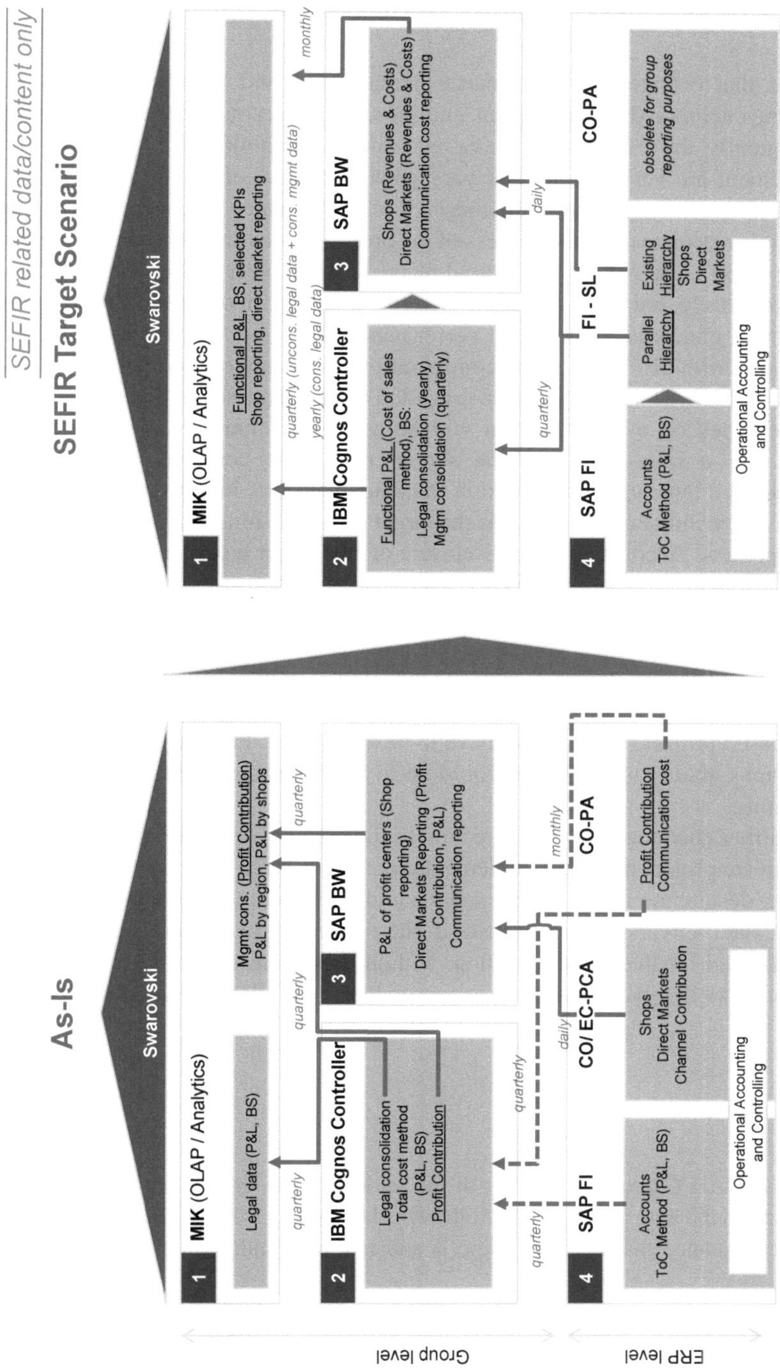

Fig. 5 Finance/reporting systems and data streams (simplified)

7 The Central Challenges of a Project for the Revision of Company Performance Management

Projects that change the performance management and reporting structures are oftentimes compared to an incision into the central nervous system of a company. Consequently, the respective interests regarding the definition of future performance management are very distinct and vary greatly. *Christ*[9] offers an overview of the various influencing factors on the redesign of performance management systems.

For this reason and for the success of the project, it was crucial to define the extent of the project clearly during the initial phase of the project and in particular, not to define to loosely, but much rather differentiate it clearly, in order to minimize project risks. Other concerns connected to performance management that were deliberately not tackled with *SEFIR* (e.g., the configuration of operative reporting, the introduction of *S/4 HANA Finance*, the modernization of the business intelligence landscape) were recorded on a roadmap and will be addressed after the implementation of SEFIR. As a result, it could be shown that these concerns did not remain unrecognized but can be addressed in the course of other initiatives/projects.

One of the initial challenges was the target of establishing a simple comparability to competitors. Accordingly, the disclosure of EBITs per business field and business unit is absolutely necessary. This necessitates either a redistribution of overheads via keys or the introduction of a differentiated settlement model that encompasses services received. In the course of this, the allocation of directly unassignable costs was chosen, in order to ensure that a settlement logic (which is already used for IT services, for instance) with an exceedingly high administrative effort, resulting in increased project risks, did not have to be introduced. In doing so, accompanying discussions about "unfair" keys could be avoided through a multilevel profit-loss accounting.

A further challenge was the transition to the predominant *ERP SAP R/3*. In order to minimize project risks, the implementation of *S/4 Hana Finance* was deliberately forgone, despite the fact that this model could have met additional requirements via the so-called universal ledgers. Instead, the possibility of "special ledgers" in *SAP R/3* was used for the implementation, without having to undertake a change—and both the risks involved in and the expenses for a new ERP financing module.

8 Conclusion

The *Swarovski Group* is currently in the middle of the implementation phase. The transition to the new structure will follow on January 1, 2017. With the transition to a new performance management logic, a substantial foundation is laid for a holistic

[9] Christ (2015), p. 221.

company management. Naturally, performance management is multifaceted and encompasses far more aspects than are covered by this contribution. Consequently, questions on planning, frequency and depth of reporting, incentive, finance, or reporting systems are related thereto.[10] After the completed definition performance management logic, the simplification of planning and in course thereof also that of calculation logic of variable compensation, which is also strongly linked to the budget, has now become the topic of discussion. The future finance and reporting system landscape will also be subjected to testing, and a concept for the consolidation of these systems is in progress.

All the above elements have great significance to company performance management, and alterations should be well-considered and planned. Due to the central importance of a functioning management and with thought to risk prevention, it is important to develop alterations sequentially rather than tackling all elements simultaneously. Furthermore, it is recommendable to first define content logic (Which performance indicators are necessary?) before subsequently adapting system landscape, planning, and incentive systems where needed.

References

Behringer S (2014) Konzerncontrolling, 2nd edn. Springer, Berlin

Christ H (2015) Redesign von Performance Management Systemen – Gestaltungsparameter und Einflussfaktoren. Shaker, Aachen

Christ H, Epple W, Hofmann F, Pedell B (2016) Systematische Performance Management System-Weiterentwicklung im Mercedes-Benz Kundencenter Sindelfingen/Rastatt. Controlling 28:36–44. https://doi.org/10.15358/0935-0381-2016-1-36

Coenenberg AG, Fischer TM, Günther T (2016) Kostenrechnung und Kostenanalyse, 9th edn. Schäffer Poeschel, Stuttgart

IAS 1, latest update 2014

Küpper H-U, Friedl G, Hofmann C, Hofmann Y, Pedell B (2013) Controlling – Konzeption, Aufgaben, Instrumente, 6th edn. Schäffer-Poeschel, Stuttgart

Niebecker J, Kirchmann M (2011) Group Reporting und Konsolidierung. Schäffer-Poeschel, Stuttgart

Paul J (2014) Beteiligungscontrolling und Konzerncontrolling. Springer Gabler, Wiesbaden

Reuter M, Zwirner C (2003) Erfolgsrechnung nach dem Umsatzkostenverfahren – Konzeption und Praxis. Betrieb und Wirtschaft 57(15):617–622

Reto Andreoli is Head of Corporate Controlling with Daniel Swarovski Corporation AG, Männedorf ZH/Switzerland.

Beate Oberholzer operates as Project Manager of SEFIR with Daniel Swarovski Corporation AG, Männedorf ZH/Switzerland.

[10]For an example Paul (2014), pp. 617–622.

Marketing and Controlling as Business Partners in the FMCG Industry

Franziska Schmiedebach-Ullner

Abstract This contribution analyzes the changing role of marketing in the FMCG industry and the corresponding implications for controllers to be real business partners. The author outlines the key marketing success factors to build and manage strong brands and deduces from these factors the required data information and controlling tools.

Keywords Brand essence · Brand positioning · Choice surplus · Consumer products industry · Data management · Differentiation

1 Introduction

Having worked as Head of Global Marketing in the consumer products industry for more than 30 years, I was more than surprised when my former finance colleague asked me whether I would write a contribution about what marketing in the FMCG industry expects from controlling[1] so that they are seen as real business partners and not as number crunchers. My first thought was: "Do marketing people really want controlling to be a business partner?" and if not, "what would controlling have to deliver, in order to be seen as a real business partner in the future?" Without doubt, both disciplines have different mindsets and different roles in the organization: marketing focusing on the consumer and controlling focusing on profits. But doesn't

An adaption of this contribution has been originally printed as Schmiedebach-Ullner, F. (2014), *Controlling als Business Partner des Marketing in der Konsumgüterindustrie*, Buttkus, M. in Controlling in der Konsumgüterindustrie: Innovative Ansätze und Praxisbeispiele, 2014, pages 91–108.

[1]The author uses the English word "controlling" to translate the German term "controlling." Please refer to the discussion in the preface.

F. Schmiedebach-Ullner (✉)
Care 4 Brands Consulting, Hamburg, Germany

M. Buttkus, R. Eberenz (eds.), *Performance Management in Retail and the Consumer Goods Industry*, https://doi.org/10.1007/978-3-030-12730-5_22

a company need both to be successful? And if both worked better together, wouldn't that be an opportunity for the company to be more successful? Success is always a team performance, in which everyone has a different role to play. The aim of this contribution is therefore to outline the changing role of marketing in the challenging FMCG industry and how controlling can be a better business partner in supporting marketing in this changing role.

2 Marketing Challenges in the Consumer Products Industry

Like every marketing person, a marketing controller needs to understand the industry in which the company is situated. What is the market? Who are the key players? What are the barriers to entry? What are the competitive challenges? What are the key factors that will lead the company or the brand to success?

The markets and challenges in the consumer products industry have changed dramatically in recent years. Technological advancement and social change are reshaping business. Factors such as the speed of innovation, social media, and corporate citizenship are having a major impact on marketing and have dramatically changed the rules of the marketing game.

One of the key challenges that marketing is facing today is an overwhelming explosion of product choices. We are living in a world of surplus: a surplus of product variants, a surplus of brands, and a surplus of manufacturers. Just think of the number of variants a consumer can choose from when standing in front of a hair care or toothpaste shelf in the supermarket. It has been estimated that an average supermarket in the USA carries 40,000 SKUs (standard stocking units), but an average family gets 80–85% of its needs from only 150 SKUs. This means that 39,850 SKUs will most probably be ignored. This complexity of choices is not only confusing for the consumer, but it also poses a key challenge for marketing. How to stand out in this mass of product and brand choices? How to be different? More than ever before, marketing needs to clearly differentiate its brand and products from those of competition. Differentiation is the cornerstone to survive in today's competitive market place. To put it bluntly: either you differentiate or die.

The key role and challenge for marketing is to find a relevant and unique point of difference for its brand, a brand positioning. Positioning is how you differentiate your product or brand in the mind of the consumer. I will come back to this later.

Despite this surplus of choices and the increasing need to differentiate in the market, new products are being launched at an ever-increasing rate. It is estimated that 30,000 new SKUs are launched in the consumer products industry in Germany every year. At most only one third of these products survive on the retailer's shelf in the first year. Approximately 70% disappear from the shelf in the first 12 months. In the perfume market alone, 200 new fragrances are launched in Germany every year. Only 10% survive the first year. With a flop rate for new products of 70%, marketing needs to find better processes and tools that ensure that new products are relevant and differentiating and can convince and bond consumers over time.

Hand in hand with an overwhelming explosion of new products, consumers are being bombarded with ever more advertising messages. Research indicates that we are exposed to 5000 brand messages per day. No wonder that people are either bored or irritated by this overflow of information and thus are avoiding or ignoring classical advertising as such. Although consumers are turning away from classical advertising, they are better informed than ever. With the Internet and the use of social media, blogs, and user reviews, it is easy for customers to compare product features and prices and to obtain user recommendations that will help them form an opinion about the quality of the product and make a purchase decision for or against a brand. The Internet has changed the way consumers make purchase decisions and the way companies need to be communicating with their users. Today consumers believe more in recommendations by friends than in advertising messages by brands. The big challenge for marketing in the consumer products industry is therefore to find new efficient ways to communicate with their target group in an authentic, inspiring, and involving way that builds credibility, trust, and desirability toward the brand, the company, and its products over time. As Interbrand's study on the Best Global Brands reveals, marketing leaders need to ensure that "brands and consumers are working in tandem to create shared value." Many companies and marketers seem not to have realized that yet.

Furthermore, marketing needs to realize that not only the consumer's opinion is increasingly shaping the image and demand for a brand but also consumer organizations like Foodwatch and Stiftung Warentest as well as NGOs like Greenpeace are increasingly watching the business practices of large corporations and critically evaluating whether these companies are behaving in an ethical and sustainable way. Corporate behavior is constantly being scrutinized to whether organizations are delivering contrary to their brand promise and corporate values. Thanks to Twitter and Facebook, misbehavior and bad performance are communicated quickly across the Internet reaching millions of consumers in a matter of seconds. If not managed properly, these mistakes can potentially ruin a company's or brand's reputation overnight. Corporate citizenship is therefore no longer a nice-to-have "add-on" but a need-to-have corporate behavior that leaders must implant in their organization to ensure that all corporate measures and activities build credibility and trust in a sustainable and long-term way.

3 The Role of Marketing in the FMCG Industry

In this dynamic and ever-changing market place, the key role and responsibility of marketing is—more than ever before—*brand leadership. Brand leadership* means the ability to successfully build and manage strong brands over time, so that they deliver long-term profitable growth for the company.

Strong brands are a company's most valuable asset. They play a significant role in enhancing a company's business performance, primarily through their influence on three key stakeholder groups: (current and potential) consumers, employees, and investors. Strong brands have the power to influence consumer choice and to create loyalty; they have the power to attract, retain, and motivate talent, and they have the power to lower the cost of financing.

Measuring the success of marketing is about measuring how successful marketing has been in building strong brands. The best internal measure of a brand's success is long-term sales and profitability. The best external measure of a brand's success is market share in the relevant segment, brand likeability, and brand loyalty. Awareness in itself does not identify the strength of a brand. The positive emotional bond the brand has with the consumer is more important: the brand likeability. For consumers to like a brand, they must first know it. Strong brands are therefore both present in consumers' minds (high awareness) and have a positive meaning (high likeability). Strong brands are trusted and evoke desirability. These are the factors that determine the strength of a brand. Therefore, these factors should also be the key performance indicators (KPIs) by which marketing is measured.

For controlling to be an effective business partner, it is decisive that they realize that for marketing, it is important to work with hard data and to achieve results. Controlling will be a real business partner when they provide marketing with the key data and tools that marketing needs to efficiently and effectively manage their business and processes. This means differentiating important facts from unimportant ones. No matter how big or small a company, controlling should not drown the organization with data and processes—that's when controlling becomes a barrier. They should be collecting and regularly monitoring the decisive facts that are important for determining how well the business is performing and giving marketing the tools to manage their business processes efficiently and effectively. These tools should be easy to handle, and the data that is generated should be prepared in such a way that it quickly and easily generates actionable, intelligent insights on how to move the business forward.

4 The Key Success Factors of Brand Leadership

For marketing to be successful at Brand Leadership, that is, to be successful at building and managing brands over time, it needs:

4.1 Consumer Understanding

Excellent consumer and market understanding is the most important prerequisite for marketing to be successful at Brand Leadership. Marketing should be obsessed with understanding their consumer. It is amazing in how many consumer products companies this is still not a given.

A company usually makes 80% of its sales with 20% of its clients. Similarly, a brand usually gets 80% of its revenue from 20% of its consumers. These are a brand's loyal user. Marketing should know everything about their loyal users, who they are in terms of sociodemographics, where they live, what they read, where they surf and buy, what they do in their free time, what other brands they use, what car they drive, etc. Marketing should generate deep insights from consumer's attitudes, usage behaviors, and needs toward the category and the brands. Of course, market research is the most important business partner for generating these insights and providing marketing with the relevant data. However, real consumer-oriented organizations do not only rely on data. They are *connected* with the consumer. They encourage their people to meet consumers in person, at the point of sale, or at the point of usage. They actively seek the consumer's opinion and experience, they let consumers share their experience on their blog, they specifically recruit users to test new products, they let consumers design packaging and improve products, and they encourage them to develop brand clips on YouTube. In summary, they connect with consumers on eye level.

It would be good for controlling, especially for marketing controllers, to connect with consumers on eye level every once in a while. This experience will make controllers realize what is important for the success of a company: brands and consumers working in tandem to create shared value. Establishing a long-term bond between consumers and the brand is the only way for a FMCG company to achieve long-term success. If controlling internalizes this in their business thinking and daily work, then they have the foundation for being a real business partner for marketing.

Deep consumer understanding also involves regular tracking and exploring of key parameters that will impact people's future lives. Demographic development is one of these key parameters. As an example, demographic trends show an increasing aging of the population in the Western world, as people are living longer and the baby boomers are getting older. This trend will increasingly impact the consumer products industry, especially industries like the health and beauty sectors, as well as the retail sector. It will influence the type of benefits that will be more relevant or the way consumers will be shopping in the future. As an illustration, by the year 2030, every second German will be 50 plus. That means antiaging products will become more relevant than anti-pimple sticks; neighborhood shopping and home delivery will become more important than driving to the big supermarket; Internet usage will increase dramatically (from 54% to 84%) in the age group 60–69 because tomorrow's 60 year olds are 40 today and 84% of them are already using the Internet. They will not be changing their online habits upon growing older. These are only a few examples of how deep consumer understanding, based both on qualitative and quantitative data, is essential for both marketing and controlling to derive valuable insights on how to better connect with consumers today and in the future. This is necessary to build long-term consumer loyalty and therewith secure the long-term profitable growth of the company.

4.2 Differentiating Positioning

In today's competitive market place with its surplus of products, brands, and suppliers, it's critically important for a successful brand to have a relevant and differentiating positioning. Positioning is defined as how you differentiate your brand in the mind of your consumer.

A good positioning starts with being very clear about the *target market* (Fig. 1) you will be competing in and the *key competitive players* you will be competing against. Secondly, and more importantly, a positioning should clearly indicate "who is my *target group*" or "who is going to buy me." I am amazed to see how many marketing people are not precise in defining their core target group. This is probably one of the biggest wastes of resources for many companies. Marketing and controllers should be aware that trying to target everyone or being too general about your target group in the hopes of getting a larger slice of the market is like shooting in the dark. You're bound to hit something after a while, but it will cost the company a lot of money and time. Being precise about the target group is the key to an excellent positioning, and it is key to an efficient and effective use of financial resources. It has influence on everything you do, your marketing strategy, your advertising strategy,

Fig. 1 Brand positioning wheel (Source: CARE 4 Brands Consulting)

and your communication material, just about anything that has to do with your brand. A clearly defined target group is the key for marketing and controlling to ensure that investments are spent in an efficient and effective way.

The *consumer insight* explains the core emotional and functional need of the target group upon which the brand is built. The *brand benefit* answers the consumer need in terms of what functional or emotional benefit the brand can deliver to meet the core consumer need. The *reason-to-believe* describes the unique features the brand has to offer—that are better than completion in delivering the benefits consumer want.

The *brand personality* describes the human characteristics and values of the brand. Brand personality has an important psychological function by either allowing consumers to identify with it or to project themselves into it. As product benefits become increasingly interchangeable, brand personality is a key tool for brands to create differentiation and relevance for the consumer. The *discriminator* pinpoints the most distinguishing brand attributes and behaviors.

Finally, the *brand essence* brings all these elements together in two or three words. It articulates the primary message you want to deliver about the brand that meets both a core consumer need and differentiates it from competition. For BMW, this core message is "the pleasure of driving," for NIVEA "feel the care," and for Coke "happiness."

Once marketing has defined the brand essence, it is their role and responsibility to make sure that every aspect of the brand's marketing activities is in line with it. If the brand promise is, for example, "safety," like it is for Volvo, then safety will be the benchmark for all new product development projects and for every marketing and communication activity of the company. Everyone in the organization—marketing, agencies, sales, R&D, production, customer service, etc.—should have a clear understanding of the brand essence and the overall positioning. The role of controlling can be key in monitoring and benchmarking how well the brand essence is being delivered in the organization. For example, how well the brand essence is delivered in the development of new products or how well it is being communicated on the website or in other advertising material. Furthermore, they can benchmark whether the marketing strategy addresses a clearly defined target group and if the media strategy, product concept, and advertising are synchronized with this target group. This is where so much marketing money is being wasted: on new product development that doesn't deliver on the brand essence or communication that doesn't resonate with the core target groups.

4.3 Convincing Product Offer

One of marketing's key roles is to ensure that the brand has a convincing product offer for its target group. In the FMCG industry, the product is at the heart of the brand. It is what the company must tell about the brand. It determines the consumer's experience with the brand. That's why designing and delivering a product that fully satisfies consumer's needs and wants is a prerequisite for successful marketing. All products within the brand portfolio must be designed, manufactured, marketed, sold, delivered, and serviced in a way that create a positive brand image and that deliver on the brand essence. Marketing controlling can help ensure that product features, which are essential to delivering the brand essence, are benchmarked and monitored throughout product development process and are tested with consumers on a regular basis.

Perceived quality and pricing plays a major role in whether a consumer is convinced of a brand's product offer and is willing to purchase it or not. On the other hand, price is the one revenue-generating element of the marketing mix. Setting the right price is therefore one of marketing's most important yet challenging roles, because it directly impacts consumers' willingness to pay and simultaneously impacts the revenues and profitability of a brand. This is where controlling can be a real business partner for marketing. Setting the right price starts with having the right data. This sounds easy, but if you have ever worked in an international corporation that works across many regions and markets, this already poses a problem. Every marketing person would dream about a data bank where at a push of the button you can see competitive prices across key markets for your category in a readable and a manageable way. Secondly, you need reliable product costs. Usually this data is easily available for existing products but not for new ones. As different departments need to calculate and estimate their part of the product cost—R&D for the formula, supply chain for the packaging, production, and logistics—this takes time and needs coordination. This is where marketing controlling can be a real support in making the data available and developing different scenarios in terms of consumer price points and impact on profitability. Excellent marketing people will try to find the highest price point the consumer is willing to pay, at the highest profitability margin for the brand because the higher the margin, the more opportunity there is to invest in marketing and sales activities. Price elasticity tests are important tools to define the optimum consumer price point. The more innovative the product, the more willingly a consumer will pay a higher price. Calculating, monitoring, and analyzing margin contribution are key tools that marketing controlling should be providing. The same applies for price setting and monitoring.

Assortment management is a further key role in which marketing needs the support of controlling. Regular monitoring and reviews of product sales performance are key to managing the portfolio. When new products are launched, they should be exchanged for weak performers. Sales benchmarks for categories and a yearly ABC analysis, to eliminate low performing products, are key tools to help reduce assortment complexity.

4.4 Consumer Involved Communication

Consumers are being bombarded with advertising messages they either do not want to hear or do not believe. A recent study by Nielsen in Germany, regarding those advertising touch points that consumers trust most, reveals that only 25% of respondents trust in the classical advertising touch points such as ads in TV, print, or radio. On the other hand, 88% of respondents trust in recommendations by friends. Sixty-four percent of respondents trust in online consumer reviews. On a worldwide basis, even 70% of respondents trust in digital word-of-mouth recommendations. Despite this fact most money is still being spent on classical advertising formats. The reason for this is the incomparably high reach that classical advertising still has. That's why it will most probably remain an important touch point for FMCG brands to reach their target audience. Nevertheless, marketing needs to find better ways to connect with consumers on eye level. Involving the consumer with the brand, letting them share their experience, actively seeking their opinion on new products, and letting them design new packaging or create their own online videos are the way forward to building a long-term relationship between the brand and its user. Communicating with consumers on eye level is what creates brand desirability and brand loyalty. FMCG companies like Procter & Gamble are spending 25–30% of their budget on online communication. Marketing and controlling need to work hand in hand in testing and monitoring what methods and touch points are the most effective and efficient ways to build this eye level connection with their target group.

4.5 An Integrated Marketing Mix

The most efficient and effective way to allocate marketing resources is to ensure that the marketing mix is fully integrated to deliver one consistent brand promise to the selected target group. Every consumer touch point, the POS, the packaging, the website, the customer service, or the online blog, should build upon the brand's core promise and help build brand desirability and brand loyalty.

Integrated marketing communication should be like a symphony. Each contact point is significant, and at the same time, it does not promote exactly the same idea as other contact points. Undoubtedly, everything should play together in a consistent way. This requires the alignment of all communication tools to ensure that the consumer experiences the brand in a consistent way in several contexts.

A fully integrated marketing communication should not implicitly use all possible points of contact, but it should consider that the classical, linear purchasing funnel from (1) awareness, (2) familiarity, (3) consideration, (4) purchase, and (5) loyalty has changed. Today the purchasing decision is more like a cycle or like a spiral as depicted in Fig. 2.

In step 1, the consumer considers an initial set of brands, based on their brand perceptions and exposure to recent touch points. In step 2, consumers gather information and actively evaluate what they want. They either add or delete brands from their relevant set. In step 3, the consumer ultimately selects a brand at the moment of purchase. In step 4, after purchasing the product, the consumer builds expectations based on his experience with the brand. If the post purchase experience was positive, it will automatically trigger the next purchasing cycle on impulse. This is the loyalty spiral.

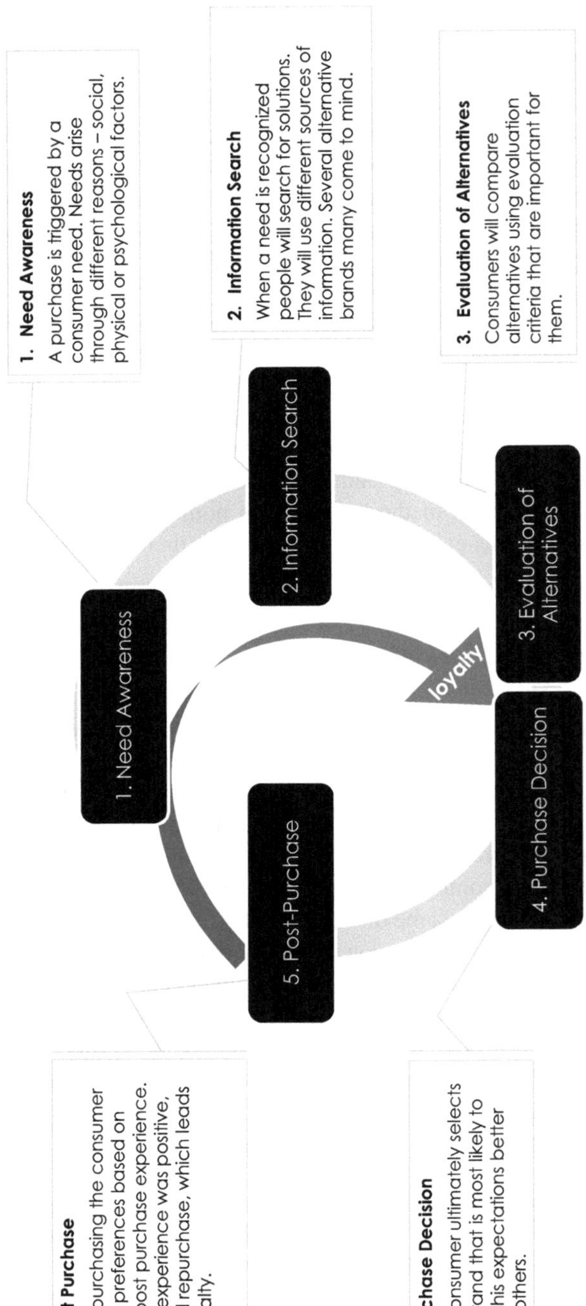

Fig. 2 The purchase cycle (Source: CARE 4 BRANDS Consulting)

The brand touch points in step 1 (advertising) and in step 3 (POS) are well known to marketing; however in today's online world, marketing needs to ensure that there are enough touch points in step 2, for consumers to actively inform themselves and evaluate the brand, and in step 4 where they can contribute and share their experience with the brand. Today you need the same impact online as offline. Similar numbers will visit a brand online as those who visit them in a store. Both the website and the store need to be as impressive and impactful as each other.

4.6 *Clarity in Strategy*

Apart from having a differentiating brand positioning and ensuring that the marketing mix is fully integrated, marketing needs to develop a clear marketing strategy for the brand. Clarity in strategy answers four very basic questions:

- Where are we now? (analysis)
- Where do we want to go? (objective setting)
- How are we going to get there? (strategy)
- How will we know we have arrived? (measuring results)

An excellent marketing strategy is based on an excellent analysis from which you draw conclusions about the activities that you need in order to drive the business forward. You measure the results of your marketing activities, analyze them, and then adjust your marketing plan based on what you have learnt. It is as simple as that. And to organize and manage that process efficiently, marketing needs controlling. Controlling will collect, analyze, and structure the relevant data in such a way that one can quickly draw conclusions on how to move the business forward.

Controlling needs to understand that marketing will not have the answers when you start out. It's about analyzing, drawing conclusions, making assumptions, measuring the results, evaluating, and then adjusting the activities based on your new findings. It's all about learning from results. Many controllers are very good at analyzing problems, but there are very few people who are diligent about analyzing success. Too often success is taken for granted. When we measure results, and find out that we are ahead of plan, we often just assume our activities were smart and right and stop looking deeper to why things have worked. Excellent managers are diligent about figuring out what has worked and why. Learning from both success and mistakes is the best way for an organization to move forward. Marketing and controlling should be sharing this learning so that the organization understands what factors are driving the success.

An excellent strategy has clear priorities. Usually a company has a portfolio of brands and works across different categories. To make the most efficient use of resources, it is critical to decide in which categories or brands the company wants to invest and grow. Controlling is an important business partner for providing marketing with the tools and data to set these business priorities. Portfolio analysis is one of these tools. It simplifies complex situations and provides a valuable overview of the strengths and weaknesses of a company's mix of businesses and products. With the help of portfolio analysis, marketing can better assess how best to identify opportunities and allocate resources across a set of products or businesses. Once the priorities are set, controlling should be tracking and monitoring resource allocation against achieved results, to ensure that priorities are delivering against expectations.

4.7 Marketing Planning

For good strategy setting, you need the right data, and you need a systematic and efficient marketing planning process.

Controlling plays a major role: on the one hand, to provide marketing with the right data for planning, and on the other hand, to manage the process across the organization as efficiently as possible (Fig. 3).

Marketing needs controlling in several phases of the process: in the marketing audit phase (3), in forecasting (8), in budgeting (9), and in the financial planning and monitoring (10) phases.

Both functions need to collect the right combination of internal and external data that is necessary for analyzing the current situation on the one hand, as well as forecasting and calculating the expected financial results that will be generated through the marketing activities and investments, on the other hand. Internal data include key performance indicators such as sales and margin data as well as predictions about cost of goods. External data include market growth forecasts, market shares, price developments, media spending levels, consumption trends, and where appropriate, key socioeconomic and demographic indicators.

Controlling must ensure that the data is reliable and that the forecasts that are made are realistic and fit into the overall company financial plan. They should be

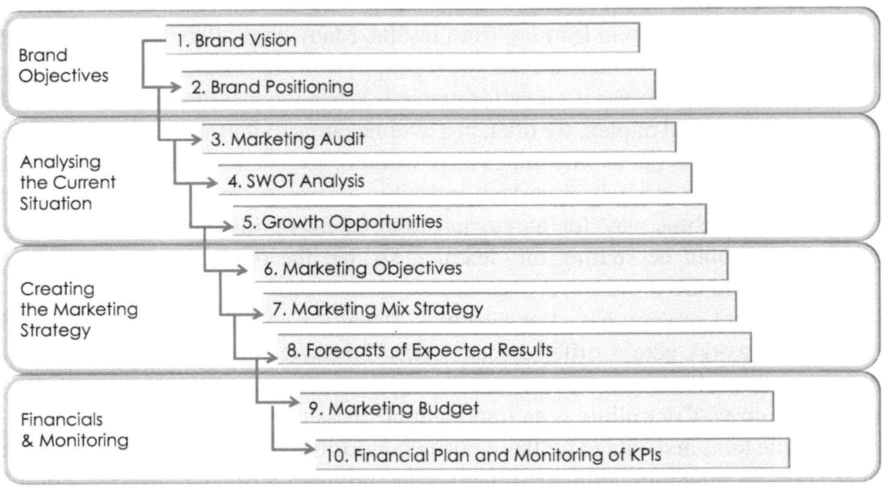

Fig. 3 Marketing planning process (Source: CARE 4 BRANDS Consulting)

validating whether response data has been generated, for example, regarding new products that marketing is planning to launch, or whether communication has been tested to see how consumers will respond to new campaigns or new communication tools. At best, controlling will have calculated different business plan scenarios for marketing to justify and validate major investments.

The financial plans should be consolidated in a common framework that is standardized across business units and countries. It is the task of controlling to ensure that this framework is easily and quickly accessible for all departments that are part of the value chain and that need the marketing plan information for their own planning process.

The planning framework should allow managers to quickly derive meaningful insights about a brand's business performance and its future marketing plans, either in a selected country or across an entire region. It is in the responsibility of controlling to ensure that these marketing plans are generated, consolidated, and communicated on time. Monitoring and communicating the results must be part of controlling's daily business so that marketing can readjust activities where necessary.

4.8 Innovation Management

In a consumer product-driven company, it is marketing that drives the innovation process, as consumer insights are at the heart of new product development. In an industry that is as fast-moving as the consumer products industry, marketing needs to strike the right balance between speed of innovation and building trust with consumers. Excellent marketers can manage the dynamics of change while carefully preserving a feeling of trust in the hearts and minds of their consumers. The speed at which change happens is thereby fast enough, so that the brand never becomes outdated or old fashioned.

But how much change does a brand need? Looking at the number of SKU's in the FMCG industry, one does not get the feeling that we are suffering from too little change. On the contrary, the opposite seems to be the case. The reason may be that young marketing professionals think it's sexier to launch new products rather than expand their loyal consumer base through existing products. "New" always has something magical. But new is not always positive. Especially loyal brand users are very sensitive when new products do not fit to the brand perception. They react very negatively to activities that dilute the core of a brand. Every new line extension or brand extension should be carefully evaluated: does it fit to the brand positioning; does it strengthen or dilute the brand essence; is it credible, convincing and easily understandable for the consumer?

Although many companies invest a lot of money in market and consumer research before they launch a new product, over 70% of new products in the FMCG industry don't survive the first 12 months on the retailer's shelf. There is probably not one recipe for successful innovation, but there are a few key questions that both marketing and controlling should be asking before filling the innovation pipeline with meaningless line extensions.

These key questions are:

1. What does our brand stand for? What is the brand essence?
2. What is our core business know-how? What is our expertise?
3. Who are our core loyal users?
4. What is changing in terms of user behavior and perception?
5. When did we last positively surprise our loyal users?

Many companies invest a lot of time and money in trying to acquire new users but neglect their current users. As mentioned earlier, usually we make 80% of our business with 20% of our clients. Marketing should be looking at these 20%. They should be aiming to make loyal users to fans and to making occasional users to loyal users. That means carefully monitoring and analyzing what is changing in user attitudes, behaviors, needs, and lifestyles. It means investing time and money in looking for ways to improve existing products and services, in surprising loyal users with a gift or with a nice promotion that helps people in need. Marketing should be communicating with their users on eye level: inviting them to share their experience or to test new products and encouraging them to contribute in improving products and services.

Managing the innovation process is undoubtedly a complex topic that needs systematic and strategic attention by both marketing and controlling. There is so much internal and external data that needs to be considered that it is easy to lose track of what is important. Furthermore, many variables like consumer attitudes and behaviors, the market and competition, the communication possibilities, and technological advancements are continuously evolving. The complexity of data and variables in the innovation development process therefore needs a structured and systematic approach. That's why many FMCG companies work with a structured stage-gate innovation process.

The stage-gate process is a tool or framework that guides the organization in their way of identifying the most promising consumer product concepts and developing breakthrough innovative products that create value for the brand and therewith for the company. It helps focus the organization on the few big ideas. The process combines leadership and professional project management from idea generation to market introduction, integrating all relevant functions in the organization (Fig. 4).

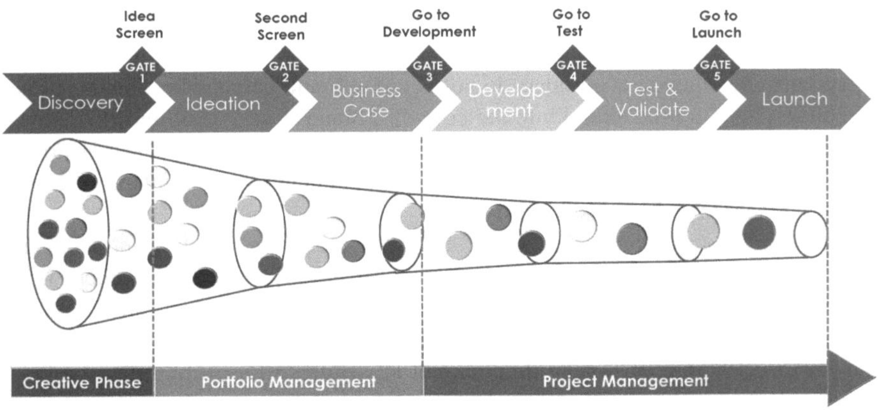

Fig. 4 Stage-gate innovation process (Source: CARE 4 BRANDS Consulting)

Marketing and controlling play the most significant roles in leading this process. While marketing will explore and validate the market and consumer opportunities of a new product or service, controlling will be focused on the cost-effectiveness of the project. Concept testing, product-in-use testing, advertising pretests, price elasticity testing, marketing mix testing, and test markets are common tools to help validate how consumers will perceive the new product. Controlling will be calculating costs and prices, verifying investments, and reviewing budgets and financial plans at various stages of the project. It is critically important that all business units work with the same tool and the same benchmarking methods. This allows controlling to consolidate results and draw important learning for improving both the projects and the process as such. The learning should be shared with all functions involved in the development process.

4.9 Leadership

As we have learnt, marketing's key role is to successfully build and manage strong brands over time, so that they deliver long-term profitable growth for the company. This is Brand Leadership. Leadership means ensuring that the entire organization knows, understands, believes, and acts upon the brand positioning, the brand values, and the brand promise. Every person working on the brand needs to understand the essentials of the brand no matter whether they are working in sales, marketing, R&D, advertising, PR, production, packaging, customer service, and merchandising or at the reception. If, for example, the promise of a brand is "care," then care is not only what every product or piece of communication must deliver to the consumer, but it is also the action standard for the way the receptionists welcome guests, the way customer service helps clients, the way the company treats its employees, and the way the company approaches topics of corporate social responsibility. The entire organization must live the brand essence.

A set of brand guidelines and principles is certainly a good starting point to ensure that the entire organization understands and delivers against the brand promise and there are certainly many different tools controlling can use to monitor and evaluate whether the organization and the products deliver against these guidelines. Brand Leadership, however, requires more than that. It requires communication, training, coaching, and most importantly top management involvement. Companies that rely on one strong brand do not delegate Brand Leadership to their marketing department only. They ensure that Brand Leadership is the core responsibility of the CEO. Apple is probably the most outstanding example of how the CEO lived Brand Leadership and made it the key success factor of the company. Especially in a fast-moving industry like that of consumer products, where change is the driving force of the market, the role of the CEO is key in taking on the Brand Leadership role and ensuring that the brand essence is the guiding principle behind every key activity in the organization. It is the CEO who should guide and coach everyone in the organization to continuously and relentlessly deliver against this promise. It is the CEO who in the end ensures that the brand essence is not diluted because he or she knows that a strong brand is a company's most important aspect.

5 Conclusion

In the FMCG industry brands are the driver of growth and profitability. The role of marketing is to successfully build and manage strong brands that deliver long-term profitable growth. This is Brand Leadership. Brand Leadership can only be successful if marketing and controlling work hand in hand.

Controlling can be a real business partner for marketing, if they understand and inhale that the key success factors to Brand Leadership are:

- Selecting and targeting a precise target group
- Consistently delivering against a clearly defined brand positioning
- Building and maintaining loyal brand consumers

Controlling also needs to understand that for marketing, it is important to work with hard data and to achieve results. Controlling will be a real business partner, if it provides marketing with the key data and tools that marketing needs to efficiently and effectively manage their business and processes. This includes:

- Key performance indicators and budgeting
- Price setting
- Assortment management
- Marketing spend efficiency
- Strategy development and priority setting
- Marketing planning process
- Innovation process

Although every department has its specific role, success is always a team performance. Oftentimes, successful companies are not better than others, but they work better together than others. So, despite the different roles of marketing and controlling, a successful team will have one common goal that they all want to achieve: to build and manage strong brands so that they deliver long-term profitable growth for the company. That is business partnership at its best.

Franziska Schmiedebach-Ullner is the founder and CEO of CARE 4 BRANDS CONSULTING, a strategic brand consulting agency. She has over 30 years of experience as marketing and brand specialist in the consumer goods industry, of which many years were spent in charge of worldwide marketing for the brand NIVEA with Beiersdorf.

Holistic Management Accounting of Brand Performance in the Consumer Goods Industry

Oliver Hupp and Franziska Rumpel

Abstract This contribution deals with the question how prospective marketing budgets can be allocated over the different communication channels as efficiently as possible. Differences between the various channels are analyzed. Measuring methods are presented, both for the effectiveness and efficiency of advertising campaigns. Besides that the author explains how to bring all of these factors into one holistic marketing steering system.

Keywords Brand · Brand image · Management accounting · Marketing · Marketing budget allocation · Marketing consumer goods industry

1 Introduction

At present, brands undoubtedly constitute the most important factor to business success. References for this can be found in the business surveys conducted by PricewaterhouseCoopers/Sattler and the GfK,[1] according to which on average the asset "brand" accounts for 50% of the corporate value. Ninety-one percent of those interviewed considered brands to be among the most important factors for business success. Consequently, an (ideally periodical) evaluation and steering of brands play a key role in securing sustained company success. It is in light of this that company practice as well as research, especially over the last decade, has increasingly focused a value-based brand management. However, it is research in particular that criticizes

An adaption of this contribution has been originally printed as Hupp, O., Rumpel, F. (2014): Ganzheitliches Controlling der Markenführung in der Konsumgüterindustrie, in: Buttkus, M., Eberenz, R., Controlling in der Konsumgüterindustrie: Innovative Ansätze und Praxisbeispiele, 2014, pp. 21–45.

[1]PricewaterhouseCoopers, Sattler GfK (1999, 2005, 2012).

O. Hupp (✉) · F. Rumpel
GfK SE, Nuremberg, Germany

M. Buttkus, R. Eberenz (eds.), *Performance Management in Retail and the Consumer Goods Industry*, https://doi.org/10.1007/978-3-030-12730-5_23

that with the available instruments, a significant and holistic brand performance management is momentarily impossible. In fact, most of the prominent research approaches within the boundaries of evaluating brand success limit themselves to attitude-oriented or sales-oriented or, rather, customer behavior-related KPIs and only focus few and distinct instruments of those marketing mix instruments actually used besides. Hence, one cannot sufficiently take account of a brand's complex system of value drivers and success indicators.

These inadequacies within brand performance analysis especially affect target-oriented planning of future measures negatively. Presently, many companies lack transparency with regard to amount and allocation of their marketing budget. Allocation is oftentimes not undertaken with considerations of profitability, but rather with rules of thumb and gut instinct and on the basis of long-standing procedures. This results in wrong decisions regarding the allocation of resources.

In light of the apparent problems of many approaches for brand management accounting,[2] it is hardly surprising—although the topic return on marketing investment (ROMI) is increasingly taking up more space in the discussions and demands of board rooms—that no systematical determination of marketing budgets exists in the majority of companies.[3] The desire for a comprehensive and effective brand management accounting system that conveys a conclusive picture of brand performance and simultaneously contributes to the management concept and optimization of the brand image will be taken up by this contribution.

In the context of the fundamental change that the consumer goods industry is facing with regard to communications politics—apart from classic communication instruments, online marketing and social media are gaining increasing significance as sources of information for the consumer—the question is how prospective marketing budgets can be distributed over the different communication channels as efficiently as possible. This research question serves as the focus of this contribution, although investments in other marketing activities (expansion of distribution, alterations of price-setting, etc.) will also be addressed marginally.

2 Foundations for an Effective Brand Management Accounting System

A slight rise in marketing costs was expected worldwide in 2013; and this despite of an unusually strong increase of over 4% in 2012 due to the Olympics. In the upcoming year, the amount of marketing costs was expected to develop comparably to the year 2012.[4]

[2]The authors use the English word "management accounting" to translate the German term "controlling." Please refer to the discussion in the preface.

[3]Kohlbacher et al. (2012), pp. 24–27.

[4]Warc, International Ad Forecast 2013/2014.

Although there were indications for a stagnation of marketing costs in Germany in 2013, it was assumed that the share of marketing costs into channels, both in 2013 and later on, would reveal similar developments to those worldwide: Investments in classic advertisement were clearly declining, and in comparison, new media such as the Internet was booming and gaining an increasingly larger portion of the cake (see Fig. 1).

In Germany, it was expected that the amount of costs spent on Internet marketing, due to a growth of approximately 7%, will be higher than that of newspapers.[5] In general, investments in print media are decreasing strongly in Germany.

The question for marketing resulting from these figures is how such budget reallocations are promising. Is the ROMI of new media significantly higher than that of classic media? Should a(n even) greater share of the available communication budget be invested in channels such as Facebook, YouTube, Internet advertisements, or even mobile games in the future? How far can classic media be forgone without negatively impacting brand success or would this possibly result in synergy benefits?

In order to supply marketing, but also company management, with reliable answers to these questions, a management accounting tool is required that takes account of both the immediately arising success factors and long-term effects of a campaign on brand success in accordance with Esch.[6] Using his brand value chain,

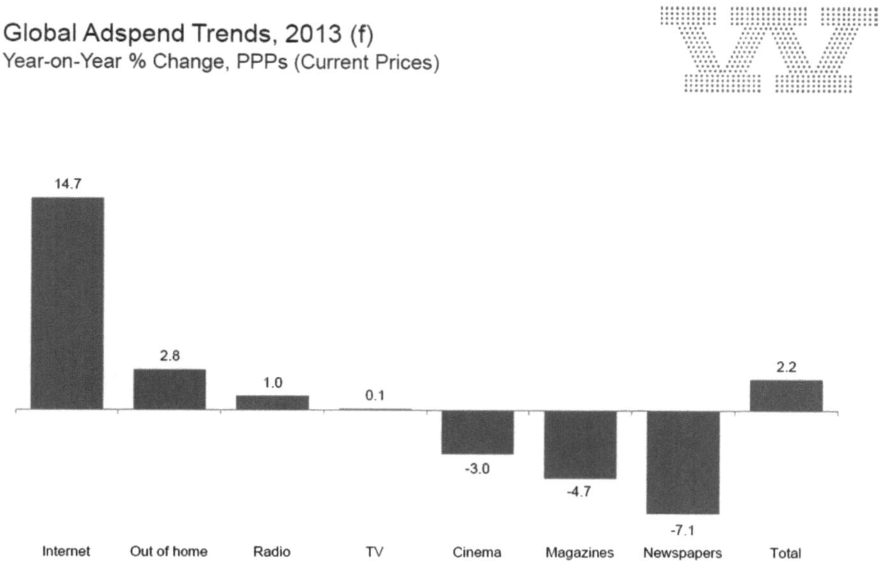

Fig. 1 Global ad spend in comparison (Warc, International Ad Forecast 2013/2014)

[5]Warc, International Ad Forecast 2013/2014.

[6]Esch (2010).

Kevin L. Keller[7] demonstratively organizes and ascertains the resulting effects of a marketing investment. He clarifies that the exclusive evaluation of the ROMI by means of monetary market success (market shares, customer reach, alterations in price elasticity) is insufficient. Additionally, effects in the consumer's mindset must be analyzed and evaluated, since these possibly underlie the (prospective) purchasing behavior and possibly even outlast them. The mindset of a consumer includes the entire knowledge and the consumer's attitude toward a brand, his thoughts, emotions, experiences, perception, images, and preferences.[8]

Figure 2 compactly summarizes the elements of a brand value chain with the subdimensions of consumer mindsets, as mentioned by Keller, and can serve as guideline for the development of a comprehensive management accounting system.

According to Keller,[9] all communicative activities should be evaluated according to their *anchorage*—the brand is remembered due to a certain experience— thereby resulting in *associations* (product-related, emotional), their general *appraisal*, as well as the subsequently resulting changes in their *attachment* to the brand.

Changes in customer mindset, resulting from an advertising campaign or other parallel marketing activities, can—in dependence of so-called market catalysts (alterations in distribution, price changes, promotional activities of their own brand or that of the competitor)—lead to an alteration of customers' purchasing behaviors, which in turn could influence the value of the brand and/or the company.

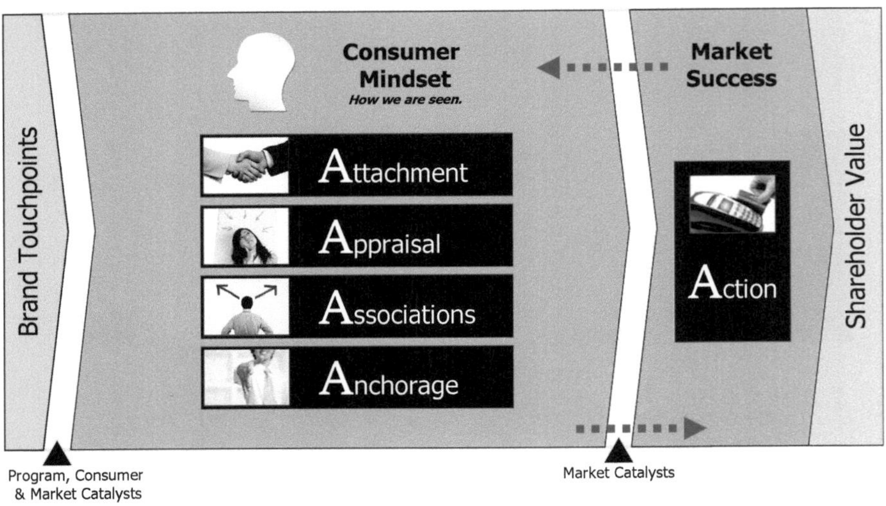

Fig. 2 Elements of the brand value chain (Source: GfK)

[7]Keller (2008).
[8]Keller (2008).
[9]Keller (2008).

Nonetheless, immediate reactions in purchasing behavior that then result in changes of mindset are possible.

In the two following chapters, relevant measurement criteria for the four dimensions of mindset, the foundation of long-term effects of a campaign, will be discussed initially. Subsequently, short-term and market success-based effects of various campaign elements will be highlighted. In accordance with business-economic understanding, short-term effects will be analyzed in light of the key-term "efficiency" and the long-term effects in light of "effectiveness." In conclusion, the evaluation of efficiency and effectiveness will be brought together using a portfolio approach, in order to offer a comprehensive perspective on the (expectable) effect of a concluded (prospective) campaign.

In the sense of a comprehensive marketing management accounting system, effectiveness and efficiency should be evaluated individually and in light of all the brand's possible touchpoints. This requirement is based on the observation that the effect of different communication channels and contents is either strengthened or undermined by parallel brand experiences, made on the brand's other touchpoints. In this respect, these touchpoints, which can partially not be influenced by the company, should be identified and understood with regard to their quality.

Particularly in view of the increasingly frequent interaction between consumers on the Internet, via blogs and discussion boards, companies must consider and evaluate a multitude of new influencing factors on the consumer's perception and thereby also the success of the brand. Furthermore, the success of entirely new advertising forms—such as online games—should be analyzed in light of management accounting processes. During the Olympic Summer Games 2012, the brand Gatorade, for instance, went online with an online game, featuring the repeated Olympic champion Usain Bolt (see Fig. 3), in order to circumvent the advertising ban imposed by the International Olympic Committee. Among other brand contacts, the online game attempted the brand placement as an alternative sports drink to water. Such market touchpoints as mentioned above should absolutely be accounted for by classic above-the-line activities (e.g., TV, print) in order to be able to depict the concrete effectiveness of all marketing activities.

Fig. 3 Example Gatorade (Source: GfK)

Fig. 4 Regulatory framework for touchpoints (Source: GfK)

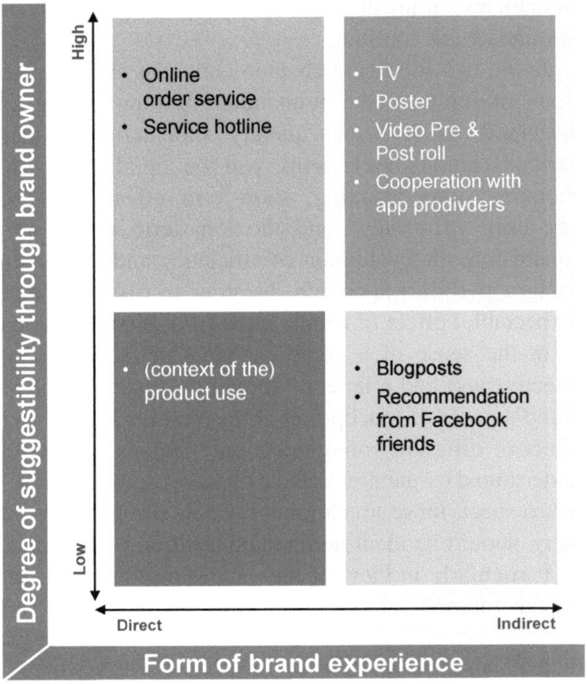

Figure 4 creates a possible regulatory framework for the multifaceted experiences, or rather, touchpoints, which a consumer is confronted with. He differentiates these touchpoints, using their suggestibility through branded companies and the form of brand contacts as criteria. The context of product usage that oftentimes impacts the consumer's quality experience cannot be influenced by the branded company, for instance. It has no influence on content found on blogs either. However, both touchpoints differ in terms of the immediacy of their brand experience. The outlined regulatory framework facilitates brainstorming on which market touchpoints should be taken into account by brand management accounting or at least monitored with regard to their influence.

3 Evaluation the Efficacy of Marketing Campaigns

On the one hand, the aim of brand management accounting is to provide marketing with a possibility of evaluating the success of transacted marketing investments. On the other, it is pointing out concrete options for improvement. Ideally, this evaluation of success is based on a specifically drafted target (e.g., a 5% growth of the present image). Deviations from set targets should be pointed out and, wherever possible, explained causally. In this case management accounting does not solely serve performance management but rather as counselling for the marketing manager.[10]

Anchorage – The effectiveness of every brand experience, and accordingly its influence on the mindset of the consumer, is initially dependent on the specific experience of the contact. A brand contact that is experienced as profound and positively impresses exerts a much stronger influence on mindset than those that are only experienced fleetingly.

If a marketing management accounting system is not limited exclusively to the illustration of performance evaluation within mindsets, but rather supplies information on the perceived quality of market contact, then it facilitates marketing's justification as to why or why not a certain investment decision led to success. In this sense, it supports the responsible brand manager in the derivation of concrete decisions in the future.

The information necessary for evaluating the specific experience of brand contact—be it a TV advertisement or a blog on the Internet—is a measurement of the recollection of this specific brand contact. At first glance, determining the recollection of the event seems trivial. However, marketing management now has a multitude of measurement approaches at their disposal that differ severely with regard to their validity.

The classic approach is determining the brand awareness with a prompted or unprompted survey—meaning with or without being given the brand name. The unprompted brand awareness is considered to be a tougher standard, as the respondent must manage remembering the event by himself (recall-test). Additionally, a so-called recognition-test could be conducted. In doing so, the respondent is shown extracts of or an entire TV spot and then asked whether he remembers it. Under the proposition that most brand contacts occurs fleetingly, without real mental effort, some market researchers consider this approach to be the most appropriate. Nonetheless, all three areas are levied and identified.

However, the realization that every explicit inquiry of brand contact can lead to misinformation has meanwhile asserted itself. The danger of confusions—the respondent states that he has seen a certain advertising poster although print was the only media used—or deliberate exaggerations or understatements of media consumption should be considered.

In light of this, implicit procedures for the determination of brand experience are meanwhile being offered. An example for this is the so-called Opportunity-to-See-Be survey approach, which does not question consumers on their media contact but rather their media behavior. They are asked to declare on which days, when during the day, and which TV or radio channel they watched or heard, respectively. Alternatively, they can be questioned as to their reading behavior of various print titles. Their answers are then compared to the actual media plan of companies. Consequently, brand contact is not measured according to the respondent's subjective memory but is rather assumed according to his media behavior.

---

[10]Esch (2010).

Associations – Which influence do those associations with a certain brand, that the consumer has through brand contact, have on the brand's desired target positioning, the so-called brand identity?

Each contact with a brand triggers certain associations within the recipient and influences the perception of the brand either positively or negatively, intensifying or diminishingly. Ultimately, however, the intended purpose behind a campaign is not to arbitrarily change brand perception in a certain way. In truth, the target should be strengthening the brand image or brand identity intended by the marketing management.

Brand identity should be the heart of every brand strategy and all activities derived from it. It is a company internal description of the most important, formative characteristics of a brand. Within it, the brand's essence and its most important character traits are prescribed. It is also in this that brand identity differs from brand image, which encompasses the brands reception with various stakeholders. Therefore, brand identity and brand image do not have to be identical.[11] Kapferer summarizes the importance of a brand identity to brand management as follows[12]: "Real brand management begins ... with ... a strategy and a consistent, integrated vision. Its central concept is brand identity, not brand image. The Identity must be defined and managed, it is the heart of brand management." In light of this, every effective brand controlling approach must give insights as to whether brand perception has improved due to previous brand activities or not.

In order to measure the influence of brand experience on brand perception (brand image), brand controlling can access various instruments for an implementation in the context of market research. These vary from the measurement of spontaneous associations to classical image batteries and to reaction-based methods. The latter form of measurement has increased in popularity during the last decade, but only gives very limited insights as regards changes of the concrete and multifaceted brand perception.

The so-called Implicit Association Test (IAT),[13] likely the most popular reaction-time-based approach, records the reaction-time and allocation of stimuli (terms) to each other and turns associations, emotions, and thoughts to a brand that is measureable separate from conscious action. However, research has shown that implicit procedures are oftentimes not problem-free and also exhibit weaknesses in comparison with many other market research approaches (Eisberg model, purchasing probability) that find application in brand management contexts. Response time procedures such as the IAT are comparably elaborate with regard to length and evaluation, require an untenable amount of time within the surveys themselves, and are consequently limited to relatively few aspects of perception.

A more pragmatic approach, in which test persons of a market research study are given the opportunity of describing a brand in their own terminology and

[11]Högl and Hupp (2010), pp. 80–104.

[12]Kapferer (2008), p. 5.

[13]Lane et al. (2007), pp. 59–102.

conceptions, is based on so-called semantic networks. These approaches support brand controlling insofar as that they produce a complete picture of brand perception as experienced by the target audiences and visually represents changes resulting from previous marketing activity. To this end, the persons surveyed are given certain themes (functional benefits, emotional associations, personality, brand signals) in a classic survey and are asked to spontaneously name respective associations they have with the focused brand. Associations that are named first are more strongly linked with the assessed brand. Changes, and therewith also accomplishments of a campaign, can be gained from a subsequent comparison with previously levied networks (see Fig. 5).

The closer referenced associations are to the brand visually, the more likely it was named by the persons surveyed, meaning "innovative" is less prominently associated with the brand than the theme "elegance." Using the aforementioned example, it is evident that price perception has changed for the worse after the campaign (expensive had risen by 11%, less cost-effectiveness decreased by 4%). In other respects, the campaign only seemed to have a limited positive effect on brand perception as well. Although quality perception, packaging, assortment competence, and the emotional associations of luxury had positive effects, the effectiveness of the campaign, regarding downward trends in emotional benefits such as wellness, well-kept appearance, and "being beautiful," should be reflected critically. Despite these changes in quality perception and emotional value (luxury, elegance) being part of

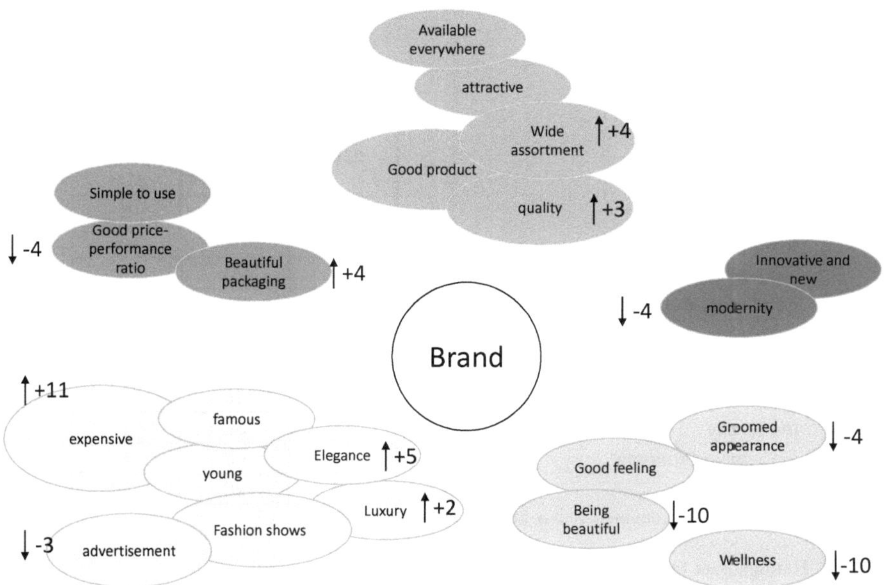

Fig. 5 Semantic network over time (numbers are the percentage change to previous year, base $n = 800$) (Source: GfK)

the campaign briefing, management should question the continuation of the campaign due to the emerging negative associations.[14]

Additionally, it should be noted that campaign success is not solely evaluated on the basis of a time series but also with a comparison of test persons that have memory of the advertising action and those that do not. Advertising memory is then either levied in a supported or unsupported manner or using the Opportunity-to-See Approach. The brand perception of both groups is then contrasted within the network.

The possibly most widespread approach to evaluating the qualitative impact of a campaign (effectiveness) is based on classic rating inquiries. With their help, changes in brand perception can be analyzed both simply and clearly, using either development over time or using a comparison of persons with and without memory of the advertisement (see Fig. 6). However, unlike the semantic networks mentioned earlier, this approach gives the persons surveyed tangible items, or rather terms, that should be evaluated with regard to a certain brand.

Figure 6 supports some of the semantic network results as shown in Fig. 5. In this case, as well as in the one before, the topic of pricing was evaluated significantly less well than in the previous period. Moreover, the brand recorded losses in the area of "uncomplicated." It is important that brand identity is mirrored just as strongly in the formulation of items as the rational or emotional benefits addressed by the campaign. The growth spanning two waves shows management accounting whether or not the campaign functioned effectively or if weaknesses exist.

The advantages of this approach lie in the accurate evaluation of intended advertising effects: How strongly can prescribed image dimensions be influenced

T2B, in %	**Brand**		
	2011	2013	Delta 2013 vs 2011
Brand competence	32	40	**8**
dynamic brand	32	31	-1
innovative products	24	23	-1
good price-performance ratio	28	20	**-8**
satisfaction with the brand	38	29	**-9**
wide assortment	38	58	**20**
beautiful packaging	27	25	-2
modernity	34	36	2
innovative products	42	46	4
simple	38	20	**-18**

Bold print=significant differences: 2013 vs. 2011 (10% Level)

Fig. 6 Ratings over time (Source: GfK)

[14]Dieckmann and Walter (2011).

positively? Was the preliminarily set degree of attainment reached? However, only such changes can be measured that are specifically inquired after.

With a combination of both approaches—semantic network and supported item batteries—in-depth analyses of qualitative advertising effects can be conducted. While top-of-mind associations within a semantic network allow for a first impression, which characteristics a consumer spontaneously associates most strongly with a brand and how these associations may have changed after a campaign, changes in key positioning areas relevant to the brand can be analyzed precisely for the time frame using prescribed items. Collectively, this results in a holistic image of the effectiveness of a brand campaign, meaning its impact on brand perception. In light of this, a holistic brand management approach should contain both unresolved issues concerning the formation of semantic networks and clear and predetermined target dimensions in the form of image features. In doing so, the ability of evaluating even unintentional effects on the brand—both the positive and the negative—is secured. This places the qualitative assessment of advertising campaigns on a conclusive level.

In the digital age, the relevance of a semantical network analysis has further increased. In these days an effective social listening program allows brand managers to reveal what consumers are thinking and feeling about a brand (and sharing with others) in real time. This helps brand managers to identify emerging situations and to react quickly and appropriately before they have a profound impact on the brands image and success.

There are quite literally millions of brand conversations happening in the social media world right now—in Twitter, blogs, forums, and message boards. Most social media listening programs allow monitoring the consumer conversation and providing an unprecedented perspective on the changing image perception of brands. A comprehensive social listening captures the content customers are sharing about competing brands and alerts to unexpected changes in conversation volumes as well as topic or sentiment changes.

The (change in) content of consumer conversations about brands can also be summarized with the help of semantical networks. However, applying deep-learning algorithms to the social media data can build these networks with less effort than in previous times.

Furthermore, especially in today's context of multichannel campaigns with online advertising instruments, it is important to understand how efficient and effective the different channels affect brand experience. Classic instruments for the measuring of efficiency, such as page impressions or click-through rates, are an often-used form of impact measurement for digital communications channels. However, these approaches do not allow for the assessment of actually induced associations or the message's appeal. In order to augment these methods of observation (passive measurement) with missing information, a combination with classic survey methods is opportune.

This can be implemented methodologically as follows:

Step 1: The participants of an online survey panel initially accept that their Internet usage is tracked by the market research institute, using so-called cookies. A cookie refers to a text file that is saved on a computer and collects and stores data concerning websites visited, without being prompted. As soon as persons come into contact with a certain advertising media, this contact is recorded (passive measurement/observation).

Step 2: The panel lists are divided into two groups in order to assess their specific advertising effect as precisely as possible. Group 1, advertising media seen; Group 2, no advertising media seen.

Step 3: The first group (test group) is further observed with focus on its brand contact frequency with the advertising media, enabling assertions regarding the effect of multiple touchpoints with a campaign at a later point in time. The second group, the control group, should be assembled identic to the first group, regarding age, income, and other socio-democratic features, however, with no touchpoints with the advertising media.

Step 4: Both groups are only questioned to their image of the brand and their purchasing behavior, after their allotments to the respective groups and after a certain timespan, in order to be able to measure the campaign's effect.

This results in insights regarding the campaign's scope, its reception (appeal, creation, touchpoint quality, product profile, image, associations, etc.), its efficiency, and its impact on brand identity.

Appraisal – In accordance with Keller, all communicative activities must be examined in their general impact on attitude (appraisal). Attitudes toward brands, but also toward respective brand contacts (TV advertisement, poster, banner), are determinants that precede changes in purchasing behavior.

Brand attitudes are attained through experiences, for instance, through various touchpoints with brands. They influence behavior and are in turn also influenced by behavior (interaction with a brand). The precondition for a change in brand attitude is that a consumer has a positive disposition toward the various brand contacts. To this extent, both dimensions should be evaluated within a brand controlling approach in order to not only assess the effects of different brand contacts but also to understand and optimize them.

In doing so, it is important to account for the complexity of attitudes using the respective measuring procedure. Attitudes are complex, as they are generally comprised by three components: (1) affective component (emotional), (2) cognitive component (rational), and (3) a behavioral component (operational term).[15] Consequently, measurement procedures should ideally assess all three dimensions.

Single dimension methods such as overall measurements regarding appeal (liking, oftentimes on rating scales "How much do you like Brand X?") or multidimensional rating scales (Likert scale) that cover multiple attributes are considered classic appraisal, or rather attitude, measurements. Multidimensional measurements allow for a better depiction of the multitude of components constituting attitudes by inquiring after emotional aspects as well as rational ones.

A prominent example is the so-called brand potential index (BPI®; see Fig. 7) which is used for an assessment of the general attractiveness of product brands in the

[15]Ajzen (2001), pp. 27–58.

Fig. 7 Brand potential index (BPI)® (Source: GfK)

Best Brands Study of the GfK SE. The BPI® is a validated indicator that assesses all relevant aspects of a brand: rational, emotional, and operational.[16]

Therefore, it is possible to validly and dependably evaluate whether or not a campaign, that is to be analyzed with regard to its effectiveness by marketing controlling, positively influences a general tendency toward the brand and consequently improves the prospective purchasing probability when using the brand potential index.

On the basis of this performance indicator and other indicators directly associated with market success, the GfK, the Trade Mark Association, the Wirtschaftswoche, the Serviceplan, and others initiated the "Best Brands Surveys," an annual compilation of ranking of the most successful German brands that could serve as a foundation for a brand controlling instrument. The "Best Brands" approach's structure has been illustrated in Fig. 8.

In order to understand the attitude or rather the disposition of a consumer to various brand contacts—does he welcome or reject them—an analogue approach is appropriate. In this case it is also necessary to measure the emotional but also rational appraisal—and in this case, also with regard to certain brand touchpoint. Apart from supported and unsupported recollection, the impression that the brand leaves on the consumer is collected to adequately answer the questions raised earlier.

The research approach developed by the GfK allows for the inclusion of both the emotional and rational effects of all possible brand experiences and then evaluating

[16]Hupp (2000), pp. 44–47.

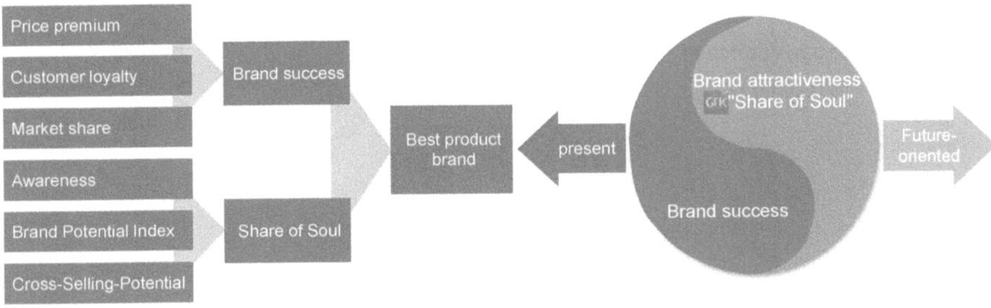

Fig. 8 Causal model "Best Brands" (Source: GfK)

and understanding them with minimal time effort. Using a two-dimensional matrix, all points of contact that a consumer has had with a brand in the past are mapped out using a drag-and-drop procedure and then subsequently evaluated.

The surveyed person is given the task of rating the intensity of the memorability of a brand experience (rational dimension) as well as its appeal (emotional dimension), simultaneously. For this purpose, he allocates icons that represent various brand experiences within the evaluation matrix provided during the interview using the drag-and-drop procedure. This matrix spans the dimensions of "memorability of touchpoint" and "impression" caused by the contact. The mathematical linking of "memorability" and "impression" can yield a comprehensive attitude-value for each brand experience. Figure 9 exemplary demonstrates an example for the banking sector.

On the basis of the allocations made by this assessment method, brand controlling can derive specific recommendations for the optimization of individual marketing activities, as shown in Fig. 10.

The prerequisite for a conclusive brand management system is that all points of contact with a brand, not only media specific ones, are evaluated and controlled. Only if all points of contact with a brand are gathered is it possible to encompass, understand, and evaluate the effect of individual activities and campaigns that include different activities. Ultimately, assertions, regarding whether contact to the campaign or other brand-initiated signals lead to measured effects, are only enabled by a holistic acquisition of all brand contacts.

Attachment – In accordance with the Keller model, brand loyalty (attachment) should be considered as a further level of impact regarding the evaluation of communication and marketing activities. This raises the question of how marketing can improve loyalty toward a brand.

A strong form of loyalty is exhibited when the willingness to replace a brand with another brand, as a result of contact with a product or a marketing campaign, is reduced and when the brand retains a strong position in the mind of the consumer even after less positive experiences with the brand (e.g., with product defects). According to Keller and Lehmann,[17] this can even lead to dedication or "addiction"

[17]Keller and Lehmann (2003), pp. 26–31.

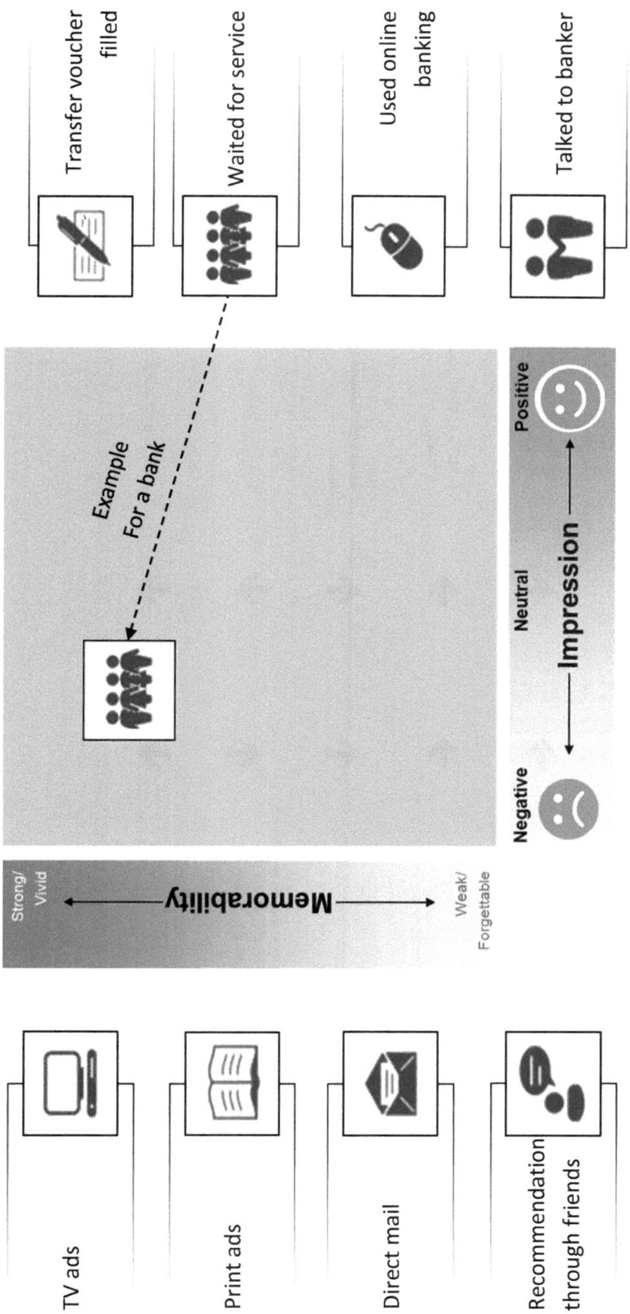

Fig. 9 Drag-and-drop system (Source: GfK)

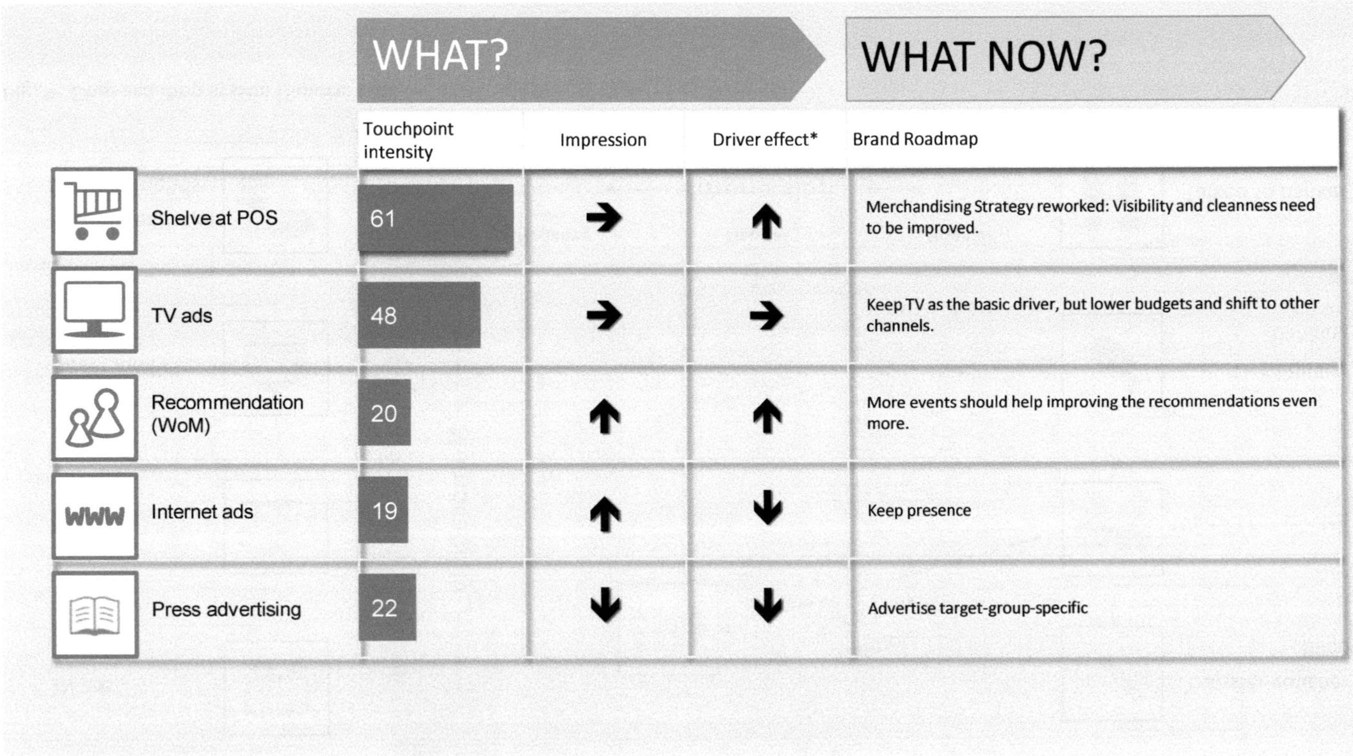

*Kontaktpunkte, die dazu beitragen, den Konsumenten von der Erwägung zur Loyalität bringen.

Fig. 10 Derivation of recommended actions (Source: GfK)

to this brand in extreme cases. Brands that invoke such a strong orientation are strong brands.

The classic measuring of the level of attachment to a brand often happens using the funnel, or rather the sales funnel, approach. This approach insinuates an ideal for the development of a consumer-brand relationship, beginning with the discovery (awareness), to greater familiarness (familiarity), to purchase and repurchases (first choice). In the case of brand controlling, it is appropriate to either observe the absolute degree on each level of the funnel model or changes in loss rates between the levels and then contrasting and relating them to the marketing activities of the past.[18]

However, the performance analysis of a brand on the individual funnel levels over time does not only indicate the success of marketing activities but opens strategic options for marketing in the future. Should prospective activities aim at expanding the brands awareness or should they strengthen customers' loyalty? The following example in Fig. 11 shows an increase on the first funnel levels after the brand had had to accept losses on the levels profile, familiarity, and probability of purchase. Nonetheless, values on higher levels (purchase, loyalty) remain low.

In light of this background, one could postulate that the previous marketing activities were successful in the sense that they returned the brand to a status where it was remade relevant to a broader group of customers. However, the prospective aim should be turning the increase of purchase contemplation into actual purchasing activities—on the basis of promotional activities or by expanding its distribution.

Activities that have the highest potential of success to this end can be found by statically interlinking the touchpoints, as evaluated in regard to their qualitative effect in Fig. 10, with the funnel performance.

The activities for which the greatest driver effect can be calculated should be used more frequently in the future—in the example above, this would mean placing a

Fig. 11 Funnel over time (Source: GfK)

	2007	2009	2011	2013
Loyalty	7	▼6	3	3
Purchase	14	▼9	6	6
Buying consideration	25	▼20	18	▲26
Brand trust	73	▼70	65	▲74
Brand awareness	85	▼80	75	▲91

[18]Critical discussion of the funnel concept, Hupp and König (2018).

stronger emphasis on shelf maintenance. Consequently, brand management is ascribed with a leading role for the future, above and beyond mere performance measurement.

4 Evaluating the Efficiency of Marketing Campaigns

However, it is ultimately of great importance for marketing controlling to recognize how strongly the various marketing activities of the past have caused changes in consumers' purchasing behavior, beyond the aforementioned changes within mindsets. The efficiency of marketing activities is best assessed by a comparison of level of investment and realized turnover effect.

Although changes in attitude are important, ultimately, marketing should always strive to improve sales—be it with the acquisition of new customers or by improving the purchasing intensity of previous customers. In order to be able to conclusively measure these important brand management KPIs, it is appropriate to use data from consumer or trade panels.

In the consumer panel, customers' purchasing decisions and behavior are monitored and analyzed continuously. Brand purchase information is gathered by scanning EAN codes of all products purchased by a consumer and supplemented with the specification of location, date, and time of purchase and price and method of transaction. The aim of this continuous collection of purchasing activities is registering and observing changes in concrete customer behavior.

Consumer panel data supplies brand management with detailed information on consumers and their purchasing activities: which brands and product variation are purchased often, where they are purchased, how much is paid for them, and which competitor's products were purchased in the past. Further, consumer panels also yield additional consumer data such as, for instance, a description of the consumer's most important sociodemographic features and his general (nonbrand-related) attitudes. Additionally, newer panel approaches offer information on which advertising activities a consumer was exposed to before his purchase.

The most important KPIs that can be supplied to brand management on the basis of a trade or consumer panel are:

- Changes in the purchasing customer reach, meaning the number of consumers that have purchased a brand
- Changes in market shares (amount or value), meaning the portion of consumers in the entire product group
- Changes in shares of loyal consumers, meaning those consumers that purchase the brand more often than the competitor's products

Each of these KPIs is directly linked with a company's sales revenues and constitutes a relevant performance indicator for brand management insofar as that they must be monitored systematically in order to evaluate marketing success.

By analytically interlinking these KPIs with other data gained from the panel, specific hints can be derived for an optimization of the marketing mix, the target group management, the shopper management, the price and promotion management, and the media management.

In order to give an answer to one of the key issues of marketing management, namely, that of maximizing the return on marketing investment (ROMI), it is important to utilize the support of panels for the evaluation of the entire media process, from strategic and tactical cross-media planning to the evaluation of certain measures.

Such analyses require using a single source panel that not only yields information on purchasing behavior but also information on media usage. Media contact is usually measured passively. In this case, passively means technical procedures rather than surveys—for example, this means installing a sound matching on the TV of the panelist (see below) or a measuring software for online channels in order to measure all advertising media touchpoints. Simultaneously, all advertising media is furnished with a tracking tag in order for all of the panelist's advertising media touchpoints to be collected. Further, all URL page views are recorded in order to retrace all touchpoints with a brand's homepage or a price comparison site. Naturally, this presumes the explicit consent of, and normally also incentives for, panel participants.

By agreeing to a "tagging" of online advertising media, panelists are not strained additionally. In addition, any effects that could possibly occur during surveys can be avoided. In this sense, the passive measurement of media contacts holds a clear advantage over classic surveying methods.

The measuring of advertising contacts within consumer panels enables a direct networking of advertising contact and purchase transaction and therefore a very valid and comparably granular measurement of advertising effects. Furthermore, newer approaches of panel research allow an analysis of digital advertising contacts such as banner advertising, social media, or SEM (search engine marketing). Additionally, the observation of specific target audiences (e.g., heavy buyers, premium shoppers) as well as the calculation of certain media coverages and contacts is possible.

The GfK's Media Efficiency Panel (MEP), which is based on the GfK Consumer Scan Consumer Panel, enables especially far-reaching applications for marketing controlling. In this panel, a measuring software has been installed on all of 13,500 households, meaning 23,000 persons' computers. This software measures all URL page views and search queries as well as the contact with tagged online campaigns (meaning advertising media marked with a tracking tag). In this way, a very complete image of panelists' online contacts can be mapped out, and the possibility of differentiating between various formats or advertising surroundings exists.

Furthermore, apart from online advertising contacts, TV advertising can be measured using an "audio sound matching" procedure. This procedure uses a mobile phone to record the audio signals of advertising relevant TV channels. Additionally, contact probability for print advertising can be calculated for the most important titles, using a panel insertion.

Apart from central sales effects, media behavior can be analyzed further, as, for instance, with the determination of an incremental customer reach capacity from online to TV or with the assessment of those websites in the relevant marketing target group used most often. Consequently, the approach is not only interesting for advertisers but also for media agencies. Furthermore, additional parameters of the marketing mix (pricing, promotional activities, distribution) can be controlled. As a result, this enables an exact attribution of effects on specific campaign elements which affords marketing management with a conclusive basis for decision-making.

However, it should be noted that a limitation exists: The activities of smaller brands and new products can only be evaluated to a limited extent, and campaigns must exhibit a certain level or GRPs (gross rating points, gross coverage) in order to be measureable, due to case number restrictions. Furthermore, a modeling of the ROMI is generally only possible for FMCG products, FMCG retailers, fashion brands, books, movies, the booking of vacations, etc.

The following figures depict exemplary evaluations and their findings for brand controlling and were yielded by a single-source approach. An analytic breakdown of the turnover realized in the assessment period is undertaken in Fig. 12. Furthermore, it illustrates which share of the realized turnover can be traced back to the media used, promotion activities, or a consumer's loyalty. Additionally, the advertising-induced turnover can further be allocated to the respective media channels, thereby creating a deeper understanding regarding their efficiency. This yields approaches for a reallocation of marketing budgets.

Figure 13 gives an overview of possible analyses and outputs that can be broken down further into relevant target groups with the help of the individual household survey. In the process, special analyses for the exclusive scope (how great was the scope created by social media alone, for instance, and how many persons were reached by classic TV advertising alone) or the classes (sales uplift according to the frequency of contact with a campaign) can be calculated in addition to the classic

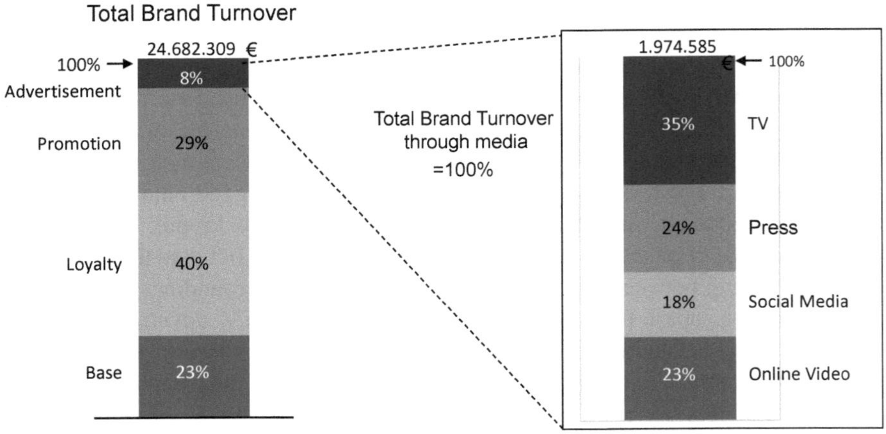

Fig. 12 Turnover through media channels—illustrative (Source: GfK)

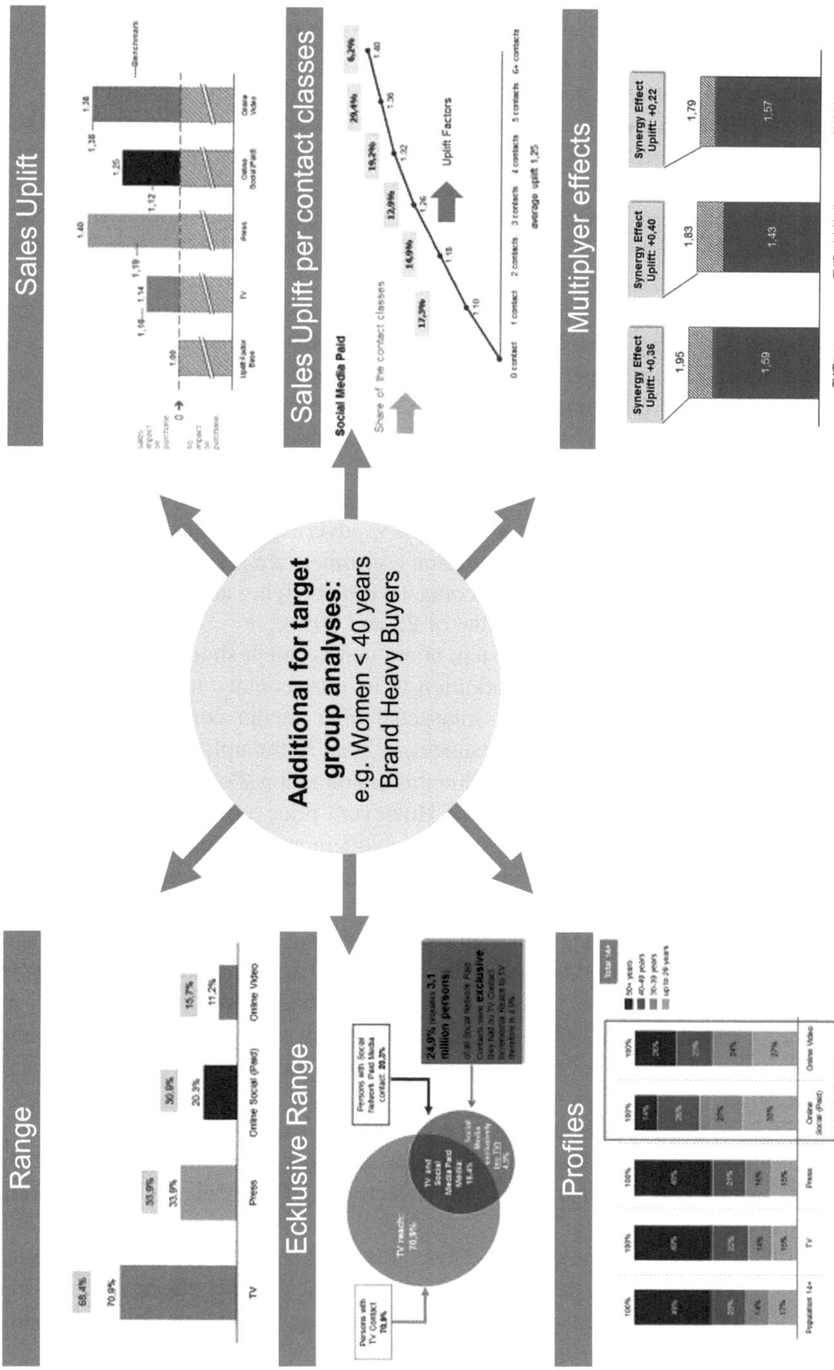

Fig. 13 Overview over analysis opportunities (Source: GfK)

analysis of scope measurements and the sales numbers. The calculated sales uplift per advertising contact allows brand controlling to optimize the expenditures of a specific advertising media. Finally, the advertiser is informed, if a significant amount of receiving persons was gained or lost by raising or lowering expenditures.

It could be of further interest to observe target group profiles for certain marketing activities. One could, for example, analyze which age group of a target audience had how much media contacts. Furthermore, multiplication effects can be calculated, giving insights as to how much more TV and social media contribute than TV and print, for example (Fig. 13 bottom right). This information could also offer valuable references for future budget allocations.

In closing, the plurality of information and relevance for advertising management will be shown using the following example: Fig. 14 illustrates that Brand A could reach almost 60% of all persons with TV advertising. Withal, each receiving person had an average of 6.1 contacts with the TV ad. Together with an online campaign started simultaneously, more than every fourth person could be reached altogether, with, however, a higher contact frequency of almost 11 contacts. This depth of information can only be measured reliably by consumer panels and not with surveys.

When observing the effect for classic TV advertising versus online advertising (Fig. 15), it becomes clear that 5.8 million consumers are reached exclusively by the online campaign (31% of all online contacts, thereby lying above the limit set by the GfK benchmark at an expected value of 25 and 30%).

In the last and most important step, brand management should evaluate a brand's specific influence on sell-off, in addition to its pure contact and experience points. The dissection of the purchases transacted after media contacts, the additional turnover gained and return on investment, as well as the uplift according to contact classes all play an important role within this examination. Possible drivers of success may well be sheer media contacts. However, price concessions, a previously established consumer loyalty, as well as sociodemographic influences also play an important role and should consequently be monitored in the course of media success evaluations.

When observing the additional turnover according to media created by Brand A, it becomes clear that in this case study (Fig. 16), Facebook paid media constitutes 23% of additional turnover during the campaign period but only expends 2.5% of the entirety of costs spent. Although TV advertising provides a greater amount of additional turnover (53.4%), it also requires a significantly higher investment expenditure.

In light of these results, marketing controlling can use this verifiable efficiency of the communications channel to advise for a higher investment in the Facebook sector. Admittedly, at this point, the effectivity of campaign elements remains unconsidered.

Lastly, the conclusion can be drawn that single-source panels offer a unique possibility of evaluating the efficiency (in the sense of sales effect) of cross-media campaign in a target-oriented manner and comparing the ROI of different channels, especially in the growing field of digital media.

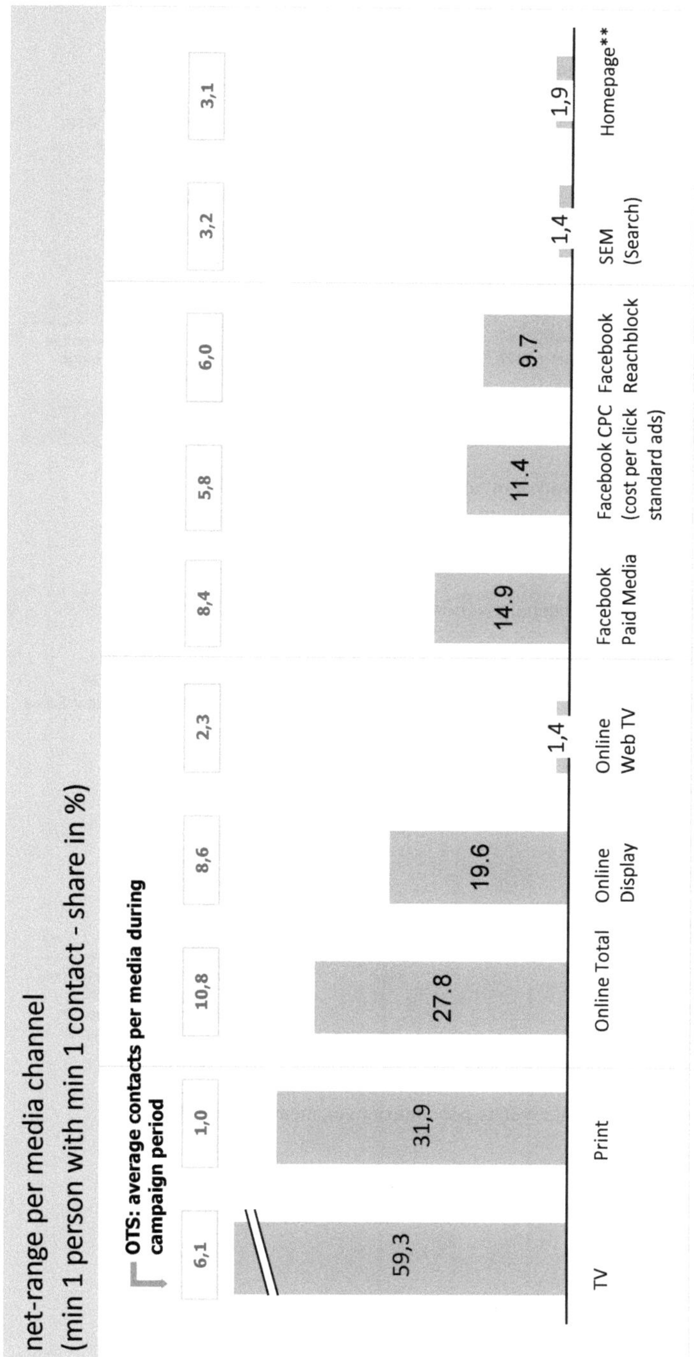

Fig. 14 Example net range per media channel (Source: GfK)

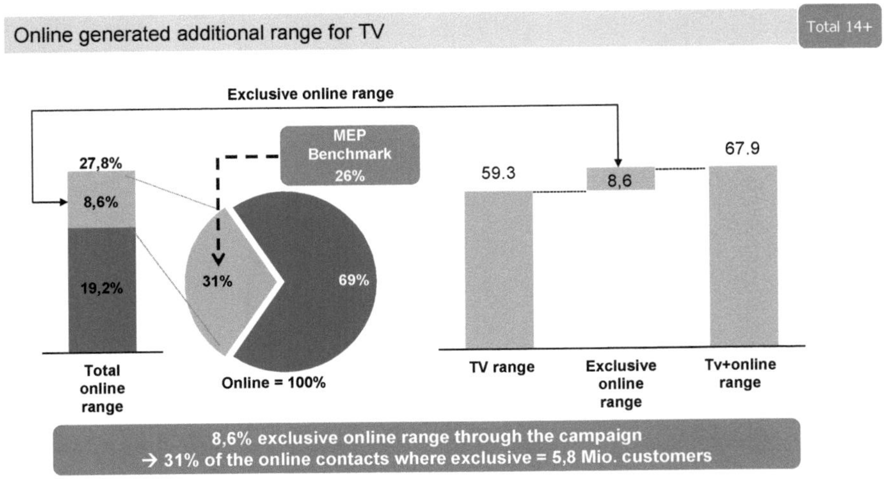

Fig. 15 Example decomposition of additional range (Source: GfK)

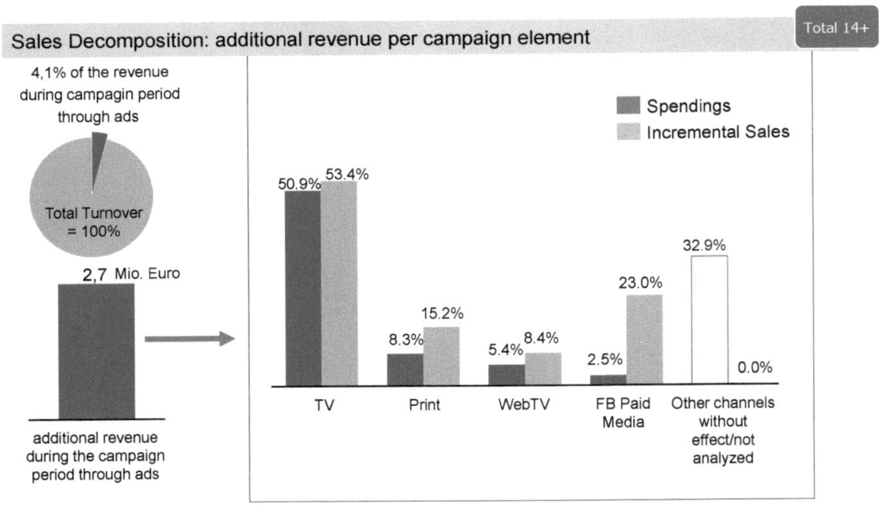

Fig. 16 Example additional revenue per campaign element (Source: GfK)

5 Conclusion

In order for brand management to evaluate to what extent marketing activities function efficiently, in the sense of sales effect, and concurrently effectively, in the sense of gained value for the brand, it is advisable to make use of the holistic and integrative brand value chain approach as a guideline. Both perspectives—efficiency and effectivity—are closely related and influence one another.

On the basis of a coalescence of the insights gained from the detailed analysis of mindset, influences on purchasing behaviors, and investments in individual marketing activities, reliable answers regarding different advertising contacts' levels of efficiency can now be derived. Thereunto, an effect matrix is created that visualizes the potential for improving brand perception (customer mindset) as well as the potential for improving impact on revenue (e.g., customer reach, action). Furthermore, assertions concern impact differences over time. Activities are then embedded in the matrix according to their level of effect, and additionally, the level of investment of individual activities is portrayed by the size of the circles. In this sense, the illustration in Fig. 17 shows that newspaper articles have no significant influence on brand perception and the number of brand customers, despite the considerable budget spent on it.

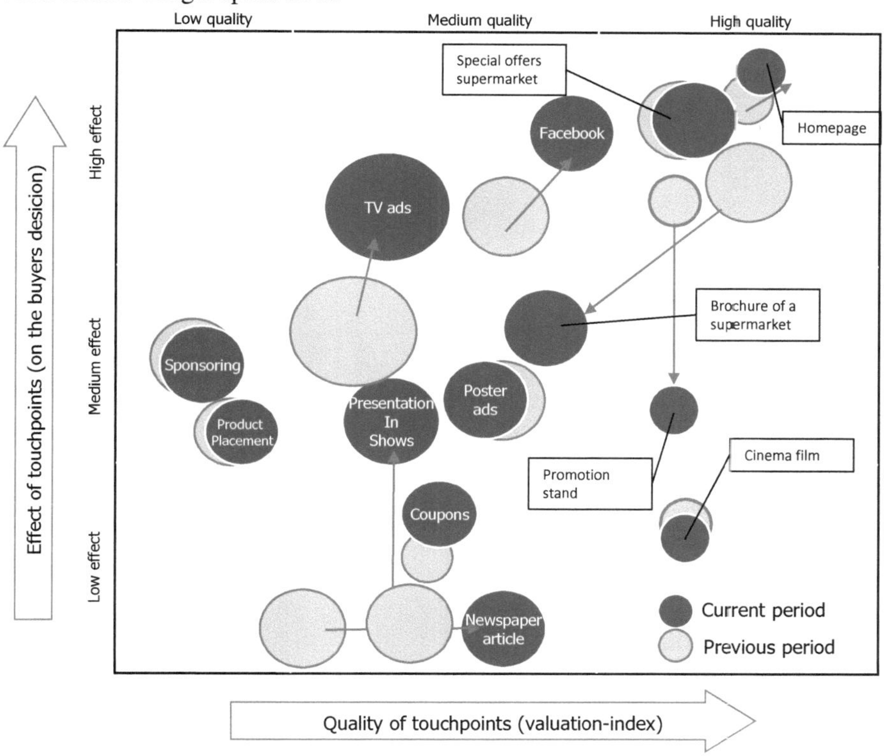

Fig. 17 Effect matrix of the two dimensions: percipience and buyers' decision (Source: GfK)

With a similarly high budget, poster advertising as classic above-the-line communications instrument can achieve a moderate effect on mindset, although a lesser one compared with the previous period (white circle). This channel must also be considered average regarding its influence on purchasing behavior. Nonetheless, an increased investment, at the expense of product placement, for example, may be worth contemplating.

TV advertising has positively changed in its effect: both regarding the improvement of brand perception and in generating new customers. Consequently, it is a viable alternative for future investments. Nonetheless, this instrument is attached to high investments. Online channels such as Facebook are gaining significance and generate (see Fig. 16) great additional sales with low investments. In this sense, an allocation that is ideally suited to the budget should be calculated using the MEP analysis mentioned above.

To help it plan prospective marketing activities holistically, brand controlling has at an approach at its disposal that is based on the previously outlined model—considering brand strength effect and sales impact.

As summary, Fig. 18 shows that many approaches must be considered in order to achieve a high degree of effectiveness and efficiency in the planning and evaluation of marketing activities. Apart from knowledge on target audiences, knowing which touchpoints with the brand influence purchasing decisions substantially is key. Based on this, an efficient allocation of advertising budgets can be determined and optimized and should be monitored constantly.

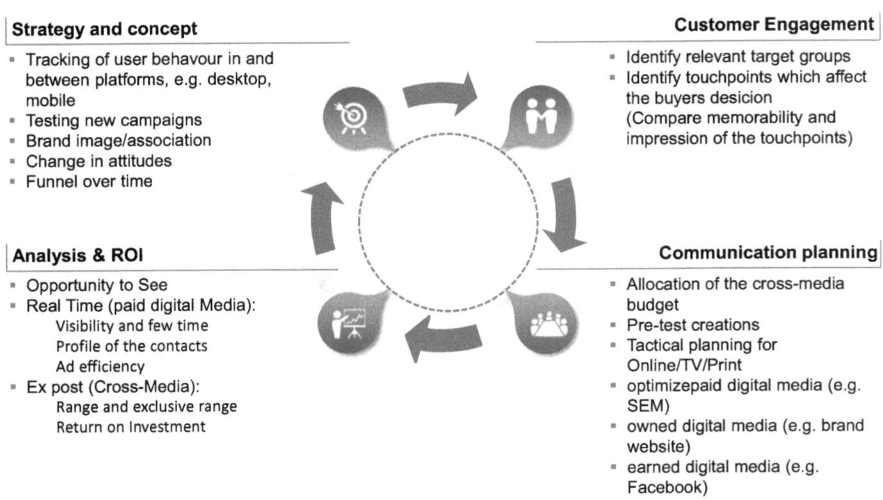

Fig. 18 Holistic analysis and consulting for raising the ROMI (Source: GfK)

References

Ajzen I (2001) Nature and operation of attitudes. Annu Rev Psychol 52:27–58
Dieckmann A, Walter K (2011) GfK internal study
Esch F-R (2010) Strategie und Technik der Markenführung. Franz Vahlen, München
Högl S, Hupp O (2010) Erfolgreiche Markenpositionierung auf Basis eines echten USP. In: Görg U (ed) Erfolgreiche Markendifferenzierung: Strategie und Praxis professioneller Markenprofilierung. Gabler, Wiesbaden, pp 80–104
Hupp O (2000) Die Validierung von Markenwerten als Voraussetzung für die erfolgreiche Markenführung. Plan Anal 5:44–47
Hupp O, König C (2018) Markterfolg, Markenbeziehungen und Markenerlebnisse. In: Esch F-R (ed) Handbuch Markenführung. Springer Gabler, Wiesbaden
Kapferer J-N (2008) The new strategic brand management. Kogan Page, London
Keller KL (2008) Strategic brand management: building, measuring, and managing brand equity, 3rd edn. Pearson, Upper Saddle River, NJ
Keller KL, Lehmann DR (2003) How do brands create value? Mark Manag 12:26–31
Kohlbacher J, Göttmann M, Meiers S (2012) RoMI: Chance für Strategische Forschung. Plan & Anal 6:24–27
Lane KA, Banaji MR, Nosek BA, Greenwald AG (2007) Understanding and using the implicit association test: IV: procedures and validity. In: Wittenbrink B, Schwarz N (eds) Implicit measures of attitudes: procedures and controversies. Guilford Press, New York, pp 59–102
PricewaterhouseCoopers, Sattler GfK (1999, 2005, 2012) Praxis von Markenbewertung und Markenmanagement in deutschen Unternehmen, Published by PricewaterhouseCoopers AG Wirtschaftsprüfungsgesellschaft. Frankfurt a. M
Warc, International Ad Forecast 2013/2014

Dr. Oliver Hupp has been working with the GfK SE since 1999. As division manager, he led the company sector Brand & Comms Consumer Goods, Services, and B2B with more than 60 staff members as well as the Methodology Department of the GfK Market Research until 2013. The team's main focus was on questions of strategic and operative brand management and marketing research. As Head, since January 2014, Oliver Hupp is responsible for the consumer goods and retail industry in Germany. Together with his team, he is comprehensively developing and advising the GfK's most important customers in the industry on the entire product range of the GfK. He is the author of numerous publications on brand management and speaker on national and international conventions and has been presented many research awards such as the ARF Great Minds Award in 2013.

Dr. Franziska Rumpel is an Account Manager in the consumer goods and retail industry Germany sectors with the GfK SE. She mainly advises international customers with a focus on advertising pretests (including measuring emotions) and validation as well as brand and communication studies.

Basket Analysis in Practice: Mathematical Models and Applications in Offline Retail

Carsten Moldenhauer and Henning Zwirnmann

Abstract The foundation of every business model is a deep understanding of the customers' preferences. Basket analysis can be used to reveal valuable insights into these preferences by analyzing massive transactional data sets that are nowadays available to bricks-and-mortar retailers. Within this contribution we review some of the requirements and mathematical methods that comprise the term basket analysis. Further, we discuss applications that leverage the discovered information and outline some of the challenges that the authors faced when applying basket analysis techniques in practice.

Keywords Basket analysis · Data analysis · Descriptive statistics · Offline retail · Shopping cart analysis · Shopping behavior

1 Introduction

Methods for the analysis of customers' preferences and purchase behavior are at the heart of interest of every retailer's sales team. Recent advances have been made in particular in online retail, where millions of products are offered to at least as many customers. This generates vast amounts of data about product considerations and purchases of customers that can be exploited using machine learning techniques; the

---

An adaption of this contribution has been originally printed as Moldenhauer, C., Lange, V., Schmidt, J., Bosch, N. (2017): Warenkorbanalyse: Kaufverhalten der Kunden mit mathematischen Modellen analysieren, Der Controlling Berater, Journal Volume 51, pp. 205–220.

C. Moldenhauer (✉)
Steering Lab, Horváth & Partners, Zurich, Switzerland

H. Zwirnmann
Steering Lab, Horváth & Partners, Munich, Germany

M. Buttkus, R. Eberenz (eds.), *Performance Management in Retail and the Consumer Goods Industry*, https://doi.org/10.1007/978-3-030-12730-5_24

most prominent example being recommender systems.[1] These techniques require big amounts of data for accuracy reasons and provide a high degree of automation.

In contrast to the online setting where all actions of the customers can be mapped to the digital space, in offline retail most of this data is unavailable. Therefore, companies based on brick-and-mortar stores have traditionally used aggregated sales data and customer surveys to gain insights on their clients. Fortunately, the data availability has changed within the last decade due to the digitization of supply and production chains with a widespread introduction of customer relationship management and enterprise resource planning systems. In particular for retailers, detailed transactional data from their point of sales are now available. This contribution describes some of the techniques that can be used to leverage the company's internal data to gain more insights on its customers. The mathematical methods described here are often referred to as parts of a *basket analysis*.

The term basket analysis covers a wide field of methods and applications. It shall be noted that statistical information about baskets has been collected and analyzed in various ways by third-party companies for a long time. The National Bureau of Statistics of Germany determines an average consumer basket every 5 years in order to measure the inflation of consumer prices.[2] Other commercial providers like The Nielsen Company (www.nielsen.com) survey consumer prices and purchased products, especially in the context of food retailing, using large-scale surveys and programs with probands. IHS Markit (www.ihs.com) offers a multitude of databases for sales and growth forecasts for various market sectors ranging from the automobile sector to the food retail sector as well as analyses on consumer trends and forecasts on possible market developments.

Analyzing consumer behavior is also part of the field of revenue and pricing management. Here, the customer's preferences and frequencies are estimated with statistical models and then used to optimize prizes and profits. Özer and Phillips (2014), Klein and Steinhardt (2008), and Talluri and Van Ryzin (2004) give comprehensive overviews on methods for revenue management that are used across various industries.[3] Most of these methods, however, make assumptions on probability distributions of some customer behavior, e.g., arrival frequencies or choice models for the willingness to pay. The parameters for these models are then estimated from historical sales data.

In contrast, due to the advances in data availability and information technology, such estimates can be avoided by using nonparametric models that operate directly with transactional data sets. See Ferreira et al. (2016) for a first implementation of nonparametric models in practice in an online setting.[4]

In this spirit, this chapter focuses on methods that can be used to answer relevant business questions by analyzing massive transactional sales data directly.

---

[1]Aggarwal (2016): see for a technical introduction.

[2]Talluri and Van Ryzin (2004).

[3]Özer and Philipps (2014), Klein and Steinhardt (2008), Talluri and Van Ryzin (2004).

[4]Ferreira et al. (2016), pp. 69–88.

Basket analysis is a very useful method particularly in the retail industry. Retailers can determine specific customer groups by segmenting them according to demographic traits such as age, income, place of residence, or current phase of life. Moreover, it is also possible to identify which additional products could be of interest for the specific target groups. These insights are then used for customized advertisement, packaging, and pricing.

Let us further note that the application of basket analyses is not restricted to retailers. Traditionally, manufacturers have had little or no access to end-customer data. However, with manufacturers opening their own retail stores, e.g., at airports or in malls, and thus bypassing traditional sales channels, these companies start to employ basket analyses as well.

In the following we will first discuss some of the prerequisites required to perform basket analyses. Then, we will elaborate on typical questions and applications that the authors have encountered in multiple projects with different companies in Sect. 2. Subsequently, the mathematical methods to answer these questions will be described in Sect. 3 which is wrapped up with a conclusion in Sect. 4.

2 Applications of Basket Analyses in Offline Retail

The objective of this contribution is to discuss some of the techniques that can be used to analyze company internal data. In particular, we focus on customer insights and list some prototypical questions that we have encountered in multiple consulting projects: the first for a luxury food producer that possesses proprietary flagship and outlet stores and thus acts similar to a retailer in these stores, the second for a toy manufacturer with an online sales channel, and the third for a retailer at airports. Finally, we also include examples from a fourth project that used a basket analysis for a car repair service provider. Let us mention that, due to the amount of data required, the subsequent methods are primarily used in business-to-consumer (B2C) business models that are characterized by frequent small transactions and many end-customers.

2.1 Required Preconditions for Application of a Basket Analysis

The basis for all subsequent methods is sales data. Most company executives seem to believe that this data is easily accessible within their enterprise. However, we have encountered a number of challenges that usually need to be addressed.

Granularity The analysis of customer preferences requires a granularity of sales data down to single transactions. Further, the single transactions must be grouped by receipts and mapped to a single customer profile. In online retail this is hardly ever a problem. However, many bricks-and-mortar stores face the challenge that they only have aggregated sales data at their disposal, e.g., sales of an item per shop per day. Manufacturers wanting to perform a basket analysis face further problems. Unless they own proprietary sales channels like flagship or outlet stores, they mostly sell their goods through intermediaries, i.e., grocery chains in the food industry. Hence, the sales data is collected at the intermediary, and in most cases, it is impossible for the manufacturer to access it.

Quality The quality of the recorded data is paramount for any subsequent analysis. The most common source for quality-related issues is different data sources. As an example, a company may use digitized cashier systems to record single sales transactions, but these systems might differ from shop to shop. Or, sales transactions are recorded in a cashier system, but the number of customers is determined by another source, e.g., with a photoelectric barrier. The inconsistencies between the data sources cause additional effort for data cleansing prior to analysis.

History and Scope To gain significant insights into the customers' behavior, the data needs to be available for multiple sales periods. For retailers, this usually means multiple years to analyze trends and seasonal patterns, e.g., sales during specific periods of the year. Companies that have started data collection early on do have a significant advantage in analyzing their customer base and leveraging this information in business decisions. Further, the scope of the collected data needs to be as extensive as possible. Most companies do have some data sources that meet the above requirements, available through online stores or flagship stores at airports. However, these points of sale are frequented by very specific customer groups, and thus their analysis is biased toward these customers. A subsequent generalization to the entire customer base can then be very difficult.

Additional Data for Steering Analysis of historical data portrays customers' previous purchasing behaviors only. Consequently, the results it generates are usually only of informative nature. In order to steer sales, additional information is required, e.g., fixed and variable production costs. Likewise, this information needs to fulfill the above criteria.

It may be noted that any analysis of historical sales data is of course biased. Hence, when introducing new sales paradigms, like new product bundles or different discount systems, it is impossible to predict the precise outcome. However, the analysis of historic data is prerequisite in designing, hopefully, most effective paradigms.

2.2 *Typical Questions Addressed by Basket Analyses*

The objective of any basket analysis is gaining insights into the behavior and needs of the customers. We have experienced in particular the following questions and applications:

Product clusters and customer segmentation *Which groups of products are often purchased together? Do there exist clusters in customer demand?*

These questions are addressed with clustering methods. When considering product clusters, they contain products that are strongly interconnected within customer demand; that means customers prefer to buy them together. This yields an alternative view on product groups or product lines which are usually determined a priori by the producer, e.g., products with similar brand, intended use, weight, size, taste, or shape. Once determined, such clusters can also be used to design new product bundles. Here, one may choose products from the same cluster to persuade customers to purchase more items, or one may choose products from non-related clusters by bundling underperforming to performing products in the hope of boosting the sales of the underperforming group. Further, the clusters can be used for product positioning at the point of sale, related products placed at the same location or explicitly far away from each other.

Clustering techniques can also be used to segment customer groups, e.g., to distinguish between premium and economy shoppers. However, to be able to use this information proactively, e.g., in a recommender system or in discount incentive systems, one needs to be able to identify the customer *before* purchase. In online retail, this is done by means of a login. In an offline setting, many retailers employ customer cards. However, personalized discounts can be perceived as highly unfair which is the reason why most retailers, particularly in physical stores, settle on discount schemes that only discriminate against non-card users.

Active sales talk and customers' buying intentions *What information about the customers' purchases can be used for commercial leverage? Are there relations between the products, e.g., customers that purchase product A oftentimes also purchase product B?*

These questions can be answered using association rule analyses. The results can be used to proactively address customers by sales personnel. However, this requires a high amount of training of the staff. In practice, we have therefore encountered that these association rule analyses are rather used for informative purposes. To motivate the sales personnel to address customers proactively, there are other effective alternatives, e.g., setting incentive systems like company internal competitions for "who can sell the most of product X."

Patterns and forecasts *Do certain purchasing patterns exist? How high is the expected customer demand?*

These questions are answered using further statistical methods, in particular time series analyses. Usually, the main focus is on forecasting the expected number of customers or expected revenue. However, these parameters are influenced by many factors such as seasonal patterns, holidays, price levels, competitors' sales and promotions, sales locations, and temperatures. Unfortunately, these company-external factors are rarely recorded, and even if they are at disposal, they would have to be forecast as well to be usable in a forward-looking scheme of the primary objective. Hence, most analyses restrict to time series forecasting based on internal data only.

These forecasts can then be used for pricing decisions. For instance, prices can be lowered to attract more customers or increased to leverage seasonal peaks. Further, they can also be used for operative purposes such as number of sales personnel required to run the shops.

Incentive systems and product portfolio *How effective are the discount systems in place? Who uses them? How do customers' choices change when the product portfolio is changed?*

Although these types of applications are usually addressed using—from a mathematical point of view simple—descriptive statistics, we still mention them here due to their immediate impact on sales and profits. For example, one may evaluate the effectiveness of discount systems and promotions by considering the distribution of customers that use them and their respective receipts. This can yield ideas on alternative discount schemes or changes in the product portfolio that can increase profitability. Further, there are other concepts like consumption-adjusted margins that can help optimizing the product portfolio. Obviously, these aspects are very much at the intersection of basket analysis, portfolio optimization, and pricing.

3 Mathematical Methods Used in Basket Analyses

In the following, we will describe some mathematical techniques that were used in the aforementioned projects. The outcomes of these methods can be used for various purposes, from bundling products, proactive sales talks, and designing discount systems to portfolio optimization and pricing. We will give some examples when considering the respective methods. The main advantage of using these methods is that they can be used to systematically analyze large data volumes and thereby reveal relations that might be overlooked by the naked eye otherwise.

3.1 Cluster Analysis

Clustering methods belong to the field of unsupervised machine learning. A cluster is a group of objects that are similar with respect to some measure. This similarity measure strongly depends on the application. For instance, in a basket analysis, two items can be similar if they have been purchased together in many receipts. Clusters are determined such that items in the same cluster are very similar and are very dissimilar from the items in other clusters.

There exists a multitude of similarity measures and many different algorithms for finding such clusters in large volumes of data.[5] As for algorithms, popular choices

[5]Hastie et al. (2009): see Sect. 14.3. for an introduction.

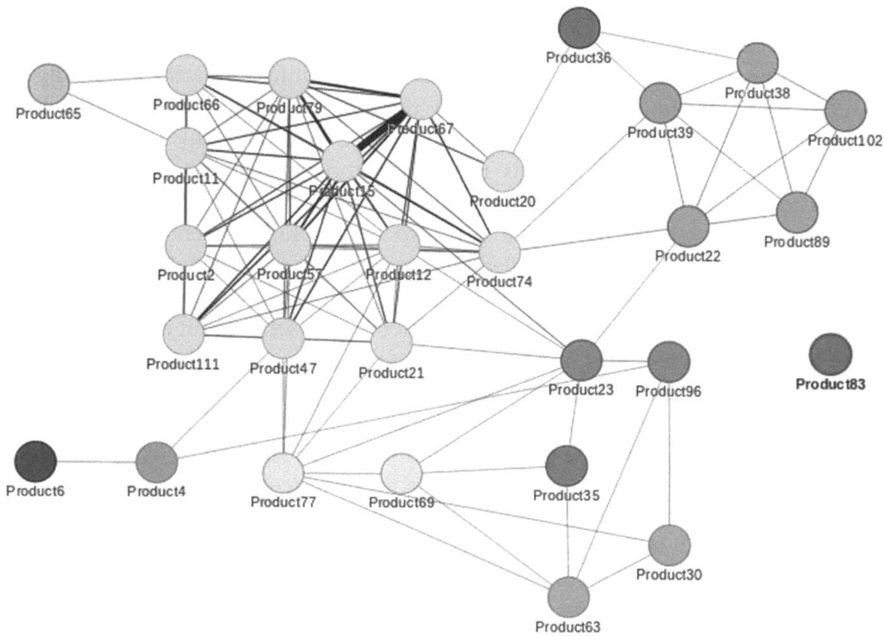

Fig. 1 Anonymized clusters on a purchase graph of the 30 most important items

are the *k-medians* algorithm and its variant *k-center*. However, for finding clusters in sales transactions composed of receipts, we have successfully used spectral clustering.[6] In the sequel we describe one possible such approach.

The objective is to cluster items, i.e., identify similar items, where similarity intuitively means that items are often purchased together. To achieve this we can build a graph consisting of nodes (vertices) and edges (connections between nodes). Each node represents an item that was sold. If two items have occurred in at least one receipt, there is an edge between their respective nodes. The weight of this edge corresponds to the frequency of purchase of these two items, i.e., the number of receipts that both items have been purchased in together. Let us call the resulting graph the *purchase graph*. To gain clusters we use spectral clustering on the purchase graph which is a technique to identify highly connected subgraphs. For how to compute such clusters mathematically, we refer the interested reader to Hastie et al. (2009).[7]

An example on anonymized transactional sales data can be found in Fig. 1. The colors indicate different clusters of items that are frequently purchased together and thereby constitute clusters of products that belong to each other.

[6]Hastie et al. (2009): see Sect. 14.5.

[7]Hastie et al. (2009): see Sect. 14.3.

From practice we have observed that the resulting clusters from such spectral analyses techniques often resemble the product structure of the retailer. As an example, in one project for a food retailer, we identified clusters consisting of products with alcoholic tastes, one with different high percentages of a main ingredient, or clusters containing articles of the same sub-brand which share a similar appearance and packaging. This is not very surprising since these products are usually located on the same shelf or very close to each other, hence the intuitive similarity. However, the technique can also be helpful to identify nonintuitive clusters. As an example, we identified clusters consisting of products with caramel and pistachio taste and clusters with orange and chili taste.

As another example, for a company that offers repair services for automobiles, we were asked to design groups of hardware and services that could be sold as bundles and thereby enable attractive pricing schemes. Given customer receipts of 15 months, we used the above algorithmic clustering method to divide possible services and hardware into clusters of three general categories: repair services of technical faults, tire replacements or purchases, and regular services required to pass mandatory inspections. Within the latter category, we found one cluster that identified the most frequent work tasks that were performed by the company's repairmen when a car failed regular checkup and needed further treatment. This cluster was solely composed of services, and we will call it C subsequently. In further analyses we found that out of 100 receipts that included a mandatory inspection, 24 also required a service from C. Further, the receipt's value increased sharply by 127% if a service from C was required and the items in C made up for roughly two fifth of this additional charge. This information was then used to design a no-worries package that worked essentially like an insurance policy. The services from C would be sold at a blended rate at the time when the customer brings in her car for inspection. If they were required, the company would provide the services from C at no additional cost. However, if the services were not needed, the company would yield additional profits.

3.2 Association Rule Analysis

The previously discussed cluster analysis induces two main disadvantages:

- Single products that are purchased very frequently dominate the results. Therefore, niche products hardly occur in the evaluations since they are purchased rarely compared to the rest of the portfolio.
- Causal relations and correlations between products remain unexplored. Products are solely clustered together, but there is no notion of which product's purchase triggered the purchase of which other product.

Association rule analysis is a means to remedy these drawbacks. In a nutshell, it examines the implications of a products' purchase or even a sales promotion. Concretely, it estimates the conditional probabilities of purchasing products given the purchase of some other products. Note that one may also consider sales promotions or discounts as dummy products here.

For example, a—fictitious—association rule for retail could be as follows: A customer that purchases chocolate also purchases wine 90% of the time. This can be extended to subsets of the products, i.e., the likelihood that a customer buys product A given she already bought B, C, and D. Further, one may also determine the product that a customer is most likely to buy next, given her current purchase.

Note that these analyses cannot be performed with clustering. To consider the fictitious example above, chocolate and wine could end up in the same cluster. However, the implication that a purchase of chocolate likely implies the purchase of wine does not mean that the contrary—purchase of wine implies purchase of chocolate—holds true! Hence the need for different methods.

Given vast amounts of sales data, it is often not obvious how to find meaningful association rules. Based on the concept of the so-called strong rules, association rule analysis was first used by Agrawal et al. (1993)[8] in order to examine the relations between the products in supermarkets.

Today, association rule analysis is performed with the help of the a priori algorithm and its variants. This algorithm uses three parameters: *support*, *confidence*, and *lift*. In the sequel we give a short description. Let X and Y be sets of products, and let us consider the rule: purchasing all products in X leads to purchasing all products in Y.

- Support describes the frequency of occurrence of all products in the rule. That is, how often all products from the union of X and Y are purchased together.
- Confidence describes the conditional probability of the rule. In our example, confidence is a measure for the conditional probability that a customer purchases all products of Y given he already has the products of X in her basket.
- Lift gives an estimate on the association measure between X and Y. In our example, how (in)dependent the purchase of all items in X is from the purchase of all items in Y.

For the mathematical backgrounds and implementation, we refer to Hastie et al. (2009) and the references therein.[9] For more applications of the a priori algorithm in practice, the interested reader is referred to Aguinis et al. (2013).[10]

As an example we depict an outcome of association rules in Fig. 2. The light blue circles refer to products. An association rule is depicted by arrows that lead from products to a dark blue circle from which one or more arrows lead to products. The size of the dark blue circle symbolizes the rule's support. The set of association rules that are to be displayed can be filtered according to support, confidence, and lift.

We provide an example of an application. In a project for a car repair service provider, we used association rule analysis to (algorithmically) find out when

[8] Agrawal et al. (1993), pp. 207–216.

[9] Hastie et al. (2009): see Sect. 14.2.2.

[10] Aguinis et al. (2013), pp. 1799–1824.

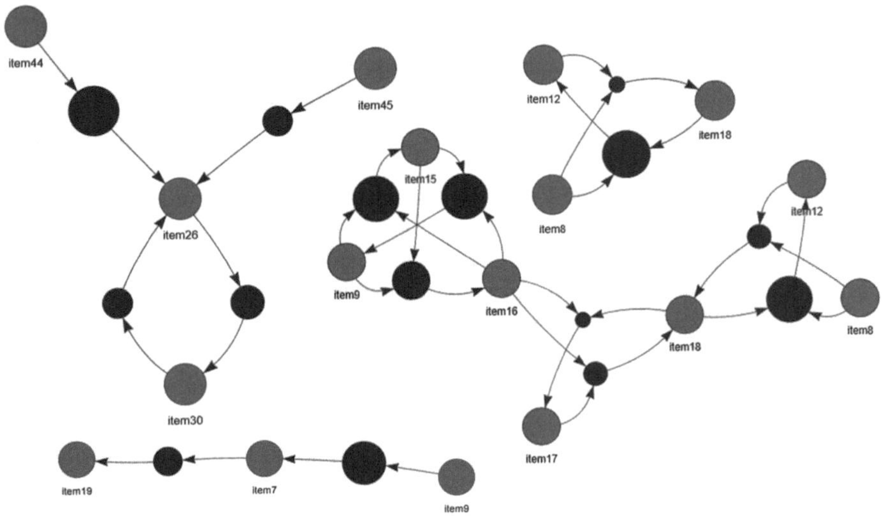

Fig. 2 Anonymized amount of association rules from shopping cart analyses in offline retail

customers required a replacement vehicle. The analysis showed that the use of a replacement vehicle was mostly preceded by an engine failure. Digging into further details, we found that about 6% of receipts that had a problem with the engine also claimed a replacement vehicle (confidence). Further, if such a vehicle was used, the average usage duration was 1.86 days with a peak of the distribution on the first day. To exploit this information, we suggested that whenever an engine problem occurred and a replacement vehicle was required, the customer would be offered a replacement immediately for an extended period of 2 days. The induced increase in rental volume could then be balanced by a discount for the second day, since statistically most customers would only require the replacement for 1 day.

3.3 Time Series Analysis

Forecasting plays a major role for the management of any retailer. There are several forecasts that most companies prepare several times a year. Most prominently, forecasts on revenue and profits are considered. Aside from these parameters that are mainly important for the finance and controlling business units, forecasts are also crucial with respect to pricing and determination of price sensitivities.

The field of time series analysis is very broad, and a comprehensive overview is beyond the scope of this chapter. Therefore, we refer to Shumway and Stoffer (2011) and Petris et al. (2009) for introductions on the mathematical methodology.[11]

[11]Shumway and Stoffer (2011), Petris et al. (2009).

Nevertheless, we would like to give some advice on typical challenges that particularly retailers face when developing forecasts.

The sales of retailers are usually predominantly influenced by the number of customers that visits the store, may it be online or offline. This number is hard to forecast since it can depend on various external aspects: weather, advertisement, competitors' actions, locations, and more. Further, business actions like aggressive promotions or widespread advertisement can have a significant influence on the number of customers. Unfortunately, quantifying the influence of these factors based on historical data is often impossible since many of them change at the same time, the history is too short, or the business situation and the customers' behavior have changed.

In any case, statistical forecasts that are based purely on historical data entail the assumption that the environment, apart from those variables already taken into account, is virtually static. A significant change in environment parameters—such as a new competitor, a push in sales, market revolutionizing new products—can lead to forecasts becoming partially or completely obsolete.

To still be able to tackle these problems, some retailers use recurrent experiments. As an example, for an airport store retailer, we conducted a series of well-designed experiments to determine the uplift obtained for several forms of promotions. Combining these statistics with an estimated trend on customer traffic, without promotion, resulted in an improved sales forecast. In our experience, well-defined experiments in confined spaces of smaller scope, i.e., in well-chosen test shops or on parts of the product portfolio only, can help to accurately estimate these influencing factors. Further, such experiments can be conducted to cross validate and, if need be, adjust current assumptions.

One frequent problem in retailers' forecasts is seasonality. Depending on the type of products, there may be several forms of seasonal effects. Most common are the summer and winter seasons with changing demands for food and clothes, e.g., ice cream in summer and chocolate in winter. Of course, this causes significant changes in the number of people buying these seasonal products. As an example, toy producers (with proprietary sales channel) make most of their revenue within the Christmas season; see Fig. 3 for a sketch of this phenomenon. This kind of seasonality can be quantified using decomposition techniques where the time series is decomposed into a general trend and seasonality patterns plus random noise.[12] Note that there can be several seasonalities including a yearly as well as a weekly pattern, e.g., more sales on Fridays and Saturdays than during the week.

Additional to the seasonality in the number of customers, there can also be seasonal effects in the number of purchased goods. As an example, we discovered in a project for a chocolate producer—in its proprietary retail stores—that the number of customers during Easter season was stable in the first weeks and only increased sharply the very few weeks before Easter Sunday. However, when considering what customers bought, we observed a steady increase during the entire

[12]Brockwell and Davis (2016): see Sect. 1.5 for an introduction.

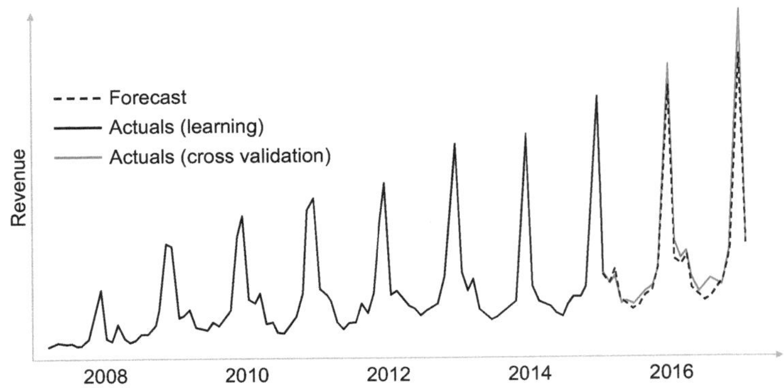

Fig. 3 Sales of a retailer that clearly depict a strong seasonality around Christmas and on closer inspection also Easter. This is a typical forecasting scenario where the data up to 2014 was used to train the forecasting model, i.e., estimate its parameters, and the forecast values are compared to the actuals in the subsequent years for cross validation

season. Most retailers also witness this phenomenon during Christmas when there are not only more people coming to the store but they also buy more.

To model these purchase seasonalities in practice, we developed the following idea: Split the sales process into two steps. The first would be a forecast of the number of customers visiting the store. The second, once a customer is in the store, consider what and the number of items she will buy. More precisely, we analyze the number of items per receipt, of a certain product, which we call *item rates*. Note that item rates are essentially a means to analyze customers' purchases independent of the number of customers which is very useful when the latter cannot be predicted. In particular, this is convenient when analyzing the effects of product relocations or changes in prices since this may only affect what people buy but not their number.

3.4 Descriptive Statistics

Aside from the aforementioned mathematical models, also descriptive statistics can be used to analyze customers' behavior. Most often this is done with the underlying objective to increase revenue and profits. There are many statistics that one may have a look at, depending on the types of goods and retail concepts. In the sequel we will give some examples from our consulting practice and some of the challenges that had to be addressed.

For a customer in the food industry, we analyzed different discount systems and designed targeted experiments to test alternatives. The discount system in place was that customers buying at least four items would get a significant discount. When considering stores that used this discount incentive with stores that did not, there was no noticeable difference between the average revenues per receipt in these stores after normalizing for the granted discount. This led to the hypothesis that the

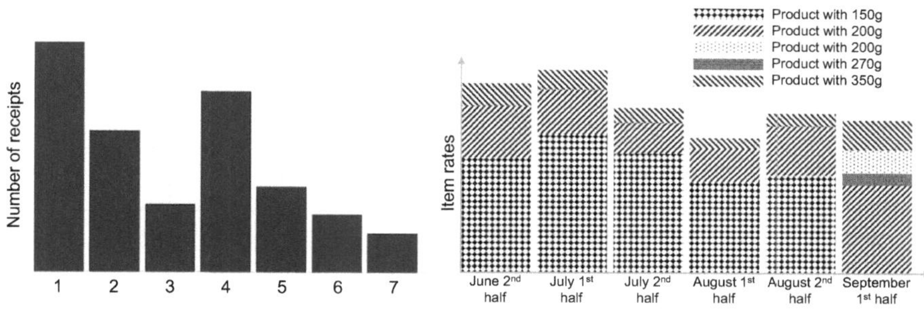

Fig. 4 Left: Histogram on the number of receipts having one to seven items. This structure is characteristic of discount incentives that offer discounts above a minimum number of purchased items (here a min. of 4). Right: With beginning of September 2018, the article of smallest size was removed from the store; hence its item rate drops to zero. Simultaneously the item rates for other packages of the same product but with different sizes grow significantly

discount system might be ineffective. However, when considering the average number of items per receipt in a discounted store, the effects were clearly visible (cf. Fig. 4 left). In particular, more than half the customers purchased at least four items.

We then proceeded to test another discount system. Customers were granted discounts progressively after passing certain monetary thresholds. More precisely, we used two thresholds, one at 10 and one at 20 Euro. When the receipt value was above these values, customers would receive certain discounts. After introduction of the new scheme, revenue per receipt jumped by 12% in the following month.

The above example exhibits one of the main challenges in the use of descriptive statistics for business decisions. The obtained values must imperatively be compared to reference periods which require historical values reaching far into the past. In particular, in the above example, the yearly seasonality would cause a natural uplift in the receipt values anyway independent of any discount system. Further, revenue per receipt is a convenient measure for most sales representatives to measure success. However, since the new discount system also changed the frequency and size of the granted discounts, it is more advisable to consider the induced profit per receipt which in turn requires good knowledge on production costs.

In another project we analyzed the customer base of a retailer that had personalized information available. Here, customers that bought multiple times throughout the year happened to be the most profitable customer group. However, most customers purchased only once per year, mainly following a strong seasonality around Christmas. In considering the time that passed between first and second purchase of a first-time buyer, we found that a quarter of all first-time buyers purchased again within only a few days and another quarter within only a few months after the initial purchase. This could be leveraged to convert first-time buyers into regular customers. If a customer does not purchase again within a few months, one may communicate product information, special offers, promotions, or coupons directly to the customer by electronic or regular mail. In particular, knowing a precise time frame for such direct contact avoids too frequent mailings that are widely regarded as spam.

There are several statistics that one could consider to analyze customers' preferences. Here are some that we have used in our projects:

- Number of items (of a certain product or product group) per receipt, i.e., item rates
- Average revenue and profit per receipt
- Most frequently purchased product or product pair within the same receipts
- Number of receipts consisting mostly of a certain group of items, e.g., number of receipts that make 70% of their revenue with seasonal items
- Number or receipts containing certain discounts and the above statistics restricted to these customer groups
- Distribution of the number of customers throughout the day
- Share of sales volume induced by certain customer groups, e.g., revenue with customer card holders
- Demographic segmentation in particular in online shops where the origin of the customer can be traced by her IP address
- Revenue and profits generated in different sales channels, e.g., via own flagship stores, retail stores, or other retailers such as Amazon

In particular item rates turn out to be a very useful tool for detecting the effectiveness of many actions like repositioning products close to the shop entrance or cashier, success of internal sales competitions of certain items, or changes in the product portfolio. As an example for the latter, one of our clients removed the item of smallest size from a product line to try to convert consumers to large-sized packages. This idea stems from the consideration of consumption-adjusted margins. It turned out that customers still kept buying nearly the same amount of goods, i.e., that the sum of item rates of over the entire product line remained stable. In fact, they did switch to slightly larger package sizes thereby increasing profits (cf. Fig. 4 right). For further practical examples, in particular with a view on pricing, we refer the interested reader to Simon (2015).[13]

In summary, descriptive statistics can be used to gain an overview of the typical customers' preferences fast. However, to estimate effects of business decisions, such as changing discounts or prices, one needs to be very careful to not overlook natural underlying trends and may need to normalize for them using advanced mathematical methods.

[13]Simon (2015).

4 Conclusion

The foundation of every business model is a deep understanding of the company's clientele and customers' needs. In pursuit of this knowledge, we have described several approaches that together yield a thorough basket analysis to reveal customers' preferences and shopping behavior.

Retailers have always striven to analyze sales data to steer their business. With the digitization of all supply and production processes, massive amounts of transactional data are now available even for most bricks-and-mortar retailers. The evaluation of this data requires mathematical and statistical methods and opens many possibilities to gain new insights that we described in this contribution.

Basket analyses are the foundation for steering a retailer's business. In particular, they can help rooting business decisions on a solid objective and quantitative basis. Applications reach from designing new products or product bundles, targeting specific customer groups, designing new discount schemes, and pricing to product portfolio optimization and targeted advertisement.

There are many further applications that utilize retailers' transactional data ranging from recommender systems to determining price sensitivities and more generally the entire profession of pricing. However, most bricks-and-mortar retailers have only begun to comprehend the analytical possibilities that lay hidden in their internal data treasury.

References

Aggarwal CC (2016) Recommender systems, the textbook. Springer, Cham

Agrawal R, Tomasz Imielinski T, Swami A (1993) Mining association rules between sets of items in large databases. In: Proceedings of the 1993 ACM SIGMOD international conference on management of data, pp 207–216

Aguinis H, Forcum L, Joo H (2013) Using market basket analysis in management research. J Manag 39:1799–1824

Brockwell PJ, Davis RA (2016) Introduction to time series and forecasting, 3rd edn. Springer, Cham

Ferreira KJ, Lee BHA, Simchi-Levi D (2016) Analytics for an online retailer: demand forecasting and price optimization. Manufacturing & Service Operations Management 18:69–88

Hastie T, Tibshirani R, Friedman J (2009) The elements of statistical learning data mining, inference, and prediction, 2nd edn. Springer, New York, NY

Klein R, Steinhardt C (2008) Revenue management, Grundlagen und Mathematische Methoden. Springer, Heidelberg

Özer Ö, Phillips R (2014) The Oxford handbook of pricing management. Oxford University Press, Oxford

Petris G, Petrone S, Campagnoli P (2009) Dynamic linear models with R. Springer, New York

Shumway RH, Stoffer DS (2011) Time series analysis and its applications with R examples, 3rd edn. Springer, Cham

Simon H (2015) Confessions of the pricing man: how price affects everything, 1st edn. Springer, Cham

Talluri KT, Van Ryzin GJ (2004) The theory and practice of revenue management. Kluwer Academic, Boston, MA

Carsten Moldenhauer is Head of Operations Research in the Horváth & Partners Steering Lab. He holds a PhD in mathematics with specialization in discrete optimization and has worked on several projects across industries with a focus on modeling businesses quantitatively. His expertise includes operations research and pricing models.

Henning Zwirnmann is Quantitative Business Modeler in the Horváth & Partners Steering Lab. He holds a master's degree in physics with specialization in computational physics and has worked on several pricing projects for clients in the retail industry. Moreover, he has a strong background in machine learning and natural language processing.

Sales Performance Management

Heiko Schulte-Oversohl

Abstract This contribution deals with the interdependency of controlling and the sales department.

The special importance of sales as an independent area for the corporate success is highlighted. This leads to the analysis of the sales department characteristics and how performance management generates value added to support the sales tasks. Relevant elements and instruments are explained in this contribution.

Keywords Controlling · Driver model · Key performance indicators · Sales organization · Sales controlling · Sales performance management

1 Introduction

The tasks of sales organizations cover much more than the distribution of goods. The sales department is much rather an independent and mighty functional area of a company. Apart from the sales-system's composition and channel-policy, sales management can further encompass sales logistics.[1] It is therefore a firm element of the company's management and plays a crucial role in the company's success. The success of upstream business areas largely depends on the sales department. The sales department uses this dependency to bundle as many competences as

An adaption of this contribution has been originally printed as Schulte-Oversohl, H. (2014): Vertriebssteuerung, Controlling in der Konsumgüterindustrie: Innovative Ansätze und Praxisbeispiele, pp. 225–243.

[1]Greiner et al. (2013).

H. Schulte-Oversohl (✉)
Management Consultant, Levanca GmbH, Hamburg, Germany

M. Buttkus, R. Eberenz (eds.), *Performance Management in Retail and the Consumer Goods Industry*, https://doi.org/10.1007/978-3-030-12730-5_25

possible and thereby safeguard its ability to self-control. This is oftentimes then used at the end of the business year to say: "Our success proves us right."

Nonetheless, even the sales department must face itself with the challenges of a dynamic economic environment. Globalized markets are in constant flux, customers' expectations and demands rise, and new channels of distribution are being opened. These challenges the sales department is faced with require an increasing measure of coordination and management in order to successfully distribute the company's own products in the future.

2 Challenges of Sales Performance Management

Apart from a modern economy, sales management is faced with other internal challenges when improving the company's sales performance. Oftentimes, a lack in distinction of central and decentral tasks can lead to tasks needlessly being processed twice or not at all. Further, individual market requirements may not be heeded sufficiently, and there is no strategic approach for performance measurement. This missing approach can be noticed in, e.g., a lacking commitment to the consolidation and cutting off of revenue or possibly the implementation of half-hearted programs to increase efficiency.

A significant characteristic of sales is oftentimes a considerably lower standardization of processes than that of other operating areas. Furthermore, individual sales channels may act without internal coordination and partially in competition with each other. There is a lack in uniform key performance indicators and incentive systems that could make the specific results of these sales areas transparent and comparable.[2]

The internal and external requirements of a modern sales organization necessitate a uniform performance measurement approach that enables management to lead the entire sales organization according to consistent, centrally defined parameters—without limiting the necessary degree of freedom of markets. For management, finding the right balance within the performance measurement approach poses a difficult task. Moreover, this approach should be integrated in a company-wide concept and should not be defined too narrowly. Sales management oftentimes only uses revenue for orientation and thereby neglects other relevant performance indicators: measuring the success of sales in a modern economic environment is not limited to using an increase in revenue. This is shown in the following contribution.

Apart from a too narrow performance management approach, positioning sales controlling[3] correctly is often a problem. The sales department tends to use sales controllers as a "number cruncher" for the board's ever-increasing demand for

---

[2]Greiner et al. (2013), Kieninger (2013).

[3]The author uses the English word "controlling" to translate the German term "controlling." Please refer to the discussion in the preface.

information. In these cases, this leads to sales controlling mostly being used as service provider for upstream processes or the corporate controlling team. Hereby, the actual function of sales controlling, to provide an effective and efficient performance management and to support the sales management in decision-making processes, is indiscernible.

2.1 *The Extent of Sales Performance Management*

Sales performance management is an original function of a company's management. It is used to break down and optimize the company's strategic aims and turn them into operative objectives for sales. The achievement of these objectives is then monitored continuously. In case of deviations, appropriate measures are developed and passed on to management for decision. In this process, sales performance management can employ different instruments.

Initially, it assumes sales planning for the coming business years. For the current business year, budgeted figures are compared with actual figures, and possible deviations are analyzed. The latter could, for instance, develop on the level of profit centers, customers, products, regions, or distribution channels. With an in-depth analysis of deviations, measures can be taken and activities planned in order to counteract these deviations. In doing so, sales performance management does not merely encompass a control function but also a design function for the sales department, which tends to be ignored by the more "classic sales representatives." During the developing and measure-taking process, there are numerous concepts for sales performance management, e.g., optimizing the distributing focus through analyses of market, competition, and product range and through benchmarks, by optimizing the organization of sales through increasing its efficiency and reducing its costs. Furthermore, sales performance management can assume an active part in the allocation of sales resources, by pointedly supporting sales employees in providing relevant information and by acting as a counterpart and sparring partner for all business matters.

In general, sales performance management can be subdivided into three levels. Direct management includes target sets, budgets, and requirements for implementations for the sales department. Sales can indirectly be controlled through a system of incentives and training seminars. Lastly, there is the level of a structural management of the sales department's organization, distribution channels, and target customers.

2.2 *Product Success and Its Allocation*

Each functional area of a company, from product management, procurement, and producing to logistics, contributes to the success of both the products and the company in general. Total sales volume and sales revenue have a collective but not synonymous factor of success. However, factors of success such as the degree of

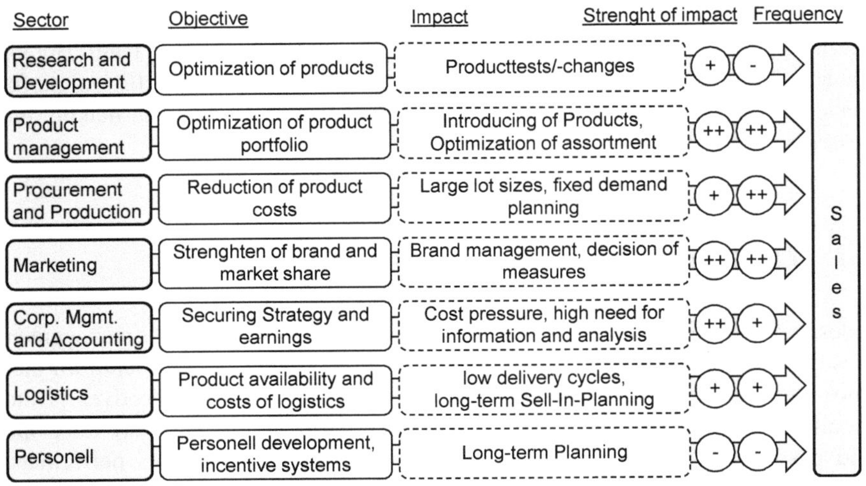

Fig. 1 Interdependencies of the sales department with other sectors of the company (Source: Own illustration)

innovation, market shares, unit pricing, product availability, or market coverage already display the specific objectives of the involved functional areas. Due to the different emphases of constituent performance indicators, participants attempt to influence sales to their own ends. The strength and frequency of this influence can vary. Figure 1 gives an overview of the interdependencies of the sales department with other sectors of the company.

The optimization of products through research and development can, for example, lead to better sales figures. In contrast, product tests and product changes must be explained to trade partners and can lead to a drop in sales. Maximizing sales volume is the most important original function of the sales department. This can be differentiated into separate steps that each represents a function in sales.[4]

The first step includes a product listing and the agreement on terms with trade partners. With a successful conclusion, the product is incorporated in trade and is available for purchase by the customer. The task the sales department is faced with following this process is reaching and saturating possible customers with the product in order to increase its presence in places of trade.

Another step is the constant improvement of product placement. The sales department must attempt to find the ideal size and positioning on shelves in order to generate sales and thereby influence trade partners. At the same time, product pricing should be set at an optimum level in order to successfully compete with other providers in the same product segment.[5] Another task included in the remit of the sales department is merchandising in order to increase or rather retain revenue over

[4]Steffenhagen (2008).
[5]Kühnapfel (2013).

time. To achieve this, promotions, special placements of products, or flyers can be used.

The objectives of each functional area are legitimate and, in case of doubt, can be derived from the company's strategy. Nonetheless, there can naturally be conflicting goals. These do not merely need to be aligned by sales performance management but must also be profitably linked. New introductions of products by a distributor and their corresponding retail price not only lead to the sectors of product management (final knowledge of the entire market and product), marketing (guiding the brand within the market), sales (final knowledge of the retail market and revenue opportunities), and corporate controlling (cost impact) being confronted with each other but also introduce the factors of possible operational restrictions through production and logistics. The impact of the influence and the frequency thereof through product management and marketing but also through procurement and the corporate management is especially high. In doing so, actions by the sales department can influence both business procedures within interlinked functional areas, as well as the processes between these. In this sense, sales performance management does not just represent the holistic management of sales in general but can serve beyond this aspect as originator for a coordination of different business processes of the company as a whole.

2.3 *Reasons for an Individual Sales Performance Management Function*

There is no generalized method on how to best organize sales performance management. Before posing the question of "centralized or decentralized?," it is necessary to ascertain whether or not an own organizational unit is appropriate.

The prerequisite of an individual organizational unit is the possibility of accordingly dividing tasks and bundling operational, sale-supportive, and strategic subtasks. However, an increase in net value added can only occur, if the entire volume of tasks is large enough and thereby justifies the introduction of an individual function. The extent of tasks is predominantly determined by the size of the company but to some extent also by its distribution type and business model. The range of tasks in a small, single-product company, selling over its own online shop, is considerably smaller than that of a full-range provider with multichannel distribution. In consequence, sales performance management in smaller companies is attached to one person, possibly the CEO, or is controlled by sales managers themselves.[6] Once a sufficient growth of the company justifies an individual organization, the matter of an optimized, organizational configuration can be solved. The clarification and analysis of this matter depends largely on the specific situation of the company. In addition, the extent to which solutions are needed plays an important role. If sales

[6]Kühnapfel (2013).

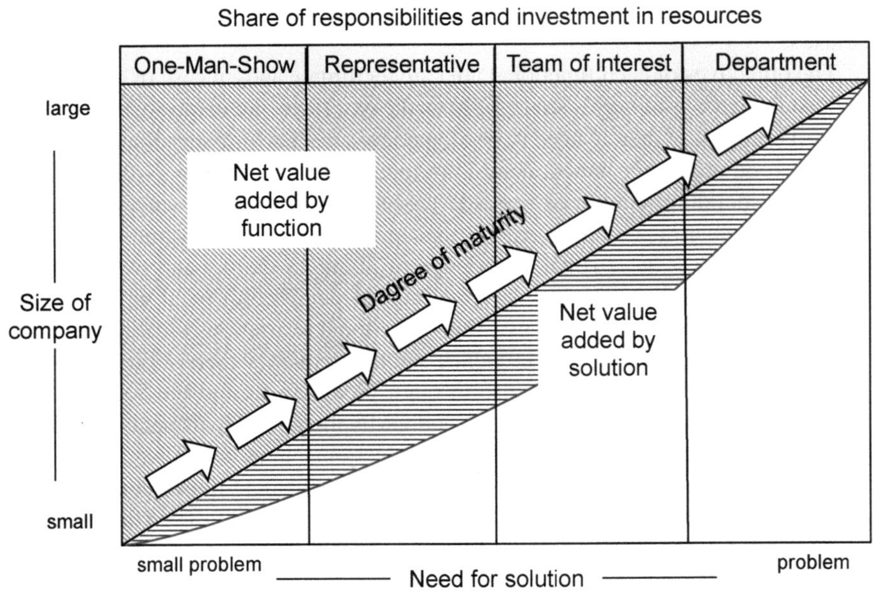

Fig. 2 Development of sales performance management over the period (Source: Own illustration)

performance management has specific issues to solve, e.g., the implementation of market entry or the optimization of sales organization, then solving these issues yields an additional increase in net value.

Even with an awareness of parameters such as company size and the demand for solutions, implementation and success of sales performance management cannot be undertaken without an analysis of existing processes, functions, and responsibilities. Hereby, the level of maturity is determined in form of expertise and the existing system infrastructure, in order to obtain conclusions for an ideal structure or expansion of sales performance management. Furthermore, an excessive strain on both the parties involved and the system landscape, right after the introduction of a sales performance management and thereby resulting obstacles, can be avoided by a preceding analysis. Figure 2 depicts solution requirements in relation to company size and demonstrates the different organizational characteristics over the period of introducing a sales performance management.

Apart from the previously mentioned criteria, as well as a detailed analysis of these processes, factors such as accountability and power—both technically and disciplinarily—play an important role in the configuration. Subsequent to the increasing institutionalization, accountability and power are bundled, and the participants will attempt to increase their influence in the company. In case of an independent organizational unit, it oftentimes becomes a part of the company's management. In order to ensure success, key people, the so-called old hands, need to be integrated into both the conceptualization and the implementation of sales performance management. In this way, potential opponents of this concept can be made promoters.

3 Elements of Sales Performance Management

If possible potential for a sales performance management within a company is perceived and the topic is broached, the company is in the state of recognition that sales has unused potential although distribution is already controlled more or less consciously. A clear organizational structure, standardized processes, and a reliable accounting are absolute prerequisites for the development and optimization of sales performance management. Only if these requirements are met, it can reach desired results with the help of key performance indicator systems and instruments such as planning, reporting, and analysis. As a result, management is not merely an addition of single elements but a temporal and contextual interlinking of individual elements and participants. These elements will be further illustrated in the following.

3.1 Unambiguous Targets

The basis of all sales performance management is the company's strategy and the objectives and measures derived from it. Along the organizational structure, strategic aims are broken down to operational subgoals and targets. These operative subgoals should be reached by the respective business functions in the running business year. The sales function has a high relevance for consumer goods companies. This is especially evident in the high number of sales staff that builds intense economic relations to multiple trade partners. If target values are transparent and convincing for each sales staff member, then a sales department can achieve success as a team. If, however, the strategy consists of a blend of multiple imprecisely defined objectives, then individual target values could be stressed incorrectly, or target values change on short notice. These developments represent a sizeable problem for sales performance management, as these new standards can possibly contradict the original ones. Aside from this fundamental strategic issue, sales performance management is only aligned in accordance with the strategy to a certain extent, and, as consequence, business objectives may not be met. Further, this reorientation causes not only a high expenditure in resources but also a loss of confidence in future standards. Especially balancing market shares and corporate results are the classic challenges of the consumer goods industry that oftentimes lead to standards not being met. Figure 3 illustrates the necessary consideration for this circumstance.

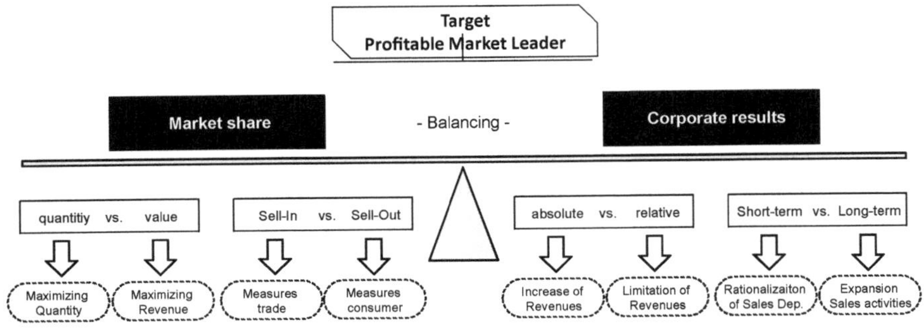

Fig. 3 Balancing market shares and corporate results (Source: Own illustration)

3.2 *Comprehensible Key Performance Indicators*

Any salesperson will consider selling a higher number of products, for a higher price than in the previous business year, as success. Initially, this success is measured exclusively by revenue, and in a positive development in revenue, failure to meet set targets in other areas is relativized. Nonetheless, it is not just the salesperson that measures his success by revenue; sales performance management oftentimes advocates the opinion that revenue can solve other problems. However, in order to achieve sustainable market success and the realization of company objectives, a functioning bundle of key performance indicators must be fixed. These key performance indicators and the deviation between budget figures and actual figures are the foundation of sales performance management. In practice however, correct key performance indicators may have been defined, but a pointed instruction of contributors is often forgotten. Application in this context means creating an understanding for how changes in parameters (e.g., list prices, promotion shares, etc.) influence specific performance indicators. Applying a so-called simplified and generalized rule of 3 has proven to be successful in this context. For example, "if the competitive price rises by ten cents, then revenue volume rises by five percent." As a consequence, sales employees are able to derive correct measures for optimization.[7] Apart from training toward a key performance indicator concept, it is advisable to implement or adapt according to IT and wage systems.

The advantage of key performance indicators is that they quantitatively and aggregately inform about relevant circumstances and developments. In this process, the consumer goods industry, for example, uses standardized key performance indicators that supply the required information in comparison with competitors. However, this entire set of key performance indicators should result from business processes, the market environment, and the company structure.[8] The premise for

[7]Stegmüller and Möller (2011).
[8]Stegmüller and Möller (2011).

effective indicators is a clear definition and that they are accepted by the recipient. In general, indicators can be divided into four groups:

- Key figures are the result at the end of a chain of effects (e.g., revenue).
- The drivers behind key performance indicators have a direct influence on performance indicators (e.g., number of listings). If the drivers can directly be influenced by the company and if they have an impact that is relevant to the set objectives, then they represent a basis for actions of the company as a control lever.
- Auxiliary indicators are intermediate variables for calculating a key performance indicator that is rarely identified.
- Market indicators oftentimes reflect estimates of variables and variations of the market with immediate effect on the company's own key performance indicators (e.g., market volume and growth).

But what is the difference between a key performance indicator (KPI) and a performance indicator? A KPI measures and depicts the progress with regard to important objectives or critical success factors within a company. This involves more of a target orientation and less of actually new figures. The importance of a system of key performance indicators can best be described with the following example: A manufacturer is represented in the market for roasted coffee with different brand names and is endeavoring to determine the effect of price changes. Hereby, the aim is increasing both market shares and the subsequent growth of the contribution margin. In theory, the price-demand relation and price and cross-price elasticity would be used to establish an Amoroso-Robinson relation and a Niehans formula.[9] However, many employees are not familiar with these theoretic approaches. Moreover, these calculations would not lead to useful results due to missing or indecisive data. In praxis, it is oftentimes relied on a combination of a driver model and the measured effect of control levers. Figure 4 constitutes an example of such a driver model, which depicts the interdependencies between the two brands A and B.

As the status quo is known and the price constitutes an explicit control lever, a change in price can be used to measure or rather evaluate this influence on specific key figures.

In the following, an example will be used for demonstration. A coffee roaster is represented on the market with the brand names A and B. The brand B produces an average NP sales volume of 40,000 pounds a week with the normal selling price (NP) set at 3.99€ and the average competitive price at 3.72€. The price gap to the competitor amounts to 27 cents and shows the brand strength. If the price gap changes, then as consequence the sales quantity will change in accordance with the price elasticity of demand. For a promotion period of 2 weeks, the selling price of brand B is now reduced by 50 cents to the promotion price of 3.49€ (PP). The price gap is thereby changed, and a PP sales volume of 100,000 pounds a week is reached,

[9]Hermann et al. (2002).

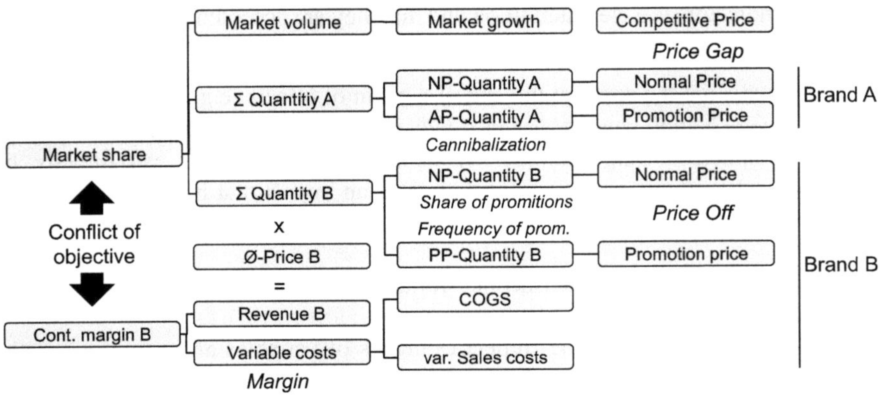

Fig. 4 Example for a driver model regarding price policy (Source: Own illustration)

a gain of 60,000 pounds. Brand A has an NP of 5.99€ and has now become more expensive compared with brand B, due to the promotion period. Its NP sales volume has dropped from 70,000 pounds to 50,000 pounds a week. Brand B's additional sales volume amounting to 60,000 pounds therefore results in a cannibalization of the own brand A (cannibalization percentage of the added sales volume = 33%). Brand A's sales volume is cannibalized by 28.6%, as consequence of the reduced price. The extent of promotions can be measured for single calendar years as share that the PP sales volume has of general sales volume (promotion shares) and also as share of weeks with promotions of total weeks in the year (promotion intensity). The cost of goods sold (production costs) of a single pound of brand B's produce amounts to 2.00€ and mostly derives from the cost of green coffee. The contribution margin (CM) per pound at NP amounts to 63 cents (3.99—VAT 7%—taxes on coffee 1.10€, cost of goods sold 2.00€) and results in a net gross profit margin of 17%. In the price off, the CM per pound reduces to 16 cents and the net gross profit margin to 5%. In order to measure success, the CM gain, resulting from added sales volumes, and the brand B's CM loss must be considered.

It is important to realistically account for the market's quantity reactions to the price change. After an initial trial-and-error phase, it should be possible to build an applicable cause-effect model, whose hypotheses can be improved increasingly with cumulative experience. In this manner, reliable sensitivities can be derived for the KPIs' market shares and contribution margins.

3.3 *Instruments of Sales Performance Management*

The basis of a target-oriented and efficient sales performance management is a deep understanding of the actual situation, the present development, and the sales department's activities. On this basis, target and incentive systems (conditioning systems for trade, payment systems for employees) can be defined and introduced. The initial point for target and incentive systems is oftentimes an income statement, in which revenue is used as a starting point. The sales department usually tends to have a declining influence on single-line items, the lower the level of the income statement. Sales performance management has different controlling instruments at its disposal that will be explained in the following. They include planning and budgeting, reporting, as well as economic modeling and the assessment of individual measures. In the process, the use of instruments will be limited to profit and loss aspects, with a corresponding detail to business sector level, product level, and customer level.

3.3.1 Planning and Budgeting

Generally speaking, planning is a proactive process. It is constituted by the setting of objectives and the selection of applicable measures to reaching these objectives as well as a continual objective and premise control. The planning process is of great importance to successful sales and can bind capacities over multiple weeks. A high level of detail, unclear target setting, poor coordination between levels of planning, and a demand for the results of overdue analyses can lead to distortions with the responsible controllers. In view of this high need for planning, these may then neglect everyday business as consequence. The basis of planning is a comprehensive annual plan. The need of purchase and production according to planned figures beyond the end of the business years can be covered by a continuous 12 or 18 months planning.

The question of the adequate planning direction—top-down or bottom-up—has in practice been outdated by the counter-current process—a combination of both.[10] In the process, management as highest planning authority makes decisions that may already encompass a preliminary draft planning. After this, the lower planning levels conduct their detail planning according to the bottom-up principle, which is then consolidated and compared to the draft planning. In case of any deviations between draft and detail planning, these could be levelled by planning measures or alterations of planning requirements. In doing so, traceable deviations of the detail planning should imperatively entail a search for solutions. If, however, there were to be a persistence on the draft planning, this planning would reveal itself as a covert top-down planning.

Oftentimes sales performance management contributes to draft planning by supplying relevant information. During the detail planning, the role of mediator between the highest planning level and the sales department is appointed to it. Sales performance management's role in this is to dissect the top-down targets into segment plans for all parties involved in planning and demand planning results at set due dates. Making the development and the importance of these requirements transparent for all participants and then offering support have proven successful.

[10] Jung (2010).

		1	2	3	4	5	6	7	8	9	10	11	12	13	14	15	16	17	18	19	20	21	22
	Month	January					February				March				April				May				
	CW	1	2	3	4	5	6	7	8	9	10	11	12	13	14	15	16	17	18	19	20	21	22
Media ATL	TV													X	X								
	Radio				X	X								X	X								
	Print							X												X			
Distribution channel	**Retail trade**																						
	Price brand A	5,99	5,99	5,99	4,99		5,99	5,99	5,99	5,99	5,99	5,99	5,99	4,49		5,99	5,79	5,79	5,79	5,79	5,79	5,79	5,79
	Price brand B	3,99	3,99	3,99	3,99	3,99	3,99	3,49		3,99	3,99	3,99	3,99	2,99		3,99	3,99	3,99	3,99	3,49		3,99	3,99
	Leaflets				X			X						X	X					X			
	Special placements													X	X								
	Display				X	X		X	X					X	X					X	X		
	Specialist Trade																						
	Price brand A	5,99	5,99	5,99	4,99		5,99	5,99	5,99	5,99	5,99	5,99	5,99	4,49		5,99	5,79	5,79	5,79	5,79	5,79	5,79	5,79
	Price brand B	3,99	3,99	3,99	3,99	3,99	3,99	3,99	3,99	3,49		3,99	3,99	2,99		3,99	3,99	3,99	3,99	3,49		3,99	3,99
	Special placements				X	X								X	X								
	Display									X	X			X	X					X	X		
	Online-Shop																						
	Price brand A	5,99	5,99	5,99	4,99		5,99	5,99	5,99	4,99	5,99	5,99	5,99	4,49		5,99	5,79	5,99	5,99	5,99	5,99	4,00	5,99
	Price brand B	3,99	3,99	3,99	3,99	3,99	3,99	3,99	3,99	3,49	3,99	3,99	3,99	2,99		3,99	3,99	3,99	3,99	3,99	3,99	3,00	3,99
					YTD				released					**to be released today**						Budget			

Fig. 5 Example for a campaign calendar (marketing activities, extract of price-political measures to be released during the year) (Source: Own illustration)

Only if every participant in planning considers his requirements as realistic, can he identify with and contribute to the planning's accomplishment.

Detail planning usually tends to proceed in successive steps. The planning of measures takes place concurrently in form of a marketing plan or a campaign calendar and in interdependency with sales planning. On the basis of the therein embedded ATL (above the line), BTL (below the line), and especially the pricing measures, the sales department can plan sales volumes. Figure 5 depicts an example of a campaign calendar encompassing all sales channels, as means of coordinated planning or sales performance management throughout the year.

The planning of sales volumes and revenue of the sales department, as foundation for the planning of the company in general, shapes the basis for planning of the sectors purchase, production, and logistics, as well as other operating areas. Therefore, planning must not only register the potentials of sales but must particularly depict a realistic forecast of business development, on which other operating areas can establish their planning. Sales performance management's task in planning is making the planning input of sales areas credible. If uncertainties are detected, its task is to define a realistic correction. In order to do this, the sales manager requires extensive knowledge of sales and marketing, as to realistically assess opportunities and risks. An exemplary sales quantity planning on the basis of calendar weeks is shown in Fig. 6. Planned promotions and their effects on sales quantity are taken into account directly.

After consolidating the planning of quantities, the budgeting procedure takes place on a higher aggregated level. Primary costs are planned that can ideally be budgeted by the sales department. Costs whose initiators come from the sales department but arise in other areas are not a direct component of sales planning. Nonetheless, these areas require data input that is provided by sales performance management for their own planning. Subsequently, performance planning of the sales department can be compiled and then reduced to the cost center planning on the one hand and on the other, used to develop a plan-result calculation.

Distribution channel specialised retail

Month	January					February				March				April				May				
CW	1	2	3	4	5	6	7	8	9	10	11	12	13	14	15	16	17	18	19	20	21	22
Campaign calendar																						
TV													X	X								
Radio				X	X								X	X								
Print							X												X			
Price Brand A	5,99	5,99	5,99	4,99		5,99	5,99	5,99	5,99	5,99	5,99	5,99	4,49		5,99	5,79	5,79	5,79	5,79	5,79	5,79	5,79
Price Brand B	3,99	3,99	3,99	3,99	3,99	3,99	3,99	3,99	3,49		3,99	3,99	2,99		3,99	3,99	3,99	3,99	3,49		3,99	3,99
Special Placement				X	X								X	X								
Display									X	X			X	X					X	X		
Quanitites (in k. pound)																						
Quantities Brand A	48	52	49	107	84	44	46	50	40	45	50	50	120	110	40	60	60	60	40	45	60	60
Quantities Brand B	42	47	46	33	37	45	47	45	90	85	39	45	120	110	35	45	45	45	90	85	40	45

Fig. 6 Example for a sales quantity planning (Source: Own illustration)

Within planning, numerous opportunities are identified, and various scenarios for sales development are assessed that are not necessarily authorized for implementation. Consequently, there remain unused alternative causes of action which could be resorted to in case of plan deviations throughout the year. To this purpose, sales performance management should accumulate and store alternative courses of action. If planning results appear to be fraught with risk, then plan coordinators can be tasked with finding alternative courses of action preventively. However, this procedure should not constitute the ordinary; it should only find application in exceptional situations.

3.3.2 Reporting

A successful sales performance management requires extensive reporting that supports its recipients in the achievement of objectives. However, these recipients—and oftentimes the creators themselves—are frequently dissatisfied. The reason for this is that the recipients' expectations toward reporting are imprecisely defined and the respective creator is insufficiently aware of business requirements.

In general, reporting is defined as the production and transmission of significant information, in form of formalized reports.[11] Further, they supply an overview of relevant key performance indicators and deviations for internal and external addressees. These key performance indicators are expected to serve the achievement of objectives in accordance with the general strategy. Some employees consider the mere supply of data as part of reporting. However, the IT department should be in charge of structuring, utilization, and detection of requested data. Nonetheless, it is the reporting coordinator's task to guarantee accurate, relevant data for key performance indicators, in close collaboration with IT.

Drafting these reports entails a high effort and is often the reason why an attempt is made to provide all addressees with a single report. However, a single report is not adequate as it reduces the acceptance of the report. A core feature of reporting is that the respective reports are both tailored and supplied to the specific addressees. Sales

[11] Göpfert (2006).

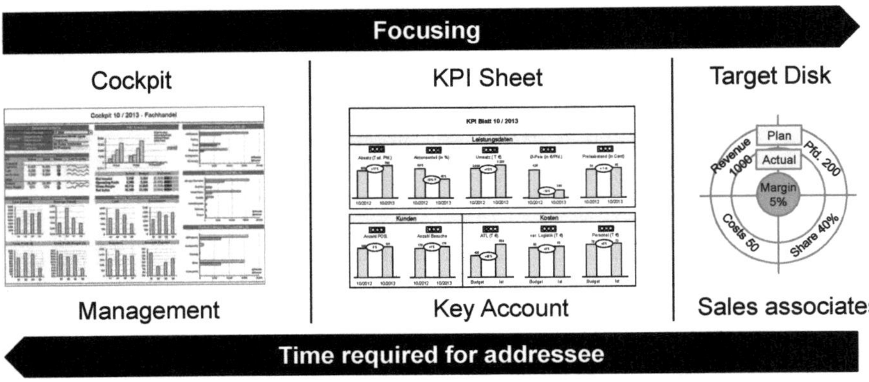

Fig. 7 Nuanced reporting in sales (example) (Source: Own illustration)

performance management should therefore create individual reports for trade partners, sales employees, and management. In this process, recipients continuously set expectations toward the reports. It is the reporting coordinator's task to delete old and unutilized key performance indicators to ensure the report's brevity. A concise one-pager should not turn into a quarterly report.

During the conception of the reports, it is necessary to take into account which addressees require a descriptive reporting and which addressees require an explanatory one. The differentiation between the two is the result of the specific responsibilities of the addressees. For example, a compact presentation of actual figures is more relevant for a sales representative, than overloading him with a management report. Further, a suitable visual representation should be chosen for information to be tailored to the addressees.

The frequency of reports depends on the nature of key performance indicators in use and the availability of final data. In case of sale volume and revenue indicators (if corresponding point-of-sale data is available), a daily report is relevant. In case of reporting profit contributions or the results of analyses, a monthly report usually appears sufficient. Whether reporting appears periodically in paper form or in "real time" with the help of IT systems is secondary. The punctual availability of information to the recipient is decisive. Figure 7 depicts an example of nuanced reporting in sales. Management receives a compact management report in form of a cockpit. The operative functions such as the key account manager and the subordinate sales associates receive detailed performance indicators and data, according to their respective requirements.

3.3.3 Modeling and Assessment of Specific Measures

The main objective of sales is increasing sales volume and revenue. It is expected of the sales manager to support the sales department in the attainment of this objective. In this process, the sales manager is tasked with identifying target-actual deviations

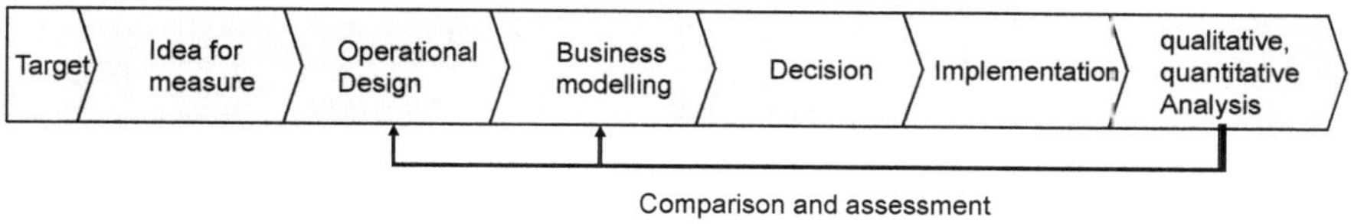

Fig. 8 Process for decisions and implementation of measures (Source: Own illustration)

at an early stage, in order to take measures for an alternate course of action and then guide this process.

Product- and POS-related measures are pillars of the campaign calendar and the instrument of reacting to target deviations. As a rule, the process depicted by Fig. 8 is valid for the aforementioned situations.

In case of strong deviations, fast responses are required which occasionally impedes a complete assessment of the situation. Subsequent to these measures, these deviations should be analyzed and evaluated with regard to their effects. The sales manager needs a fundamental understanding for the measures taken. During the implementation of measures, it is the sales manager's task to guide the drafting of these measures through a business-economic modeling of the cause-effect relations and then validly analyzing its success after its execution. Subsequently, it is his task to make these results transparent to the sales department. In practice, errors may occur during this process due to incomplete evaluation designs, lacking peer groups, or the disregard of trends.

In order to achieve more valid results, it is advisable to utilize long observation periods and large groups of reference. Reality is characterized by unpredictable and hardly assessable external effects, as well as a rarely complete design. The sales controller's task is making assessments according to premises and hypotheses. Over the course of time, sales controlling will compile a collection of measures that the marketing and the sales department can use for orientation, depending on the intended effect and willingness to bear costs. Consequently, as mentioned previously, decisions made at short notice should be validated continuously. The results of these analyses can then be used for future reference. Ideally a tool kit solution can be constructed (Fig. 9).

Different promotions should not be employed simultaneously, the duration of the promotion should lie between 3 and 4 weeks, and a promotion type should not be repeated more frequently than once every 8 to 10 weeks. Throughout this process, increasing or decreasing the normal price does not constitute a promotion in its actual sense.

It is expected of sales performance management to deliver a complete assessment that has previously been coordinated with all participants. It is advisable to use a default template that has been filled out with the expected values and is then updated with actual values and deviations after its implementation. Such a default template is portrayed in Fig. 10. Apart from the quantitative and qualitative assessment, it is important to deliver recommended actions for the future.

Measure			Impact: Quantity (net impact in %) ATL-imp.	Impact by measure	Max.	Result (effect on profit) in k. €		Brand (qualitative)	Feasibility (fast, complex)
Measure	Price-reductive	Price-Off	TV 1,6 Radio 1,3 Print 1,1	each 10ct. +5% Thresholdprice-factor 1,2	+20%	TV -100 Radio -20 Print -10	On balance measures before ATL 20 to -100	- - -	+ + +
		Bundle	TV 1,4 Radio 1,2 Print 1,1	2er (2 for 1,5) +70% 3er (3 for 2) +120% 4er (3+1) +60%		TV -100 Radio -20 Print -10	On balance measures before ATL 10 to -40	-	- -
		Collection points	TV 1,3 Radio 1,2 Print 1,1	value high +20% value middle +10% value low +5%		TV -100 Radio -20 Print -10	On balance measures before ATL 0 to -20	+	- -
	Non price-reductive	Addition	Radio 1,2 Print 1,1	+10% - +30%		individual		+ +	- - -
		Samples, Tasting		+10% - +20%		individual		+ +	- - -
		Lottery	Radio 1,2 Print 1,1	+5% - +20%		individual		+ +	- -
	supportive	Special placement		1,20		poss. WKZ		+ +	- -
		Leaflet		1,15		poss. WKZ		+ +	-
		Display		1,10		-10 to -20		+ +	+
	Adjustment normal price			each 10 ct. Price gap +/-5%		Profit-Margin +/- 2%-P			

Fig. 9 Example of a tool kit solution of measures (Source: Own illustration)

STANDARD-Assessment marketing actions

ACTION **Packaging bundle Brand A "4 for 3"**

Date **Woche 26-27 2013**

post
after action
before follow-up

PREMISE **Action without ATL**
Special Placement and leaflets

	Action	Base: kPound	Ø-Price	Ø GM	GM	Effect	Actual Result: kPound	Ø-Price	Ø GM	GM	Difference: kPound	Ø-Price	Ø GM	GM
Brand A	X	50	5,99	3,08	154	210%	105	4,49	1,68	177	55	-1,50	-1,40	23
Brand B		45	4,99	2,15	97	70%	32	4,99	2,15	68	-14	0,00	0,00	-29
Sum		95	5,52	2,64	251	144%	137	4,61	1,79	244	42	-0,91	-0,85	-7

Primary Effects

Difference	
Quantities kPound	**42**
Price / Pound	-0,91
GM / Pound	-0,85
GM	-7

Additional costs		
Costs of action	Assembly	-20,0
	Labeling of Goods - Trade	-10,0
	Logistic and Distribution	-15,0

Result k€	
GM Effect	-7
Costs	-45
= Result	**-52**

Secondary Effects

Effect Stockpilling not yet avaluable: each 1 kPound Effect GM -3 k€

Assessment

Quantities-Budget	120	GM-Effect	-52	Due to missing secondary placement budget was missed by 12%
Quantities-Actual	105	Ø each ΔPound	-1,24	Cannibalization rather low. Hope for a positive trend.
Plan achieved	88%			Low effect on sales volume does not justify costs - volume bought dearly.
Cannibalization	25%			Conclusion:
Net effect	42			**Without ATL action is not foreseen in the future**

Fig. 10 Example for a default template for assessment of marketing actions (Source: Own illustration)

3.3.4 Trusting Controlling Tools in the Sales Department

Lastly, a particular aspect will be highlighted in detail. A successful sales performance management requires not only quantitative information on the development of sales. Sales performance management much rather creates a broad understanding of decisions and measures taken by the sales department. Further, it must anticipate future developments at an early stage in order to recognize opportunities and risks for the company in time. For this purpose, sales performance management must communicate intensively and trustfully with the sales department and its management. Supply of information and communications with the parties involved should therefore be a high priority of sales performance management. Moreover, it must build trust in their data and instruments, not only to the end of strengthening their own position in the sales department but also to be able to gather confidential information and insider knowledge from the operative functions. This does not represent an easy task in a sales environment. It is often insinuated that a controller would like to control and direct everything—which does per se coincide with the definition of controlling. However, controlling and trust are two concepts that seem incompatible for most employees. A potential controlling claim can quickly be understood as interference and manipulation. However, there are multiple approaches to creating mutual trust.

If sales performance management wants to obtain information from potential sellers and operative units, then it should explain to the addressees why the information is required and who has access to them. Moreover, sales performance management should ensure that possibly confidential data is not passed on to third parties, or accessible to them. In practice, it is often difficult to ensure that these procedures are adhered to, due to procedural reasons. Nonetheless, the importance of retrieving the necessary expertise from the sales department becomes evident by the first wrong decision at the latest. Therefore, sales performance management should in no way make the impression that it is controlling sales out of distrust. As counteraction, it is beneficial to lay open the motives and reasons for one's own actions and communicate these.[12] Further, using authoritative measures to demand information and statements and then blaming possible data errors on the sales department should be avoided. Sales controllers need to develop a sense for an adequate means of communication. He must be successful in creating control that can be understood and accepted through a mutually confidential method.

Sales performance management should find and emphasize common ground. Reaching their respective subgoals within the boundaries of the company's general objectives is the task of both the operational level of the sales department and sales performance management. As previously clarified—with according authority—sales performance management can add value to the sales department. If, however, sales performance management and the sales department do not work in accordance with each other, then tasks could unnecessarily be faced twice, or synergy potentials may remain unused. Controllers are expected to demonstrate the added value of cooperation to sales employees. A good cooperation and a positive working relation can be promoted by a joint *Jour fixe*, collaborative projects, or the controller joining employees in field work. Nonetheless, in an ideal cooperation, the controller can and should be able to maintain an objective and rational sales performance

[12]Eberenz (2012).

management of the sales department, without his objectivity being questioned—as consequence of his "good relation" with the sales department.[13]

4 Conclusion

Sales performance management has increasingly gained importance to company success over the last years, and many companies and their sales departments have introduced and expanded on performance management approaches. As shown in practice, these processes oftentimes entail problems in the cooperation between the sales department and controlling. In order to be successful and to create an acceptance of sales performance management, controllers need to take the characteristic features of the sales department into account. The sales department possesses a distinct role and self-perception, as it generates revenue and is key to the company's success. As a result of this self-perception, the sales department usually attempts keeping external influences on the own business activity at a minimum.

The company management's and its controller's task is representing a controlling approach that is oriented toward the sales department's concerns and creates added value for the sales department and the company's management. This is no easy task. The elements and instruments for successful sales performance management have been illustrated in this contribution. Further, it has been exemplified how important good communication and a lively exchange of information between controlling and sales department is. Recognizing the needs of the sales department, making own approaches and objectives transparent, and striving for cooperation are the controller's main tasks in this. In doing so, sales performance management can create trust, in order to gain relevant data and assessments from the sales department. Finally, this data, the analysis thereof, and successful cooperation are the foundation for the sales performance management's success and its acceptance within the company.

References

Eberenz R (2012) Controlling im Spannungsfeld von Vertrauen und Kontrolle. In: Nordakademie (ed) Forschung für die Wirtschaft. Cuvillier, Göttingen

Göpfert I (2006) Berichtswesen. In: Handelsblatt (ed) Wirtschaftslexikon, 2nd edn. Oldenbourg Wissenschaftsverlag, Stuttgart

Greiner O, Hiendlmeier S, Dauter R (2013) Potenziale systematisch erschließen. Wie eine wirksame Vertriebssteuerung gelingt. In: Horváth AG (ed) The Performance Architect: Das Kundenmagazin von Horváth & Partners, Edition 1/2013: Schwerpunkt Vertriebsexzellenz: Wie eine wirksame Vertriebssteuerung gelingt. Horvath & Partners, Stuttgart

Herrmann R, Möser A, Werner E (2002) Neue empirische Befunde zur Preissetzung und zum Verbraucherverhalten im Lebensmitteleinzelhandel. Agrarwirtschaft 51(2):99–111

[13]Eberenz (2012).

Jung H (2010) Allgemeine Betriebswirtschaftslehre, 12nd edn. Oldenbourg Verlag, München
Kieninger M (2013) Den Vertrieb richtig steuern. In: Horváth AG (ed) The Performance Architect: Das Kundenmagazin von Horváth & Partners, Ausgabe 1/2013: Schwerpunkt Vertriebsexzellenz: Wie eine wirksame Vertriebssteuerung gelingt. Horvath & Partners, Stuttgart
Kühnapfel J (2013) Vertriebscontrolling: Methoden im praktischen Einsatz. Springer Gabler, Wiesbaden
Steffenhagen H (2008) Marketing: Eine Einführung, 6th edn. Kohlhammer, Stuttgart
Stegmüller W, Möller K (2011) Trends im Vertriebscontrolling. In: Beck CH (ed) Controlling, Magazine 7. München

Heiko Schulte-Oversohl mainly operates as Management Consultant for retail and consumer goods companies. He has gained long years of expertise in sales controlling as Division Manager of Service & Finance Sales Department with the Tchibo GmbH, with the Otto Group, and with Thomson Consumer Electronics.

Digitized Performance Management Along the Supply Chain

Christian Daxböck, Jochen Kröber, and Markus Bergmann

Abstract The following contribution illustrates effects and potentials that digitization has on the supply chain. Digitization creates new possibilities for a closer interlinking of participants as well as wide-ranging potentials for an optimization of supply chain planning and management. The potentials and control levers of a digital supply chain are largely situated in logistics, production, and the superordinate supply chain management.

Keywords Digital supply chain · Digitization · Industry 4.0 · Performance management · New technologies · Supply chain management

1 An Introduction to Supply Chain Management

1.1 Definition and Significance of Supply Chain Management

In a dynamic market environment that is characterized by a high degree of competition, companies must be able to react flexibly to permanently changing factors of influence. Consequently, the concept of supply chain management (SCM) aims at

---

An adaption of this contribution has been originally printed as Daxböck, C., Kröber, J., Bergmann, M. (2017): Digitalisierte Steuerung entlang der Supply Chain, in Kieninger, M., Digitalisierung in der Unternehmenssteuerung, 2017, pp. 139–159, Schäffer-Poeschel, Stuttgart.

C. Daxböck (✉)
Organization & Operations, Horváth & Partners, Vienna, Austria

J. Kröber
Organization & Operations, Horváth & Partners, Stuttgart, Austria

M. Bergmann
Industrial Goods and High Tech, Horváth & Partners, Munich, Germany

M. Buttkus, R. Eberenz (eds.), *Performance Management in Retail and the Consumer Goods Industry*, https://doi.org/10.1007/978-3-030-12730-5_26

optimizing business processes within the supply chain in order to reach an adaptation to dynamic market requirements.

The particularities of SCM are best summarized by the following definition: SCM is the company-wide coordination of both material and data flow along the entire supply chain with the aim of organizing the entire process at optimal time and cost efficiency—from raw material extraction, over all individual refining processes, until the final customer.[1]

This interface-spanning efficient cooperation of all network participants creates transparency along the entire supply chain, avoids information deficits between companies, improves cost and performance structures, and what is more, optimizes the results of involved companies.

1.2 Requirements Concerning Supply Chain Management

The increasing globalization of markets represents a permanently increasing complexity of business processes for all companies. Due to collaborative manufacturing and trade processes in particular, multilevel international supply chains emerge. Additional influencing factors such as an increasing individualization of demand and continuously decreasing batch sizes further support the trend toward progressively complex supply chains. In order to be able to control the material and data flows underlying SCM, a comprehensive view in the sense of an end-to-end (E2E) process consideration is necessary. In this process, the integration of all involved organizational units as well as continuous standardization and optimization encompassing all levels, functions, and interfaces is paramount. Only when this comprehensive view is given, decisions and their consequences for upstream or downstream processes can be evaluated and used for overall optimization.

As requirements concerning supply chains and value networks continuously rise due to the influences named above, the significance and necessity of SCM as companies' organizational and management instrument intensifies. Therefore, the ability of meeting increasing requirements concerning flexibility, efficiency, and risk aversion is emerging as decisive competitive advantage. With its cross-section and integrational functions, SCM must continuously evolve in order to comprehensively coordinate and optimize information and material flows. The present development toward a digitization of supply chains offers substantial impulses for mastering the requirements concerning SCM and even leads to a fundamental reconfiguration of the supply chain.

[1]Scholz-Reiter, B., Jakobza, J. (1999), p. 7.

2 Data Technological Preconditions as Driving Forces Behind Digital Supply Chains

Technologies developed for a more comprehensive and more efficient use of data have long been a significant element in SCM, as many optimization approaches and methods only became applicable in practice with data availability and usage thereof. There are many examples for this, such as the automatized acquisition of shipping data per RFID, with which the status of shipments can be tracked via defined registration points, or the GPS-based optimization of transport routes for the minimization of transportation time and the prevention of unloaded mileage for vehicles. Further developments of ERP systems have also strongly furthered cross-functional and cross-system harmonization of processes over the last few years, while simultaneously differentiating supply chains according to market-specific and product-specific properties. Through the further progress of digital technologies and their improved and more economical use, supply chains are becoming more transparent and more manageable through available information. Hence, the flexibility for all participants is improved, costs can be reduced further, and supply chain pace can be improved by this automatization of processes (e.g., RFID).

The digitization of the supply chain therefore considerably supports the improvement of both the adaptability and capacity for development in the entire supply chain organization. Supply chain management and planning also contribute, thanks to a continuous information and data flow as well as the possibility of processing enormous incidental data quantities with technologies such as “big data analytics.” Due to enhanced computing performance concerning storage and processing of data, real-time control is no longer wishful thinking. It much rather enables a faster adaptation of production and logistic capacities that are globally spread to customer’s demands that are changing rapidly.

Due to the interplay and the general usage of digital technologies for data management and the according processes, SCM takes a major leap in development, through which cost and performance are considerably improved. Four fundamental factors are primarily necessary for a complete digital saturation of the supply chain:

1. **Data Acquisition:** Sensors or scanners track all relevant data along the entire supply chain, such as status information of transported goods, means of transportation, or carriers permanently and in real time. This consistent transparency serves as the ideal foundation for optimization and management of the digital supply chain.
2. **Data Transfer:** By means of an automated and standardized communication between all participants of the supply chain, for instance per electronic data interchange (EDI), data transfer takes place immediately between consignors and consignees and thereby realize an interlinking of processes. New communication and data technologies, such as transaction platforms that offer the transfer and cultivation of much larger data volumes and exceed simple data transfer, offer further developments. With the technical possibilities of permanently transferring logistic status information, valuable performance management impulses are gained for the optimization of commodity flow and logistic processes.

3. **Data Processing:** In order to process these vast data volumes, high-performance processors in combination with big data/smart data technologies such as SAP HANA are necessary. It is only with the use of these technologies that the enormous data volumes, from orders placed by customers or real-time data collection via sensors, for example, are processed sensibly.
4. **Data Storage:** Available data capacities have multiplied exponentially. Thus, levied data is stored simply, and for example, through cloud technologies. They are used independently, both location-wise and organizationally, in order to be able to react both rapidly and flexibly along the entire supply chain.

These four factors lay the foundation for the use and implementation of a digital supply chain. Technologies for the application of cloud and big data/smart data technologies are already being used successfully in some areas. However, applications are oftentimes used in a manner where they are isolated from each other, the result being that their full potential remains unreached. The key factor of success lies in the continuous usage of data, from its acquisition and transmission until its processing and storage, along the entire supply chain. This is the only way to secure a real networking and the realization of respectively resulting advantages, such as data transparency in real time.

However, the challenges of the implementation of digital technologies are not simply restricted to their technical use, but rather lie in the implementation of open standards within the company as well as along the entire supply chain. Accordingly, acceptance of these standards has great importance in the implementation process and necessitates clear regulations that ensure a balanced distribution of effort (e.g., in data acquisition) and benefit (e.g., effective and efficient processes), as well as aim at permanent cooperation.

In addition, digital technologies often face the obstacle that the companies involved in the supply chain do not follow uniform strategies for digitization. Further, companies frequently possess different technological preconditions concerning data processing or the usage of IT systems and their respective interfaces.

Before beginning the technical implementation and the problem-solving process of individual solutions, a strategy and target objective should be formulated. Concrete individual applications and possibilities for data usage derived from this strategy, e.g., for product-specific demand data, can be integrated into a performance management concept, with which a target aim should be reached and put into practice, and finally, purposefully promoted.

For example, high data transparency only reaches its full potential, if it is clearly regulated which rules apply when bottlenecks or target conflicts between sourcing, production, and logistics ensue, and if these rules are also enforced.

Provided the four aforementioned fundamental factors and the outlined requirements are met, new possibilities result through the usage of digital technologies for comprehensive cooperation within the supply chain. This is exemplified in the following:

- Improved skills for the recognition of actual customer demands, by means of comprehensive sales data and analyzed demand correlation.

- Heightened reaction speed in volatile markets, due to consistently controllable and scalable processes and structures along the supply chain.
- Continuous processes, due to comprehensive cooperation and collaboration between suppliers, producers, and customers (end-to-end).

3 Impacts of Digitization on Supply Chains

Digitization's effects will impact whole companies and thereby lead to a fundamental change of the supply chain. In the course of technological developments, mass data is created. If used accordingly, these lead to new possibilities in the management and optimization of processes via new solutions and systems. Through digitization, a strong interlinking with customers and a close data exchange, such as demand data and purchase order data, is achieved. Companies expand on their range of services and better and more appropriately align their products and services to customer requests with the aid of this data. This alignment is then analyzed in a target-oriented manner and transformed into competitive advantages by an intelligent usage of customer data in the sense of smart data. An example is the prediction on the expected sales volume or customer preferences. Capacities are planned according to demand, and costs are optimized accordingly and in compliance with the extent of customer requirements. In this way, the range of services is specifically tailored to individual customer requests with the help of additional customer-relevant data, in order to adapt logistic services automatically to customers and their respective concrete requests in the delivery of products, for example. In this process, a delivery profile, gained from previously delivered orders, provides an automatized decision, whether a customer is given a premium or standard delivery, if a previously defined time frame must be met, or if additional requests concerning the delivery or packaging processes exist—to name some examples. With regard to customers' willingness to pay extra for precisely these services, the company achieves a significantly better range of services or additional revenue potentials.

The digitization of supply chains also creates new application possibilities and business models in the production sector. Primarily, these are connected with technological developments in serial mass production, as well as the reduction of batch sizes and consequently also the realization of customer individual manufacturing. Additional applications include the further development to intelligent products that supply certain data, as well subsequent service offers such as preventive maintenance for an automatized detection of wear. Hence, necessary maintenance and repair is detected and conducted at an early stage in order to avoid machine failure and thereby enabling a higher degree of utilization.

A key element of this is the digital transformation of processes, systems, and organizations. For this, fundamental questions need answering. For example:

- What is the company's digitization structure?
- Which products and which services are going to be offered on the market and which supply chain is necessary for them?

- Which strategic objectives could be reached by a digital supply chain?
- How should projects and measures be structured in order to reach the most effective and efficient solutions for the entire supply chain?
- How should processes, organization, and systems be aligned, in order to reach the previously set target vision?
- Which competences do employees need for the management of a digital supply chain?

Companies face ever-increasing changes in market environment and increasingly short cycles of technical development. Therefore, repeatedly evaluating all alterations, with regard to innovations and risks and their influence on the supply chain, is a significant factor of success in the implementation of a digital supply chain.

4 Potentials and Control Levers of a Digital Supply Chain

The supply chain illustrates all events and participants from the supplier to the customer and encompasses the fundamental functions of sourcing, production, and distribution.[2] A supervisory supply chain management is responsible for a successful interplay and the optimization of these three functions. The following models are inspired by this structure and reference logistics, production, and supply chain management.

4.1 Digitization Approaches for Logistics

Digitization plays an enormous part in logistics and leads to a significant further development regarding effectivity ("implementing the correct methods") and efficiency ("correctly implementing the methods"). A substantial use is optimized performance management, which operates on the basis of data processing and thereby resulting transparency, essentially contributing to the improvement of processes and the performance of logistics, as well as the entire supply chain. For example, status information gained from sensors or scanners gives concrete indications as to whether an intervention or countermeasures are necessary or not. As a consequence, a downstream, reactive observation is replaced with a predictive, active steering of processes and services. Furthermore, growth stimuli are derived as the result of new enhanced performances and services. In order to be able to use these growths in effectivity and efficiency to their full potential, a comprehensive examination of the preconditions and consequences of digitization and new technologies on the supply chain becomes necessary.

---

[2] Pfohl, H.-C. (2004), p. 28.

4.1.1 Digitization Approaches for Supply Logistics

There are several established digital applications existing for supply logistics that lead to significant growth in efficiency. This includes applications such as time slot control management for incoming goods, securing that incoming trucks are processed in a predefined order, thereby avoiding bottlenecks and high standby times. If a truck is early, it must wait until loading bay is cleared. If a truck is late, decisions must be made according to urgency, whether an immediate offloading can take place, or if the truck must return to the end of the line of waiting vehicles. All deliveries are monitored and companies are informed on sanctions in order to secure compliance with timeframes. In these processes, digitization begins with the allocation of time frames, the recognition of certain distance radii of incoming trucks via GPS systems, and the monitoring of process quality. What is new is not the logistic process, but much rather the possibilities of its management that digitization yields. With an interlinking of participating partners, data-driven, automatized decision-making processes are drafted to follow clearly defined regulations. Further successful applications are transaction and communication-based platforms that enable an efficient data exchange and the permanent collection, as well as offer retrieval of status information in real time. This enables communication between various participants, each using different IT systems, along the entire supply chain. Its particularity lies in the usage of platforms as mediator between different systems and data standards, leading to a significant step toward an integrated supply chain. Processing times are shortened, manual labor is avoided, and the use of interchanged data leads to optimized decisions.

4.1.2 Digitization Approaches for Distribution Logistics

A fast and efficient delivery of goods is of paramount importance for distribution logistics. In future, new forms of commissioning technology will play an important role to this end. For quite some time now, technologies such as Pick-by-Voice have successfully been in use. In this process, the commissioner is guided to the correct storage space via headphones and is given the details regarding the picking quantity of the respective item. New developments have gone a step further by guiding the commissioner on his or her commissioning tour, using smart glasses. Consequently, both hands are free exclusively for the extraction process and despite quality securing processes (e.g., photographing the item through a nod of the head as confirmation), a high degree commissioning performance can be reached. However, people are a limiting factor of this new technology with regard to his or her ability to concentrate and his or her expectations toward a pleasant working environment. Momentarily, a deployment of these new technologies is only conceivable in case of large order loads during peak periods. Therefore, development tendencies toward a stronger automatization of commissioning technology through the use of robots and robot-supported technologies are far more likely. These technologies that are presently under development in some companies can, for instance, ensure that whole shelving units with rarely used items, as an example, are brought to the commissioners via transport robots. The commissioner can then retrieve the item from a nearby storage unit without either having to leave his/her workspace or having to walk too great a distance. With the use of new data processing technologies, distribution processes (e.g., delivery services) can be simplified permanently and designed to be more efficient. Through connectivity with recipients, delivery rates can be improved significantly and the costs for unsuccessful delivery reduced—while simultaneously improving customer satisfaction. If, for instance, the recipient is able to choose a time frame in which he or she wishes the shipment to be delivered, a direct connection between the delivery service's route planning, which has the aim of an ideally rapid and efficient delivery, and preferences and particularities of the recipient. On the basis of intelligent networking, the recipient can decide whether he or she wishes a delivery at the earliest possible point of time or a delivery within a time frame that is defined by him or her. Through the integration of recipient data with further new technologies or services, order deliveries can be aligned perfectly to requirements; for the shared advantage of both customer and logistics service providers. Included in these new technologies is the usage of drones for the delivery to remote areas, as well as for extremely urgent deliveries of medication or replacement parts. Furthermore, first cooperation projects between delivery service providers and automobile manufacturers exist, designing the installation of devices that could enable a direct delivery into car trunks by the delivery man/woman. A further example is the delivery in inner-city areas via delivery robots. Through the use of digital processes, delivery can be organized to be more efficient, more sustainable, and faster. A decisive factor in this will be choosing the correct solution for each service yielded (e.g., delivery speed), depending on the customer's willingness to cover costs (e.g., paying a surcharge).

4.1.3 Use Case: Digitization Approaches for Process Cost Accounting in Logistics

Process cost accounting is a groundbreaking instrument for logistics as it enables a cause-related allocation of costs to processes and subprocesses. Through this allocation, process cost accounting can offer substantial impulses for a holistic optimization of logistic systems or for the organization of ranges of goods. The concept of process cost accounting was previously limited by numerous limitations that primarily resulted from a lacking assignability and, consequently, a generalized cost allocation. On one hand, this occurred due to standards of internal cost accounting and, on the other hand, due to lacking possibilities of gathering, processing, and storing relevant data. The significantly improved performance of data processing available today, as well as further developments in cost accounting, now creates the preconditions for reaching an actual end-to-end observation and thereby enter a new dimension of processing transparency and performance management. By means of permanently being able to gather data through sensor or scanner technology, simple processing steps can be dissected into ascertainable units and then evaluated according to different characteristic values. In doing so, actual differences in processing can be depicted as costs by cause. From these results, decisions such as those concerning the allocation of products within a location network, concerning the choice of logistic processes and supply chains, and concerning minimum lot sizes or packaging units can be derived. The thereby resulting transparency can be used to make decisions on a matter-of-fact and data-based level. These decisions can then be evaluated on the basis of certain scenarios or planning parameters in all their consequences, such as their effects on capacity or resource requirements.

4.2 Outlook and Paths of Development Towards Digital Logistics

Digitization can already be ound in logistics today and will increase in prevalence due to the progressing developments of technological possibilities. By already existing digital logistics applications such as RFID sensors, further interlinking, such as between logistics and production processes, is generally implementable. Investments in logistic pilot projects or measures for further interlinking of digital processes can therefore be rapidly amortized and can serve as drivers of a comprehensive distribution of digital applications in companies. Furthermore, digitized logistic processes are an essential key element of digital production, as no integrated digital production processes in the sense of a smart factory can be reached without taking logistic material and information flows into account. Implementations must therefore build on the fact that developments augment each other and are expedited under joint coordination. Finally, data standards, IT systems, and data security should be unified in order to make these usable for all processes along the supply chain.

4.3 Digitization Approaches for Production

Digitization in production is usually understood as the various application possibilities of Industry 4.0. Industry 4.0 is defined as the fourth industrial revolution and also as an interplay of production technology and Internet technology toward an interlinking of machines, humans, and production resources. Potential applications of Industry 4.0 aim at an increase in efficiency and efficacy in the production of goods and services. In this process, increasing flexibility and economic production of small batch sizes are mainly targeted. From a strategic point of view, the development, or rather the expansion, of the existing production system to a digital production system has high relevance.[3]

A study conducted by Horváth & Partners in 2015 evaluated the momentary and future importance of Industry 4.0 with respect to increasing efficiency and company

[3]Bauer, W. et al. (2014), p.10.

growth (see Fig. 1). While in future the aspect of growth will increase in significance, presently, companies included in the study were mostly conducting projects with regard to increased efficiency. At present, the main areas of application concentrate on the acquisition of operational data, on agility and adaptability of production, as

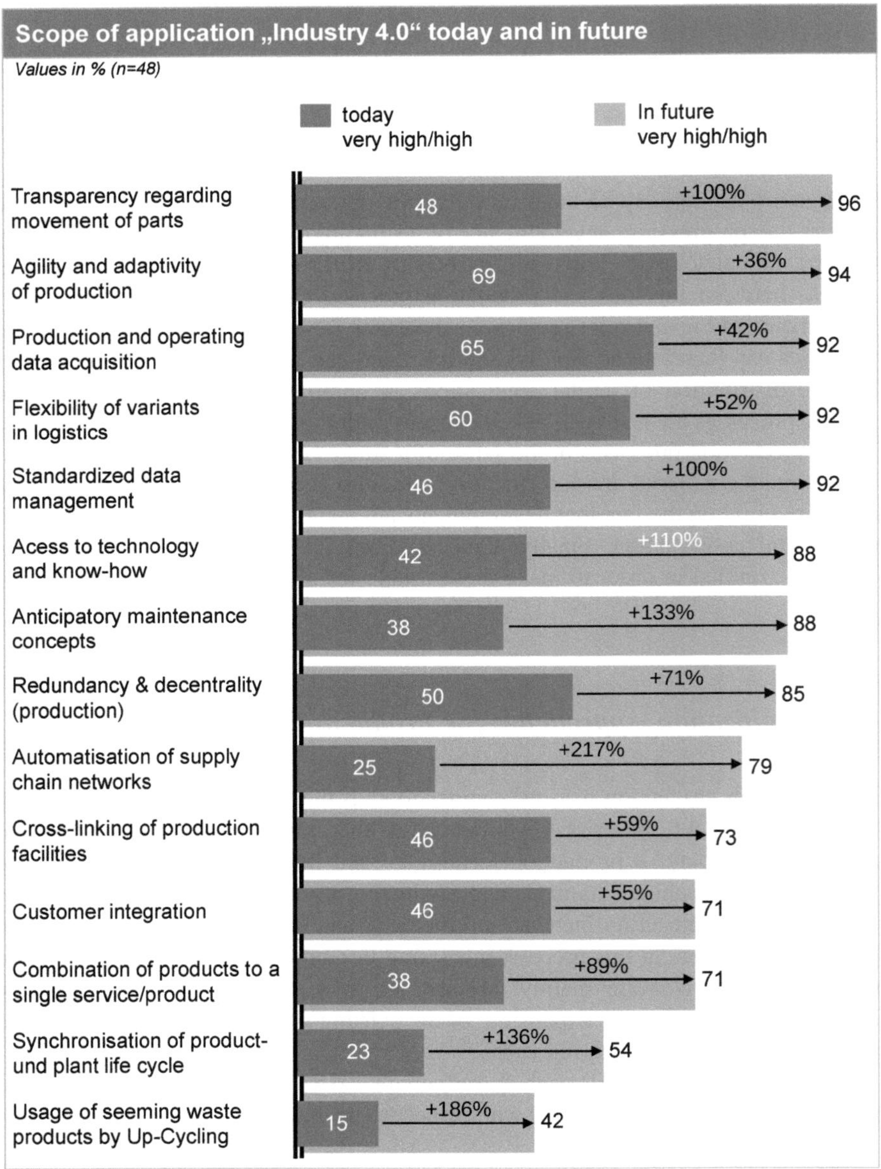

Fig. 1 Scope of application industry 4.0 today and in future

well as on variant flexibility. In future, applications for automatization of all supply chain networks will gain greater significance.[4] However, this requires an extensive integration of enterprise resource planning (ERP) systems, as well as manufacturing execution systems (MES) and machine control such as storage-programmable steering units (SPS) along the supply chain.[5]

5 Smart Factory as Version of the Future

This optimal combination of application possibilities for Industry 4.0 illustrates the scenario of a smart factory (see Fig. 2). This intelligent factory can control and optimize itself on the basis of information from interlinked objects available in real time, of which the processing is enabled through algorithms. In this case, a digital production system is especially relevant. It controls the smart factory in a general context. All restrictions of the factory are ledged within the digital production system and its algorithms that are necessary for control (e.g., which machines are not suitable for certain final product varieties, due to their quality standards). According to the concept of cyber physical systems, all real objects and activities of this production system are digitally portrayed.[6] The production system processes and supplies data from logistic processes, material flow, as well as multi-step production

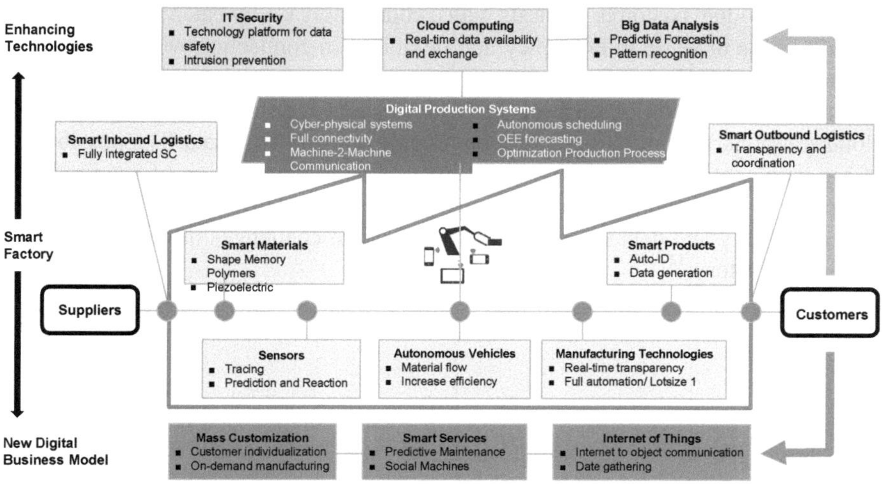

Fig. 2 Digitalization & industry 4.0—smart operations scenario and selected applications

---

[4]Daxböck, C., Bergmann, M. (2016), p. 7.
[5]Ziemke, A. et al. (2016), p. 54.
[6]Bauer, W. et al. (2014), p. 20.

processes. A decentralized, autonomic control of machines via algorithms and in interplay with the production system is enabled with adherence to predefined rules. Machines undertake a stand-alone detailed planning of production order and machine utilization, while taking all technical restrictions into account. All material movement necessary for production processes are undertaken and secured by autonomous or partly autonomous transport vehicles. In this situation, the automatized supply of components allows for the realization of a respective efficiency.[7]

A further precondition for the smart factory to function is the interlinking of machines, humans, and production means. This interlinking enables communication and data transfer concerning location, machine status, and the processing status of individual objects. Data transfer is available through the generation and storage of necessary data via sensors attached to materials, production means, and products, through communications technologies such as RFID. Information yielded by all sensors enable a real-time portrayal of all processes within the factory, thereby ensuring a compete transparency of production processes.[8]

Furthermore, this digital production system leads to a drastic change in work environment for employees in production. Due to digitization and the control system derived from it, employees' main task is now the monitoring of production systems. Actual physical interference is only required and necessary in exceptions, such as during disturbances or maintenance. In case of machine failure, e.g., in case of a tool breakage, the production system itself reorganizes and proposes an alternative way, provided this is possible.[9]

A smart factory will in the future be able to flexibly react to shifting demands and react to individual customer requests with a comparably cheap batch size of "one" as a result of the increase in efficiency and flexibility in connection with new production technologies.[10]

An implementation of such an intelligent factory requires technologies such as cloud solutions, machine-to-machine communication, and big data. The possibilities of big data applications' help with the analysis and interpretation of acquired data and recognized patterns then influence control processes of the production system. Data sensibility and data security are therefore great challenges of Industry 4.0 and the Smart Factory.[11]

[7]Ziemke, A. et al. (2016), p. 59.

[8]Bauer, W. et al. (2014), p. 19.

[9]Spath, D. et al. (2013), p. 52.

[10]Spath, D. et al. (2013), p. 17.

[11]Bauer, W. et al. (2014), p. 22.

6 Industry 4.0 and Existing Production Systems

In business practice, the interplay or possible conflicts between Industry 4.0 and established production systems, such as the Toyota Production System (TPS), is an issue of concern. The main characteristics of both traditional as well as digital production systems are slim processes in the sense of lean management that secure speed, sustainability, reduction of waste, and flexibility. In doing so, the flow principle is applied: work content is leveled and processing steps are interlinked using the pull principle. The result is that existing processes have little overlap and a high degree of standardization, which secures stable operations. Furthermore, the production system is aimed at reducing the reaction time in various demand situations (e.g., multiple varieties, seasonal fluctuations). The principles of Industry 4.0 and interlinking play a significant role to this end and enable a smooth interplay of interfaces and increasingly standardized processes, thereby reducing waste within production processes. Consequently, no inconsistencies exist between Industry 4.0 and established production systems. The flexibility and the adaptability of production systems are significantly increased by Industry 4.0 applications via a stronger interlinking, greater transparency, and possibilities of analysis of large data quantities.[12]

7 Outlook and Paths of Developments Toward an Industry 4.0 Factory

The previously outlined scenario of an intelligent factory is purely a scenario of the future for many companies. Apart from the new construction of a factory on a green grass field in which presently available technologies are already integrated, the question of which path of development is best suited for existing production sites is raised. The following two application scenarios can offer first steps toward a smart factory in the case of an existing production site and also create the necessary preconditions.

1. Creating transparency via the site's performance with the help of defined indicator systems such as OEE (Overall Equipment Effectiveness) and their portrayal in dashboards as well as real-time monitoring of the facilities. This is definitely possible with an upgrade of machine control and the respective time logging with the machines.
2. Usage of existing data to find patterns via "predictive analytics" and "big data applications" and derivatives of, for example, an OEE forecast for the active management and improvement of system availability, optimization of occupancy time, and quality enhancement such as avoiding waste.

[12]Bauer, W. et al. (2014), p. 35.

These steps can be supported and implemented with the use of a manufacturing execution system (MES); thereby first potentials in the sense of Industry 4.0 can be levied:

- Practice shows that very often data is still processed and reported using spreadsheet calculations. An increased efficiency in processing and presentation can be reached by a reduction of manual activities and the creation of a consistent database.
- More efficient machine usage through improved and automatized detail planning on the basis of relevant process and status data.
- Use and further development of insights on the sites which will undergo development toward a digital production system and will flow into respective algorithms.

During the implementation process on the basis of a pilot project, the following steps should be undertaken:

- Setting up an automatized interface for the use of work schedules of the ERP system in order to conduct the detail planning for resources of a production line.
- Collecting the data of relevant machines and productive applications, in order to be able to find errors, downtime, etc., in the "Control Panel."
- Setting up a model for finding patterns in the conduct of resources with algorithms, in order to verify the OEE prognosis. This is applied as the basis for proactive decisions concerning production detail planning and OEE prognoses are made for the next planning period.

8 Digitization in Supply Chain Management

Applications of Predictive Analytics

Opportunities for digitization in SCM mainly arise from the prognosis of future demand developments that are both identifiable and assessable through certain demand patterns and demand correlations. In this process, large, structured or unstructured data volumes are analyzed and researched from previously unrecognized correlations of certain factors and features. The potential lies in the vast possibilities of correlations that are yielded from data analysis and can then be transferred. In doing so, classical mathematical-statistic methods, as well as methods of data mining (such as cluster processes, selection of variables, and explorative data analysis) and even the application of neuronal networks (for instance, for the solving of multi-variant, multiple nonlinear regressions), can be used to search for approaches to the developments of algorithms. These algorithms can then be used to gain insights into future quantities or future developments. Using the results, data-driven decisions such as stockpiling or inventory allocation within the network can be generated and can contribute significantly to economic success. Due to the incalculability of demand and the complexity of global supply chains, precise demand forecasts represent one of the biggest challenges SCM is faced with. A solution can be found in the applications bundled within the term "predictive analytics." All applications have in common that prognoses continuously and automatically adapt to changed general conditions and thereby contribute to the fundamental optimization of business processes. Consequently, procurement decisions are directly synchronizable with demand and inventory is reduced to the required minimum, without jeopardizing delivery capability. From this, automatized order proposals are generated, synchronized delivery processes are realized, and unexpected "jumps" in demand are covered. Predictive analytics goes above and beyond previously existing business intelligence applications and requires companies to change their perspective. The focus has shifted from the evaluation of past-related data, and in some cases also gut instinct, to future-oriented and reliable results derived from concrete data patterns. In this approach, different scenarios can be simulated, thus ensuring accurate decisions and improved management.

In the following, applications and potentials that enable digitization of the supply chain and predictive analytics are highlighted and exemplified:

- Improved sales forecasts on the level of individual products, as well as an improved consideration of promotional and seasonal products through a systematical detection of need and requirement patterns.
- Improvement of availability and prevention of out-of-stock situations through automatized, self-steering disposition processes with regard to a life-span-based determination of parameters.
- Optimization of inventory through an exact determination of optimal replenishment quantities according to demand forecasts.
- Exact determination of process- or product-related logistics costs for different planning scenarios or decision cases according to process cost accounting in connection with predictive analytics.

The ability of analyzing large quantities of structured or unstructured data is a key prerequisite for the achievement of the aforementioned potentials: on one hand, with regard to data infrastructure and, on the other hand, with regard to the ability of identifying correlations and of formulating powerful algorithms that enable a data-driven deduction of prognoses and thereby also of founded decisions. In order to use the methods of predictive analytics in a target-oriented and beneficial manner, transparent data structures must be established and powerful systems for the analysis of data must be available. A significant focus should lie on customer data, as they are necessary to gaining a further understanding of customer requests and ordering behavior.

9 Outlook and Paths of Development Toward Digital Supply Chain Management

In SCM, the potentials of data-driven models in the sense of predictive analytics can be illustrated clearly. Companies that undertake a data-driven analysis of their customer data will better understand their customers and use this knowledge for concrete product and service offers. Further, specific requirements are met adequately in the supply chain. Using suggestion lists, with similar to or fitting with products and respective accessories, during online shopping is already customary today. This is used to animate the customer toward further purchases. The customer data from one's own purchasing processes are thereby condensed and used for direct customer address, with the aim of additional sales and increased revenue, according to recognized patterns and deduced probabilities. How a holistic integration of supply chain partners can be advantageous to all partners can be exemplified by this. The customer is possibly content to have purchased a useful accessory product to go with his actual purchase and the operator of the online shop increases revenue or can consolidate shipping, thereby keeping logistics costs low. With the help of powerful algorithms, these possibilities will develop further and are used more specifically. This indicates that companies that are able to read their customer data correctly and link them to a general context have a distinct advantage over those that are not. Consequently, a large amount of the potentials of a data-driven orientation of SCM is appropriable.

10 Success Factors for the Digital Transformation of Supply Chains

The digitization of supply chains is in full swing and will expand to other areas of the supply chain with great rapidity over the next few years. The technologies necessary partially exist already. However, they must be brought to a running application in a holistic digitization strategy. The main features of the digital supply chain can be described with the comprehensive availability of information, mobility of processes and services, as well as an increased performance of technologies. Especially the complex interplay of all supply partners should be considered when dealing with the supply chain. In doing so, a standard-based communication system is given a central role. A general target set for all participants, as well as measures derived thereof, can make general solutions for the entire supply chain a reality. A key prerequisite for its success is the development of a new target operating model. This model can serve as the basis for future digital processes and structures within an organizing framework and thereby enables a coordination of all measures within a single company, but also for an overall context. Relevant issues are found in the key areas: organization, personnel, processes/IT and infrastructure, as well as the control factors: governance

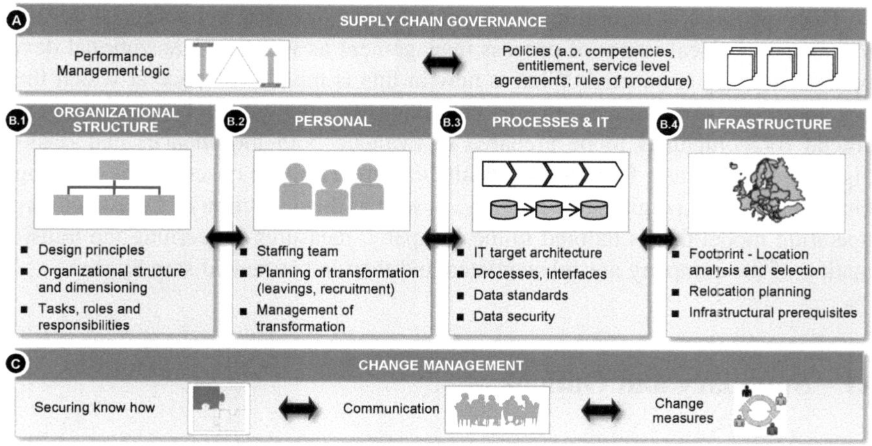

Fig. 3 Approach for a digital performance management of the supply chain

and change management (see Fig. 3). Taking these six factors into account enables the transition into digital performance management of the supply chain.

What this means in specific is that single factors concerning digitization must be developed and that the respectively necessary capacities for their application must be developed. To this end, IT is an essential precondition and must be primed—regarding its technology—to be able to process and store enormous data volumes. This can be implemented using data warehouse solutions or via a virtual data integration (e.g., using collaborative platforms or cloud solutions), although the security of data must be guaranteed at all times. Processes must be standardized and in order to enhance or reduce content that makes the use of gains in efficiency and flexibility possible. Concerning infrastructure, a general coordination and interlinking of the elements of the supply chain will increasingly move to the fore. Consequently, organization requires a stimulation and a permanent adaptation to new circumstances. For this digitized target operating model to take full effect, additional management requirements within governance must be adapted to individual functions. Furthermore, preconditions should be created for a change in organization and acting personnel within change management.

Initially, the adjustment of the business model and, consequently, also the adjustment of processes should be focused for a digital transformation. This procedure can be exemplified by the introduction of 3D printing. By introducing this printing procedure at the emergence of concrete demand, the entire supply chain is altered in the sense that fundamental processes such as demand planning, inventory management goods storage, and distribution are drastically reduced or may even fall away altogether. In the automotive industry, as well as in mechanical and plant engineering, many applications have been successfully implemented. Accordingly, 3D printing technology is ascribed a central driver role that is significantly responsible for the further development toward digital supply chains.

The process of transforming the supply chain shows that technological developments and classical issues of process management as well as organizational development must be connected. What is new in this is mainly the pace at which these developments take place, as well as the dimensions that ensue. Consequently, it is crucial for companies to be prepared to evaluate both the chances and risks of digitization and create frameworks. With the help of holistic observations of changes brought about by a digitization strategy, as well as the deduction of a digitized target operating model that is tailored to the company, measures concerning the transformation of the company are substantiated and then implemented step by step.

11 Summary and Outlook

The digitization of supply chains has already found its way into some companies and is only a matter of time before previously established business models can no longer function without digital processes. Digitization fundamentally revolutionizes the way in which companies produce new service offers and business models. Companies are faster, more efficient, and more innovative. Better strategic decisions are made, more exact sales and demand prognoses are generated, and a more exact cost management is introduced. Especially companies that are able to implement these new technologies to their advantage at an early stage and also create a common basis for company processes generate a competitive advantage. Due to a greater understanding of the customer, the foundation for lasting revenue is laid.

In order to secure a successful implementation, significant challenges must be met: on the one hand, technical preconditions, meaning technological infrastructure and standardization of data for participants of the supply chain, must be created. On the other hand, a comprehensive data security system, meaning the safeguarding of personal data protection through anonymization of data as well as the establishment of a secure data infrastructure that protects from unauthorized access, must be guaranteed.

Even though companies still have some challenges to meet, there are some lighthouse and pilot projects toward a digitization of the supply chain, such as, 3D print technologies, predictive analytics, or transaction platforms. From SCM especially, countless opportunities can be gained from integrated processes and data-driven decision models, as this impacts the core of underlying decision processes. Consequently, SCM will remain a significant driver of digitization and will create further digital innovations. In order to integrate these innovations successfully into processes and organization, a comprehensive management is necessary. This management must enable a transformation of the established processes to a digitization and utilization of these new technologies.

Apart from securing the management support necessary, a significant factor of success for the introduction of a digital supply chain is the development of a digitization strategy according to a target operating model. The necessary appreciation of employees for the change requirements concerning processes, organization, and management can only be reached by a clear specification of the strategy and these requirements themselves. Therefore, the development of the digital supply chain encompasses not only a technological transition but also a fundamental change in consciousness. This means going away from the isolated fulfillment of customer demands and delivery order toward the development and use of new, groundbreaking possibilities in the cooperation of supply chain partners. Seizing these opportunities will be a decisive criterion for future business success. Therefore, an early commencement of necessary steps on the path toward a digital supply chain is imperative.

References

Bauer W, Schlund S, Marrenbach D, Hanschar O (2014) Industrie 4.0 - Volkswirtschaftliches Potenzial für Deutschland. BITKOM Bundesverband Informationswirtschaft, Telekommunikation und neuer Medien e.V.

Daxböck C, Bergmann M (2016) Studienbericht "Industrie 4.0" – Bedeutung für zukünftige Effizienzsteigerung und Wachstum

Pfohl H-C (2004) Logistiksysteme - Betriebswirtschaftliche Grundlagen. Springer, Heidelberg

Scholz-Reiter B, Jakobza J (1999) SCM - Überblick und Konzeption. HDM Praxis der Wirtschaftsinformatik 207:7–15

Spath D, Ganschar O, Gerlach S, Hämmerle M, Krause T, Schlund S (2013) Produktionsarbeit der Zukunft - Industrie 4.0. Frauenhofer Verlag, Munich

Ziemke A, Stöckel T, Thomsen L (2016) Produktion 4.0.: Neue Wege für die Automobilindustrie, Media-Manufaktur GmbH

Christian Daxböck is a Partner with Horváth & Partners and head of Business Unit Operations Manufacturing Industries. He supervises international companies and medium-sized customers on the topic areas of digitization in purchase, production, and supply chain management.

Jochen Kröber is a Principal with Horváth & Partners in the Business Segment Supply Chain Management. He directs projects for the development and optimization of supply chain management and the implementation of digitization strategies along the supply chain.

Markus Bergmann is a Principal with Horváth & Partners in the Business Segment Production and Development. He directs projects for the realignment of production management as well as the optimization and digitization of production processes.

Opportunities for Supply Chain Processes by SAP S/4HANA

Dominik Fuchs, Mathias Haas, Julian Dombrowski, and Nicolas Göpfert

Abstract A current processual challenge for players of the retail industry is represented by the approach of omnichannel sales, which must not only be systemically enabled, but at the same time also secured by correct processes in the operations area.

In this regard, modern cloud-based system solutions do offer an opportunity to better respond to operational challenges of dynamic market environments. Simultaneously, they enable a further enhancement of the operational excellence of individual functional areas by providing novel system functionalities.

However, the transformation of individual corporate divisions is also accompanied by a large diversity of adaptive needs. The current example of an international retail client provides an exemplary insight in this regard.

Keywords Integrated business planning · Omnichannel management · Predictive analytics · Process management · SAP S/4 HANA · Supply chain planning

An adaption of this contribution has been originally printed as Fuchs, D., Haas, M., Dombrowski, J., Göpfert, N. (2018): Supply Chain Management: Auswirkungen von SAP S/4Hana im Einzelhandel, Der Controlling Berater, Volume 53, pp. 145–168.

Sources: Freely available information from SAP SE (SAP PartnerEdge) as well as project related information and experiences.

D. Fuchs (✉)
Organization & Operations, Horváth & Partners, Munich, Germany

M. Haas · N. Göpfert
Organization & Operations, Horváth & Partners, Stuttgart, Germany

J. Dombrowski
Organization & Operations, Horváth & Partners, Dusseldorf, Germany

M. Buttkus, R. Eberenz (eds.), *Performance Management in Retail and the Consumer Goods Industry*, https://doi.org/10.1007/978-3-030-12730-5_27

1 Supply Chain Process Efficiency in Retail

1.1 General Relevance of Integrated Process Operations

Effective integration and, in particular, the management of partners and functional processes along the supply chain have traditionally been a critical challenge for companies in all sectors. It can still also provide competitive advantages, if properly executed.

A crucial element in this regard is that for any company, process flows must be coordinated in the overall context of the respective company-specific business model, in order to be sustainable in a cost-effective manner and, ultimately, not to result in isolated process lines. Especially in the latter case, additional coordinating efforts may become necessary to control dispersed planning operations or overarching process flows across functions. The complexity of doing so may even increase further, as retail companies carry out their own production processes for in-house goods. In times of highly dynamic business environments, such avoidable process inefficiencies can cost valuable time and therefore reduce overall efficiency as well as sales potentials.

Retail companies in particular, as they have a low degree of self-generated added product value, rely on correctly functioning and coordinated processes for planning, procurement, or logistics, in order to be able to offer customers an optimum range of products at any time of the day or business. Nowadays, in the absence of specific goods, it is possible for potential customers to switch directly to alternative retail providers without additional efforts, due to today's constant worldwide transparency via online comparison portals. While doing so, customers generally do not have to accept any losses in terms of product offer, delivery times, buying experience, or the actually realized final product price. Given the fact that suppliers and products are oftentimes easily substitutable, the availability of goods and delivery information must therefore be secured continuously by coordinated process flows as a basic prerequisite for competitive business.

1.2 The Processual Effect of Omnichannel Integration

In this context, the increasing digitalization of the business world represents both a potential and a challenge for the various providers of the retail sector. In terms of the sales function, opportunities for the customization of products or personalized offer communications, which can serve as differentiation approaches to the competition or customer retention mechanisms, are constantly opening up.

However, as a result of rising customer demands to the digital buying experience, retailers are also faced with the overall challenge of and need to digitally transform their traditional business models. The classic purchase event has gradually developed from a rather linear experience to a dynamic as well as individualized

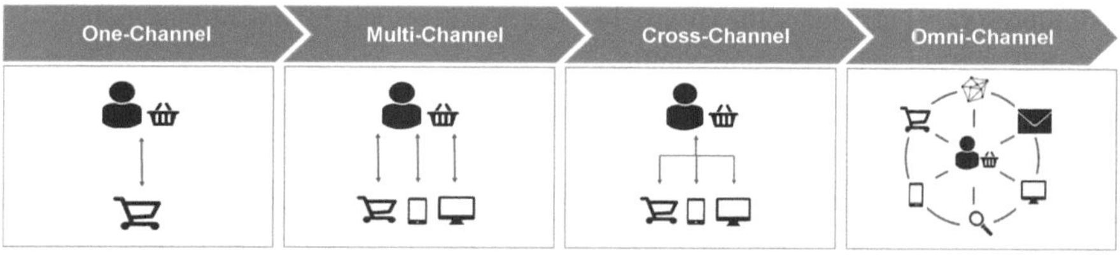

Fig. 1 Illustration of one-channel, multichannel, crosschannel, and omnichannel

experience. This is generally resulting in a blurring or even disappearing of boundaries between marketing and actual sales processes, no matter if online or stationary. As part of this sales process, customers no longer only expect to be free in deciding when and where to buy a product, but also which channels they will use to a certain extent.

Retailers are responding to these changing customer requirements by extending and integrating existing sales channels. Since the 2000s, the approach of omnichannel distribution has developed as a consequence, following the stages of multichannel and crosschannel distribution. In contrast to the latter two forms, the omnichannel concept fully integrates all sales channels and does not execute them independently of each other. Thus, it currently presents the highest maturity format of distribution integration. A prerequisite for an omnichannel approach and the associated optimization of the customer communication is the intelligent linking of different channels and their respective data. In future, the interaction process with the customer must therefore be completely standardized within all touch points along an individual customer journey. On the sales side alone, it must therefore be ensured that, for example, uniform price (omnichannel pricing) or delivery information is always available to the customer both in the local shop and in mobile applications (Fig. 1).

However, one consequence of such high levels of service and information quality is that an already high level of dynamics and complexity is constantly being driven upward from inside the company itself. This, in turn, leads to new or increasing challenges for operational processes and a holistic steering approach in meeting constantly changing customer needs. Thus, at the same time, the implementation of an omnichannel strategy must consider its potential effects and adaption requirements for warehouse or supply chain planning systems as well as overarching supply chain process flows.

Furthermore, at the level of overarching supply chain control, traditional logistics and warehouse concepts quickly reach their limits when it comes to the pursuance of an omnichannel approach. Depending on the business model, storage locations, for example, must be fundamentally realigned for a simultaneous serving of all sales channels. The requirement of making the availability of goods transparent to the customer at any time, at any place, and via any booking medium means that the digitization of the supply chain and up-to-date planning results are indispensable. Continuous transparency regarding possible delivery bottlenecks or storage risks will therefore be crucial in the future, in order to keep such a constantly dynamic and complex supply network controllable.

1.3 Integrated Planning as a Core Operations Process

With regard to supply chain planning, omnichannel sales integration, among other things, means that data from a constantly increasing number of sources must be taken into account in regular demand and logistics planning procedures. At the same time, opportunities arise for the evaluation of complex data volumes by means of systemic planning algorithms, which in turn may support the achievement of an overall higher planning quality. A development in the discipline of supply chain management is therefore especially represented by the leveraging of predictive analytics solutions. Even in this rather systemically driven approach, planning results must be effectively integrated and harnessed within the overall operational process landscape. Thus, data integration is becoming even more a key component in this context (Fig. 2).

The challenge of an effective and integral supply chain planning is therefore especially related to the harmonization of requirements and objectives of different business units or relevant customer specifications.

The central process in this context is represented by the sales and operations planning, in which all kinds of information from the areas of sales planning, stock planning, procurement, and, if relevant, production converge. Its general objective is to take a proactive approach regarding planning and execution of all downstream operational processes in the medium term, by fundamentally acting on the basis of

Fig. 2 Current trends in supply chain planning

projected sales expectations. It is no longer just a short-term response to incoming customer requirements, which are served by increased safety stocks. Instead, production and procurement processes are fully organized in advance, according to a company's business expectations. Through a targeted operational orientation, the adequate goods can be pre-produced or procured in an appropriate amount and thus storage quantities are kept within an acceptable range. In this context, the new possibilities offered by predictive analytics system solutions (e.g., SAP UDF), which can further strengthen a proactive orientation of the overall operational control system and thus offer significant potential, are worth mentioning (Fig. 3).

However, in order to keep an overarching entrepreneurial perspective at all times, these rather operationally based planning processes should also be linked directly and adjusted to requirements of the overall corporate financial and strategic planning, which is often only partly realized due to time restrictions of the daily business. In this way, the linkage to a financial planning perspective at an overarching level can support the derivation of long-term business decisions, as financial simulations can be directly based on most current operational planning values.

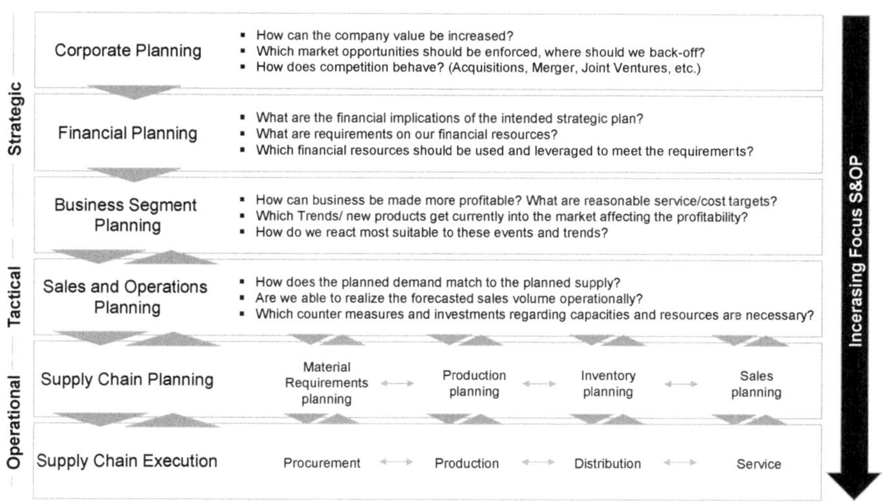

Fig 3 Central questions as part of the tactical and operational supply chain planning

2 SAP S/4HANA: New Potentials for Supply Chain Management and the Retail Industry

2.1 *Infrastructural Challenges Resulting from Process Complexities*

As organizational divisions and companies in general develop with regard to their operational process designs and customer service offerings, this goes well in hand with new requirements regarding enhanced functional support and infrastructural performance.

With respect to the aforementioned omnichannel sales renovation, a major challenge of digitally transforming existing sales concepts is to create the right technical prerequisites to handle the escalating processual complexity. So far, heterogeneous system landscapes in which product characteristics, classifications, price information, or inventory data are maintained redundantly and often inconsistently, rather enhance complexity further, and reduce the controllability of modern sales strategies and subsequent operational planning.

Regarding the latter, the need for digitalization of processes and data integration into operational supply chain management has, however, not just emerged recently. Nevertheless, in this regard, traditional database-based ERP systems offer only limited functionalities and, in particular, only limited computing power in order to fully leverage the possibilities of the new digitally driven age from a system perspective. Companies must prospectively recognize that a decisive advantage for more effective operational and sales planning processes can already be found in their internally collected data. However, depending on the volume of these datasets, traditional heterogeneous system solutions are often limited in terms of timely processing and analysis. Frequently, data has to be collected from different parts of the company in a time-consuming manner and is analyzed using individualized approaches (e.g., Excel). This oftentimes nonexistent data integration employing a uniform system interface or coherent data structure makes an end-to-end supply chain planning time-consuming and sometimes even impossible.

On the other hand, modern ERP systems of the most recent age of development, such as SAP S/4HANA, offer significantly more computing power with their in-memory database technology. In future, this will be a fundamental prerequisite in order to cope with the increasing flood of data volumes and the digitization of even basic processes. Thus, among other things, faster data processing supports a continuous execution of planning processes in real time, which will make it possible to implement new approaches for more transparent monitoring and well-timed adjustments in case of deviations or risks. At the same time, the possibility of efficiently handling and including exponentially increasing data volumes also supports a further sophistication of planning approaches, as more diverse data sources can be leveraged.

With respect to the retail and commerce sector in particular, S/4HANA Retail for merchandise management represents SAP's complementary industry solution. It was

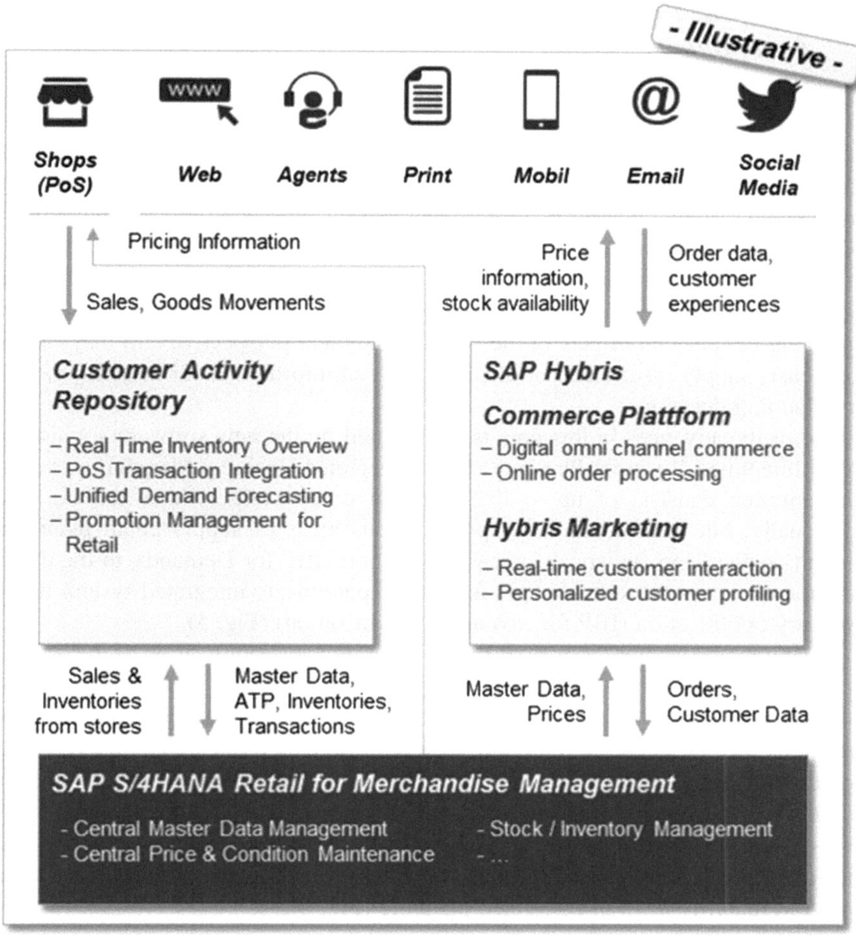

Fig. 4 Omnichannel system landscape (in reference to SAP SE)

developed natively on the basis of SAP HANA and its simplified data model. It thus combines the enhanced system performance and possibility of using sophisticated analytical applications with industry-specific functionalities and data structural designs. In interaction with specialized modules, such as the SAP Hybris platform, omnichannel order processing can be enabled by, among other things, centrally recording all order information and leveraging these as part of inventory cross-checks that can be provided to the customer in real time (Fig. 4).

In the following, you will be introduced to two specific system solutions and functionalities of S/4HANA, which, based on the SAP HANA in-memory technology, will prospectively offer significant potentials for the optimization of processes in the retail industry and for the management of supply chains in general.

2.2 Integrated Business Planning Functions as Process Components

The traditional planning process is usually based on the processing of heterogeneous data sources, whereby various data structures and aggregation levels hinder an effective coordination of strategic, operative, and financial planning processes over time. Due to different data formats and separated systems, an efficient simulation of possible planning scenarios is often only possible to a limited extent by harnessing customized solutions such as MS Excel. In the tactical planning process of sales and operations planning, the use of limited or obsolete information often leads to a neglecting of financial effects in the overall analytical perspective and may, in the worst case, supply insufficient or already outdated information for currently necessary planning decisions.

One of the advances in this area is represented by the new software solution of SAP's Integrated Business Planning (IBP). Integrated Business Planning as a software solution consists of up to five different components, which can be used individually, but each cover very specific focus areas of supply chain planning. Contents range from statistical forecasting support (IBP for Demand), to the determination of very short-term changes in demand patterns, to integrated system-based inventory optimization (IBP for Inventory Optimization) (Fig. 5).

In general, the aspiration of SAP IBP is a significant simplification of the holistic supply chain planning process, thereby building on the benefits of HANA in-memory database technology. The Integrated Business Planning for sales and operations thereby generally functions as a uniform data basis, collaborative working platform, and central data interface between operations, sales, and finance functions. It thus enables linking longer-term financial and strategic planning with short- to medium-term operational planning of production, procurement, or sales. The approach of the traditional sales and operations planning can thus be raised to an improved maturity level of integrated planning (Fig. 6).

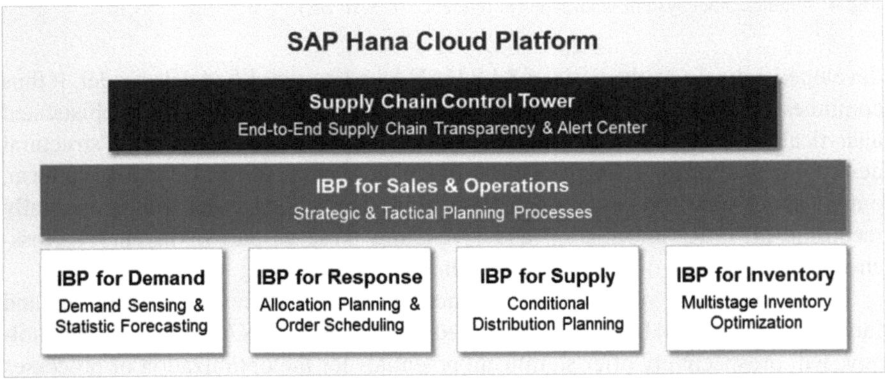

Fig. 5 Components of the SAP integrated business planning (in reference to SAP SE)

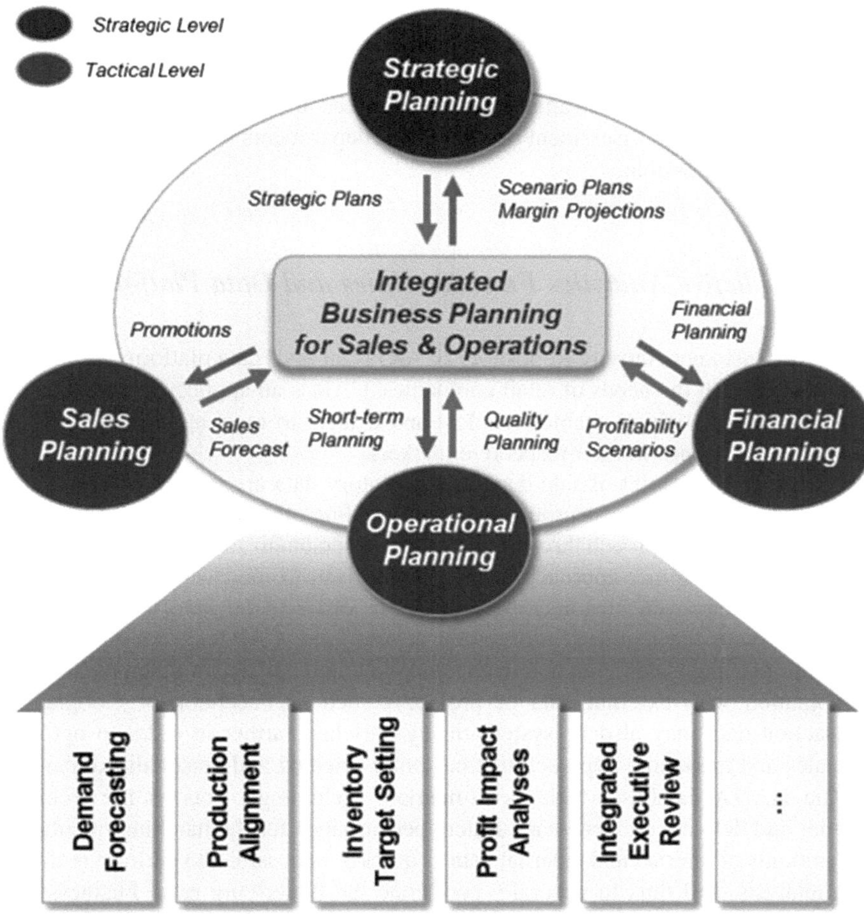

Fig. 6 Illustration of the IBP for sales and operations by SAP (in reference to SAP SE)

The integration of up-to-the-minute information makes it possible to build complex data models and, through the use of a uniform integrated platform, enables an efficient integration of various stakeholders throughout the planning process. At the same time, data models can be evaluated in real time and dedicated simulations ("What if?" scenarios) can be created on short notice, supporting necessary decision-making processes. By linking the various operative and strategic data sources, it is possible to analyze financial effects directly on the basis of individual demand or supply scenarios and to include them in an evaluation. Accelerated decision-making processes, involving different perspectives, are thus made possible and in turn are then also based on the most up-to-date data.

Homogeneous datasets additionally reduce efforts for data collection and data preparation. This should significantly increase overall process efficiency and reduce the time and effort involved in complex alignment cycles. Integrated Business Planning for S&OP supports the efficient execution of an operative sales and operations planning and at the same time elevates it to a higher maturity level. Overall financial objectives can be considered linked to operational S&OP planning cycles, and an overall assessment of all relevant departments with resulting financial effects is made possible.

2.3 Predictive Analytics Functionalities and Data Platforms

The SAP Customer Activity Repository (CAR) is an SAP data platform specifically designed to meet the needs of retail companies. CAR is an application based on the HANA database, which enables retailers and dealers to react appropriately to the fast-moving changes in their respective markets.

Customer data, point-of-sale data, and inventory data are pooled and processed centrally using CAR. The centralization and bundling of data enables a targeted and efficient customer approach through an improved personalization of customer offers. An improved customer approach in turn should lead to increasing customer satisfaction and improved customer perception. In order to be able to provide end customers with the required information at any time, CAR uses transaction data from all existing sales channels (omnichannel) and all existing interactions. In combination with external data of providers such as Facebook or Google, the transaction data may also be systematically enriched further in order to optimize the sales and marketing approach in a customer-oriented and personalized manner.

The HANA database, with its in-memory technology, acts as the technical enabler and delivers the necessary system performance for the handling of substantial amounts of internal and external data as quickly as possible, to perform real-time data analysis, and thus to generally accelerate the underlying retail business processes. In using the CAR, merchants are given the possibility of obtaining fast comprehensive transparency on their processes, of having a real-time overview on stock situations, and of actually obtaining insights on current consumer needs. In turn, increased transparency of customer requirements and customer demands improves forecasting accuracy and enables a better planning of future requirements.

With state-of-the-art forecasting algorithms, merchants can analyze point-of-sale data on the basis of predictive analytics and then use these insights to generate forecasts and planning models that predict future consumer buying behavior. With these functionalities, it becomes possible to procure stocks optimally and store them at the right place in the logistics chain so that they are available for the end customer's needs at the right place. Working capital is reduced and product availability at the point of sale is optimized. Figure 7 illustrates the SAP CAR as well as its interfaces to other SAP modules and applications.

A core functionality of the Customer Activity Repository is, among other things, a solution for the creation of demand forecasts. It is based on the Demand Data Foundation module and represents more than just a basic forecasting software, it is

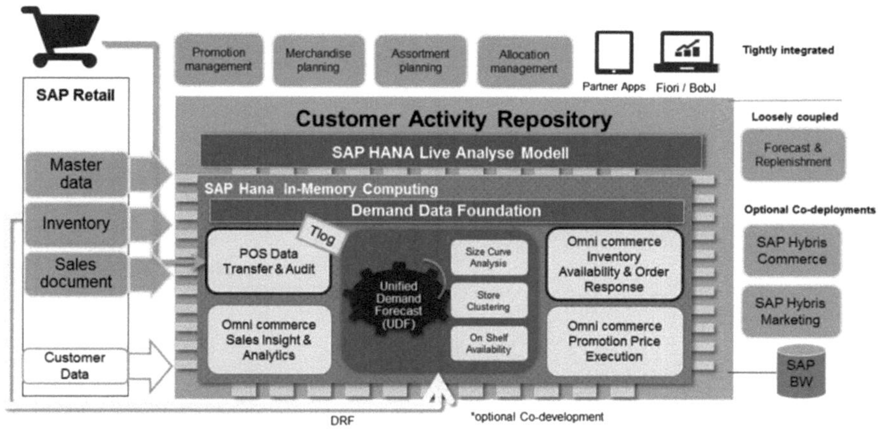

Fig. 7 Customer Activity Repository as central data platform for retail (in reference to SAP SE)

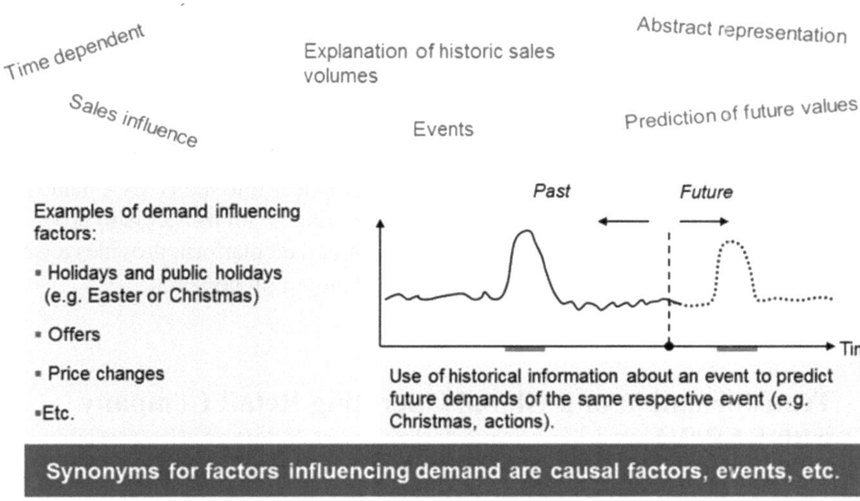

Fig. 8 Explanation and illustration of demand influencing factors (in reference to SAP SE)

called Unified Demand Forecast (UDF). On the basis of real-time information and historical data analyses, the UDF delivers future demand values down to the daily base level. As an option, it is possible to enrich demand values by so-called demand influencing factors, as for example through advertising and promotion activities. A demand influencing factor in this sense is an external factor that has a significant effect on future demand and sales levels. The generated demand forecasts can ultimately be used to create a variety of planning scenarios (Fig. 8).

By means of data modeling, employing statistical-stochastic methods, the UDF also integrates so-called priors into the modeling process and enables the derivation of insufficient or missing, but essential, data volumes on the basis of historical events

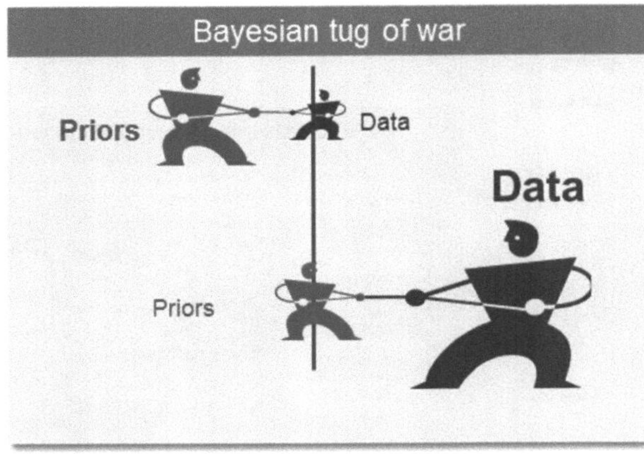

Fig. 9 Prior application in case of limited availability of historical data (in reference to SAP SE)

and effects. Priors basically represent "best guesses" and are based on the Bayesian paradigm. In situations with little or no historical data available, the defined priors of a prediction model are more important than the existing real data. Over time and with increasing data availability, the influence of the defined priors on the prediction accuracy is gradually reduced. This relationship is also known as the "Bayesian tug of war" (Fig. 9).

The result of future demand modeling and forecasting can also be used by other system modules via the implementation of a CAR module into the HANA database, thus simplifying production and replenishment planning. With its access to point-of-sales data and its predictive capability, CAR's central data platform provides a well-founded database for higher-level supply chain planning processes.

3 Transformation of a Global Operating Retail Company with SAP S/4

3.1 Customer, Initial Situation and Objectives

In the following chapter, we will offer an insight to the transformation of a fundamental end-to-end supply chain management approach of a global operating retail company.

Like many other participants in the global retail market, the client company has been confronted with a variety of current megatrends that necessitated far-reaching changes in the overarching operational steering approach of the company. In addition to fundamental technological trends, the continuous change in customer behavior with regard to preferred sales channels was a major trigger for an extensive process optimization program (Fig. 10).

On the sales side, the development of an integrated omnichannel management system was the central starting point for securing sustainable customer loyalty and

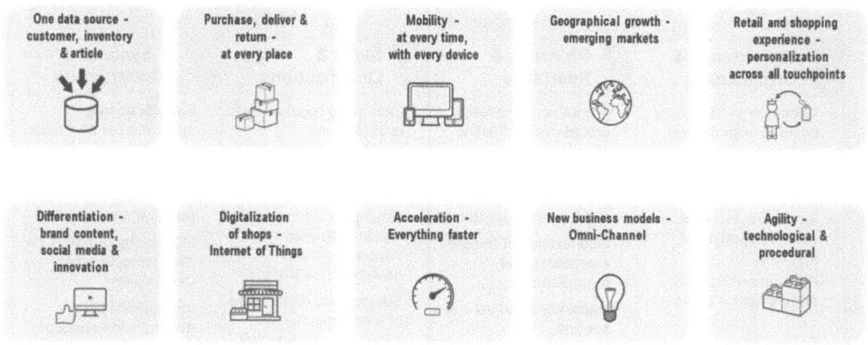

Fig. 10 Current trends of the retail industry

the associated sales growth in an increasingly competitive environment. Targeted and customized marketing plays a decisive role in this context. The aim is to offer customers an individually tailored and context-specific range of product and service offerings across all sales channels.

On the operational side, on the other hand, the focus was on establishing a regular demand management in order to ensure the availability of goods in all sales areas and thus to be able to fully exploit all available sales potentials. Complexity drivers for the company in this connection, in particular, are a comprehensive range of products with highly fluctuating seasonal effects. In light of the holistic omnichannel transformation of all sales-related processes, the optimization of established planning processes was identified as an appropriate starting point.

Initially, a large number of separate sub-projects were started to optimize process flows within individual departments. After an initial start-up phase, however, these were consolidated into a comprehensive optimization program.

The aim here is to enable an end-to-end process integration across all areas which, on the one hand, enable omnichannel interaction with customers and, on the other hand, enable all existing data to be used for a proactive operative planning and usage in the supply chain. In order to stay ahead of the competition, it was decided not to push forward with the objectives on the basis of the existing system architecture. Instead, a holistic transformation of the system landscape based on state-of-the-art SAP S/4 Hana applications was initiated.

Comprehensive technical transformations usually influence almost every process and operational aspect of a company. Based on the approach of the target operating model, we would like to present some of the conceptual changes to the considered company in the following, as results of its S/4 Hana transformation (Fig. 11). These extend along the four model dimensions:

- Governance and organization
- Processes and interfaces
- Skills and qualifications
- IT systems and infrastructure.

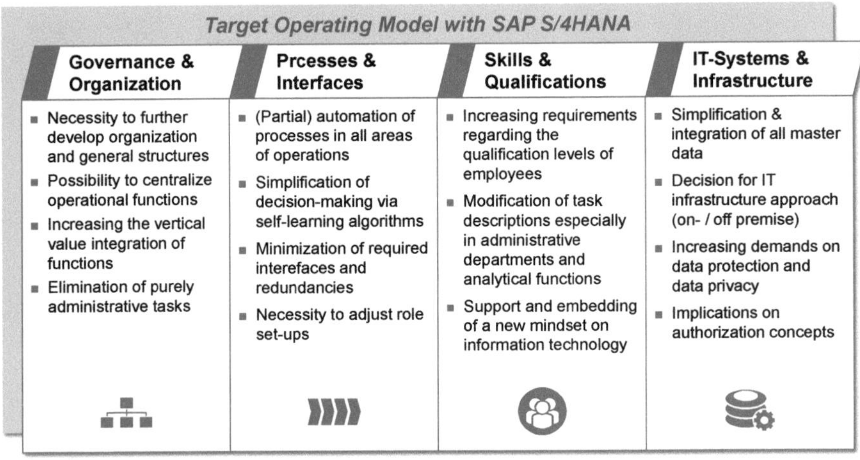

Fig. 11 Target operating model with SAP S/4-Hana

3.2 Governance and Operations: Target Processes and Master Data as a Basic Framework for System Transformations

For the realization of a new integrated system landscape based on S/4-Hana, the underlying process landscape forms the basic framework. In this context, it is generally crucial not to pursue existing, possibly inefficient, actual processes without optimization. Rather, existing improvement potentials and hidden optimization potentials must be identified in the first step. On this basis, the client company has developed an optimized target picture, taking into account new potentials of the S/4 system. At the same time, it was possible to derive specifications for required system functionalities. A direct comparison of designed target process flows with the testing of system functionalities makes it possible to initiate necessary process or system optimizations at an early stage and ensures the consideration of special user requirements on the basis of specific business models.

A fundamental challenge in the current implementation phase is the correct definition of harmonized master data, which can be used and applied across all systems. As one example, the future system landscape of the client company will consider the complete integration of all sales-related customer interfaces as a basic element.

In this case, the SAP Customer Activity Repository serves as a central system platform, by consolidating data information of various applications such as stationary POS systems, Hybris Webshop, Hybris Marketing, and the CRM system. Prospectively, this alone has clear efficiency potentials in terms of required master data definition and related maintenance efforts. Prices, product names, GTINs, as well as customer master data are maintained centrally and transferred uniformly within all channels and systems. On the one hand, this leads to significant time savings and more consistent data, while simultaneously ensuring a uniform data basis, consisting originally of separate data pools.

In the first step, the resulting consistency of customer transaction and movement data will lay the foundation for an integrated marketing planning so that customers will be able to receive customized communication and product offers in the future. At this point in time, it can be said that the master data subject will become even more important for the efficient feasibility of business processes in the future. At the same time, it is foreseeable that in the final state, fewer employees will be required for pure data maintenance efforts in the future, so that qualified personnel will have to be employed for other tasks in the company.

3.3 Processes and Interfaces: Organizational Structure as Enabler for Effective Planning Control

The definition of required target states also provides interesting insights for necessary organizational changes and supplemental requirements. With regard to the described transformation project, this means that it was recognized that an expansion and centralization of the demand planning competence was becoming increasingly necessary. In the existing format, it was often only possible to take reactive actions in order to counteract short-term supply bottlenecks. The situation was further complicated by a high volume of articles, which consisted of a changing standard, as well as of high-frequency special assortments. In particular, the switch to an omnichannel sales orientation would, however, further increase the already existing dynamics and complexity, since demand patterns of different sales channels have to be taken into account simultaneously.

For this reason, the organizational unit of a demand management function that was previously nonexistent was conceptually designed and launched parallel to the overall start of the transformation project. With help of the demand management division, planning and procurement processes that are often separated from each other should be harmonized and bundled centrally in one place. The tasks and objectives that the new department had to pursue as target from the beginning included, among other things:

- Introduction of a uniform forecasting approach for the planning of regular as well as unscheduled additional demands from different sales channels
- Regular assessment of planning quality and accuracy via plan/ as-is comparisons
- Reorganization of historical disposition and demand planning processes
- Adaptation of responsibilities as well as organizational and operational structures in line with optimized inventory management processes

At the same time, the development of proactive-oriented planning concepts was started, which was meant to enable a targeted proactive control of critical article units. It is important to mention that all initiated measures of the demand management division are intended to lead to effective results, independent of the overall transformation project.

Nevertheless, all developed concepts and processes already take into account the future target state under S/4-Hana. Intermediate solutions are generally developed and introduced for the transition phase of the transformation, but new potentials, such as a Unified Demand Forecast (UDF), are taken into account for developing the organizational structure.

3.4 *Skills and Qualifications: Advancing from Planner to Business Analyst*

As far as qualifications and role profiles are concerned, there will be far-reaching changes for every company triggered by systemic transformations and the digitalization in general. With regard to the illustrated project example, the demand management division, or the demand planner function, presents an interesting example.

On this occasion, in particular, the switch to a systemically driven demand planning will require substantial change adaptions. The integrated forecasting capabilities of the Unified Demand Forecast (UDF) enable the determination of the effects of individual demand influencing factors on the basis of existing historical transactions, price, or promotion data and integrate them into complex predictive forecasting models. In future, forecasts of individual SKU demands will no longer be based solely on the extrapolation of historical seasonality observations and the experience of individual supply and demand planners. Instead, links between all possible influencing factors that are concealed in the company's available data are taken into account in a forward-looking manner.

What will this mean for the required roles and qualifications in demand management?

In particular, the role of the traditional planner, who consolidates, reviews, and adjusts various bottom-up forecasts, will change significantly. Rather, these tasks will no longer be necessary in future, as they are largely taken over by the system. A classical bottom-up demand planning will be replaced, for example, by the predictive planning of a UDF. Planners therefore have to transform themselves into analysts who are able to make sense of the increasingly complex data structures of the company. A core qualification here will be to not only understand the predictive models of a UDF in parts, but also to modify them if necessary and to create own forecast models. Companies must therefore be prepared to adapt their existing role profiles accordingly or to involve and promote individuals with the existing potential in the transformation process at an early stage, as is the case with our client company.

A change that does not only have to take place in functions such as demand management, but affects an entire company is a fundamental cultural change. In future, all planning related areas will have to trust system applications so that manual intervention in systemic predictions can be minimized. In contrast to the system, these are often subjective and experience has shown that they distort results in a mostly negative way.

In the considered transformation project, this is tackled by an accompanying change management, a factor that cannot be emphasized enough in the context of such large-scale transformation projects.

3.5 *IT Systems and Infrastructure: Choosing Between On-premise Systems and Cloud Transformations*

Contrary to other parts of the TOM, changes with regard to the company's own IT infrastructure and associated systems usually already occur within the overall conceptual phase and business case calculation. In recent years, the balance between the possibilities of traditional in-house-driven one-premise software solutions and fully cloud-based software-as-a-service (SaaS) offerings has generally grown rapidly. The same applies to SAP, which has steadily driven its transformation to a cloud-based provider.

For the company under consideration, the question of whether a switch to a cloud-based system landscape would be a viable way forward was also raised in the phase prior to the transformation. In addition to existing extensive internal IT infrastructure and long-term cost effects, the topic of customer information's data security played a decisive role as part of the decision weighing.

While system maintenance costs and a significantly reduced level of internal IT support required a clear change to a cloud-only solution, the aspect of data security in particular assumed a counter position. Ultimately, the decision was made to keep a self-powered on-premise solution. Data security in particular was the decisive factor here, as sensitive customer and transaction information should not be separated from the company's own resources and direct control.

As can be seen, a large number of different factors often play a role when considering which infrastructure solution to pursue. Experience has shown that these are often driven by a subjectively critical feeling toward a complete system change to a cloud application. A radical system change to the cloud thus appears rather feasible for smaller companies, which were based on their own rather limited IT infrastructure until now.

4 Success Factors and Lessons Learned

In conclusion, it can be said that the innovations and inherent system performance of the SAP S/4HANA solutions bear quite a great potential for operating business units of any company. Planning approaches are easier to harmonize and can be optimized by employing predictive methodologies. Depending on the maturity degree of process interactions within a company, this offers good opportunities for further vertical integration, so that downstream functions such as logistics can also be controlled predictively and in an organized manner.

At the same time, a variety of challenges await companies along such a development path, which, ideally, one should want to be prepared for. Based on previous project experiences, we see that a cross-functional end-to-end approach should be pursued in particular. Potentials of integrated systemic processes can only be achieved if they are not conceptualized and improved in a discipline-isolated manner, but are considered in their entirety and in the overall operational context of the company. The presented approaches of an integrated business planning offer a good starting point for achieving this.

In order to be able to take industry-specific requirements of the various departments into account at an early stage of the system modeling, they should be integrated as early as possible, by being part of developing functional requirements and user designs. For this purpose, experts of the respective areas should be won over, which are accepted as well-respected representatives of their individual functions and can bring about decisions efficiently.

A factor that sounds rather simple, but must not be neglected in the case of long-lived and at the same time extensive system transformations, is a partnership-based cooperation of all involved stakeholders. With the help of dedicated change management initiatives, all employees should be involved early on in the change process, in order to secure support for the project from within the company itself. In this regard, communication tools such as information days or newsletters can ensure that the entire workforce remains well informed and is involved in the overall process as part of the larger whole, with little effort involved.

Dominik Fuchs is a Principal with Horváth & Partners and responsible for the Business Segment Business Transformation by S/4HANA. Due to his previous professional employments and long-term consulting experience, he possesses profound expertise in the context of operations and supply chain planning.

Mathias Haas is a Principal with Horváth & Partners and responsible for the Business Segment Business Transformation by S/4HANA. He acts as expert for the functional discipline of operations and production management as well as the optimization and digitization of production processes.

Julian Dombrowski is a Managing Consultant with Horváth & Partners within the Business Segment Supply Chain Management. His consulting work is focused on projects regarding business and operations planning for small and medium-sized companies as well as major corporations.

Nicolas Göpfert is a Managing Consultant with Horváth & Partners within the Business Segment Production & Development. Based on his previous project engagements, he acquired broad expertise with respect to organizational transformation and digitization in operations management.

MIX
Papier aus verantwortungsvollen Quellen
Paper from responsible sources
FSC® C105338

If you have any concerns about our products,
you can contact us on
ProductSafety@springernature.com

In case Publisher is established outside the EU,
the EU authorized representative is:
Springer Nature Customer Service Center GmbH
Europaplatz 3, 69115 Heidelberg, Germany

Printed by Libri Plureos GmbH
in Hamburg, Germany